Lecture Notes in Computer Science　　7379

Commenced Publication in 1973
Founding and Former Series Editors:
Gerhard Goos, Juris Hartmanis, and Jan van Leeuwen

Judith Masthoff   Bamshad Mobasher
Michel C. Desmarais   Roger Nkambou (Eds.)

User Modeling,
Adaptation,
and Personalization

20th International Conference, UMAP 2012
Montreal, Canada, July 16-20, 2012
Proceedings

 Springer

Volume Editors

Judith Masthoff
University of Aberdeen
Dept. of Computing Science
Meston Building, King's College, Aberdeen AB24 3UE, UK
E-mail: j.masthoff@abdn.ac.uk

Bamshad Mobasher
DePaul University
School of Computing, College of Computing and Digital Media
243 South Wabash Avenue, Chicago, IL 60604, USA
E-mail: mobasher@cs.depaul.edu

Michel C. Desmarais
Polytechnique Montreal
Génie informatique et génie logiciel
C.P. 6079, succ. Centre-Ville, Montreal, QC, Canada, H3C 3A7
E-mail: michel.desmarais@polymtl.ca

Roger Nkambou
UQÀM
Dépt. d'informatique
201, av. Président-Kennedy, local PK-4150 Montreal, QC, Canada
E-mail: nkambou.roger@uqam.ca

ISSN 0302-9743   e-ISSN 1611-3349
ISBN 978-3-642-31453-7   e-ISBN 978-3-642-31454-4
DOI 10.1007/978-3-642-31454-4
Springer Heidelberg Dordrecht London New York

Library of Congress Control Number: Applied for

CR Subject Classification (1998): H.5.2-4, H.3.3, H.5, H.3, I.2, H.4, K.4.4

LNCS Sublibrary: SL 3 – Information Systems and Application, incl. Internet/Web
and HCI

Typesetting: Camera-ready by author, data conversion by Scientific Publishing Services, Chennai, India

Printed on acid-free paper

Springer is part of Springer Science+Business Media (www.springer.com)

Preface

The 20th International Conference on User Modeling, Adaptation and Personalization (UMAP 2012), chaired by Michel Desmarais and Roger Nkambou, took place in Montreal, Canada, during July 16–20, 2012. It was the fourth annual conference under the UMAP title, which resulted from the merger in 2009 of the successful biannual User Modeling (UM) and Adaptive Hypermedia (AH) conference series. Approximately 500 researchers from 38 countries were involved in creating the technical program, either as authors or as reviewers.

The Research Paper Track of the conference was chaired by Judith Masthoff from the University of Aberdeen, UK, and Bamshad Mobasher from DePaul University, USA. They were assisted by an international Program Committee of 95 leading figures in the AH and UM communities as well as highly promising younger researchers. Papers in the Research and Industry Paper Tracks were reviewed by three or more reviewers. The conference solicited Long Research Papers of up to 12 pages in length, which represent original reports of substantive new research. In addition, the conference solicited Short Research Papers of up to 6 pages in length, whose merit was assessed more in terms of originality and importance than maturity and technical validation. The Research Paper Track received 101 submissions, including 75 long and 26 short papers. Of these, 22 long and 7 short papers were accepted, resulting in an acceptance rate of 29% for long papers, 27% for short papers, and 29% overall. Many authors of papers that were not accepted were encouraged to revise their work and to resubmit it to conference workshops or to the Poster and Demo Tracks of the conference.

The Research Paper Track included sessions on a variety of established as well as emerging topics in user modeling, adaptation, and personalization. Among these were sessions on user engagement; trust; user motivation, attention, and effort; recommender systems (including topics such as matrix factorization, critiquing, noise and spam in recommender systems); user-centered design and evaluation; educational data mining; modeling learners; user models in microblogging; and visualization.

The Industry Paper Track was chaired by Ido Guy, from IBM Research in Israel, and Diego Zapata-Rivera, from ETS in USA. This track covered innovative commercial implementations or applications of UMAP technologies, and experience in applying recent research advances in practice. Submissions to this track were reviewed by a separate Industry Paper Committee with 11 leading industry researchers and practitioners. Of five submissions that were received, three were accepted (two long and one short papers).

The conference also included a Doctoral Consortium, a forum for PhD students to get feedback and advice from a Doctoral Consortium Committee of 17 leading UMAP researchers. The Doctoral Consortium was chaired by Lora Aroyo from the University of Amsterdam, The Netherlands, and Robin Cohen,

University of Waterloo, Canada. This track received 18 submissions of which 11 were accepted.

The Poster and Demo Session of the conference was chaired by Li Chen, Hong Kong Baptist University, China, and Stephan Weibelzhal, National College of Ireland, Ireland. As of the time of writing, the number of acceptances was still unknown. It was expected that this session would feature dozens of lively posters and system demonstrations. Summaries of these presentations will be published in online adjunct proceedings.

The UMAP 2012 program also included Workshops and Tutorials that were selected by Chairs Eelco Helder, L3S Researh Center, Germany, and Kalina Yacef, University of Sydney, Australia.

The following tutorials were offered as part of the UMAP 2012 program:

- Empirical Evaluation of User Modeling Systems, by David Chin
- Evaluation of Adaptive Systems, by Stephan Weibelzahl, Alexandros Paramythis and Judith Masthoff
- Designing and Evaluating New-Generation User Modeling, by Frederica Cena and Cristina Gena

The following workshops were organized in conjunction with UMAP 2012:

- AUM: Second Workshop on Augmented User Modeling, chaired by Fabian Abel, Vania Dimitrova, Eelco Herder and Geert-Jan Houbert
- FactMod: Matrix Factorization Techniques for Student Skills and User Preference Modeling, chaired by Michel Desmarais, Neil Heffernan, Tomas Horvath, Thai-Nghe Nguyen, and Zacharia A. Pardos
- PALE: Personalization Approaches in Learning Environments, chaired by Milos Kravcik, Olga C. Santos, Jesus G. Boticario and Diana Perez-Marin
- PATCH: Fourth International Workshop on Personal Access to Cultural Heritage, chaired by Tsvi Kuflik, Lora Aroyo, Anthony Collins, Eyal Dim, Judy Kay and Bob Kummerfeld
- Personalized Knowledge Modeling with Big (Usage and Context) Data, chaired by Doreen Cheng, Lora Aroyo, Deborah McGuinness and Daniel Park
- SASWeb: Semantic and Adaptive Social Web, chaired by Lora Aroyo, Federica Cena, Antonina Dattolo, Pasquale Lops and Julita Vassileva
- SRS: Third International Workshop on Social Recommender Systems, chaired by Ido Guy, Li Chen and Michelle Zhou
- TRUM: Trust, Reputation and User Modeling, chaired by Julita Vassileva and Jie Zhang
- TVM^2P: International Workshop on TV and Multimedia Personalization, chaired by Shlomo Berkovsky and Luiz Pizatto

Two keynote speakers were invited to share their influential contributions in the field of adaptive interfaces: Francesco Ricci from the University of Bozen-Bozano (Italy), and Ryan S.J.d. Baker from Worcester polytechnic Institute (USA). A panel was organized by Alfred Kobsa, the editor of the UMUAI journal, to commemorate two decades of research in our field.

In addition to all the contributors mentioned above, we would also like to thank the Local Arrangements Chair Jacqueline Bourdeau from TÉLUQ, Canada, and the Publicity Chair Cristóbal Romero from Universidad de Córdoba in Spain. A number of indispendable student volunteers also contributed to the organization, of which Pierre Chalfoun from the University of Montreal, and Daniel Capelo Borges from TÉLUQ, Canada, were involved from the start. We are also grateful to UQÀM for providing enthusiastic administrative and secretarial help from Jocelyne Blanchard and Louise Tremblay.

We deeply acknowledge the conscientious work of the Program Committee members and the additional reviewers, who are listed on the next few pages. We also gratefully acknowledge our sponsors who helped us with funding and organizational expertise: User Modeling Inc., ACM SIGART, SIGCHI and SIGIR, the Chen Family Foundation, Microsoft Research, the U.S. National Science Foundation, Springer, Polytechnique Montréal, and the Université du Québec à Montréal. Finally, we want to acknowledge the use of EasyChair for the management of the review process and the preparation of the proceedings.

April 2012

Judith Masthoff
Bamshad Mobasher
Michel C. Desmarais
Roger Nkambou

Organization

UMAP 2012 was organized by the Université du Québec à Montréal, Canada, in cooperation in cooperation with Polytechnique Montreéal, User Modeling Inc., ACM/SIGIR, ACM/SIGCHI and ACM/SIGART.

Organizing Committee

General Co-chairs

Michel C. Desmarais	Polytechnique Montréal, Canada
Roger Nkambou	UQÀM, Canada

Program Co-chairs

Judith Masthoff	University of Aberdeen, UK
Bamshad Mobasher	DePaul University, USA

Industry Track Co-chairs

Ido Guy	IBM Research, Israel
Diego Zapata-Rivera	ETS, USA

Workshop and Tutorial Co-chairs

Eelco Herder	L3S Research Center, Germany
Kalina Yacef	University of Sydney, Australia

Doctoral Consortium Co-chairs

Lora M. Aroyo	University of Amsterdam, The Netherlands
Robin Cohen	University of Waterloo, Canada

Demo and Poster Co-chairs

Li Chen	Hong Kong Baptist University, China
Stephan Weibelzahl	National College of Ireland, Ireland

Local Arrangements Chair

Jacqueline Bourdeau	TÉLUQ, Canada

Publicity Chair

Cristóbal Romero	Universidad de Córdoba.

Research Track Program Committee

Fabian Abel	TU Delft, The Netherlands
Kenro Aihara	National Institute of Informatics, Japan
Esma Aimeur	Université de Montréal, Canada
Sarabjot Anand	University of Warwick, UK
Liliana Ardissono	Università degli Studi di Torino, Italy
Lora Aroyo	VU University, The Netherlands
Ryan S.J.d. Baker	Worcester Polytechnic Institute, USA
Mathias Bauer	Mineway, Germany
Joseph Beck	Worcester Polytechnic Institute, USA
Shlomo Berkovsky	CISRO, Australia
Maria Bielikova	Slovak University of Technology, Slovakia
Jesus G. Boticario	Tu Universidad, Spain
Jacqueline Bourdeau	TÉLUQ, Canada
Peter Brusilovsky	University of Pittsburgh, USA
Susan Bull	University of Birmingham, UK
Robin Burke	DePaul University, USA
Sandra Carberry	University of Delaware, USA
Rosa M. Carro	Universidad Autónonoma de Madrid, Spain
Federica Cena	Università degli Studi di Torino, Italy
Li Chen	Hong Kong Baptist University, China
David Chin	University of Hawaii, USA
Mihaela Cocea	University of Portsmouth, UK
Cristina Conati	University of British Columbia, Canada
Ricardo Conejo	Universidad de Málaga, Spain
Albert Corbett	Carnegie Mellon University, USA
Alexandra Cristea	University of Warwick, UK
Paul de Bra	Eindhoven University of Technology, The Netherlands
Vania Dimitrova	University of Leeds, UK
Peter Dolog	Aalborg University, Denmark
Benedict Du Boulay	University of Sussex, UK
Rosta Farzan	Carnegie Mellon University, USA
Alexander Felfernig	Technische Universität Graz, Austria
Cristina Gena	Università degli studi di Torino, Italy
Floriana Grasso	University of Liverpool, UK
Eduardo Guzmán	Universidad de Málaga, Spain
Neil Heffernan	Worcester Polytechnic Institute, USA
Nicola Henze	University of Hannover, Germany
Eelco Herder	L3S Research Center, Germany
Haym Hirsh	Rutgers University, USA
Geert-Jan Houben	TU Delft, The Netherlands

Anthony Jameson	DFKI, Germany
Dietmar Jannach	TU Dortmund, Germany
W. Lewis Johnson	Alelo Inc., USA
Judy Kay	University of Sydney, Australia
Alfred Kobsa	University of California at Irvine, USA
Milos Kravcik	RWTH Aachen University, Germany
Antonio Krueger	DFKI, Germany
Tsvi Kuflik	University of Haifa, Israel
Paul Lamere	Music Machinery, USA
James Lester	North Carolina State University, USA
Frank Linton	MITRE, USA
Mark Maybury	MITRE, USA
Gordon McCalla	University of Saskatchewan, Canada
Lorraine McGinty	University College Dublin, Ireland
Alessandro Micarelli	Roma Tre University, Italy
Tanja Mitrovic	University of Canterbury, New Zeland
Riichiro Mizoguchi	Osaka University, Japan
Yoichi Motomura	Institute of Advanced Industrial Science and Technology, Japan
Michael O'Mahony	University College Dublin, Ireland
Helen Pain	University of Edinburgh, UK
Georgios Paliouras	NCSR Demokritos, Greece
Alexandros Paramythis	Johannes Kepler University, Austria
Cecile Paris	CSIRO, Australia
Mykola Pechenizkiy	TU Eindhoven, The Netherlands
Francesco Ricci	Free University of Bozen-Bolzano, Italy
John Riedl	University of Minnesota, USA
Cristobal Romero	Universidad de Córdoba, Spain
Lloyd Rutledge	Open University, The Netherlands
Melike Sah	Trinity College Dublin, Ireland
Olga C. Santos	AdeNu, Spain
Barry Smyth	University College Dublin, Ireland
Carlo Tasso	Università di Udine, Italy
Nava Tintarev	University of Aberdeen, UK
Alexander Tuzhilin	New York University, USA
Julita Vassileva	University of Saskatchewan, Canada
Yang Wang	Carnegie Mellon University, US
Gerhard Weber	Pädagogische Hochschule Freiburg, Germany
Stephan Weibelzahl	National College of Ireland, UK
Kalina Yacef	University of Sidney, Australia
Markus Zanker	University Klagenfurt, Austria
Diego Zapata-Rivera	ETS, USA
Jie Zhang	Nanyang Technological University, Singapore
Ingrid Zukerman	Monash University, Australia

Industry Track Program Committee

Fabian Abel	L3S Research Center
Mathias Bauer	Mineway, Germany
Vanessa Frias-Martinez	Telefonica Research, Spain
Enrique Frias-Martinez	Telefonica Research, Spain
Abigail Gertner	Mitre, USA
Werner Geyer	IBM, USA
Gustavo Gonzalez-Sanchez	Mediapro, Spain
Maxim Gurevich	Yahoo, USA
George Magoulas	Birkbeck University of London, UK
Jalal Mahmud	IBM, USA
Bhaskar Mehta	Google, Switzerland
David Millen	IBM, USA

Doctoral Consortium Reviewers

Liliana Ardissono	Università degli Studi di Torino, Italy
Federica Cena	Università degli Studi di Torino, Italy
Cristina Conati	University of British Columbia, Canada
Darina Dicheva	Winston-Salem State University, USA
Benedict Duboulay	University of Succex, UK
Michael W. Fleming	University of New Brunswick, Canada
Edward Lank	University of Waterloo, Canada
Gordon McCalla	University of Saskatchewan, Canada
Cecile Paris	CSIRO, Australia
Francesco Ricci	Free University of Bozen-Bolzano, Italy
Thomas T. Tran	University of Ottawa, Canada
Julita Vassileva	University of Saskatchewan, Canada
Neil Yorke-Smith	American University of Beirut, Lebanon
Jie Zhang	Nanyang Technological University, Singapore
Ingrid Zukerman	Monash University, Australia

Additional Reviewers

Shaikhah Al Otaibi	University of Saskatchewan, Canada
Michal Barla	Slovak University of Technology in Bratislava, Slovakia
Claudio Biancalana	Università degli Studi di Roma Tre, Italy
Steven Bourke	University College Dublin, Ireland
Matt Dennis	University of Aberdeen, UK
Qi Gao	TU Delf, The Netherlands
Sandra Garcia Esparza	University College Dublin, Ireland
Fabio Gasparetti	Università degli Studi di Roma Tre, Italy

Maurice Hendrix	Coventry University, UK
I-Han Hsiao	University of Pittsburgh, USA
Charles Hélou	Université de Montréal, Canada
Johnson Iyilade	University of Saskatchewan, Canada
Julia Kiseleva	TU Eindhoven, The Netherlands
Bart Knijnenburg	University of California at Irvine, USA
Michal Kompan	Slovak University of Technology in Bratislava, Slovakia
Hitoshi Koshiba	National Institute of Informatics, Japan
Aris Kosmopoulos	IIT NCSR Demokritos, Greece
Tomáš Kramár	Slovak University of Technology in Bratislava, Slovakia
Thomas Largillier	University of Saskatchewan, Canada
Danielle H. Lee	University of Pittsburgh, USA
Eleni Mangina	University College Dublin, Ireland
Kevin Mccarthy	University College Dublin, Ireland
Sabine Moebs	Dublin City University
Rita Orji	University of Saskatchewan, Canada
Zach Pardos	Worcester Polytechnic Institute, USA
Terry Peckham	University of Saskatchewan, Canada
Dimitrios Pierrakos	IIT NCSR Demokritos, Greece
Arthur Pitman	Alpen-Adria University Klagenfurt, Austria
Shaghayegh Sahebi	University of Pittsburgh, USA
Giuseppe Sansonetti	Università degli Studi di Roma Tre, Italy
Natalia Stash	TU Eindhoven, The Netherlands
Ke Tao	TU Delft, The Netherlands
Amit Tiroshi	University of Haifa, Israel
Jozef Tvarozek	Slovak University of Technology in Bratislava, Slovakia
Fabiana Vernero	Università degli studi di Torino, Italy
Dimitrios Vogiatzis	IIT NCSR Demokritos, Greece

Table of Contents

Long Papers

Short Papers

Doctoral Consortium

Personalized Network Updates: Increasing Social Interactions and Contributions in Social Networks

Shlomo Berkovsky[1,2], Jill Freyne[1], and Gregory Smith[1]

[1] CSIRO ICT Centre,
Marsfield, NSW, Australia
firstname.lastname@csiro.au
[2] NICTA,
Alexandria, NSW, Australia
firstname.lastname@nicta.com.au

Abstract. Social networking systems originally emerged as tools for keeping up with the daily lives of friends and strangers. They have established themselves as valuable resources and means to satisfy information needs. The challenge with information seeking through social networks is that their immense success and popularity is also a weakness. The data deluge facing users has surpassed comfortably managed levels and can impact on the quality and relevance of the information consumed. We developed a personalized model for predicting the relevance of news feed items, in order to facilitate personalized feeds. Results of a live analysis show that our approach successfully identifies and promotes relevant feed items, with the knock-on effects of increasing interaction between users and the contribution of user generated content.

1   Introduction

Social media refers to online services and portals that foster user interaction and a sense of community, allowing their users to establish and maintain relationships, share information, and express opinions. Social media evolved into a class of applications that build on the foundations of Web 2.0 and allow the creation and exchange of user-generated content [9]. Among other social media applications, social networking sites (or, in short, social networks – SNs) have gained remarkable popularity, and are fast becoming locations, where content is shared and found. Facebook alone reports more than 800 million active users (more than half of which log on daily), with an average user connected to 80 communities and events, having 130 friends, and using the system for about one hour a day [4].

The volume of content generated by SN users is enormous, and there seems to be no foreseen limits to the growth and diversity of this content. The initial mechanism devised for keeping users abreast of the activities of others is the News or Activity Feed, a reverse chronologically ordered list showing the activities of friends or followees (see two popular examples in Figure 1). The feed typically communicates updates and activities carried out by all of a user's friends and followees in one list. While simple and easy to understand, the feed was not designed to cope with the huge number of friends and followees, or the volume and diversity of content contributed nowadays to SNs, and is crumbling under the pressure being placed upon it.

J. Masthoff et al. (Eds.): UMAP 2012, LNCS 7379, pp. 1–13, 2012.

Fig. 1. Example news feeds: Facebook (left) and Twitter (right)

In response to this growing issue, we investigate in this work the use of personalization algorithms, which are common solutions in other information overload situations, in order to identify the content of news feeds that is most valuable for each user. We extend earlier works [7,14] and exploit the observable activities of SN users to predict the degree of relevance of the feed items for users. We judge the relevance of the feed items using two factors: user-to-user relationship strengths and user-action interest scores. Then, we filter the feed to separating relevant news items from noise.

This paper follows up on earlier work [1] and evaluates the developed feed personalization approach as part of a large-scale live user study of an experimental eHealth portal. We present an extensive analysis of the uptake of the feeds, as well as of user interactions resulting from the feed clicks. The results show that the personalization successfully highlights relevant SN activities, assists users in establishing and maintaining online friendships, and increases contribution of content (wall comments and blog posts). Hence, the pivotal contribution of this work is the thorough investigation of the impact of personalized activity feeds on user behaviour on a SN site, in particular on content contribution and friending.

The rest of this paper is structured as follows. Section 2 surveys related work on personalization of SN feeds. Section 3 provides an overview of the Online TWD Portal. Section 4 presents our feed personalization algorithms. Section 5 presents the experimental evaluation and discusses the obtained results. Finally, Section 6 concludes the paper and outlines our future research directions.

2   Related Work

To facilitate a reorganisation of the news feed, a robust mechanism capable of judging the relevance of the users and actions in each feed item is required [3]. Recently, we have seen works on predictive models that examine the relationships between users and items on SNs, which are ideal for this purpose. Although these works concentrate on the development of the models, they pave the way to the application of these models in personalized algorithms, in order to alleviate the data deluge facing SN users.

Gilbert and Karaholios developed the tie strength model [7], which classified the strength of a relationship between Facebook users as weak or strong based on 74 factors, divided into seven categories: intensity, intimacy, duration, reciprocal service, structure, emotion, and social distance. Paek *et al.* used SVM-based classifiers to elicit a set of most predictive features and then exploited these features to compute the importance of activities included in Facebook news feeds [12]. These works evaluated their predictive models with small cohorts of users and, although the models were accurate in both cases, the factors included in the models were specific to the SN system on which they were generated.

Wu *et al.* developed a model for computing professional, personal, and overall closeness of users of an enterprise SN [14]. 53 observable SN factors were derived and divided into five categories: user factors, subject user factors, direct interaction factors, mutual connection factors, and enterprise factors. Freyne *et al.* developed an approach for recommending SN activities of interest based on long- and short-term models of content viewing and activities performed by users [5]. They simulated feed personalization using offline logs and simulated the events from these logs. Guy *et al.* proposed to consider the content of the activity feeds for profiling users of an enterprise SN [8]. These works judged the strength or closeness of users based on their online behaviour, observed interactions, and content of their feeds. Our work expands the existing models to include activity interest and illustrates a high-value use case of personalized news feeds in a live SN.

3   The Online Total Wellbeing Diet Portal

The evaluation of the proposed feed personalization approach was conducted as part of a large-scale user study of an experimental eHealth portal. The portal aimed to support people embarking of the CSIRO Total Wellbeing Diet (TWD) program [11] and contained dietary information and tools, as well as typical SN functionalities (see Figure 2). The online information mirrored the content of the TWD book and included recipes, exercises, menu plans, shopping lists, and other health links. In addition, the portal included several tools, such as a meal planer and weight tracker, which provided users with real-time feedback on decisions and progress [6].

The goal of the SN was to provide online mutual support for dieters. Each user was represented by a profile page, which contained personal information, an image

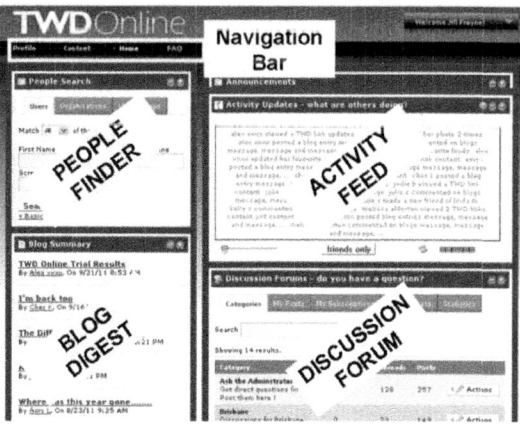

Fig. 2. TWD Online portal

gallery, a personal message board (wall) and a blog. The blogs were free-text diaries, to which the users could contribute as often as they wished. Privacy restrictions of the blogs were set by their owners, but public blogs could be seen by any user. To facilitate community-based information sharing, the portal contained a discussion forum. Here, the users could ask questions, provide support, seek advice, and discuss ideas and thoughts with the community. The forum was monitored by domain experts, who answered health-, exercise-, and nutrition-related questions posted by users.

A key goal of the portal was to support and encourage dieters by exposing them to the thoughts and activities of others on the diet. By highlighting activities, like meal planning, weighing in, browsing recipes and exercises, and reading/writing blogs, we aimed to encourage users to also carry out these activities. By showing the users who carries out the activities, we introduced them to like-minded people on which they can call for support. Similarly, by providing links to blog and forum, we allowed users to provide feedback, support each others, and be inspired to contribute. To this end, it was important to make the activities and contributions of others highly visible. Hence, our portal included an activity feed, which aggregated the interactions of users with the content, tools, and SN (see the interface of the feed in Figure 3).

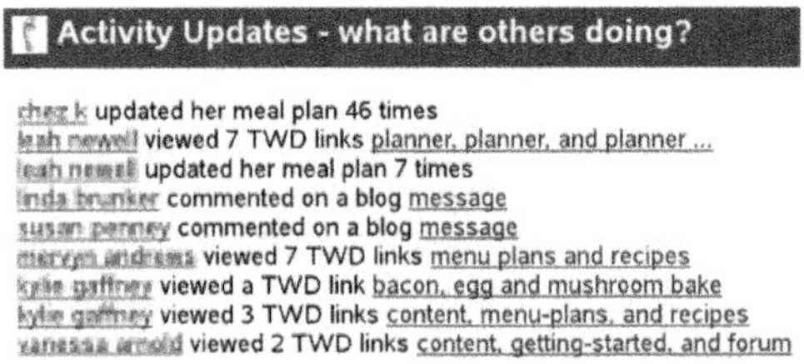

Fig. 3. SN activity feed

4   Personalized News Feeds

The feed presented a target user u_t with a list of activities performed by others. Each item i_x included in the feed references two components: the subject user u_x who performed the activity and the action a_x that was performed, e.g., wall comments, forum posting, or content viewing. When the feed was visualised, both the user name and action were hyperlinked, such that clicks on u_x, i.e., *user clicks*, provided access to the profile page of the user who performed the activity, whereas clicks on a_x, i.e., *action clicks*, led to the content viewed/contributed by the activity.

Our personalization algorithm assigns to each feed item a relevance score $S(u_t, i_x)$, which represents the predicted level of interest that a target user u_t will have in item i_x and is computed as a weighted linear combination of a user-to-user score $S_u(u_t, u_x)$ and a user-action score $S_a(u_t, a_x)$, where w_u and w_a denote the relative weights of the two components as seen in Equation 1:

$$S(u_t, i_x) = w_u S_u(u_t, u_x) + w_a S_a(u_t, a_x) \qquad (1)$$

Following the feed mechanisms applied by the popular SNs (see examples in Figure 1), we presumed that activities of users with which u_t had closer relationships would attract higher interest than activities involving actions of importance to users. Hence, we assigned static weights of $w_u=0.8$ and $w_a=0.2$, which emphasise activities performed by relevant users.

The user-to-user relevance score $S_u(u_t,u_x)$ reflects the closeness of a target user u_t and a subject user u_x, derived solely from their online interactions. To compute this relevance score, we deployed a modified variant of the tie strength model developed in [7], adapted according to the closeness factors proposed in [14]. Some of the original factors of [14] were related to the enterprise environment and were found inapplicable to the TWD Online portal. Hence, we used four categories of factors:

- User factors (UF) – online behaviour and activity of the target user u_t.
- Subject user factors (SUF) – online behaviour and activity of the subject user u_x.
- Direct interaction factors (DIF) – direct interactions between u_t and u_x.
- Mutual connection factors (MCF) – interaction between u_t and $\{u_y\}$ and between u_x and $\{u_y\}$, where $\{u_y\}$ is the set of mutual friends of u_t and u_x.

The user-to-user relevance score $S_u(u_t,u_x)$ was computed as a linear combination of the scores of these four categories of factors:

$$S_u(u_t,u_x)=w_{uf}S_{uf}(u_t,u_x)+w_{suf}S_{suf}(u_t,u_x)+w_{dif}S_{dif}(u_t,u_x)+w_{mcf}S_{mcf}(u_t,u_x) \qquad (2)$$

Since the functionality and the components of the enterprise SN presented in [14] were similar to those offered by the TWD Online portal, we assigned to the scores of these four categories relative weights that are proportional to the original weights derived in [14]: $w_{uf}=0.178$, $w_{suf}=0.079$, $w_{dif}=0.610$, and $w_{mcf}=0.133$.

Category scores $S_{uf}(u_t,u_x)$, $S_{suf}(u_t,u_x)$, $S_{dif}(u_t,u_x)$, and $S_{mcf}(u_t,u_x)$ were computed as a linear combination of the scores of the factors belonging to each category. For the UF and SUF categories, we derived 32 factors that reflect the individual behaviour of u_t and u_x. These include the number of forum/blog/wall posts they initiated/answered/rated, the number of active sessions/days, the number of times they updated/viewed the content/images in their profiles, and others. Also, we derived 28 factors for the DIF and MCF categories that, respectively, reflect the direct interaction between u_t and u_x, and their interaction with the set of their mutual friends $\{u_y\}$, i.e., the users who friended both u_t and u_x. These factors included the number of answers/ratings to each other's forum/blog/wall posts, number of sessions/days they interacted with each other, whether they friended each other, duration of their friendship, and others.

The scores of the factors were computed using the observed frequencies of various user interactions with the TWD Online portal and normalised[1] to the [0,1] range. The scores of the UF and SUF factors were computed in the same manner, but using the frequencies observed for users u_t and u_x, respectively. The scores of the DIF factors were computed using the frequencies of direct interactions between the two users. The scores of the MCF factors were computed[2] by averaging the individual DIF scores computed for the two users u_t and u_x across their mutual friends, i.e., across a set of users $\{u_y\}$, who are online friends of both u_t and u_x. Table 1 presents four factors with the highest weight within each category.

---

[1] The scores of the UF and SUF factors were normalised by dividing the observed frequency of the user by the maximal frequency observed for any other user. The scores of the DIF and MCF factors, which involve multiple users, were normalised using Jaccard's similarity coefficient. Due to space limitations, the details of the normalisation are omitted.

[2] Due to space limitations, the details of this computation are also omitted.

Table 1. User-to-user relevance factors and their weights

UF		SUF		DIF		MCF	
factor	weight	factor	weight	factor	weight	factor	weight
# forum posts added by u_t	0.02031	# forum posts added by u_x	0.00899	has u_t friended u_x	0.07627	has u_t friended $\{u_y\}$	0.01656
# posts in u_t's blog	0.02031	# posts in u_x's blog	0.00899	# days u_t interacted with u_x	0.04576	# days u_t interacted with $\{u_y\}$	0.00994
# u_t's comments in blogs of others	0.01015	# u_x's comments in blogs of others	0.00449	# u_t's posts in u_x's blog	0.03814	# posts in $\{u_y\}$'s blog	0.00828
# images in u_t's profile	0.01015	# images in u_x's profile	0.00449	# mutual friends of u_t and u_x	0.02670	# mutual friends of u_t and $\{u_y\}$	0.00580

In a similar manner, we calculated the user-action interest score $S_a(u_t, a_x)$. This score reflects the importance of action a_x for user u_t and is informed by the frequency of performing the action a_x and the frequencies of performing other actions [2]. The user-action relevance score $S_a(u_t, a_x)$ is calculated as shown in Equation 3, where $f(u_t, a_x)$ is the frequency of user u_t performing a_x, $f(u_t)$ is the average frequency of all actions performed by u_t, $f(a_x)$ is the average frequency of all users performing a_x, and $f()$ is the average frequency of all actions performed by all users.

$$S_a(u_t, a_x) = \frac{f(u_t, a_x)}{f(u_t)} / \frac{f(a_x)}{f()}$$

(3)

This computation quantifies the relative importance of a_x for u_t and normalises it by the relative importance of a_x for all users. The user-action score $S_a(u_t, a_x)$ computed using Equation (3) and the user-to-user score $S_u(u_t, u_x)$ computed using Equation (2) are aggregated into the overall feed item score $S(u_t, i_x)$, as shown by Equation (1). Items having the highest predicted scores were included in the feed.

5   Evaluation

Over 8000 individuals were recruited to participate in a large scale study of the TWD Online portal over a period of 12 weeks in late 2010. The study mainly focused on health-related outcomes, such as weight loss and engagement with the diet. 5279 users participated in the study, but only a portion of these were relevant to the presented analyses, as not all users had access to the activity feeds and not all those who had access interacted with the portal when the personalization became active (after a bootstrapping period of one week). Of those who had access to the feeds, each user was randomly allocated to an experimental group at recruitment time, such that half were exposed to personalized and half to non-personalized feeds. Users in the personalized group were shown personalized feeds, in which the items were scored as described in Section 3, while users in the non-personalized control group were presented with chronologically ordered feeds. By default, the feeds included 20 items (with the highest scores or most recent timestamps), but the users could adjust this parameter.

5.1 Activity Feed Uptake

Overall, the level of user interaction with the news feed was lower than expected, with 137 users generating 530 feed clicks over the course of the study[3]. Table 2 summarises the number of users who interacted with the feed, i.e., clicked on feed items, the number of sessions that included feed clicks, the overall number of logged clicks and their breakdown into user clicks (on the user name) and action clicks (on the action that was carried out), and the user- and session-based click through rates, CTR_u and CTR_s [13], computed as the ratio between the overall number of clicks and the number of users and sessions, respectively, as observed for both groups.

Table 2. Feed uptake

	users	sessions	clicks$_u$	clicks$_a$	clicks	CTR_u	CTR_s
personalized	64	125	159	87	246	3.844	1.968
non-personalized	73	159	155	129	284	3.890	1.786

We note that users interacted more with the non-personalized feeds (both the number of users and overall numbers of clicks), but the observed CTR_u was comparable. However, the personalized feeds appear to provide more relevant information, as communicated by their higher session-based CTR_s. Note that the percentage of user clicks in the personalized feeds was 64.6%, in comparison 54.6% in the non-personalized feeds. That is, users in the personalized group were more interested in the subject users who performed the activities than users in the non-personalized group. This can be explained by the weighting mechanism of Equation (1), which assigned 80% of the overall weight to $S_u(u_t,u_x)$ and only 20% to $S_a(u_t,a_x)$. Thus, activities of users with high user-to-user score dominated over activities with high user-action score, and this was reflected by the higher percentage of user clicks.

We compared the average number of feed clicks per session with clicks for each group. Table 3 shows the percentage of sessions, in which N (from 2 to 12) feed clicks or more occurred. For example, in 42.4% of sessions where personalized feeds were presented and at least one feed click was logged, two or more feeds clicks were recorded, while for the non-personalized feeds two or more clicks were recorded in 37.1% of sessions. The percentage of sessions with multiple clicks in the personalized group was consistently higher than those observed in the non-personalized group, although no statistically significant difference was detected[4]. Overall, the higher CTR_s and rate of sessions with multiple clicks show that the personalized feeds attracted more user attention and, thus, deemed more relevant than the non-personalized feeds.

---

[3] A small portion of clicks were omitted from the analyses due to technical issues that resulted in unreliable user logs.

[4] All statistical significance results refer to a two tailed t-test assuming equal distribution.

Table 3. Multiple feed clicks in a session

N – number of clicks	2	3	4	5	6	7	8	9	10	11	12
personalized [%]	42.4	20.0	15.2	12.8	8.0	7.2	5.6	5.6	4.0	4.0	1.6
non-personalized [%]	37.1	17.6	9.4	7.6	6.3	4.4	3.1	1.8	1.2	1.2	1.2

5.2   Feed Ranking

The motivation for personalizing activity feeds was to assist users in finding relevant information by re-ranking the feed and promoting items in which they are likely to be interested. Hence, we compared the distribution of the clicked items across the two feeds, to verify whether the personalization affected the positioning of user clicks within the feeds [13]. The average rank of the clicked items in the personalized feeds was 4.00 in comparison to 4.46 (smaller numbers indicate higher rank) in the non-personalized feeds, and the difference was statistically significant, $p<.05$, illustrating the influence of personalization in promoting relevant feed items. We computed the average rank of the clicked items, as observed for weeks 2 to 9 (week 1 was bootstrapping and weeks 10-12 did not attract sufficient clicks). As can be seen in Figure 4, the personalized feeds consistently outperformed the non-personalized ones and presented relevant items closer to the top of the feed. The difference between the two groups was statistically significant, $p<.05$.

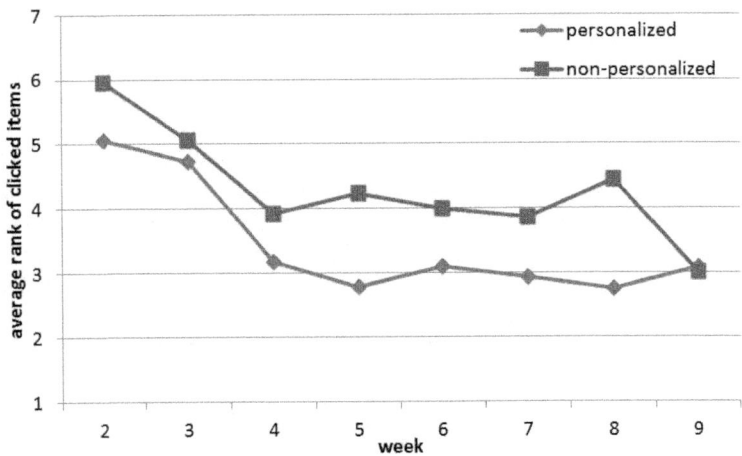

Fig. 4. Average rank of the clicked items over time

We also assessed the impact of personalization on the distribution of feed clicks. Figure 5 details the percentage of clicks observed for positions 1 to 10 in the feed for both groups. In the non-personalized feeds, a comparable distribution of 10-15% across the top seven positions was observed. Thus, users showed a similar level of interest in a large group of items, rather than only in the top-ranked most recent items. In the personalized feeds, we note a preference for items in the top position,

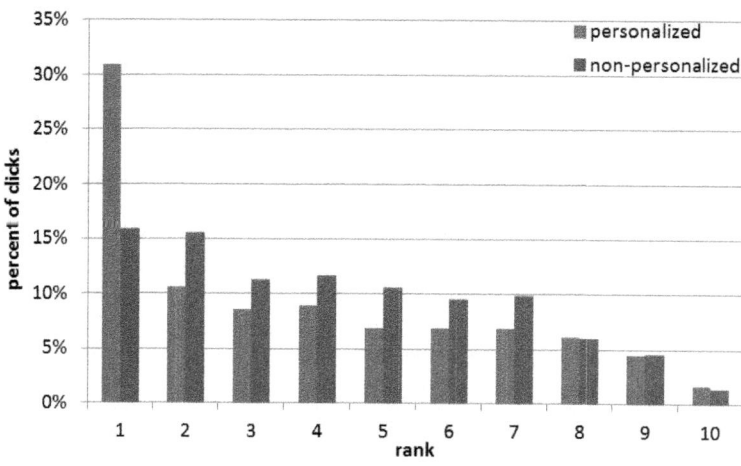

Fig. 5. Rank of the clicked items

which attracted 30.9% of clicks – double that of the top position in the non-personalized feeds. The observed click patterns clearly show that users found the personalized top items to be more relevant than the non-personalized ones. Hence, the personalization successfully promoted relevant items and making relevant information easier to find.

5.3   Impact on User Activities

Another aim of the activity feed was to highlight activities of others, in order to spark social relationships and social learning. To understand the extent to which this was achieved, we examined the activities carried out by users in the sessions where they interacted with the activity feed. Focusing on the social interactions sparked by the feed, we examined the number of blog and forum activities, profile views, wall postings, and the overall session length observed in each session that included feed clicks. In addition, we split the blog and forum activities into contribution activities (posting, responding) and consumption activities (viewing), as shown in Table 4.

Table 4. Sessions with feed clicks

	blog	bl-cont	bl-cons	forum	f-cont	f-cons	profile	wall	session
personalized	10.35	5.54	4.81	5.58	1.00	4.58	7.35	0.71	48.19
non-personalized	9.77	3.92	5.84	5.04	0.28	4.76	4.16	0.31	45.12

The personalization increased (although not significantly) the overall session length from 45.12 to 48.19 activities. This was reflected by more blog, forum, profile viewing, and wall posting activities. Out of all these, the profile viewing and wall posting were statistically significant, both $p<.01$. It must be noted that these two activities were not independent, as the wall is located on a user's profile page, such that all wall postings are preceded by a profile view. That said, less than 10% of profile views resulted in wall posts, showing that users view profiles not only when they intend to write wall messages. Furthermore, significant increases in the contribution to blogs and forums were made by users viewing personalized feeds, when compared to non-personalized feeds. Thus, personalization sparked social interactions with other users and encouraged contribution of content to blogs and forums, as intended.

Refining this analysis and concentrating on activities immediately following the feed clicks, Table 5 summarizes the average number of SN-related activities recorded within five user activities following a feed click[5]. We note similar trends: higher levels of blog and forum contributions, profile views, and wall posts within the immediate activities following clicks. The most frequent activity to follow a click was profile viewing. Note that in this case, the majority of forum and blog activities were consumption rather than contribution. This is in line with prior research, which showed that consumption of user-generated content normally exceeds contribution [10].

Table 5. Five activities following feed clicks

	blog	bl-cont	bl-cons	forum	f-cont	f-cons	profile	wall
personalized	0.760	0.187	0.573	0.407	0.041	0.366	1.825	0.037
non-personalized	0.630	0.095	0.535	0.394	0.007	0.387	1.429	0.018

Overall, the personalization of activity feeds had a prolific impact on activities carried out on the TWD Online portal. It increased the volume of traffic to the user profiles, social interactions through message walls, and contribution of user-generated content to blogs and forum. Thus, personalization played an important role in the sustainment of the social features of the portal. The contribution of user-generated content is pivotal for the sustainability of any SN, as it invites users to return for further interactions with the portal and increases user engagement. Likewise, it is important in facilitating social support for users embarking on the diet, which, from the health perspective, was the primary goal of the TWD Online portal.

5.4   Feeds and Friending

The developed relevance scoring mechanism inherently presumes that users are more interested in the information pertaining to the actions of their articulated group of online friends in preference to information relating to other portal users. To this end, we examined the links between online relationships and feed clicks. It should be noted that the TWD Online portal is not a typical friendship-based SN reflecting offline friendships; very few users were familiar with other participants prior to the study.

Of the 246 clicks logged in the personalized feeds, in 79 cases (or 32.1%) the target and subject user established an online friendship over the course of the study. In the non-personalized feeds, this happened in 78 cases out of the 284 logged clicks (or 27.4%). Thus, the ratio of clicks on items representing activities of friends in the personalized feeds was higher than in the non-personalized feeds. We hypothesise that

---

[5] Feed clicks themselves were excluded and only five activities after the click were analysed. The sum of each row is less than 5, as health- and content-related activities were excluded.

the effect of the personalized ordering of feeds brought the actions of friends to the attention of users by promoting them to the top of the activity feeds.

This finding brings to the fore the issue pertaining to the 'personalization bubble'. In other words, does the personalization and its inherent focus on promoting the actions of those a user is close to limit the user's awareness of activities of other SN users? To answer this question, we measured the ratio of feed items involving activities of friends. Note that this ratio refers to the entire feed presented to a user rather than to clicked items only, which were addressed in previous analysis. Overall, the ratio of friend activities in the feeds increased over time in both groups. This is explained by the observed user attrition and skewed distribution of the established friendships. The attrition of users was stable over the course of the study: from week 2 onwards, about 20% of users who interacted with the portal in any given week, never returned to the portal in the following weeks. On the contrary, close to half of all the observed friendships were established in the first week only and the friending rate steadily declined afterwards. Thus, the density of the friendship network increased over time, as well as the percentage of feed items including activities performed by friends.

Figure 6 details the percentage of feed items involving activities of friends, as observed for weeks 2 to 9 for both groups. In the non-personalized feeds, the ratio between the number of friend and non-friend activities increased steadily from 3.1% in week 2 to 25% in week 9. However, in the personalized feeds this ratio did not increase and hovered around the 20% mark until week 6. Hence, the feeds still included closely to 80% of activities performed by non-friends and did not severely limit the user's awareness of activities of others. Afterwards, the friendship network became dense and the percentage of friend activities in the personalized feeds increased.

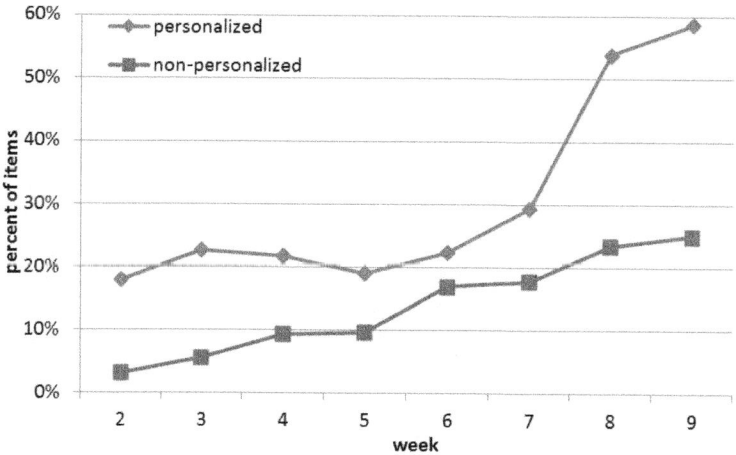

Fig. 6. Ratio of friend activities in the feeds over time

6   Conclusions and Future Work

This work was motivated by the aggravating information overload problem in SNs, which is only exacerbated by the simplistic nature of network news feeds. We developed a personalized model for predicting the relevance of news feed items to an individual and applied this model to produce personalized news feeds to participants of a live study of an online diet portal. This paper discusses the observed impact of the personalization on user interactions with the portal and other participants.

The results show that the uptake of the personalized feeds was higher than of the non-personalized ones, which had a prolific impact on the sustainability of the SN. Firstly, the personalized feeds appears to promote items of higher relevance within the news feeds, assisting the users in the identification of relevant activities. Secondly, it was found that the personalized feeds increased the contribution of user-generated content to the forum, blogs, and walls. This was observed both for immediate activities following the feed clicks and for the entire duration of the sessions. Thirdly, the personalized feeds highlighted the activities performed by online friends, while not limiting user awareness of activities of other SN users.

In the future, we plan to revise the scoring model and investigate the appropriateness of its adaptation to the domain and application in hand. We also plan to ascertain the accuracy of the user-action scoring, as it was not based on extensive prior research. We intend to extensively evaluate these in a large-scale live user study.

Acknowledgment. This research is jointly funded by the Australian Government through the Intelligent Island Program and CSIRO. The authors thank Stephen Kimani, Nilufar Baghaei, Emily Brindal, and Mac Coombe for their contributions to this work.

References

1. Berkovsky, S., Freyne, J., Kimani, S., Smith, G.: Selecting Items of Relevance in Social Network Feeds. In: Konstan, J.A., Conejo, R., Marzo, J.L., Oliver, N. (eds.) UMAP 2011. LNCS, vol. 6787, pp. 329–334. Springer, Heidelberg (2011)
2. Bohnert, F., Zukerman, I., Berkovsky, S., Baldwin, T., Sonenberg, L.: Using Collaborative Models to Adaptively Predict Visitor Locations in Museums. In: Nejdl, W., Kay, J., Pu, P., Herder, E. (eds.) AH 2008. LNCS, vol. 5149, pp. 42–51. Springer, Heidelberg (2008)
3. De Choudhury, M., Counts, S., Czerwinski, M.: Identifying Relevant Social Media Content: Leveraging Information Diversity and User Conginition. In: Proceedings of HT, Eindhoven (2011)
4. Facebook Statistics, http://www.facebook.com/press/info.php?statistics (accessed December 2011)
5. Freyne, J., Berkovsky, S., Daly, E.M., Geyer, W.: Social Networking Feeds: Recommending Items of Interest. In: Proceedings of RecSys, Barcelona (2010)
6. Freyne, J., Berkovsky, S., Baghaei, N., Kimani, S., Smith, G.: Personalized Techniques for Lifestyle Change. In: Peleg, M., Lavrač, N., Combi, C. (eds.) AIME 2011. LNCS, vol. 6747, pp. 139–148. Springer, Heidelberg (2011)

7. Gilbert, E., Karahalios, K.: Predicting Tie Strength with Social Media. In: Proceedings of CHI, Boston (2009)
8. Guy, I., Ronen, I., Raviv, A.: Personalized Activity Streams: Sifting through the "River of News". In: Proceedings of RecSys, Chicago (2011)
9. Kaplan, A.M., Haenlein, M.: Users of the World, Unite! The Challenges and Opportunities of Social Media. Business Horizons 53(1), 59–68 (2010)
10. Muller, M.J., Freyne, J., Dugan, C., Millen, D.R., Thom-Santelli, J.: Return On Contribution (ROC): A Metric for Enterprise Social Software. In: Proceedings of ECSCW, Vienna (2009)
11. Noakes, M., Clifton, P.: The CSIRO Total Wellbeing Diet. Penguin Publ. (2005)
12. Paek, T., Gamon, M., Counts, S., Chickering, D.M., Dhesi, A.: Predicting the Importance of Newsfeed Posts and Social Network Friends. In: Proceedings of AAAI, Atlanta (2010)
13. Shani, G., Gunawardana, A.: Evaluating Recommendation Systems. In: Ricci, F., Rokach, L., Shapira, B., Kantor, P.B. (eds.) Recommender Systems Handbook. Springer (2011)
14. Wu, A., DiMicco, J.M., Millen, D.R.: Detecting Professional versus Personal Closeness using an Enterprise Social Network Site. In: Proceedings of CHI, Atlanta (2010)

Realistic Simulation of Museum Visitors' Movements as a Tool for Assessing Sensor-Based User Models

Fabian Bohnert, Ingrid Zukerman, and David W. Albrecht

Faculty of Information Technology,
Monash University, Clayton, VIC 3800, Australia
{Fabian.Bohnert,Ingrid.Zukerman,David.Albrecht}@monash.edu

Abstract. We present a realistic simulation framework to examine the impact of sensor noise on the performance of user models in the museum domain. Our contributions are (1) models to simulate noisy visit trajectories as time-stamped sequences of (x, y) positional coordinates which reflect *walking* and *hovering* behaviour; (2) a discriminative inference model that distinguishes between hovering and walking on the basis of (simulated) noisy sensor observations; (3) a model that infers viewed exhibits from hovering coordinates; and (4) a model that predicts the next exhibit on the basis of inferred (rather than known) viewed exhibits. Our staged evaluation assesses the effect of these models (in combination with sensor noise) on inferential and predictive performance, thus shedding light on the reliability attributed to inferences drawn from sensor observations.

1 Introduction

Recent advances in sensor technology and mobile computing [7,8] have fostered increased interest in the construction of user models from sensor-based data [11]. When applied to the museum domain, the introduction of sensors enables unobtrusive visitor tracking, but it poses modeling challenges, as the viewed exhibits are not known with certainty. In fact, the best we can hope for is a time-stamped trajectory of (x, y) coordinates (sampled at a particular rate), which may diverge from the true positions of the visitor by some sensor error. A likely sequence of exhibits must then be inferred from the sensor observations. In this paper, we offer a *realistic* simulation framework that enables the assessment of the impact of sensor-based data on user models. We focus on the inference of viewed exhibits (required for streaming information), and the prediction of exhibits to be viewed (required for making recommendations).

In previous research, we offered a preliminary simulation framework which focused on the impact of different sensing technologies on the performance of user models [12]. However, that work made strong simplifying assumptions that affected the realism of the framework, and hence the significance of its results, viz (1) sensors can detect, with some error, a *single* square (in a grid representation of the museum space) where a visitor is *statically positioned* while viewing an exhibit i_k; and (2) the previously viewed exhibits $i_1, \ldots, i_{k-1}$ are *known* when predicting the next exhibit i_{k+1}. However, in reality, people do not 'teleport' between squares on the floor, and tend not to remain stationary at an exhibit. Rather, they *walk* between exhibits, and often *hover* around an exhibit to view it from different perspectives. Further, the previously viewed exhibits are often not known with certainty – there are only observations of previous (noisy) coordinates.

J. Masthoff et al. (Eds.): UMAP 2012, LNCS 7379, pp. 14–25, 2012.

In this paper, we eschew the above assumptions, and significantly extend our previous work by offering: (1) models that simulate noisy visit trajectories as time-stamped sequences of (x, y) coordinates which reflect *walking* and *hovering* behaviour; (2) a discriminative inference model that distinguishes between walking and hovering on the basis of noisy sensor observations; (3) a model that infers likely viewed exhibits from time-stamped sequences of hovering coordinates (instead of a single static grid square per exhibit); and (4) a model that predicts the next exhibit on the basis of these inferred (rather than known) viewed exhibits. In addition, we present the results of a *staged* evaluation which examines the effect of the above models, in combination with sensor noise, on inferential and predictive performance.

This paper is organised as follows. Section 2 discusses related research, and Sect. 3 summarises our previous simulation framework. Our simulation of coordinate-based visit trajectories appears in Sect. 4, and our inference and prediction models in Sect. 5. Section 6 presents the results of our evaluation, and Sect. 7 offers concluding remarks.

2   Related Research

Many research projects have studied the development of user models for visitors of physical spaces, in particular museums, e.g., [1,10,14]. In this section, we focus on projects that incorporate wireless technology or sensor networks. The *GUIDE* project [4] developed a hand-held tourist guide for visitors to the city of Lancaster, UK. It employed user models obtained from explicit user input to generate dynamic and user-adapted city tours. The project used wireless access points to stream content data to a visitor's device, but did not employ the wireless network to localise the user. Both the *PEACH* project [13] and the augmented audio reality system for museums *ec(h)o* [6] consulted their user models to generate personalised presentations for museum visitors, and adapted their models on the basis of implicit observations of a visitor's interactions with a mobile device. Additionally, although both systems employed localisation technology, only *ec(h)o* used the information obtained from sensors to adapt its user model, while *PEACH* employed explicit user feedback. However, *ec(h)o* did not investigate the effect of localisation accuracy on the quality of the resultant user model.

In contrast to the above research, this paper investigates the impact of using sensing technology as a means for acquiring a user model. It significantly extends the work of Schmidt *et al.* [12] by refining the modeled user behaviours, and presents additional detail and results to those published in [2].

3   Prerequisites

This section summarises four key components of the simulation framework introduced by Schmidt *et al.* [12]: (1) *Transition Model*, (2) *Spatial Exhibit Viewing Model*, (3) generation of exhibit tours, and (4) generation of exhibit squares.

A *frequency-based Transition Model*, implemented as a 1-stage Markov model, represents visitors' movements between exhibits. $\Pr_{i,j}$, the transition probability from exhibit i to j, is estimated from frequency counts of observed transitions.

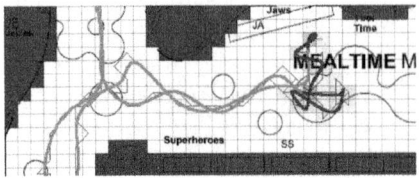 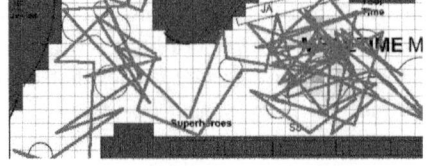

(a) Smooth representation (ground truth)   (b) Noisy representation ($\nu = 2$ metres)

Fig. 1. Two representations of a simulated visitor pathway

A *probabilistic grid-based Spatial Exhibit Viewing Model* divides the museum space into a grid of squares (for the Marine Life Exhibition, the grid size is $47 \times 61 = 2,867$ squares, where a square is approximately $30\,cm \times 30\,cm$; Fig. 1). This model specifies a discrete viewing probability distribution $\Pr(i\,|\,x,y)$, which represents the probability of a visitor viewing an exhibit i from a square at position (x,y). The probabilities are derived from frequency counts of observed viewing events.

A *tour of viewed exhibits* comprises a sequence of tuples $\langle i_k, T_{i_k} \rangle$, where i_k is an exhibit identifier ($k = 1, 2, \ldots$), and T_{i_k} is the time spent at exhibit i_k. The tour is iteratively generated by sampling each consecutive exhibit from a categorical distribution specified by the transition probabilities. Each viewing time T_{i_k} is generated by randomly drawing from an exponential distribution, i.e., $T_{i_k} \sim \mathrm{Exp}(\lambda_{i_k})$, where the average viewing time λ_{i_k} at exhibit i_k is estimated from observed tours.

Once a tour of exhibits has been simulated, Schmidt *et al.* [12] generate a *single viewing square* at position (x,y) for each viewed exhibit i_k in the tour. This is done by sampling from the categorical distribution $\Pr(x,y\,|\,i_k)$ over all exhibit squares ($\Pr(x,y\,|\,i_k)$ is derived by applying Bayes' theorem to the probabilities obtained from the Spatial Exhibit Viewing Model). In this work, we use Schmidt *et al.*'s approach to generate the *first* hovering square for each viewed exhibit (Sect. 4.2), which provides the skeleton for simulating coordinate-based visit trajectories as discussed below.

4   Simulation of Coordinate-Based Visitor Pathways

In this section, we refine the one-square-per-exhibit tour generated in the previous section by simulating (smooth and noisy) coordinate-based visit trajectories which encapsulate two types of behaviour: *walking* between exhibits, and *hovering* at exhibits. Our approach comprises the following four steps: (1) generation of natural connected paths of *walking* squares between exhibits (Sect. 4.1); (2) generation of natural connected paths of *hovering* squares to simulate viewing behaviour at exhibits (Sect. 4.2); (3) smoothing of the obtained square trajectory (Sect. 4.3); and (4) simulation of noisy sensor observations from this smooth pathway representation (Sect. 4.4).

Figure 1 depicts two representations of a simulated visit trajectory. Figure 1(a) shows the trajectory obtained after simulation (walking is represented by a red/grey line, hovering by a blue/dark-grey line on pink/shaded squares, and wall squares are coloured in blue/dark-grey; Sects. 4.1 to 4.3), and Fig. 1(b) shows the representation obtained after applying Gaussian sensor noise of $\nu = 2$ metres (Sect. 4.4).

4.1 Generating Walking Squares

To produce a realistic trajectory for a visitor, we build a path that links Schmidt *et al.*'s "viewing" squares [12] of two consecutive exhibits. The natural walking patterns of museum visitors are simulated by incorporating stochastic effects into the shortest path between two exhibits. Specifically, we model the probability of moving into a square as being proportional to the (smoothed) probability of viewing the destination exhibit from this square, moderated by the visitor's propensity to avoid walls and to meander, which is controlled through parameters (Eqn. 1). The generation of a sequence of walking squares between two exhibits in a tour is implemented as follows.

Let (x_s, y_s) denote the end square of the previous exhibit (i.e., the *source square*), and (x_d, y_d) the starting square of the current exhibit i (i.e., the *destination square*). We start by employing Dijkstra's algorithm [5] to generate a distance matrix $\mathbf{D}$ whose elements $D_{x,y}$ correspond to the shortest-path distances from each square (x, y) of the museum space to the destination square (x_d, y_d).

We now place the visitor at the source square (x_s, y_s). Treating diagonal squares as adjacent, a visitor may move into one of eight surrounding squares, i.e., the squares $(x_s + \delta x_j, y_s + \delta y_j)$, $j = 1, \ldots, 8$, where

$$\delta \boldsymbol{x} = (-1, -1, -1, \quad 0, \quad 0, \quad 1, \quad 1, \quad 1)$$
$$\delta \boldsymbol{y} = (-1, \quad 0, \quad 1, -1, \quad 1, -1, \quad 0, \quad 1)$$

Each next square (x_{n+1}, y_{n+1}) that a visitor moves into while walking is randomly sampled from among the eight candidate squares $(x_n + \delta x_j, y_n + \delta y_j)$, provided that the move does not take the visitor further away from (x_d, y_d), i.e., for $j = 1, \ldots, 8$,

$$\Pr(x_{n+1} = x_n + \delta x_j, y_{n+1} = y_n + \delta y_j) \propto \begin{cases} e^{\phi_1 w_j} (p_j + \varepsilon) & \text{for } d_j < D_{x_n, y_n} \\ e^{\phi_1 w_j} (p_j + \varepsilon)/\phi_2 & \text{for } d_j = D_{x_n, y_n} \\ 0 & \text{for } d_j > D_{x_n, y_n} \end{cases} \quad (1)$$

where

- $\phi_1 > 0$ and $\phi_2 > 0$ control the trajectory of the visitor (in our experiments, we use $\phi_1 = 8$ and $\phi_2 = 4$):[1] ϕ_1 controls the visitor's aversion to walk near walls — the larger ϕ_1, the less likely the visitor is to move into a square that is close to a wall; and ϕ_2 controls the erraticness of a visitor's path — the smaller ϕ_2, the more likely the visitor is to move to a square that is equidistant from (x_d, y_d).
- w_j denotes the distance (in squares) from a candidate square to the nearest wall,
- $d_j = D_{x_n + \delta x_j, y_n + \delta y_j}$ is the distance between a candidate square and the destination square (x_d, y_d) (obtained from $\mathbf{D}$),
- D_{x_n, y_n} is the distance between the square currently occupied by the visitor and (x_d, y_d) (obtained from $\mathbf{D}$),
- $p_j = \Pr(x_n + \delta x_j, y_n + \delta y_j \,|\, i)$ for $j = 1, \ldots, 8$ is the probability that a visitor is standing in square $(x_n + \delta x_j, y_n + \delta y_j)$ when viewing exhibit i (Sect. 3), and
- ε is a small smoothing constant.

---

[1] An alternative to using fixed parameters is to sample them for each trajectory simulation. Also, certain parameter values in combination with different transition models may yield the different types of museum visitors reported in [15] *inter alia*.

The visitor moves in this fashion until s/he reaches (x_d, y_d). At that point, the trajectory between (x_s, y_s) and (x_d, y_d) is complete, and time stamps are iteratively added as follows (for $n = s, \ldots, d - 1$):

$$t_{n+1} = t_n + \frac{1}{v_w} \sqrt{(x_{n+1} - x_n)^2 + (y_{n+1} - y_n)^2} \qquad (2)$$

where v_w is the visitor's walking speed (we assume a constant walking speed).

4.2   Generating Hovering Squares

When observing an exhibit, visitors typically move around to examine the exhibit from different perspectives. We simulate this *hovering* behaviour by varying the movement model defined in Eqn. 1 so that a visitor is more likely to move towards a square from which an exhibit is easier to observe, but may not move at all. To this effect, we redefine δx and δy by including the current square as a candidate square at index $j = 5$:

$$\delta x = (-1, -1, -1, \quad 0, \quad 0, \quad 0, \quad 1, \quad 1, \quad 1)$$
$$\delta y = (-1, \quad 0, \quad 1, -1, \quad 0, \quad 1, -1, \quad 0, \quad 1)$$

The probability of moving to square $(x_n + \delta x_j, y_n + \delta y_j)$ is then given by

$$\Pr(x_{n+1} = x_n + \delta x_j, y_{n+1} = y_n + \delta y_j) \propto \begin{cases} p_j + \varepsilon & \text{for } j = 5 \\ (p_j + \varepsilon)/\phi_3 & \text{for } j \neq 5 \end{cases}$$

where $p_j = \Pr(x_n + \delta x_j, y_n + \delta y_j \,|\, i)$, ε is a small smoothing constant, and $\phi_3 > 0$ controls a visitor's tendency to move (smaller ϕ_3s yield higher mobility; we use $\phi_3 = 2$).

Time stamps are added to the generated hovering squares by using Eqn. 2, while assuming a hovering speed of $v_h < v_w$ (as for the walking case, we assume a constant hovering speed). If the visitor hovers in place (i.e., $x_{n+1} = x_n$ and $y_{n+1} = y_n$), we assume a hovering distance of one square. The hovering behaviour continues until the sampled viewing time T_i (Sect. 3) for the current exhibit i is exceeded.

4.3   Smoothing the Trajectory of Squares

Alternately generating walking squares (Sect. 4.1) and hovering squares (Sect. 4.2) yields a time-stamped trajectory of squares $(\langle t_n, x_n, y_n \rangle; n = 1, 2, \ldots)$ for a visitor's tour. To obtain a smooth positional pathway from such a trajectory, we fit piecewise cubic splines to the coordinate-individual trajectories $\langle t_n, x_n \rangle$ and $\langle t_n, y_n \rangle$ (one piecewise cubic spline each). This approach uses the method of least squares to fit splines with reduced degrees of freedom,[2] generating a smooth representation of the trajectory (i.e., (x, y), $(\dot{x}, \dot{y})$ and $(\ddot{x}, \ddot{y})$ are continuous in time). The resultant continuous representation of the visit trajectory enables us to obtain a visitor's position at any point in time (Fig. 1(a) depicts one such smooth visit trajectory).

---

[2] We use spline fitting rather than spline interpolation, as fitting yields 70% less spline pieces than interpolation, and interpolation may produce trajectories with unnatural oscillations.

4.4 Simulating Sensor Noise

The final step of our simulation consists of generating the output of sensors that track the smooth and continuous visitor path produced so far. We explore sensor noise that may be attributed to *range-based positioning technology*, e. g., WiFi and ultra-wide band (UWB) [7]. We follow a widely accepted model for sensor noise which assumes that the *measured* coordinates (x', y') are obtained by distorting the true coordinates (x, y) through Gaussian noise and sampling at regular time intervals (for our experiments, we use a sampling rate of 1 second). Specifically, the measured coordinates are generated by sampling from a bivariate normal distribution $N((x, y), \sigma^2 I)$ with mean (x, y) and covariance $\sigma^2 I$, where σ is a constant that reflects the expected accuracy of the sensors, and I is the identity matrix. For example, if the sensors have an accuracy of ν metres 95% of the time, then setting $\sigma = \nu/2$ places approximately 95% of the probability mass of the normal distribution within the circle defined by $(x' - x)^2 + (y' - y)^2 = \nu^2$. Figure 1(b) depicts a noisy visit trajectory sampled by following this procedure for the pathway in Fig. 1(a) at a sampling rate of 1 second with $\nu = 2$ metres.

5   Inference and Prediction of Viewed Exhibits from Coordinates

The sensors that track a visitor's movements yield a sequence of (typically noisy) time-stamped (x, y) coordinates (Sect. 4.4).[3] In order to model this visitor's actions (and interests), we must first detect when a visitor is hovering (and hence viewing an exhibit), i. e., we must identify sub-sequences of (x, y) hovering coordinates (Sect. 5.1). From these sub-sequences, we can infer which exhibit the visitor is viewing (Sect. 5.2), and in turn predict which exhibit the visitor is likely to view next (Sect. 5.3).

5.1 Classification-Based Inference of Walking and Hovering

To infer walking and hovering behaviour from positional (x, y) coordinates, we employ a classifier which receives as input $2\omega + 7$ features from a window comprising the previous ω sensor observations. These features are: $\omega - 1$ velocities, minimum and maximum velocity, mean and median velocity, standard deviation of the velocities, $\omega - 2$ accelerations, minimum and maximum acceleration, mean and median acceleration, and standard deviation of the accelerations.[4] Prior to deriving these features, we smooth the noisy sensor observations $\langle t, x, y \rangle$ by fitting piecewise cubic splines to the $\langle t, x \rangle$ and $\langle t, y \rangle$ trajectories, and sampling from these splines at the original time stamps (similarly to Sect. 4.3, but here we fit the splines to the coordinates returned by sensors).

In our experiments (Sect. 6), we use support vector machines (SVM) to train the classifier. We employ C-SVC SVMs with an RBF kernel from LIBSVM [3], using features derived from the previous five observations ($\omega = 5$).

---

[3] To simplify notation, we henceforth denote measured coordinates by (x, y) instead of (x', y').

[4] It is worth noting that the input velocities are variable as a result of the smoothing of the square trajectories (Sect. 4.3) and the sampling of noisy (x, y) trajectories (Sect. 4.4).

5.2 Score-Based Inference of Exhibits

After inferring a visitor's activity (walking or hovering) for each sensor observation $\langle t, x, y \rangle$, we first extract from the complete (x, y) sequence all sub-sequences of (x, y) coordinates classified as "hovering". For each hovering sub-sequence, we then calculate a probability distribution which specifies how likely a visitor is to view each exhibit. To this effect, we first compute the score for each exhibit as follows:

$$\text{score}(i) = \prod_{(x,y)} \Pr(i \mid x, y) \quad \text{for all exhibits } i \qquad (3)$$

where $\Pr(i \mid x, y)$ is the probability of a visitor viewing exhibit i while hovering within the square at (x, y) (Sect. 3). To smooth out possible errors introduced in the classification step, we delete walking labels that separate two consecutive hovering sub-sequences for which the same exhibit has the highest score, and remove hovering sub-sequences of length 1. The exhibit scores for any affected sub-sequences of hovering labels are then recomputed, and all scores are normalised to obtain probabilities.

5.3 Model-Based Prediction of Exhibits

The (inferred) viewed exhibits can now be used to predict $\Pr_{\text{next}}(i \mid x, y)$, the probability of viewing exhibit i next for each (x, y) position at which the visitor is hovering.[5] However, as seen in the previous section, there is some uncertainty regarding which exhibit the visitor is actually viewing. To address this problem, we use the *Weighted* approach [12] to predict the next exhibit from positional information:[6]

$$\widehat{\Pr}_{\text{next}}(i \mid x, y) = \sum_{j=1}^{M} \left\{ \Pr(j \mid x, y) \times \Pr_{j,i} \right\}$$

where $\Pr_{j,i}$ is the transition probability from exhibit j to exhibit i, which is weighted by $\Pr(j \mid x, y)$, the probability that the user is viewing exhibit j when standing within the square at position (x, y) (Sect. 3).

6   Evaluation

Our dataset of exhibit tours (also used in [12]) was obtained at the Marine Life Exhibition of Melbourne Museum (Melbourne, Australia). It consists of a (manually collected) record of the exhibits viewed by 44 visitors, and the viewing times at the exhibits. On average, each visitor viewed 7.2 of the $M = 22$ exhibits. The data for the Spatial Exhibit Viewing Model described in Sect. 3 were obtained separately by manually annotating a grid-based map to record the positions of visitors to the exhibition. These datasets were employed by the method described in Sect. 4 to generate 1000 simulated visits,

---

[5] Predictions of a visitor's next exhibits may be combined with inferences about the user's interests to recommend exhibits that may be overlooked if the predicted next exhibits are visited.

[6] According to Schmidt *et al.* [12], this approach yields better predictions than using *Argmax*.

Table 1. Our models and their experimental conditions

Models	Time & (x, y)	Walk/Hover	Exhibits Previous	Current
TL_{all}	sequence of $\langle t, x, y\rangle$	Inferred	Inferred	Inferred
TLA_{all}	sequence of $\langle t, x, y\rangle$	Given	Inferred	Inferred
$\mathrm{Exh}_{prev}\mathrm{TLA}_{curr}$	sequence of $\langle t, x, y\rangle$	Given	Given	Inferred
Schmidt *et al.*	one $\langle x, y\rangle$ *per exhibit*	*N/A*	*Given*	*Inferred*
Exh_{all}	sequence of $\langle t, x, y\rangle$	Given	Given	Given

where each visit comprises time-stamped sequences of (typically noisy) (x, y) coordinates. When generating the visits, we assumed a walking speed of $v_w = 3$ km/h and a hovering speed of $v_h = 1$ km/h.

Current range-based positioning systems are often based on processing radio signals, e. g., WiFi and ultra-wide band (UWB). The accuracy of WiFi-based technology is typically between 2-3.5 metres [8], while that of UWB-based systems is expected to be between 0-0.15 metres [7]. We therefore considered accuracy levels of $\nu = 0$ to 4.5 metres for the sensors. Our sampling rate was one observation per second.

6.1 Experiments and Results

To evaluate our models, we employed *bootstrapping* [9] as follows. We split the 1000 generated visits into a training set of 100 visits and a test set of 900 visits. 200 *bootstrap* test samples were then generated from the test set; each test sample was constructed by sampling 900 times from the 900 visits with replacement (200 is the recommended upper bound on the number of test samples for bootstrapping [9]). The training set remained the same for all samples.[7] Our results are averaged over the bootstrap samples.

We conducted three different experiments with these training and test sets to separately evaluate the three stages of the inference and prediction process: (1) walking/hovering classification; (2) inferring exhibits from positional hovering coordinates; and (3) predicting the next exhibit. All performance differences between models were found to be statistically significant with $p \ll 0.001$ for all results that are averaged across exhibits (evaluated using two-tailed paired t-tests on the bootstrap samples).

Table 1 summarises the models used in our experiments, indicating the inferred versus given information (only the first two models, i. e., those with grey background, are used in our first two experiments). The top model TL_{all} (*Time-Location* for *all* observations) is the most realistic, as its information is akin to that obtained from sensor readings (i. e., a sequence of time-stamped (x, y) coordinates). The models then become progressively less realistic, starting with TLA_{all} (*Time-Location-Action* for *all* observations), where the walking/hovering labels are considered given, up to Exh_{all}, where the walking/hovering labels, previous exhibits and current exhibit are given. The top three models employ the *Weighted* approach from Sect. 5.3 to predict the next exhibit, while Exh_{all} directly applies the transition matrix from Sect. 3. To contextualise

---

[7] We employed bootstrapping, because it models only the variation of the test data, compared to cross validation, which conflates the variation in the training and test data.

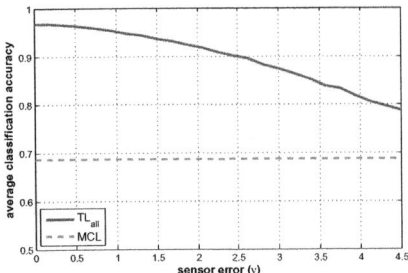 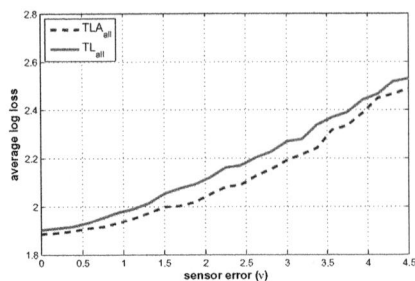

Fig. 2. Average walking/hovering classification accuracy against sensor error

Fig. 3. Average log loss of actually viewed exhibits against sensor error

our work, Table 1 also lists Schmidt *et al.*'s model [12] (typeset in *italics*), but the results pertaining to that model are excluded from our evaluation, as it does not handle positional trajectories or temporal information.

Walking/Hovering Classification. The input to our walking/hovering SVM classifier (Sect. 5.1) comprised sequences of times and positions ($\langle t_n, x_n, y_n \rangle; n = 1, 2, \ldots$). For each walking/hovering classification, we considered the five positional observations made within the last four seconds ($\omega = 5$). As visitors hover slightly less than 69% of the time, and walk between exhibits for the rest of the time, we under-sampled the hovering portion of the training data to balance the classes.[8]

Figure 2 depicts classification accuracy as a function of sensor error, where the majority class baseline (MCL) assumes that a person is always hovering (the results are averaged over the 22 exhibits of the Marine Life Exhibition). Our results show that for no sensor error, our SVM classifier is able to infer whether a visitor is walking or hovering with approximately 97% accuracy. As expected, classification accuracy decreases, but only to about 79%, as sensor error increases to 4.5 metres.

Inferring Exhibits from Positional Hovering Coordinates. The input to our inference mechanism (Sect. 5.2) comprises sequences of times and positions ($\langle t_n, x_n, y_n \rangle$; $n = 1, 2, \ldots$) and walking/hovering labels (one label for each element in the sequence). The probabilities of viewed exhibits were calculated once for given (known) walking/hovering labels, and once for labels inferred by the SVM classifier (Sect. 5.1). For each sub-sequence of hovering labels, our mechanism yielded a probability distribution of the exhibit being viewed by a visitor.

Figure 3 depicts the average *log loss* (negative log of the probability of the actually viewed exhibit), averaged over the 22 exhibits, as a function of sensor error. It compares the performance obtained for inferred walking/hovering labels (TL_{all}) versus that obtained for known labels (TLA_{all}). The comparison was done for the time stamps where the inferred and given hovering labels overlap, but the exhibit scores

---

[8] We under-sampled the larger class, rather than over-sampling the smaller class, in order to retain the variation in the latter class. We also experimented with unbalanced data, but the performance was inferior to that obtained with the balanced data.

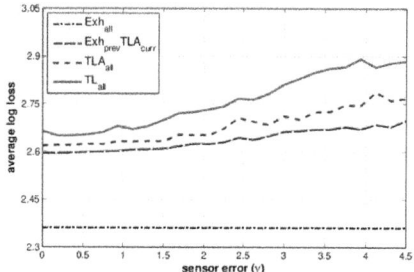
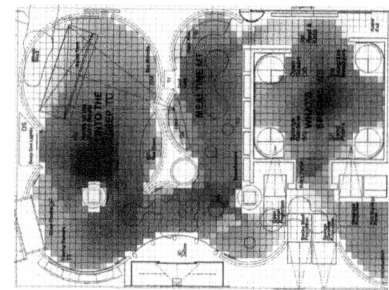

Fig. 4. Average log loss of predicted next exhibits against sensor error

Fig. 5. Entropy map for the Marine Life Exhibition [12]

used in the comparison were calculated for *all* the inferred or given hovering labels in each continuous sub-sequence of hovering labels. This explains the (expected) slight drop in performance for inferred hovering labels, since, as seen in the first experiment, the inferred labels are sometimes wrong. Also, as expected, performance deteriorates as sensor error increases (from an approximate log loss of 1.9 for accurate sensor readings to approximately 2.5 for sensor noise of $\nu = 4.5$ metres). Interestingly, the difference in performance between given and inferred walking/hovering labels remains relatively small (but statistically significant) even for large sensor errors.

Predicting the Next Exhibit. This experiment determines the effect of available information on predictive accuracy. We consider our four models from Table 1, whose information ranges from time-stamped positional sensor logs (TL_{all}) to a sequence of visited exhibits (Exh_{all}). In line with Schmidt *et al.* [12], for all four models the next exhibit was predicted using the transition matrix learned from the 44 tours observed at the Marine Life Exhibition (Sect. 3). For Exh_{all}, we used the transition matrix directly, while for the other models, we used the *Weighted* approach (Sect. 5.3).

Figure 4 shows the average log loss (averaged over the 22 exhibits) for the four models described in Table 1 as a function of sensor error. For this experiment, log loss is the negative log of the probability with which the exhibit viewed *next* is predicted. As seen in the figure, the higher the uncertainty about a visitor's behaviour, the higher the log loss (statistically significant), and, as expected, log loss increases with sensor error. Notice, however, that Exh_{all} is invariant to sensor noise, as all the information is known (Table 1). Interestingly, the differences in performance between the three lower-information models (TL_{all}, TLA_{all} and $Exh_{prev}TLA_{curr}$) are relatively small, and their performance profiles are quite flat (especially up to $\nu = 1.5$ metres). This means that one can expect acceptable predictive performance from sensor-based systems.

Figure 6 shows the average log loss for each of the 22 exhibits separately (in ascending order of log loss): Fig. 6(a) for accurate sensor readings ($\nu = 0$ metres), and Fig. 6(b) for sensor noise of $\nu = 3$ metres. Note that there are no results for exhibits 1 and 7 for the two lower-information models (TL_{all} and TLA_{all}) due to the fact that these models may not infer that certain exhibits have been viewed, even though they appear in the simulated trajectory. As expected, exhibit-specific performance is usually worse for $\nu = 3$ than for $\nu = 0$ for the three lower-information models. Additionally,

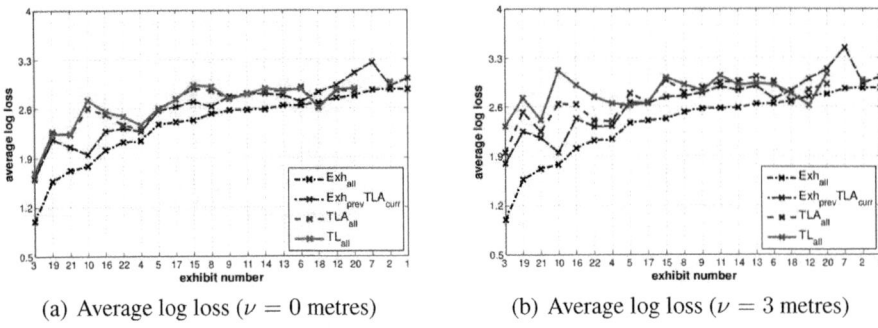

(a) Average log loss ($\nu = 0$ metres)   (b) Average log loss ($\nu = 3$ metres)

Fig. 6. Predictive performance of the four models against exhibit numbers

performance varies between exhibits, which may be explained by the spatial layout of the Marine Life Exhibition. Schmidt *et al.* [12] derived an entropy map of the Marine Life Exhibition (Fig. 5) from the Spatial Exhibit Viewing Model (Sect. 3) to visually assess the clutter in the museum space: darker exhibition squares indicate high entropy (i. e., a cluttered space where many exhibits are equally likely to be viewed), and lighter squares suggest low entropy (i. e., an uncluttered space with few exhibits). Linking performance with entropy, the exhibits where performance is better (left-hand side of the figures) tend to be located in areas of the exhibition with less clutter, while the exhibits where performance is worse (right-hand side) tend to reside in the more cluttered areas.

7   Conclusions

This paper offers a comprehensive framework for examining the impact of sensor observations on the performance of user models in physical spaces. Our framework comprises a simulation model that generates realistic visit trajectories which include walking and hovering behaviours, and provides inference and prediction models based on sensor observations. We also investigated the effect of different assumptions regarding available information on inferential and predictive performance. The obtained results shed light on the reliability of inferences drawn from sensor observations, and may be used to guide the layout of sensor networks and exhibits in a museum.

As expected, predictive performance deteriorates for every inferred (rather than given) experimental parameter, and as sensor error increases. However, performance remains quite stable for sensor accuracies of up to 1.5 metres, which is an encouraging result for real-world systems. These findings in combination set an upper bound on the inferential and predictive performance of sensor-based user modelling systems. Further, our exhibit-specific results (Fig. 6) indicate that exhibits in cluttered areas are more sensitive to sensor error than exhibits in uncluttered areas. We expect that our model can be reliably used to plan the configuration of sensors in a museum jointly with the layout of exhibits, thereby controlling the reliability of the inferences drawn from sensors.

Acknowledgements. This research was supported in part by grant DP0770931 from the Australian Research Council. The authors thank Timothy Baldwin, Liz Sonenberg and Carolyn Meehan for fruitful discussions and their support; and David Abramson, Jeff Tan and Blair Bethwaite for their assistance with the computer cluster.

References

1. Bohnert, F., Zukerman, I.: Non-intrusive Personalisation of the Museum Experience. In: Houben, G.-J., McCalla, G., Pianesi, F., Zancanaro, M. (eds.) UMAP 2009. LNCS, vol 5535, pp. 197–209. Springer, Heidelberg (2009)
2. Bohnert, F., Zukerman, I., Albrecht, D.W., Baldwin, T.: Modelling and predicting movements of museum visitors: A simulation framework for assessing the impact of sensor noise on model performance. In: Proc. of the IJCAI 2011 Workshop on Intelligent Techniques for Web Personalization and Recommender Systems (ITWP 2011), Barcelona, Spain, pp. 49–56 (2011)
3. Chang, C.C., Lin, C.J.: LIBSVM: A library for support vector machines (2001), software, http://www.csie.ntu.edu.tw/~cjlin/libsvm
4. Cheverst, K., Mitchell, K., Davies, N.: The role of adaptive hypermedia in a context-aware tourist GUIDE. Communications of the ACM 45(5), 47–51 (2002)
5. Dijkstra, E.W.: A note on two problems in connexion with graphs. Numerische Mathematik 1, 269–271 (1959)
6. Hatala, M., Wakkary, R.: Ontology-based user modeling in an augmented audio reality system for museums. User Modeling and User-Adapted Interaction 15(3-4), 339–380 (2005)
7. Hazas, M., Scott, J., Krumm, J.: Location-aware computing comes of age. IEEE Computer 37(2), 95–97 (2004)
8. Lassabe, F., Canalda, P., Chatonnay, P., Spies, F.: Indoor Wi-Fi positioning: Techniques and systems. Annals of Telecommunications 64, 651–664 (2009)
9. Mooney, C.Z., Duval, R.D.: Bootstrapping: A Nonparametric Approach to Statistical Inference. Sage Publications, Newbury Park (1993)
10. Petrelli, D., Not, E.: User-centred design of flexible hypermedia for a mobile guide: Reflections on the HyperAudio experience. User Modeling and User-Adapted Interaction 15(3-4), 303–338 (2005)
11. Philipose, M., Fishkin, K.P., Perkowitz, M., Patterson, D.J., Fox, D., Kautz, H., Hahnel, D.: Inferring activities from interactions with objects. IEEE Pervasive Computing 3(4), 50–57 (2004)
12. Schmidt, D.F., Zukerman, I., Albrecht, D.W.: Assessing the Impact of Measurement Uncertainty on User Models in Spatial Domains. In: Houben, G.-J., McCalla, G., Pianesi, F., Zancanaro, M. (eds.) UMAP 2009. LNCS, vol. 5535, pp. 210–222. Springer, Heidelberg (2009)
13. Stock, O., Zancanaro, M., Busetta, P., Callaway, C., Krüger, A., Kruppa, M., Kuflik, T., Not, E., Rocchi, C.: Adaptive, intelligent presentation of information for the museum visitor in PEACH. User Modeling and User-Adapted Interaction 18(3), 257–304 (2007)
14. Wang, Y., Aroyo, L., Stash, N., Sambeek, R., Schuurmans, Y., Schreiber, G., Gorgels, P.: Cultivating personalized museum tours online and on-site. Interdisciplinary Science Reviews 34(2), 141–156 (2009)
15. Zancanaro, M., Kuflik, T., Boger, Z., Goren-Bar, D., Goldwasser, D.: Analyzing Museum Visitors' Behavior Patterns. In: Conati, C., McCoy, K., Paliouras, G. (eds.) UM 2007. LNCS (LNAI), vol. 4511, pp. 238–246. Springer, Heidelberg (2007)

GECKOmmender: Personalised Theme and Tour Recommendations for Museums

Fabian Bohnert, Ingrid Zukerman, and Junaidy Laures

Faculty of Information Technology, Monash University,
Clayton, VIC 3800, Australia
{Fabian.Bohnert,Ingrid.Zukerman}@monash.edu,
junaidylaures@gmail.com

Abstract. We present GECKO*mmender*, a mobile system for personalised theme and tour recommendations in museums, based on a digital site-map representation. Star ratings provided by visitors for seen exhibits are used to predict ratings for unvisited exhibits. The predicted ratings in turn form the basis for recommendations. These recommendations are presented in one of three display modes: StarMap – stars on the site map, HeatMap – colours from green to red that indicate the interestingness of exhibits (from interesting to not interesting respectively), and TourPlan – directed personalised tours through the museum. GECKO*mmender* was evaluated in a field study at Melbourne Museum (Melbourne, Australia). Our results show that (1) most participants enjoyed GECKO*mmender*, (2) GECKO*mmender*'s recommendations often reflected the participants' personal interests, and (3) HeatMap was the most popular display mode.

1 Introduction

Advances in user modelling have enabled technology that can help museum visitors select personally interesting exhibits. Typically, such technology utilises information about a visitor's interests (i. e., ratings) to generate personalised exhibit recommendations based on rating predictions, e. g., [3,7,9]. In this paper, we present GECKO*mmender*, our system for personalised recommendation of *exhibit themes* (sets of exhibits) and *museum tours* (sequences of exhibits). GECKO*mmender* takes as input a visitor's explicit ratings of exhibits, which are used to predict the ratings for the unvisited exhibits. The predicted ratings in turn form the basis for theme/tour recommendations.

The physicality of the museum domain offers the opportunity to utilise its spatial layout when delivering recommendations. We do so by showing the recommendations on a digital site map of the museum, which supports an intuitive presentation of the recommendations relative to a visitor's current location in the museum. This paper investigates three approaches for the presentation of recommendations: (1) StarMap, where stars are used to indicate the level of interestingness of *particular* exhibits; (2) HeatMap, where colours are used to indicate the level of interestingness of *all* exhibits; and (3) TourPlan, where personalised tours through the museum are shown.

GECKO*mmender* was evaluated by means of a field study in June 2011, where 41 visitors to Melbourne Museum (Melbourne, Australia) used GECKO*mmender* during their museum visit. The participants were free to use GECKO*mmender* for as long as they

J. Masthoff et al. (Eds.): UMAP 2012, LNCS 7379, pp. 26–37, 2012.

liked, and toggle GECKO*mmender*'s display mode as often as they wanted. We collected both quantitative and qualitative data by logging the participants' usage of GECKO*mmender*, and asking them to fill a post-visit questionnaire. Our evaluation had three objectives, viz to determine (1) whether museum visitors enjoy GECKO*mmender*, (2) GECKO*mmender*'s predictive accuracy and perceived recommendation quality, and (3) which display mode is preferred. The results from our evaluation indicate that the majority of participants enjoyed GECKO*mmender*. Additionally, GECKO*mmender* achieved a normalised root-mean-square error of 0.270 compared to an error of 0.307 obtained by a non-personalised baseline (thereby outperforming the baseline by 12.1%), and the majority of participants felt that the recommendations often reflected their interests. Our results also indicate that the **StarMap** mode was explored most often, and that the **HeatMap** mode was the best-received GECKO*mmender* display mode.

This paper is structured as follows. Section 2 discusses related research, and Sect. 3 describes GECKO*mmender*. The design of our field study and results from our evaluation are presented in Sect. 4. Section 5 concludes the paper.

2   Related Research

In previous work, Bohnert and Zukerman described user models that predict exhibits of interest to museum visitors [1,2]. This paper studies the impact of our recommendation system as a whole, focusing on techniques for *delivering* personalised theme/tour recommendations to museum visitors on the basis of their predicted interests.

Many research projects have studied the development of user models for visitors of physical spaces, in particular museums, e. g., [1,8,9]. In this section, we focus on user models and recommendation delivery methods of related recommender systems for the tourism and museum domains.

The following projects developed personalised hand-held city guides that generate recommendations: *GUIDE* for Lancaster, UK [3]; *Deep Map* for Heidelberg, Germany [6]; and *DTG (Dynamic Tourist Guide)* for Görlitz, Germany [5]. The three systems use knowledge-based techniques for interest prediction, with *Deep Map* also employing content-based and collaborative techniques. *GUIDE* and *DTG* require explicit input about users' preferences or interests, while *Deep Map* also employs implicit user feedback and usage data. In terms of delivery mode, *GUIDE* delivers theme and tour recommendations as lists, while *Deep Map* and *DTG* display tours on digital city maps.

Hippie/HIPS (Hyper-Interaction within Physical Space) [7] and *CHIP (Cultural Heritage Information Personalization)* [9] focus on museums. The rule-based *HIPPIE/HIPS* system (tested at the Civic Museum in Sienna, Italy) recommends personally interesting exhibit lists on the basis of several sources, such as interaction history and movement through the museum. By contrast, *CHIP* (partnered with the Rijksmuseum in Amsterdam, The Netherlands) uses a content-based approach coupled with semantic web techniques to generate personalised tours from visitors' explicit ratings of artworks. The tours are delivered via digital museum maps.

GECKO*mmender* resembles *CHIP* in that it receives explicit ratings as input and it uses a content-based user model, but differs from all the above systems in its consideration of three different map-based modes of recommendation delivery.

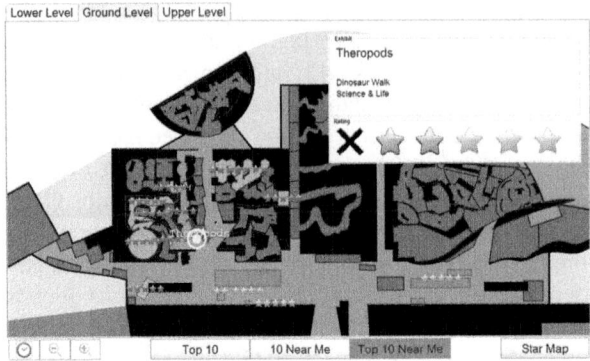

Fig. 1. Rating "Theropods" of the Dinosaur Walk in the StarMap mode, Top10NearMe view

3 Personalised Exhibit Theme and Tour Recommendations

This section describes the functionality and presentation modes of GECKO*mmender*, our system for presenting personalised theme and tour recommendations for museums.

3.1 Core Functionality

GECKO*mmender* typically resides on portable devices, such as tablets, hand-held computers or smart phones. Its main component is a digital site map of the museum, where each exhibit area is represented by a clickable polygon, and a visitor's current location is indicated by a circled white dot (Fig. 1).[1] To avoid relying on localisation technology, in this study, visitors click on the site map to update their location, which causes GECKO*mmender* to re-centre the map. The site map may be navigated by dragging it, and may be zoomed by using the − and + buttons in the bottom-left corner of the interface. Maps (i. e., floor levels) may be switched by selecting one of the tabs at the top of the interface. In the Melbourne Museum case, the visitor may choose from the three floor levels "Lower level", "Ground level" and "Upper level".

Ratings. After viewing an exhibit, a visitor may give it a star rating. This is done by clicking on the exhibit on the site map, which brings up a rating panel (Fig. 1). The visitor then clicks on the desired number of stars (we use a 5-star rating scale, where 1 star means "not at all interesting", and 5 stars mean "very interesting"). The rating given by the visitor then appears as yellow stars on the rating panel and site map, and may be adjusted by repeating the rating procedure.

If a visitor dislikes an exhibit, s/he may click the black × symbol to the left of the rating stars to avoid getting recommendations about similar exhibits.[2] After the ×

---

[1] The colours in the screenshots have been adjusted for better visibility in greyscale proceedings.

[2] The similarity between exhibits is derived from keyword-based representations of the exhibits [2]. The level of similarity that enables the exclusion of an exhibit is configurable, and is currently set to 0.13 (empirically determined).

symbol is clicked, the system greys out the excluded exhibits on the site map, and marks them with an × symbol (left-hand side of Fig. 2): a red × indicates "explicitly excluded by the visitor", and a black × means "excluded due to similarity with an explicitly excluded exhibit". An exclusion may be undone by re-clicking on the × symbol on an exhibit's rating panel.

Recommendations. GECK*Ommender* starts making recommendations as soon as three ratings have been provided.[3] These recommendations are based on the predicted ratings of unseen exhibits, which are updated as the visitor rates additional exhibits. The ratings of unseen exhibits are predicted using a nearest-neighbour *Content-Based Filter (CBF)* [2] by computing the weighted average of the visitor's ratings for the seen exhibits, where the weights for each unseen exhibit are calculated from its content-based similarity with the seen exhibits.[4] The content-based model comprises a list of keywords and multi-word phrases for each exhibit (on average, 11 distinct words per exhibit). These were obtained through an annotation process involving several independent annotators, who after engaging with each exhibit area in the museum, proposed words and phrases that best reflect the exhibit's content.

3.2   Recommendation Presentation

When starting up GECK*Ommender*, a visitor must select one of the three display modes described below: StarMap (Fig. 2), HeatMap (Fig. 3) or TourPlan (Fig. 4). The display mode may be changed by clicking on the *display-mode* button in the bottom-right corner of the interface (this button also indicates the current display mode).

In addition, on start-up, the visitor needs to set the time available for the museum visit. This duration is used in the TourPlan mode as the maximum length of a tour recommendation. The time is automatically reduced as the visit progresses, and may also be manually adjusted by the visitor by clicking the *clock* button in the bottom-left corner of the GECK*Ommender* interface.

Star Map. In this mode, the exhibit recommendations are indicated as red stars on red-coloured exhibit areas (a visitor's ratings have yellow stars), where 5 stars mean "very interesting", and 1 star means "not at all interesting" (Figs. 1 and 2). Using stars to represent the level of interest is the classical way for visualising recommendations (e. g., www.amazon.com, rogerebert.suntimes.com).

The StarMap mode has four views: Top10, 10NearMe, Top10NearMe and All. A view may be selected by clicking on the *view* buttons under the site map (the current view is highlighted in green). The All view, which shows predictions for *all* exhibits, may be chosen by toggling off the currently selected view. The default view is Top10, which presents the ten personally most interesting exhibits across the entire museum, i. e., on all floor levels. By contrast, the 10NearMe view (Fig. 2) indicates the ten exhibits that are spatially closest to the visitor's current location, irrespective of their star ratings. The

---

[3] The minimum number of required ratings is configurable.

[4] We chose a content-based prediction method for this study, as it exhibits good performance while eschewing reliance on other visitors [2].

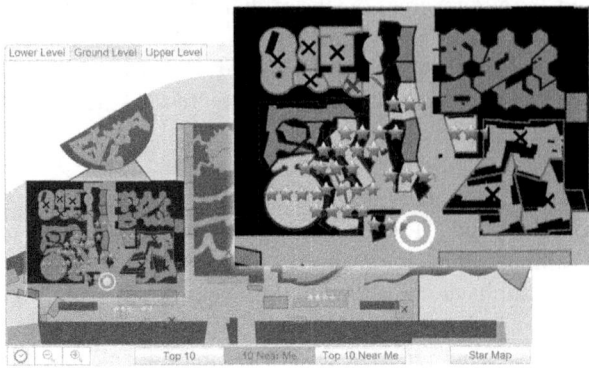

Fig. 2. GECKO*mmender*'s StarMap mode – 10NearMe view

Top10NearMe view (Fig. 1) combines the Top10 and 10NearMe views by presenting ten fairly interesting exhibits that are relatively close to the visitor's current location. For this view, the predicted rating for each exhibit is multiplied by a number that reflects the proximity of the exhibit to the visitor's location, so that close but relatively uninteresting exhibits may be assigned lower scores than more distant but interesting exhibits. The resultant exhibit scores are then used to re-rank the exhibits prior to presentation. Thus, the Top10NearMe view tends to show exhibits that are slightly farther away than those displayed in the 10NearMe view, but have higher predicted ratings. For the Top10 and Top10NearMe views, only exhibits with a predicted rating of at least three stars are presented.

Heat Map. This mode shows the predicted level of interestingness of *all* exhibits, where the level of interest is indicated by different colour shades in the red-green spectrum (green represents the most interesting exhibits, and red the least interesting ones; Fig 3). A legend in the bottom-right corner of the site map shows the possible colour shades together with their interpretation. The motivation for the HeatMap mode is that it provides a comprehensive visualisation that enables a visitor to quickly gain an understanding of the locations of personally interesting museum sections. As for the StarMap mode, yellow stars show the ratings previously given by the visitor.

Figure 3 shows GECKO*mmender*'s heat map for two situations in Melbourne Museum that are almost identical but for the rating for "Aboriginal Artefacts" near the visitor's current location (indicated by a circled white dot in the bottom-right quarter of the site map). This rating, which is 5 stars in Fig. 3(a) and 2 stars in Fig. 3(b), has a substantial effect on the predicted ratings for the museum sections that relate to Aboriginal content (e. g., the right-hand side of the ground level). Specifically, a 5-star rating for "Aboriginal Artefacts" causes these sections to turn green/dark-grey (indicating high interest), while a 2-star rating yields red/light-grey colours (indicating little interest).

Tour Plan. This mode generates fully personalised *tours* that take into account a visitor's interests and time available for the museum visit. These tour recommendations, which are selective and directional, are more explicit than the *theme* recommendations

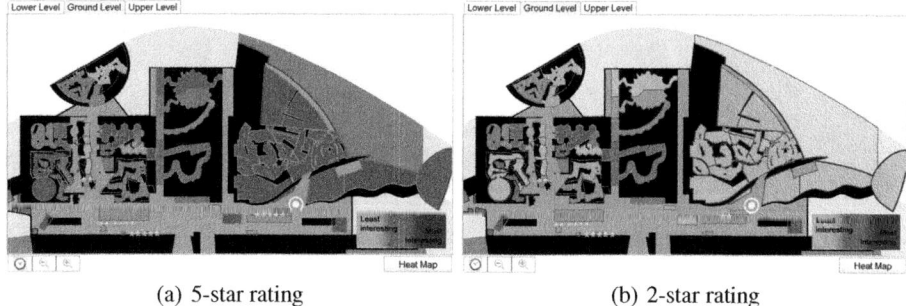

(a) 5-star rating   (b) 2-star rating

Fig. 3. GECKO*mmender*'s HeatMap mode for different ratings of one exhibit (5 stars vs. 2 stars)

of the StarMap and HeatMap modes, which make only implicit suggestions (by show-ing stars or colours respectively).

The problem of generating a personalised tour may be cast as the *orienteering prob-lem (OP)* [4] – a variation of the standard *travelling salesman problem (TSP)*, where each stop is associated with a reward (i. e., satisfied interest), but not all possible stops (i. e., exhibit areas) must be visited. The objective is to find a subset of stops such that the total collected reward is maximised, under the constraint that the maximum travel cost (i. e., the time limit) is not exceeded. Like the standard TSP, the OP is NP-hard. The OP has been extensively studied in the literature, and both exact and approximate solution algorithms have been devised. For GECKO*mmender*, we adopted a heuristic procedure that starts with a greedy solution, and repeatedly applies the following four basic operations until the tour cannot be further improved [4]: (1) adding an exhibit to the tour, (2) deleting an exhibit from the tour, (3) reordering the exhibits in the tour, and (4) replacing an exhibit in the tour with an exhibit outside the tour. This procedure receives the following inputs: the predicted ratings and exclusions for all unvisited ex-hibits (the former indicate the rewards that are collected at the exhibits, and the latter are never included in a tour), the walking distances between all pairs of unvisited ex-hibits, a constant walking speed (we assume a walking speed of 2 km/h), the average exhibit viewing times (derived from a dataset of visitor pathways through Melbourne Museum [1]), and the current time limit. Due to the computational complexity of re-planning a tour, we opted for a configuration where a visitor must request tour up-dates (rather than automatically updating the tour when the rating predictions change). This provides the visitor with the opportunity to update their tour only when desired, and is done by clicking the *update* button in the middle under the site map (Fig. 4).

In GECKO*mmender*, a recommended tour starts at the exhibit that was rated last, and ends at the main entrance of the museum. The exhibits that are part of the tour are colour-shaded like in the HeatMap mode, and the tour is shown as a white line with white dots at the included exhibits, where the dot size decreases as the distance between the corresponding exhibit and a visitor's location increases (Fig. 4). Using differently-sized dots in this way indicates the direction of the tour. Level changes are indicated by special icons (arrows for escalators, and "lift" symbols for elevators, e. g., Fig. 4(b)). Figure 4 illustrates the effect of available time on personalised tour recommendations for two situations with identical ratings but different time availability: 1h (Fig. 4(a)),

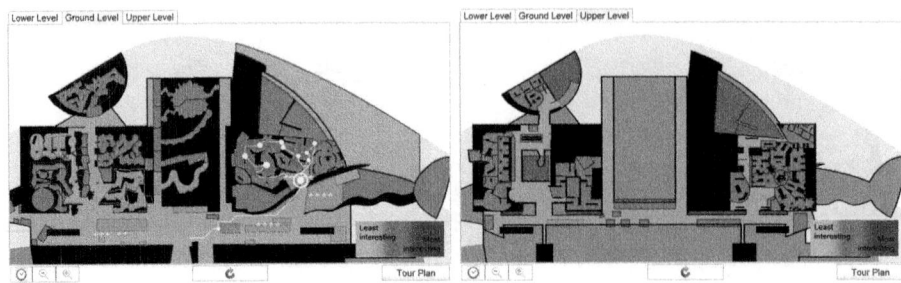

(a) Planned 1h tour (ground level and upper level – no exhibits were selected at this level)

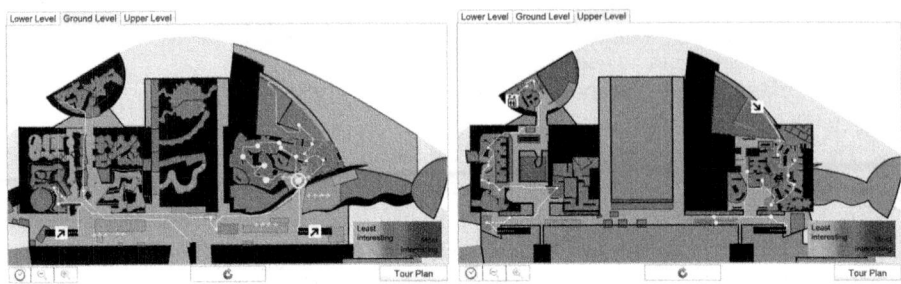

(b) Planned 2.5h tour (ground level and upper level)

Fig. 4. GECKO*mmender*'s TourPlan mode for two tour lengths (1h and 2.5h)

and 2.5h (Fig. 4(b)). As seen in Fig. 4, the recommended 1h tour takes the visitor only to a small, spatially confined section of Melbourne Museum, while the 2.5h tour extends across both sides and levels of the museum.

4 Evaluation

To evaluate GECKO*mmender*, we conducted a field study at Melbourne Museum in June 2011. The museum comprises two main floors of nearly 8,000 square metres each, and exhibits a few thousand objects distributed over eight themed galleries. Its large size and diverse collection makes it ideal for evaluating personalised technology for museums.

41 visitors participated in the field study, for which we used ten tablet computers with touch-screen display. Nine tablets were used by the participants, and the tenth device was used for demonstrating and explaining GECKO*mmender*.

4.1 Field Study Procedures

Participants were recruited by approaching suitable visitors near the main entrance of Melbourne Museum, and explaining the project and trial. Visitors were considered suitable if they were adults visiting either alone or in a small group. Table 1 lists the visitors' break-down in terms of age, gender, whether they visited the museum before, were alone, or had limited time in the museum.

Table 1. Participant details

Age	18–24:	25 (61.0%)	25–34:	10 (24.4%)
	35–44:	5 (12.2%)	55–64:	1 (2.4%)
Gender	Male:	30 (73.2%)	Female:	11 (26.8%)
Visited before	Yes:	5 (12.2%)	No:	36 (87.8%)
Visited alone	Yes:	18 (43.9%)	No:	23 (56.1%)
Limited time	Yes:	22 (53.7%)	No:	19 (46.3%)

After a visitor agreed to participate in the trial, we explained the functionality of GECKO*mmender* and answered clarification questions. We then gave the visitor the tablet computer with GECKO*mmender*. For each participant, we set the *initial* display mode (i. e., StarMap, HeatMap or TourPlan) and the time *initially* available for the visit. We advised the participants that they could use GECKO*mmender* for as long as they wanted, and that they could toggle the display mode and adjust the remaining time available for their visit.

Visitors' GECKO*mmender* usage was automatically logged during their visit. Upon completion, each participant filled out a post-visit questionnaire, which included 29 questions (some with several items), comprising 12 Likert-scale (different scales were used as appropriate, ranging from 0–3 to 0–6), 13 closed and 11 open-ended questions. 11 questions were about the visitors' demographics and their museum-visiting habits, and 18 questions pertained to the current museum visit and the usage of GECKO*mmender* in the context of this visit.

4.2   Results

In this section, we present the results for (1) GECKO*mmender* in general, (2) its predictions and recommendations, and (3) its display modes. The results were obtained by analysing the GECKO*mmender* usage data and the questionnaire answers of our 41 participants. Where possible, we correlate in our analysis the participants' questionnaire answers with figures derived from the logged GECKO*mmender* usage data.

GECKO*mmender* in General. Our results indicate that the majority of participants enjoyed GECKO*mmender*. Specifically, 31 participants (76%) said that they used GECKO*mmender* either often, very often or always during their visit, and 25 participants (61%) answered that they liked playing with GECKO*mmender* (98% were either neutral or positive about playing with GECKO*mmender*). Additionally, 20 participants (49%) said that using GECKO*mmender* made their visit more enjoyable (90% answered that using GECKO*mmender* either had no impact on their enjoyment or improved it), and 22 participants (54%) said that GECKO*mmender* made it easier to find exhibits (93% said that GECKO*mmender* either had no effect on their ability to find exhibits or improved it).

GECKO*mmender*'s Predictions and Recommendations. To evaluate the predictive accuracy of GECKO*mmender*, we implemented a *post-trial* non-personalised baseline that predicts the rating a visitor gives to an exhibit as the average of the other participants' ratings for this exhibit.[5] This baseline achieves a *normalised root-mean-square error (NRMSE)* of 0.307.[6] In comparison, GECKO*mmender*, which uses our *CBF* for prediction generation [2], achieves an NRMSE of 0.270 (thereby outperforming the baseline by 12.1%). These NRMSE values were computed from the logged data (specifically, 1120 rating-prediction pairs) by comparing the actual ratings given by the 41 participants with the predicted ratings.

We obtained the following results regarding GECKO*mmender*'s perceived quality of recommendations.

- 25 participants (61%) said that GECKO*mmender*'s recommendations reflected their interests either often or very often, 13 (32%) said that their interests were reflected at most sometimes, and three (7%) did not answer this question. Surprisingly, there is a small positive correlation of 0.17 between the participants' perceptions of how well the recommendations reflect their interests and their NRMSEs for star ratings (i.e., higher errors occur when the perceptions are more positive). A possible explanation for this result is the ambiguity of the phrase "reflect interests". This problem may have been circumvented (at least for the StarMap mode) by posing a more precise question about how well predicted and actual ratings match.
- 14 participants (34%) liked the recommendations (93% were at least neutral regarding the recommendations), one participant (2%) disliked the recommendations, and two participants (5%) did not answer this question. We checked whether there are any associations between the participants' liking of recommendations and age, gender, group size, level of education, and time limitations in the museum. All associations are not statistically significant at the 5% level according to a Fisher's exact test, but there is a subtle trend for age (*p-value* = 0.175): participants under 25 years of age tended to like the recommendations more than older participants. Also, we measured a medium positive correlation of 0.37 between the perceived follow-up of recommendations and the liking of recommendations.
- 22 participants (54%) said that they followed the recommendations at least sometimes, 18 (44%) said that they did so at most rarely, and one participant (2%) did not answer this question. Our data show a small positive correlation of 0.21 between the perceived follow-up of recommendations and the per-participant percentage of exhibits that were rated immediately after they were recommended.
- 27 participants (66%) used GECKO*mmender*'s exclusion functionality described in Sect. 3.1. This suggests that GECKO*mmender*'s assessment of similarity between exhibits was found useful by most participants.

Overall, the vast majority of the reactions to GECKO*mmender*'s recommendations ranged from neutral to positive, with a substantial number of reactions falling in the positive band. Most participants found the recommendations at least appropriate, about one third liked them, and about half followed them at least sometimes. These are encouraging results for the usefulness and acceptance of recommender systems in museums.

---

[5] Since there is no clear non-personalised baseline for *CBF*, we did not perform a non-personalised, display-only experiment within the trial. However, the questionnaire attempts to separate the effect of the display from that of the recommendations.

[6] We also considered as a baseline a method that predicts a rating as the rating-scale average of three stars, but this method yields an NRMSE of only 0.315.

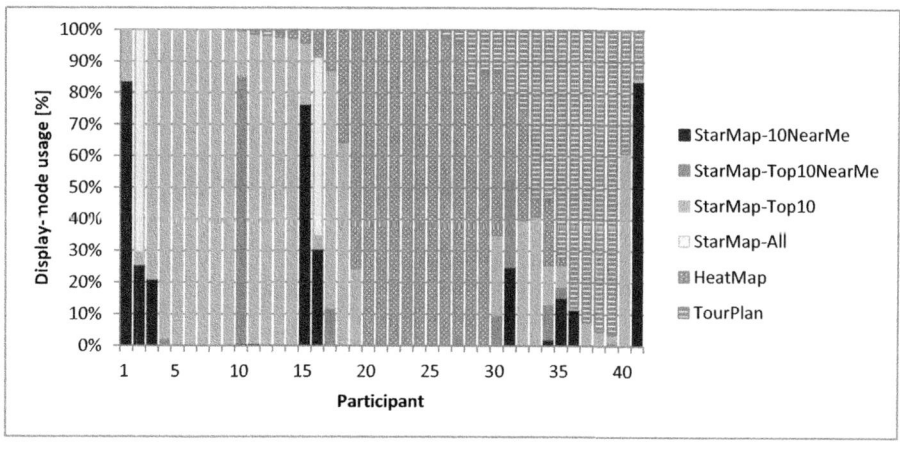

Fig. 5. Display-mode usage percentages by participant

GECKO*mmender*'s Display Modes. The results regarding GECKO*mmender*'s display modes are shown in Fig. 5 and summarised in Table 2 (*D* indicates "from the logged data" and *Q* indicates "from the questionnaire answers"). Figure 5 depicts the percentage of time spent by each of the 41 participants in the various display modes and StarMap views. For instance, participant 41 (rightmost bar) spent 84% of the visit in StarMap-10NearMe, 15% in TourPlan, and 1% in StarMap-Top10.

- 23 participants (56%) were started in the StarMap mode (Top10 view), 15 (37%) were started in HeatMap, and only three (7%) were started in TourPlan (Table 2, row 1). We skewed the start-up modes in this manner, as we wanted visitors to feel at ease with a familiar, automatically updated representation (StarMap, followed by HeatMap), avoiding the more complex TourPlan mode until they gained familiarity with the system.
- 27 participants (66%) spent most of the time in the starting mode. Still, most participants (73%) explored different display modes or StarMap views, with 11 participants (27%) exploring two StarMap views to some extent (more than 5% of their visit), and five participants (12%) using all three display modes and 11 (27%) two display modes at some length (Fig. 5).
- The StarMap mode was used for the longest time and most often, followed by HeatMap and TourPlan (Table 2, rows 2 and 3).[7] The logged usage results match the perceived usage results (Table 2, row 4), as the participants remembered correctly their mode usage 80% of the time.
- 27 (87%) of the 31 participants who used the StarMap mode employed the Top10 view, ten (32%) used 10NearMe, five (16%) used Top10NearMe, and two (6%) used All. The Top10 view was also used for the longest time (by 15 of the 22 participants who spent most of the time in the StarMap mode), with each of the other

---

[7] We considered a display mode as used by a participant if s/he spent more than 3.5 minutes in that mode. This threshold is based on observations of engagement with a display mode.

Table 2. Display-mode statistics

		StarMap	HeatMap	TourPlan
Display mode at start-up (logged)	D	**23 (56%** /41)	15 (37% /41)	3 (7% /41)
Display mode with longest time (logged as most time spent)	D	**22 (54%** /41)	12 (29% /41)	7 (17% /41)
Display-mode usage (logged as used)	D	**31 (76%** /41)	20 (49% /41)	15 (37% /41)
Display-mode usage (perceived as used)	Q	**34 (83%** /41)	23 (56% /41)	14 (34% /41)
Display-mode liking (perceived at least as liked)	Q	25 (74% /34)	**19 (83%** /23)	11 (79% /14)
Most useful display mode (perceived)	Q	13.5 (40% /34)	**16 (70%** /23)	7.5 (54% /14)

views being used most of the time by only a few participants. This may be explained by the fact that Top10 was the start-up view, combined with the observation that participants seemed less curious about views than about modes. Specifically, only 22 (71%) of the StarMap users experimented with different views, compared to 28 (90%) who tried other modes.

- 25 (74%) of the 34 participants that reported using the StarMap mode, 11 (79%) of the 14 TourPlan mode users, and 19 (83%) of the 23 HeatMap mode users either liked the mode's look or liked it a lot (Table 2, rows 4 and 5). These results match the perceived usefulness results (Table 2, row 6).[8] Thus, although all three modes were positively regarded, the StarMap mode was the least preferred in terms of appearance and usefulness, despite its frequent usage (which may be attributed to its start-up frequency). Finally, the majority of the participants (73%) spent most of the time in the mode they found most useful, which validates the intuition that display-mode usage is a good indicator of perceived usefulness.

Overall, our results show that although the StarMap display mode was used most often, the participants preferred the other two modes, with the HeatMap mode being the best-received and considered the most useful. The results for the different views of the StarMap mode indicate that the participants preferred an overall museum view (Top10), which informs visitors of the personally most interesting exhibits regardless of location, and a view of nearby exhibits (10NearMe), which enables visitors to determine their level of interest in the current area.

5   Conclusions

This paper offered the GECKO*mmender* system for personalised exhibit theme and tour recommendations in museums. GECKO*mmender* employs a *CBF* to predict exhibit ratings, and has three modes to display recommendations: StarMap (with four views), HeatMap and TourPlan.

---

[8] Two participants found two display modes most useful. Hence, we assigned 0.5 instead of 1 to each display mode. Four participants did not answer this question.

The results from our field study at Melbourne Museum indicate that most participants used GECKO*mmender* fairly regularly during their visits, enjoyed playing with it, and explored different display modes. The majority of the participants were positive about the recommendations, noting that the recommendations reflected their interests and that they followed the recommendations at least sometimes. Finally, while the StarMap display mode was used most often, the HeatMap mode was best liked, and was considered the most useful mode.

Overall, our results show that map-based visualisations are suitable for presenting recommendations in physical spaces, such as museums, and that recommendation systems running on mobile platforms are a promising option for museums.

Acknowledgements. This research was supported in part by grant DP0770931 from the Australian Research Council. The authors thank Carolyn Meehan and her team from Museum Victoria for fruitful discussions and their support, and the eEducation team at Monash University for the use of the tablet computers.

References

1. Bohnert, F., Zukerman, I.: Non-intrusive Personalisation of the Museum Experience. In: Houben, G.-J., McCalla, G., Pianesi, F., Zancanaro, M. (eds.) UMAP 2009. LNCS, vol. 5535, pp. 197–209. Springer, Heidelberg (2009)
2. Bohnert, F., Zukerman, I.: Using Keyword-Based Approaches to Adaptively Predict Interest in Museum Exhibits. In: Nicholson, A., Li, X. (eds.) AI 2009. LNCS, vol. 5866, pp. 656–665. Springer, Heidelberg (2009)
3. Cheverst, K., Mitchell, K., Davies, N.: The role of adaptive hypermedia in a context-aware tourist GUIDE. Communications of the ACM 45(5), 47–51 (2002)
4. Feillet, D., Dejax, P., Gendreau, M.: Traveling salesman problems with profits. Transportation Science 39(2), 188–205 (2005)
5. ten Hagen, K., Modsching, M., Kramer, R.: A location aware mobile tourist guide selecting and interpreting sights and services by context matching. In: Proceedings of the 2nd Annual International Conference on Mobile and Ubiquitous Systems: Networking and Services (MobiQuitous 2005), Washington, DC, pp. 293–304 (2005)
6. Malaka, R., Zipf, A.: Deep Map – Challenging IT research in the framework of a tourist information system. In: Proceedings of the 7th International Conference on Information and Communication Technologies in Tourism (ENTER 2000), Barcelona, Spain, pp. 15–27 (2000)
7. Oppermann, R., Specht, M.: A Context-Sensitive Nomadic Exhibition Guide. In: Thomas, P., Gellersen, H.-W. (eds.) HUC 2000. LNCS, vol. 1927, pp. 127–142. Springer, Heidelberg (2000)
8. Stock, O., Zancanaro, M., Busetta, P., Callaway, C., Krüger, A., Kruppa, M., Kuflik, T., Not, E., Rocchi, C.: Adaptive, intelligent presentation of information for the museum visitor in PEACH. User Modeling and User-Adapted Interaction 18(3), 257–304 (2007)
9. Wang, Y., Aroyo, L., Stash, N., Sambeek, R., Schuurmans, Y., Schreiber, G., Gorgels, P.: Cultivating personalized museum tours online and on-site. Interdisciplinary Science Reviews 34(2), 141–156 (2009)

Property-Based Interest Propagation in Ontology-Based User Model*

Federica Cena, Silvia Likavec, and Francesco Osborne

Università di Torino, Dipartimento di Informatica, Torino, Italy
{cena,likavec,osborne}@di.unito.it

Abstract. We present an approach for propagation of user interests in ontology-based user models taking into account the properties declared for the concepts in the ontology. Starting from initial user feedback on an object, we calculate user interest in this particular object and its properties and further propagate user interest to other objects in the ontology, similar or related to the initial object. The similarity and relatedness of objects depends on the number of properties they have in common and their corresponding values. The approach we propose can support finer recommendation modalities, considering the user interest in the objects, as well as in singular properties of objects in the recommendation process. We tested our approach for interest propagation with a real adaptive application and obtained an improvement with respect to IS-A-propagation of interest values.

1 Introduction

Recommender systems, both collaborative and content-based, usually suffer from cold-start and diversity problems. The *cold start* problem [20] happens at the beginning of the interaction when the system does not have enough user data to provide appropriate adaptation. The *diversity problem* [14] occurs when recommendation results, although similar to the initial object are also very similar to each other, thus lacking diversity and not providing the user with the satisfying alternatives. In the last years, several approaches have been proposed to address such problems.

Regarding the cold start problem, the most common solutions are [21]: displaying non-personalized recommendations until the user has interacted enough, asking the users directly for their interests or demographic features, clustering users in stereotypes, sharing the user models among adaptive applications [3], importing user profiles from social web applications [1]. Using ontology structure to propagate user interest values starting from a small number of initial concepts to other related concepts in the domain has proven to be a valuable tool in resolving the cold-start problem [7,4]. Following this direction, we develop an approach for propagating user interests which enables incremental update of the user model starting from initial user feedback on domain objects.

As far as the diversity problem is concerned, the following solutions were proposed [23]: bounded greedy selection strategy where a diverse retrieval set is built starting from the concepts most similar to the initial query and choosing the additional candidates for recommendation according to their similarity *and* diversity; ordered-based retrieval where cases for recommendation are ordered based on their similarity to

---

* This work has been supported by PIEMONTE Project - People Interaction with Enhanced Multimodal Objects for a New Territory Experience.

J. Masthoff et al. (Eds.): UMAP 2012, LNCS 7379, pp. 38–50, 2012.

ideal features; compromise-driven strategy where a subset of compromises is involved. To contribute to the resolution of diversity problem, we develop an approach for propagation of user interest values based on relatedness also among distant concepts.

The main contribution of the paper is a novel algorithm for propagation of user interests to other similar and related objects which takes into account the properties of the objects in the domain and their corresponding values. Our approach helps solve the cold start problem, enabling efficient propagation even in the presence of user feedback for a small number of items. It also alleviates the diversity problem, since it allows not only propagation to similar objects, but also to related but more distant objects which share some property that the user may find desirable [23].

The approach is based on the following:

- a *semantic representation of the domain knowledge* using an OWL ontology where domain concepts are taxonomically organized, related to each other (object type properties) and enriched with data type properties;
- a methodology for calculating the *similarity (and relatedness) of domain objects* considering common properties for the objects and their corresponding values;
- a *user model* defined as an overlay on the domain ontology;
- a *strategy for building and updating the user model*, that automatically detect preferences for objects' properties starting from the user feedback.

Although our approach can be used as a preliminary step for enabling any type of recommendation, it is especially suitable for *case-based recommendation* [23], where user interest in object properties is calculated in order to select objects to recommend. However, the investigation of recommendation strategies is out of the scope of this paper.

In our previous work [7], we presented an effective approach for propagation of user interests in an ontology, following the IS-A relationships among concepts. This approach required an ontology with an explicit, well-built taxonomy of classes and subclasses. Such vertical propagation was limited to certain portions of the ontology (sub-ontologies). The approach presented in this paper is different since it is suitable for ontologies which do not have explicit and deep hierarchical structure, and where the classes are defined with restrictions on properties. Considering the properties of concepts, the propagation algorithm can reach the nodes in different sub-ontologies (hence different and sometimes distant) which would not be reachable using only IS-A propagation, allowing to solve in this way the diversity problem.

We tested this approach with a real social semantic application, WantEat [15], in order to asses the accuracy of the user model built with our approach. We also validated the advantages of our propagation mechanism, w.r.t. the vertical propagation approach presented in [7].

The rest of the paper is organized as follows. In Sect. 2, we describe the domain representation requirements, with a brief description of the treatment of properties in OWL. In Sect. 3 we describe how to calculate the similarity and relatedness between concepts in the domain ontology. We describe our user modelling approach and specific algorithm for the propagation of user interests in an ontology in Sect. 4. The results of a preliminary evaluation are given in Sect. 5. In Sect. 6 we present some related work. Finally, we conclude and give some directions for future work in Sect. 7.

2   Background: Properties in OWL

To develop our approach, the domain knowledge must be represented semantically by means of ontologies expressed in OWL[1]. Ontologies represent a hierarchy of domain concepts and the features of such concepts are defined as their properties. OWL distinguishes two kinds of properties: (i) *object properties* relating objects among themselves and ii) *data type properties* relating objects to data type values. We are primarily interested in object properties, since they describe objects in terms of relations with other objects, i.e. they allow to define relations that are not IS-A. In particular, we consider OWL classes defined with restrictions on property values.

Defining Classes with Property Restrictions. Properties can be used to define classes by means of *local anonymous classes*, i.e. collections of objects satisfying certain restrictions on certain properties. For example, Mortadella can be defined as a subclass of an anonymous class that has its *hasMeatKind* property restricted to Pork, *preparationType* property restricted to Cooked and *isMinced* property restricted to Yes. There are three ways of expressing the restrictions on the *kind* of the value[2]: (i) owl:hasValue states a specific value that the property must have; (ii) owl:allValuesFrom specifies the class of possible values the property can take (it is possible not to have any); (iii) owl:someValuesFrom specifies the class of values for at least one of the values for the property (at least one must exist). Hence, we can consider each of the concepts in our ontology, to have certain properties defined for it. These properties further describe the concepts in the ontology and can be used to calculate their mutual similarity.

Defining Instance Properties. The instances in the ontology inherit the properties of the classes they belong to (IS-A relation). Hence, in OWL the properties of the instances are defined by associating to each property its specific value.

3   Property-Based Similarity and Relatedness of Domain Elements

Property-based similarity regards the similarity of classes defined with restrictions. For example, in an ontology describing cold cuts, certain concepts can have these properties: *hasMeatKind, preparationType, isMinced*. Consider the following cold cuts from this ontology: Mortadella, Cooked_Ham and Raw_Ham. Mortadella is made with pork, is cooked and minced, Cooked_Ham is made with pork, is cooked and not minced and Raw_Ham is made with pork, is not cooked and not minced. If we simply count the properties which certain cold cuts have in common, we see that Mortadella is more similar to Cooked_Ham than to Raw_Ham, since Mortadella and Cooked_Ham have two properties in common, whereas Mortadella and Raw_Ham have only one property in common. But, it can happen that for a certain property, two values are given. For example, for Salame_Pavese, the property *hasAddedMeat* has two values: veal and chicken.

There are three kinds of restriction declarations used to define properties for certain classes: (i) owl:hasValue; (ii) owl:allValuesFrom; (iii) owl:someValuesFrom. When

---

[1] http://www.w3.org/TR/owl-ref

[2] It also is possible to express *cardinality restrictions* on the property, by using minCardinality, maxCardinality and cardinality. We are not dealing with cardinality restrictions here.

calculating the property-based similarity of two domain elements N_1 and N_2 [3], we start from Tversky's feature-based model of similarity [24], where similarity between objects is a function of both their common and distinctive characteristics:

$$\text{SIM}_T(N_1, N_2) = \frac{\alpha(\psi(N_1) \cap \psi(N_2))}{\beta(\psi(N_1) \setminus \psi(N_2)) + \gamma(\psi(N_2) \setminus \psi(N_1)) + \alpha(\psi(N_1) \cap \psi(N_2))}$$

where $\psi(N)$ is the function describing all the relevant features of N, and $\alpha, \beta, \gamma \in \mathbb{R}$ are parameters permitting to treat differently various components. By taking $\alpha = 1$ we obtain maximal importance of the common features of the two concepts and by taking $\beta = \gamma$ we obtain non-directional similarity measure. We will use $\alpha = 1$ and $\beta = \gamma = 1$.
  So we have to calculate

- *common features of N_1 and N_2:* $\text{CF}(N_1, N_2) = \psi(N_1) \cap \psi(N_2)$,
- *distinctive features of N_1:* $\text{DF}(N_1) = \psi(N_1) \setminus \psi(N_2)$ and
- *distinctive features of N_2:* $\text{DF}(N_2) = \psi(N_2) \setminus \psi(N_1)$.

To this aim, for each property p, we calculate CF_p, DF_p^1 and DF_p^2, which denote how much the property p contributes to common features of N_1 and N_2, distinctive features of N_1 and distinctive features of N_2, respectively. We distinguish the following six different cases based on how the restrictions on properties are defined for N_1 and N_2:

1. The property p is defined with owl:hasValue in N_1 and N_2. If p has h' different values in N_1 and h'' different values in N_2, and we denote by k the number of times P_1 and P_2 have the same value for p, then $\text{CF}_p = \frac{k^2}{h'h''}$ $\text{DF}_p^1 = \frac{h'-k}{h'}$ $\text{DF}_p^2 = \frac{h''-k}{h''}$.
2. The property q is defined in N_1 with $\langle$owl:allValuesFrom rdf:resource="#A$_1$"$\rangle$ at most once and in N_2 with $\langle$owl:allValuesFrom rdf:resource="#A$_2$"$\rangle$ at most once. Let a_1 (resp. a_2) be the number of sub-classes of A_1 (resp. A_2). If A_1 and A_2 are equivalent or equal, $a_1 = a_2$ and $\text{CF}_q = \frac{1}{(a_1+1)^2}$. Otherwise $\text{DF}_q^1 = \frac{1}{a_1+1}$ and $\text{DF}_q^2 = \frac{1}{a_2+1}$.
3. The property r is defined in N_1 $\langle$owl:someValuesFrom rdf:resource="#S$_1$"$\rangle$ at most once and in N_2 with $\langle$owl:someValuesFrom rdf:resource="#S$_2$"$\rangle$ at most once. Let s_1 (resp. s_2) be the number of sub-classes of S_1 (resp. S_2) and w be the number of classes in the whole domain. If S_1 and S_2 are equivalent or equal, $s_1 = s_2$ and $\text{CF}_r = \frac{1}{(s_1+1)^2w^2}$. Otherwise $\text{DF}_r^1 = \frac{1}{(s_1+1)w}$ and $\text{DF}_r^2 = \frac{1}{(s_2+1)w}$.
4. The property t is defined m times in N_1 with owl:hasValue and once in N_2 with $\langle$owl:allValuesFrom rdf:resource="#A$_3$"$\rangle$. If a_3 is the number of sub-classes of A_3, then $\text{CF}_t = \frac{1}{m(a_3+1)}$, $\text{DF}_t^1 = \frac{m-1}{m}$ and $\text{DF}_t^2 = \frac{1}{a_3+1}$.
5. The property x is defined n times in N_1 with owl:hasValue and once in N_2 with $\langle$owl:someValuesFrom rdf:resource="#S$_3$"$\rangle$. If s_3 is the number of sub-classes of S_3 and w is the number of classes in the whole domain then $\text{CF}_x = \frac{1}{n(s_3+1)w}$, $\text{DF}_x^1 = \frac{n-1}{n}$ and $\text{DF}_x^2 = \frac{1}{(s_3+1)w}$.
6. The property y is defined once with $\langle$owl:allValuesFrom rdf:resource="#A$_4$'''"$\rangle$ in N_1 and once with $\langle$owl:someValuesFrom rdf:resource="#S$_4$'''"$\rangle$ in N_2. Let a_4 (resp. s_4) be the number of sub-classes of A_4 (resp. S_4) and w be the number of classes in the whole domain. Then $\text{CF}_y = \frac{1}{(a_4+1)(s_4+1)w}$, $\text{DF}_y^1 = \frac{1}{a_4+1}$ and $\text{DF}_y^2 = \frac{1}{(s_4+1)w}$.

---

[3] We consider equal the properties defined with EquivalentProperty.

Finally, to calculate all common and distinctive features of N_1 and N_2 we repeat the above process for each property defined for N_1 and N_2, obtaining:

$$\text{CF}(N_1, N_2) = \Sigma_{i_p=1}^{n_p} \text{CF}_{p_{ip}} + \Sigma_{i_q=1}^{n_q} \text{CF}_{q_{iq}} + \Sigma_{i_r=1}^{n_r} \text{CF}_{r_{ir}} + \Sigma_{i_t=1}^{n_t} \text{CF}_{t_{it}} + \Sigma_{i_x=1}^{n_x} \text{CF}_{x_{ix}} + \Sigma_{i_y=1}^{n_y} \text{CF}_{y_{iy}}$$

$$\text{DF}(N_1) = \Sigma_{i_p=1}^{n_p} \text{DF}_{p_{ip}}^1 + \Sigma_{i_q=1}^{n_q} \text{DF}_{q_{iq}}^1 + \Sigma_{i_r=1}^{n_r} \text{DF}_{r_{ir}}^1 + \Sigma_{i_t=1}^{n_t} \text{DF}_{t_{it}}^1 + \Sigma_{i_x=1}^{n_x} \text{DF}_{x_{ix}}^1 + \Sigma_{i_y=1}^{n_y} \text{DF}_{y_{iy}}^1$$

$$\text{DF}(N_2) = \Sigma_{i_p=1}^{n_p} \text{DF}_{p_{ip}}^2 + \Sigma_{i_q=1}^{n_q} \text{DF}_{q_{iq}}^2 + \Sigma_{i_r=1}^{n_r} \text{DF}_{r_{ir}}^2 + \Sigma_{i_t=1}^{n_t} \text{DF}_{t_{it}}^2 + \Sigma_{i_x=1}^{n_x} \text{DF}_{x_{ix}}^2 + \Sigma_{i_y=1}^{n_y} \text{DF}_{y_{iy}}^2.$$

where n_p (resp. n_q, n_r, n_t, n_x and n_y) is the number of properties defined in each of six possible ways. Finally, we calculate the similarity between two entities N_1 and N_2 defined with restrictions as follows:

$$\text{SIM}(N_1, N_2) = \frac{\text{CF}(N_1, N_2)}{\text{DF}(N_1) + \text{DF}(N_2) + \text{CF}(N_1, N_2)}.$$

Not all the features have the same importance in defining a concept. For example, it is possible to account for relevance of properties by providing the relevance factors (either as a-priori expert values or as user preferences) $R_{i_p}^p$, $i_p = 1, \ldots, n_p$, for each property p (and analogously for all the others). In this way, some properties become more important than the others, e.g. in case of cold cuts ontology *hasMeatKind* can be considered more important than *isSpicy*. In this case the formula for calculating the mutual similarity between domain items N_1 and N_2 becomes:

$$\text{SIM}^r(N_1, N_2) = \frac{\text{CF}^r(N_1, N_2)}{\text{DF}^r(N_1) + \text{DF}^r(N_2) + \text{CF}^r(N_1, N_2)}$$

where $\text{CF}^r(N_1, N_2) = \Sigma_{i_p=1}^{n_p} R_{i_p} \text{CF}_{p_{ip}} + \ldots + \Sigma_{i_y=1}^{n_y} R_{i_y} \text{CF}_{y_{iy}}$ and similarly for $\text{DF}^r(N_1)$ and $\text{DF}^r(N_2)$.

Another feature we want to take into account is the presence of equivalent classes, even though they are not defined as restrictions. We assume that two classes declared equivalent with equivalentClass would have similarity based on properties equal to 1.

As far as individuals are concerned (instances of the classes) we simply compare the values-property pairs declared for each instance. This is a simple case, analogous to the first case in the above discussion.

As opposed to similarity, which finds the elements similar to each other, relatedness helps find the elements that are *related* to each other. For example, if a certain product is *producedBy* a certain company and another product is *soldBy* the same company, these two products might not be similar but are definitely related. Finding related elements in the domain, permits us to cover different sub-ontologies of the domain, which are not reachable only with similarity, hence helping to resolve the diversity problem.

In order to calculate the property-based relatedness of domain elements we apply similar reasoning as for calculating similarity, but considering the values that are the same, for the different properties having the same ancestor. More precisely, considering completely unrelated properties would lead to relating very different elements and that is not our goal. Instead, we choose the properties that are in some way related (for example all are descendants of the same class) and calculate relatedness based on these properties. Lack of space does not allow us to go into more details on relatedness.

4   User Model

In this section we describe our approach to model users. We start with the definition of the user model (Sect. 4.1), followed by the description of the user feedback and how we use it (Sect. 4.2), to conclude with our technique for user model update and interest propagation (Sect. 4.3).

4.1   User Model Definition

As described above, the domain is represented by means of an OWL ontology, with the explicit specification of the concepts' properties. The user model is defined as an overlay on such an ontology (*ontology-based user model*), in order to represent the user interests for the domain concepts. More precisely, each ontological user profile is an instance of the domain ontology, where each node in the ontology has an interest value associated to it. This means that each node N in the domain ontology can be seen as a pair $\langle N, I(N) \rangle$, where $I(N)$ is the interest value associated to node N. Hence, the user model contains the values of user interests for the concepts in the ontology. Notice that at the beginning of the interaction the model is empty and the interest values will be inserted in the further update phases. The user model contains not only the information about the user's interest in domain objects, but also in all the objects' properties.

4.2   User Feedback

We chose not to directly ask the users about their preferences, but to automatically detect user preferences for properties according to users' behavior. The system records implicitly the user actions, inferring from them the interest for the object the action is performed on, and uses it to incrementally create and update the user model by modifying the interest values for certain domain objects.

Table 1. Weights associated to user actions

Action	Weight
Bookmarking an object	0.9
Tagging an object	0.7
Commenting on an object	0.5
Selecting an object	0.3
Rating an object	0.1*vote

Following Kobsa [11], each type of user feedback can be a signal of different user interest and as such can have different impact on the user model. We consider 5 possible most common typologies of generic user feedback in an adaptive social system[4]: (i) selecting an object, (ii) tagging, (iii) commenting, (iv) rating/voting on $1 - 5$ scale, or (v) putting an item into favorites/bookmarking it. Each of these actions is assigned a certain weight f, following the approach in [6] (see Table 1). These values are registered in the log files and analyzed further to calculate the user interest in both, the objects receiving the feedback and in their properties, as described in Sect. 4.3.

---

[4] The choice of actions to consider depends on a particular domain and application being used.

4.3   User Model Update and Interest Propagation

Adapting the approach in [7], each time a user provides a feedback, we first calculate the user *direct interest* $I_D(N)$ for the node N receiving the direct feedback as a weighted sum of old interest and sensed interest: $I_D(N) = \sigma_1 I_O(N) + \sigma_2 I_S(N)$, $\sigma_1, \sigma_2 \in \mathbb{R}$ such that $\sigma_1 + \sigma_2 = 1$. **Old interest** I_O is the old value for the user interest (initially equal to zero). The **sensed interest** I_S is the value obtained from the direct feedback of the user. It depends on the user feedback for the node and the position of the node in the ontology, since the nodes lower down in the ontology represent specific concepts, and as such signal more precise interest than the nodes represented by upper classes in the ontology, expressing more general concepts. In order to calculate the interest sensed by a given node N, we use the sigmoid function

$$I_S(N) = \frac{l(N)}{\text{MAX}(1 + e^{-f(N)})}$$

where $l(N)$ is the level of the node receiving the feedback, MAX is the level of the deepest node in the ontology and $f(N)$ is the feedback obtained from the user for the node N.

In our previous work [7] we used a power law with a negative exponent to weight the feedbacks. We now use the sigmoid function since it allows negative feedbacks, moves between -1 and 1 and does not need any constant.

In addition to being used for updating the direct interest value for the domain objects, sensed interest is also used to update the interest values for the object properties in the user model. Let $N_1, \ldots, N_k$ be the nodes that have a certain property p defined for them and each of them has $p_1, \ldots, p_{n_k}, n_k \in \mathbb{N}$ total properties defined. If the corresponding sensed interest values are $I_S(N_1), \ldots, I_S(N_k)$, then the interest value for the given property p is calculated as follows:

$$I(p) = \frac{1}{k} \Sigma_{i=1}^{k} \frac{I_S(N_i)}{n_i}.$$

If the relevance for the properties is provided in the system, then the above interest value is multiplied by the relevance value for that property.

Moreover, this value is also used for the subsequent propagation phase, in which the *inferred* interest values for the similar objects can be calculated as: $I_I(M) = \pi_1 I_O(M) + \pi_2 I_P(N, M)$ where **propagated interest** I_P is the value obtained by property-based propagation and $\pi_1, \pi_2 \in \mathbb{R}$, such that $\pi_1 + \pi_2 = 1$. We use the properties of each of the domain elements to calculate their mutual similarity (see Sect. 3) and decide to which elements to propagate the user interest. This propagation does not have any particular direction (as opposed to the one described in [7]) and permits us to propagate the user interests to various (sometimes quite distant) nodes of the ontology. The value of propagated interest value is calculated using the hyperbolic tangent function as follows:

$$I_P(N, M) = \frac{e^{2\text{SIM}(N,M)} - 1}{e^{2\text{SIM}(N,M)} + 1} I_S(N)$$

where $I_S(N)$ is the sensed interest of the node N receiving the feedback and $\text{SIM}(N, M)$ is the *similarity* between the node N receiving the feedback and the node M receiving the propagated interest (see Sect. 3). It is possible to propagate the user interest also to related nodes, using relatedness instead of similarity. We keep these two interest values, $\mathcal{I}_D$ and $\mathcal{I}_I$ separated for each concept, but the total interest for each concepts is obtained as: $\mathcal{I}(N) = \epsilon_D \mathcal{I}_D + \epsilon_I \mathcal{I}_I$, where $\epsilon_D, \epsilon_I \in \mathbb{R}$ and $\epsilon_D + \epsilon_I = 1$. By varying the constants ϵ_1 and ϵ_2 it is possible to assign different level of importance to either $\mathcal{I}_D$ or $\mathcal{I}_I$.

5 Evaluation

We evaluated our approach in *WantEat* application[15], where food such as cold cuts and wines, but also shops, restaurants etc, are intelligent objects able to provide recommendations. The domain is represented using a set of OWL ontologies, and the user model is defined as an overlay on such ontologies. For the experimental evaluation we selected the portion of the ontology regarding cold cuts (see Fig. 1), since it is fairly well balanced and easy for users to provide feedback. The system shows an adaptive behavior, ordering the objects returned by a search or displayed during the navigation according to user interest.

Hypothesis and Experimental Design. We assumed that our algorithm can help us generate ordered lists of objects having good correlation with the user preferences. Furthermore, we wanted to compare the present *property-based* propagation approach with the *vertical* propagation approach developed in [7] where the propagation is based on the lengths of the edges between classes.

We designed a questionnaire to collect users' preferences regarding cold cuts. In the first part, labelled U, the users voted for 8 non-leaf classes (e.g. Minced_ Cooked_ ColdCuts) on 1-10 scale. In the second part, labelled L, the users chose 4 leaf classes (e.g. Wurstel, Speck etc.) they "like very much" and 4 leaf classes they "like enough" among the total of 15 leaf classes.

We initially started with 100 subjects, 19-45 years old, recruited according to an availability sampling strategy[5]. Later, we restricted the initial sample to 87 users, eliminating all the users who assigned the same vote to 5 out of 7 classes, this being a strong indicator of random preferences assignment.

Measures and Material. We distinguished two phases in the evaluation process:

(i) *Exhaustive propagation evaluation*, where we generated an ordered list of both upper and leaf classes starting from one half of the two lists generated by the user and comparing the generated list with the remaining half

(ii) *Upward propagation evaluation*, where we generated an ordered list of upper classes using the list L and we compared them with the classes in the list U.

We used Spearman's rank correlation coefficient ρ to compute the association between the original user's list and the algorithm generated list, since it allows to address the possible ties in the ordered lists. $\rho = 1$ occurs when no repeated values exist and the two list are in the same order, $\rho \geq 0.5$ points to a "fair direct correlation", $\rho \geq 0.7$ to a "good direct correlation" and $\rho \geq 0.9$ to a "strong direct correlation".

---

[5] Much research in social science is based on samples obtained through non-random selection, such as the availability sampling, i.e. a sampling of convenience, based on subjects available to the researcher, often used when the population source is not completely defined.

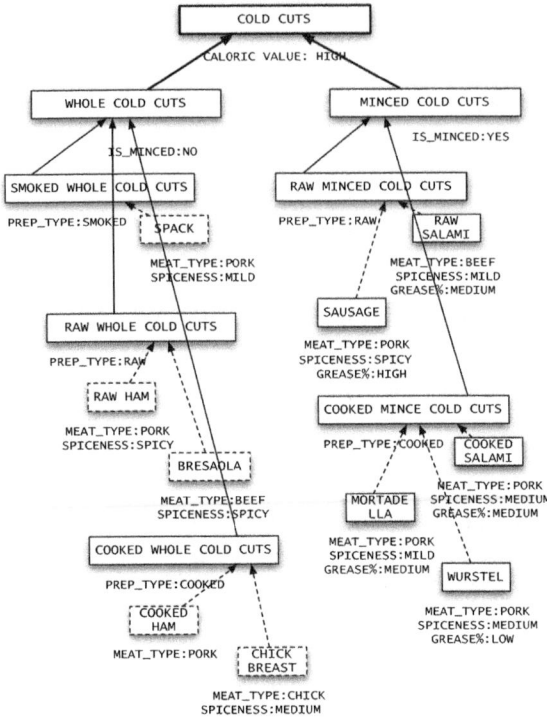

Fig. 1. The part of domain ontology describing cold cuts

Results. We computed the Spearman's coefficient ρ for 87 pairs of lists using both the property based propagation (red line) and the vertical propagation (dashed blue line) [7].

Exhaustive propagation. Using the property-based propagation technique we obtained the results shown in Figure 2. In 90% of the cases we acquired a list with a positive association with the user preferences. More impressive, in 25% of the cases we computed a list with a good positive association ($\rho \geq 0.7$). Only in 2% of the cases we obtained a list with a moderate inverse correlation ($\rho \leq -0.5$). On the other hand, applying the vertical propagation yields the results not much better then random. In fact, the ability to propagate interests also horizontally is required.

Upward propagation. Figure 3 shows the distribution of the values of ρ for the 87 pair of lists compared. We can see that in 86% of the cases with the *property-based* propagation and in 62% of the cases with the *vertical* propagation we generated a list with a positive association with the user preferences. Therefore, the flexibility of property-based

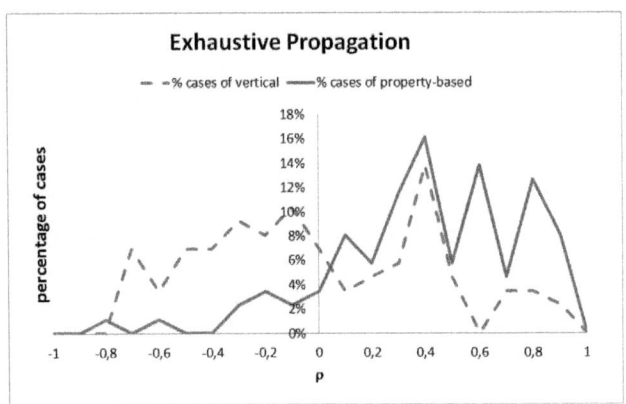

Fig. 2. Distribution of cases for various values of ρ for the exhaustive propagation

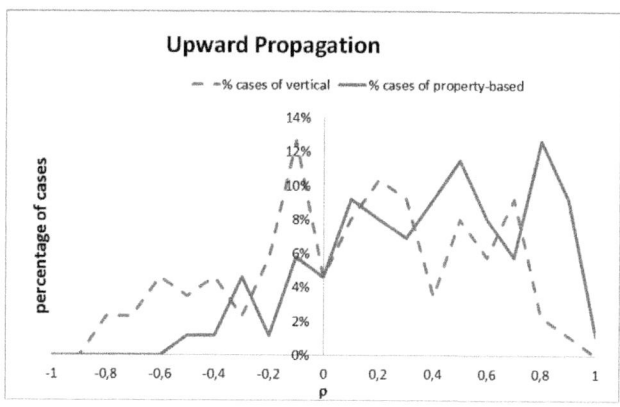

Fig. 3. Distribution of cases for various values of ρ for the upward propagation. A comparison between the *property-based* and the *vertical* approach.

propagation allows for a better overall performance. Moreover, after only providing the feedback eight times, we are able to obtain a "good correlation" ($\rho \geq 0.7$) in 28% of the cases with property-based propagation, as opposed to 12% for the vertical propagation. The number of misleading cases with $\rho \leq -0.5$ is 1% for the property-based propagation and 13% for the vertical one.

Discussion. The results show that the *property-based* approach works well, both for he exhaustive and upward propagation. It appears to perform better then *vertical* technique since it allows for the exhaustive propagation and it also yields better result in the upward case. We were able to generate lists with a good correlation ($\rho \geq 0.7$) in more then one forth of the cases after small amount of feedback. The risk of suggesting a misleading list to the user is also very low for both tests. Therefore, our technique, while learning the user preferences very quickly, rarely misfires or introduces anomalies in the user model. Thus it can safely be applied alone or in combination with other methods to address the cold start and the diversity problems.

6   Related Work

Since our approach requires the use of ontologies to represent domain knowledge and the user model is represented as an overlay on such ontologies, it is similar to *ontology-based recommender* [13,22,5,9]. Similarly to these works we take advantage of the enhanced semantics representation, and user profiles are compared at a finer level than in usual recommender systems. What is different in our approach is the way we compute item-item similarity based on properties. [13] and [22], in order to update the interest values in the ontology, exploit only IS-A relationships. In the approach in [5], the concept, item, and user spaces are clustered in a coordinated way, and the resulting clusters are used to find similarities among individuals at multiple semantic layers. [9] take into account the semantic relatedness between different concepts in terms of semantic words relations (synonymy, hyponymy, and meronymy).

Notice that in this paper we use the term "ontology-based user model" in a different sense with respect to other works [8], that define ad hoc ontology to represent the user features in the user model. Differently, we only use the ontology to model the domain, and the user model is defined as an overlay over the domain ontology, as it has been done for a long time in educational systems [4,18]

In similar fashion to us, other approaches make use of ontological structure to calculate similarity among concepts. In addition to Tversky's feature-based model of similarity [24], semantic similarity can be calculated in two general modes. Resnik's notion of semantic similarity [19] is based on information content in an IS-A taxonomy, given by the negative logarithm of the probability of occurrence of the class in a text corpus. The closest class subsuming compared concepts provides the shared information for both and gives the measure of their similarity. Rada et al. [17] use the ontology graph structure, using the distance between nodes (the number of edges or the number of nodes between the two nodes) to calculate the similarity. These three basic measures of similarity gave rise to many combined approaches. In Jiang and Conrath [10] distance based approach is improved with the information content one. The semantic similarity introduced by Pirró and Euzenat in [16] combines the feature-based model of similarity with the information theoretical one, where Lin [12] introduces an information-theoretic definition of similarity based on a set of assumptions about similarity, calculated as the ratio between the amount of information that two concepts have in common and the amount of information needed to fully describe them. Smyth [23] takes into account individual features of concepts and each feature has its own similarity function defined for it. Similarly to us, they also introduce the weights which help distinguish the importance of individual features when calculating similarity.

7 Conclusions and Future Work

This paper presents a novel approach for the propagation of user interest values in a domain ontology, considering similarity (and relatedness) of the domain concepts, based on their properties values. This approach advances the current state of the art by supporting finer recommendation modalities (e.g. case-based or item-based recommendations), since it is able to take user interests in object properties into account, thus calculating similarity among objects in a more precise way. The evaluation of the approach in gastronomic domain proved its effectiveness in improving the user model accuracy.

Notice that, when calculating similarity, we consider the values of the concept's properties, both data type and object type ones. In the first case, we do not consider the values represented as textual descriptions. In case of object-type properties, we only take into account the presence or absence of the same values of properties. Further possible development would be to give a priori similarity values between properties (e.g. soft cheese would be more similar to medium than to hard cheese). We also do not take into account cardinality restrictions, as well as restrictions defined as intersections, unions and complements, leaving these aspects for future work.

In addition, we intend to combine our approach with the vertical propagation of user interests presented in [7], obtaining a complete approach for dealing with missing user interest values. Also, it should be possible to extend the propagation of interests also to similar users. Furthermore, we want to make the user model more dynamic by taking in consideration the timing of the feedbacks and the context. We aim also at adding a confidence measure to propagation, i.e. to know how much the inference of user interest is reliable. Finally, we intend to test the user model created with our approach with different recommendation algorithms which take user preferences for properties into account to calculate recommendations, such as *case-based recommendation* [23]. In this way, we would be able to recommend restaurants and shops, based on user feedback on food products, starting from food features. Our approach could be also used to provide *multi-criteria item-based collaborative filtering recommendation* [2] where recommendations are computed by finding items similar to the other items the user likes.

References

1. Abel, F., Araújo, S., Gao, Q., Houben, G.-J.: Analyzing Cross-System User Modeling on the Social Web. In: Auer, S., Díaz, O., Papadopoulos, G.A. (eds.) ICWE 2011. LNCS, vol. 6757, pp. 28–43. Springer, Heidelberg (2011)
2. Adomavicius, G., Manouselis, N., Kwon, Y.: Multi-criteria recommender systems. In: Recommender Systems Handbook, pp. 769–803 (2011)
3. Aroyo, L., Dolog, P., Houben, G.-J., Kravcik, M., Naeve, A., Nilsson, M., Wild, F.: Interoperability in personalized adaptive learning. Educational Technology & Society 9(2), 4–18 (2006)
4. Brusilovsky, P., Millán, E.: User Models for Adaptive Hypermedia and Adaptive Educational Systems. In: Brusilovsky, P., Kobsa, A., Nejdl, W. (eds.) Adaptive Web 2007. LNCS, vol. 4321, pp. 3–53. Springer, Heidelberg (2007)
5. Cantador, I., Bellogín, A., Castells, P.: A multilayer ontology-based hybrid recommendation model. AI Communications 21(2-3), 203–210 (2008)
6. Carmagnola, F., Cena, F., Console, L., Cortassa, O., Gena, C., Goy, A., Torre, I., Toso, A., Vernero, F.: Tag-based user modeling for social multi-device adaptive guides. User Modeling and User-Adapted Interaction 18, 497–538 (2008)
7. Cena, F., Likavec, S., Osborne, F.: Propagating User Interests in Ontology-Based User Model. In: Pirrone, R., Sorbello, F. (eds.) AI*IA 2011. LNCS, vol. 6934, pp. 299–311. Springer, Heidelberg (2011)
8. Heckmann, D., Schwartz, T., Brandherm, B., Schmitz, M., von Wilamowitz-Moellendorff, M.: GUMO – The General User Model Ontology. In: Ardissono, L., Brna, P., Mitrović, A. (eds.) UM 2005. LNCS (LNAI), vol. 3538, pp. 428–432. Springer, Heidelberg (2005)
9. IJntema, W., Goossen, F., Frasincar, F., Hogenboom, F.: Ontology-based news recommendation. In: 2010 EDBT/ICDT Workshops. ACM Int. Conf. Proc. Series. ACM (2010)
10. Jiang, J., Conrath, D.: Semantic similarity based on corpus statistics and lexical taxonomy. In: International Conference on Research in Computational Linguistics, pp. 19–33 (1997)
11. Kobsa, A., Koenemann, J., Pohl, W.: Personalized hypermedia presentation techniques for improving online customer relationship. The Knowledge Engineering Review 16(2), 111–155 (2001)
12. Lin, D.: An information-theoretic definition of similarity. In: 15th International Conference on Machine Learning ICML 1998, pp. 296–304. Morgan Kaufmann Publishers Inc. (1998)
13. Middleton, S.E., Shadbolt, N.R., De Roure, D.C.: Ontological user profiling in recommender systems. ACM Transactions on Information Systems 22, 54–88 (2004)
14. O'Sullivan, D., Smyth, B., Wilson, D.C.: Preserving recommender accuracy and diversity in sparse datasets. Int. Journal on Artificial Intelligence Tools 13(1), 219–235 (2004)

15. PIEMONTE Team: Interacting with a social web of smart objects for enhancing tourist experiences. In: ENTER 2012 Conference, Helsingborg (2012)
16. Pirró, G., Euzenat, J.: A Feature and Information Theoretic Framework for Semantic Similarity and Relatedness. In: Patel-Schneider, P.F., Pan, Y., Hitzler, P., Mika, P., Zhang, L., Pan, J.Z., Horrocks, I., Glimm, B. (eds.) ISWC 2010, Part I. LNCS, vol. 6496, pp. 615–630. Springer, Heidelberg (2010)
17. Rada, R., Mili, H., Bicknell, E., Blettner, M.: Development and application of a metric on semantic nets. IEEE Trans. on Systems Management and Cybernetics 19(1), 17–30 (1989)
18. Razmerita, L., Angehrn, A., Maedche, A.: Ontology-based User Modeling for Knowledge Management Systems. In: Brusilovsky, P., Corbett, A.T., de Rosis, F. (eds.) UM 2003. LNCS, vol. 2702, pp. 213–217. Springer, Heidelberg (2003)
19. Resnik, P.: Semantic similarity in a taxonomy: An information-based measure and its application to problems of ambiguity in natural language. Journal of Artificial Intelligence Research 11, 95–130 (1999)
20. Salton, G., McGill, M.: Introduction to Modern Information Retrieval. McGraw-Hill Book Company (1984)
21. Schein, A.I., Popescul, A., Ungar, L.H., Pennock, D.M.: Methods and metrics for cold-start recommendations. In: 25th Annual International ACM SIGIR Conference on Research and Development in Information Retrieval, SIGIR 2002, pp. 253–260. ACM (2002)
22. Sieg, A., Mobasher, B., Burke, R.: Web search personalization with ontological user profiles. In: 16th ACM Conference on Information and Knowledge Management, CIKM 2007, pp. 525–534. ACM (2007)
23. Smyth, B.: Case-Based Recommendation. In: Brusilovsky, P., Kobsa, A., Nejdl, W. (eds.) Adaptive Web 2007. LNCS, vol. 4321, pp. 342–376. Springer, Heidelberg (2007)
24. Tversky, A.: Features of similarity. Psychological Review 84(4), 327–352 (1977)

EEG Estimates of Engagement and Cognitive Workload Predict Math Problem Solving Outcomes

Federico Cirett Galán and Carole R. Beal

The University of Arizona, Department of Computer Science, School of Information, Science, Technology and Arts, Tucson, AZ 85721-0077
{fcirett,crbeal}@email.arizona.edu

Abstract. The study goal was to evaluate whether Electroencephalography (EEG) estimates of attention and cognitive workload captured as students solved math problems could be used to predict success or failure at solving the problems. Students (N = 16) solved a series of SAT math problems while wearing an EEG headset that generated estimates of sustained attention and cognitive workload each second. Students also reported on their level of frustration and the perceived difficulty of each problem. Results from a Support Vector Machine (SVM) training indicated that problem outcomes could be correctly predicted from the combination of attention and workload signals at rates better than chance. EEG data were also correlated with students' self-report of problem difficulty. Findings suggest that relatively non-intrusive EEG technologies could be used to improve the efficacy of tutoring systems.

Keywords: Machine Learning, Electroencephalography, Math, Intelligent Tutoring Systems, physiology, behavior.

1 Introduction

The vision of a personalized experience for every user relies on the ability of adaptive systems to collect appropriate data in order to estimate the user's state and respond accordingly. Considerable progress has been made over the last decade in integrating models generated from behaviors such as keyboard clicks and inter-action latencies with real-time sensors indicating users' affective states. These models have produced significant advances in intelligent tutoring systems (ITS) research, leading to more adaptive systems that should ultimately be able to intervene to optimize learning for individuals. However, when considering the typical classroom situation, feasibility of data collection becomes an important constraint to consider: Although more information about the user's state would clearly be better in terms of creating accurate student models, there is also a limit to the instrumentation that we can apply to the user, at least outside a laboratory situation.

The present study was conducted to investigate the potential value of Electroencephalography (EEG) data about students' engagement and workload during problem solving. Engagement includes estimates of cognitive activities such

J. Masthoff et al. (Eds.): UMAP 2012, LNCS 7379, pp. 51–62, 2012.

as information gathering, visual scanning and sustained attention, and Workload is a measure of effortful cognitive activity [15]. However, the application of EEG in educational research is relatively recent. If we could establish that EEG data could provide a reliable indication of the student's progress in learning, such data might eventually be incorporated into a real-time system that could intervene if the learner is predicted to be on an unproductive path.

2   Prior Work

Researchers in the Intelligent Tutoring Systems (ITS) community have investigated several approaches to investigate the state of the learner. One approach is to use behaviors such as the time between clicks and rapid activation of instructional scaffolding (e.g., repeatedly clicking on the "help" button) to estimate whether the student is actually engaged with trying to solve a problem or is avoiding effort, perhaps by "gaming the system" by deliberately entering wrong answers in order to move on quickly [4]. Beal, Mitra and Cohen [5] used a Hidden Markov Model (HMM) to infer the level of engagement of the student to predict behavior in the next problem. The results showed that students had distinct trajectories of engagement, and that the HMM estimates were strongly related to independent estimates of individual students' mathematics motivation, based on students' self-report and reports provided by their teachers, and mathematics proficiency (grades, test scores). Johns and Woolf [11] also reported that an HMM provided good predictions about students' motivation while solving a series of problems in a math tutoring system, predicting a student correct response 72% of the time (versus 62% of the baseline) with a Dynamic Mixture Model based on Item Response Theory. More recently, Arroyo, Mehranian and Woolf [2] tested 600 students on an ITS for mathematics, estimating in real time the effort the student invested on solving each problem and using the results to choose the next problem with the same level or greater level of difficulty if the student is engaged, and an easier one otherwise. Students using the experimental effort-based selector scored significantly better than those that got problems served by a random problem selector (57% vs. 42% accuracy in post-tests).

Another approach has been to use direct sensors that can capture more direct physical indications of the learner's state. Kapoor, Burleson and Picard [12] used an array of sensors (eye tracking, mouse sensitivity, skin conductance, chair pressure) in a laboratory setting to track students' level of frustration and reported that they could predict when a user was about to give up with a 79% accuracy, using Support Vector Machines (SVM) and SVM with Gaussian Process Classification (GP). Arroyo et al [3] used a suite of sensors, including facial expression recognition, skin conductance, mouse pressure, and back pressure, as well as feedback from participants to estimate students' emotional state as they solved math problems in an authentic classroom context. They report predicting more than 60% of the variance of students' emotional states. Fincham et al [10] tested subjects with functional Magnetic Resonance Imaging (fMRI) equipment while solving problems in an ITS. Then they applied a cognitive model to predict distribution of problem solution times from measures of problem complexity, and used fMRI data to predict when students were actively engaged in problem solving. With a Hidden Markov Model based on these two data sets, they could predict the mental state of the subject with up to 83% of accuracy.

Although these results have been encouraging, the need to apply multiple sensors to instrument the learner may prove challenging. Certainly, obtaining fMRI data is still quite costly and not likely to be feasible for use in classroom situations. Another issue is that research to date has focused mostly on estimating the learner's affective or motivational state, rather than on the amount of cognitive effort being expended during problem solving.

An alternative that has attracted attention is the use of EEG to assess cognitive workload. Technology for capturing EEG signals has progressed considerably, to the point where the user can wear a lightweight recording unit that transmits data for analysis. The recording unit is sufficiently non-intrusive and it is being used in a variety of tasks that require sustained attention and cognitive effort, including long-haul truck driving, missile tracking and submarine systems control. For example, Berka and Levendowski [7] found that officers tracking missiles in a simulated environment Aegis Combat System had a high or extreme cognitive workload 25 to 30% of the time and achieved a detection efficiency of almost 100%. Education researchers have begun to use this type of device to track students' cognitive activity during problem solving. Stevens, Galloway, Berka, Johnson and Sprang [17] compared novices and experts as they solved a series of chemistry problems, and reported that the two groups showed distinct patterns of attention that correlated with problem solving time and accuracy. Mostow, Chang and Nelson [13] used a single-channel EEG recorder with both adults and children as they read difficult and easy text passages. The EEG data were used to train a classifier, and results were significantly better than chance at discriminating the reading of adults and children, as well as predicting the difficulty of the text. Chaouachi, Jraidi and Frasson [8] recorded EEG activity with a six-channel unit as users solved cognitive tasks varying in difficulty, and verified that their estimates of the users' mental workload were correlated with the difficulty of the tasks. Thus, initial results appear to suggest that EEG might be a valuable technology for directly assessing a student's level of cognitive effort.

3   Methodology

In the present study, we followed a similar approach: EEG data were recorded as students solved a series of easy and difficult math problems. Estimates of engagement (sustained attention) and cognitive workload derived from the EEG signals were used to train a classifier to predict the outcome of the problem: correct or incorrect answer. We were also interested in learning if the EEG estimates would be different for easy and hard problems, as suggested by the results of Chaouachi et al. [8], and if the estimates would be related to the students' self-report of how difficult the problem was. There were 16 participants in the study (8 males, 8 females). Participants were college students who were at least 18 years old and gave active written consent for participation. They

Table 1. The problems in the study were of multiple choice with 4 possible options. *Correct answers are* **c** *and* **b**.

Difficulty	Name	Problem
Easy	Classroom	In a class of 78 students 41 are taking French, 22 are taking German and 9 students are taking both French and German. How many students are not enrolled in either course? a.)6 b.)15 c.)24 d.)33
Hard	Triangle	A triangle has a perimeter 13. The two shorter sides have integer lengths equal to x and x + 1. Which of the following could be the length of the other side? a.)4 b.)6 c.)8 d.)10

received either a small stipend or course credit for participation. Each person participated in a 90 minute session, which included informed consent procedures, fitting the EEG headset, completing a 15 minute baseline calibration task, and solving eight multiple-choice math problems presented at the computer while wearing the EEG headset. Math problems were taken from a set of released SAT items; there were four easy problems and four hard problems, with difficulty level determined by information from the College Board. Each problem had four answer options. The items were presented to students within an online tutoring system that recorded the time on the problem (initial presentation on the screen to first answer selection) as well as the outcome (correct, incorrect answer chosen). Problems were presented in one of two sequences (easy, easy, hard, hard, easy, easy, hard, hard or hard, hard, easy, easy, hard, hard, easy, easy) across subjects.

3.1   EEG Data Acquisition

The electroencephalogram (EEG) data were recorded from nine sensors integrated into a mesh cap covering the upper half of the head, along with two reference signals attached to the mastoid bones (behind the ears) and two sensors attached to the right clavicle and to the lowest left rib to record the heart rate (although the heart rate data were not used in the study). The location of each sensor was determined by the International 10-20 System [14] to ensure standardized reproduction of tests. This cap was equipped with a small wireless transmission unit. A small USB dongle received the wireless transmissions to a PC computer with Windows (XP/Vista/7) 32 bit operating system. Each second, 256 EEG signals were transmitted and converted to Theta, Alpha, Beta and Sigma wave signals (ranging from 3 Hz to 40 Hz). These signals were processed by Advanced Brain Monitoring proprietary software from B-Alert [1] to produce classifications of mental states, meaning the probability that the participant was in a particular state in epochs of one second. States included Engagement, Distraction, Drowsiness and Cognitive Workload [6]. Engagement includes estimates of cognitive activities such as information gathering, visual scanning and sustained attention, and Workload is a measure of effortful

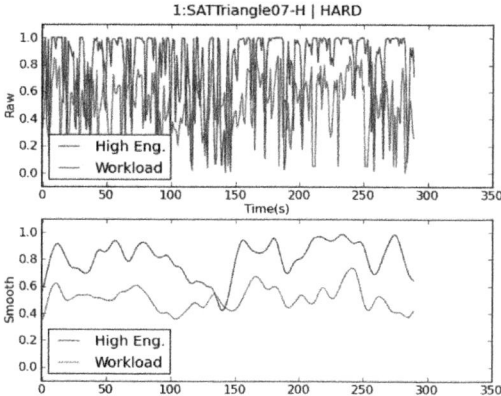

Fig. 1. Signals at the top are considered *'raw'* and show high variability. The same signals smoothed for visual presentation are shown at the bottom. X-axis represents time in seconds.

cognitive activity [15]. The Engagement and Workload data were selected for our analyses because levels of Drowsiness were almost non-existent in the present study, and Distraction is essentially the inverse of Engagement.

3.2   Self Report

Participants were provided with an eight-page paper booklet to use as they solved the math problems. Each page included an area for working out the problem on paper (if needed). After completing each problem, participants were also asked to rate the difficulty of the problem, how confident they felt about their performance, and their level of frustration. Ratings were made on a five-point Likert-type scale.

4   Data Analysis

We first investigated whether the EEG data could be used to predict the outcome (right or wrong answer) of a math problem. Of the 16 participants, 15 completed all eight problems and one completed seven of the eight items. The outcome data set thus consisted of 127 completed math problems, with 49 answered incorrectly (38.6%). One participant aced the problems, another one failed in just one, while 6 participants only erred on two. The rest got wrong answers on 3, 4, 5 and up to 6 problems.

4.1   Data Processing

The Engagement signals (one per second) were processed by converting each raw signal into one of three equal-sized bins, with limits set at 0.333 and 0.666

of the Cumulative Distribution Function. The count of signals below 0.333 were considered as the Low State, values between 0.333 and 0.666 as the Medium state, and those between 0.666 and 1.0 as the High state. By doing this, we assure a normalization between all the participants. Then the Engagement signal sequence was scanned and tagged to produce a transition probability table (tpt). The tpt consisted of nine cells representing the transition probabilities between the three states. The tpt was then tagged with the problem outcome (+1 for a correct answer and -1 for an incorrect one). A file was constructed with 16 records (one for each participant) including the outcome tag and nine features to serve as input to a Support Vector Machine (SVM). Because the sample size was small (each problem had only 16 records) libsvm [9] was used with leave-one-out cross-validation enabled. A similar method was used to process the Workload signals.

4.2   SVM Classification

Several experiments were conducted with SVM classification: First, we used files with nine features as described above. Second, we constructed files that included the best three transitions with better information gain [16], where the features that have the higher probability of describing an outcome were chosen based by finding an Optimum Decision Tree. Third, we built files with only three specific features: High to High, Medium to Medium and Low to Low transitions. As will be shown in the next section, the best results were obtained using the latter method. We also compared the predictions for different segments of the EEG data. First, we used the full sequence of data for the entire problem (Engagement, Workload and Engagement & Workload together) for each participant. Of course, the time on each problem varied across participants. In an effort to reduce the potential confound of overall time on the problem, we also considered only the first n seconds of the signal after the subject started answering the problem, as well as using only the last n seconds of the signal just before the subjected answered the problem. To obtain the optimal n value of seconds, a series of SVM experiments with 10, 15, 20 and 25 seconds was conducted. Of these, the best predictions resulted from using the data from the first 20 seconds after the problem was presented on the screen, and the last 20 seconds before the problem was answered.

5   Results

5.1   SVM Predictions

Prediction accuracies are shown in Table 2 for each math problem, along with the base rate of performance (how many times the problem was answered correctly) and the average time per problem. As may be seen in Table 2, the SVM predictions were consistently higher than chance (25%, or one answer out of four possible) and also higher than the base rate of performance for each problem.

That is, relying on the EEG data would provide a better estimate of the problem outcome than simply knowing that, i.e., there is a 56% chance of a correct solution to the Towns problem, based on the actual performance of the problem solvers. Using the most informative (Max) signals from both the Engagement and Workload data streams provided an overall prediction accuracy of 87%.

Table 2. SVM cross validation results for each problem and their averages by difficulty. Average solving time is in seconds.

			Cross validation accuracy			
Easy problems	Average time	Base rate Accuracy	Engagement	Workload	Eng.& Wkld.	Max(Eng, Wkld)
Bows	124	75%	75%	88%	88%	88%
Class	139	50%	88%	69%	75%	88%
Summation	37	75%	75%	88%	88%	88%
Village	177	44%	75%	81%	63%	81%
Average	**119**	**65%**	**83%**	**83%**	**80%**	**87%**
Hard problems	Average time	Base rate Accuracy	Engagement	Workload	Eng.& Wkld.	Max(Eng, Wkld)
Bus	119	62%	75%	75%	69%	75%
Fence	247	62%	81%	69%	63%	81%
Towns	230	56%	81%	63%	69%	81%
Triangle	259	50%	75%	63%	63%	75%
Average	**214**	**57%**	**78%**	**67%**	**66%**	**78%**
Both	**167**	**62%**	**80%**	**75%**	**73%**	**83%**

As shown in Table 2, there were some differences for the easy versus the hard problems: On average, the SVM classifier performed better on the easy problems, with the Engagement and Workload signals being equally good predictors (83% both). Combining the Engagement & Workload signals (six features in total) as input for the SVM actually reduced the classification accuracy slightly (80%). On hard problems, the Engagement signal was a better predictor than the Workload signal (78% vs. 67%). Using the maximum value between the result of the SVM classification of the Engagement and Workload signals increments the cross validation accuracy for the easy problems up to 87% and for the hard problems to 78% (Figure 2). One reason that the predictions were somewhat less accurate for the hard problems may be that students took longer on the hard problems, meaning that the signals were longer and possibly nosier.

We also tried to predict the outcome of the problems with reduced information. First, we assumed that the initial 20 seconds the Engagement signal might provide a useful signature of the initial comprehension phase of problem solving. Second, we considered the last 20 seconds of the Workload signal, which we thought might correspond to the cognitive activity involved in computing the solution to the problem. However, as shown in Figures 3 and 4 (shown in page 58), prediction accuracy did not improve. Using only the first and last 20 seconds of the signal to predict a correct or incorrect outcome gives us a prediction rate of 77% and 79% overall.

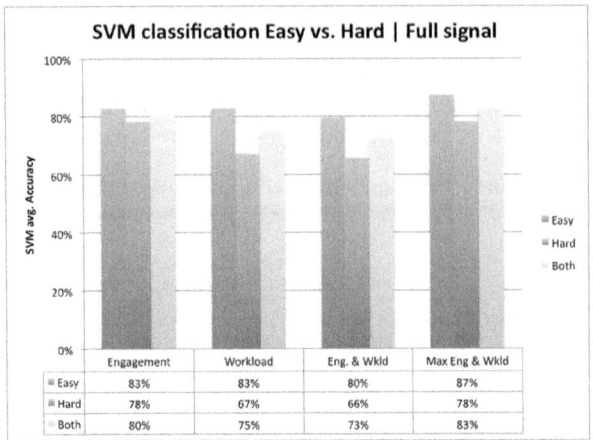

Fig. 2. SVM accuracy for easy vs. hard problems using the full EEG signal for each problem

5.2 Relation of EEG and Self-report Data

We were interested in whether students' experiences during problem solving might be related to their cognitive workload as indicated by the EEG estimates. We started by attempting to verify that the hard problems actually were more challenging. Results are shown in Table 3. As may be seen in Table 3, participants took more time to answer the hard problems than the easy ones. A matched-pairs t-test indicated that this difference was significant, $(t(15) = 3.746, p<.01)$. Subjects rated themselves as more frustrated on hard problems than on easy

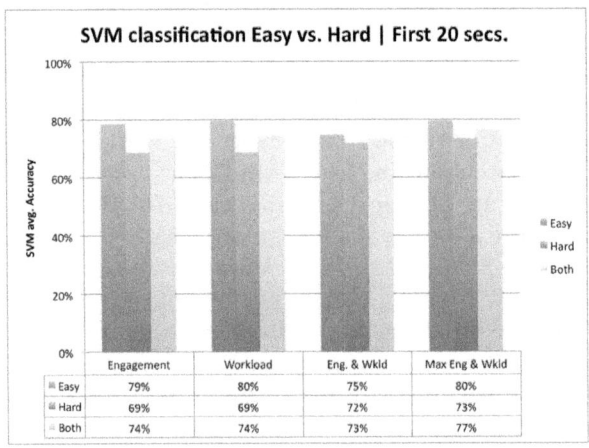

Fig. 3. SVM accuracy for easy versus hard problems using the first 20 seconds of the EEG signal for each problem

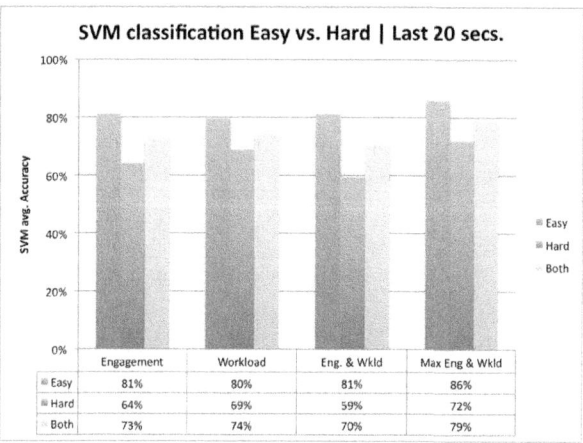

Fig. 4. SVM accuracy for easy versus hard problems using the last 20 seconds of the EEG signal for each problem

Table 3. Mean scores by problem difficulty. Standard deviations are shown in parentheses. The * at the right hand column indicates a significant difference in a matched-pairs t-test.

	Easy problems	Hard problems	
Behavior			
Time (seconds)	119.5 (66.9)	213.8 (110)	*
Use of scratch area	0.81 (0.17)	0.83 (0.29)	
Self report			
Difficulty rating	2.07 (0.57)	2.91 (0.79)	*
Frustration	1.86 (.56)	2.42 (0.69)	*
Confidence	3.73 (.89)	3.21 (1.17)	

problems, $t(14) = 2.84$, p<.05, and rated hard problems as more difficult than easy problems, $t(12) = 6.273$, p<.01. In absolute terms, participants reported less confidence in their answers on hard problems than on easy problems, but the difference was not significant. There was no difference in participants' use of scratch paper for hard problems and easy problems. Mean scores for Engagement and Workload are shown in Table 4 by problem difficulty. There was no difference for Engagement, but Workload scores were significantly higher for difficult problems than for easy problems. The effect was admittedly not strong in absolute terms, but the finding that workload was higher on average on the more challenging problems is consistent with the participants' self-reports suggesting that they experienced those problems as more difficult. Our investigation into the relation of self-report with EEG data was limited by our relatively small sample size. However, in an exploratory analysis, we first considered the extent to which the reports of problem difficulty, frustration and confidence were correlated. Results are shown in Table 5.

60 F.C. Galán and C.R. Beal

Table 4. Mean scores for Engagement and Workload by problem difficulty. Standard deviations are shown in parentheses. The * at the right hand column indicates a significant difference (p<.05) in a matched-pairs t-test.

	Easy problems	Hard problems	
Engagement	0.52 (.18)	0.50 (.19)	
Workload	0.65 (.14)	0.69 (.14)	*

Table 5. Correlations for self-reports of confidence, frustration and problem difficulty. * p<.05, ** p<.01.

	Confidence	Frustration	Difficulty
Confidence	1	-0.65*	-0.81
Frustration	-0.65*	1	0.64*
Difficulty	-0.81**	0.64*	1

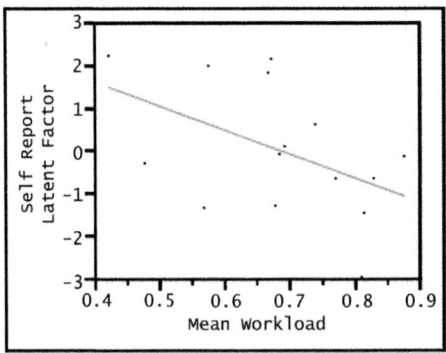

Fig. 5. Relation of workload and latent factor representing the user's self-reported experience of a problem as challenging

The strong intercorrelations suggested a principal components analysis, which indicated that there was one underlying factor that accounted for 72% of the variance in the self-report responses. Therefore, we extracted the estimate for this latent factor for each participant, and then used the mean workload scores to predict these estimates. Results are shown in Figure 5 in page 60. The figure indicates the suggestion that for individuals with higher average workload scores, the self-reported experience was one of reduced confidence, greater frustration and the perception that the problems were more challenging. However, the relation was not statistically significant, F(1,13) = 3.875, p<.07, perhaps due to the incomplete data from two participants.

6 Discussion

These preliminary results suggest that using the estimates of Engagement and Workload from EEG data predicts the problem outcome better than base rate of problem performance and on average the predictions are comparable to prior work, like Johns and Woolf [11] 72% correct prediction of outcome using only behavioral data, Kapoor et al.[12] 79% rate prediction of frustration, and Fincham et al.[10] 83% correct prediction of mental state of test subjects. It is worth mentioning that prior work was focused on behavioral data while our experiment focused on cognitive activity.

In this study, problems labeled as *Easy* were solved in less time than those tagged as *Hard* problems and the SVM got a better accuracy predicting the former. We suspect that as the time to answer a problem increments, so does the noise in the EEG signals of Workload & Engagement and the accuracy to predict the correct outcome drops.

In future work a predictor module for ITS could be developed, using nonintrusive EEG caps and SVM classification on the first 20 seconds of Engagement and Workload signals to help the students stay interested on the interactive session with the ITS. A possible area of research would include the use of Theta, Alpha, Beta and Sigma wave signals of brain activity (the basis for obtaining the Engagement & Workload signals) with different techniques as SVM, k-nn clustering and Multi-Event Dependency Detection (MEDD), to obtain patterns of activity in different locations of the brain surface while subjects are solving math problems, and test if we can do a better rate of classification of outcome.

Acknowledgements. The research was supported by National Science Foundation HRD 0903441. We would like to thank the staff at Advanced Brain Monitoring for their support, as well as the students who participated in the research.

References

1. Advanced Brain Monitoring, BAlert X10 (2011),
   http://www.b-alert.com/x10.html
2. Arroyo, I., Mehranian, H., W.B.P.: Effort-based Tutoring: An Empirical Approach to Intelligent Tutoring. In: Baker, R.S.J.d., M. A. P. P. J. E. (eds.), Proceedings of the 3rd International Conference on Educational Data Mining (2010)
3. Arroyo, I., Cooper, D.G., Burleson, W., Woolf, B.P., Muldner, K., Christopherson, R.: Emotion Sensors Go To School. In: Proceeding of the 2009 Conference on Artificial Intelligence in Education, pp. 17–24. IOS Press (2009)
4. Baker, R.S.J.d., Walonoski, J., Heffernan, N., Roll, I., Corbett, A., Koedinger, K.: Why students engage in gaming the system behavior in interactive learning environments. Journal of Interactive Learning Research 19, 185–224 (2008)
5. Beal, C., Mitra, S., Cohen, P.R.: Modeling learning patterns of students with a tutoring system using Hidden Markov Models. In: Proceeding of the 2007 Conference on Artificial Intelligence in Education, pp. 238–245. IOS Press (2007)

6. Berka, C., Levendowski, D.J., Lumicao, M.N., Yau, A., Davis, G., Zivkovic, V.T., Olmstead, R.E., Tremoulet, P.D., Craven, P.L.: EEG correlates of task engagement and mental workload in vigilance, learning, and memory tasks. Aviat Space Environ. Med. 78(5 suppl.), B231–B244 (2007)

7. Berka, C., Levendowski, D.J., Ramsey, C.K., Davis, G., Lumicao, M.N., Stanney, K., Reeves, L., Regli, S.H., Tremoulet, P.D., Stibler, K.: Evaluation of an EEG workload model in an Aegis simulation environment. In: Caldwell, J.A., Wesensten, N.J. (eds.) Society of Photo-Optical Instrumentation Engineers (SPIE) Conference Series, vol. 5797, pp. 90–99 (2005)

8. Chaouachi, M., Jraidi, I., Frasson, C.: Modeling Mental Workload Using EEG Features for Intelligent Systems. In: Konstan, J.A., Conejo, R., Marzo, J.L., Oliver, N. (eds.) UMAP 2011. LNCS, vol. 6787, pp. 50–61. Springer, Heidelberg (2011)

9. Fan, R.-E., Chen, P.-H., Lin, C.-J.: Working Set Selection Using Second Order Information for Training Support Vector Machines. J. Mach. Learn. Res., JMLR.org 6, 1889–1918 (2005)

10. Fincham J.M., Anderson J.R., B.S., J., F., Using Neural Imaging and Cognitive Modeling to Infer Mental States while Using an Intelligent Tutoring System. In: Baker, R.S.J.d., M. A. P. P. J. (eds.) Proceedings of the 3rd International Conference on Educational Data Mining, vol. 3, pp. 51–60 (2010)

11. Johns, J., Woolf, B.P.: A dynamic mixture model to predict student motivation and proficiency. In: Proceedings of the AAAI. IOS Press, Boston MA (2006)

12. Kapoor, A., Burleson, W., Picard, R.W.: Automatic prediction of frustration. International Journal of Human-Computer Studies 65(8), 724–736 (2007)

13. Mostow, J., Chang, K.-M., Nelson, J.: Toward Exploiting EEG Input in a Reading Tutor. In: Biswas, G., Bull, S., Kay, J., Mitrovic, A. (eds.) AIED 2011. LNCS, vol. 6738, pp. 230–237. Springer, Heidelberg (2011)

14. Niedermeyer, Ernst, D.S.F.H.L., Ovid Technologies, I.: Electroencephalography Basic Principles, Clinical Applications, and Related Fields, p. 140. Lippincott Williams & Wilkin, Philadelphia (2005)

15. Poythress, M., et al.: Correlation between Expected Workload and EEG Indices of Cognitive Workload and Task Engagement. Augmented Cognition: Past, Present and Future, 32–44 (2006)

16. Quinlan, J.R.: Induction of Decision Trees. Machine Learning 1, 81–106 (1986)

17. Stevens, R.H., Galloway, T., Berka, C., Johnson, R., Sprang, M.: Assessing students' mental representations of complex problem spaces with EEG technologies. In: Proceedings of the 52nd Annual Meeting of the Human Factors and Ergonomic Society, New York, NY (2008)

Preference Relation Based Matrix Factorization for Recommender Systems

Maunendra Sankar Desarkar, Roopam Saxena, and Sudeshna Sarkar

Department of Computer Science and Engineering,
Indian Institute of Technology Kharagpur, India
{maunendra,roopam.saxena,sudeshna}@cse.iitkgp.ernet.in

Abstract. Users in recommender systems often express their opinions about different items by rating the items on a fixed rating scale. The rating information provided by the users is used by the recommender systems to generate personalized recommendations for them. Few recent research work on rating based recommender systems advocate the use of preference relations instead of absolute ratings in order to produce better recommendations. Use of preference relations for neighborhood based collaborative recommendation has been looked upon in recent literature. On the other hand, Matrix Factorization algorithms have been shown to perform well for recommender systems, specially when the data is sparse. In this work, we propose a matrix factorization based collaborative recommendation algorithm that considers preference relations. Experimental results show that the proposed method is able to achieve better recommendation accuracy over the compared baseline methods.

Keywords: User feedback, Preference relations, Latent factors, Matrix Factorization.

1 Introduction

Recommender systems gather feedback from the users about different items to understand the interest profile of the users. This information is then used to generate personalized recommendations for them. User feedbacks about items may come either directly (in the form of ratings), or indirectly (by observing the user behavior using traces or click logs etc.) [1]. Direct or explicit feedback gathering is often used by several recommender systems for recommending movies, music items, books etc. In this work, we concentrate on recommendation algorithms for such explicit feedback based systems.

It is understood that recommender systems looking at pure ratings only have some drawbacks. A user may prefer one item over another item, but may have no choice but to give the same rating to both the items due to the limited rating scale [2]. Moreover, it might be difficult to pick a particular rating for an item, whereas given two different items it is probably easier to say which one is better (or both are equally good) [3]. The mood and the context also may influence the rating a user assigns to an item. [4]. Again, even users having similar interests for items tend to rate the same items differently. This is because rating is subjective, and

J. Masthoff et al. (Eds.): UMAP 2012, LNCS 7379, pp. 63–75, 2012.
© Springer-Verlag Berlin Heidelberg 2012

users have different levels of leniency while rating items [3]. This poses problems for the collaborative recommender systems as they attempt to exploit the rating patterns of *similar users*.

Once the system has the user feedbacks in some form (ratings, preference relations, implicit data etc.), it can use those for item recommendation. The *content based recommendation approaches* consider the different attributes of the items. The attributes may be the item categories (genres for movie items or songs, categories for books etc.), the authors (for books), singers (for music), actors and directors (for movies), language etc. If for an item, (some or all of) its attributes are known, and a user's interest in those attributes are also known, then the system may use that information for recommending items to the user.

However, detailed attribute information of items are often not available. Recommendation algorithms based on *latent feature model* assume that there exist some attributes or features of the items, but those are hidden to the system. The algorithms try to find the user and item representations in this latent feature space. In a sense, such features provide an automated alternative to the aforementioned human created item attributes. For movies, the discovered features might measure obvious dimensions as mentioned above; or less well-defined dimensions such as depth of character development, oddity, good vs weak narration; or completely uninterpretable dimensions. For users, each feature measures how much a user likes movies that score high on the corresponding feature [5]. Latent feature model based recommenders first learn the user and item features from the available data. The learned features are then used to find the items' utilities or values to different users.

One of the most widely used realizations of latent feature models is obtained via Non-negative Matrix Factorization (NMF). NMF has been shown to give good results even when the data is *sparse*. Also, it allows the system to represent the users and items using a small number of features and hence is computationally efficient. In this paper, we propose an NMF based recommendation algorithms that uses preference relations instead of actual ratings. To the best of our knowledge, this is the first research work that aims at solving the recommendation problem by using preference relations in matrix factorization framework. As there is no publicly available recommendation dataset containing preference relations provided by users, we use a rating database for experimentation. From the absolute ratings provided by the users, we induce the preference relations and use that data for testing the algorithms. Experimental results show that even when absolute ratings are available, using the induced preference relations may result in better recommendation performance.

2   Related Work

There have been some work that use preference relations instead of actual ratings for recommender systems. According to a user survey presented in [4] users do favor giving feedbacks in the form of preference relations instead of absolute ratings. The survey also found that preference relations are more stable in nature.

[2] presents a collaborative filtering algorithm for rating prediction and uses it for making recommendations. Positions of an item in the preference lists of the *similar users* are used to get an utility estimate of the item. Recommendation list is constructed by ordering the items in decreasing order of their estimated utilities. Another collaborative filtering based rating prediction framework that uses preference relations is proposed in [3]. It views each user's rating profile as a preference graph, where items are represented as nodes. For the target user, the algorithm builds an aggregate preference graph by considering the preference graphs of the most similar users. Each preference edge in the aggregate graph indicates the strength of the corresponding preference relation, as obtained from the similar users. Integer ratings are picked for each unrated item so that the induced preference relations have maximal agreement with the aggregate preference graph. As the predicted ratings are integers from a fixed rating scale, there will be lots of ties when the items are sorted according to their predicted scores. It is not clear how to break those ties. Hence it is difficult to generate recommendations from these predicted ratings.

Existing work on recommendation algorithms using preference relations have mainly concentrated upon user-based or item-based collaborative filtering approaches. Another type of recommendation algorithms, namely Non-negative Matrix Factorization (NMF) based algorithms, also have been shown to work well on real world data. NMF has been found to be a good alternative to collaborative filtering approach, specially when the data is sparse. NMF algorithms model each user and each item as d-dimensional vectors. For an item, the d dimensions are viewed as the latent classes that the items may belong to. For users, the dimensions correspond to their interests in those latent classes. [5] mentions several NMF based algorithms used for rating prediction problems. Items are often sorted according to the predicted ratings to produce the recommendation list [6]. Research is also being done for faster convergence of NMF algorithms [7], techniques like efficient initializations [8], using hierarchies and side information [9] for improving the recommendation accuracy etc. Although a rich literature is available for NMF techniques, all the methods discussed in literature use the absolute rating data, but not preference relations.

3   Using Preference Relations in the Matrix Factorization Framework

As discussed in Section 1, there are some recent research that studies the use of preference relations instead of actual ratings for recommender algorithms. The results are promising and motivate the use of preference relations for generating effective recommendations. On the other hand, the Non-negative Matrix Factorization (NMF) framework has been successfully applied to solve various problems related to recommender systems. However, for explicit rating based systems, the framework has been used with actual ratings only. In this work, we propose an algorithm that uses preference relations in the matrix factorization framework to solve the problem of personalized recommendation generation.

4   Preliminaries and Problem Definition

Let U be the set of users and I be the set of the items. In rating based recommender systems, feedbacks of the users are of the form r_{ui}, which indicates that user u has given a rating r_{ui} to item i. If we have preference relations as user feedbacks, then the feedbacks are of the form $\pi(u, i, j)$. It indicates that for the ordered item pair (i, j), the strength of user u's preference relation is $\pi(u, i, j)$. Generally, $\pi(u, i, j)$ has the following properties:

1. $\pi(u, i, j) \in [0, 1]$.
2. $\pi(u, j, i) = 1 - \pi(u, i, j)$.

If the users provide the preference relations directly, then the values of $\pi(u, i, j)$ are readily available. If only absolute ratings are available, then we can induce preference relations from it by modeling $\pi(u, i, j)$ using some function $\pi(u, i, j) = f(r_{ui}, r_{uj})$. However, $f(\cdot)$ has to satisfy the above properties of preference relations.

Given a set of preference relations, we want to develop a recommendation strategy that can output a recommendation list R_u for any user $u \in U$. The length of R_u is often fixed to some predefined constant K.

We solve the problem using the Non-negative Matrix Factorization framework. Details of the algorithm are presented in the subsequent sections.

5   Details of Our Approach

We now describe how the problem of personalized item recommendation can be solved using preference relation based matrix factorization. Like any standard matrix factorization based algorithm, the suggested approach has to first model each user and each item as a point in a d-dimensional space. The value of d is often chosen beforehand and is independent of the actual user or items. Generally, if m and n are the numbers of users and items respectively, then $d \ll m, n$. The d-dimensional feature representation of an item suggests the item's belongingness to the d hidden categories. Similarly, the d-dimensional feature representation of a user suggests the user's affinities to those d categories. The model learning part that computes the user and item features is performed offline. Once the feature representations are available, the system may predict the items' utilities to different users. This information is then used to generate the recommendations. This recommendation generation part is performed online when the user accesses the system or explicitly asks the system to recommend items for him/her. Both the tasks of model learning and recommendation generation are described below.

5.1   Learning the Factorization Model

In this task, the goal is to develop a factorization model that is able to predict the users' preference relations for different item pairs. If i and j are two items, then the preference relation for a user u and the item pair (i, j) is defined using the following function:

$$\pi(u, i, j) = \begin{cases} 0 & \text{if } u \text{ prefers } j \text{ over } i, \\ 0.5 & \text{if } i \text{ and } j \text{ are equally preferable to } u, \\ 1 & \text{if } u \text{ prefers } i \text{ over } j. \end{cases} \tag{1}$$

If the users provide the values of the preference relations, then the values of π can be obtained directly. However, there can be applications where users do not directly provide the values of the pairwise preference relations. For example, in a movie recommender system, users provide ratings for the movies they have watched. In this case, if a user's rating for movie i is greater than that for movie j, then it can be inferred that the user prefers movie i over movie j and $\pi(u, i, j)$ can be set accordingly.

In the proposed factorization model, we represent each user u by a d-dimensional feature vector $p_u \in \mathbb{R}^d$. Each item i is also represented in the same d-dimensional feature space $q_i \in \mathbb{R}^d$. As in the basic Matrix Factorization model, users' likings for different items are modeled as inner products in this shared feature space. For example, item i's value for user u is estimated as $p_u q_i^T$.

Given a pair of items i and j, their values for the user u are $p_u q_i^T$ and $p_u q_j^T$ respectively. If $p_u q_i^T > p_u q_j^T$, it can be said that i has more value than j for u. In other words, u prefers item i over item j. The *strength of this preference relation* can be estimated as $p_u (q_i - q_j)^T$. As $\pi(\cdot)$ is bounded between 0 and 1, it is necessary to bound the values of the predicted preference relations $\hat{\pi}(\cdot)$ between 0 and 1. In order to bound the value of the strength of this preference relation, we model it using the *inverse-logit* function. To summarize, given a user u and a pair of items i and j, the estimated strength of the preference relation is computed as:

$$\hat{\pi}(u, i, j) \overset{def}{=} \frac{e^{p_u (q_i - q_j)^T}}{1 + e^{p_u (q_i - q_j)^T}}. \tag{2}$$

The values of the user and item features p_u and q_i need to be learned from the training data. Each entry in the training data S is of the form $\langle u, i, j, \pi(u, i, j)\rangle$. It means that for user $u \in U$, strength of the preference relation for the item pair $(i, j) \in I \times I$ is $\pi(u, i, j)$. The learned values of p and q should be such that the induced preference relations $\hat{\pi}(\cdot)$ are as close as possible to the actual preference relations $\pi(\cdot)$. For the entire dataset, the error in estimating $\pi(\cdot)$ is defined as:

$$\mathcal{E} = \frac{1}{2} \sum_{\substack{\langle u,i,j,\pi(u,i,j)\rangle \\ \in S \\ \wedge (i<j)}} (\pi(u, i, j) - \hat{\pi}(u, i, j))^2. \tag{3}$$

The goal of the modeling step is to find the p^* and q^* vectors such that the prediction error in Equation 3 is minimized. However, trying to minimize the prediction error on the training set may lead to overfitting. To avoid overfitting, we add a regularization term $\mathcal{R}(p, q)$ with Equation 3. This leads to the following optimization task:

$$\min_{p,q} \frac{1}{2} \sum_{\substack{\langle u,i,j,\pi(u,i,j)\rangle \\ \in S \\ \wedge(i<j)}} (\pi(u,i,j) - \hat{\pi}(u,i,j))^2 + \mathcal{R}(p,q). \tag{4}$$

The regularization term is taken to be $\mathcal{R}(p,q) = \lambda_p \sum_{u\in U} ||p_u|| + \lambda_q \sum_{i\in I} ||q_i||$. We can now define the learning problem as an optimization task.

Model fitting as an optimization task: Let U be the set of users and I be the set of items. Let S be the set of preference relations. Each entry in S is of the form $\langle u,i,j,\pi(u,i,j)\rangle$, which means that for user $u \in U$, the strength of the preference relation for the item pair $(i,j) \in I \times I$ is given by $\pi(u,i,j)$. Find the matrices $p^{|U|\times d}$ and $q^{|I|\times d}$ containing user and item features such that the following objective function is minimized:

$$f(p,q) = \frac{1}{2} \sum_{\substack{\langle u,i,j,\pi(u,i,j)\rangle \\ \in S \\ \wedge(i<j)}} (\pi(u,i,j) - \hat{\pi}(u,i,j))^2 + \lambda_p \sum_{u\in U} ||p_u||^2 + \lambda_q \sum_{i\in I} ||q_i||^2, \tag{5}$$

where $\hat{\pi}(u,i,j)$ is given in Equation 2.

We use stochastic gradient descent to solve the optimization problem. For each observation $\langle u,i,j,\pi(u,i,j)\rangle$ from the training set S, the contribution to the objective function (given in Equation 5) is:

$$l_{uij} = \frac{1}{2}\epsilon^2_{uij} + \lambda_p||p_u||^2 + \lambda_q||q_i||^2, \tag{6}$$

where $\epsilon_{uij} = \left(\pi(u,i,j) - \frac{e^{p_u(q_i-q_j)^T}}{1+e^{p_u(q_i-q_j)^T}}\right)^2$. By computing the gradients of l_{uij} w.r.t. p_u, q_i and q_j, the update rules can be found as:

$$p_u = p_u + \gamma\left(\frac{\epsilon_{uij}\hat{\pi}(u,i,j)(q_i-q_j)}{1+e^{p_u(q_i-q_j)^T}} + \lambda_p p_u\right) \tag{7}$$

$$q_i = q_i + \gamma\left(\frac{\epsilon_{uij}\hat{\pi}(u,i,j)p_u}{1+e^{p_u(q_i-q_j)^T}} + \lambda_q q_i\right) \tag{8}$$

$$q_j = q_j - \gamma\left(\frac{\epsilon_{uij}\hat{\pi}(u,i,j)p_u}{1+e^{p_u(q_i-q_j)^T}} + \lambda_q q_j\right) \tag{9}$$

5.2   Recommendation Generation

Once the user and item features are computed, the system can generate recommendations for the users. Intuitively, if for a particular user u, an item i is (predicted to be) better than many other items, then i can be recommended to u. Based on this observation, we assign to each item i a score ($x_u(i)$) defined as:

$$x_u(i) = \sum_{j\in I\setminus\{i\}} p_u(q_i-q_j)^T \tag{10}$$

If we view $p_u(q_i - q_j)^T$ as the algorithm's *trust* on the preference relation i *is better than* j for user u, then $x_u(i)$ can be interpreted as the total *preference score* of the item i. The items are sorted in decreasing order of their scores to produce the recommendation list. Top-K items from this list are displayed to the user.

It is observed that the list generated by $x_u(\cdot)$ is same as the list generated by another scoring function $y_u(i)$ defined below. This is formally proved later in Theorem 1.

$$y_u(i) = p_u q_i^T \qquad (11)$$

Theorem 1. *The item orderings generated by the scoring functions x_u and y_u are the same.*

Proof. According to the definition of $x_u(\cdot)$ given in Equation 10, we have:

$$
\begin{aligned}
x_u(i) = \sum_{j \in I \backslash \{i\}} p_u(q_i - q_j)^T &= \sum_{j \in I} p_u(q_i - q_j)^T - p_u(q_i - q_i)^T \\
&= \sum_{j \in I} p_u q_i^T - \sum_{j \in I} p_u q_j^T \\
&= n p_u q_i^T - C \\
&= n y_u(i) - C \qquad (12)
\end{aligned}
$$

We have assumed that the number of items $|I| = n$. Also the term $\sum_{j \in I} p_u q_j^T$ is independent of i and is replaced by the constant C. The last line is obtained by replacing $p_u q_i^T$ by $y_u(i)$. Following Equation 12, it is now easy to see that:

$$y_u(i) > y_u(j) \iff n y_u(i) - C > n y_u(j) - C \iff x_u(i) > x_u(j).$$

Hence the item orderings induced by $x_u(.)$ and $y_u(.)$ are same. $\qquad \square$

The algorithm should look at all item pairs (i, j) to compute the score $x_u(i)$. However, if $y_u(\cdot)$ is used as the scoring function, then it only has to consider the feature representations of the user and the item, and the score can be computed in lesser time. Moreover, the recommendation lists generated by both these scoring functions are exactly same. Hence, we use $y_u(\cdot)$ as the scoring function to generate the recommendation list. We did not use $\hat{\pi}(\cdot)$ for scoring the items as for this phase it is not necessary to bound the preference relations in a fixed range. Also, directly using $\hat{\pi}(\cdot)$ for this phase would require looking at all item pairs (i, j) and hence would have higher computational complexity.

5.3   Complexity of the Approach

Let m and n be the number of users and items respectively. Careful observation of the algorithms reveal that the complexity for the model fitting phase is $O(kdmn^2)$, if k passes over the training dataset are made. Recommendation generation can be done in $O(nd + n \log n)$ time. We leave the details due to the space limitations.

6   Evaluation

6.1   Dataset Used

We used a sample of the Netflix dataset for testing the proposed approach. The sample dataset was created by considering the first 1500 movies from the original Netflix data. Some ratings were then eliminated so as to have a dataset where each user has rated at least 20 movies and at most 500 movies. The resultant dataset contains 124,637 ratings assigned by 3999 users to 1255 movies. The data was sorted in increasing timestamp order. The first 75% of the sorted data was used as training data. The remaining 25% data was used for testing.

6.2   Algorithms Compared

We compared our algorithm with two alternative algorithms proposed in literature and also use NMF as the baseline for our method.

- **NMF:** The first baseline algorithm uses standard NMF for recommendation. If the available feedbacks are of the form $\langle u, i, r_{ui} \rangle$, then the algorithm first learns the user and item factors (p_u and q_i respectively) by minimizing the following objective function:

$$\min_{p,q} \sum_{\langle u,i,r_{ui} \rangle} (r_{ui} - p_u q_i^T)^2 + \lambda_1 \sum_{u \in U} \|p_u\|^2 + \lambda_2 \sum_{i \in I} \|q_i\|^2. \qquad (13)$$

  Predicted ratings are computed using the formula $\hat{r}_{ui} = p_u q_i^T$. K best items according to the predicted ratings are recommended to the user.
- **RtCF:** The next algorithm uses vector similarity based collaborative filtering approach [10]. Let I_u denote the set of items rated by u. C_{uv} denotes the set of items rated by both the users u and v. Similarity weight between users u and v is defined as:

$$sim(u, v) = \sum_{i \in C_{uv}} \frac{r_{u,i}}{\sqrt{\sum_{l \in I_u} r_{u,l}^2}} \frac{r_{v,i}}{\sqrt{\sum_{l \in I_v} r_{v,l}^2}}. \qquad (14)$$

  If $\widehat{U}(u, i, k)$ is the top-k neighborhood of u for the item i, then the predicted rating for unrated items are computed using the following formula:

$$\hat{r}_{ui} = \frac{\sum_{v \in \widehat{U}(u,i,k)} sim(u, v) \cdot r_{vi}}{\sum_{v \in \widehat{U}(u,i,k)} sim(u, v)} \qquad (15)$$

  K items with highest predicted scores are displayed as recommendation.
- **PrCF:** Our next baseline is the Preference based Collaborative Filtering (PrCF) algorithm proposed in [2]. It produces preference relations between items following Equation 1. Similarity weight between u and v is defined as:

$$sim(u, v) = \frac{|\{(i, j) : i, j \in C_{uv} \wedge \pi(u, i, j) = \pi(v, i, j)\}|}{\sqrt{|I_u||I_v|}}. \qquad (16)$$

For a user v, utility of a product i (denoted as $ut_v(i)$) that he/she has rated is defined as:

$$ut_v(i) = \frac{-\#_{v,i}^{\oplus} + \#_{v,i}^{\ominus}}{\#_{v,i}^{\oplus} + \#_{v,i}^{\approx} + \#_{v,i}^{\ominus}}, \qquad (17)$$

where $\#_{v,i}^{\oplus}$, $\#_{v,i}^{\approx}$ and $\#_{v,i}^{\ominus}$ stand for the number of items given higher rating, same rating and lower rating respectively than i by v. Predicted utility of item i for user u is computed using Equation 15, after replacing r_{vi} and $\widehat{r}_{ui}$ by $ut_v(i)$ and $\widehat{ut}_u(i)$ respectively. We then sorted those items based on their predicted utilities. Top-K items from that sorted list are displayed to the test user as recommendation.

The method proposed in this paper is referred to as Preference relation based NMF, or **PrefNMF**. For PrefNMF, values of λ_p and λ_q were taken as 0.001 and 0.0005 respectively. For **NMF**, both λ_1 and λ_2 were set to .001.

6.3   Experimental Results

Here we compare the results of the proposed method and the other algorithms. Precision@5 and Precision@10 were used as the evaluation metrics. For PrCF and RtCF, we used 20, 40 and 80 as neighborhood sizes. For each of these algorithms, the best precision scores (over the different neighborhood sizes) are considered for comparison. For NMF and PrefNMF, we generated the recommendations using 60 features. Table 1 compares the metric values for this experiment.

Table 1. Comparing Precision scores for *all users*

Algorithm	Precision@5	Precision@10
RtCF	0.0049	0.0085
PrCF	0.0208	0.0223
NMF (60 features)	0.0257	0.0245
PrefNMF (60 features)	0.0280	0.0258

Though PrefNMF gave the best results among the algorithms that we tested, we wanted to see the effect of the number of features used on the performance of PrefNMF. For this, we ran both NMF and PrefNMF for 40, 60, 80, 100, 120, 150, 200 and 250 features. Table 2a presents the values of Precision@5 for both the algorithms. It shows that the performances of both NMF and PrefNMF improve initially with the number of features. PrefNMF does better than NMF when lesser number of features are used. As the number of features goes beyond 120, the performance does not improve much, and degrades in some cases. This might be due to overfitting. Similar observation can be made from Table 2b, which compares the values of Precision@10 for the algorithms. For 100 features, NMF does better than PrefNMF. Figure 1 shows the comparisons graphically.

PrefNMF uses preference relations for modeling the users and items. If the number of preference relations available for a user is less, then PrefNMF may

72   M.S. Desarkar, R. Saxena, and S. Sarkar

Table 2. Comparing Precisions for all users for PrefNMF and NMF

(a) Precision@5

#Features	20	40	60	80	100	120	150	200	250
NMF	0.0135	0.0234	0.0257	0.0287	0.0299	0.0301	0.0289	0.0289	0.0276
PrefNMF	0.0190	0.0252	0.0280	0.0296	0.0309	0.0301	0.0308	0.0312	0.0288

(b) Precision@10

#Features	20	40	60	80	100	120	150	200	250
NMF	0.0139	0.0223	0.0245	0.0271	0.0280	0.0282	0.0274	0.0272	0.0261
PrefNMF	0.0184	0.0236	0.0258	0.0274	0.0281	0.0275	0.0279	0.0279	0.0256

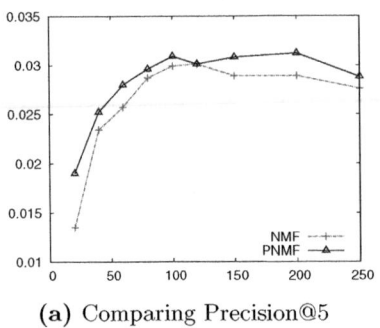
(a) Comparing Precision@5

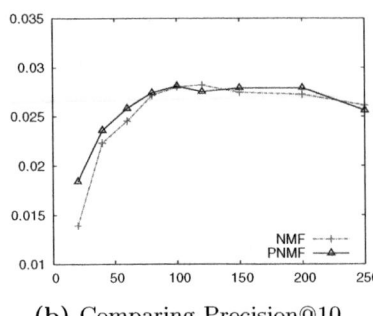
(b) Comparing Precision@10

Fig. 1. Comparing Precision values. x-axis represents the number of feature dimensions. y-axis represents the precision values.

not be able to model the user properly. On the other hand, for users who have provided more number of preference relations, it is easier to model them more accurately. We term this later group of users as the *dense users*. As more data is available for the *dense users*, both NMF and PrefNMF benefit from it as the user features can be modeled more accurately. PrCF and RtCF also would perform better since for such users it is easy to find the similar users with higher confidence. In the following experiment, we compared the performances of all four algorithms for the *dense users*. We considered the users who have entered 35 or more ratings as *dense users*.

Values of Precision@5 and Precision@10 for this experiment are presented in Table 3. For NMF and PrefNMF, this table shows the results obtained using 60

Table 3. Comparing Precision scores for the *dense users*

Algorithm	Precision@5	Precision@10
RtCF	0.0076	0.0164
PrCF	0.0260	0.0281
NMF (60 features)	0.0280	0.0258
PrefNMF (60 features)	0.0360	0.0329

features. Comparison of the values in this table with the corresponding values in Table 1 reveals that all the algorithms perform better for the dense users.

When we observed the effects of the number of features on NMF and PrefNMF for this experiment, we found that PrefNMF did outperform NMF consistently for all feature dimensions that we tried. Precision@5 and Precision@10 values for these two algorithms are shown in Table 4a and Table 4b respectively. The comparisons are shown graphically in Figure 2.

Table 4. Comparing Precisions for *dense users*

(a) Precision@5

#Features	20	40	60	80	100	120	150	200	250
NMF	0.0190	0.0252	0.0280	0.0296	0.0309	0.0301	0.0308	0.0312	0.0288
PrefNMF	0.0267	0.0350	0.0360	0.0388	0.0410	0.0416	0.0421	0.0432	0.0429

(b) Precision@10

#Features	20	40	60	80	100	120	150	200	250
NMF	0.0184	0.0236	0.0258	0.0274	0.0281	0.0275	0.0279	0.0279	0.0256
PrefNMF	0.0245	0.0318	0.0329	0.0357	0.0387	0.0382	0.0390	0.0387	0.0384

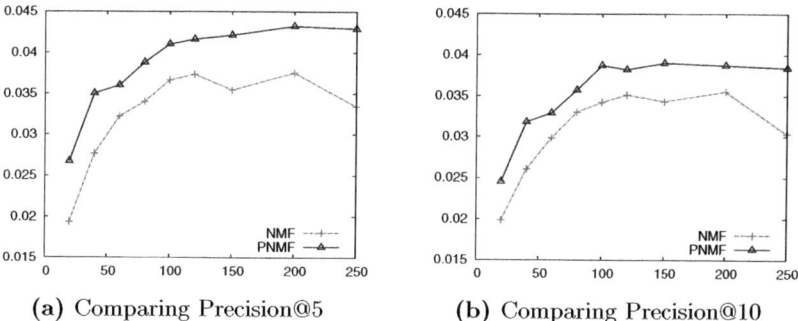

(a) Comparing Precision@5   (b) Comparing Precision@10

Fig. 2. Comparing Precision values for the *dense users*. x-axis represents the number of feature dimensions. y-axis represents the precision values.

6.4 Discussion on the Results

We compared the performance of our algorithm (PrefNMF) with that of three other algorithms. Two of them, RtCF and PrCF, use the neighborhood based framework. RtCF uses this framework with rating data, and PrCF uses this framework with preference relation data. The other algorithm, NMF, uses the Matrix Factorization framework. PrefNMF performed better than all these algorithms as measured by the Precision@5 and Precision@10 metrics.

When we compare the performance of PrefNMF with the NMF algorithm, the observations are two folds. Firstly, it indicates that using preference relations may lead to better recommendations. Secondly, the Matrix Factorization framework can be efficiently adapted to support preference relations as well. PrefNMF outperformed NMF in almost all the cases. If lesser number of features are used, PrefNMF does much better than NMF. As the number of features is increased, performances of both PrefNMF and NMF improve initially. If the number of features are increased further, overfitting occurs and the performances degrade.

When we considered only the users who have rated high number of movies, PrefNMF did much better than NMF for all the feature values. This is because more number of preference relations are available for the *dense users*. So for such users, PrefNMF is able to learn the feature representations more accurately.

It can be seen that the precision scores are quite low for both the algorithms. In reality, users may be interested in several movies, but due to various reasons, they might be actually viewing a small fraction of those movies. Moreover, both the algorithms consider each movie in the dataset as a candidate for recommendation. It might be useful to do a filtering beforehand that considers some of the aspects like user demography, the current popularity of the items, the recent interest profile of the user etc. Only the filtered items can then be considered as recommendation candidates.

7   Conclusion

We have proposed an algorithm that produces recommendations by considering preference relations from users. Matrix factorization framework is used to learn the user and item features. Item utilities for users are estimated using alignment of the user and item vectors in the joint feature space. Empirical evaluations performed on a benchmark dataset show that the proposed method is able to achieve better recommendation accuracy compared to the alternative algorithms.

Acknowledgements. The first author is supported by a PhD Fellowship grant from Microsoft Research India. The authors like to thank Dr. Deepak Agarwal, Yahoo Research for providing initial ideas and pointers to relevant literature.

References

[1] Gemmis, M.D., Iaquinta, L., Lops, P., Musto, C., Narducci, F., Semeraro, G.: Preference learning in recommender systems. In: Preference Learning (PL 2009) ECML/PKDD-09 Workshop, pp. 41–55 (2009)

[2] Brun, A., Hamad, A., Buffet, O., Boyer, A.: Towards preference relations in recommender systems. In: Preference Learning (PL 2010) ECML/PKDD 2010 Workshop (2010)

[3] Desarkar, M.S., Sarkar, S., Mitra, P.: Aggregating preference graphs for collaborative rating prediction. In: RecSys 2010, pp. 21–28 (2010)

[4] Jones, N., Brun, A., Boyer, A.: Comparisons instead of ratings: Towards more stable preferences. In: IEEE/WIC/ACM International Conference on Web Intelligence and Intelligent Agent Technology, vol. 1, pp. 451–456 (2011)

[5] Koren, Y., Bell, R., Volinsky, C.: Matrix factorization techniques for recommender systems. Computer 42, 30–37 (2009)

[6] Koren, Y.: Factorization meets the neighborhood: a multifaceted collaborative filtering model. In: KDD 2008, pp. 426–434 (2008)

[7] Pilászy, I., Zibriczky, D., Tikk, D.: Fast als-based matrix factorization for explicit and implicit feedback datasets. In: RecSys 2010, pp. 71–78 (2010)

[8] Zhang, L., Agarwal, D., Chen, B.-C.: Generalizing matrix factorization through flexible regression priors. In: RecSys 2011, pp. 13–20 (2011)

[9] Menon, A.K., Chitrapura, K.-P., Garg, S., Agarwal, D., Kota, N.: Response prediction using collaborative filtering with hierarchies and side-information. In: KDD 2011, pp. 141–149 (2011)

[10] Breese, J.S., Heckerman, D., Kadie, C.M.: Empirical analysis of predictive algorithms for collaborative filtering. In: UAI 1998, pp. 43–52 (1998)

A Framework for Modeling Trustworthiness of Users in Mobile Vehicular Ad-Hoc Networks and Its Validation through Simulated Traffic Flow

John Finnson[1], Jie Zhang[2], Thomas Tran[3], Umar Farooq Minhas[1],
and Robin Cohen[1]

[1] U. Waterloo, Canada
[2] Nanyang Tech. U., Singapore
[3] U. Ottawa, Canada

Abstract. In this paper, we present an approach for modeling user trustworthiness when traffic information is exchanged between vehicles in transportation environments. Our multi-faceted approach to trust modeling combines priority-based, role-based and experience-based trust, integrated with a majority consensus model influenced by time and location, for effective route planning. The proposed representation for the user model is outlined in detail (integrating ontological and propositional elements) and the algorithm for updating trust values is presented as well. This trust modeling framework is validated in detail through an extensive simulation testbed that models vehicle route planning. We are able to show decreased average path time for vehicles when all facets of our trust model are employed in unison. Included is an interesting confirmation of the value of distinguishing direct and indirect observations of users.

1 Introduction

Modeling the trustworthiness of users has been a topic of research within the multiagent systems community for some time now [5,6], for applications such as electronic commerce (both modeling the reputability of sellers and the trustworthiness of buyers providing advice about those sellers, in the marketplace (where the users are represented by intelligent agents)) [8,11]. It is especially challenging to properly model trustworthiness over time, learning how best to adjust one's representation of this part of the user model, by reasoning about past experiences with the user, towards future interactions.

In this paper, we focus on modeling trust in the context of mobile vehicular ad-hoc networks. This is explored for the purpose of enabling users to make effective travel decisions, based on traffic reports from peers. We propose a multi-faceted trust model in order to cope with challenges of data sparsity, dynamically changing parameters, the need for real-time decision making and the important influences of location and time for effective user modeling. From here, we distinguish whether the advice that is provided has been directly or indirectly observed, proposing formulae for modeling trust sensitive to this distinction.

J. Masthoff et al. (Eds.): UMAP 2012, LNCS 7379, pp. 76–87, 2012.

Enabling effective exchange of traffic reports in these environments requires a framework for messaging: determining both how to represent the reports that are provided in order to reason about travel as well as an appropriate algorithm for when messages should be exchanged. Towards this end, we offer a specific proposal that employs an ontological representation with propositional elements, along with a provision for both pull and push-based communication. This constitutes our decision for when to begin the construction of the user model, populated with a representation of user trustworthiness and when to make use of that model, towards decision making in the environment.

We demonstrate the effectiveness of our trust modeling and our proposed construction of the user model by introducing a detailed simulation framework that enables simulating traffic flow in an environment, with vehicles making travel decisions based on their reasoning about the traffic reports that have been received from other vehicles. In particular, we demonstrate the relative benefit of allowing for the distinction of direct and indirect reporting in our modeling, compared to decisions made without this distinction. The end result is a validation of our proposed VANET ((mobile) vehicular ad-hoc network) trust modeling framework. We discuss the benefit of our approach in contrast with related work and conclude with a view to possible future research.

2 Multi-faceted Trust Model

We consider the driver of each vehicle in our VANET environment to be a user. In order for each vehicle on the road to make effective traffic decisions, information is sought from other vehicles (about the traffic congestion on a particular road). As a result, for each driver an intelligent agent constructs and maintains a user model for each of the other vehicles. Travel decisions are then made based on a multi-faceted model of user trustworthiness. In particular, we propose a core processing algorithm to be used by each user that seeks advice from other vehicles in the environment as summarized below.

Algorithm 1. Computation Steps

```
while on the road do
    Send requests and receive responses;
    if in need of advice then
        Choose n; //number of users to ask for advice
        //according to roles and experiences
        Prioritize n users;
        if response consensus > acceptable ratio then
            Follow advice in response;
        else
            Follow advice of user with highest role and highest trust value;

    Verify reliability of advice;
    Update users' trust values;
```

In order to cope with possible data sparsity, various facets of each user are taken into consideration when reasoning about travel, including the user's role, location and inherent trustworthiness (determined on the basis of past experiences with this particular user - i.e. whether past advice has proven to be trustworthy). Each of these facets of the user is stored within the user model.

We first acknowledge that certain vehicles in the environment may play a particular role and, on this basis, merit greater estimates of trustworthiness. For example, there may be vehicles representing the police and other traffic authorities (authority) or ones representing radio stations dedicated to determining accurate traffic reports by maintaining vehicles in the vicinity of the central routes (expert). Or there may be a collection of users representing a "commuter pool", routinely traveling the same route, sharing advice (seniority).

Consideration of any past personal experiences with users allows the model to include any learning about particular users due to previous encounters, specifically modeling trustworthiness each time and adjusting the level of trust to be higher or lower, based on the outcome of the advice that is offered. Experience-based trustworthiness is represented and maintained following the model of [8] where $T_A(B) \in (-1, 1)$ represents A's trust in B (with -1 for total distrust and 1 for total trust) which is incremented by α if B's advice is found to be reliable or decremented by β if unreliable, with $|\beta| > |\alpha|$ to reflect that trust is harder to build up but easier to tear down. Distinct from the original model of [8], the values of α and β can be set to be event-specific. For example, when asking about a major accident, these values may be set high, to reflect considerable disappointment with inaccurate advice. We also incorporate a requirement for users to reveal whether the traffic information they are providing has been directly observed or only indirectly inferred from other reports that user has received. The critical distinction of direct or indirect reporting then influences the values set for α and β, introducing greater penalties for disappointment with direct advice. In [4] we discuss at greater length the incentives to honesty that are introduced within this framework; for brevity, we omit that discussion in this paper.

2.1   Majority Consensus

A central calculation to influence the travel decision of each user is the determination of majority consensus amongst the users providing advice about a particular road. The user maintains, as part of her model of other users, a list of users to ask for advice. This list is ordered from higher roles to lower roles with each group G_i of users of similar roles being ordered from higher experience-based trust ratings to lower ratings. The user sets a value n and asks the first n users[1] from her ordered list the question (thus using priority-based trust), receives their responses (reports), and then performs majority-based trust measurement. Suppose that q of these n users declare that their reports are from direct experience. The requesting user determines whether there are sufficient direct witnesses such that she can make a decision based solely on their reports.

If $q \geq N_{min}$, then the requesting user will only consider the reports from the q direct witnesses if a majority consensus on a response can be reached,

---

[1] This integrates task-based trust. For instance, a user may set n to be fairly small, say $n \leq 10$, if she needs to make a quick driving decision, or set a larger n if she has time to process responses.

up to some tolerance set by the requester (e.g. the user may want at most 30% of the responders to disagree), then the response is taken as the advice and followed. If $q < N_{min}$, then there are insufficient direct witnesses; the user will consider reports from both direct and indirect witnesses, assigning different weight factors to them, computing and following the majority opinion. (Once the actual road conditions are verified, the requesting user adjusts the experience-based trust ratings of the reporting users: It penalizes (rewards) more those users who reported incorrect (correct) information in the direct experience case than those users with incorrect (correct) information in the indirect experience case.) If a majority consensus cannot be reached, then instead, the user relies on role-based trust and experience-based trust (e.g., taking the advice from the user with highest role and highest experience trust value). Note that in order to eventually admit new users into consideration, the user will also ask a certain number of users beyond the nth one in the list. The responses here will not be considered for decision, but will be verified to update experience-based trust ratings and some of these users may make it into the top n users, in this way.

The computation of majority consensus adheres to the set of formulae outlined as follows: Suppose user A receives a set of m reports $\mathcal{R} = \{R_1, R_2, ..., R_m\}$ from a set of n other users $\mathcal{B} = \{B_1, B_2, ..., B_n\}$ regarding an event. User A will consider more heavily the reports sent by users who have higher level roles and larger experience-based trust values. When performing majority-based process, we also take into account the location closeness between the reporting user and the reported event, and the closeness between the time when the event has taken place and that of receiving the report. We define C_t (time closeness), C_l (location closeness), T_e (experience-based trust) and T_r (role-based trust). Note that all these parameters belong to the interval $(0, 1)$ except that T_e needs to be scaled to fit within this interval.

For each user B_i ($1 \le i \le n$) belonging to a subset of users $\mathcal{B}(R_j) \subseteq \mathcal{B}$ who report the same report $R_j \in \mathcal{R}$ ($1 \le j \le m$), we aggregate the effect of its report according to the above factors. The aggregated effect $E(R_j)$ from reports sent by users in $\mathcal{B}(R_j)$ can be formulated as follows (per [4]):

$$E(R_j) = \sum_{B_i \in \mathcal{B}(R_j)} \frac{T_e(B_i)T_r(B_i)}{C_t(R_j)C_l(B_i)W(B_i)} \qquad (1)$$

$W(B_i)$ is a weight factor set to 1 if user B_i who sent report R_j is an indirect witness, and $W(B_i)$ is set to a value in $(0, 1)$ if user B_i is a direct witness[2].

A majority consensus can be reached if

$$\frac{M(R_j)}{\sum_{R_j \in \mathcal{R}} E(R_j)} \ge 1 - \varepsilon \qquad (2)$$

where $\varepsilon \in (0, 1)$ is set by user A to represent the maximum error rate that A can accept and $M(R_j) = \max_{R_j \in \mathcal{R}} E(R_j)$. A majority consensus can be reached if

---

[2] For example, setting $W(B_i) = 1/2$ for the case of direct witnesses indicates that the requesting user values direct evidence two times more than indirect evidence.

the percentage of the opinion (the effect among different reports) over all possible opinions is above the threshold set by user A.

The trust modeling framework described so far clarifies the algorithms that lead to the calculation of the trustworthiness value which would then be stored in each user model. Trip planning decisions of a vehicle would then be made in light of these particular user models. Two elements that require further clarification are the detailed representation of the user model and a proposal for when updates to the user model should occur. These are elaborated in the section that follows.

3   Messaging in Support of Trust Modeling

Vehicles on the road receive traffic reports from other vehicles as part of their trip planning. In this context, the messages that take place between vehicles follow a format established from our framework. Messages typically are composed of a request, such as *vehicle: Location?*, and a reply, such as *replyingVehicle: Specific-highway, Congestion Value*. Upon receiving the reply, the requester processes it and updates their user model of the replying vehicle, updating location information and the agent's trustworthiness value, when appropriate.

The frequency with which vehicles message each other in the environment determines when user model variables are updated. In our case, it is desirable to allow for both pull-based and push-based communication. In the pull-based case, vehicles requiring information for their trip planning will poll other vehicles in the environment with a certain frequency, receiving reports that then result in updating the user models of the replying vehicles. For push-based communication, the vehicles in the environment broadcast their location and congestion information with a certain frequency and this information is then received by other vehicles, leading to an updating of the sending vehicle's trust values. In our simulation framework described in the next section, this is in fact enacted as pull-based only with one message in every 6-15 seconds.

The knowledge representation selected for the mobile vehicular environment consists of combination of ontological information and propositional information. Each individual user maintains her own knowledge base that respects the same ontological structure but is populated unique instances and values. The knowledge base stores a model of each other user they have come in contact with as well as domain information. The ontology is designed as the combination of two separate ontologies, a modified version of the Knowledge Provenance (KP) ontology from [2] shown in Figure 1, and a new ontology called Vont, which contains all previous and new semantic information from the VANET trust model and is shown in Figure 2.

An important additional concept that is introduced to the ontologies used by this model is the use of classes that represent propositions. A proposition is an atomic piece of information that is annotated with provenance information. It is through these KP propositions that our model can provide specific information such as the source user and domain specific data such as, in our application, road congestion values, to be be used in trust and certainty evaluations.

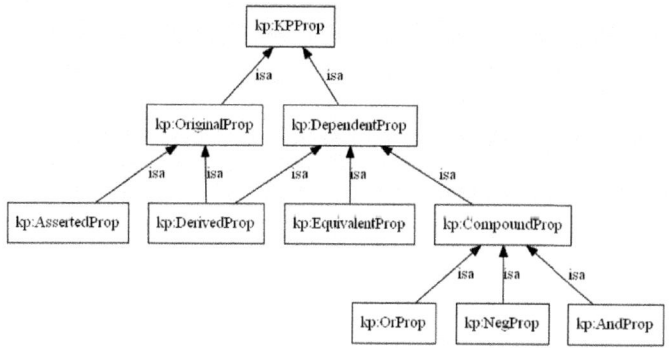

Fig. 1. Knowledge Provenance Ontology

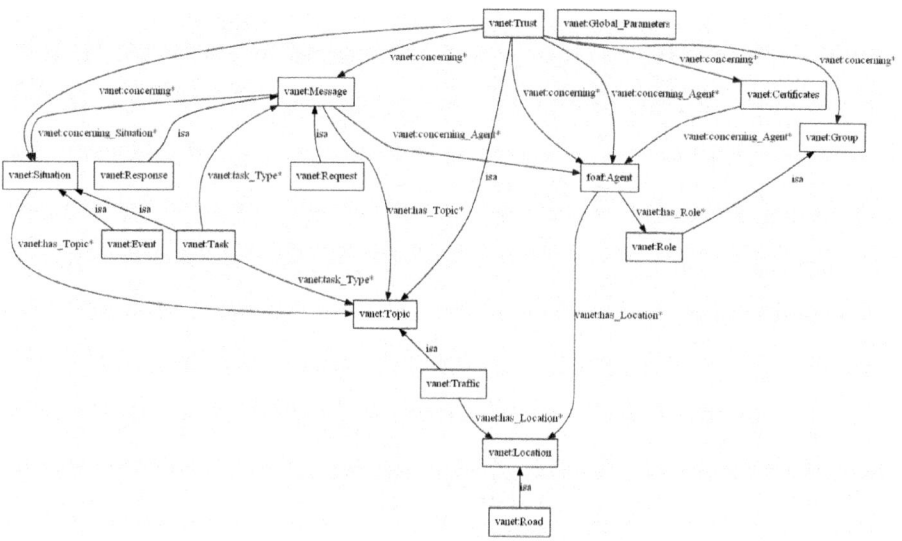

Fig. 2. VANET Vont Ontology

The dual ontology nature of the model allows for the propositions of the KP ontology to use the descriptive language of the other ontology, defined in this paper as Vont, to describe its contents. KP proposition instances reference Vont instances. An example would be a KP asserted proposition instance referencing an instance of *Vont:Traffic* which represents a traffic report of a location, reported by a user defined in a variable of the proposition.

The necessity of using Vont to describe the content of KP proposition instances stems from the need for a computer to be capable of understanding the content of a KP proposition for analytical purposes, such as a reasoner analyzing the content of a traffic report proposition to understand the road it's concerning and the reported congestion. Vont forms the basic descriptive level which is used by the KP ontology to describe its content, but still remains fundamentally disjoint. Messaging enables the combined Knowledge Base to be populated with instances, to then have that data used as part of the path planning of the vehicle. Figure 2 shows the Vont Ontology that is unique to and created from our trust model. The figure ontologically describes most of the important components and relations previously defined by our VANET trust modeling framework in Section 2. Instances of the classes shown are used by the KP ontology to describe its contents. Agent refers to each user.

4 Simulation Framework

This section describes the simulation framework for VANET, which enables the simulation of traffic flow with vehicles acting as autonomous agents. The simulated vehicles make travel decisions based on their reasoning about the traffic reports that have been received from other vehicles through the messaging described in Section 3. The implementation is designed as a VANET extension to an existing real time traffic simulator. Each vehicle within the simulation is representative of an individual agent that implements the proposed VANET framework. This means in a 100 car simulation there are 100 instances of the framework, including 100 knowledge bases and 100 VANET-Reasoners.

The implementation makes use of the following third party software, JiST/SWANS, vans, DUCKS, and Protege. JiST stands for Java in Simulation Time; it is a high-performance discrete event simulation engine that runs over a standard Java Virtual Machine (JVM). SWANS stands for Scalable Ad-hoc Network Simulator; it is built on top of the JiST platform and serves as a host of network simulation tools. Vans is a project comprising the geographic routing and the integrated Street Random Waypoint model (STRAW). STRAW utilizes an A* search algorithm to calculate shortest path to a destination. DUCKS is a simulation execution framework, which allows for a Simulation Parameters file to be provided to define the simulation. Protege is a free, open source ontology editor and knowledge base framework.

To reflect the majority opinion calculation from Algorithm 1 in the simulation, it was important to introduce new specific elements. While that algorithm was originally designed to model majority opinion for Boolean responses (yes or no when asked whether a road was congested), in our case responses from users indicate specific congestion values. This then required us to continuously build an average congestion value from trusted users, labelling as suspicious those agents at odds with the majority and failing to incorporate their congestion value into the running average. As in Algorithm 1, we follow majority advice when, considering n user reports, there is consensus (i.e. the reported congestion values are within a certain standard deviation of each other) and that consensus is above a desired threshold as calculated using formulae 1 and 2.

Algorithm 2 describes the pull-based protocol and the two different types of requests that can be sent by users. The algorithm is triggered according to the communication frequency (6-15 seconds). The two different types of messages are a request for an agent's location and congestion or a specific request for congestion information concerning a specific road. The concept of a priority road facilitates messaging (and hence the updating of user models). A priority list is constantly maintained which stores a road and the number of times advice and information has been retrieved for the road since it was added to the list. Roads are added to this list when the pathing algorithm looks for congestion information about a road and either none exists or the data is very old. Roads are removed from the list when a set number of retrievals has been done.

Algorithm 2. Send requests and receive responses

```
while on the road do
    if Triggered according to communication frequency then
        //Get road to request advice about and agent to request from
        if priority road exists then
            Choose highest priority road;
            Get trustworthy agent;
            if Trustworthy agent exists then
                └ Send request to trustworthy agent for advice concerning the high priority road;
            else
                └ Send request to random agent for advice concerning the high priority road;
        //Send request for current location and congestion to a random agent
        └ Send random request for current location and congestion;
```

---

5 Simulation Evaluation

This section describes the simulation tests performed to compare and contrast the effectiveness of our model's implementation against a system that does not use traffic information in routing; a best case scenario; the inclusion of time, location, and indirect advice.

The simulation was set to poll cars every 6-15 seconds; with 100 cars in total, experience with every other car would be gained quickly. In order to simulate environments with low experience-based trust, we introduce a variable called sparsity. For example, 80% sparsity resembles having a lack of previous experience with 80% of the agents. In the simulation, this variable effectively ignores updates of trust values, thus hindering experience-based trust.

These graphs chart the performance of simulations that either use trust modeling (i.e. profiling) (Hon #) or not (no P, Hon #). Agent honesty represents the percent of honest agents in the simulation (i.e. 0.5 is 50% honesty). Role-based trust (Role #) represents the percent of agents in the simulation that have been assigned a role (i.e. 0.2 will have 20% of agents assigned a role). Sparsity (Spars #) represents the percent sparsity in the simulation (i.e. 0.8 will have 80% sparsity). Dishonest lie percentage (Lie #) represents the percent of the time which a dishonest agent will lie (i.e. 0.8 means dishonest agents will lie 80% of the time)(set at 100% if unspecified). By default, trust modeling uses at least experience and majority based trust. The other trust model components individually indicated are time closeness (Time), location closeness (Loc), and indirect advice (Indir). (Full) indicates when all multidimensional trust components are being used. The VANET trust modeling results are also compared against two additional simulations: the first is a worst case scenario where traffic is ignored (no traffic)[3], and the other is a best case omnipresent version (omni) which simulates the ability for any car to look up the exact congestion of any road at anytime. All simulation tests results are averaged over 5 runs.

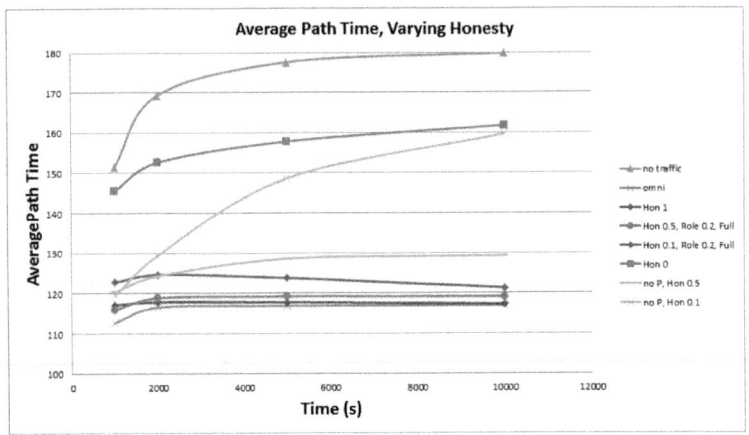

Fig. 3. Avg Path Time comparison of our model vs. best and worst case scenarios

Figure 3 compares the worst case scenario against the best case scenario and various simulations which use our VANET system with different degrees of honesty. As seen in the figure, all of the simulations that used our trust modeling framework (Full) or the omnipresent setup averaged close to the same path time at the end of the 10000 second simulation. The other simulations produced a predictably declining performance as the honesty percentage approached the worst case scenario. The VANET trust modeling simulations show approximately a 35% decrease in average path time over the worst case scenario. The curves in the scenarios are representative of the simulations approaching a steady state. Another observed trend is the tendency for the profiling-enabled simulations to reach a steady state faster than the other simulations.

Figure 4 demonstrates the increased effectiveness of each of the multidimensional trust component described in previous sections. The incremental components demonstrated are the base system (experience and majority based trust), then role based trust, time and location closeness, and indirect advice. These simulations also simulate honesty at 50%, data sparsity at 50%, and additionally compare them to the best case scenario. As seen in the figure, the incremental addition of trust components demonstrated predictable and substantial increases in performance. The simulation with sparsity enabled showed a predicably worse performance than its counterpart. This reflects the fact that when one has little experience-based trust, one makes poorer decisions. The simulation with role-based trust enabled show a dramatic increase in performance, which demonstrates the impact roles have in situations with data sparsity. The best

---

[3] Routing without traffic just uses a shortest path calculation.

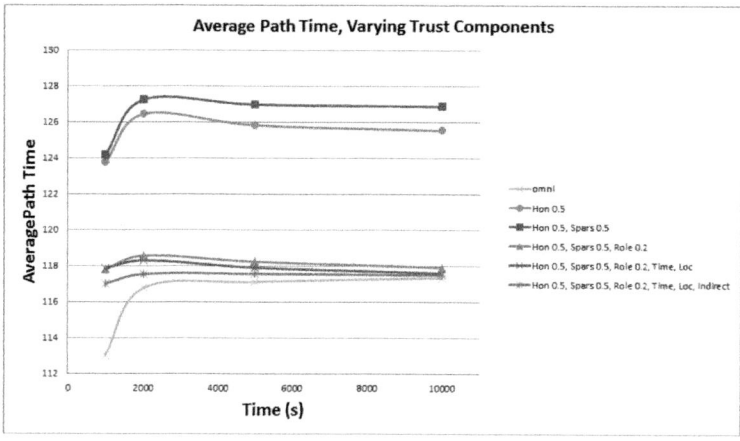

Fig. 4. Avg Path Time comparison, multidimensional trust component variations

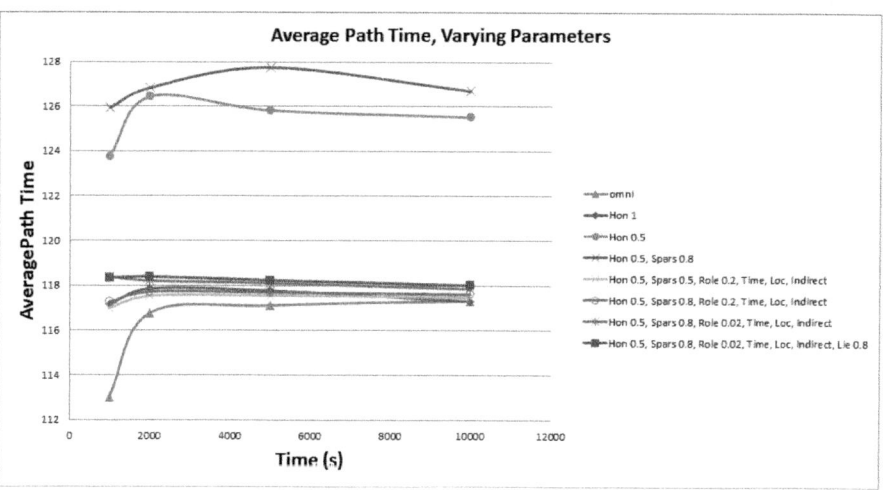

Fig. 5. Avg Path Time comparison, multidimensional parameter variations

case scenario and the simulations with the higher number of trust components averaged close to the same path time at the end of the 10000 second simulation. The curves in the scenarios are representative of the simulations approaching a steady state. Another observed trend is the tendency for the component-enabled simulations to have a steadier state than the other simulations.

Finally, Figure 5 compares the improvement in average path time that results with varying values for sparsity, role, degrees of honesty and lie percentage. We note that, even if there are very few roles assumed or if dishonest agents lie inconsistently, our framework is able to adapt and yield excellent performance. When using all dimensions (Full), being more challenged with experienced-based trust (higher sparsity) degrades performance slightly as does having less role-based trust to rely on.

6   Discussion

In this paper, we have proposed a framework for modeling users in VANET environments that includes a detailed derivation of user trustworthiness (along with a representation of user location and role). Our trust calculation takes as a starting point an experience-based calculation; however, motivated by the VANET demands of data sparsity and the need for frequent updates of information for real-time decision making, we augment the trust calculation to include role-based, location-based, time-based and priority-based trust. We also integrate a majority consensus calculation to make use of collective reports on a given road but distinguish direct and indirect reporting, penalizing misleading direct reports considerably more (to promote honesty) and allowing path decisions to rely more heavily on direct advice.

The design of a detailed knowledge representation supports effective tracking of the time and location of reports provided by users (along with their trustworthiness) and the design of a messaging solution then clarifies the conditions under which user modeling updates occur. The value of this multi-faceted trust modeling framework is confirmed through simulated traffic flow in a detailed simulation testbed which supports tracking 100 cars at once. The simulation is adjusted to allow for the modeling of low direct experience, few designated roles, and high dishonesty and in all cases the average path time of vehicles that follow our proposed algorithms is demonstrably good, approaching the performance achieved with perfect knowledge and far surpassing travel decisions made without the modeling of trust. Each proposed trust component is shown to improve the path decisions that are made.

Our experience-based trust is motivated by the design of [7] reflecting an implicit acquisition of the value of this user modeling parameter, derived by learning from experience with that user. This framework has already proved to be effective when espousing the position that trust is hard to build up, but easy to tear down and we incorporate this in our setting of trust adjustment parameters. In contrast with [7], however, we have valuable distinctions between direct and indirect reporting of trust (and the contribution derived from modeling this parameter is demonstrated through our simulation results).

Other researchers have proposed trust modeling frameworks that integrate majority opinion [3,11]. We integrate here imporant consideration of time and location as well, in order to value more highly the reports from users closer to the destination. In so doing, we are able to weight the combination of majority and experience based considerations more appropriately. Others have employed a social network for trust modeling (e.g. [10] consider trust propagation in a network but this is less relevant in our sparsely populated environment) and others propose the use of stereotypical trust [1] (but in our domain a small set of roles can be used to reflect levels of trust.) [9] also describe trust as multi-faceted; this work is more focused on having trust calculated differently in distinct contexts. In addition, their selection of peer advice is based on similar preferences; for our domain, location of the user and the time of its report are more critical determinants. For future work, we will be using our extensive simulation testbed to discern the relative value of different trust modeling conditions; we also plan to explore the trust levels required of various traffic scenarios, possibly leading to more detailed user modeling in support of path planning.

References

1. Burnett, C., Norman, T., Sycara, K.: Sources of stereotypical trust in multi-agent systems. In: Proceedings. AAMAS Trust Workshop, Trust 2011 (2011)
2. Huang, J.: Knowledge Provenance: An Approach to Modeling and Maintaining the Evolution and Validity of Knowledge. Ph.D. thesis, University of Toronto (2007)
3. Josang, A., Ismail, R.: The beta reputation system. In: Proceedings of the 15th Bled Electronic Commerce Conference (2002)
4. Minhas, U.F., Zhang, J., Tran, T.T., Cohen, R.: Intelligent agents in mobile vehicular ad-hoc networks: Leveraging trust modeling based on direct experience with incentives for honesty. In: Proceedings of the IEEE/WIC/ACM International Conference on Intelligent Agent Technology, IAT (2010)
5. Ramchurn, S.D., Huynh, D., Jennings, N.R.: Trust in multi-agent systems. The Knowledge Engineering Review 19(1), 1–25 (2004)
6. Teacy, W.T.L., Patel, J., Jennings, N.R., Luck, M.: TRAVOS: Trust and reputation in the context of inaccurate information sources. Autonomous Agents and Multi-Agent Systems 12(2), 183–198 (2006)
7. Tran, T.: Protecting buying agents in e-marketplaces by direct experience trust modelling. Knowledge and Information Systems (KAIS) 22, 65–100 (2010)
8. Tran, T., Cohen, R.: Modelling Reputation in Agent-based Marketplaces to Improve the Performance of Buying Agents. In: Brusilovsky, P., Corbett, A.T., de Rosis, F. (eds.) UM 2003. LNCS, vol. 2702, pp. 273–282. Springer, Heidelberg (2003)
9. Wang, Y., Vassileva, J.: Bayesian network-based trust model. In: Proceedings IEEE/WIC International Conference on Web Intelligence, WI 2003, pp. 372–378 (October 2003)
10. Yu, B., Singh, M.P.: Detecting deception in reputation management. In: Proceedings of the Second International Joint Conference on Autonomous Agents and Multiagent Systems, AAMAS 2003, pp. 73–80. ACM, New York (2003), http://doi.acm.org/10.1145/860575.860588
11. Zhang, J., Cohen, R.: A framework for trust modeling in multiagent electronic marketplaces with buying advisors to consider varying seller behavior and the limiting of seller bids. ACM Transactions on Intelligent Systems and Technology (ACM TIST) (2011) (to appear)

A Comparative Study of Users' Microblogging Behavior on Sina Weibo and Twitter

Qi Gao[1], Fabian Abel[1], Geert-Jan Houben[1], and Yong Yu[2]

[1] Web Information Systems, Delft University of Technology
{q.gao,f.abel,g.j.p.m.houben}@tudelft.nl
[2] APEX Data & Knowledge Management Lab., Shanghai Jiaotong University
yyu@apex.stju.edu.cn

Abstract. In this article, we analyze and compare user behavior on two different microblogging platforms: (1) Sina Weibo which is the most popular microblogging service in China and (2) Twitter. Such a comparison has not been done before at this scale and is therefore essential for understanding user behavior on microblogging services. In our study, we analyze more than 40 million microblogging activities and investigate microblogging behavior from different angles. We (i) analyze how people access microblogs and (ii) compare the writing style of Sina Weibo and Twitter users by analyzing textual features of microposts. Based on semantics and sentiments that our user modeling framework extracts from English and Chinese posts, we study and compare (iii) the topics and (iv) sentiment polarities of posts on Sina Weibo and Twitter. Furthermore, (v) we investigate the temporal dynamics of the microblogging behavior such as the drift of user interests over time.

Our results reveal significant differences in the microblogging behavior on Sina Weibo and Twitter and deliver valuable insights for multilingual and culture-aware user modeling based on microblogging data. We also explore the correlation between some of these differences and cultural models from social science research.

Keywords: user modeling, microblogging, comparative usage analysis.

1   Introduction

Microblogging services such as Twitter allow people to publish, share and discuss short messages on the Web. Nowadays, Twitter users publish more than 200 million posts, so-called *tweets*, per day[1]. In China, Sina Weibo[2] is leading the microblogging market since Twitter is unavailable. Both Sina Weibo and Twitter basically feature the same functionality. For example, both services limit the lengths of microposts to 140 characters and allow users to organize themselves in a follower-followee network, where people follow the message updates of

---

[1] http://blog.twitter.com/2011/06/200-million-tweets-per-day.html
[2] http://www.weibo.com/

J. Masthoff et al. (Eds.): UMAP 2012, LNCS 7379, pp. 88–101, 2012.
© Springer-Verlag Berlin Heidelberg 2012

other users (unidirectional relationship). Sina Weibo and Twitter provide (real-time) access to the microposts via APIs and therefore allow for investigating and analyzing interesting applications and functionality such as event detection [1,2] or recommending Web sites [3].

By analyzing individual microblogging activities, it is possible to learn about the characteristics, preferences and concerns of users. In previous work, we therefore introduced a semantic user modeling framework for inferring user interests from Twitter activities and proved its efficiency in a news recommendation system [4]. In this paper, we extend this Twitter-based user modeling framework to also allow for sentiment analysis and user modeling based on Chinese microblog posts. We conduct, to the best of our knowledge, the first comparative study of the microblogging behavior on Sina Weibo and Twitter and relate our findings to theories and models from social science. The main contributions of our work can be summarized as follows.

– We extend our framework for user modeling based on usage data from microblogging services with functionality for sentiment analysis and semantic enrichment of Chinese microblog posts.
– We conduct intensive analyses based on more than 40 million microblog posts and compare the microblogging behavior on Sina Weibo and Twitter regarding five dimensions: (i) access behavior, (ii) syntactic content analysis, (iii) semantic content analysis, (iv) sentiment analysis, (v) temporal behavior.
– We relate our findings to theories about cultural stereotypes developed in social sciences and therefore explain how our insights can allow for culture-aware user modeling based on microblogging streams.

2   Related Work

Various types of research efforts have been conducted on Twitter data recently ranging from information propagation [5,6] to applications such as Twitter-based early warning systems [1]. Furthermore, user modeling and personalization research started to study Twitter. Chen et al. investigate recommender systems on Twitter that consider social network features or the popularity of items in the Twitter network [3]. In previous work, we developed a Twitter-based user modeling framework for inferring user interests [4] and studied different applications that exploit the framework for personalization [7].

Research on cultural characteristics of user behavior on the Social Web has also been initiated. For example, Mandl [8] investigates how blog pages, especially the communication patterns between bloggers and commentators, from China differ from the ones from Germany. He correlates his findings to cultural dimensions proposed by Hofstede et al. [9]. Chen et al. analyze the tagging behavior of two user groups from two popular social music sites in China and Europe respectively [10] and observe differences between the two cultural groups, e.g. Chinese users have a smaller tendency to apply subjective tags but prefer the usage of factual tags. So far, there exists little knowledge about the differences and commonalities regarding the microblogging behavior of users from different cultural groups. Yu et al. compare popular trending topics on Sina Weibo with those on Twitter [11], but only compare global trends and do not study individual user behavior. In this paper, we close this gap: based on our extended user modeling framework, we conduct a large-scale analysis and comparison of users' microblogging behavior on Sina Weibo and Twitter.

3   Research Methodology and Evaluation Platform

In this section, we detail our research questions and present our enhanced user modeling environment that allows us to investigate the research questions.

3.1   Research Questions

Our research goal is to analyze and compare user behavior on Sina Weibo and Twitter to gain insights for user modeling on microblogging streams. Therefore, we investigate (1) how people access microblogging services, (2) the content, (3) semantics and (4) sentiment of microblog posts and (5) the temporal behavior of users' microblogging activities.

Analysis of Access Behavior. Microblogging services such as Sina Weibo and Twitter can be accessed via different client applications from both mobile devices and desktop devices. User behavior that can be observed on a microblogging service may be influenced by the way in which a user accesses the service. We thus first study the following research questions:

– *RQ1:* How do people access Sina Weibo and Twitter respectively to publish microposts?
– *RQ2:* To what extent do individual users access a microblogging service from different client applications?

Syntactic Content Analysis. Both Sina Weibo and Twitter limit the length of posts to 140 characters. This limitation impacts the writing style of microblog users and may result in characteristic usage patterns that we would like to compare between Sina Weibo (Chinese) and Twitter (English):

– *RQ3:* How does the usage of hashtags, URLs and other syntactic patterns (e.g. punctuation) differ between Sina Weibo and Twitter for both (i) the entire user population and (ii) individual users?
– *RQ4:* To what extent is the usage of hashtags and URLs influenced by the users' access behavior?

Semantic Content Analysis. To better understand the meaning of the messages that users post on microblogging services, we analyze the semantics and investigate the following aspects:

– *RQ5:* What kind of topics and concepts do users mention and discuss on Sina Weibo and Twitter respectively?
– *RQ6:* To what extent do the types of concepts that users mention in their posts depend on the client applications via which they publish their posts?

Sentiment Analysis. Microblogs allow users to express and discuss their opinions about topics that people are concerned with. We therefore analyze the sentiment of Chinese and English messages and study the following questions:

- *RQ7:* To what extent do users reveal their sentiment on Sina Weibo and Twitter respectively?
- *RQ8:* To what extent does the sentiment correlate with the type of topics and concepts that people mention in their Sina Weibo and Twitter messages?

Analysis of Temporal Behavior. The users' microblogging behavior may change over time and may, for example, differ between working hours and leisure time. Therefore, we investigate the following research questions:

- *RQ9:* How does the posting behavior of users, particularly regarding the type of topics that the users mention, change between weekdays and weekends on Sina Weibo and Twitter?
- *RQ10:* How do individual user interests change over time in the two microblogging services?

3.2   Evaluation Platform

Extended User Modeling Framework for Microblogging Services. In previous work, we developed a Twitter-based user modeling framework for inferring user interest from tweets [4,7]. Our framework monitors Twitter activities of a user and enriches the semantics of her Twitter messages by extracting meaningful concepts and topics (e.g. named entities) from the messages' content and by linking posts to external relevant Web resources such as new articles. Different weighting schemes such as time-sensitive or term-frequency-based functions allow for estimating to what extent a user might be interested in a given concept at a particular point in time. The generated user profiles can therefore be considered as a set of weighted semantic concepts.

In this paper, we extend our framework with three core features: (1) functionality for monitoring microblogging activities and collecting microposts published on Sina Weibo, (2) named entity recognition for Chinese microposts and (3) sentiment analysis for both Chinese and English microposts. We use ICTCALS[3] as part-of-speech tagger for Chinese text and extract named entities such as locations, organizations and persons from Chinese posts. We implemented a baseline approach to analyze the sentiment of Chinese and English microposts as proposed in [12]. Given these additional features, we are able to apply the same user modeling techniques on both microblogging services Sina Weibo and Twitter and can therefore analyze and compare user characteristics and behavior on the Asian and Western microblogging platforms.

Data Collection. Given the framework, we collected microposts over a period of more than two months via the Sina Weibo Open API and the Twitter Streaming API respectively. For Twitter, we started from a seed set of 56 Twitter users

---

[3] http://ictclas.org/

Table 1. Number of posts published via different categories of access clients

type of access	fraction of posts Weibo Twitter	
posted on a Web or desktop application	54.9	66.2
posted on a mobile application	45.1	33.8
primary product of microblogging activity	90.6	96.7
byproduct of an activity on another platform	9.4	3.3

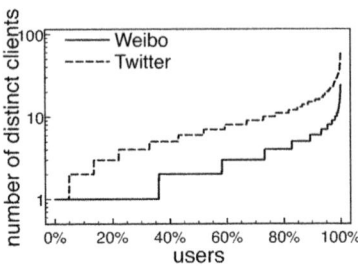

Fig. 1. Number of distinct access clients for individual users

and then we gradually extended this set in a snowball manner. Overall, we collected more than 24 million tweets published by more than 1 million users. For Sina Weibo, since it does not provide functionality similar to Twitter's Streaming API, we monitored the most recent public microposts and finally collected more than 22 million microposts published by more than 6 million users. Twitter posts and Sina Weibo posts were then processed by our framework in order to enrich the semantics of the posts (e.g. entity extraction, sentiment analysis). To better understand the behavior on the level of individual users, we extracted a sample of 1200 active Twitter users (who post in English) and 2616 active Sina Weibo users. The majority of the Twitter users (more than 80%) is – according to their Twitter profile – from the United States while the great majority of the Sina Weibo users (more than 95%) is located in China. For a detailed description on the dataset characteristics we refer the reader to [4] and [2] respectively.

4   Analysis of User Behavior on Sina Weibo and Twitter

Based on the more than 40 million posts that we collected from Sina Weibo and Twitter and processed with our user modeling framework, we study the users' behavior on the two platforms and answer the research questions regarding the five dimensions ranging from access behavior to temporal behavior.

4.1   Analysis of Access Behavior

Results. We first analyzed the most popular client applications that people use to publish posts on Sina Weibo and Twitter. On both platforms, the Web interface is the most popular way to access the microblogging services: 43.1% of the posts are published via the Web on Sina Weibo and 38.5% on Twitter. Other popular clients on Sina Weibo are mainly designed for mobile devices such as the iPhone (7.6%) and Nokia devices (9.4%). Among the most popular Twitter clients are many desktop-based applications such as *TweetDeck*, via which 10.7% of the posts are published. Moreover, we observe on both platforms that people

Table 2. Comparison of syntactic content analysis

syntactic characteristics posts that contain:	proportion of posts Weibo	Twitter
hashtags	6.3%	20.0%
URLs	14.8%	29.1%
question marks "?"	9.9%	18.6%
exclamation marks "!"	26.1%	20.7%
"?" and "!"	3.1%	3.5%

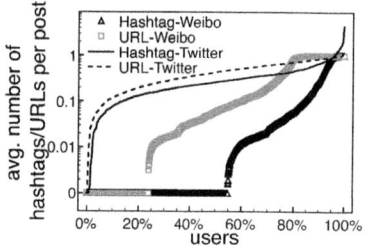

Fig. 2. Comparison of writing style for individual users

publish posts that are rather byproducts of activities the users perform on other platforms. For example, 1.3% of the posts in our Twitter dataset are published via *Twitterfeed*, an application that allows for publishing announcements on a user's Twitter timeline whenever she publishes a new blog article.

In Table 1, we overview the type of client applications that people use to publish microblog posts. We therefore manually categorized the 50 most popular clients, that generate more than 90% of the posts on both microblogging services. We observe that the fraction of posts that are published via mobile devices is significantly higher on Sina Weibo (45.1%) in comparison to Twitter (33.8%). Furthermore, we discover that the fraction of posts which are rather byproducts of other Web activities of the users – hence where the intent of the actual user activity was not targeted towards Sina Weibo or Twitter – is almost three times higher on Sina Weibo (9.4%) than on Twitter (3.3%).

In Fig. 1, we plot for each of the sample users the number of distinct applications which they utilize for publishing microposts. We see that on Twitter more than 95% of the people use more than one client application while on Sina Weibo around 65% of the users switch between different clients.

Findings. From the results above, we conclude the analysis of access behavior with two main findings, referring to the research questions *RQ1* and *RQ2*:

- *F1:* On both platforms, the major way to accessing the microblogging services is via the official Web interfaces or desktop-based applications. Chinese users seem to differ from the English-spoken Twitter users regarding two core aspects: (i) they use mobile applications more extensively and (ii) publish microposts more often as a byproduct of their other Social Web activities.
- *F2:* The results regarding the individual users' access behavior illustrate that Twitter users switch between different clients more often than the users on Sina Weibo. This difference in behavior could be explained by the lower overall number of valuable Sina Weibo client applications (e.g. in our dataset: 3015 different Sina Weibo clients versus 5468 Twitter clients).

4.2   Syntactic Content Analysis

Results. In Table 2, we compare the syntax of messages posted on Sina Weibo and Twitter and particularly the usage of hashtags and URLs. Overall, 20% of the Twitter messages contain hashtags and 29.1% of the tweets feature a URL. Therefore, the usage of hashtags and URLs on Twitter is 3.2 times and 1.97 times respectively more intensive than on Sina Weibo. The analysis of special characters implies that users on Twitter ask more than twice as many questions than users on Sina Weibo (see question marks in Table 2). In contrast, Sina Weibo users make more extensive use of exclamation marks and therefore more often put extra emphasis on their statements.

To further analyze the usage of hashtags and URLs, we also plot for each individual user in our samples the average number of hashtags and URLs per post. From Fig. 2, we infer that a considerably high fraction of Sina Weibo users does not mention hashtags or URLs at all. For 55% of the Chinese microbloggers on Sina Weibo, we did not observe any hashtag. In contrast, on Twitter the people make more frequently use of hashtags or URLs. For example, for more than 85% of the Twitter users, the average number of hashtags per post is at least 0.1, i.e. at least every tenth micropost mentions a hashtag, and 3.9% of the users mention, on average, even more than one hashtag per tweet.

In Table 3 we analyze the influence of the access behavior (see Sect. 4.1) on the usage of hashtags and URLs. For both services, we observe that the usage of hashtags and URLs decreases slightly when people publish microposts from their mobile devices instead of their desktop computers. This difference is more significant on Sina Weibo. For example, on Sina Weibo the number of posts that contain a URL and are issued from a desktop application (17.8%) is more than three times higher than the one for mobile devices (5.2%). On Twitter, the usage of URLs on desktop devices is only 1.57 times higher than on mobile devices. Regarding the type of activity that a user performed to publish a micropost, we observe that 97.9% of the tweets that were generated as byproducts of other activities (e.g. publishing an article in a blog or "check-in" activities on *Foursquare*) contain URLs. In contrast, for the conventional microblogging, only 25.3% of the Twitter messages contain URLs. A similar increase can be observed on Sina Weibo. The number of hashtags is slightly less influenced by the type of activity that caused a micropost (see Table 3).

Findings. Given the results above, we can answer *RQ3* and *RQ4* as follows:

- *F3:* Overall, the results show that hashtags and URLs are less frequently applied on Sina Weibo than on Twitter. This finding holds for both (i) the

Table 3. Impact of the access behavior on the syntactic characteristics of microposts

Syntactic characteristics posts that contain:	proportion of posts			
	Weibo		Twitter	
	Desktop/Mobile	Microblog/Byproduct	Desktop/Mobile	Microblog/Byproduct
hashtags	6.5%/3.5%	3.8%/17.9%	20.7%/18.6%	19.9%/21.3%
URLs	17.8%/5.2%	5.7%/73.5%	31.6%/20.1%	25.3%/97.9%

entire user population and (ii) individual users. In fact, we observe that a large fraction of users on Sina Weibo does not make use of hashtags which implies that hashtag-based user profiles, as discussed in [4], or topic modeling based on hashtags, as proposed by Romero et al. [6] do not seem to be appropriate on Sina Weibo. The usage statistics regarding question marks indicate that Twitter users ask twice more questions than Sina Weibo users.

– *F4:* The usage of hashtags and URLs is moreover influenced by the access behavior. We discover that (i) users are more likely to use hashtags and URLs when they post messages via desktop applications than via mobile applications. Furthermore, (ii) whenever messages are published as a byproduct of another activity – where the primary intention of the user is rather the promotion of an activity that the user performed on another platform – the probability that a micropost contains a hashtag or URL increases. A large fraction of these *byproduct microposts* seems to be automatically generated based on the activity the user performed on another platform. For user modeling those posts offer means to further contextualize the microblogging activities by following the URLs that are contained in the posts (cf. [4]).

4.3 Semantic Content Analysis

Results. Based on the semantic enrichment provided by our user modeling framework, we analyze and compare the types of concepts and topics that people mention in their microposts on Sina Weibo and Twitter respectively. In Table 4 we compare the usage of three types of entities (location, people and organization). Most of the extracted semantic concepts refer to locations (e.g. cities, points of interests): 58.4% for Sina Weibo and 44.6% for Twitter. On Twitter, posts that refer to organizations (e.g. companies, institutions) are more than four times more likely to appear than on Sina Weibo. Examples of entities that were trending on Twitter include different types of entities such as "Mubarak" (person), the former president of Egypt, or "Republican Party" (organization). In contrast, the most popular entities on Sina Weibo are related to locations such as "Beijing" or "United States".

Fig. 3 depicts the average number of entities that can be extracted per post for the individual users in our sample. For 24.8% of the Sina Weibo users, one can detect, on average, more than one entity per post. Moreover, the fraction of users for whom no entity can be extracted is 7.9% in contrast to 10.1% on Twitter. The semantics of the users' messages posted on Sina Weibo are therefore easier to deduce than on Twitter. Based on a comparison of a sample of individual Chinese and English microposts, we hypothesize that this is caused by the expressivity of the Chinese language: while Twitter users are often forced to leave out entities or use abbreviations to refer to entities, Sina Weibo users can exploit the 140 characters more effectively.

Table 4 illustrates how the access behavior influences the semantics of the microposts. When users publish posts from their mobile devices, then it becomes less likely, in comparison to access via desktop (tailored Web) applications, that a message mentions an entity. For microposts that are byproducts of other Web

Table 4. Semantic analysis overall and impact of access behavior on the semantics

type of posts	proportion of posts	
	Weibo	Twitter
Location	58.4%	44.6%
Organization	3.3%	16.0%
Person	38.3%	39.4%

Impact of the access behavior on the type of concepts mentioned in the posts

	Desktop/ Mobile	Microblog/ Byproduct	Desktop/ Mobile	Microblog/ Byproduct
Location	11.2%/6.6%	15.5%/4.0%	9.3%/8.4%	8.9%/13.7%
Organization	0.7%/0.6%	0.9%/0.4%	3.5%/2.9%	3.3%/4.5%
Person	12.4%/12.3%	17.4%/4.9%	8.1%/6.7%	7.6%/8.7%

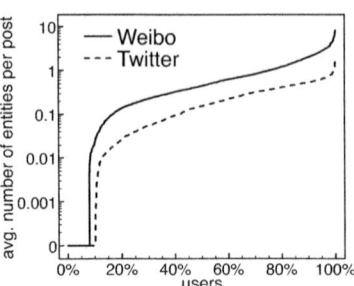

Fig. 3. Semantic analysis for individual users

activities (e.g. activities on *Foursquare*), we observe that it becomes more likely that entities and particularly location entities are mentioned in a post on Twitter. In contrast, on Sina Weibo users mention more entities in context of their standard microblogging activities.

Findings. The results of the analysis illustrate the commonalities and differences regarding the semantic meaning of the microposts that users publish on Sina Weibo and Twitter respectively (see *RQ5* and *RQ6* in Sec. 3.1):

- *F5:* The topics that users discuss on Sina Weibo are to a large extent related to locations and persons. In contrast to Twitter, users on Sina Weibo avoid talking about organizations such as political parties or other institutions. Overall, the semantics of Sina Weibo messages can be better extracted than the semantics of tweets. Consequently, when modeling the microblogging activities for individual users, entity-based user profiles [4] can more successfully be generated for Sina Weibo users: for 92.1% of them one can identify at least one entity of interest in comparison to 89.9% on Twitter.
- *F6:* The type of applications via which users access the microblogging services, affects the occurrence of semantic concepts in the microposts. On mobile devices people tend to mention less entities than on desktop devices. Furthermore, microposts on Twitter are more likely to mention entities and locations particularly if the post was generated as a byproduct of an activity performed on another platform.

4.4 Sentiment Analysis

Results. The sentiment analysis provided by our framework classifies microblog posts as either positive, negative or neutral. Overall, 83.4% and 82.4% of the Sina Weibo and Twitter posts respectively were classified as neutral. Table 5 overviews the sentiment polarities of those posts that have been classified as positive or negative. On Sina Weibo the portion of positive posts (78.8%) is clearly higher than on Twitter (70.5%). In Fig. 4 we plot the ratio of positive

Table 5. Sentiment expressed in (i) overall posts
and (ii) posts that mention certain types of topics

type of posts	proportion of positive/negative posts	
	Weibo	Twitter
Overall posts	78.8%/21.2%	70.5%/29.5%
posts that mention certain types of entities:		
Location	82.7%/17.3%	65.6%/34.4%
Organization	78.5%/21.5%	70.1%/29.9%
Person	82.8%/17.2%	65.7%/34.3%

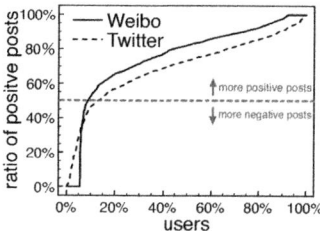

Fig. 4. The ration of positive posts on two microblogging services

posts with respect to all posts, which either have a positive or negative sentiment, for individual users: 92.5% of the users publish more positive messages than negative ones on Sina Weibo in comparison to 86.4% for the Twitter users. On Sina Weibo, we also discover a considerable fraction of users for whom the non-neutral posts are always positive (8.0%) or always negative (5.6%).

In Table 5 we moreover analyze the sentiment revealed in the microposts that mention certain types of entities. Again, the proportion of positive posts exceeds the proportion of negative posts clearly and Sina Weibo users tend to be more positive towards mentioned entities than Twitter users. Interestingly, whenever locations or persons are mentioned in Sina Weibo messages then the likelihood that the post is positive increases on Sina Weibo (from 78.8% to 82.7% and 82.8% respectively) while on Twitter the opposite can be observed (decrease from 70.5% to 65.6% and 65.7% respectively).

Findings. Regarding the research questions *RQ7* and *RQ8* about the sentiment that users express in their microposts, we conclude the following:

- *F7:* We observe that on both platforms there are significantly more positive posts than negative ones. Moreover, users on Sina Weibo have a stronger tendency to publish positive messages than Twitter users. In fact, the probability for positive messages is 11.8% higher on Sina Weibo than on Twitter.
- *F8:* The sentiment that is expressed in microposts correlates with the type of concepts that are mentioned in the posts. On Sina Weibo posts that mention locations or persons are more likely to be positive than posts containing organizations. While on Twitter, the opposite can be observed: people talk more positively about organizations than about persons or locations.

4.5 Analysis of Temporal Behavior

Results. In Table 6 we first compare the posting behavior of users between working days and weekend days by calculating the ratio between the average number of posts per day published during the weekends (Saturday-Sunday) and the one during the week (Monday-Friday). For Sina Weibo this ratio is 1.19,

Table 6. Ratio between weekend posts and weekday posts = the average number of posts per day on a weekend divided by the average number of posts per weekday

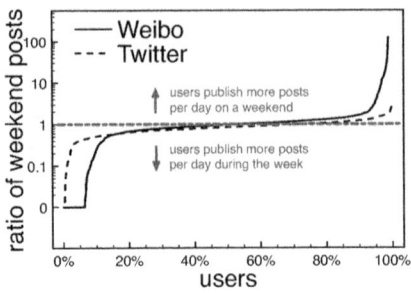

Fig. 5. Weekend-weekday ratio per user

posts per weekend day / posts per weekday		
	Weibo	Twitter
Overall posts	1.19	0.89
posts that mention certain types of entities:		
Location	0.81	1.05
Organization	1.50	0.91
Person	1.19	0.97

which means that Sina Weibo user publish, on average, 19% more messages per day on the weekend than they do during the week. On the other hand, the users on Twitter publish, on average, 11% less posts during the weekend. Therefore, it seems that microblogging in China has not penetrated the daily (possibly work-related) routines as strongly as it does in Western countries.

In Fig. 5 we plot the weekend-weekday ratio for the individual users. While the overall amount of microblogging activities per day on Sina Weibo is higher on the weekends than during the day, we also discover that 1.2% of the Sina Weibo users perform microblogging activities solely during the weekend (ratio of weekend posts is infinite). For about 50% of the users on Sina Weibo the weekend-weekday ratio is greater than 1 which means that they publish more frequently during the weekend. In contrast, on Twitter we identify only 28% of the users who publish more tweets per day on a weekend than during a weekday.

As depicted in Table 6, the occurrence of organizations and persons is more likely during the weekend than during the week on Sina Weibo whereas locations appear more likely during a weekday. On Twitter, the opposite characteristics can be observed. For example, Twitter users mention locations more frequently during the weekend than during the week. These differences in mentioning entities during weekends/weekdays on Sina Weibo and Twitter respectively may relate to different life styles that Chinese and Western people follow. Investigating the particular reasons for them can be interesting for future work.

Furthermore, we study how individual user interests change over time by calculating the standard deviation of the timestamps of microposts that mention a certain topic (entity). The higher the standard deviation of a certain topic the longer the time period over which the topic is mentioned in the posts. In Fig.6 we plot for each user the average standard deviation of the topics which a user mentioned at least once, and group the average standard deviations by the type of the topics. Overall, we observe that topics on Sina Weibo seem to fluctuate stronger than on Twitter. Sina Weibo users often mention certain concepts only once. For example, for more than 80% of the Sina Weibo users of

Table 7. Hofstede's cultural index for China and United States

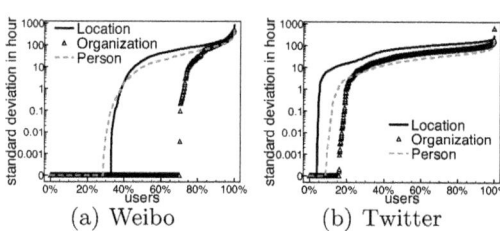

(a) Weibo   (b) Twitter

Fig. 6. Comparison of topic drift

	China	US
Power distance	80	40
Individualism	20	91
Masculinity	66	62
Uncertainty avoidance	40	46
Long term orientation	118	29

our sample, the standard deviation of the organization-related topics is 0. These users mention thus organizations only once in their posts. On both platforms the location-related concepts are, on average, mentioned over a longer period of time than organization-related and person-related concepts.

Findings. The main findings from the analysis of the temporal behavior (research questions *RQ9* and *RQ10*) can be summarized as follows:

- *F9:* On both platforms, the users posting behavior during weekdays differs the one during weekend: while users on Sina Weibo are more active on the weekends, Twitter users tend to be more active during weekdays. Moreover, user interests change between weekends and weekdays. Again, this change of interests differs between Sina Weibo and Twitter users: while for Sina Weibo users we observe a rising interest in persons and organizations during the weekend, the interests of Twitter users focus more on locations. These findings imply that it is beneficial to adapt user interest profiling to the temporal as well as to the cultural context.
- *F10:* User interests change over time. On Sina Weibo, the user interests seem to have a shorter lifespan than on Twitter. Especially, the individual users interests regarding organization-related topics vanish quickly on Sina Weibo while locations feature the longest span of interests.

5   Discussion

Some of our findings can be explained also by cultural differences between the Chinese Sina Weibo users and the Twitter users who are mainly located in the U.S. (more than 80% of the Twitter sample users are located in the United States). According to Hofstede's cultural index [9], people in China can, for example, be characterized by a higher *power distance* than people from the U.S. (see Table 7). This difference might explain our finding *F1* regarding the access behavior (see Sec. 4.1): Sina Weibo users more frequently generate microposts as a byproduct of their other Social Web activities. Therefore, it seems that they are, in comparison to the people who use Twitter, less afraid of disclosing information about themselves. Given the high power distance that is specific to the Chinese culture, we assume that this behavior can be observed because Chinese users do not attribute much impact to their individual activities, i.e. the impact of disclosing information is less because of the high power distance. The more intensive usage of hashtags and URLs which is characteristic for the Twitter users (*F3*, see Sec. 4.2), may relate to both the lower *power distance* and the higher degree of *individualism* of American people (see Table 7). By mentioning a hashtag, microbloggers ensure that their message will appear in the public discussions. Twitter users seem to be more eager to let their posts appear in the public discussion. Hence, they seem to have a stronger belief that their post makes a difference (power distance) and possibly also a higher demand to profile themselves in the public discussions (individualism).

We also observed that Sina Weibo users less frequently mention organizations in their posts than Twitter users (*F5*, see Sec. 4.3). This observation is in line with Hofstede's observation that "employee commitment to an organization is low" in China[4], which is one of the typical indicators for a high *long term orientation*. The sentiment analysis (see Sec. 4.4), which showed that the Chinese Sina Weibo users are more positive than the Twitter users from the U.S. (*F7*), further supports this cultural difference regarding the long term orientation. In the context of the sentiment analysis, we furthermore discovered that Sina Weibo users are more positively talking about persons than Twitter users (*F8*) which again supports the Chinese tendency for *collectivism* rather than *individualism*.

The temporal analysis (see Sec. 4.5) revealed that Sina Weibo users are less actively publishing microblog posts during the working days and particularly mention less frequently organizations than during the weekend. This can be interpreted as an indicator for *long term orientation* as it implies a rather low commitment for the organization that the user is working for. Sina Weibo users also seem to change their interests rather quickly in comparison to Twitter users (*F10*). While this seems to contradict to the long term orientation of Chinese people, it also reveals that Chinese people adapt faster to new topics which may be interpreted as "an ability to adapt traditions to changed conditions", one of the characteristics of cultures with high long term orientation.

We have given an innovative basis for analyzing microblogging behavior on Sina Weibo and Twitter. Further interpretation and validation of our first set of conclusions can be done in future work, with research questions that follow our conclusions. Independent from these interpretations, we believe that our findings already provide valuable insights for the application of user modeling techniques that are provided by our user modeling framework.

References

1. Sakaki, T., Okazaki, M., Matsuo, Y.: Earthquake shakes Twitter users: real-time event detection by social sensors. In: WWW 2010, pp. 851–860. ACM (2010)

---

[4] http://geert-hofstede.com/china.html

2. Long, R., Wang, H., Chen, Y., Jin, O., Yu, Y.: Towards Effective Event Detection, Tracking and Summarization on Microblog Data. In: Wang, H., Li, S., Oyama, S., Hu, X., Qian, T. (eds.) WAIM 2011. LNCS, vol. 6897, pp. 652–663. Springer, Heidelberg (2011)

3. Chen, J., Nairn, R., Nelson, L., Bernstein, M., Chi, E.: Short and tweet: experiments on recommending content from information streams. In: CHI 2010, pp. 1185–1194. ACM (2010)

4. Abel, F., Gao, Q., Houben, G.-J., Tao, K.: Analyzing User Modeling on Twitter for Personalized News Recommendations. In: Konstan, J.A., Conejo, R., Marzo, J.L., Oliver, N. (eds.) UMAP 2011. LNCS, vol. 6787, pp. 1–12. Springer, Heidelberg (2011)

5. Kwak, H., Lee, C., Park, H., Moon, S.: What is twitter, a social network or a news media? In: WWW 2010, pp. 591–600. ACM (2010)

6. Romero, D.M., Meeder, B., Kleinberg, J.: Differences in the mechanics of information diffusion across topics: Idioms, political hashtags, and complex contagion on twitter. In: WWW 2011. ACM (2011)

7. Gao, Q., Abel, F., Houben, G.J.: GeniUS: Generic User Modeling Library for the Social Semantic Web. In: JIST 2011. Springer (2011)

8. Mandl, T.: Comparing Chinese and German Blogs. In: HT 2009. ACM (2009)

9. Hofstede, G., Hofstede, G.J.: Cultures and Organizations: Software of the Mind. McGraw-Hill (2005)

10. Chen, L., Tsoi, H.K.: Analysis of user tags in social music sites: Implications for cultural differences. In: CSCW 2011. ACM (2011)

11. Yu, L., Asur, S., Huberman, B.A.: What trends in chinese social media. CoRR abs/1107.3522 (2011)

12. Go, A., Bhayani, R., Huang, L.: Twitter sentiment classification using distant supervision. Technical report, Stanford University (2009)

Modeling Multiple Distributions of Student Performances to Improve Predictive Accuracy

Yue Gong, Joseph E. Beck, and Carolina Ruiz

Computer Science Department, Worcester Polytechnic Institute,
100 Institute Road, Worcester, MA, 01609, USA
{ygong,josephbeck,ruiz}@wpi.edu

Abstract. In this paper, we propose a general approach to improve student modeling predictive accuracy. The approach was designed based on the assumption that student performance is sampled from multiple, rather than only one, distribution and thus should be modeled by multiple classification models. We applied k-means to identify student performances sampled from those multiple distributions, using no additional features beyond binary correctness of student responses. We trained a separate classification model for each distribution and applied the learned models to unseen students to evaluate our approach. The results showed that compared to the base classifier, our proposed approach is able to improve predictive accuracy: 4.3% absolute improvement in R^2 and 0.03 absolute improvement in AUC, which are not trivial improvements considering the current state of the art in student modeling.

Keywords: student modeling, predictive accuracy, multiple classifiers, multiple distributions of student performances, performance factors analysis.

1 Introduction

Predicting student behaviors is a very important task for computer tutors. Accurately predicting student performances enables the tutor to be aware of a student's mastery status, so that the tutor can determine the necessity of more practice [7]. By accurately assessing student bad behaviors, such as "off-task" or "abusing help", the tutor is better able to intervene at the right time and place so as to decrease student disengagement [2]. Student modeling plays a key role in prediction and further drives decision-making in computer tutors. The model in use should be able to accurately predict a student's *individual* behaviors at the problem level (i.e., how the student will behave in the next problem). The model must also be able to make predictions about new students, for whom it has no historical data.

Unfortunately, predicting individual trials is a difficult task with model-fit statistics generally being fairly low. For predicting student individual correctness, we have found R^2 values ranging from 7.2% to 16.6% [3, 6] on data sets from different computer tutors using common student modeling approaches. This lack of model fit is not specific to our data; psychology studies predicting student individual response time, a continuous value and thus easier to see incremental improvements in

J. Masthoff et al. (Eds.): UMAP 2012, LNCS 7379, pp. 102–113, 2012.

performance, R^2 values ranged from 5.4% 67.9% [4] on 40 sets of data representing learning series. Most existing student models fail to produce satisfyingly high predictive accuracy [5, 6].

The knowledge tracing model (KT) [7], which emerged over a decade ago, has been established as a standard to evaluate new models and is being used in real applications [1]. KT has been shown, by studies on a variety of data sets sampled from different populations, to have predictive accuracy generally between 0.65 and 0.70 in AUC (Area Under the Curve) of the ROC (Receiver Operating Characteristic) curves [5, 6]. More frustratingly, although there have been a number of attempts dedicated to improving accuracy, none have dramatically improved model fit.

One class of attempts, which attracts a large amount of attention, is tweaking existing models [5, 8, 9, 10, 11, 12]. In the evaluations of predicting unseen students' problem-level performances, these models generally performed similarly to the original KT, and some even underperformed KT. Several papers have reported performance improvements in terms of AUC. The *prior per student* model, enhancing KT by incorporating individualization, resulted in an improvement of 0.007 [5]. The contextual guess and slip model, fitting KT by contextually-computed *guess* and *slip* parameters, resulted in negative improvement of -0.21 [5]. KT-gaming, adding student gaming status into the model, led to no gain in accuracy [11]. It appears that none of the methods of tweaking models worked well.

Another class of attempts, which is relatively less common, is to construct new modeling approaches. Performance Factors Analysis (PFA) is an alternative of KT [13]. However, its predictive performance relative to KT varies. Gong et al. [6] found that PFA worked substantially better than KT, on a data set from ASSISTments, with 0.071 gains of absolute value in AUC. Baker et al. [5] found the model did not perform as well as KT, about 0.033 worse in absolute value in AUC, on a data set from the Cognitive Tutors. Therefore, it seems that attempts on building new models have not resulted in clear and consistent improvement.

As neither class of efforts have provided impressive results, it seems that improving accuracy of student models is not straightforward. This paper presents a new approach to tackling this difficult problem. Unlike other approaches that are tailored to some specific model's shortcomings and only deal with that model, our approach targets a common weakness of both KT and PFA, aiming to have generalizability across other established student models.

1.1   Motivation

Our prior work examined KT and PFA, two popular student modeling techniques [6]. When visualizing their classification performances in confusion matrices, we found a common characteristic of both: a large number of false positives. A confusion matrix, seen in Table 1, is an approach for visually understanding a classifier's performance. A confusion matrix summarizes performance with four elements: true positive (TP), false negative (FN), false positive (FP) and true negative (TN). Traditionally, for binary classification, the rare class is often denoted as the positive class, while the majority class is denoted as the negative class [14]. In our case, however, the class of correct student performances is denoted as the positive class, as conveys more semantic meaning (i.e., positives indicate correct answers).

Table 1. The confusion matrix of the baseline PFA model used in this analysis

		Predicted class	
		Positive	Negative
Actual class	Positive	16206 (TP)	2399 (FN)
	Negative	5899 (FP)	3965 (TN)

Table 1 shows the confusion matrix of the PFA model on the data set used in our previous work [6] and for this study. There are two types of errors: false positive (FP) and false negative (FN). The bottom-left cell, FP, corresponds to the number of incorrect responses wrongly predicted as correct (5899) by the classification model; while FN (2399) denotes the number of correct responses misclassified by the model as incorrect. In this work FP is much higher than FN, and we also found this trend to be true for KT, as well as for KT's and PFA's variants [6]. This result inspired us with an idea that a promising approach for improving accuracy is to reduce FP.

This imbalanced FP/FN ratio is a consequent of positive student responses being the majority class in our data set. However, the phenomenon that correct responses are the majority is not unique to our data set, but is fairly common in most of the student performance data sets that are being used in the field (e.g. [5, 9, 13]). This imbalance makes sense, as in most learning environments students will get more than half the items correct in order to prevent frustration. Consequently, we believed that placing our efforts on decreasing FP is meaningful.

1.2   The Base Classifier: Performance Factors Analysis

We used PFA, rather than KT, as the modeling approach for this study. The rationale is that we have observed that PFA has been the most accurate at predicting student problem-level performances on our data [6]. Using this model prevents the improvement, if found in this study, from being attributed to a less fair comparison, where a weaker model is used as the baseline.

The Performance Factors Analysis model is a student modeling method that takes the form of logistic regression with student performance (correctness) as the dependent variable [13]. Equation 1 shows the expression of the logit, m, which by the function of $1/(1-e^{-m})$ can be transformed to a probability, representing how likely a student i is to correctly answer a question q. The PFA model takes question identifiers as an independent variable and estimates a parameter (β_q) for each question, representing its difficulty. In the equation, $s_{i,j}$ and $f_{i,j}$ are two observed variables, representing the numbers of the prior successful and failed practices done by student i on one of the required skills, j. The corresponding two coefficients (γ_j and ρ_j) are estimated to respectively capture the effects of a prior correct response and a prior incorrect response of skill j on how likely the student is going to answer the current question correctly.

$$m(i \in \text{students}, q \in \text{questions}, s, f) = \beta_q + \sum_{j \in \text{required skills for } q} (\gamma_j s_{i,j} + \rho_j f_{i,j}) \qquad (1)$$

2   Approach

2.1   Rationale: Modeling Multiple Distributions of Student Performances

We have established our goal as reducing the error rate, by reducing the FP rate, of student models. In order to find a means of *how* to reduce FP, a reasonable first step is to analyze *why*. In particular, what possibly causes high FP? We hypothesized that high FP could be due to the insufficiency of using a single classification model to classify student performances. We proposed that a solution could be to learn multiple classification models, with the purpose of modeling multiple distributions of student performances (MMD-SP). The pseudo code of MMD-SP is listed in Table 2.

Using a single classification model implies that instances were sampled from a single distribution and thus can be modeled with a single classifier. Contrariwise, using multiple classification models assume that instances were sampled from multiple distributions and thus should be modeled separately representing each of the distributions.

If there are multiple distributions, while using a single classification model to fit, then a high false positive is not unexpected. More specifically, suppose we have a naïve student model, where the target is the correctness of a student performance and the only independent variable is the question the student was solving. We then learn a single classification model based on the naïve model. As a result, all instances would be mapped to *correct* or *incorrect* using the same function. As long as it deals with the same question, the model believes that its difficulty is perceived equally across all students, even though the question could be harder to a subgroup of students. If on the question, the majority of student responses happen to be *correct*, the model tends to predict correct for every instance of the question. For those students who have high difficulty in answering this question, a false positive occurs.

2.2   Distinguish Samples of Multiple Distributions

In order to accomplish MMD-SP, we need to first identify samples of each of those multiple distributions. We used k-means cluster analysis to partition student performances into clusters, each of which represents the sample of a distribution. The corresponding pseudo code is from line 2 to line 12 in Table 2.

We assumed that being sampled from the same distribution, student performances should share common characteristics and be different from student performances from another distribution. That is to say, student performances from a distribution should be able to form a mathematically meaningful group. We used clustering as we did not know how to separate the groups, and chose k-means as the algorithm is straightforward and a prominent clustering method.

To classify a student performance, a set of attributes describing that performance is needed. We use normalized confusion matrices, so the counts in Table 1 are normalized so that all elements of the matrix sum to 1. The proportion of FP in the data is 0.21, FN is 0.08, TP is 0.57, and TN is 0.14.

Table 2. Pseudo code of the MMD-SP algorithm

```
MMD-SP Algorithm

1: Let D denote the training data, D[i] denote the i^th student's
       data, D[i][j] denote the j^th instance in D[i], CM[i] denote
       the i^th student's confusion matrix, T denotes the test
       data, T[i] denote the i^th student's data, T[i][j] denote
       the j^th instance in T[i], and k denote the number of
       clusters specified.
2:    PFA_0 = train_PFA(D).
3:    for i=1 to D.length do (i.e., for each student)
4:       Initialize CM[i]. //CM[i].TN=0,CM[i].FP=0,CM[i].FN=0,
                                      CM[i].TP=0
5:       for j=1 to D[i].length do
6:          NCM[i] = normalize (CM[i]).
7:          Attributes[i][j] = {NCM[i].TN, NCM[i].FP, NCM[i].FN}.
8:          apply_PFA(PFA_0, D[i][j]).
9:          update CM[i] according to the result from line #8.
10:      end for
11:   end for
12: Clusters[] = K-means(Attributes, k).
13: for c=1 to k do
14:    D_c = instances D[][] ∈ Clusters[c].
15:    PFA_c = train_PFA(D_c).
16: end for
17: for l=1 to T.length do
18:    for j=1 to T[l].length do
19:       PFA_x=select model from {PFA_0...PFA_k} for T[l][j].
20:       apply_PFA(PFA_x, T[l][j]).
21:    end for
22: end for
```

Rather than using a single confusion matrix to summarize a model's overall classification performance, for each student performance, we calculated a confusion matrix that summarized the model's classification performance so far on that student. More specifically, a base classifier, PFA, was induced from training data. Before a student's first instance, the student's confusion matrix is initialized to be four zeros, indicating no observations so far in his TN, FP, FN or TP. Then the algorithm computes the normalized confusion matrix. Since the four normalized values sum up to 1, the dimensions of the attribute set can be reduced to 3, and so we used the tuple <TN, FP, FN> as the attributes of the instance. Then the algorithm applies the base classifier to the instance, resulting in either a TN, FP, FN or TP, and the algorithm updates the confusion matrix. For example, suppose that our algorithm is about to generate a confusion matrix for the *j*th performance of the student *i*. It looks at his performances from 1 to j-1, and calculates the normalized confusion matrix. We use this normalized confusion matrix as the attribute set to perform the clustering.

Although using confusion matrices are an odd choice for features for clustering, it was not a haphazard decision. We chose confusion matrices for two reasons.

First, we prefer general attributes that require nothing beyond the binary response data normally required to train a student model. Our proposed approach is designed to be widely applicable to solve the problem of high false positives. Using confusion matrices as attributes perfectly matches our goal, as they can be calculated on any sequential user data. Therefore, our approach can be easily applied to any other modeling techniques and data sets, without requiring certain attributes exclusive to a specific data set (such as in [15]).

Second, we think that using confusion matrices as the attributes helps distinguish samples from multiple distributions. A confusion matrix is informative in reflecting the model's performance and capturing a student's proficiency, and thus represents exactly the constructs we are interested in analyzing. In the aspect of capturing a student's proficiency, a confusion matrix shows how well the student performed previously, and shows which instances the base classifier confuses and how it misclassifies them. For example, if the confusion matrix of an instance shows large FP, it suggests that the instance is not suitable to be modeled by the base classifier; rather it might be sampled from a distribution where the class of negative is the majority, perhaps reflecting relatively weaker students.

2.3   Learn Multiple Classification Models

Applying k-means, we partitioned the training data into K portions, one for each cluster, which presumably represents each of the multiple distributions. Now for each distribution, we learn a separate classification model. The corresponding pseudo code is from line 13 to line 16 in Table 2.

All classification models were learned on the basis of the same approach, PFA. In particular, we fit each portion of the data to a PFA model and learned a classification model. As a result, we had K classification models.

We decided to use PFA as the student model for all classification models, as we wanted to test the effectiveness of the proposed approach, MMD-SP, in isolation. We controlled other factors that possibly result in improvement, especially the use of another student modeling approach that may improve accuracy. In this way we can ensure that the parameter estimates of K classification models capture differences between different distributions. For example, if a question's difficulty parameter is high in one model but low in another, perhaps some aspect of instruction varies that causes two groups of students to respond to the same question very differently.

2.4   Select a Classification Model for an Unknown Instance

For each instance in the test data, we need to estimate from which distribution it was drawn, or equivalently, select the best model to use for predicting this instance.

The corresponding pseudo code is from line 17 to line 22 in Table 2. We implemented two methods for selecting which model to use when making a prediction.

Least Distance. A test instance should be similar to the training instances sampled from the same distribution. Following the k-means cluster analysis, the instance should be assigned to a cluster whose centroid is closest to this instance's attributes. We followed the same procedure as we did for the training data, and used the base classifier to generate a confusion matrix for each unknown instance and compared it to each of the cluster centroids. We then selected the classification model corresponding to the cluster having the least distance from its centroid to the instance.

Least error associates test instances with clusters that have performed well for this student in the past. For an unknown instance of a student, we computed which classifier, so far, has had the lowest error rate for this student. In this method, no confusion matrices are needed during the testing process.

In addition, to overcome the cold-start problem, for the first three instances of each student, we used the base classifier.

3   Experiment and Results

3.1   Data and Performance Metrics

We used data from ASSISTments (http://www.assistments.org), a web-based math tutoring system,. The data are from 445 8th-grade (generally twelve- through fourteen- year old) students in urban school districts of the Northeastern United States. These data consisted of 113,979 problems completed in ASSISTments during Nov. 2008 to Feb. 2009. There are 31 skills in the data set, such as understanding-data-generation-techniques, understanding-polygon-geometry, etc. ASSISTments logged performance records of each student chronologically.

We performed a 4-fold crossvalidation at the level of students, and tested our models on unseen students. We randomly separated data at the student level since it results in a more independent test set. In addition, testing on unseen students can examine the generalizability of the induced multiple models. It is particularly important for our proposed approach, as we assume that test data should also be sampled from the same multiple distributions, which have been modeled while using training data. Evaluating on unseen students examines this assumption and shows how the approach performs for a number of students who have never been seen in model training.

We used two metrics to measure predictive accuracy, Efron's R^2 and AUC. Efron's R^2 is a measure of how well a model performs in terms of accurately predicting values for each test instance. Efron's R^2 presents a relative measure against a naïve model, which uses the mean to predict every instance. $R^2=1$ indicates perfect prediction, while a 0 indicates no better prediction than the naïve model. AUC of ROC curve evaluates the model's performance on classifying the target variable which has two categories. It is a classic metric in classification tasks, and also being broadly used in the field. In our case, it measures the model's ability to differentiate students' positive and negative responses. AUC = 0.5 is the baseline, which suggests random prediction (i.e., there is no relationship between the predicted value and the true value), while AUC=1 indicates perfect prediction.

3.2   Results

In this section, we evaluate our proposed approach. We compared the predictive accuracy of the multiple classifiers induced by the approach and the predictive accuracy of the base classifier. We used the k-means cluster analysis in SPSS. We used the value of K from 2 to 5 without specifying initial cluster centers. To evaluate the models, we perform paired-sample two-tailed t-tests using the results from the crossvalidation with degrees of freedom of N-1, where N is the number of folds (4).

Table 3. Cross-validated of predictive accuracy of the base and multiple classifiers

No. of classifiers	R^2		AUC	
	Least distance	Least error	Least distance	Least error
Base (PFA)	16.2%		0.740	
2	19.6%	20.5%	0.765	0.770
3	19.7%	20.1%	0.766	0.769
4	19.5%	19.8%	0.766	0.768
5	18.5%	19.3%	0.761	0.765

Table 3 compares predictive accuracy of multiple classifiers against the base classifier. The first row shows the predictive accuracy of the base classifier, a single PFA model, on the test data. From the second row downwards are the multiple classifiers induced by our proposed approach with the number of classifiers varying from 2 to 5, one for each cluster. We report results for least distance and least error.

We noticed that multiple classifiers induced by our approach all outperformed the base classifier, with a 4.3% absolute improvement in R^2 (20.5% - 16.2% = 4.3%) and 0.03 absolute improvement in AUC (0.770 - 0.740 = 0.03) achieved with the best setting. Based on the paired-sample t-tests (df=3) using the results from the crossvalidation, all differences in two metrics using multiple classifiers and the base classifier are significant with $p<0.01$.

We also found that the two model selection methods performed fairly consistently. Both resulted in similar predictive accuracy, though using least error as the selection metric generally achieved slightly higher predictive accuracy, but not noticeably so. Furthermore, least error is superior to least distance due to its low complexity, as, unlike least distance, it does not require building confusion matrices for the test data.

Interestingly, we found that introducing more classifiers does not help for boosting predictive accuracy further. Two classifiers resulted in the peak when using least error, while three classifiers did the best when using least distance. Three possible reasons could cause these results. First, the student performances are not from *many* distributions, but rather from a small number of distributions. Therefore, modeling 2 or 3 distributions of student performances is sufficient, while modeling extra distributions causes over-fitting. Second, the presence of more classifiers confuses the model selection methods, for both least error and least distance. Classifying an instance using an improper classifier caused the drop of predictive accuracy. The third possibility is we do not have sufficient training data to train 5 classification models with well-estimated parameters. In fact, a classification model may have not seen some questions at all while being trained, and also could be required to predict an unknown instance involving the question. Perhaps more training data would enable the use of additional classifiers?   To resolve these issues, we examined the classifiers' predictive accuracy on training data, as shown in Table 4.

Table 4. Comparisons of predictive accuracy of the classifiers on the training and test data

No. of classifiers	R^2	
	Training	Test (least error)
Base (PFA)	18.0%	16.2%
2	23.2%	20.5%
3	25.1%	20.1%
4	25.5%	19.8%
5	25.6%	19.3%

Comparing the two values of the base classifier, 18.0% vs. 16.2%, we found that the PFA model generalizes well to unseen students. We also noticed that the presence of more classifiers doesn't help much on the training data either, with only a 2.4% improvement from using 2 classifiers (23.2%) to using 5 classifiers (25.6%). Thus the third explanation is not plausible, as sparse training data should produce strong model-fit statistics on the training data.   The second explanation is less plausible, since no heuristic is required to determine which cluster to use.   Thus, our results suggest that a small number (2 or 3) of distributions, at least as derived by k-means for our set of features, are the more likely explanation for the asymptote in performance relative to the number of clusters.

Since the accuracy measure treats all classes as equally important, it may not be suitable for analyzing imbalanced data sets, such as the one we used. Therefore, we used confusion matrices to evaluate the classifiers derived from our approach. In this paper, due to limited space, we chose to show FP and FN in graphs, shown in Fig. 1, rather than all elements of a confusion matrix.

Fig. 1 shows the percent of false positives and the percent of false negatives, generated from the test data and using least error to select the classifiers. The x-axes in the two charts represent the number of classifiers (= the number of clusters). The first one, with label 1, corresponds to the base classifier, PFA. The y axes in the two charts have the same unit of 1%, so that it is fair to compare the lines across the graphs. Take 21.10% in the first chart as an example, the value indicates 21.10% of the entire data was misclassified as correct responses, while in fact they are incorrect responses. As we can see, the PFA model produced about 2.5 times as many FPs as FNs. In addition, we showed that our proposed approach, targeting the goal of reducing FP, has succeeded. Moreover, the error of FN increases much less than the decreases of FP. Finally, we found that from 3 classifiers afterwards, the two errors did not change much. This result suggests there is little benefit to adding additional clusters, as since neither error is improved, ensembling models with more clusters will probably not be beneficial in improving the error rate.

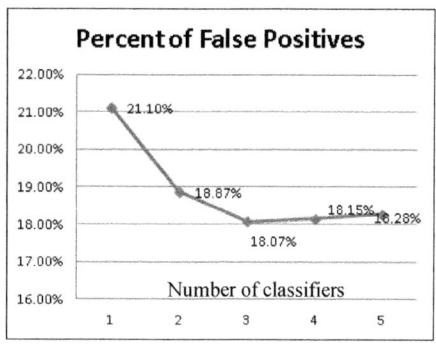
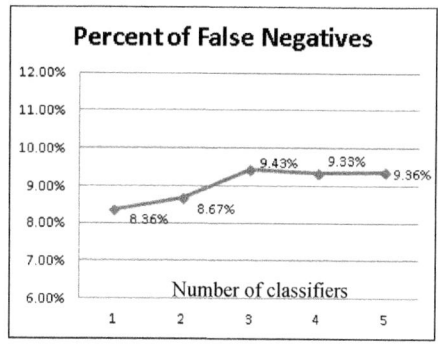

Fig. 1. False positive and false negative percentages across different numbers of classifiers

4   Contributions

This paper made several contributions to student modeling.

We pointed out a common issue of student modeling: models tend to produce many false positives when used to predict student performances. There have been many efforts on improving predictive accuracy and some of them certainly work [5, 6, 8, 9, 10, 11]. However, all of them improved the accuracy without seeing where the real weakness lies. In particular, they worked on certain models and enhanced the models based on their hypotheses as to what the models' specific drawbacks are. Our work started with looking at what the typical misclassifications were, and have identified a fruitful area of research. We believe that this approach is helpful for efficiently allocating our future efforts.

Trivedi et al. presented an approach which also uses clustering and multiple classification models [15]. However, this work does not attempt to predict student individual responses, but focuses on student performance in an annual state-wide test. Also, this work clusters students on the basis of knowledge-engineered features specific to the ASSISTments tutor, whereas we focus on generic properties of student performance that apply to a variety of systems. Their work also differs in that their clusters represent student traits, in that students are the unit of cluster membership. Our work looks at student performance and allows students to belong to different clusters if their performance changes over time.

Although other work has used clustering for student modeling (e.g. [15]), our work assumes no additional features are used for the clustering. Although using no information beyond the classifier itself and the student performance data at first sounds limiting, we found it enables noticeable gains in predictive accuracy. Furthermore, due to not requiring any additional information, this approach is more broadly applicable than a technique that relies on domain-specific features. The notion of creating a confusion matrix from predicted performance can apply to any sequential user modeling task, not just those for educational systems. Thus, this technique is applicable to, for example, recommendation systems.

We presented a general approach implementing the idea of MMD-SP. Our evaluation results showed that the approach successfully improved predictive accuracy. Comparing to a student model, PFA, which has been found to be the most accurate on our data set, our approach resulted in 4.3% absolute improvement in R^2 and 3% absolute improvement in AUC. Considering other work on improving accuracy [5, 6, 8, 9, 10, 11] has often found limited improvements, these results are not trivial.

5   Future Work and Conclusions

In our approach, to model multiple distributions, we used k-means to identify corresponding samples in training data. We explored several values of k in this study, but having a means to determine the optimal value of k would be very helpful for the approach. In addition, as a center-based cluster analysis, k-means partitions the data into clusters in which each point is closer to the center to its cluster than to the center of any other clusters. That is to say partition is done based on distance in the data space. However, perhaps the real data distribution has some characteristics leading to a necessity of other types of clustering techniques, such as density-based clustering or spectral clustering. Exploring data to find a possibly better-suited method to find the distributions could possibly refine the approach.

MMD-SP is a general idea and its implementation presented in this paper is applicable to many other student models. It is interesting to understand how it performs when applied to other student models, especially knowledge tracing, as KT also tends to produce high FP. Whether this approach helps KT will help determine MMD-SP's generalizability. In addition, replicating this study on different data sets also helps further explore MMD-SP's generalizability.

An important open question is how to design a student model that is better at distinguishing true positives from false positives. Although this work reduced false positives, it is still the majority of classification errors. This work is significant due to the increasing importance of ensemble methods (e.g. [5]). The power of ensembling comes from the variability of predictions from different classifiers. However, the current problem is that most classifiers agree with each other to a large amount, and make similar errors leading to a high number of false positives. Therefore, there is currently fairly small gains from ensembling [5].

In this work we introduced the idea of MMD-SP, modeling multiple distributions of student performances, aiming to solve the problem of high false positives. We questioned the assumption that a single distribution samples the entire student data, and found that 2 or 3 distributions of student performances appear to be more plausible, which suggests the idea of one-model-fits-all is not a good assumption for student modeling. Using the performance factors analysis model to compare the assumption of multiple distributions vs. a single distribution, we found that R^2 was increased 4.3% in absolute and AUC was improved 0.03 in absolute improvement. In addition, we found that the approach worked well on reducing false positives.

Furthermore, our idea of modeling multiple distributions has the advantage of generalizing beyond student modeling. Rather, many user modeling tasks could use this idea and possibly benefit from it. It is plausible that users or user behaviors vary greatly, so it is logical to hypothesize that they are sampled from multiple distributions. Modeling those multiple distributions, rather than forcing all users to be fit a single model, seems more appropriate.

References

1. Koedinger, K.R., Anderson, J.R., Hadley, W.H., Mark, M.A.: Intelligent Tutoring Goes to School in the Big City. Int. J. Artificial Intelligence in Education (1997)
2. Baker, R.S., Corbett, A.T., Koedinger, K.R.: Responding to Problem Behaviors in Cognitive Tutors: Towards Educational Systems Which Support All Students. National Association for the Dually Diagnosed (NADD) Bulletin 9(4), 70–75 (2006)
3. Gong, Y., Beck, J.: Items, Skills, and Transfer Models: Which Really Matters for Student Modeling? In: Proceedings of the 4th International Conference on Educational Data Mining, pp. 81–90 (2011)
4. Heathcote, A., Brown, S., Mewhort, D.J.K.: The Power Law repealed: The case for an Exponential Law of Practice. Psychonomic Bulletin & Review (2002)
5. Baker, R.S.J.d., Pardos, Z.A., Gowda, S.M., Nooraei, B.B., Heffernan, N.T.: Ensembling Predictions of Student Knowledge within Intelligent Tutoring Systems. In: Konstan, J.A., Conejo, R., Marzo, J.L., Oliver, N. (eds.) UMAP 2011. LNCS, vol. 6787, pp. 13–24. Springer, Heidelberg (2011)
6. Gong, Y., Beck, J.E., Heffernan, N.T.: How to Construct More Accurate Student Models: Comparing and Optimizing Knowledge Tracing and Performance Factors Analysis. International Journal of Artificial Intelligence in Education (2010) (in press)
7. Corbett, A.T., Anderson, J.R.: Knowledge Tracing: Modeling the Acquisition of Procedural Knowledge. User Modeling and User-Adapted Interaction 4, 253–278 (1995)
8. Pardos, Z.A., Heffernan, N.T.: Modeling Individualization in a Bayesian Networks Implementation of Knowledge Tracing. In: De Bra, P., Kobsa, A., Chin, D. (eds.) UMAP 2010. LNCS, vol. 6075, pp. 255–266. Springer, Heidelberg (2010)
9. Pardos, Z.A., Heffernan, N.T.: KT-IDEM: Introducing Item Difficulty to the Knowledge Tracing Model. In: Konstan, J.A., Conejo, R., Marzo, J.L., Oliver, N. (eds.) UMAP 2011. LNCS, vol. 6787, pp. 243–254. Springer, Heidelberg (2011)
10. Baker, R.S.J.d., Corbett, A.T., Aleven, V.: More Accurate Student Modeling through Contextual Estimation of Slip and Guess Probabilities in Bayesian Knowledge Tracing. In: Woolf, B.P., Aïmeur, E., Nkambou, R., Lajoie, S. (eds.) ITS 2008. LNCS, vol. 5091, pp. 406–415. Springer, Heidelberg (2008)
11. Gong, Y., Beck, J.E., Heffernan, N.T.: Understanding the impact of student seriousness on learning in a computer tutor. Journal of Educational Psychology (2011) (submitted)
12. Xu, Y., Mostow, J.: Using Logistic Regression to Trace Multiple Subskills in a Dynamic Bayes Net. In: Proceedings of the 9th International Conference on Educational Data Mining, pp. 241–246 (2011)
13. Pavlik, P.I., Cen, H., Koedinger, K.: Learning Factors Transfer Analysis: Using Learning Curve Analysis to Automatically Generate Domain Models. In: Proceedings of the 2nd International Conference on Educational Data Mining, pp. 121–130 (2009)
14. Tan, P., Steinbach, M., Kumar, V.: Introduction to Data Mining. Addison-Wesley, Boston (2005)
15. Trivedi, S., Pardos, Z.A., Heffernan, N.T.: Clustering Students to Generate an Ensemble to Improve Standard Test Score Predictions. In: Biswas, G., Bull, S., Kay, J., Mitrovic, A. (eds.) AIED 2011. LNCS, vol. 6738, pp. 377–384. Springer, Heidelberg (2011)

A Simple But Effective Method to Incorporate Trusted Neighbors in Recommender Systems

Guibing Guo*, Jie Zhang, and Daniel Thalmann

School of Computer Engineering
Nanyang Technological University, Singapore
{gguo1,zhangj,danielthalmann}@ntu.edu.sg

Abstract. Providing high quality recommendations is important for on-line systems to assist users who face a vast number of choices in making effective selection decisions. *Collaborative filtering* is a widely accepted technique to provide recommendations based on ratings of similar users. But it suffers from several issues like *data sparsity* and *cold start*. To address these issues, in this paper, we propose a simple but effective method, namely "Merge", to incorporate social trust information (i.e. trusted neighbors explicitly specified by users) in providing recommendations. More specifically, ratings of a user's trusted neighbors are merged to represent the preference of the user and to find similar other users for generating recommendations. Experimental results based on three real data sets demonstrate that our method is more effective than other approaches, both in accuracy and coverage of recommendations.

1 Introduction

Recommender systems are heavily used in e-commerce to provide users with high quality, personalized recommendations to help them find satisfactory items (e.g. books, movies, news, music, etc.) among a huge number of available choices. Collaborative filtering (CF) [7] is the most commonly used technique to generate recommendations. The heuristic is that the items appreciated by those who have similar taste will also be appreciated by the active user (the user who needs recommendations). However, CF suffers from several inherent drawbacks like *data sparsity* and *cold start*. Data sparsity arises due to the fact that users in general only rate a small portion of items. Cold start refers to the dilemma that accurate recommendations are expected for new users whereas they often rate only a few items that are difficult to reveal their preferences.

To mitigate the problems suffered by CF, trust-aware recommender systems (TARSs) have been proposed to incorporate social trust information (i.e. trusted neighbors of users) [2,5]. For example, Massa et al. [5] suggest that trust information is more meaningful to bootstrap recommender systems than item-rating information. Both implicit trust (e.g. [6,9]) and explicit trust (e.g. [2,5,1,8]) have

---

* Would like to thank the Institute for Media Innovation (IMI) at Nanyang Technological University (NTU) for providing a PhD grant.

J. Masthoff et al. (Eds.): UMAP 2012, LNCS 7379, pp. 114–125, 2012.
© Springer-Verlag Berlin Heidelberg 2012

been utilized in the literature whereas explicit trust is more accurate than the implicit one. Although the overall performance of recommendation can be improved to some extent by the trust-aware recommender systems [12], the mitigation for the cold-start problem is still limited [10].

In this paper, we propose a simple but effective method called "Merge" to incorporate trusted neighbors explicitly specified by users in recommender systems to improve the overall performance of recommendation and mitigate the cold-start problem. Specifically, we merge the ratings of an active user's directly trusted neighbors by averaging the neighbors' ratings for their commonly rated items according to how much the neighbors are trusted by the active user. The merged rating set is then used to represent the active user's preference and find similar other users for the active user. Finally, the ratings provided by both the similar users and the trusted neighbors are used to predict item ratings for the active user. Experiments on three real data sets are conducted to verify the effectiveness of our method. The results show that it can achieve promising accuracy and coverage for recommendation, and is especially useful for cold-start users, compared with other approaches. Our method thus shades light on incorporating trusted neighbors for building an effective trust-aware recommender system.

2   Related Work

Trust has been extensively studied in recommender systems, that is trust-aware recommender systems. The intuition is that trusted users may share similar taste. In fact, researchers have found that trust has a positive and strong correlation with preference [11].

O'Donovan et al. [6] indicate that trust is useful to decrease recommendation error. They define *profile-level* and *item-level* trust as the percentage of correct predictions from the view of general profile and specific items, respectively. In our work, we focus on explicit trust relations as they are directly specified by users and more accurate than implicit ones. Jamali and Ester [3] design the *Trust-Walker* approach to randomly select neighbors in the trust network formed by users and their trusted neighbors. Trust information of the selected neighbors is combined with an item-based technique to predict item ratings. On the contrary, our work focuses on generating predictions by combining trust information with a user-based technique. Liu and Lee [4] report that more accurate prediction algorithms are possible by incorporating trust information into traditional collaborative filtering. They do not directly use trust to substitute similarity but rather amplify similarity measurement by taking into account the number of messages exchanged among users. Thus this approach is message specific.

The closest approaches to ours are as follows. Massa and Avesani [5] analyze the drawbacks of CF-based recommender systems and describe how and why trust can mitigate those problems. They propose *MoleTrust* [5], which performs depth-first search, to propagate and infer trust in the trust network. Empirical results show that the coverage is significantly enlarged but the accuracy remains comparable when propagating trust. Besides, Golbeck [2] proposes a breadth-first search method *TidalTrust* to infer and compute trust value, but the performance of them is close [12]. Hence, we only consider MoleTrust for comparison in this paper. Chowdhury et al. [1] propose to enhance CF by predicting the ratings of similar users who did not rate the concerned items according to the ratings of their trusted neighbors, so as to incorporate more users for recommendation. However, it performs badly for cold-start users, which is the main concern of this work. Another recent work using the trust network is proposed by Ray and Mahanti [8]. They improve the prediction accuracy by reconstructing the trust network. More specifically, they remove the trust links between two users if their correlation is lower than a threshold. Empirical results show that good performance is achieved at the cost of poor coverage.

In addition, although many trust-aware recommender systems have been proposed to exploit explicit trust for effective recommendations, most of them are evaluated on only one data set. These approaches often achieve improvements in either accuracy or coverage, but not both. More importantly, the cold-start problem has not been well addressed yet. Therefore, how to incorporate trust information for effective recommendations remains a big challenge [10]. The purpose of our work is to take a step further in addressing this challenge by proposing a simple but effective method to incorporate trusted neighbors in TARSs.

3   The Merge Method

Our Merge method incorporates trusted neighbors of an active user for recommendations by taking the following three steps: 1) merging the ratings of trusted neighbors to represent the preference of the active user; 2) finding similar users according to the merged rating set; and 3) predicting the ratings of items for the active user based on the ratings for the items provided by the similar users and trusted neighbors. The detailed and formal description as well as the insights of the Merge method are given in the subsequent sections.

3.1   Merging the Ratings of Trusted Neighbors

Let U and I denote the sets of all users and items in the system, respectively. Let $r_{v,i}$ be the rating of an item $i \in I$ provided by a user v. For an active user $u \in U$ who has not rated an item $j \in I$, the task is to predict a rating for the item j that the active user u will likely provide, denoted by $\hat{r}_{u,j}$.

In the system, the active user u has identified a set of trusted neighbors TN_u. For a trusted neighbor $v \in TN_u$, user u also specifies a trust value $t_{u,v}$ indicating the degree to which user u trusts user v. We assume that the active user u should fully trust herself because the ratings of items provided by herself should accurately represent her own preference on the rated items. Thus, user u herself is also included in the set TN_u of her trusted neighbors, and $t_{u,u} = 1$ if the highest possible degree of trust is 1.

For an item $i \in I$ that is rated by at least one trusted neighbor in TN_u, we merge the ratings of item i provided by the trusted neighbor(s). More specifically, we average the ratings according to the trust values of the trusted neighbors specified by the active user u, as follows:

$$\tilde{r}_{u,i} = \frac{\sum_{v \in TN_u} t_{u,v} r_{v,i}}{\sum_{v \in TN_u} t_{u,v}} \tag{1}$$

where $\tilde{r}_{u,i}$ is the merged rating for the active user u on item i, according to the ratings of her trusted neighborhood TN_u (including herself).

We perform the process of merging ratings for every item in I that is rated by at least one trusted neighbor in TN_u. We denote the set of such items as $\tilde{I}_u$. In the end, we have a set of merged ratings, each of which is for an item in $\tilde{I}_u$. This merged rating set is used to represent the preference of the active user u.

3.2   Incorporating with Collaborative Filtering

Given the merged rating set on the items in $\tilde{I}_u$, which represents the preference of the active user u, we then apply the collaborative filtering technique to predict the rating of the item j that is not rated by u. More specifically, we first find a set of similar users (i.e. a set of nearest neighbors denoted as NN_u) for the active user u based on the merged rating set. The rating of item j is then predicted by aggregating the ratings for the item j provided by the nearest neighbors in NN_u and the trusted neighbors in TN_u.

For finding a set of similar users for the active user u, we adopt the popular Pearson Correlation Coefficient (PCC) to compute the similarity between user u and another user v who is not in TN_u, as follows:

$$s_{u,v} = \frac{\sum_{i \in I_{u,v}} (\tilde{r}_{u,i} - \bar{r}_u)(r_{v,i} - \bar{r}_v)}{\sqrt{\sum_{i \in I_{u,v}} (\tilde{r}_{u,i} - \bar{r}_u)^2} \sqrt{\sum_{i \in I_{u,v}} (r_{v,i} - \bar{r}_v)^2}} \tag{2}$$

where $I_{u,v} \subseteq \tilde{I}_u$ is the set of the items in $\tilde{I}_u$ that are also rated by user v, $\tilde{r}_{u,i}$ is the merged rating for the active user u on item i calculated using Equation 1, $\bar{r}_u$ is the average of the merged ratings for the active user u on the items in $\tilde{I}_u$, and $\bar{r}_v$ is the average of the ratings of all the items rated by user v.

A group of similar users, or *nearest neighbors*, is then selected as follows:

$$NN_u = \{v | s_{u,v} > \theta, v \in U\} \tag{3}$$

where θ is a predefined similarity threshold, and NN_u denotes the nearest neighborhood of the active user u.

Finally, the predicted rating $\hat{r}_{u,j}$ of item j for the active user u is generated by aggregating the ratings of item j provided by the nearest neighbors in NN_u and the trusted neighbors in TN_u weighted by their similarity values and trust values respectively, as follows:

$$\hat{r}_{u,j} = \frac{\sum_{v \in NN_u} s_{u,v} r_{v,j} + \sum_{v \in TN_u} t_{u,v} r_{v,j}}{\sum_{v \in NN_u} s_{u,v} + \sum_{v \in TN_u} t_{u,v}} \tag{4}$$

The neighbors who have larger similarity with the active user u or are trusted more by user u will have higher impact on the predicted rating.

3.3   The Insights of the Merge Method

One common characteristic of the *data sparsity* and *cold-start* problems is that the small number of commonly rated items between users makes it difficult to accurately compute user similarity and hence difficult to find effective nearest neighbors for the active users. In many cases, there is even no commonly rated items between two users because of data sparsity, causing their similarity not computable. In our method, we merge the ratings of the active user u's trusted neighbors to represent the preference of user u. Since the merged rating set usually covers a larger number of items than the active user u's own rating set (i.e. $|\tilde{I}_u| > |I_u|$), the number of the items in $\tilde{I}_u$ that are also rated by another user v, which is $|I_{u,v}|$, is also likely to be larger. This is especially true for cold-start users who have not rated many items yet. As a result, the similarity between a larger number of users can be computed accurately. In this way, our method mitigates the data sparsity and cold-start problems.

Many trust-based approaches (for example, the MoleTrust algorithm in [5] and the approach proposed in [8]) predict ratings for items based only on the ratings provided by the trusted neighbors. In contrast, our Merge method not only makes use of the ratings provided by the trusted neighbors, but also considers the ratings of similar users (NN_u) found based on the merged rating set of trusted neighbors (see Equation 4). Thus, the number of neighbors used for rating prediction is certainly larger in our method, resulting in the improvement in both accuracy and coverage of rating prediction that will be confirmed by the experimental results in Section 4.3.

Due to relying only on the ratings provided by the trusted neighbors for rating prediction, the trust-based approaches may also suffer from the similar cold-start problem where some users may only specify a small number of other users as their trusted neighbors. This issue could be a common case for many social systems, especially when users are lack of incentives to be pro-active. Thus, the performance is limited since only a few neighbors can be incorporated for recommendation. Our Merge method addresses this problem by also making use of the ratings of the active user u herself if any. In particular, the active user u is considered as a fully trustworthy neighbor to herself when merging the ratings of trusted neighbors. When user u has no trusted neighbors but rated a certain number of items, the merged rating set will be the same as her own rating set because the only trusted neighbor is herself. The whole procedure will be exactly the same as the traditional collaborative filtering technique. In this way, our method is competent to mitigate the cold-start problem.

To cope with the cold-start problem for trusted neighbors, some work (e.g. [6]) also proposes approaches to infer implicit trust from users' rating profiles. However, implicit trust is not as accurate as explicit trust that is directly specified by users. Trust propagation [5] has also been widely used to cope with the cold-start problem by inferring the trust between two users based on the trust network formed by any available trusted neighborhood relationships. However, it has several shortcomings: 1) the best propagation length is difficult to be determined for different networks; 2) trust propagation makes it possible to incorporate less valuable users, especially when the propagation length is long, and hence may decrease the prediction accuracy; 3) it is often costly and time-consuming to propagate trust, especially when the trust network is dense. Our method makes use of only direct trusted neighbors. We will also show in Section 4.3 that trust propagation does not bring any benefit to our method.

4 Experimental Validation

In order to verify the effectiveness of the Merge method, we conduct experiments on three real data sets. We aim to find out: 1) how the performance of our Merge method is in comparison with other approaches; 2) whether it is effective to propagate trust for our method; and 3) how the performance changes when tuning the similarity threshold θ in Equation 3.

4.1 Data Acquisition

Three real data sets are used in our experiments, including FilmTrust[1], Flixster[2] and Epinions[3]. FilmTrust is a trust-based social site in which users can rate and review movies. Since there is no publicly downloadable data set, we crawled one in June 2011, collecting 1,986 users, 2,071 movies and 35,497 ratings (scaled from 0.5 to 4.0 with step 0.5). Besides, it also contains 1,853 trust ratings that are issued by 609 users. The trust ratings in FilmTrust are binary where 1 means "trust" and 0 otherwise. Flixster is also a social movie site in which users can make friends and share their movie ratings. The original data set[4] is very large. For the simplicity, we sample a subset by randomly choosing 53K users who issued 410K item ratings (scaled from 0.5 to 4.0 with step 0.5) and 655K trust ratings. The trust ratings in Flixster are scaled from 1 to 10 but not available in the data set. We assign the trust value 1 to a user who is identified as a trusted neighbor, and 0 otherwise. Epinions is a website in which consumers can express their opinions by assigning numerical ratings to items. The data set[5] is generated by Massa and Avesani [5], consisting of 49K users who issued 664K ratings (scaled from 1 to 5 with step 1) over 139K different items and 478K trust ratings. The trust ratings in Epinions are also binary (either 1 or 0).

4.2 Experimental Settings

In our experiments, we compare Merge with the following approaches:

- **TrustAll** simply trusts every user and predicts a rating for an item by averaging all ratings of those who have rated the item.

---

[1] http://trust.mindswap.org/FilmTrust/
[2] http://www.flixster.com/
[3] http://www.epinions.com/
[4] http://www.cs.sfu.ca/~sja25/personal/datasets/
[5] http://www.trustlet.org/datasets/downloaded_epinions

- **CF** computes user similarity using the PCC measure, selects the users whose similarity is above the threshold θ, and uses their ratings for prediction.
- **MT**x ($x = 1, 2, 3$) are the implementations of the MoleTrust algorithm [5] in which trust is propagated in the trust network with the length x. Only trusted neighbors are used to predict ratings for items.
- **RN** denotes the approach proposed in [8] that predicts item ratings by reconstructing trust network. We adopt their best performance settings where the correlation threshold is 0.5, propagation length is 1, and the top 5 users with highest correlations are selected for rating prediction.
- **TCF2** denotes the approach proposed in [1] that enhances CF by predicting the ratings of the similar users who did not rate the items according to the ratings of the similar users' trusted neighbors, so as to incorporate more users for recommendation. In [1], the best performance is achieved when trust propagation length is 2. We adopt the same setting in our experiments.
- **Merge2** is a variation of the Merge method where the trust propagation length is 2, to also incorporate the trusted neighbors of the trusted neighbors. The purpose is to investigate the impact of trust propagation.

In addition, we split each data set into different views in the light of user-related or item-related properties as defined in [5]:

- **All** represents the whole data set.
- **Cold Users** are those who rated no more than 5 items.
- **Heavy Users** are those who rated more than 10 items.
- **Opinionated Users** are those who rated more than 4 ratings, and the standard deviation of the ratings is greater than 1.5.
- **Black Sheep** rated more than 4 ratings, and the average difference between their average rating and the mean rating of each item is greater than 1.
- **Controversial Items** are those which received ratings with standard deviation greater than 1.5.
- **Niche Items** are those which received less than 5 ratings.

We focus on the performance in the views of **All** and **Cold Users**, which indicate the effectiveness to mitigate the data sparsity and cold-start problems.

The evaluation is proceeded by applying the *leave-one-out* technique [5] on every user rating. The results are analyzed according to the performance in terms of accuracy and coverage. In particular, the predictive accuracy is evaluated using *Mean Absolute Error* (MAE), the degree to which a predicted rating is close to the ground truth. *Rating coverage* (RC) is measured as the percentage of all items that are predictable.

4.3   The Performance of the Merge Method

In this set of experiments, we evaluate the performance of our Merge method, in comparison with the other approaches presented in the previous section. We fix the similarity threshold θ to be 0. Tables 1, 2 and 3 summarize the results on the FilmTrust, Flixster and Epinions data sets, respectively.

We obtain very close results on the Epinions data set in Table 3 as those in [5] and [1]. The similar trends of results are also obtained on the other two data sets, as shown in Tables 1 and 2. From all these results, we can see that our Merge method achieves consistent and better performance both in accuracy and coverage whereas other approaches expose their limitations in either accuracy or coverage. More specifically, CF results in benchmark performance and large diversity across three data sets, which can be explained by [7] that its effectiveness is heavily associated with the distributions of ratings of similar users. The trust-based approaches (MTx) are able to increase rating coverage to a large extent, but the accuracy is quite low. The RN method accomplishes good accuracy but covers the smallest portion of items since only the ratings of the users who have a large number of trusted neighbors and high rating correlation with others are possible to be predicted. Although TCF2 achieves relatively good results and improves both accuracy and coverage over CF, RN and MTx, its performance varies on different data sets. Comparing with TCF2, the accuracy of our Merge method is similar on Epinions but much better on FilmTrust and Flixster, and the coverage of our method is much better on Flixster but worse on Epinions. Therefore, we can conclude that in general our Merge method outperforms the other approaches. It consistently achieves high accuracy and large coverage, demonstrating its effectiveness in mitigating the data sparsity problem.

Table 1. The Performance on FilmTrust

Views	MAE/RC								
	Approaches								
	CF	MT1	MT2	MT3	TrustAll	RN	TCF2	Merge	Merge2
All	0.703	0.852	0.795	0.771	0.726	0.571	0.683	0.612	0.624
	93.83%	21.20%	27.95%	30.38%	98.17%	0.74%	96.85%	95.36%	95.52%
Cold Users	0.744	0.853	0.880	0.819	0.753	NaN	0.740	0.604	0.634
	39.64%	17.11%	23.19%	23.85%	98.19%	0.00%	41.12%	68.91%	69.90%
Heavy Users	0.705	0.854	0.797	0.772	0.728	0.571	0.684	0.617	0.628
	94.95%	21.53%	28.25%	30.75%	98.13%	0.80%	98.06%	95.82%	95.97%
Opin. Users	1.469	1.268	1.156	1.194	1.105	NaN	1.405	1.210	1.213
	87.63%	14.43%	15.46%	15.46%	94.85%	0.00%	91.75%	93.81%	93.81%
Black Sheep	1.237	1.228	1.243	1.269	1.255	NaN	1.244	1.130	1.140
	90.63%	19.94%	24.82%	26.13%	99.86%	0.00%	92.22%	90.94%	90.98%
Contr. Items	2.106	2.358	2.418	2.265	2.380	0.500	1.482	1.947	2.056
	62.58%	16.04%	21.38%	27.36%	100.0%	0.31%	89.31%	66.35%	71.38%
Niche Items	0.986	1.031	1.011	0.962	1.009	0.485	0.574	0.915	0.940
	53.92%	14.04%	19.35%	25.36%	79.51%	0.66%	85.17%	61.67%	63.44%

More importantly, none of previous approaches works well in the view of *Cold Users*. CF covers very limited percentage of items (around 3% in Flixster and Epinions) with very poor accuracy. MTx methods can alleviate this problem relative to CF in these two data sets. However, it performs worse than CF in FilmTrust because the performance of MTx depends on the number of trusted neighbors and this value is very small in FilmTrust (around 3 trusted neighbors

Table 2. The Performance on Flixster

Views	MAE/RC								
	Approaches								
	CF	MT1	MT2	MT3	TrustAll	RN	TCF2	Merge	Merge2
All	0.928	1.060	0.932	0.862	0.855	0.858	0.811	0.664	0.776
	68.56%	12.36%	71.37%	90.71%	98.11%	0.38%	86.82%	94.19%	95.86%
Cold	1.153	1.127	1.005	0.934	0.918	NaN	0.930	0.723	0.784
Users	3.27%	8.11%	52.69%	79.55%	99.03%	0.00%	21.42%	82.73%	88.75%
Heavy	0.913	1.046	0.917	0.846	0.839	0.858	0.797	0.654	0.776
Users	85.59%	13.29%	75.55%	93.29%	97.70%	0.52%	98.74%	95.92%	96.83%
Opin.	1.494	1.574	1.487	1.457	1.447	1.095	1.419	1.098	1.272
Users	74.80%	12.65%	72.37%	92.50%	99.23%	0.55%	98.61%	98.03%	98.65%
Black	1.320	1.300	1.288	1.273	1.279	1.258	1.248	0.977	1.145
Sheep	76.21%	13.59%	75.53%	93.46%	99.42%	0.23%	94.64%	97.92%	98.47%
Contr.	1.830	1.847	1.833	1.873	1.951	1.167	1.373	1.549	1.709
Items	30.64%	2.33%	27.63%	76.94%	100.0%	0.10%	85.00%	68.68%	82.15%
Niche	1.068	1.195	1.021	1.057	1.073	1.400	0.409	1.016	1.029
Items	11.77%	0.66%	11.23%	43.73%	61.60%	0.02%	81.42%	35.01%	46.10%

Table 3. The Performance on Epinions

Views	MAE/RC								
	Approaches								
	CF	MT1	MT2	MT3	TrustAll	RN	TCF2	Merge	Merge2
All	0.876	0.845	0.852	0.832	0.821	0.673	0.691	0.708	0.775
	51.24%	26.34%	57.64%	71.68%	88.20%	9.87%	87.46%	77.94%	81.87%
Cold	1.032	0.756	0.916	0.890	0.857	NaN	0.936	0.670	0.738
Users	3.22%	6.57%	22.06%	41.73%	92.92%	0.00%	10.52%	47.22%	57.56%
Heavy	0.873	0.847	0.848	0.827	0.818	0.673	0.677	0.713	0.780
Users	57.41%	29.28%	62.40%	75.36%	87.50%	11.48%	95.24%	80.95%	84.07%
Opin.	1.120	1.060	1.124	1.110	1.105	0.774	1.022	0.879	0.990
Users	49.99%	19.99%	52.02%	68.79%	92.80%	5.34%	86.79%	80.77%	85.09%
Black	1.246	1.199	1.259	1.252	1.255	0.852	1.205	0.989	1.123
Sheep	55.72%	20.06%	53.73%	70.98%	97.03%	4.50%	89.85%	85.67%	89.57%
Contr.	1.598	1.481	1.646	1.707	1.741	0.953	1.389	1.326	1.553
Items	45.40%	22.87%	57.81%	78.19%	100.0%	7.47%	86.15%	81.19%	88.91%
Niche	0.835	0.743	0.811	0.829	0.829	0.598	0.282	0.775	0.802
Items	12.16%	7.84%	23.65%	39.37%	55.39%	2.14%	79.81%	37.42%	46.17%

per user on average). The MAE value of the RN method is NaN (not-a-number), meaning that it is unable to predict any rating. This is because only the users who have at least 4 commonly rated items with others will be kept in the trust network [8]. This is conflicting with the setting for cold users. TCF2 also covers only a limited range of items because it depends on the number of similar users, which is very small for cold users. This limitation also causes low accuracy. These results confirm that the cold-start problem remains a big challenge for recommender systems. Both CF and previous trust-aware methods cannot achieve good accuracy or coverage and even perform worse than TrustAll. On the contrary, our Merge method is especially effective for the cold users. The improvement in accuracy reaches up to 18.82%, 37.29% and 35.08% relative to CF, and 18.38%, 22.26% and 28.42% relative to TCF2 according to the results in Tables 1, 2 and 3, respectively. The amount of increment in coverage is even larger. This is because after merging, even the rating set of the cold users could cover a large number of items, hence they can find many similar users.

We also compare the Merge method with its variation Merge2 where the trust propagation length is 2. We find that the increment in coverage is very limited but the accuracy is much worse. The reason is that although propagating trust is able to incorporate more neighbors to represent user's preference, it does not guarantee that the merged rating set will cover more items than the one without propagation, especially when the active users initially have many trusted neighbors. In addition, propagation will increase the possibility to incorporate less valuable users which may decrease the accuracy. Furthermore, the Merge method has already covered a good range of items hence it is not necessary to propagate trust. Overall, trust propagation is not necessary for our method.

4.4 The Effect of the Similarity Threshold θ

The similarity threshold θ plays an important role in CF-based methods. It is used to select a group of similar users as recommenders for rating prediction (see Equation 3). Intuitively, when the similarity threshold is set high, a smaller number of less similar users (unreliable recommenders) will be selected. The prediction accuracy should be better, but the coverage may decrease. Therefore, to explore the effect of the similarity threshold, we tune the θ value from 0 to 0.9 with step 0.1. The results are illustrated in Figures 1, 2 and 3.

Surprisingly, the results show that the accuracy of CF does not increase as expected, rather, it becomes worse with the increment of θ. We attribute this counter-intuitive phenomenon to the overestimation problem of the PCC similarity measure. That is, when the number of commonly rated items between users is small, the computed PCC value tends to be high, which makes it difficult to distinguish reliable users from unreliable ones via the similarity threshold. Although RN achieves good accuracy when $\theta \geq 0.6$ on FilmTrust and Epinions, the results are not representative because it covers too few items (less than 10%). The performance of TCF2 is not much affected by the similarity threshold.

Our method works in the way as expected. With the increment of θ, the accuracy first goes up and then drops down. More specifically, the best accuracy for our method can be achieved when the similarity threshold is set to be 0.4, 0.6 and 0.8 for FilmTrust, Flixster and Epinions, respectively. Besides, the amount of increment in accuracy is around 4.81%, 2.61% and 8.33% for cold users for three data sets, respectively, comparing with the case where the similarity threshold is 0. In general, when the similarity threshold θ is set to be 0.4 $\sim$ 0.8, better performance can be achieved for our method, and at the same time, its coverage does not decrease much. In addition, by tuning the similarity threshold, the Merge method significantly outperforms TCF2 on all data sets.

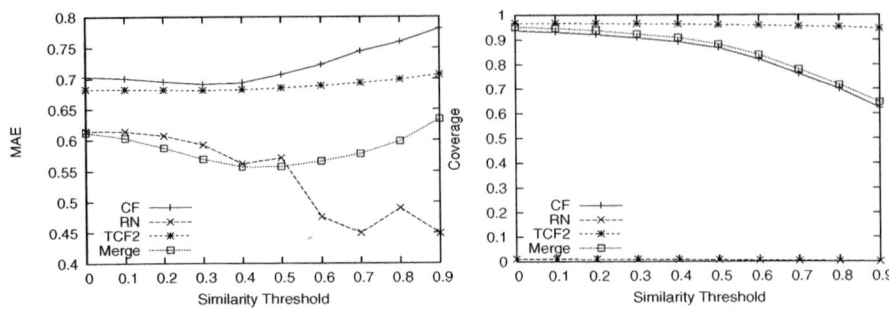

Fig. 1. The Effect of Similarity Threshold on FilmTrust

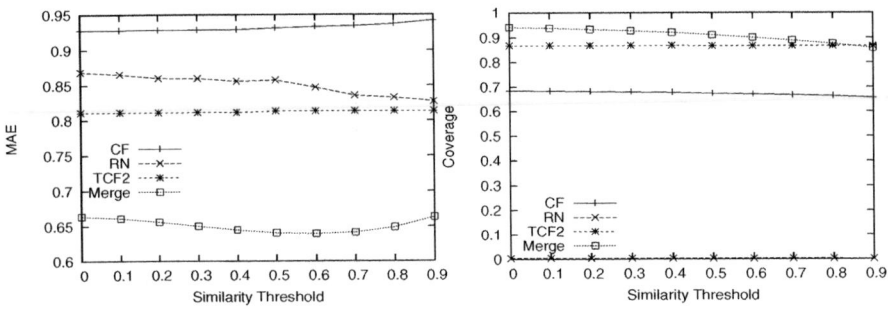

Fig. 2. The Effect of Similarity Threshold on Flixster

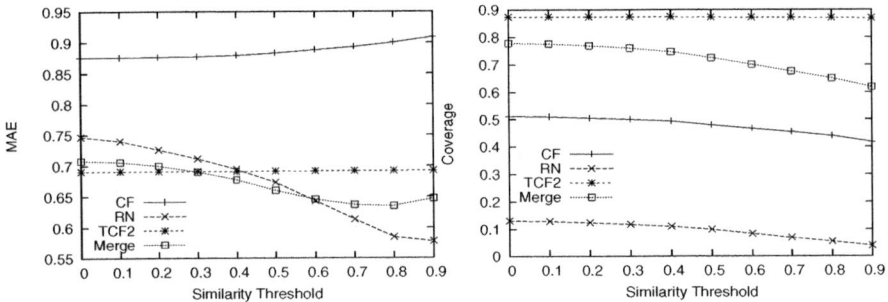

Fig. 3. The Effect of Similarity Threshold on Epinions

5   Conclusion and Future Work

Aiming to overcome the data sparsity and cold-start problems for recommender systems, we proposed a simple but effective method to incorporate trusted neighbors that are directly specified by users. The ratings of trusted neighbors are merged to represent the preference of the active user, based on which we then find similar users and generate recommendations. We conducted experiments on three real data sets and the results show significant improvement against other methods both in accuracy and coverage. We also demonstrated that it is not necessary for our method to propagate trust since incorporating direct trusted neighbors works well enough. Furthermore, by tuning the similarity threshold, better performance can be achieved for our method.

Our Merge method merges the ratings of trusted neighbors by a weighted average strategy (see Equation 1), which is shown effective in the scenario of sparse distribution of ratings. However, for the items that receive many ratings from trusted neighbors, the majority strategy that assigns the majority as the merged rating may work better, especially when the ratings are diverse (i.e. the standard deviation is large). For future work, we will investigate how the majority strategy can possibly improve the performance of our method.

References

1. Chowdhury, M., Thomo, A., Wadge, B.: Trust-based infinitesimals for enhanced collaborative filtering. In: Proceedings of the 15th International Conference on Management of Data, COMAD (2009)
2. Golbeck, J.: Computing and applying trust in web-based social networks. Ph.D. thesis (2005)
3. Jamali, M., Ester, M.: Trustwalker: a random walk model for combining trust-based and item-based recommendation. In: Proceedings of the 15th ACM SIGKDD International Conference on Knowledge Discovery and Data Mining, pp. 397–406
4. Liu, F., Lee, H.: Use of social network information to enhance collaborative filtering performance. Expert Systems with Applications 37(7), 4772–4778 (2010)
5. Massa, P., Avesani, P.: Trust-aware recommender systems. In: Proceedings of the ACM Conference on Recommender Systems, pp. 17–24 (2007)
6. O'Donovan, J., Smyth, B.: Trust in recommender systems. In: Proceedings of the 10th International Conference on Intelligent User Interfaces (IUI), pp. 167–174.
7. Rafter, R., O'Mahony, M.P., Hurley, N.J., Smyth, B.: What Have the Neighbours Ever Done for Us? A Collaborative Filtering Perspective. In: Houben, G.-J., McCalla, G., Pianesi, F., Zancanaro, M. (eds.) UMAP 2009. LNCS, vol. 5535, pp. 355–360. Springer, Heidelberg (2009)
8. Ray, S., Mahanti, A.: Improving prediction accuracy in trust-aware recommender systems. In: Proceedings of the 43rd Hawaii International Conference on System Sciences (HICSS), pp. 1–9 (2010)
9. Seth, A., Zhang, J., Cohen, R.: Bayesian Credibility Modeling for Personalized Recommendation in Participatory Media. In: De Bra, P., Kobsa, A., Chin, D. (eds.) UMAP 2010. LNCS, vol. 6075, pp. 279–290. Springer, Heidelberg (2010)
10. Shi, Y., Larson, M., Hanjalic, A.: How Far Are We in Trust-Aware Recommendation? In: Clough, P., Foley, C., Gurrin, C., Jones, G.J.F., Kraaij, W., Lee, H., Mudoch, V. (eds.) ECIR 2011. LNCS, vol. 6611, pp. 704–707. Springer, Heidelberg (2011)
11. Singla, P., Richardson, M.: Yes, there is a correlation: from social networks to personal behavior on the web. In: Proceedings of the 17th International Conference on World Wide Web, pp. 655–664 (2008)
12. Victor, P., Cornelis, C., De Cock, M., Teredesai, A.: Trust- and distrust-based recommendations for controversial reviews. In: Proceedings of the WebSci 2009: Society On-Line. No. 161 (2009)

Exploring Gaze Data for Determining User Learning with an Interactive Simulation

Samad Kardan and Cristina Conati

Department of Computer Science, University of British Columbia
2366 Main Mall, Vancouver, BC, V6T1Z4, Canada
{skardan,conati}@cs.ubc.ca

Abstract. This paper explores the value of eye-tracking data to assess user learning with interactive simulations (IS). Our long-term goal is to use this data in user models that can generate adaptive support for students who do not learn well with these types of unstructured learning environments. We collected gaze data from users interacting with the CSP applet, an IS for constraint satisfaction problems. Two classifiers built upon this data achieved good accuracy in discriminating between students who learn well from the CSP applet and students who do not, providing evidence that gaze data can be a valuable source of information for building user modes for IS.

Keywords: Eye-tacking, Eye Movement Data, Interactive Simulation Environments, User Classification, User Modeling.

1   Introduction

In recent years, there has been increasing interest in using interactive simulations (IS) for education and training. The idea underlying these environments is to foster experiential learning by giving students the opportunity to proactively experiment with concrete examples of concepts and processes they have learned in theory. One possible drawback of IS is that not all students learn well from this rather unstructured and open-ended form of interaction (e.g., [1]). These students may benefit from having additional guidance when they interact with an IS. The long-term goal of our research is to devise mechanisms to provide this guidance in real-time during interaction, personalized to the needs of each individual student. Detecting these needs, however, is challenging because there is still limited knowledge of which behaviours are indicative of effective vs. non-effective interactions with an IS. In previous work [2], we showed that it is possible to build user models that can classify successful vs. unsuccessful learners in a IS using logs of user interface actions. In this paper, we investigate student gaze data as an additional source of information to give to a user model for assessing how well a user learns with an IS. Initial results on the value of eye-tracking data in user-modeling for IS were presented in [3] and [4]. They looked at gaze information related to the occurrence of a simple gaze pattern defined a priori as being relevant for learning with an IS for mathematical functions. We extend this work by looking at a much broader range of general eye-tracking features, in the context of a different IS. This is an important contribution to research in user modeling

J. Masthoff et al. (Eds.): UMAP 2012, LNCS 7379, pp. 126–138, 2012.
© Springer-Verlag Berlin Heidelberg 2012

for IS, because pre-defining gaze patterns that indicate learning (as was done in [4, 3]) may not always be easy or possible, due to the often unstructured and open-ended nature of the interaction that IS support. Furthermore, such pre-defined patterns are task specific, and may not directly transfer to a different IS. In contrast, our approach is more general and can be applied to a variety of IS. It relies on giving to a classifier user model a broad range of standard eye-gaze features that are either task indepen-dent or based solely on identifying the main components of the target IS interface. Then, it is left to the classifier to identify patterns that are indicative of users' learning with that IS. An additional difference of our work from [4, 3] is that, in [4, 3], gaze data was integrated with information on action logs, whereas we look at gaze data only, to directly evaluate its value in assessing learning in IS. We discuss the perfor-mance of two gaze-based classifiers for modeling users who interact with the CSP applet, an IS that demonstrates the workings of an algorithm for constraint satisfaction problems (CSP). We show that these classifiers achieve good accuracy in discriminat-ing between students who learn well from the CSP applet and students who do not, thus providing further evidence of the value of gaze data for user modeling in IS.

In the rest of the paper, we first discuss related work. Next, we describe the CSP applet, and the study we ran to collect the necessary eye-tracking data. After discuss-ing data pre-processing, we illustrate the performance of two different classifiers built on this data. We conclude with a discussion of the future work.

2   Related Work

Using eye tracking to understand cognitive constructs such as intentions, plans or behaviour has received a lot of attention in psychology (e.g., [5, 6]). Researchers in human computer interaction and intelligent interfaces also started looking at gaze data as a source of information to model relevant cognitive processes of users during spe-cific interaction tasks. For instance, gaze data has been investigated to capture users' decision making processes during information search tasks (e.g., [7, 8]), for activity recognition during working with a user interface (e.g., [9]), to predict word relevance in a reading task [10], to predict how well users process a given information visualiza-tion (e.g., [11]), and to estimate mental workload in relation to evaluating users' inter-ruptibility (e.g., [12]). Muldner et al. [13] looked at pupil dilation to detect relevant user affective states and meta-cognitive processes during the interaction with a learn-ing environment that supports analogical problem solving. Knoepfle et al. [14] used eye-tracking data for comparing existing theories of how users learn to play strategies in normal-form games. The theories were compared in terms of how they could pre-dict users' moves and attention to relevant information during interaction with a com-puter card game, with all theories showing limited predictive power.

In our work, we are interested in investigating whether a user's gaze patterns dur-ing interaction with an IS can be used to assess if the student is learning. We were inspired by existing research showing that it is possible to identify distinctive patterns in the gaze data of successful vs. unsuccessful users during simple problem solving and question answering tasks (e.g., [15–18]). In this body of work, the attention pat-terns analyzed related mainly to processing the problem description [15] or supporting visual material [16–18]. The main finding was that successful problem solvers pay more attention to information relevant to answer correctly, while unsuccessful problem solvers show more scattered attention patterns. Eivazi and Bednarik [19] went a step further showing that it is possible to build a classifier that relies solely on gaze data to predict users' performance during an interactive 8-tile puzzle game. Conati and Merten [3] and Amershi and Conati [4] present results that are even more relevant for our work, since they also looked at gaze-data to model student reasoning and learning during interaction with an IS. As explained earlier, the student models in [4, 3] combine simple gaze-pattern information with information on the user's interface actions, whereas in this paper we focus on gaze data only, in a broader and more generalizable manner, to better isolate its potential as a source of information for user modeling in IS.

3   The AISpace CSP Applet

The Constraint Satisfaction Problem (CSP) Applet is one of a collection of interactive tools for learning Artificial Intelligence algorithms, called AIspace [20]. Algorithm dynamics are demonstrated via interactive visualizations on graphs by the use of color and highlighting, and graphical state changes are reinforced through textual messages.

CSP consists of a set of variables, variable domains and a set of constraints on legal variable-value assignments. Solving a CSP requires finding an assignment that satisfies all constraints. The CSP applet illustrates the Arc Consistency 3 (AC-3) algorithm for solving CSPs represented as networks of variable nodes and constraint arcs. AC-3 iteratively makes individual arcs consistent by removing variable domain values inconsistent with a given constraint, until all arcs have been considered and the network is consistent. Then, if there remains a variable with more than one domain value, a procedure called domain splitting can be applied to that variable to split the CSP into disjoint cases so that AC-3 can recursively solve each case.

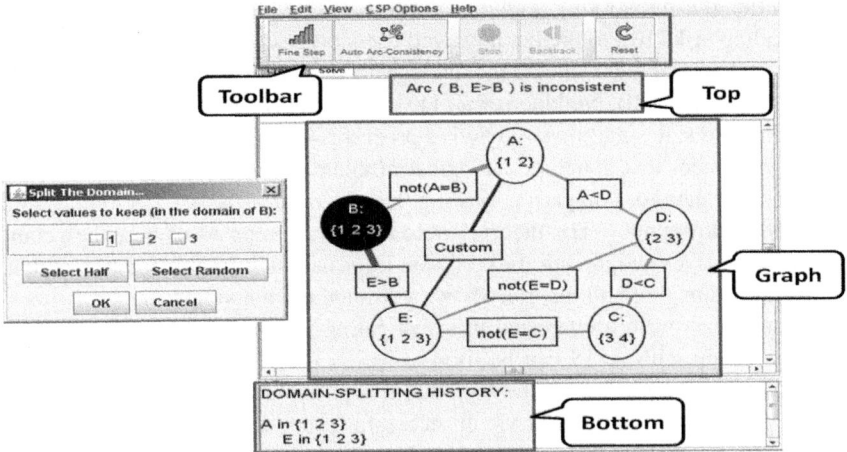

Fig. 1. CSP applet with example CSP problem

The CSP applet provides several mechanisms for the interactive execution of the AC-3 algorithm on a set of available CSP problems. These mechanisms are accessible through the toolbar shown at the top of Fig. 1 or through direct manipulation of graph elements. The user can, for instance: (*i*) use the *Fine Step* button to see how AC-3 goes through its three basic steps (selecting an arc, testing it for consistency, removing domain values to make the arc consistent); (*ii*) automatically fine step through the completion of the problem (*Auto Arc Consistency* button); (*iii*) pause auto arc consistency (*Stop* button); (*iv*) select a variable to split on, and specify a subset of its values for further application of AC-3 (see popup box in the left side of Fig. 1). Alternative sub-networks can be recovered by clicking on the *Backtrack* button on the toolbar. As a student steps through a problem, the message panel above the graph panel reports a description of each step. Another message panel situated below the graph panel reports the history of domain spitting decisions made by the user, i.e., which value-variable assignment has been selected at each domain splitting point.

The CSP applet currently does not provide any explicit support to help students learn at best from the mechanisms described above. Research however, shows that students may benefit from this support, since unaided exploration of interactive simulations often fails to help students learn [1]. The purpose of the study described in the next section was to collect data to investigate whether a user's attention patterns can be indicators of effective vs. non-effective learning with the CSP applet, to be eventually used in a user model that can drive personalized support when needed.

4   User Study

Fifty computer science students participated in the study. The data for 5 users was not usable due to technical issues, reducing the dataset to 45 users. All participants were required to have taken a set of courses ensuring that they would have the prerequisites to study Constraint Satisfaction Problems as discussed below. Participants were run one at the time, and each experimental session was structured as follows. First, participants were asked to study a text book chapter on Constraint Satisfaction Problems and the AC3 algorithm. This part was allotted 45 minutes and all the participants reported finishing the material in the given time. Then, participants wrote a pre-test designed to evaluate their understanding of the CSP concepts covered in the chapter they had studied. Next, participants were shown a video that explained the functionalities of the CSP applet.

The main part of the experiment was run on a Pentium 4, 3.2GHz, with 2GB of RAM with a Tobii T120 eye-tracker as the main display. Tobii T120 is a remote eye-tracker embedded in a 17" display, providing unobtrusive eye-tracking (as opposed to what head-mounted devices do). In addition to the user's gaze data, Tobii also records video data of the user's face. After undergoing a calibration phase for the eye-tracker, the participants started working with the applet to solve two CSP problems: first an easier problem involving 3 variables, 3 constraints and at most 2 domain splitting actions to find its unique answer; next, a more difficult problem involving 5 variables, 7 constraints and a minimum of 5 domain splitting actions to find its two solutions.

Participants were instructed to find both of these solutions. All relevant instructions for this phase were provided on a written instruction sheet. No time limit was given for this phase, which lasted on average 16.7 (SD = 9.0) minutes. The study ended with a post-test analogous to the pre-test.

5   Data Preparation and Preprocessing

Eye-tracking data can be rather noisy when collected with eye-trackers that, like the Tobii T120, do not constrain the user's head movements [21]. In this section, we briefly explain the process we used to deal with two sources of noise in our dataset. This validation process is crucial to ensure that the data reliably reflects the attention patterns that users generated while working with the CSP applet.

The first source of noise relates to the eye-tracker collecting invalid samples while the user is looking at the screen, due to issues with calibration, excessive user movements or other user-related matters (e.g., eyeball's shape). Thus, gaze data for each user needs to be evaluated to ascertain whether there are enough valid samples to retain this user for analysis. The second source of noise relates to users looking away from the screen either for task-related reasons (e.g., looking at the instruction sheet) or due to getting distracted. During the looking-away events, the eye-tracker reports invalid samples similar to when there is a tracking error on the user gaze, even if there was no gaze to track. Thus, sequences of invalid samples due to looking-away events must be removed before starting the validation process of actual user's gaze samples. Looking-away events were automatically detected when the user gaze moved out of the screen gradually, by calculating the trajectory of fixations heading outside the screen. Automatic detection, however, is not possible when the user's gaze moves away from the screen suddenly. These events were manually identified by an investigator using videos of the user recorded during the study.

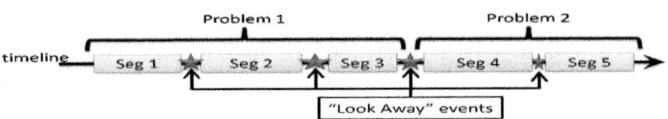

Fig. 2. A sample timeline showing segments and "look away" events

Detection of looking-away events resulted in the partitioning of the remaining gaze samples into sequences occurring between two such events (*segments* from now on, see Fig. 2). The next step was to analyze the validity of these gaze segments. In particular, we needed to set a threshold to define, for each user in our dataset: (*i*) whether there are enough valid samples in the user's complete interaction, represented by the aggregation of her eye-gaze segments; (*ii*) if so, whether there are sufficient valid samples in each segment. This second step is to avoid situations in which a large number of the invalid samples in an overall valid interaction are concentrated in few segments, making the gaze data in these segments unreliable.

We determined the threshold by plotting the percentage of segments that get discarded for different threshold values. The threshold value of 85% was selected, because it is where the percentage of discarded segments starts to rise sharply (Fig. 3). Fig. 4 shows the percentage of samples left after discarding the invalid segments based on the 85% threshold. For all users except one, more than 90 percent of the samples were kept. The average duration of each user's interaction with the CSP applet only changed from 16.7 (SD = 9.0) to 16.3 (SD = 8.8) minutes. Next, we will explain the eye gaze features calculated for each user.

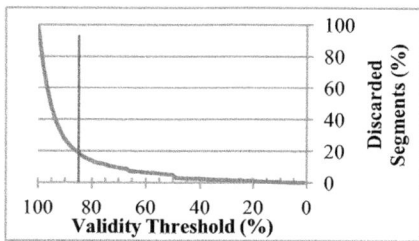

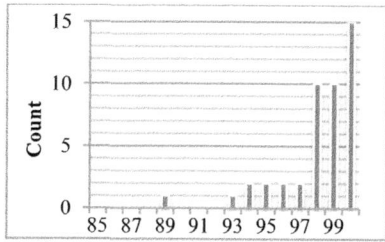

Fig. 3. Percentage of segments discarded for different threshold values

Fig. 4. Histogram of users with different percentage of segments left after removing the invalid segments

6   Eye Gaze Features

An eye-tracker provides eye-gaze information in terms of *fixations* (i.e., maintaining eye-gaze at one point on the screen) and *saccades* (i.e., a quick movement of gaze from one fixation point to another), which are analyzed to derive a viewer's attention patterns. As mentioned in the related work section, previous research on using gaze information for assessing learning in IS relied on tracking one specific attention pattern, predefined a priori [4, 3]. In contrast, in our analysis we use a large set of basic eye-tracking features, described by [21] as the building blocks for comprehensive eye-data processing. These features are built by calculating a variety of statistics upon the basic eye-tracking measures described in Table 1. Of these measures, *Fixation rate*, *Number of Fixations* and *Fixation Duration* are widely used (e.g., [11, 15–17]); we also included *Saccade Length* (e.g., distance d in Fig. 5), *Relative Saccades Angle* (e.g., angle y in Fig. 5) and *Absolute Saccade Angle* (e.g., angle x in Fig. 5), as suggested in [21], because these measures are useful to summarize trends in user attention patterns within a specific interaction window (e.g., if the user's gaze seems to follow a planned sequence as opposed to being scattered). Statistics such as sum, average and standard deviation can be calculated over these measures with respect to: (*i*) the full CSP applet window, to get a sense of a user's overall attention; (*ii*) specific areas of interest (AOI from now on) identifying parts of the interface that are of specific relevance for understanding a user's attention processes.

Table 1. Description of basic eye tracking measures

Measure	Description
Fixation rate	Rate of eye fixations per milliseconds
Number of Fixations	Number of eye fixations detected during an interval of interest
Fixation Duration	Time duration of an individual fixation
Saccade Length	Distance between the two fixations delimiting the saccade (d in Fig. 5)
Relative Saccade Angles	The angle between the two consecutive saccades (e.g., angle y in Fig. 5)
Absolute Saccade Angles	The angle between a saccade and the horizontal (e.g., angle x in Fig. 5)

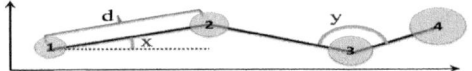

Fig. 5. Saccade based eye measures

We defined four AOIs for our analysis, corresponding to the areas that provide conceptually different functionalities in the CSP applet. Rectangles corresponding to these AOIs are shown in Fig. 1. One AOI covers the region of the applet toolbar that includes action buttons (*toolbar* AOI); one covers the main graph panel (*graph* AOI); one covers the part of the top panel where the description of every step of the algorithm is displayed (*top* AOI); the last covers the part of the bottom panel that displays domain splitting information (*bottom* AOI).

Table 2. Derived eye tracking features for the full CSP applet window

Fixation rate
Total Number of Fixations
Sum of Fixation Durations
Mean and Std. Dev. of Fixation Durations
Mean and Std. Dev. of Saccade Length
Mean and Std. Dev. of Relative Saccade Angles
Mean and Std. Dev. of Absolute Saccade Angle

Table 3. Derived eye tracking features for each of the four AOIs

Fixation rate
Total Number of Fixations
Proportion of Total Number of Fixations
Mean Fixation Durations
Proportion of Total of Fixation Durations
Highest Fixation Duration
Number of Transitions between pairs of AOIs
Proportion of Transitions between pairs of AOIs

Table 2 shows the set of gaze features calculated from the eye movement measures in Table 1 over the full CSP applet window. Table 3 shows the set of features calculated for each of the four AOIs. As the table shows, the two sets are different. For the AOIs, we added features that measure a user's relative attention to each AOI: *Proportion of Total Number of Fixations* and *Proportion of Total Fixation Duration* give the percentage of the overall number of fixations and fixation time, respectively, that were spent in each AOI. We also added features that quantify gaze transitions between different pairs of AOIs [21] (including from an AOI to itself), as a way to capture the dynamics of a user's attention patterns. Transitions are represented both in terms of total number (*Number of Transitions between pairs of AOIs in Table 3*), as well as a proportion of all transitions (*Proportion of Transitions between pairs of AOIs*). Adding the aforementioned AOI-specific features substantially increases the overall number of features considered. In order to keep this number manageable, for the AOIs we did not compute saccade-based features, which are less commonly used than fixation-based features in eye-tracking research. In total, we included 67 features, 11 for the full CSP window, and 56 for AOI.

7   Classifying Learners Based on Gaze Data

To ascertain whether a user's success in learning with the CSP applet can be identified using his/her eye movement data, we built two different classifiers using this data. The first classifier uses the eye-tracking features described in section 6, computed over the complete interaction of a student with the CSP applet (*Whole Interaction dataset* from now on). Thus, this classifier relies on features that describe a user's overall attention patterns during the study task. The second classifier uses features that reflect the *changes* in the user's attention patterns between solving the first and the second problem (*Interaction Evolution* dataset). Each classifier is built to discriminate between two classes of users, High Achievers (HA) and Low Achievers (LA), defined based on the median split of Proportional Learning Gain (PLG) from pre-test to post-test. PLG is defined as the ratio of a student's actual learning from pre-test to pos-test, over the student's maximum possible learning (in percent). Thus, PLG provide a better way to compare learning between students with high and low pre-test scores than absolute learning gains do.

The median PLG is 45.83, resulting 23 LA and 22 HA. The average PLG overall is 41.25 (SD = 35.31). It is 68.27 (SD = 12.39) for the HA and 15.40 (SD = 30.29) for the LA group. In the next two sections, we discuss each classifier and its performance results.

7.1   User classification Based on the *Whole Interaction* Dataset

This classifier aims to predict a user's class label (HA vs. LA) using the *Whole Interaction* dataset, i.e., the 67 features that describe a user's overall attention patterns during the study task. We tried 6 different classifiers from the different classifier types available in the Weka data mining toolkit (Decision Tree based, Support Vector Machine, Linear Ridge Regression, Binary Logistic Regression and Multilayer Perceptron), using feature-selection and leave-one-out cross-validation. The classifier with the highest accuracy is a Decision Tree based Classifier generated using the C4.5 algorithm (DTC from now on). The accuracy of the DTC for each class and overall is shown in Fig. 6 (we will discuss the RRC classifier shown in the picture in the next section). The figure also reports the accuracy of a baseline classifier that always selects the most likely class (LA in our case), thus failing in all cases of the other class. The DTC achieves 71.1% overall accuracy, which is significantly higher than baseline (χ^2 (1) = 16.01, $p < 0.001$). DTC does not have very high accuracy (63.3%) for the HA class, but achieves 78.3% accuracy for the LA class, showing that it can recognize those students who may need help to better learn with the CSP applet. These results clearly show the potential of using eye movement data as a source of information to classify learning performance.

The structure of the decision tree, shown in Fig. 7, indicates which features contribute to discriminate between high and low achievers with the CSP applet. In Fig. 7, each node represents a feature with a partitioning value that DTC uses to separate users into two groups, one with values higher than the partitioning value (right branch of the node) and one with values that are lower (left branch of that node). The numbers next to each branch specify how many HA and LA datapoints are found in the corresponding subgroup. The leaves of the tree assign a class label to all the users in the corresponding subgroups. For simplicity, we will only look at the top three nodes of the tree The partition of datapoints created by the root node (*prop_Total_fixations_Bottom* in Fig. 7) shows that LA tend to have a higher proportion of fixations in the Bottom AOI than HA. The Bottom panel is only used for displaying domain splitting information, which becomes relevant only when a CSP graph has been made arch consistent. Thus, showing a higher proportion of fixations in this panel may be an indication that LA are looking at irrelevant information due to confusion or not knowing which action to perform next. Interestingly, the partition created by the left child of the root node, (*Bottom_fixation_rate* in Fig. 7), shows that most HA in this branch have higher fixation rate in the Bottom AOI, suggesting that, although HA look at the bottom panel less often than LA, when they do look they seem to pay more attention.

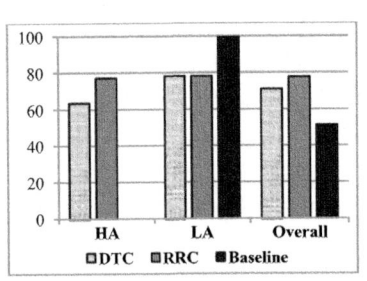

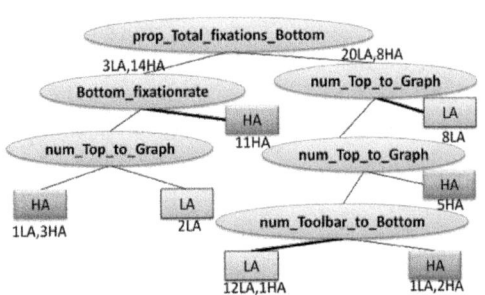

Fig. 6. The classifier performance (percent) for each class and overall

Fig. 7. The Decision Tree Classifier

Thus, it appears that HA know the value of the information displayed in the Bottom panel and only use it when it is relevant. These results are consistent with the findings in problem solving research indicating that successful problem solvers show selective attention to relevant information, while unsuccessful problem solvers tend to get distracted by irrelevant information [17, 18]. The right child of the root node (*num_Top_to_Graph*) generates a partition based on the number of transitions between Top and Graph AOIs, and it appears twice in the right subtree. At the second level of the tree it identifies a subgroup of LA who show a high number of transitions, while at the third level it identifies a subgroup of HA who show this pattern. Since the Top panel is used for displaying the outcome of any action related to stepping through the AC-3 algorithm, for the HA sub-group the high number of transitions between the two AOIs could be a sign of focused attention to the workings of the algorithm, which helped them learn from the interaction. For LA, on the other hand, the high number of transitions from top to graph panel, may be another indication of confusion, for instance if they happened in a few clusters as opposed to regularly after every action. A more detailed gaze-data analysis at the level of user actions would be necessary to gain further insights on what is happening with this group of LA.

7.2   User classification Based on the *Interaction Evolution* Dataset

For our second classifier, we wanted to explore whether *changes* in the user's attention patterns from the first to the second problem (P1 and P2 from now on) could be predictors of learning. We calculated the 67 features described in section 6 for each of the two periods during which the user was interacting with P1 and P2, respectively, and then we compared the values obtained to verify whether any difference actually existed. A battery of paired t-tests on the values for each feature in P1 and P2 resulted in 44 features that are significantly different, indicating that users' attention patterns do change to some extent when solving these two problems.

We used these 44 features, with values assigned to be the difference between their corresponding values for P1 and P2 (*Interaction Evolution* dataset), to train a second classifier of LA vs. HA. As with the previous dataset, we tried 6 different classifiers, with the classifier using Ridge Regression (RRC from now on), obtaining the highest accuracy. The RRC's performance of for each class and overall, is shown in Fig. 6. The RRC achieves 77.8% accuracy overall, which is significantly higher than baseline (χ^2 (1) = 29.17, $p < 0.001$). The overall accuracy of the RRC is also higher than DTC's, but the difference is not significant. It should be noted, however, the RRC achieves significantly higher accuracy than DTC on the HA class (χ^2 (1) = 8.408, $p = 0.004$), thus yielding a much better balance between the accuracy of the HA and LA classes (77.3% and 78.3% respectively). These results indicate that changes in a user's gaze patterns as the interaction with the CSP proceeds and the user attempts more difficult problems can be even more informative than overall attention patterns for predicting learning with this IS.

Table 4. Regression features with non-zero coefficients

Feature	Change (P1 to P2)	Stand. Coef.	Feature	Change (P1 to P2)	Stand. Coef.
Bottom_num_fixations	Increase	1.3837	Total_num_fixations	Increase	-0.2487
num_Toolbar_to_Toolbar	Increase	0.6519	Top_longest_fixation	Decrease	-0.3498
prop_Graph_to_Graph	Increase	0.5857	num_Graph_to_Toolbar	Increase	-0.4110
num_Toolbar_to_Top	Decrease	0.3441	num_Graph_to_Top	Decrease	-0.5729
Top_fixationrate	Increase	0.3177	num_Graph_to_Bottom	Increase	-0.8279
			SD_absolute_saccade_angles	Decrease	-0.8783

As we did with the classifier described in the previous section, we now discuss some of the features that contribute to distinguish LA from HA in our second classifier. The complete set of features with non-zero coefficients in the regression model is shown in Table 4. The table also reports, for each feature, the direction of change between P1 and P2, as well as its standardized coefficient. Here we discuss some of the most intuitive features with high impact in the regression (as measured by the standardized coefficients). The strongest positive indicator of learning in Table 4 is an increase in the number of fixations on the Bottom AOI (*Bottom_num_fixations*) from P1 to P2. As discussed in the previous section, the Bottom panel shows domain splitting information. Domain splitting is required more often in P2 than in P1, so the trend found shows that HA change the amount of attention they devote to the bottom panel accordingly while LA fail to do so. Table 4 also shows that one of the highest *negative* predictors of learning is an increase in the number of transitions between Graph and Bottom panels from P1 to P2 (*num_Graph_to_Bottom*), i.e., the number of transitions from the Graph to the Bottom panel increases from P1 to P2 for LA. However, except for the times when domain splitting is performed, there is no new information presented in the bottom panel, so these results could be further evidence that LA tend to look at the bottom panel when it is not relevant, as indicated by the results discussed in the previous section. Another strong negative indicator of learning is an increase in the number of transitions from the Graph to the Toolbar AOI (*num_Graph_to_Toolbar*). As users gain more experience with the interface, it is expected that they would shift their attention less often between the Graph and Toolbar. Thus, an increase in number of transitions can be interpreted as a sign that, during the interaction with the second more complex problem, LA were more often at loss about what action to perform next and looked frequently at the Toolbar for inspiration. In contrast, Table 4 shows that the number of gaze shifts staying in the Toolbar buttons area (*num_Toolbar_to_Toolbar*) is positively associated with learning. This feature shows the process of making decisions about which action to perform next. A likely reason for HA to go back and forth between the items on the toolbar more often during P2 than during P1 is that more actions are relevant at the same time for solving P2 (e.g., continuing to step through the solution of a sub-case resulting from domain splitting vs. deciding to backtrack to an alternative sub-case because the current one does not look promising) and HA are carefully considering the available options.

To summarize, the good classification performance on the Interaction Evolution dataset shows that taking into account temporal information on how attention patterns evolve during logical units of interactions (e.g., different problems in our case) can further improve the potential of eye-tracking data for user modeling for IS.

8   Conclusion and Future Work

We presented results on using eye-tracking data to assess user learning with an interactive simulation for constraint satisfaction problems (the CSP applet). We showed that a classifier using solely information on a user's overall attention patterns during a complete session with the CSP applet can achieve good accuracy in distinguishing students who learned well from students who did not. Adding information on how students' attention patterns changed while solving two different problems of increasing difficulty further improved classification accuracy.

Classification in this work was done after the interaction, as a proof of concept for the value of eye-tracking data in user modeling for IS. As a next step, we want to leverage the results discussed here to increase the accuracy of an online classifier of user learning we previously developed based solely on interface actions [2]. The goal is to have a user model for the CSP applet that integrates both gaze and action data to classify users *during* the interaction. We also plan to investigate techniques to further exploit the temporal nature of attention patterns, such as clustering of scanpaths (sequences of consecutive saccades). Finally, we are investigating how to design adaptive interventions for the CSP applet, to be provided to users when the user model detects that they are not learning well from the interaction.

References

1. Shute, V.J.: A comparison of learning environments: All that glitters. In: Computers as Cognitive Tools, pp. 47–73. Lawrence Erlbaum Associates, Inc., Hillsdale (1993)
2. Kardan, S., Conati, C.: A Framework for Capturing Distinguishing User Interaction Behaviours in Novel Interfaces. In: Proc. of the 4th Int. Conf. on Educational Data Mining, Eindhoven, The Netherlands, pp. 159–168 (2011)
3. Conati, C., Merten, C.: Eye-tracking for user modeling in exploratory learning environments: An empirical evaluation. Knowledge-Based Systems 20, 557–574 (2007)
4. Amershi, S., Conati, C.: Combining Unsupervised and Supervised Classification to Build User Models for Exploratory Learning Environments. Journal of Educational Data Mining, 18–71 (2009)
5. Keith, R.: Eye movements and cognitive processes in reading, visual search, and scene perception. In: Eye Movement Research Mechanisms, Processes, and Applications, pp. 3–22. North-Holland (1995)
6. Rayner, K.: Eye movements in reading and information processing: 20 years of research. Psychological Bulletin; Psychological Bulletin 124, 372–422 (1998)
7. Rong-Fuh, D.: Examining the validity of the Needleman–Wunsch algorithm in identifying decision strategy with eye-movement data. Decision Support Systems 49, 396–403 (2010)
8. Simola, J., Salojärvi, J., Kojo, I.: Using hidden Markov model to uncover processing states from eye movements in information search tasks. Cognitive Systems Research 9, 237–251 (2008)
9. Courtemanche, F., Aïmeur, E., Dufresne, A., Najjar, M., Mpondo, F.: Activity recognition using eye-gaze movements and traditional interactions. Interacting with Computers 23, 202–213 (2011)
10. Loboda, T.D., Brusilovsky, P., Brunstein, J.: Inferring word relevance from eye-movements of readers. In: Proc. of the 16th Int. Conf. on Intelligent User Interfaces, pp. 175–184. ACM, New York (2011)
11. Loboda, T.D., Brusilovsky, P.: User-adaptive explanatory program visualization: evaluation and insights from eye movements. User Modeling and User-Adapted Interaction 20, 191–226 (2010)
12. Iqbal, S.T., Adamczyk, P.D., Zheng, X.S., Bailey, B.P.: Towards an index of opportunity: understanding changes in mental workload during task execution. In: Proc. of the SIGCHI Conf. on Human Factors in Computing Systems, pp. 311–320. ACM, New York (2005)

13. Muldner, K., Christopherson, R., Atkinson, R., Burleson, W.: Investigating the Utility of Eye-Tracking Information on Affect and Reasoning for User Modeling. In: Houben, G.-J., McCalla, G., Pianesi, F., Zancanaro, M. (eds.) UMAP 2009. LNCS, vol. 5535, pp. 138–149. Springer, Heidelberg (2009)

14. Knoepfle, D.T., Wang, J.T., Camerer, C.F.: Studying Learning in Games Using Eye-tracking. J. of the European Economic Association 7, 388–398 (2009)

15. Hegarty, M., Mayer, R.E., Monk, C.A.: Comprehension of Arithmetic Word Problems: A Comparison of Successful and Unsuccessful Problem Solvers. J. of Educational Psychology 87, 18–32 (1995)

16. Canham, M., Hegarty, M.: Effects of knowledge and display design on comprehension of complex graphics. Learning and Instruction 20, 155–166 (2010)

17. Jarodzka, H., Scheiter, K., Gerjets, P., van Gog, T.: In the eyes of the beholder: How experts and novices interpret dynamic stimuli. Learning and Instruction 20, 146–154 (2010)

18. Tsai, M.-J., Hou, H.-T., Lai, M.-L., Liu, W.-Y., Yang, F.-Y.: Visual attention for solving multiple-choice science problem: An eye-tracking analysis. Computers & Education 58, 375–385 (2012)

19. Eivazi, S., Bednarik, R.: Predicting Problem-Solving Behavior and Expertise Levels from Visual Attention Data. In: The 2nd Workshop on the Eye Gaze in Intelligent Human Machine Interaction, Palo Alto, California, USA, pp. 9–16 (2011)

20. Amershi, S., Carenini, G., Conati, C., Mackworth, A.K., Poole, D.: Pedagogy and usability in interactive algorithm visualizations: Designing and evaluating CIspace. Interacting with Computers 20, 64–96 (2008)

21. Goldberg, J.H., Helfman, J.I.: Comparing Information Graphics: A Critical Look at Eye Tracking. Presented at the BELIV 2010, Atlanta, GA, USA (2010)

Studies to Determine User Requirements Regarding In-Home Monitoring Systems

Melanie Larizza[1], Ingrid Zukerman[2], Fabian Bohnert[2], R. Andrew Russell[3],
Lucy Busija[4], David W. Albrecht[2], and Gwyn Rees[1]

[1] Centre for Eye Research Australia, Royal Victorian Eye and Ear Hospital,
East Melbourne, VIC 3002, Australia
{mlarizza,grees}@unimelb.edu.au
[2] Faculty of Information Technology
[3] Faculty of Engineering,
Monash University, Clayton, VIC 3800, Australia
{Ingrid.Zukerman,Fabian.Bohnert,Andy.Russell,
David.Albrecht}@monash.edu
[4] Melbourne EpiCenter and Melbourne Brain Center, The Royal Melbourne Hospital,
The University of Melbourne, Parkville, VIC 3050, Australia
lbusija@unimelb.edu.au

Abstract. The ageing of the world population is leading to an increased number
of elderly people remaining in their homes, requiring different levels of care. MIA
is a user-centric project aimed at monitoring elderly people in order to help them
remain safely in their homes, where the design of the system is informed by the
requirements of the stakeholders. In this paper, we present the results of two user
studies that ascertain the views of elderly people and their informal carers regarding the acceptability and benefits of in-home monitoring technologies: (1) concept mapping coupled with brainstorming sessions, and (2) questionnaires. We
then discuss how these requirements affect the design of our monitoring system.

1   Introduction

The proportion of people aged over 60 worldwide will increase from 10% in 2000
to 20% in 2050 [12]. This shift, together with current trends in health-care services,
underscores the need for solutions that support older adults in their own homes [6].
Furthermore, older adults prefer to remain in their homes, living as independently as
possible, even when faced with conditions that challenge their independence [4,5,15].
In fact, there is already an increase in the number of older people living in their homes,
with restrictions in daily living activities, reduced independence, and curtailed participation in meaningful activities and social networks [1]. This situation is exacerbated
by vision impairment – a common disability associated with ageing, which affects 185
million people over the age of 50 worldwide [9].

These issues have motivated a plethora of projects that focus on providing computer-
based assistance for different aspects of the ageing process (e. g., specific medical conditions or general safety) [12]. Many of these projects consist of in-home monitoring
systems, which are equipped with sensors that monitor the residents, and share the collected information with the residents or their caregivers, e. g., [2,8,13]. These systems

J. Masthoff et al. (Eds.): UMAP 2012, LNCS 7379, pp. 139–150, 2012.

may include "heavy" options, such as sensor gloves [11], which detect fine-grained activities (e. g., slicing bread), or "lightweight" options, which detect coarse-grained activities (e. g., presence in the kitchen) [8].[1] Although research shows that technological aids are discarded when they do not meet users' needs and preferences [2], only a few of the current projects have adopted a user-centric approach, and only for particular aspects (e. g., *Agnes* for communication, http://agnes-aal.eu/, and *Bedmond* for the early detection of Alzheimer's disease, http://www.bedmond.eu).

The *MIA* project (*Monitoring, Interacting and Assisting*) proposes to develop sensor-based systems that will help elderly people remain safely in their homes. A central objective of our project is to ascertain our stakeholders' requirements in order to develop systems that are useful and well received. Although the envisaged system is expected to be useful to elderly people in general, in this project we focus on vision-impaired people for two reasons: (1) as indicated above, visual impairment is common in elderly people, and (2) focusing on a specific population enables us to develop more targeted models, which can later be tailored to different populations.

In this paper, we present the results of the first stage of our project, which comprises two user studies that consider the requirements of different stakeholder groups (older adults, informal carers and health-care professionals), and canvass (1) the stakeholders' views regarding benefits of in-home monitoring systems, (2) their concerns about these systems, and (3) their opinion about the acceptability and importance of actions performed by these systems. Our first study, which consists of concept mapping coupled with brainstorming sessions, yielded general characteristics of a monitoring system that are of interest to the stakeholders. Our second study, in the form of detailed questionnaires, revealed attitudes towards specific aspects of the system. The obtained information, which guides the design of our system (Sect. 6), will be validated against actual acceptance as the system is developed.

This paper is structured as follows. Section 2 discusses related research. Sections 3, 4 and 5 describe our user studies, analysis methodology and results respectively. Section 6 discusses the impact of our results on system design and concludes the paper.

2   Related Research

Many projects explore smart-home technologies for the elderly, e. g., [4,8,11,12,15]. However, most are developed from a technological point of view, often overlooking the needs and preferences of the target users [12]. This is problematic, since the adoption of a system relies on its acceptance by the target users [2]. For example, Courtney *et al.* [2] found that surveyed residents of a continuing care retirement community deemed certain in-home monitoring technologies to be inappropriate (e. g., image-based technologies) or redundant (e. g., a stove sensor), which negatively affected their willingness to adopt these technologies. Further, Fisk *et al.* [5] noted that age-related factors that pose additional challenges to people's use of technology (such as cognitive, mobility and sensory impairments) must be taken into account during system design.

---

[1] A list of current European projects appears in
http://www.aal-europe.eu/projects

Recently, researchers have begun to assess the attitudes of users towards smart-home technologies, focusing on user attitudes towards specific technologies, factors influencing the adoption of smart-home technologies, and user concerns, e. g., [4,6,7,13,15,16]. Overall, older adults have been found to have a positive attitude towards smart-home technologies [4,6], and reported maintaining independence, detecting cognitive decline, sharing information and monitoring health [15], and having an increased sense of safety and security [13] as some of the benefits of this technology. At the same time, they indicated that smart-home technology must be user friendly, reliable, non-intrusive, affordable, must be able to detect a range of emergency situations, and must require minimal action on the part of the user [4,7].

Despite the wealth of knowledge provided by these studies, they variously suffer from the following limitations: small sample sizes [2], exploring the views of one user group only (generally the older adult) [6], obtaining the views of individuals who may not be in need of this technology (e. g., young people) [16], consulting users after the product is finished [7], or assessing user views on specific aspects of the technology (preventing them from openly expressing their views about other aspects) [6]. The *TigerPlace* project [3,4] overcomes some of these limitations, demonstrating to some extent how multiple stakeholders (i. e., the older adult, family members and health-care professionals) may be involved in all aspects of system design.

Following [3,4], we consider these three stakeholder groups in order to obtain a broad range of views about in-home monitoring systems,[2] while focusing on older adults with vision impairment, which supports the development of targeted models. From a methodological perspective, in addition to classical questionnaires, we employ concept mapping coupled with group-based brainstorming sessions [14], which enable participants to express their ideas freely about any aspect of the technology.

3   User Studies

Our studies assess the views of older people with vision impairment (hereafter called 'patients'), informal caregivers and health-care professionals regarding in-home monitoring systems. To this effect, we employed two methodologies: (1) concept mapping (Sect. 4.1) coupled with brainstorming sessions, and (2) questionnaires. The former was used to find themes that are relevant to the envisaged system, and to determine their importance to the stakeholders. During the brainstorming sessions, the participants offered statements that reflected their views about in-home monitoring systems. They then assessed the relative importance of these statements, and sorted them into conceptually homogeneous categories, yielding general themes that describe the main characteristics of a monitoring system from the point of view of the participants. The questionnaires provide a structured way to canvass the views of larger groups of people regarding specific system-related questions.

3.1   Study Population and Recruitment

Owing to our focus on vision-impaired elderly people, we recruited patients aged 60 years or older who presented with a visual acuity of less than half the nominal acuity

---

[2] Our questionnaire is yet to be completed by enough health-care professionals.

Table 1. Participants in the user study

	Patient	Caregiver	Professional	Total
Brainstorming	16	8	7	31
Sorting & Rating	10	7	7	24
Questionnaire	78	25	5	108
Total	78	25	12	115

(i. e., 6/12 in metres or 20/40 in feet) in the better eye. Informal caregivers and health-care professionals were aged 18 years or older, where a caregiver was identified as the person the patient 'usually turns to for help'.

Eligible patients and caregivers were recruited from eye clinics of the Royal Victorian Eye and Ear Hospital (Victoria, Australia). Health-care professionals were recruited from Able Australia (an organisation that offers community-based support services to people with a vision or hearing impairment) and the Centre for Eye Research Australia (CERA). Staff included service coordinators, team managers and orthoptists. All concept-mapping sessions were conducted at CERA, but participants had the option of completing the questionnaire at CERA or over the telephone.

In total, 115 participants were recruited for this study: 78 patients, 25 caregivers and 12 health-care professionals. Table 1 shows a breakdown of the number of participants who completed the three tasks associated with the study: (1) brainstorming, (2) sorting and rating, and (3) questionnaire. Brainstorming sessions were attended by 31 partici-pants, of which 15 also completed the sorting/rating task; 9 additional participants were recruited for this task (yielding a total of 24). The questionnaire was completed by 108 participants (of whom 11 had participated in the brainstorming sessions only, 9 in the sorting/rating task only, and 15 in both activities).

3.2   Brainstorming Sessions and Statement Assessment

The brainstorming sessions and sorting/rating tasks generate the input for the concept-mapping component. Four brainstorming sessions were conducted for patients and care-givers, and a fifth session was held for health-care professionals. All five sessions were attended by 5-7 participants, each session taking approximately 1.5 hours. Four addi-tional participants (one patient, one caregiver and two health-care professionals) who could not attend any of the sessions were interviewed separately.

At the beginning of each brainstorming session, a facilitator gave a detailed expla-nation of the study, showed sample sensors, and presented a short film (made in-house) demonstrating the proposed technology.[3] Participants were then invited to generate statements in response to the following two seeding prompts: (1) *How can an in-home monitoring system be used to enhance quality of life in people with low vision?*, and (2) *Concerns people may have related to the use of such technologies include* . . . .

---

[3] Prior to these trials, we conducted a pilot study where participants were given the same detailed explanation and shown the sensors, but no film was shown. The subsequent brainstorming session revealed that the participants had failed to understand the functionality of the proposed system. To overcome this problem, we made a film, whose screening significantly improved understanding. The results from the pilot study are excluded from this paper.

In total, 376 statements were generated from the brainstorming sessions and individual interviews (between 50-69 statements per group in total). The statements were reviewed by two researchers, who (by consensus) removed unclear or irrelevant statements (e. g., "The kitchen is a dangerous place"), and combined repetitive or overlapping statements into single statements. 293 statements were removed in this manner, of which 204 (70%) were repetitions. This amount of repetition indicates that the data from the brainstorming sessions have reached saturation. When necessary, the remaining 83 statements were rephrased to express requirements, e. g., "I am worried that maintenance will be too expensive" was rephrased as "maintenance costs should be low". This was done so that the participants would consider only one sentence style when performing the sorting/rating task.

To ascertain the stakeholders' views regarding the importance of the resultant statements and their perceptions about the relationship between the statements, participants were recruited for the sorting/rating task (15 had participated in the brainstorming sessions, and 9 were new). In the sorting task, each participant was asked to group the statements into categories (in any way the participant thought made sense), and to give the categories titles that best describe their contents. This grouping information is the basis for the distance metric used in the clustering process of concept mapping (Sect. 4.1). In the rating task, each participant rated the relative importance of each statement (for supporting independent living of older people with vision impairment) on a 5-point Likert scale (1 = "relatively unimportant" and 5 = "extremely important").

3.3   Questionnaires

We developed three formative, semi-structured questionnaires (which include multiple-choice and open-ended questions) for patients, caregivers and health-care professionals to assess their perceptions regarding the envisaged technology, and their needs and preferences.[4] Specifically, we sought to ascertain the stakeholders' views regarding (1) features of in-home monitoring systems, (2) reasons for accepting/rejecting a system, (3) usefulness and appropriateness of reporting different types of information, and (4) who should have access to the obtained information (i. e., particular people or agencies); and (5) their concerns regarding the envisaged system (e. g., privacy). We also obtained personal information, such as living arrangements, familiarity with technology, socio-demographic characteristics, and clinical and personal circumstances.

4   Methodology

We employed two main techniques to process the gathered information: concept mapping and traditional statistical analysis.

4.1   Concept Mapping

Originally, concept maps were graphical visualisation tools for organising and representing information [14]. These tools have been developed into a methodology which

---

[4] The questionnaires differ in aspects that are relevant to particular groups, e. g., "What is your relationship with the older adult you care for?" is relevant only to caregivers.

combines information gathering and statistical analysis. The information-gathering part combines brainstorming sessions with a sorting/rating exercise (Sect. 3.2). During statistical analysis, multi-dimensional scaling (MDS) is applied to position the participants' statements on a point map, followed by hierarchical cluster analysis to cluster these statements. This was done with the *Concept Systems (CS)* software package (http://www.conceptsystems.com/). The distance metric used for MDS is based on the frequency with which two statements were sorted into the same category by the participants (the higher the frequency, the shorter the distance). For instance, statement 64 ("Maintenance costs should be low") and 46 ("The cost of the sensors, computer and installation of these devices should be affordable for pensioners") were assigned to the same category by 23 users. Hence, they were positioned closer together than statements 64 and 1 ("Safety should be monitored in all rooms of the house, including hallways"), which were never assigned to the same category. Although in principle, the statements may be grouped manually, clustering the statements by the frequency with which participants assign them to the same category reduces researcher bias [14].

4.2 Questionnaires

We mainly applied simple descriptive statistics (proportions and means) to gain insights regarding the views of patients and caregivers about the benefits and acceptability of in-home monitoring systems, and their concerns about these systems. Significance tests were performed and correlations calculated for specific observations.

5 Results

We report on the clustering and rating results followed by the questionnaire results.

5.1 Clustering

The CS package was set to generate 14 cluster configurations, ranging from 2 to 15 clusters (this setting is configurable). Two researchers, who jointly reviewed these configurations, selected a 9-cluster solution, which has a stress value of 0.22 (a favourable stress value is considered to be < 0.35).[5] Table 2 lists the nine clusters, and shows two highly-ranked statements within each cluster.[6] The first column shows the cluster/statement number, the second column contains the title (and the number of statements in a cluster), and the third column shows the average importance rating for all participants on a scale from 1 to 5 (1 = "relatively unimportant" and 5 = "extremely important"). Figure 1 shows the grouping of the 83 statements into these clusters, where each dot represents a statement, and the relative position of two statements reflects how often they were assigned to the same category during the sorting task (Sect. 3.2). Each

---

[5] Stress represents the amount of variance in the raw data (results of individual sorting tasks) which is unexplained by the multidimensional scaling solution – a small amount of unexplained variance yields a low stress value [10].

[6] It is worth noting that a few statements did not have a good conceptual fit with their cluster, e. g., "Safety is monitored in all rooms of the house, including hallways" was assigned to *C9*.

Table 2. Nine clusters and two highly-ranked statements per cluster

#	Statement	Avg. Rating
C1	**Affordability (7 statements)**	**4.31**
46	The costs of the sensors, computer and installation of these devices should be affordable for pensioners.	4.63
47	Financial support should be provided to users of this system for the purchasing, installation and running of the system.	4.46
C2	**Implications of the users' reliance on the system (4 statements)**	**4.13**
9	The limitations of the system should be clearly communicated to the older adult.	4.46
60	The older adult and/or caregiver should be given clear instructions about what to do if the system should stop working.	4.38
C3	**Simplicity of installing, operating and maintaining the system (8 statements)**	**4.09**
13	The system should be easy to operate.	4.46
57	The battery life of the sensors should be long.	4.33
C4	**System integrity and reliability (11 statements)**	**4.09**
40	The system should continue to work during blackouts.	4.63
2	The system should be able to reliably tell the difference between emergency and non-emergency situations	4.42
C5	**Detecting falls and monitoring safe movement in the home (8 statements)**	**4.08**
35	The system can detect if the older adult has a fall in the home.	4.54
39	The system can monitor the older adults' safety in the bathroom and toilet.	4.42
C6	**User customisation (5 statements)**	**4.07**
32	The older adult should nominate how they would like alerts issued in their home (i. e., audio, visual, vibration).	4.17
24	The system should monitor activities and safety concerns that are specific to the older adult.	4.13
C7	**User preferences regarding information delivery to caregivers (12 statements)**	**4.00**
48	A follow-up alert should be issued to a second caregiver when the primary caregiver does not respond.	4.46
19	Information about the older adult should be secure, kept private and shared only with people it is intended for.	4.33
C8	**Caregiver alerts based on abnormal length of stay (7 statements)**	**3.70**
10	The system can let the caregiver know when the older adult has been locked out of the house.	4.00
51	The system can let the caregiver know when the older adult has stayed too long in the bathroom or toilet.	3.92
C9	**Personal alerts and notifications for the older adult (21 statements)**	**3.33**
80	The system allows for a personal safety device that the older adult can press in an emergency.	4.54
68	The system can let the older adult know if they leave the stove or gas on for too long.	4.38

bounded area represents a cluster of similar statements, and is accompanied by its title and average importance rating. Similar themes are located close to each other within the map (the absolute positions of the statements are not important, i. e., the graphic may be turned in any direction). These results highlight the key features that, according to our participants, are required for a monitoring system to be acceptable and beneficial.

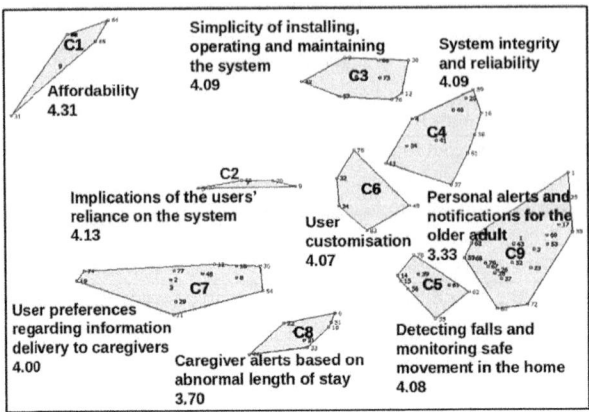

Fig. 1. Clusters produced by concept mapping

5.2   Rating

As seen in Table 2 and Fig. 1, overall, *Affordability* (*C1*) was considered the most important cluster, and *Personal alerts and notifications for the older adult* (*C9*) the least important. We computed the Pearson correlation between the average ratings of the three
pairs of groups regarding statement importance, which is strong between patients and
caregivers ($r = 0.86$) and between patients and health-care professionals ($r = 0.78$),
but only moderate between caregivers and professionals ($r = 0.60$). Figure 2 shows the
association between the views of the three stakeholder groups about cluster importance.
All three groups agreed that *C9* is the least important cluster, but there are discrepant
cluster ratings which reflect the concerns of each stakeholder group. Specifically,

- patients and caregivers considered *Affordability* (*C1*) to be of the highest importance, compared to professionals, who gave it a medium rating;
- patients rated *Simplicity of installing, operating and maintaining the system* (*C3*)
  higher than caregivers and professionals;
- caregivers rated *Caregiver alerts based on abnormal length of stay* (*C8*) higher than
  patients and professionals; and
- professionals rated *User customisation* (*C6*) and *Implications of the users reliance
  on the system* (*C2*) higher than patients and caregivers.

5.3   Questionnaires

Below we present the main insights obtained from the patients' and carers' responses
to the questionnaires, broken down by the topics presented in Sect. 3.3. Most of the
results indicate percentages (statistical significance, computed with Fisher's exact test,
is noted when present). It is worth mentioning that caregivers use technology more than
patients (statistically significant, $p = 0.002$) and are more comfortable with technology
($p = 0.006$). This makes intuitive sense, as the patients are older and vision impaired.
However, we found no statistically significant difference in perceptions regarding in-
home monitoring systems when we compared different usages of technology.

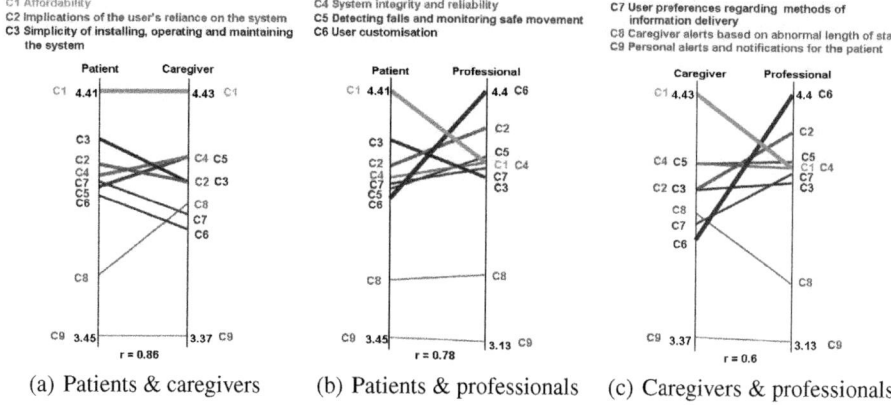

C1 Affordability
C2 Implications of the user's reliance on the system
C3 Simplicity of installing, operating and maintaining the system

C4 System integrity and reliability
C5 Detecting falls and monitoring safe movement
C6 User customisation

C7 User preferences regarding methods of information delivery
C8 Caregiver alerts based on abnormal length of stay
C9 Personal alerts and notifications for the patient

(a) Patients & caregivers   (b) Patients & professionals   (c) Caregivers & professionals

Fig. 2. Associations between importance ratings of patients and caregivers, patients and health-care professionals, and caregivers and health-care professionals

In-Home Monitoring Systems. All the caregivers thought that a monitoring system would be of benefit (now or in the future), while 14% of the patients deemed it to be of no benefit. Further, 72% of the caregivers felt that the system would enable them to take better care of the patients, while only 58% of the patients felt that this was the case. At the same time, about 70% of the patients and carers felt that the system would enable patients to lead a safer life and live independently for longer, and 76% of the carers felt the system would give them peace of mind. Both patients and caregivers felt that the decision to install the system should be made by the patients alone (32%) or by patients and caregivers together (40%), and both groups were willing to be trained in the use of the system (but the patients were slightly less enthusiastic: 70% versus 80%).

Reasons for Accepting/Rejecting an In-Home Monitoring System. Carers mainly had safety concerns: the most frequent reasons for accepting the system were *detecting falls and dangerous situations* (96%) and *safety* (91%), which correspond to cluster C5. These reasons were also ranked as the most important by patients and carers. 85% of the patients shared the carers' concern for *falls and dangerous situations*, but the reason nominated most frequently by the patients (87%) was *maintaining independence*, which was mentioned by only 57% of the carers (statistically significant, $p = 0.05$).

Over half the caregivers found no reason to reject the system, while only 28% of the patients agreed with this view. The most often cited reasons for rejection were *cost* (carers and patients) and the system being *unnecessary at this stage* (patients). Further, 76% of the patients and 88% of the carers deemed cost to be "important" to "critical", which agrees with the high priority of the *Affordability* cluster (*C1*).

Usefulness and Appropriateness of Reporting Different Types of Information. When asked about specific activities, about 2/3 of the patients found it acceptable to have their presence at home, movements around the house and use of the bathroom monitored, while only 1/3 agreed with their use of the toilet and the telephone being monitored. The main point of disagreement between patients and carers pertained to the patients' use of the toilet (which about half the carers found acceptable to monitor). Interestingly, when asked an open-ended question about activities or places that are *not* acceptable to monitor, all the caregivers replied that everything would be acceptable, while 17% of the patients nominated some unacceptable locations, mainly toilet and bedroom.

In line with the reasons for accepting a monitoring system, both patients and caregivers agreed that the most useful notifications pertain to alarms regarding falls and to safety issues. None of the carers found such alarms useless, while 12 (15%) of the patients indicated that they would not be useful. In addition, both patients and caregivers thought it was "important" or "very important" for *them* to be able to select what is being monitored and when (70% and 80% respectively for patients and carers). Interestingly, this point was never explicitly raised in the brainstorming sessions, which highlights the advantages of adopting a mixed-method approach for our user study.

Who Should Have Access to the Obtained Information. 96% of the caregivers thought that they should have access to the information about the patient. This largely matched the patients' views, who mainly nominated their spouse or adult child (comprising 89% of the primary caregivers) to receive this information.

Concerns Regarding the Envisaged System. As one would expect, patients expressed a greater concern than caregivers about the privacy and security of the information about themselves, while caregivers were substantially more concerned about the equipment making mistakes. Additionally, 76% of the patients and 68% of the carers thought that it was "important" to "very important" for the need for action to be minimal, which agrees with the *Simplicity of installing, operating and maintaining* cluster (*C3*).

Summary. The participants' replies regarding access to information, privacy and security confirm the results obtained from concept mapping, while their views on in-home monitoring systems and their reasons for acceptance/rejection provide further insights into their expectations from such systems. The answers to questions about usefulness and appropriateness of reporting different types of information add detail to the results obtained from concept mapping, highlight the importance of the patients being able to control the activities being monitored, and bring to the fore disagreements between patients and caregivers regarding these activities.

6   Discussion

In-home monitoring systems aim to identify situations that require the intervention of a remotely located caregiver. In principle, all activities can be monitored to any useful level of precision. However, in practice there are significant limitations on the sensors used in these systems in terms of acceptability to the patient and cost effectiveness.

We used a mixed-methods approach to ascertain the views of three stakeholder groups about the acceptability of in-home monitoring systems for the elderly. We found that the majority of older adults, caregivers and health-care professionals have a positive attitude towards such systems, and feel that these systems could help older adults maintain independence in the home, and ensure the detection of, and response to, immediate needs, especially falls. Several of our specific findings corroborate those in the literature. Like [4,7], we found that users view smart-home technology as beneficial and acceptable when it is affordable (*C1*), reliable (*C4*), non-intrusive (questionnaire), is able to detect a range of emergencies (*C5*), and requires minimal action from the user (*C3*). Like [6,7], we found that the two main barriers to the adoption of an in-home monitoring system are cost and self-perception of need. However, contrary to [15], which reports a mixed response to family members receiving monitoring information, a large proportion of our patients nominated their spouses and adult children as recipients.

Our results also yield novel insights regarding implications of an in-home monitoring system on patients' lives (*C2*), and older adults' ability to customise the system (*C6*), producing specific findings regarding activities to be monitored (questionnaire) and methods for delivering information and alerts about the patients (*C7-C9*). Overall, our results suggest that in-home monitoring systems must be evaluated on an on-going basis and include all stakeholders during design and implementation.

Below we describe how our user studies affect the design of our system.

Most of the system's hardware is based on burglar-alarm system components for the following reasons. Firstly, the burglar alarm market is large with economies of scale, and alarm components are designed for economical power usage, thus addressing the *affordability* theme (*C1*). Second, burglar-alarm systems are designed for *ease of installation, operation and maintenance* (*C3*), and do not require special actions on the part of the users, although skilled installers are still needed. Thirdly, burglar-alarm hardware has high *integrity and reliability* (*C4*); specifically burglar-alarm sensors are reliable, rugged and usually battery powered, incorporating battery monitoring. This level of integrity and reliability must be matched by the monitoring software.

On the grounds of acceptability, it is important for the system to be non-intrusive (questionnaire). A system without image-based technologies or wearable devices may *monitor safe movement* (*C5*) and *detect abnormal length of stay* (*C8*) through standard sensors of burglar-alarm systems. For example, motion sensors can detect a user getting out of bed or going into the bathroom (and staying for a while). *Fall detection* (*C5*) is more indirect, as it involves detecting the absence of expected motion. Clearly, a more precise identification of falls is technically possible, but this affects cost and (sensor) intrusiveness, which conflicts with high-priority patient requirements.

User preferences regarding information delivery to caregivers (*C7*) and many of the *caregiver* (*C8*) and *personal* (*C9*) alerts can be addressed through decision procedures implemented in the software on the basis of input from existing sensors (e. g., the patient has stayed too long in the bathroom (*C8*) or the fridge door has been left open (*C9*)). However, some alerts nominated under *C8* (e. g., the patient remaining too long in bed, which could still trigger a motion sensor) or *C9* (e. g., the cook-top being left on) require additional types of sensors, thus affecting cost and intrusiveness. *User customisation* (*C6*) and the selection of activities to be monitored (questionnaire) require a combination of software and hardware, e. g., to allow the patient to disable the monitoring of certain locations at will, and to issue an alert when the monitoring of an essential activity has been disabled for too long. Finally, *implications of the users' reliance on the system* (*C2*) will be addressed through user studies while the system is being trialed.

At present, a trial sensor network is deployed and gathering data in the home of one of the authors. Next, we will obtain additional questionnaire results from professional health-care providers, and we will proceed to build models of users' behaviour on the basis of data gathered at the author's home and other sites.

Acknowledgements. This research was supported in part by grant LP100200405 from the Australian Research Council, and endowments from Meticube, Portugal, VicHealth and the Helen McPherson Smith Trust.

References

1. Burmedi, D., Becker, S., Heyl, V., Wahl, H., Himmelsbach, I.: Emotional and social consequences of age-related low vision: A narrative review. Visual Impairment Research 4(1), 15–45 (2002)
2. Courtney, K., Demiris, G., Rantz, M.: Needing smart home technologies: The perspective of older adults in continuing care retirement communities. Informatics in Primary Care 16(3), 195–201 (2008)
3. Demiris, G., Oliver, D., Dickey, G., Skubic, M., Rantz, M.: Findings from a participatory evaluation of a smart home application for older adults. Technology and Health Care 16(2), 111–118 (2008)
4. Demiris, G., Rantz, M., Aud, M., Marek, K., Tyrer, H., Skubic, M., Hussam, A.: Older adults' attitudes towards and perceptions of 'smart home' technologies: A pilot study. Medical informatics and the Internet in Medicine 29(2), 87–94 (2004)
5. Fisk, A.D., Rogers, W.A., Charness, N., Czaja, S.J., Sharit, J.: Designing for Older Adults: Principles and Creative Human Factors Approaches, 2nd edn. CRC Press, Boca Raton (2009)
6. Mann, W.C., Belchoir, P., Tomita, M.R., Kemp, B.J.: Older adults' perception and use of PDAs, home automation system, and home health monitoring system. Topics in Geriatric Rehabilitation 23(1), 35–46 (2007)
7. McCreadie, C., Tinker, A.: The acceptability of assistive technology to older people. Ageing and Society 25(1), 91–110 (2005)
8. Ohta, S., Nakamoto, H., Shinagawa, Y., Tanikawa, T.: A health monitoring system for elderly people living alone. Journal of Telemedicine and Telecare 8(3), 151–166 (2002)
9. Pascolini, D., Mariotti, S.P.: Global estimates of visual impairment: 2010. British Journal of Ophthalmology (December 2011)
10. Petrucci, C., Quinlan, K.: Bridging the research-practice gap: Concept mapping as a mixed methods strategy in practice-based research and evaluation. Journal of Social Service Research 34(2), 25–42 (2007)
11. Philipose, M., Fishkin, K.P., Perkowitz, M., Patterson, D.J., Fox, D., Kautz, H., Hahnel, D.: Inferring activities from interactions with objects. IEEE Pervasive Computing 3(4), 50–57 (2004)
12. Pollack, M.E.: Intelligent technology for an aging population: The use of AI to assist elders with cognitive impairment. AI Magazine 26(2), 9–24 (2005)
13. Sixsmith, A.: An evaluation of an intelligent home monitoring system. Journal of Telemedicine and Telecare 6(2), 63–72 (2000)
14. Trochim, W., Kane, M.: Concept mapping: An introduction to structured conceptualization in health care. International Journal for Quality in Health Care 17(3), 187–191 (2005)
15. Wild, K., Boise, L., Lundell, J., Foucek, A.: Unobtrusive in-home monitoring of cognitive and physical health: Reactions and perceptions of older adults. Journal of Applied Gerontology 27(2), 181–200 (2008)
16. Ziefle, M., Röker, C., Holzinger, A.: Medical technology in smart homes: Exploring the user's perspective on privacy, intimacy and trust. In: SAPSE 2011 – The 3rd IEEE International Workshop on Security Aspects of Process and Services Engineering, Munich, Germany, pp. 410–415 (2011)

Improving Tensor Based Recommenders with Clustering

Martin Leginus, Peter Dolog, and Valdas Žemaitis

Department of Computer Science, Aalborg University,
Selma Lagerlofs Vej 300
{mleginus,dolog}@cs.aau.dk, valdas.zemaitis@gmail.com
http://iwis.cs.aau.dk/

Abstract. Social tagging systems (STS) model three types of entities
(i.e. tag-user-item) and relationships between them are encoded into a
3-order tensor. Latent relationships and patterns can be discovered by
applying tensor factorization techniques like Higher Order Singular Value
Decomposition (HOSVD), Canonical Decomposition etc. STS accumu-
late large amount of sparse data that restricts factorization techniques
to detect latent relations and also significantly slows down the process
of a factorization. We propose to reduce tag space by exploiting clustering techniques so that the quality of the recommendations and execution time are improved and memory requirements are decreased. The
clustering is motivated by the fact that many tags in a tag space are
semantically similar thus the tags can be grouped. Finally, promising
experimental results are presented.

Keywords: tensor factorization, HOSVD, clustering.

1 Introduction

The state of the art tag-based recommenders are based on tensor factorizations
[9, 11] which are a concern of this study. Tensor based recommenders build 3-
dimensional matrix (tensor) by reflecting relationships between all users, items
and tags from STS. Afterwards, a factorization technique is performed on the constructed tensor. The tensor approximation usually reveals latent relations between
the involved objects. They outperform other tag-aware state-of-the-art recommendation algorithms as was shown in [9, 11]. They generate recommendations of
items, tags or users from the same approximated tensor [11] – a factorization needs
to be computed only once for all types of recommendations. However, there are
many practical difficulties that restrict usage of tensor based recommenders in real
world applications. Following significant problems are addressed in this paper: A
factorization is computationally demanding process and most of the tensor based
recommenders [9, 11] calculate tensor approximation in the offline mode. When
new users, items or taggings are inserted into a system there is a need to recom-
pute factorization so the appropriate recommendations are generated. Moreover, a
sparse STS data restricts factorization technique to detect latent relations hence a

J. Masthoff et al. (Eds.): UMAP 2012, LNCS 7379, pp. 151–163, 2012.
© Springer-Verlag Berlin Heidelberg 2012

recommender is not always able to generate appropriate recommendations. A particular topic in STS is represented with various tags assigned by different users. Therefore, user preferences can be too specific due to the nature of tags diversity. In consequence, a factorization technique cannot correctly detect important interests of a user as these preferences can be defined differently by other users. Also a factorization has excessive memory demands when large datasets are used. In order to generate accurate recommendations there is a need for a tuning process of factorization parameters which is time-consuming.

Our approach addresses above mentioned problems with exploitation of the clustering techniques that reduce the size of a tag space. We follow the assumption that majority of the STS contain a lot of related tags which can be grouped (clustered). The cluster representative is then used instead of a number of tags which is the reason why the tag space is reduced. To find out which techniques performs the best under the aforementioned assumptions, we explore 4 different clustering techniques and evaluate various similarity and distance measures. We also introduce a heuristic method to speed-up parameters tuning process for HOSVD recommenders. The main contribution of this paper is twofold:

- Precision of recommendations is improved by $\sim 11\%$ for Bibsonomy and $\sim 1\%$ for Movielens dataset.
- Execution time of a tensor approximation is significantly decreased. The approach speeds up time performance by $\sim 66\%$ for Bibsonomy and $\sim 64\%$ for Movielens.

In consequence, memory requirements are significantly decreased. Also, the factorization can be recomputed more often and recommendations will embrace the new entered objects. To the best of our knowledge, we are the first who introduce clustering of tag space to reduce a dimension of the tensor to improve precision and execution time of the factorization for recommender systems.

2   Related Work

Tensor Based Recommenders. Symenonidis et al. [11] introduce a recommender based on HOSVD where each tagging activity for a given item from a particular user is represented by value 1 in the initial tensor, all other cases are represented with 0. The HOSVD factorization of a tensor results into an approximated tensor which reveals the latent relationships and patterns of the users. The initial tensor is split into three mode matrices by applying different perspectives to the initial tensor. The Singular Value Decomposition (SVD) is the factorization method used for all the three mode matrices. The approximated tensor is computed by multiplying the results from SVD of the mode matrices. The recommendations are obtained from the approximated tensor by inspecting the entries that belong to a given user, item and tag. We utilize this recommendation system and use it as a baseline for the comparison of precision and time performance with our proposed techniques. [9] presents different factorization technique that can be also extended with clustered tag space.

Parameters Tuning for HOSVD Recommenders. For HOSVD based recommenders, there must be provided a number of preserved top singular values for each mode matrix. Symeonidis et. al [11] analyze the impact of the parameters on the precision of the recommendations. According to their empirical results, a 70 % of original diagonal matrices provides the best quality of recommendations. Rendle et. al [9] also describe that HOSVD is sensitive to small changes of the parameters. In both works, the parameters are manually tuned and this naive approach searches through a defined parameters space that requires executing 3 inner loops as there is no correlation between the parameters. We utilize genetic algorithm (GA) to speed up the selection of the optimal parameters as it can explore faster the parameters search space.

Clustering Techniques. They are commonly utilized within recommendation and personalization algorithms.Begelman et al.[1] group tags into clusters to improve search, exploration and subscription of content.The technique builds similarity matrix where an affinity between two tags is based on their co-occurrence (amount of items that were annotated with given tag pair). Afterwards, the spectral clustering is performed. Our method similarly computes affinities between tag pairs however, we exploit different similarity measures (Dice coefficient, Jaccard and Cosine similarities).In [3], tags are expressed as feature vectors and in such way a tag space is clustered. Each tag is encoded as a vector over the set of items and a tag frequency for the particular item is used as a weight on the corresponding position in the vector. Clustering techniques Mean Shift and K-means also utilize the same approach. There exist also linguistic approaches (stemming, lemmatization) that cluster tag space based on linguistic resources such are dictionaries or ontologies. The drawback of linguistic techniques is their expensiveness and language dependency. [10] expresses each tag with a tag signature that is a vector with the frequencies of the terms from the documents of the given tag. Such approach is unfeasible in this work because of the utilized datasets i.e movies from Movielens dataset do not have textual description and electronic articles from Bibsonomy would be expensive to process.

3   Clustered Tag Space and GA

We propose to utilize a cluster analysis on the tag space to group similar tags into clusters. Clustered tag space overcomes tags diversity, reduces sparsity and better expresses users' preferences in STS. As consequence, it improves a precision of the recommendations. Moreover, a reduced tag space causes smaller initial tensor thus time performance is improved while lower memory demands are achieved. Before describing technical details of our method, we provide motivation for clustering and describe our approach with the illustrative example.

3.1   Motivation

The majority of tags used within the social tagging systems are assigned and used rarely. In [6] authors have shown that around 30 % of all distinct tags were used only once within the Delicious system. The analysis shows that synonyms, acronyms and spelling variations occur frequently among tags. Many tags differ only in the spelling variations – upper or lower case initial letters of tags, singulars or plurals, spelling mistakes. Majority of the rare tags can be grouped with the more frequent ones because of the mentioned reasons.

To better understand the issue, let us present the following motivational example with the 4 users (*u1, u2, u3, u4*), 4 web items (*cars.com, bmw.com, automobile.de, java.com*) and 4 distinct tags (*car, cars, bmw, programming*). The tagging posts of the users assigned to the web items are depicted in the Table 1. Obviously, the tags *car, cars, bmw* are semantically related and our

Table 1. Tagging posts of the motivational example and results of the factorization (only new relations are presented) with the revealed associations between user *u2* and web items *cars.com, automobile.de*

User	Web item	Tag	Weight
u1	cars.com	car	1.0
u2	bmw.com	bmw	1.0
u1	automobile.de	car	1.0
u3	automobile.de	cars	1.0
u3	cars.com	cars	1.0
u4	java.com	programming	1.0

User	Web item	Tag	Weight
u1	bmw.com	car cluster	0.0116
u1	bmw.com	car cluster	0.9287
u2	cars.com	car cluster	0.0116
u2	automobile.de	car cluster	0.0551
u3	bmw.com	car cluster	1.0

approach groups them into one cluster *car cluster* = {*car, cars, bmw*}. Grouping the similar tags into the cluster provides new relations such that all the weights related to tags from *car cluster* are agregated and represented only by one value (i.e., user *u1* annotated resource *cars.com* with tag *car* from *car cluster* and it is represented with weight 1; for the user *u2* and the resource *bmw.com* and tags from *car cluster* is also set weight to 1 as only one tag was assigned by the given user). Before the HOSVD factorization is computed, we find the number of preserved top singular values for each mode matrix with GA method. Once the tensor is approximated, the scores in Table 1 are obtained for the given triplets.

HOSVD factorization reveals latent relations between the user *u2* and the web items *automobile.de, cars.com*. Therefore, the system recommends item *automobile.de* and *cars.com* to the user *u2*. The clustering of similar tags improves a precision of the recommendations as obtained clusters represent latent topics expressed by tags in the STS. Without grouping similar tags web items *automobile.de* and *cars.com* would not be recommended to the user *u2*. Such clusters consist of various semantically related tags assigned by different users and it allows to overcome tags diversity. Therefore, it better represents preferences of the users accross the STS. Moreover, our approach removes 2 slices of the tensor and in consequence it improves time performance of the factorization and decreases memory requirements.

3.2   Higher-Order Singular Value Decomposition (HOSVD)

HOSVD is an extended version of the SVD [7] applied to the multi-dimensional matrices. HOSVD of 3rd order tensor is defined as:

$$\mathcal{A}' = \mathcal{S} \times_1 U_{c1}^1 \times_2 U_{c2}^2 \times_3 U_{c3}^3 \tag{1}$$

where U_{c1}^1, U_{c2}^2 and U_{c3}^3 are matrices with the top c_i left singular vectors from the SVD of $1, 2, 3$ mode matrices respectively [7]. Core tensor S is obtained according to:

$$\mathcal{S} = \mathcal{A} \times_1 (U_{c1}^{(1)})^T \times_2 (U_{c2}^{(2)})^T \times_3 (U_{c3}^{(3)})^T \tag{2}$$

The factorized tensor $\mathcal{A}'$ is the approximation of the initial tensor $\mathcal{A}$.

The usage data of a recommender are represented by 3rd order tensor – $\mathcal{A}$ where for a particular user with a selected information item and an assigned tag is stated a weight 1 and for all other cases where is not created relation a weight is 0. From the approximated tensor $\mathcal{A}'$, the recommendation system is able to suggest tags or information items with the highest weights to a given user.

3.3   Cluster Analysis of Tags

We exploit and evaluate 4 different clustering techniques that are adjusted to group similar tags into clusters. The general proposed approach consists of the following steps:

1. Perform cluster analysis of a tag space with the selected clustering method from the 4 proposed techniques.
2. Build an initial tensor where a tag dimension has the same size as the amount of obtained clusters. A tagging performed by a user u to a item i with a tag t is a triplet (u, i, t). All such triplets are encoded to corresponding positions in the initial tensor with the initial weight 1 and a tag t is mapped to the matching cluster. When two or more triplets share the same item and user – differ only in tags and these tags belong to the same one cluster a final weight in the tensor is the amount of such triplets, e.g. given two triplets: (u, i, t_1), (u, i, t_2) and tags t_1, t_2 belong to the same tag cluster, then an initial tensor will contain weight 2 at the position (a row for a user u, a column for a item i and slice corresponding to tag cluster with tags t_1, t_2).
3. Find the optimal parameters for the recommender with the proposed GA based heuristic method.
4. Compute tensor factorization for the constructed initial tensor. Finally, items recommendations are generated according to the sorted weights from the factorized tensor for the given user and all not observed items.

In the following sections, we describe 4 different clustering techniques which were selected to inspect advantages of expressing tags relations with 2 different models. The former one (Correlated Feature Hashing, Spectral K-means clustering) clusters tags according to their co-occurrence based similarities. The latter one (K-means and Mean shift algorithms) considers each tag from a tag space as feature vector.

Correlated Feature Hashing. We propose to reduce a tag space with hashing function. The idea is to share and group tags with the similar meaning. We sort the tags used within the system according to the frequency of usage such that t_1 is the most frequent tag and t_T is the least frequent. For each tag $t_i \in 1, \ldots, T$ is calculated *DICE* coefficient with respect to each tag $t_j \in 1, \ldots, K$ among the top K most frequent tags. The *DICE* coefficient is defined as:

$$\text{DICE}(t_i, t_j) = \frac{2.\text{cocr}(t_i, t_j)}{\text{ocr}(t_i) + \text{ocr}(t_j)} \quad (3)$$

where $\text{cocr}(t_i, t_j)$ denotes the number of co-occurrences for tags t_i and t_j, $\text{ocr}(t_i)$ and $\text{ocr}(t_j)$ is the total number of tag t_i, t_j assignments respectively. For each tag t_i, we sort the K scores in descending order such that $S_p(t_i) \in 1, \ldots, K$ represents the tag of the p-th largest DICE score $\text{DICE}(t_i, S_p(t_i))$. We can then use hash kernel approximation as defined in [7] The described approach is replacing each tag t_i with the tag $S_1(t_i)$. Obviously, we have reduced tag space from all T tags to the K most frequent tags.

Spectral K-means Clustering. In the second approach we utilize Spectral K-means clustering technique. Firstly, we encode tag relations into the affinity matrix W, such that $w_{i,j}$ entry represents affinity between tag t_i and tag t_j. The similarity matrix can be also interpreted as undirected weighted graph G where tags represent nodes and weights are expressed as similarities between given tags. We exploit Jaccard (4) and Cosine (4) similarity measures denoted as $\text{JAC}(t_i, t_j)$ and $\text{COS}(t_i, t_j)$.

$$\text{JAC}(t_i, t_j) = \frac{\text{cocr}(t_i, t_j)}{\text{ocr}(t_i) + \text{ocr}(t_j) - \text{cocr}(t_i, t_j)} \quad \text{COS}(t_i, t_j) = \frac{\text{cocr}(t_i, t_j)}{\sqrt{\text{ocr}(t_i) \times \text{ocr}(t_j)}} \quad (4)$$

where $\text{cocr}(t_i, t_j)$ is the sum of all co-occurrences for tags t_i and t_j, $\text{ocr}(t_i)$ and $\text{ocr}(t_j)$ is the total number of tag t_i, t_j occurrences respectively. *DICE* similarity (3) is also explored. Once the similarity matrix W is created, we then proceed to find (sub) clusters of tags that address the same topic. To obtain clusters, we rely on a spectral clustering algorithm which input is the undirected weighted graph G. The spectral clustering algorithm (more described in [7]) partitions the graph G based on its spectral decomposition into sub graphs. We obtained disjoint groups of similar and related tags and we are able to build initial tensor with the reduced tag dimension and then proceed with the factorization.

K-means. The K-means is a simple well known clustering technique that groups objects from a given set into k clusters (given a priori). The algorithm starts with generating k random centroids. Then for each object from a dataset, i.e., for a tag from T, the nearest centroid is found. Thus the given tag is associated with a particular centroid. When all tags are processed, centroids have to be recomputed such that new centroid is the mean value of the vectors for the given cluster. Again for all objects the nearest centroids are identified and objects are clustered with them. This process repeats until locations of centroids do not change.

More formally, we denote $T = \{t_1, t_2 \ldots, t_{|T|}\}$ as the set of all distinct tags that are clustered and $R = \{res_1, res_2 \ldots res_n\}$ the set of all items that are tagged with tags from T. Let $f(t, res_i)$ be equal to a frequency of a tag t assignments to item res_i otherwise it is equal to 0. Then, the feature vector representation of tag t is:

$$t = (f(t, res_1), f(t, res_2), \ldots, f(t, res_n)) \tag{5}$$

Once, tags from T are expressed as n-dimensional vectors, we proceed with the cluster analysis.

We obtained k disjoint clusters of tags so we can proceed with the tensor factorization. The results of K-means algorithm depend on used distance measure - we exploit Cosine, Manhattan, Euclidean and Jaccard distances.

Mean Shift Clustering. The Mean shift [2] is a nonparametric clustering as it does not require a prior definition of the number of clusters.

In the context of tags clustering, for each tag that is expressed as d-dimensional vector a window is placed around a given tag such that a window size is conditioned with parameter h and a given point is centroid of that window. Mean shift computes mean for all tags within the given window (mean shift vector points to the computed mean). Centroid of the window is moved to the obtained mean and this repeats until window position stabilize. The main advantage of this technique is to automatically determine the number of clusters, however this depends on the window size which is given by bandwidth parameter h and it has to be tuned. The smaller parameter is set more final clusters are obtained. The drawbacks are computational expensiveness and when a feature space with large amount of dimensions is considered it is demanding to identify points that belong within the particular window.

3.4   GA - Tuning Tensor Based Recommenders

We propose a method based on Genetic Algorithm (GA) [8] that identifies the optimal parameters for HOSVD based recommenders so that the best possible accuracy is attained. GA is adapted to our search problem in the following way: The parameters c_1, c_2, c_3 are genes that are together encoded in a chromosome. A population of possible solutions consists of k different chromosomes. Fitness function is the average precision for considered users and for the provided chromosome (parameters c_1, c_2, c_3). Once the searching process is finished, GA returns a chromosome with the best average precision (result of the fitness function). The given chromosome contains the optimal parameters c_1, c_2, c_3 that are used in the Formulas 1,2.

4   Experiments

We investigate the prediction quality and time performance of the techniques and compare it with the baseline results of the HOSVD recommender [11]. The proposed techniques are evaluated on the BibSonomy dataset and the snapshot of MovieLens dataset. Similarly, as in [11] the datasets are preprocessed with p-core filtering so that data are more dense. P-core constraints data such that each user, item and tag has to appear at least p times in the dataset. For the Bibsonomy a p-core value was set to 5 and the dataset contains 116 distinct users, 361 items and 412 tags. The total number of tagging posts is 10148. The snapshot of Movielens dataset contains 250 most active users and 326 unique tags and 382 movies assigned by selected users that satisfy p-core filtering with the p-core value set to 50. The total number of tagging posts is 11144. All the experiments are conducted on Ubuntu Server 11.10 64-bit operating system running on Intel Xeon X3460 CPU 2.8GHz with 8 GB RAM. The HOSVD and clustering techniques are implemented in Java 6 and source code and all results are available on our website[1]. The same methodology is followed as in [11] in order to compare the enhancements of our approaches. For a test user we split his tagging posts into training and evaluation set in the ratio 50 %:50 %. The task of the recommender is to predict the items that correspond to the tagging posts in the evaluation set. The models are trained on the training set and the recommendations quality is measured on the test set. The prediction quality is evaluated according to the following common evaluation metrics. Precision P_N is the ratio of the number of recommended relevant items (we consider only items that correspond to the tagging posts in the evaluation part of the data set - denoted as rel items) from the top-N list of entries to N. Recall R_N is the ratio of the number of recommended items from the top-N list of entries to the total number of items for a given user from the evaluation part of data set.

$$P_N = \frac{|\{\text{rel items}\} \cap \{\text{top-N items}\}|}{|\{\text{top-N items}\}|} \quad R_N = \frac{|\{\text{rel items}\} \cap \{\text{top-N items}\}|}{|\{\text{rel items}\}|} \quad (6)$$

We measure precision and recall for different top-N lists (N is between $[1..10]$).

4.1   Baseline

We conduct experiments using the HOSVD recommender without clustering. The results are used as the baseline for the comparison with our proposed techniques. For the BibSonomy dataset the average precision P_5 for all 116 users is 0.2827 and the average recall R_5 is 0.114. We achieve the similar precision for the BibSonomy dataset as is reported in [11], however the achieved recall is worse, because the BibSonomy dataset contains significantly more items (+115) and the amount of users is similar. The splitting into training and evaluation set is performed with ratio 50 % : 50 %, therefore the evaluation set of a test user contains many items and in consequence the recall is lower. The average precision P_5 for MovieLens dataset is 0.18, and the average recall R_5 is 0.064. The quality of recommendations is lower for Movielens in comparison with Bibsonomy because considered users have posted a few tags to the items constrained by p-core. The average execution time of HOSVD factorization for BibSonomy is 224 s and 378 s for MovieLens.The recommendations were generated when top $(60, 105, 225)$ singular values and corresponding left singular vectors were preserved for the 1st, 2nd and 3rd mode matrices respectively for the BibSonomy dataset. For the MovieLens dataset the following top singular values were used $(73, 86, 211)$.

---

[1] http://people.cs.aau.dk/$\sim$mleginus/umap2012/

4.2   Clustered Tag Space

We evaluate the quality of the recommendations and the execution time of the factorization when a tag space is clustered and the sets of users and items have the original size. HOSVD is applied on such compressed tensor where tags dimension is reduced from the original size to the certain number of clusters. The goal is to find the best trade-off between the accuracy of recommendations and time performance.

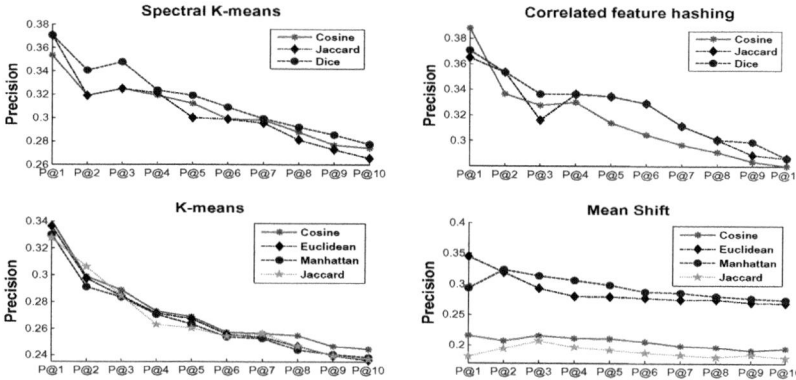

Fig. 1. Comparison of distance and similarity measures and their impact on the recommendations quality when number of clusters is set to 50 % of the original tag space for Bibsonomy

Distance and Similarity Measures. Before performing clustering, a tag space has to be preprocessed so that tags are expressed either as feature vectors (K-means, Mean Shift) or in the affinity matrix where each entry represents similarity between two tags (Spectral Clustering, Correlated Feature Hashing).

When a tag space is clustered with K-means algorithm and Mean Shift, we explore and compare Cosine, Euclidean, Manhattan and Jaccard distance measures on Bibsonomy dataset. The impact of a given distance measure on the quality of recommendations is depicted in the Figure 1.

The cosine distance produces the best recommendations results. Many tags are placed into one large cluster when Euclidean and Manhattan distances are used thus the quality is decreased. The observation is similar to the [5] as authors identify Cosine similarity as the most suitable. It is sensitive to the small variations in more elements. Euclidean and Manhattan distances are more sensitive to significant changes in a few elements of feature vectors. Therefore, we use the Cosine similarity for all K-means clustering computations.

Euclidean and Manhattan distances perform better than Cosine and Jaccard measures for Mean Shift clustering. Kernel density estimation approximate probability density function better when distances between tag vectors belong to the larger interval. Results of Cosine and Jaccard distance measures are always in the interval $[0, 1]$. Therefore, we have decreased the window size to obtain better

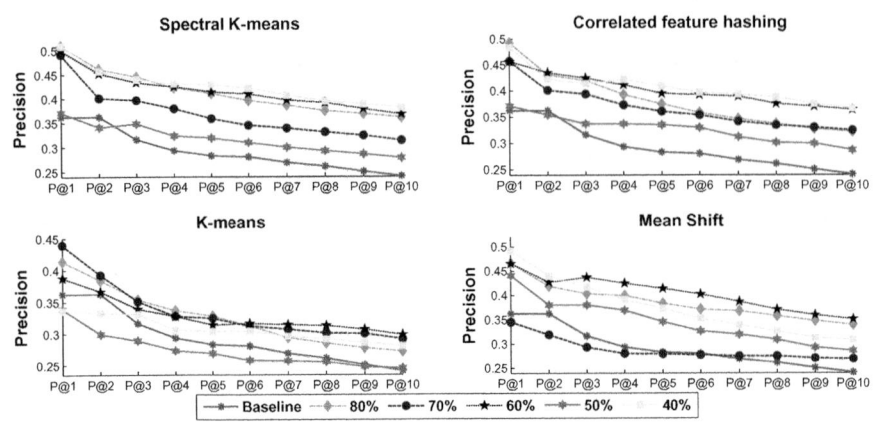

Fig. 2. Precision comparison of clustering techniques for Bibsonomy

estimated probability density function but the quality of recommendations was not improved significantly. Due to the mentioned facts, Euclidean distance is utilized in all Mean shift computations.

For the spectral K-means clustering and Correlated feature hashing, a co-ocurrence similarity has to be computed for each tag pair in the original tag space. We evaluate Dice (3), Jaccard (4) and Cosine (4) similarity measures. For both clustering techniques the highest precision is achieved when Dice coefficient is utilized then follows Jaccard and the worst is Cosine similarity. Dice and Jaccard similarity measures reflect the ratio of tag pair co-occurrences to the sum or union of tags occurrences. Dice similarity more emphasizes tag pairs co-occurrences which better distinguishes between semantically related tags and those which are not similar enough. The denominator of Cosine similarity is the square root of multiplicated tags occurrences. It restricts clustering techniques to differentiate similar tags from not related as changes in tags occurrences are not reflected enough. Therefore, we utilize only Dice similarity for both clustering techniques.

Results. For each technique, the number of clusters is iteratively changed: starting from the 40 % of the original tag space size, after each iteration amount of clusters is increased by 10 % until 80 %. We plot the precision value versus amount of clusters in Figure 2. The spectral K-means outperforms Correlated feature hashing, K-means and also Mean Shift almost in all cases. Correlated feature hashing and Mean Shift have similar results however, the latter technique requires time-consuming and sensitive tuning of window size parameter. The K-means attains the worst precision for all number of clusters as the distribution of tags in clusters is not uniform.

All clustering techniques improve precision in comparison with baseline technique. Generated clusters aggregate tags with similar meanings. Appropriate

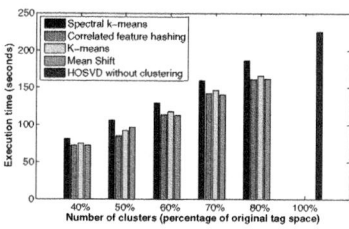
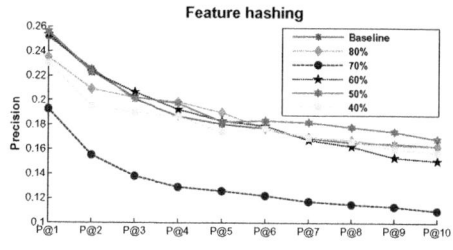

Fig. 3. Execution time of tensor factorization for Bibsonomy and precision comparison of clustering techniques for Movielens

clusters represent character and nature of documents in more general way. Instead of concrete tags, documents are represented with clusters that have particular topics. Also preferences and interests of users are more generalized. These facts enable a factorization technique to better reveal and propagate important patterns in STS's data which are by nature very sparse. A sparse data of STS restricts factorization technique to detect latent relations in data. Therefore, a recommender is not always able to generate appropriate recommendations. Our results show that clustering reduces sparsity of data and in consequence also with reasonably generated clusters improves the quality of recommendations. The enhancement of precision is also caused by finding reduction coefficients with GA as a factorization process is highly sensitive to correctly set parameters.

We also measure improvement of time performance. The execution time of the factorization is decreased as is showed in the following Figure 3. The best trade-off between accuracy and execution time is reached when the number of clusters is 40 % of the original tag space. In such case the average precision for all users is increased with ~ 0.13 for Spectral k-means, ~ 0.11 for Correlated feature hashing and ~ 0.09 for Mean Shift. The execution time is decreased about $\sim 66\,\%$.

Based on these findings, we evaluate only the most applicable clustering method – Correlated feature hashing on the Movielens dataset (Figure 3). The quality of recommendations is slightly improved in comparison to the baseline. The precision is not enhanced so significantly as the considered tag space contains very frequent tags which are semantically diverse. Another reason is the nature of this dataset, there are many tags with general meaning like: *movie to see, own, want...* Such tags can belong to semantically different clusters of tags. The best performance is attained when the tags dimension is equal to 50 % of the original tag space. The precision is improved with ~ 0.01 and the execution time is decreased about $\sim 64\,\%$.

Discussion and Limitations. One could argue that applying clustering to reduce tag dimension before computing the tensor factorization is unnecessary as HOSVD is also dimensional reduction technique. However, the low rank approximation [4] is not reducing tag dimension in the same sense as clustering. The low rank SVD is only removing noisy data, so that approximated tensor better reflects the patterns in the data. The importance of clustering is to shrink tag space in such way that an initial tensor contains less slices and the factorization is faster. Once the tag space is clustered each mode matrix is smaller. In case only the low rank SVD is applied user and item mode matrices reflect the original tag space and only the tag mode matrix is reduced.

GA improves a process of estimating appropriate parameters for HOSVD factorization. In all cases of clustered tag space the quality of recommendations was improved. However, this search heuristic sometimes only reaches a local maximum in the search space and it negatively affects final precision of recommendations. Such case can be observed for Bibsonomy dataset when the number of clusters is set to 50 % and the precision is lower than for 60 % and 40 % clustered tag space. The same case occurs for Movielens dataset when a tag space is reduced to 70% of the original tag space. To avoid this, GA should be executed in more independent iterations when initial genes are seeded with various random values but this requires additional computational time.

5   Conclusion and Future Work

In this work, we propose to utilize clustering techniques for reducing tag space that improves the quality of recommendations and also the execution time of the factorization and decreases the memory demands. Two approaches of computing tags similarities are investigated. The former one utilizes tag pair co-occurrence similarity measures. The latter expresses tags as feature vectors and uses standard distance measures. Techniques that employ co-occurrence tag pair similarity perform better than methods based on feature vectors. The best prediction quality is achieved with the Spectral K-means however, due to the time complexity we consider Correlated feature hashing as the most applicable technique. The best trade-off between prediction accuracy and execution time is when the number of clusters equals to 40 % for Bibsonomy or 50 % for Movielens of the original tag space size. Such reduced tag space improves time performance of a factorization and the prediction quality is enhanced. As a future work, we intend to extend the clustering techniques with ability to detect tags with multiple meanings (polysemy).

Acknowledgements. This work has been supported by FP7 ICT project M-Eco under grant No. 247829 and Otto Mønsteds Fond.

References

1. Begelman, G., Keller, P., Smadja, F.: Automated tag clustering: Improving search and exploration in the tag space. In: CWT at WWW 2006, Edinburgh, Scotland, pp. 15–33. Citeseer (2006)
2. Comaniciu, D., Meer, P.: Mean shift: A robust approach toward feature space analysis. IEEE Transactions on Pattern Analysis and Machine Intelligence (2002)
3. Gemmell, J., Shepitsen, A., Mobasher, B., Burke, R.: Personalization in folksonomies based on tag clustering. Intelligent Techniques for web Personalization & Recommender Systems 12 (2008)

4. Hansen, P.: The truncatedsvd as a method for regularization. BIT Numerical Mathematics 27(4), 534–553 (1987)
5. Huang, A.: Similarity measures for text document clustering. In: Proceedings of NZCSRSC 2008, Christchurch, New Zealand, pp. 49–56 (2008)
6. Kipp, M., Campbell, D.: Patterns and inconsistencies in collaborative tagging systems: An examination of tagging practices. Proceedings of the American Society for Information Science and Technology 43(1), 1–18 (2006)
7. Leginus, M., Zemaitis, V.: Speeding up tensor based recommenders with clustered tag space and improving quality of recommendations with non-negative tensor factorization. Master's thesis, Aalborg University (2011)
8. Mitchell, M.: An introduction to genetic algorithms. The MIT Press (1998)
9. Rendle, S., Balby Marinho, L., Nanopoulos, A., Schmidt-Thieme, L.: Learning optimal ranking with tensor factorization for tag recommendation. In: Proceedings of the 15th ACM SIGKDD Conference on Knowledge Discovery and Data Mining. ACM (2009)
10. Solskinnsbakk, G., Gulla, J.: Mining tag similarity in folksonomies. In: Proceedings of the 3rd International Workshop on Search and Mining User-Generated Contents, pp. 53–60. ACM (2011)
11. Symeonidis, P., Nanopoulos, A., Manolopoulos, Y.: A unified framework for providing recommendations in social tagging systems based on ternary semantic analysis. IEEE Transactions on Knowledge and Data Engineering (2009)

Models of User Engagement

Janette Lehmann[1], Mounia Lalmas[2], Elad Yom-Tov[3], and Georges Dupret[4]

[1] Universitat Pompeu Fabra Barcelona, Spain
janette.lehmann@gmx.de
[2] Yahoo! Research Barcelona, Spain
mounia@acm.org
[3] Yahoo! Research New York, USA
eladyt@yahoo-inc.com
[4] Yahoo! Labs Sunnyvale, USA
gdupret@yahoo-inc.com

Abstract. Our research goal is to provide a better understanding of how users engage with online services, and how to measure this engagement. We should not speak of one main approach to measure user engagement – e.g. through one fixed set of metrics – because engagement depends on the online services at hand. Instead, we should be talking of models of user engagement. As a first step, we analysed a number of online services, and show that it is possible to derive effectively simple models of user engagement, for example, accounting for user types and temporal aspects. This paper provides initial insights into engagement patterns, allowing for a better understanding of the important characteristics of how users repeatedly interact with a service or group of services.

Keywords: diversity of user engagement, models, user type, temporal aspect.

1 Introduction

User engagement is the quality of the user experience that emphasises the positive aspects of the interaction, and in particular the phenomena associated with being captivated by a web application, and so being motivated to use it. Successful web applications are not just used, they are engaged with; users invest time, attention, and emotion into them. In a world full of choice where the fleeting attention of the user becomes a prime resource, it is essential that technology providers design engaging experiences. So-called *engagement metrics* are commonly used to measure web user engagement. These include, for example, number of unique users, click-through rates, page views, and time spent on a web site. Although these metrics actually measure web usage, they are commonly employed as proxy for online user engagement: the higher and the more frequent the usage, the more engaged the user. Major web sites and online services are compared using these and other similar engagement metrics.

User engagement possesses different characteristics depending on the web application; e.g. how users engage with a mail tool or a news portal is very different.

J. Masthoff et al. (Eds.): UMAP 2012, LNCS 7379, pp. 164–175, 2012.

However, the same engagement metrics are typically used for all types of web application, ignoring the diversity of experiences. In addition, discussion on the "right" engagement metrics is still going on, without any consensus on which metrics to be used to measure which types of engagement. The aim of this paper is to demonstrate the diversity of user engagement, through the identification and the study of *models of user engagement*. To this end, we analysed a large number of online sites, of various types (ranging from news to e-commerce to social media). We first show the diversity of engagement for these sites. To identify models of engagement, we cluster all sites using various criteria (dimensions) of engagement (e.g. user types, temporal aspects). Our results are two-fold. First, we can effectively derive models of user engagement, for which we can associate characteristics of the type of engagement. Second, by using various criteria, we gain different but complementary insights into the types of engagement.

The paper is organised as follows. Section 2 provides related work. Section 3 describes the data and engagement metrics used. Section 4 demonstrates the diversity of user engagement. Section 5 presents the methodology adopted to identify models of user engagement, and the outcomes. Section 6 looks at relationships between models, providing further insights into types of engagement. We finish with our conclusions and thoughts for future work.

2   Related Work

Approaches to measure user engagement can be divided into three main groups: self-reported engagement, cognitive engagement, and online behaviour metrics. In the former group, questionnaires and interviews (e.g. [7,4]) are used to elicit user engagement attributes or to create user reports and to evaluate engagement. They can be carried out within a lab setting, or via on-line mechanisms (including crowd-sourcing). However, these methods have known drawbacks, e.g. reliance on user subjectivity. The second approach uses task-based methods (e.g. dual-task [8], follow-on task), and physiological measures to evaluate the cognitive engagement (e.g. facial expressions, vocal tone, heart rate) using tools such as eye tracking, heart rate monitoring, and mouse tracking [3].

Measures in the second group, although objective, are suitable for measuring only a small number of interaction episodes at close quarters. In contrast, the web-analytics community has been studying user engagement through online behaviour metrics that assess users' depth of engagement with a site. For instance, [5] describes *engagement metrics* that indicate whether or not users consume content slowly and methodically, return to a site, or subscribe to feeds. Widely used metrics include click-through rates, number of page views, time spend on a site, how often users return to a site, number of users, and so on. Only online behaviour metrics are able to collect data from millions of users. Although these metrics cannot explicitly explain why users engage with a service, they act as proxy for online user engagement: the higher and the more frequent the usage, the more engaged the user. Indeed, two millions of users accessing a service daily is a strong indication of a high engagement with that service. Furthermore, by

Table 1. Engagement metrics used in this paper

Metrics	Description
Popularity	(for a given time frame)
#Users	Number of distinct users.
#Visits	Number of visits.
#Clicks	Number of clicks (page views).
Activity	
ClickDepth	Average number of page views per visit.
DwellTimeA	Average time per visit (dwell time).
Loyalty	(for a given time frame)
ActiveDays	Number of days a user visited the site.
ReturnRate	Number of times a user visited the site.
DwellTimeL	Average time a user spend on the site.

varying specific aspects of the service, e.g. navigation structure, content, functionality, and measuring the effect on engagement metrics can provide implicit understanding on why users engage with the service. Finally, although this group of measures is really accounting for "site engagement", we retain the terminology "user engagement" as it is commonly used by the online industries. We look at models of user engagement based on this third group of metrics.

3   Metrics and Interaction Data

Engagement Metrics. The metrics used in this paper are listed in Table 1. As our aim is to identify models of user engagement, we restrict ourselves to a small set of widely reported metrics. We consider three types of engagement metrics, reflecting, *popularity*, *activity*, and *loyalty*. Popularity metrics measure how much a site is used, e.g. total number of users. The higher the number, the more popular the corresponding site. How a site is used is measured with activity metrics, e.g. average number of clicks per visit across all users. Loyalty metrics are concerned with how often users return to a site. An example is the return rate, i.e. average number of times users visited a site[1]. Loyalty and popularity metrics depend on the considered time interval, e.g. number of weeks considered. A highly engaging site is one with a high number of visits (popular), where users spend lots of time (active), and return frequently (loyal). It is however the case, as demonstrated next, that not all sites, whether popular or not, have both active and loyal users, or vice versa. It does not mean that user engagement on such sites is lower; it is simply different. Our conjuncture is that user engagement depends on the site itself.

---

[1] A user can return several times on a site during the same day, hence this metric is different to the number of active days.

Interaction Data. This study required a large number of sites, and a record of user interactions within them. We collected data during July 2011 from a sample of approximately 2M users who gave their consent to provide browsing data through the Yahoo! toolbar. These data are represented as tuples (timestamp, bcookie, url). We restrict ourselves to sites with at least 100 distinct users per month, and within the US. The latter is because studying the engagement of sites across the world requires to account for geographical and cultural differences, which is beyond the scope of the paper. This resulted in 80 sites, encompassing a diverse set of sites and services such as news, weather, movies, mail, etc.

4   Diversity in Engagement

Sites. Figure 1 reports the normalized engagement values for the eight metrics and the 80 sites under study. All original values v_i of metric v are translated into an ordinal scale and then normalized (μ_v is the mean of the ordinal v_i values, and σ_v is the corresponding standard deviation value): $v_i' = (v_i - \mu_v)/\sigma_v$. The average value (ordinal) of an engagement metric becomes then zero. The y-axes in Figure 1 order the sites in terms of number of users (*#Users*). Finally, *MergeUE* is the linear combination of *#Users*, *DwellTimeA*, and *ActiveDays*.

We can see that sites differ widely in terms of their engagement. Some sites are very popular (e.g. news sites) whereas others are visited by small groups of users (e.g. specific interest sites). Visit activity also depends on the sites, e.g. search sites tend to have a much shorter dwell time than sites related to entertainment (e.g. games). Loyalty per site differs as well. Media (news, magazines) and communication (e.g. messenger, mail) have many users returning to them much more regularly, than sites containing information of temporary interests (e.g. buying a car). Loyalty is also influenced by the frequency in which new content is published (e.g. some sites produce new content once per week). Finally, using one metric combining the three types metrics (*MergeUE*) also shows that engagement varies across sites.

Metrics. To show that engagement metrics capture different aspects of a site engagement, we calculate the pair-wise metrics correlations using Kendall tau (τ) rank correlation on the ordinal values. The resulting average intra-group correlation is $\tau = 0.61$, i.e. metrics of the same groups mostly correlate; whereas the average inter-group correlation is $\tau = 0.23$, i.e. metrics from different groups correlate weakly or not at all. This shows that the intuition we followed when we grouped the metrics is confirmed in practice.

The three popularity engagement metrics show similar engagement type for all sites, i.e. high number of users implies high number of visits ($\tau = 0.82$), and vice versa. For the loyalty metrics, high dwell time per user comes from users having more active days ($\tau = 0.66$), and returning regularly on the site ($\tau = 0.62$). The correlation between the two activity metrics is lower ($\tau = 0.33$). There are no correlation between activity and, popularity or loyalty metrics. High popularity does not entail high activity ($\tau = 0.09$). Many site have many

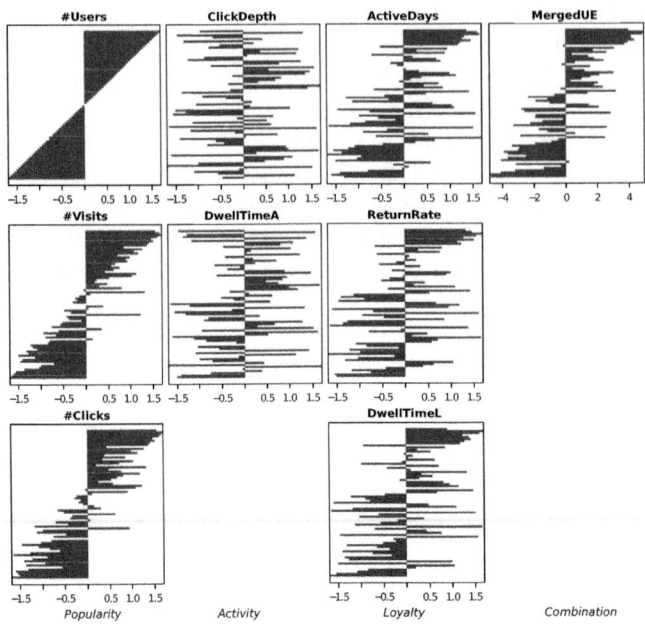

Fig. 1. Normalized engagement values per site (y-axes order sites by #Users)

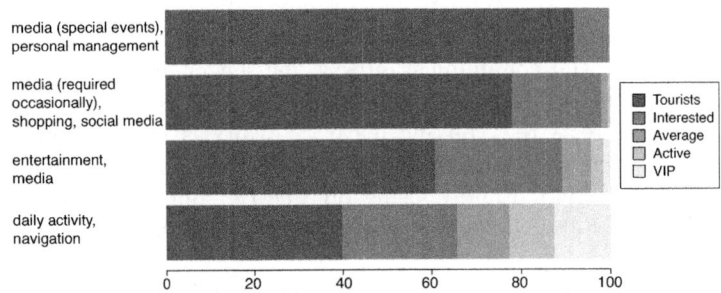

Fig. 2. User groups (Tourists, Interested, Average, Active, VIP)

users spending little time on them; e.g. a search site is one where users come, submit a query, get the result, and if satisfied, leave the site. This results in a low dwell time even though user expectations were entirely met. The same argument hold for a site on Q&A, or a weather site. What matters for such sites is their popularity. Finally, we observe a moderate correlation ($\tau = 0.49$) between loyalty and popularity metrics. This is because popular sites are those to which users return regularly. The same reasoning applies for the other metrics of these two groups.

Users. Studies have shown that users may arrive in a site by accident or through exploration, and simply never return. Other users may visit a site once a month, for example a credit card site to check their balance. On the other hand, sites such as mail may be accessed by many users on a daily basis. We thus looked at how active users are within a month, per site. The number of days a user visited a site over a month is used for this purpose. We create five types of user groups[2]:

Group	Number of days with a visit
Tourists :	1 day
Interested :	2-4 days
Average :	5-8 days
Active :	9-15 days
VIP :	≥ 16 days

The proportion of the user groups for each site is calculated, then sites with similar proportion of user groups are clustered using k-means. Four cluster were detected and the cluster centers calculated. Figure 2 displays the four cluster centers, i.e. the proportion of user groups per cluster. The types of sites in each cluster are shown, as illustration. We observe that the proportion of tourist users is high for all sites. The top cluster has the highest proportion of tourist users; typical sites include special events (e.g. the oscars) or those related to configuration. The second from the top cluster includes sites related to specific information that are occasionally needed; as such they are not visited regularly within a month. The third cluster includes sites related to e-commerce, media, which are used on a regular basis, albeit not daily. Finally, the bottom cluster contains navigation sites (e.g. landing page) and communication sites (e.g. messenger). For these sites, the proportion of VIP users is higher than the proportion of active and average users. The above indicates that the type of users, e.g. tourist vs. VIP, matters when measuring engagement.

Time. Here, we show that depending on the selected time span different types of engagement can be observed. We use #Users to show this. Using the interaction data spanning from February to July 2011, we normalized the number of users per site (#Users) with the total number of users that visited any of the sites on that day. The time series for each site was decomposed into three temporal components: periodic, trend and peak, using local polynomial regression fitting [1]. To detect periodic behaviour we calculated the correlation between the extracted periodic component and the residual between the original time series and the trend component. To detect peaks, the periodic component was removed from the time series and peaks were detected using a running median.

Figure 3 shows graphically the outcomes for four sites (under examples). Possible reasons for a periodic or peak behaviours are given (under influence). Finally, sites for which neither periodic behaviour nor peak were found are given (under counter-example). The engagement pattern can be influenced by external and internal factors. Communication, navigation and social media sites tend to be more "periodically used" than media sites. Access to media sites tends to be

---

[2] The terminology and the range of days is based on our experience in how user engagement is studied in the online industry. For instance, a VIP user is one that comes on average 4 days per week, so we chose the value 16 days within a month.

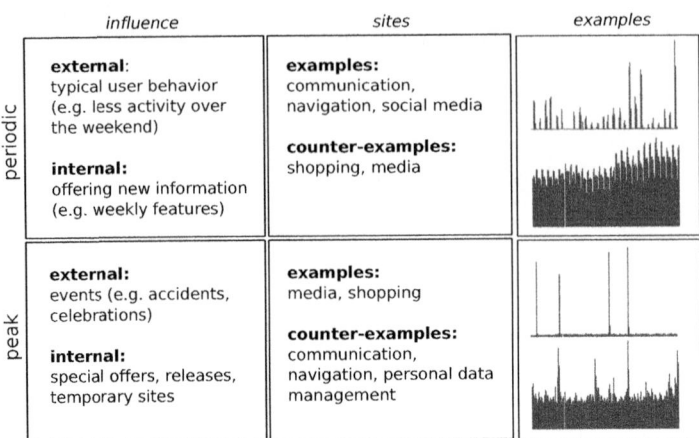

Fig. 3. Engagement over time using #Users (February – July 2011)

influenced by external factors (important news) or the frequency of publishing new information. Interesting is the fact that sites with a periodic behaviour tend to have no peaks and sites with peaks tend not to be periodic. Thus accounting for time is likely to bring important insights when measuring site engagement.

5   Models of User Engagement

The previous section showed differences in site engagement. We study now these differences to identify patterns (models) of user engagement. The base for all studies is a matrix containing data from the 80 sites under study. Each site is represented by eight engagement metrics. A metric can be further split into several dimensions based on user and time combinations. The values of each metric are transformed into an ordinal scale to overcome scaling issues. We clustered the sites using the kernel k-means algorithm [2], with a Kendall *tau* rank correlation kernel [6]. The number of clusters are chosen based on the eigenvalue distribution of the kernel matrix. After clustering, each cluster centroid is computed using the average rank of cluster members (for each metric). To describe the centroids (the models), we refer to the subset of metrics selected based on the correlations between them and the Kruskal-Wallis test with Bonferonni correction, which identifies values of metrics that are statistically significantly different for at least one cluster (compared to the other clusters).

Three sets of models are presented, based on the eight engagement metrics (general), accounting for user groups (user-based), and capturing temporal aspects (time-based). Although all dimensions could be used together to derive one set of models (e.g. using dimensionality reduction to elicit the important characteristics of each model), generating the three sets separately provides clear and focused insights into engagement patterns. When presenting each model, we give

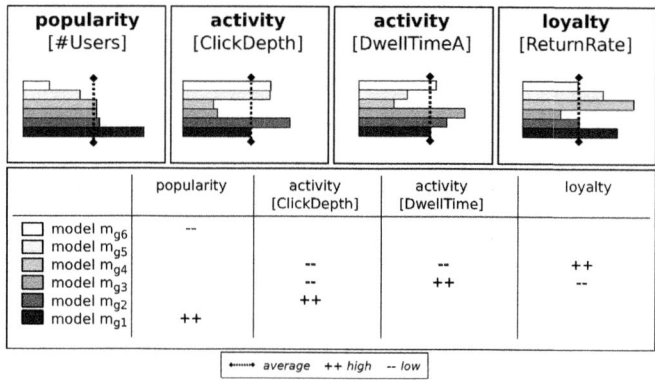

Fig. 4. General models of engagement – Top panels display the cluster (model) centers. Bottom panels provide the corresponding model descriptions.

illustrative examples of the types of sites belonging to them. It is not our aim to explain why each site belongs to which model, and the associated implications.

5.1   General Models

We look at models of user engagement, without accounting for user type or temporal aspect. We refer to them as "general models". Our eight metrics generate six "general" models of user engagement, visualized in Figure 4. As the three popularity metrics exhibit the same effect, only #Users is reported. The same applies for the loyalty metrics, i.e. only *ActiveDays* is reported. The two activity metrics yield different behaviours, hence are both shown.

In **model m_{g1}**, high popularity is the main factor; by contrast, low popularity characterizes **model m_{g6}**. Media sites providing daily news and search sites follow **model m_{g1}**; whereas **model m_{g6}** captures interest-specific sites. The main factor for **model m_{g2}** is a high number of clicks per visit. This model contains e-commerce and configuration (e.g. profile updating) sites, where the main activity is to click. By contrast, **model m_{g3}** describes the engagement of users spending time on the site, but with few click and with low loyalty. The model is followed by domain-specific media sites of periodic nature, which are therefore not often accessed. However when accessed, users spend more time to consume their content[3]. Next, **model m_{g4}** is characterized by highly loyal users, who spend little time and perform few actions. Navigational sites (e.g. front pages) belong to **model m_{g4}**; their role is to direct users to interesting content in other sites, and what matters is that users come regularly to them. Finally, **model m_{g5}** captures sites with no specific engagement patterns.

---

[3] Looking further into this, it seems that the design of such sites (compared to mainstream media sites) leads to such type of engagement, since new content is typically published on their front page. Thus users are not enticed to reach (if any) additional content in these sites. This is the sort of reasoning that becomes possible by looking at models of user engagement, as investigated in this paper.

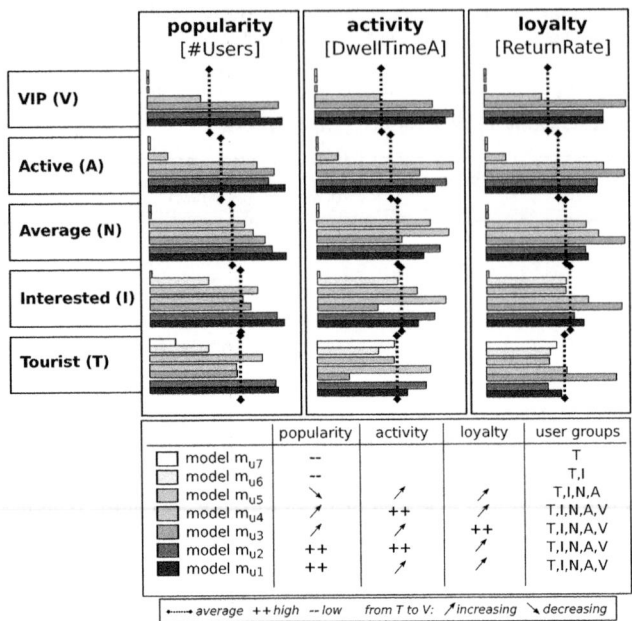

Fig. 5. User-based models of engagement – Top panels display the cluster (model) centers. Bottom panels provide the corresponding model descriptions.

5.2   User-Based Models

We investigate now models of user engagement that account for the five user groups elicited in Section 4. The eight metrics were split, each into five dimensions, one for each user group, i.e. VIP to Tourists. This gives 40 engagement values per site. A site without a particular user group get 0 values for all metrics for that group. We obtain seven "user-based" models (clusters), visualized in Figure 5. We only report the results for one metric of each group (#Users, *DwellTimeA* and *ReturnRate*), as these are sufficient for our discussion.

The first two models, **model m_{u1}** and **model m_{u2}** are characterised by high popularity across all user groups. Activity is high across all user groups for **model m_{u2}**, whereas it increases from Tourist to VIP users for **model m_{u1}**. Finally, both models are characterised by an increase in loyalty from Tourist to VIP users. Popular media sites belong to these models. The next two models, **model m_{u3}** and **model m_{u4}**, exhibit the same increase in popularity from Tourist to VIP users. High loyalty across all groups and an increase in activity from Tourist to VIP users further characterise **model m_{u3}**. Sites falling in this model include navigation pages (e.g. front pages). High activity across all user groups apart for VIP and an increasing loyalty from Tourists to Active users is an important feature of **model m_{u4}**, which typically include game and sport sites. Interestingly, **model m_{u4}** is characterised by a low number of VIP users, compared to the three previous models.

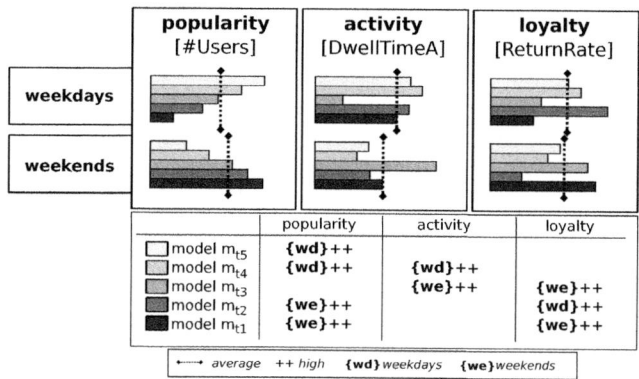

Fig. 6. Time-based models of engagement – Top panels display the cluster (model) centers. Bottom panels provide the corresponding model descriptions.

Third, **model m$_{u5}$** model caters for the engagement of Tourist, Interested and Average users. Loyalty increases going from Tourist to Average users, which makes sense as loyalty is used to determine the user groups. More interestingly is that activity augments the same way, whereas popularity decreases. Shopping and social media sites belong to this model. Finally, **model m$_{u6}$** and **model m$_{u7}$** are concerned with the low engagement (popularity) of Interested and Tourist users, and only Tourist users, respectively. They correspond to sites on very particular interests or of a temporary nature; as such popularity for these two groups of users is low compared to other models. Moreover, **model m$_{u7}$** indicates that when on site, the activity of Tourist users is not negligible. By contrast, **model m$_{u6}$** highlights a higher activity of Interested users than Tourist users.

5.3   Time-Based Models

We look now at models of user engagement that account for the temporal aspect. For simplicity, we consider two time dimensions, *weekdays* and *weekends*. Each site becomes associated with fourteen metrics; seven of our engagement metrics are split into these two time dimensions (*ActiveDays* is not used, as it has a different time span). To elicit the differences in engagement on weekdays vs. weekends, we transformed the absolute engagement values into proportional ones, e.g. the proportional *ReturnRate* is ReturnRate$_{weekdays}$ / (ReturnRate$_{weekdays}$ + ReturnRate$_{weekend}$). The same methodology as that used for the other types of models was then applied. This led to the identification of five "time-based" models of engagement (clusters), shown in Figure 6.

We can see that **model m$_{t1}$** and **model m$_{t2}$** describe sites with high popularity on weekends; loyalty is also high on weekends for **model m$_{t1}$**, whereas it is high on weekdays for **model m$_{t2}$**. Both models characterize sites related to entertainment, weather, shopping and social media. The loyalty in **model m_{t2}** is more significant on weekdays, because it contains sites for daily use, whereas **model m_{t1}** contains sites relating to hobbies and special interests. Second, **model m_{t3}** characterizes sites that are highly active, and to which users return frequently on weekends. Sites following this model include event related media sites (e.g. sport), search and personal data management (e.g. calendar, address book). Finally, **model m_{t4}** and **model m_{t5}** are similar as they both are characterised with high popularity during weekdays, and **model m_{t4}** is further characterised by high activity during weekdays. The models are followed by sites related to daily and particular news and software; **model m_{t4}** exhibits higher activity because it contains sites used for work issues.

6   Relationship between Models

We checked whether the three groups of models describe different engagement aspects of the *same set* of sites or that they are largely unrelated. We calculate the similarity between the three groups using the *Variance of Information*. The outcome is shown in Table 2 (5.61 is the maximal difference). We observe the highest (albeit low) similarity between the general and user-based models. The user- and time-based models differ mostly. Overall, all groups of models are independent i.e. they characterize different if not orthogonal aspects of user engagement, even though the matrices used to generate them are related.

We cannot show here all the relationships between each model of each group. Instead, we discuss two cases. For **model m_{g1}**, a general model characterizing popular sites, 38% of its sites belong to **model m_{u1}** (high popularity and increasing activity and loyalty from tourists to VIP users), and 31% follow **model m_{u5}** (no VIP users, decreasing popularity and increasing activity and loyalty from tourists to active users). We now look at the user-based **model m_{u2}** characterizing sites with high popularity and activity in all user groups and an increasing loyalty from Tourists to VIP users. Sites following this model are split into two time-based models, **model m_{t2}** (50%) (high popularity on weekends and high loyalty on weekdays), and **model m_{t3}** (50%) (high activity and loyalty on weekends). This comparison provides different angles into user engagement, allowing to zoom into particular areas of interests, e.g. further differentiating the "high loyalty" associated with **model m_{u2}** into weekdays vs. weekends.

Table 2. Intersections of the models – cluster similarities

	General	User	Time	(Range [0,5.61])
General	0.00	3.50	4.23	
User	3.50	0.00	4.25	
Time	4.23	4.25	0.00	

7   Conclusions and Future Work

Our aim was to identify models of user engagement. We analysed a large sample of user interaction data on 80 online sites. We characterised user engagement in terms of three families of commonly adopted metrics that reflect different aspects of engagement: popularity, activity and loyalty. We further divided users according to how often they visit a site. Finally, we investigated temporal behavioural differences in engagement. Then using simple approaches (e.g. k-means clustering), we generated three groups of models of user engagement: general, user-based and time-based. This provided us different but complementary insights on user engagement and its diversity. *This research constitutes a first step towards a methodology for deriving a taxonomy of models of user engagement.*

This paper did not study why a site follows one engagement model. However, while analysing our results, we observed that sites of the same type (e.g. mainstream media) do not necessarily belong to the same model(s) of engagement. It would be interesting to understand the reasons for this, e.g. is it the type of content, the structure of the site, etc? Furthermore, other aspects of user engagement should be considered. Accounting for user demographics (e.g. gender, age) and finer-grained temporal aspects (e.g. time of the day) are likely to bring additional and further insights into modelling engagement. Incorporating geographical location will bring perspectives related to culture and language. Finally, we must revisit engagement metrics. Indeed, the description of models often referred to only some of the metrics employed. A major next step will be to map the most appropriate metrics to each model of engagement.

Acknowledgements. Janette Lehmann acknowledges support from the Spanish Ministry of Science through the project TIN2009- 14560-C03-01.

References

1. Cleveland, R.B., Cleveland, W.S., McRae, J.E., Terpenning, I.: A seasonal-trend decomposition procedure based on loss. Journal of Official Statistics 6, 3–73 (1990)
2. Dhillon, I., Guan, Y., Kulis, B.: A unified view of kernel k-means, spectral clustering and graph cuts. Technical report (2004)
3. Huang, J., White, R.W., Dumais, S.T.: No clicks, no problem: using cursor movements to understand and improve search. In: CHI (2011)
4. OBrian, H., Toms, E., Kelloway, K., Kelley, E.: The development and evaluation of a survey to measure user engagement. JASIST 61(1), 50–69 (2010)
5. Peterson, E.T., Carrabis, J.: Measuring the immeasurable: Visitor engagement. Technical report, Web Analytics Demystified (2008)
6. Sabato, S., Yom-Tov, E., Tsherniak, A., Rosset, S.: Analyzing system logs: a new view of what's important. In: USENIX Workshop on Tackling Computer Systems Problems with Machine Learning Techniques (2007)
7. Sauro, J., Dumas, J.S.: Comparison of three one-question, post-task usability questionnaires. In: CHI (2009)
8. Schmutz, P., Heinz, S., Métrailler, Y., Opwis, K.: Cognitive load in ecommerce applications: measurement and effects on user satisfaction. Advances in Human-Computer Interaction, 3:1–3:9 (2009)

Improving the Performance of Unit Critiquing

Monika Mandl and Alexander Felfernig

Institute for Software Technology, Graz University of Technology,
Inffeldgasse 16b, A-8010 Graz, Austria
{monika.mandl,alexander.felfernig}@ist.tugraz.at

Abstract. Conversational recommender systems allow users to learn and adapt their preferences according to concrete examples. Critiquing systems support such a conversational interaction style. Especially unit critiques offer a low cost feedback strategy for users in terms of the needed cognitive effort. In this paper we present an extension of the experience-based unit critiquing algorithm. The development of our new approach, which we call nearest neighbor compatibility critiquing, was aimed at increasing the efficiency of unit critiquing. We combine our new approach with existing critiquing strategies to ensemble-based variations and present the results of an empirical study that aimed at comparing the recommendation efficiency (in terms of the number of critiquing cycles) of ensemble-based solutions with individual critiquing algorithms.

Keywords: Recommender Systems, Conversational Recommendation, Critiquing Systems.

1 Introduction

Critiquing-based recommender systems belong to the group of conversational recommender – users of such systems provide feedback by critiquing attributes of recommended items in a directional way [1]. A major advantage of this feedback strategy is that the user can constrain a particular product attribute without providing a specific value [13]. For example, a user of a holiday recommender might express that she wants to see a holiday package that is *cheaper* than the actual recommendation by critiquing the corresponding price attribute. Research on human decision making has shown that users are rarely able to provide complete and accurate preferences at the beginning of a recommendation session but become aware of latent preferences when recommended products violate them – therefore the feedback can be inconsistent and contradictory [2]. This fact is typically integrated in the incremental refinement of the user preference model (see e. g. [3]).

There exist different approaches to integrate critiquing in a decision support tool. *Unit critiques* operate on a single product attribute in each critiquing cycle and typically facilitate a "more", "less", or "other" type of feedback. *Compound critiques* provide the possibility to critique multiple product attributes during each critiquing cycle [1]. Different knowledge sources are exploited to calculate

J. Masthoff et al. (Eds.): UMAP 2012, LNCS 7379, pp. 176–187, 2012.

such critiques. *Static compound critiques* are generated according to the system's knowledge of the product domain (see e. g. [4]) – the items are equipped with a fixed set of critiques. An example of such a compound critique is the *sportier* critique in the Car Navigator system [4], which implies several changes to the feature set: engine size, acceleration and price are all increased. *Dynamic compound critiques* are generated according to the system's knowledge of the remaining items (see e. g. [5]). Such critiques are a selection of individual feature critiques that represents the differences between the actual recommendation and the remaining items [5]. For example, a user in the PC domain can express that she is interested in a product that is cheaper and equipped with a faster CPU compared to the current recommendation by selecting the corresponding *lower price, faster CPU* compound critique. *Incremental critiquing* [3] extends the dynamic critiquing approach by exploiting previous user critiques to influence future recommendations. Zhang and Pu [6] have introduced an approach where compound critiques are generated according to the system's knowledge of the user's preferences. The calculation of such compound critiques is based on the multi-attribute utility theory (MAUT) [16]. An in-depth discussion of critiquing techniques can be found in [17].

In this paper we focus on improving the efficiency (in terms of critiquing cycles) of unit critiquing. We introduce an extension of the *experience-based unit critiquing approach* developed by McCarthy, Salem, and Smyth [7]. The basic idea of experience-based critiquing is that successful critiquing experiences – critiquing sessions which led to a purchase decision – may imply critiquing patterns that are similar to the current user's critiquing session and therefore might help to short-cut the critiquing process for the current user [7]. Experience-based critiquing systems search for the user with the most similar critiquing history compared to the current user (nearest neighbor) and use the corresponding accepted final item as new recommendation. We adopt this idea and recommend that item in nearest neighbor's critiquing history that best matches the current user's requirements. The new recommendation represents an item that has been presented to a past user with a similar critiquing history but not necessarily the final purchase decision. We call this new approach *nearest neighbor compatibility critiquing*. To further reduce the number of interaction cycles needed to successfully complete a critiquing session, we combine this approach with conventional and experience-based critiquing to corresponding ensemble-based variations.

2   Unit Critiquing Based Recommendation

Research has shown that unit critiques result in significant lower cognitive costs for users compared to compound critiques. The reason for this is that it is more difficult to evaluate and understand compound critiques [1]. Although the usage of compound critiques can result in shorter critiquing sessions users are more willing to apply unit critiques [1]. In the following we will present basic concepts of existing approaches to unit critiquing.

2.1   Conventional Critiquing – Tweaking

One of the earliest systems that deployed the conventional critiquing approach, were the FindMe Systems [12]. In such systems the user critiques are handled as a *"show me more like this, but..."* type of feedback. When the user applies a critique c_i to a recommended item r_i the applied recommendation strategy is to find an item which is compatible with the current user critique c_i and which is maximally similar to the critiqued item r_i. Algorithm 1 shows a simplified version of conventional critiquing. First the algorithm filters out those items that are incompatible with the current user critique and then selects the next recommendation from the remaining cases.

Algorithm 1. Conventional Critiquing

Input:

     – c_u current user's critique
     – CB item catalog
     – r_i actual recommendation

$CB' \leftarrow \{r \in CB \mid satisfies(r, c_u)\}$
$CB' \leftarrow sort\ cases\ in\ CB'\ in\ decreasing\ order\ of\ their\ similarity\ to\ r_i$
$r_i \leftarrow most\ similar\ item\ in\ CB'$
return r_i

2.2   Experience-Based Critiquing

The experience-based critiquing approach [7] is based on the idea of determining recommendations by exploiting information from the critiquing sessions of past users. A user's critiquing session s_u can be defined as a sequence of recommendation critique pairs p_i (see Formulae 1, 2).

$$s_u = \{p_i, ..., p_n\} \tag{1}$$

$$p_i = (r_i, c_i) \tag{2}$$

r_i represents the recommended item in critiquing cycle i and c_i represents the critique that was applied to that item. A critique can be defined as a triple that is composed of the item's attribute f_i that is the focus of the critique, the value v_i of that attribute, and the *type* of the applied critique (typically $<, >, =, <>$, *accept*, where *accept* marks the item as final decision) (see Formula 3).

$$c_i = (f_i, v_i, type) \tag{3}$$

If the user applies a new critique to a recommended item the system typically checks this critique against the critiquing session of the user. If the new critique contradicts or refines an old critique, the old critique is deleted from the critiquing history before the new critique is added [7].

The experience-based critiquing approach [7] exploits information about critiquing experiences of past system users to calculate recommendations for the current user. The algorithm first extracts those previous sessions where the accepted final item is compatible with the current user's critique (see Algorithm 2). These previous user sessions are then ranked according to the similarity of their critiquing history to the (partial) critiquing history of the current user. The session of the top ranked candidate (nearest neighbor) is then used to recommend the corresponding accepted final item to the current user.

Algorithm 2. Experience Based Critiquing

Input:

- c_u current user's critique
- s^u current user's critiquing session
- S^P previous users' critiquing sessions
- r_i actual recommendation
- $r_{p,final}$ accepted final item in session p
- t threshold for number of overlapping critiques

$SP' \leftarrow \{s^p \in S^P \mid satisfies(r_{p,final}, c_u)\}$
$SP' \leftarrow sort\ cases\ in\ SP'\ in\ decreasing\ order\ of\ their\ similarity\ to\ s^u$
$s_i \leftarrow session\ with\ highest\ similarity\ in\ SP' > t$
$r_i \leftarrow r_{p,final}\ in\ s_i$
return r_i

After this introduction to the basic unit critiquing strategies, we will now focus on our new approach – nearest neighbor compatibility critiquing.

3   Algorithm: Nearest Neighbor Compatibility Critiquing

The incremental critiquing approach [3] extends the ideas of conventional critiquing. The algorithm focuses on finding an item that is compatible with the current user critique and satisfies most of the user's previous critiques in the critiquing history. We combine this approach with the ideas of experience-based critiquing [7] and exploit previous users' critiquing experiences to find that item in nearest neighbor's critiquing history that best matches the current user requirements. For each item that was critiqued in the nearest neighbor's critiquing session we calculate a compatibility score for the user's critiquing history. That item in the nearest neighbor's critiquing history that satisfies the actual user critique and that has the highest compatibility score will serve as recommendation to the current user. We denote this new approach *Nearest Neighbor*

Compatibility Critiquing. In Algorithm 3 the basic steps of this critiquing approach are shown[1]. Note that in the case that there is no relevant item to recommend, then we revert to conventional critiquing.

Algorithm 3. Nearest Neighbor Compatibility Critiquing

Input:

- c_u current user's critique
- s^u current user's critiquing session
- S^P previous users' critiquing sessions
- CS compatibility scores for items
- r_i actual recommendation
- t threshold for number of overlapping critiques

$SP' \leftarrow$ *sort cases in S^P in decreasing order of their similarity to s^u*
$s_i \leftarrow$ *session with highest similarity in $SP' > t$*
for each critique c_i **in** s^u **do**
   for each recommendation r_i **in** s_i **do**
      if $satisfies(r_i, c_i)$ **then**
         $CS \leftarrow updateCompatibilityScore(CS, r_i)$
      end if
   end for
end for
$CS' \leftarrow \{r \in CS \mid satisfies(r_i, c_u)\}$
$r_i \leftarrow$ *item with highest compatibility score in CS'*
return r_i

A simple example for the application of *nearest neighbor compatibility critiquing* is the following. Table 1 contains six products (digital cameras). Table 2 contains three successful critiquing sessions s_1, s_2, and s_3 from previous users. Let us assume that the current user has already applied the critiques $s^u = \{c_0: manufacturer \mathrel{!=} HP, c_1: price > 160, c_2: MPix < 12\}$. The nearest neighbor compatibility critiquing approach will identify session s_2 as the nearest neighbor session for this combination of critiques (the critiques on the attributes *manufacturer* and *MPix* are identical to the critiques in s^u). The next step is to find the item in the critiquing history of the nearest neighbor session that best satisfies the current user's critiques. In the nearest neighbor session s_2 products p1, p2, p3, and p4 were critiqued (see Table 2). p1, p3, and p4 satisfies the currents user's critique on the manufacturer attribute ($c_0: manufacturer \mathrel{!=} HP$), p1, p2, and p4 satisfies the critique on price ($c_1: price > 160$), and p1 and p3 satisfies the critique on the MPix attribute ($c_2: MPix < 12$). Therefore the nearest neighbor compatibility critiquing approach will present *p1* as recommendation since it best satisfies the current user's critiques.

---

[1] Note that in our implementation we used a simple similarity approach, where only direct matches of critiques are considered as similar.

Table 1. Available digital cameras in working example

	price	manufacturer	MPix
p1	170	Canon	10
p2	250	HP	12
p3	150	Canon	8
p4	190	Nikon	12
p5	280	HP	16
p6	160	Nikon	10

4 Ensemble-Based Variation

The basic idea of ensemble-based methods is to combine the results of several recommendation algorithms to improve the overall prediction quality [8]. Research has shown that this approach has the potential to outperform corresponding individual strategies – some of the top-ranked teams in the Netflix competition applied an ensemble based approach [9,10,11].

In the following we will describe our approach to combine different unit critiquing algorithms to an ensemble-based solution in order to reduce the number of critiquing cycles.

Table 2. Example: successful critiquing sessions from previous users

user session	critiqued product	critique
s_1	p3	$c_0=$(price, 150, $>$)
	p1	$c_1=$(manufacturer, Canon, $!=$)
	p4	$c_2=$(MPix, 12, $=$)
	p2	$c_3=$accept
s_2	p2	$c_0=$(manufacturer, HP, $!=$)
	p4	$c_1=$(MPix, 12, $<$)
	p1	$c_2=$(price, 170, $<$)
	p3	$c_3=$accept
s_3	p6	$c_0=$(price, 160, $>$)
	p4	$c_1=$(manufacturer, Nikon, $!-$)
	p2	$c_2=$(MPix, 12, $>$)
	p5	$c_3=$accept
s^u	p5	$c_0=$(manufacturer, HP, $!=$)
	p6	$c_1=$(price, 160, $>$)
	p4	$c_2=$(MPix, 12, $<$)

Identifying an Ensemble-Based Solution. In order to calculate an ensemble-based recommendation we combine *nearest neighbor compatibility critiquing* with *conventional critiquing* [12] and *experience-based critiquing* [7]. We select the k

best-ranked items of each algorithm and weight them according to their ranking positions in the individual algorithm rankings (see Formula 4).

$$ensembleranking_{a_i} = \sum_{i=1}^{n} \sum_{j=1}^{k} itemranking(a_{ij}) * rankingweight(j) \quad (4)$$

In Formula 4, $itemranking(a_{ij})$ specifies the item which is ranked on position j by algorithm i (see Table 3), and $rankingweight(j)$ defines the weight of a specific ranking position j in the result list (see Table 4). E.g., itemranking(2,1) is p3 since p3 has been ranked on position 1 by experience based critiquing, and the weight of ranking position 1 is 100.

Let us assume that the current user s^u has applied the following critique to product $p4$ in the current critiquing cycle: $c_a=\{MPix<12\}$ (see Table 2). *Conventional critiquing* will rank product $p6$ on the first position (see Table 3) since p6 satisfies the user's critique and it is most similar to the critiqued product $p4$. *Experience-based critiquing* will select product $p3$ as top-ranked since in session s_2 (session with the critiquing history most similar to the current session s^u) p3 has been selected (e.g., purchased) by the user (see Table 2). *Nearest neighbor compatibility critiquing* will calculate $p1$ as best recommendation since it is that item in nearest neighbor session s_2 that best matches the current user's critiques.

As shown in Table 5, the product with the highest ensemble-based ranking is product $p3$ which will be used as next recommendation to the current user.

Table 3. Product ranking of individual critiquing algorithms

	ranking		
algorithm	**1**	**2**	**3**
conventional critiquing	p6	p1	p3
experience-based critiquing	p3	-	-
nearest neighbor compatibility critiquing	p1	p3	-

Table 4. Weights of ranking positions

ranking position	1	2	3
weight of ranking	100	10	1

For our evaluation we combine the individual algorithms to 3 ensemble-based variations (see Table 6): *variation 1* assembles *conventional* with *experience-based critiquing*, *variation 2* assembles *conventional* with *nearest neighbor compatibility critiquing*, and *variation 3* includes all three algorithms.

Table 5. Ensemble-based ranking of possible recommendations in the next critiquing cycle

product	overall rating
p1	1*100+1*10 + 0*1= 110
p2	0*100+0*10 + 0*1= 0
p3	1*100+1*10 + 1*1= **111**
p4	0*100+0*10 + 0*1− 0
p5	0*100+0*10 + 0*1= 0
p6	1*100+0*10 + 0*1= 100

Table 6. Ensemble based variations

	conventional	experience-based	nearest neighbor compatibility
Variation 1	x	x	
Variation 2	x		x
Variation 3	x	x	x

5 Evaluation

In our evaluation we compare the ensemble-based solutions with the performance of the individual critiquing algorithms. We will use the well-known *Travel* dataset (available from http://www.ai-cbr.org/), that consists of over 1000 vacation cases. Each case is described in terms of 9 features – 6 nominal, and 3 numeric features – including *Price, Region, Transportation, Hotel*. On the basis of this dataset, we performed an offline experiment which follows the leave-one-out approach described by e.g. McCarthy, Salem, and Smyth [7]. In this evaluation method each case in the item case base (the Travel dataset) is temporarily removed and used as *target* of a critiquing session. A critiquing session consists of two steps: In the first step the target case is extracted from the dataset and a random subset of five of the target item's features are taken to form the initial query that represents the user requirements. This query is used to find the first recommendation among the remaining cases in the case base – that item that best matches the user requirements. In the second step the target item is included in the case base again. In order to simulate a user critique we randomly select one of the nine features of the vacation cases that serves as focus attribute to critique. For each recommended case a critique is generated that is compatible with the target item. For example, if the current recommended holiday has a duration of 7 days and the target holiday has a duration of 14 days, a "*more*" critique is applied. The critiquing session terminates when the target item is selected as recommendation. Therefore the *number of critiquing cycles* that were needed until the target item was recommended serves as performance measure to compare the different critiquing strategies.

Experience-based critiquing as well as *nearest neighbor compatibility critiquing* reuse past critiquing sessions to calculate recommendations for the current user.

For this purpose we use the critiquing sessions generated with the *conventional critiquing* algorithm. We generated three different initial queries for the 1024 travel cases in the dataset and applied the resulting critiquing sessions as a session case base for the experience-based and nearest neighbor compatibility critiquing techniques.

6   Results

For our evaluation we recorded the number of critiquing cycles (session length) needed until the target item was recommended and averaged these results for each algorithm. Therefore the key performance measure is the *average number of critiquing cycles* (see Figures 1, and 2).

An average critiquing session where the conventional critiquing algorithm is used requires 42 critiquing cycles to recommend the target item (see Figure 1). As mentioned by McCarthy, Salem, and Smyth [7] for the experience-based approach the impact of the threshold value t (specifies the minimum amount of overlapping critiques) has a strong impact on the performance results of the algorithm. In our setting we found that the experience-based approach performed best with $t=8$ (critiquing sessions must have at least three overlapping critiques). This agrees with the findings of McCarthy, Salem, and Smyth who indicate that thresholds of 8 and greater can lead to shorter average session lengths compared to conventional critiquing [7]. Correspondingly, the performance of the nearest neighbor compatibility approach also depends on the selection of an appropriate threshold. Figure 1 exemplifies the results with threshold values 8 for the experience-based and the nearest neighbor compatibility approaches. With the experience-based algorithm 33 cycles, and with the nearest neighbor compatibility approach 28 cycles are needed on average. Our strategy to recommend that item that was of interest for the nearest neighbor user but not necessarily the user's final purchase decision can lead to better recommendations for the current user. Since our results are based on artificially generated data they have to be considered as preliminary and need to be verified in an online experiment with real users. But as McCarthy, Salem, and Smyth [7] point out, exploiting the information of past users' critiquing history can be promising in the field of critiquing systems, leading to less effort for users to find their target item.

The results of the ensemble-based variations are illustrated in Figure 2. If two algorithms are combined to calculate an ensemble-based recommendation the number of critiquing cycles can be reduced – variation 1, where conventional critiquing is combined with experience based critiquing, shows a similar performance as our nearest neighbor compatibility approach (28 cycles are needed on average until the target item is recommended). Variation 2 – the combination of conventional and nearest neighbor compatibility critiquing – shows the best performance of the ensemble-based variations (25 cycles are needed on average until the target item is recommended). Variation 3 – the combination of all three individual algorithms – cannot take advantage of the item candidates recommended by the individual algorithms. This variation requires on average 31 critiquing cycles to recommend the target item.

An in-depth analysis of these results, to see how the individual algorithms move towards the target item and therefore influences the ensemble-based solution, lies within future work.

7   Related Work

Conversational recommender systems help users to quickly navigate to suitable products in the product space by supporting an incremental construction of user preferences [12],[4]. Different strategies for capturing user feedback on recommended items have been explored, which can be categorized in four types: value elicitation, tweaking/critiquing, preference-based, and ratings-based feedback (see e.g. [14]). We set the focus of our paper on critiquing-based recommender systems. In such systems users provide feedback by critiquing particular product attributes of a presented recommendation in a directional way.

The simplest form of critiquing is *unit critiquing*, where users can constrain one single product attribute in each recommendation cycle. In the first systems that implemented this approach (e.g. the *FindMe* systems [12]) the response to a user critique was to recommend a new item, that is compatible with the actual critique and that is maximally similar to the critiqued item. While this approach works well in domains that are reasonably sparse it can lead to protracted critiquing sessions in domains that are dense since critiques lead to relatively minor changes in the quantity of item attributes, which means that new recommendations are not really very different from the critiqued product [15]. To overcome this problem, and to make larger jumps in the product space, the concept of *compound critiques* has been introduced, that provides the possibility to critique multiple features within a single critiquing cycle (see e. g. [4],[5],[6]). Research has shown that compound

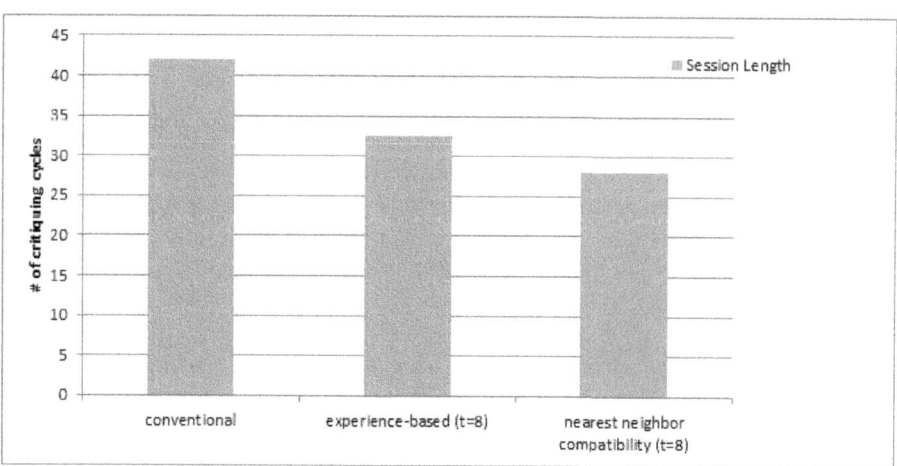

Fig. 1. Evaluation results for the individual algorithms – average session lenghts (# critiquing cycles) recorded for each of the algorithms

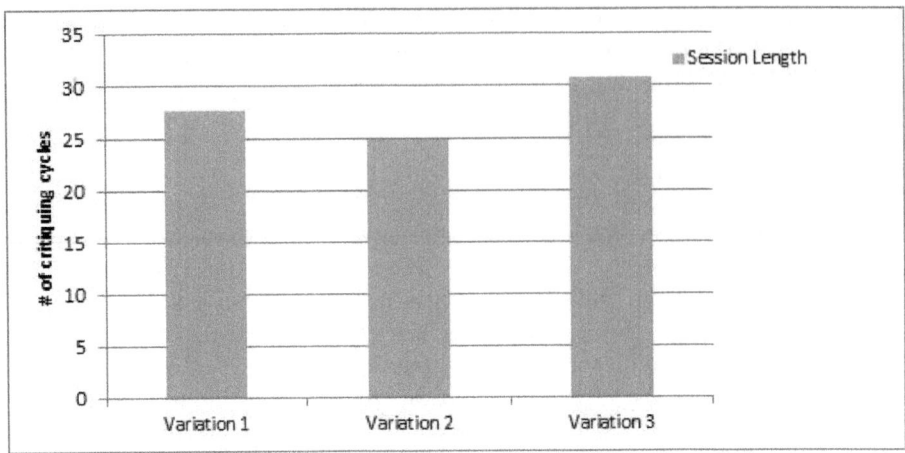

Fig. 2. Evaluation results for the ensemble-based variations – average session lengths (# critiquing cycles) recorded for each of the algorithms

critiques have the potential to outperform the unit critiquing technique in terms of less critiquing cycles, but the application of compound critiques significantly increases the cognitive load for the user [1].

McCarthy, Salem, and Smyth [7] introduced a new approach to improve the efficiency of unit critiquing. They exploit critiquing experiences of past system users to calculate recommendations for the current user (*experience-based unit critiquing*). We adopted the idea of McCarthy et al. [7] and introduced a new approach (*nearest neighbor compatibility critiquing*) to item selection which can potentially reduce critiquing session length. In addition, we introduced the concept of ensemble-based critiquing which has to potential to further reduce the number of needed critiquing cycles.

8 Conclusion

In this paper we introduced a new unit critiquing based approach which exploits the information of successfully completed critiquing sessions to identify an item from a nearest neighbor critiquing history that best matches the current user's critiques. We combined our nearest neighbor compatibility approach with the conventional critiquing algorithm [12] and the experience-based approach [7] to ensemble-based critiquing variations and conducted an offline experiment to compare the performance of the different critiquing algorithms. The results of our experiment indicate that our new nearest neighbor compatibility critiquing approach as well as ensemble-based variations thereof have the potential to reduce the number of critiquing cycles in critiquing sessions.

Acknowledgments. The work presented in this paper has been conducted within the scope of the research projects IntelliReq(829626) and Casa Vecchia (825889) funded by the Austrian Research Promotion Agency.

References

1. McCarthy, K., McGinty, L., Smyth, B.: Dynamic Critiquing: An Analysis of Cognitive Load. In: Proceedings of the 16th Irish Conference on Artificial Intelligence and Cognitive Science, pp. 19–28 (2005)
2. Reilly, J., Zhang, J., McGinty, L., Pu, P., Smyth, B.: Evaluating compound critiquing recommenders: a real-user study. In: Proceedings of the 8th ACM Conference on Electronic Commerce, pp. 114–123 (2007)
3. Reilly, J., McCarthy, K., McGinty, L., Smyth, B.: Incremental Critiquing. In: Research and Development in Intelligent Systems XXI, pp. 101–114 (2005)
4. Burke, R.D., Hammond, K.J., Young, B.C.: The FindMe Approach to Assisted Browsing. IEEE Expert, 32–40 (1997)
5. McCarthy, K., Reilly, J., McGinty, L., Smyth, B.: On the Dynamic Generation of Compound Critiques in Conversational Recommender Systems. In: De Bra, P.M.E., Nejdl, W. (eds.) AH 2004. LNCS, vol. 3137, pp. 176–184. Springer, Heidelberg (2004)
6. Zhang, J., Pu, P.: A Comparative Study of Compound Critique Generation in Conversational Recommender Systems. In: Wade, V.P., Ashman, H., Smyth, B. (eds.) AH 2006. LNCS, vol. 4018, pp. 234–243. Springer, Heidelberg (2006)
7. McCarthy, K., Salem, Y., Smyth, B.: Experience-Based Critiquing: Reusing Critiquing Experiences to Improve Conversational Recommendation. In: Bichindaritz, I., Montani, S. (eds.) ICCBR 2010. LNCS, vol. 6176, pp. 480–494. Springer, Heidelberg (2010)
8. Rokach, L.: Taxonomy for characterizing ensemble methods in classification tasks: A review and annotated bibliography. Computational Statistics & Data Analysis (2009) (in press, corrected proof)
9. Bell, R.M., Koren, Y., Volinsky, C.: The BellKor solution to the Netflix Prize (2007)
10. Piotte, M., Chabbert, M.: The Pragmatic Theory Solution to the Netflix Grand Prize. Netflix Prize Documentation (2009)
11. Töscher, A., Jahrer, M.: The BigChaos Solution to the Netflix Prize 2008 (2008)
12. Burke, R.D., Hammond, K.J., Young, B.C.: Knowledge-Based Navigation of Complex Information Spaces. In: AAAI/IAAI, vol. 1, pp. 462–468 (1996)
13. Salamó, M., Smyth, B., McCarthy, K., Reilly, J., McGinty, L.: Reducing critiquing repetition in conversational recommendation. In: Proceedings of the IJCAI 2005 Workshop on Multi-Agent Information Retrieval and Recommender Systems, pp. 55–61 (2005)
14. Smyth, B., McGinty, L.: An Analysis of Feedback Strategies in Conversational Recommender Systems. In: Proceedings of the Fourteenth National Conference on Artificial Intelligence and Cognitive Science (AICS 2003), pp. 211–216 (2003)
15. Burke, R.D.: Interactive Critiquing for Catalog Navigation in E-Commerce. Artificial Intelligence Review 18, 245–267 (2002)
16. Keeney, R.L., Raiffa, H.: Decisions with Multiple Objectives: Preferences and Value Tradeoffs. John Wiley & Sons, New York (1976)
17. Chen, L., Pu, P.: Critiquing-based recommenders: survey and emerging trends. In: User Modeling and User-Adapted Interaction, pp. 1–26 (2011)

Enhanced Semantic TV-Show Representation for Personalized Electronic Program Guides

Cataldo Musto[1], Fedelucio Narducci[1], Pasquale Lops[1],
Giovanni Semeraro[1], Marco de Gemmis[1],
Mauro Barbieri[2], Jan Korst[2], Verus Pronk[2], and Ramon Clout[2]

[1] Department of Computer Science, University of Bari "A. Moro", Italy
{cataldomusto,narducci,lops,semeraro,degemmis}@di.uniba.it
[2] Philips Research, Eindhoven, The Netherlands
{mauro.barbieri,jan.korst,verus.pronk,ramon.clout}@philips.com

Abstract. Personalized electronic program guides help users overcome information overload in the TV and video domain by exploiting recommender systems that automatically compile lists of novel and diverse video assets, based on implicitly or explicitly defined user preferences. In this context, we assume that user preferences can be specified by *program genres* (documentary, sports, ...) and that an asset can be labeled by one or more program genres, thus allowing an initial and coarse preselection of potentially interesting assets. As these assets may come from various sources, program genre labels may not be consistent among these sources, or not even be given at all, while we assume that each asset has a possibly short textual description. In this paper, we tackle this problem by considering whether those textual descriptions can be effectively used to automatically retrieve the most related TV shows for a specific program genre. More specifically, we compare a statistical approach called *logistic regression* with an enhanced version of the commonly used vector space model, called *random indexing*, where the latter is extended by means of a negation operator based on quantum logic. We also apply a new feature generation technique based on *explicit semantic analysis* for enriching the textual description associated to a TV show with additional features extracted from Wikipedia.

Keywords: Personalized Electronic Program Guides, Explicit Semantic Analysis, Vector Space Model, Random Indexing, Logistic Regression.

1 Introduction

The world of television has changed dramatically in the last few years. People used to have access to a few tens of television channels. Then, with the advent of digital satellite receivers, these few tens channels became a few hundred channels. More recently, the number of channels has become practically unlimited if we count the billions of videos that websites such as YouTube offer. We have never seen so many options for finding and accessing videos. While having some options is more desirable than having no choice, it is known that having too many choices

J. Masthoff et al. (Eds.): UMAP 2012, LNCS 7379, pp. 188–199, 2012.
© Springer-Verlag Berlin Heidelberg 2012

leads eventually to dissatisfaction [12]. One possible solution to this overload problem is represented by *personalized electronic program guides* (EPGS).

Personalized EPGs help users find relevant (TV and Web) video content by using recommender systems. A possible approach for realizing a personalized EPG [19] is to divide the task into two steps. A first step consisting of a coarse filtering of the available assets in predefined categories, followed by a ranking step based on the application of a recommender system employing a learned user profile specific for each category. For the first filtering step, it is common practice to classify TV shows by labeling them with one or more *program genre* labels, such as *documentary, sports*, etc.

This two-step approach also helps overcoming scalability issues that arise if we want to consider the suitability of each individual asset for each individual user. More specifically, if N is the number of available videos and M is the number of users, we want to avoid that we have to consider each of the $N \cdot M$ combinations in looking for matches.

As digital video asset originate from various sources (e.g. YouTube, broadcast TV, video-on-demand libraries) we may not expect that assets are consistently labelled with one or more program genres. While some sources may not even provide labels, we do expect that each video asset has associated a title and a possibly short textual description.

We believe it makes sense to use program genres as intermediate specification medium to make a first, coarse preselection of potentially interesting assets. In this paper we focus on the problem of automatically mapping the textual descriptions of video assets to program genres. We compare two machine learning methods used to compile a ranked list of TV shows for each program genre. We also investigate how to enrich short textual descriptions with more informative keywords using knowledge automatically extracted from Wikipedia. Our experimental results are obtained on a large collection of TV-show descriptions.

2 Motivating Scenario

This research is carried out in the context of APRICO Solutions, a software company that is part of Philips Electronics (see www.aprico.tv), which develops video recommender and targeting technology, primarily for the broadcast and Internet industries. The EPG data used in this research is provided by Axel Springer (see www.axelspringer.de), a strategic partner of APRICO Solutions.

One of the concepts developed at APRICO Solutions is the concept of *personal channels*. A user can create a personal channel by selecting a TV show or an Internet video asset as seed. Based on the seed attributes, similar TV shows and Internet videos are automatically selected and aggregated into a playlist that can be viewed as a linear channel next to the traditional broadcast TV channels. The order of the videos in the playlist of a channel is typically based on time of broadcast or relevance of the content to the channel. Users can add and delete programs from the playlist at will. The basic architecture of a personal channel is shown in Figure 1. Each channel has a boolean filter that preselects TV shows

and Internet videos based on the characteristics of the video seed used to create
the channel. The shows that pass the filter are prioritized by a recommender that
learns from the interaction of the user with the channel and through explicit
ratings. Note that in this concept, users are not explicitly modeled, but their
multiple interests and preferences are captured by the multiple personal channels,
each having a dedicated recommender.

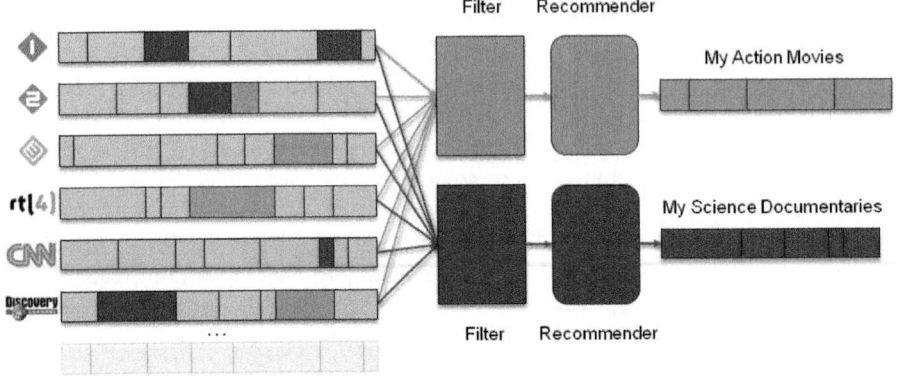

Fig. 1. The personal channel concept

An important attribute used by the boolean filters to preselect shows for a
personal channel is the *program genre*. Examples of program genres are *movie*,
sports, *documentary*, and *TV series*. Given that many video assets do not have
associated an explicit program genre (e.g. videos from Internet video portals),
the problem addressed in this paper is: given a program genre, automatically
retrieve a ranked list of TV shows and Internet videos that match the given
program genre. More formally, we define the problem as follows:

TV-show ranked retrieval task. Given $S = \{s_1, \ldots, s_n\}$ a set of TV-show
descriptions, and given a program genre $p \in P = \{p_1, \ldots, p_m\}$, where P is a set
of program genres, return a ranked list of k TV-show descriptions from S that
best match program genre p.

3 TV-Show Representation Using Explicit Semantic Analysis

A simple and convenient way to represent textual descriptions of TV shows is
called *bag of words* (BOW), in which each item is represented by the set of words
in the text, together with their number of occurrences. In this work we compare the classical BOW representation with an enhanced one (E-BOW) built by
enriching the classical BOW model with additional features automatically extracted from Wikipedia. To this purpose we exploited a technique called *explicit*

semantic analysis (ESA) [11] that allows to represent terms and documents using Wikipedia pages (concepts). In order to describe how ESA works, we assume that each article in Wikipedia is a concept. Given a set of concepts $C_1, C_2, ..., C_n$ and a set of associated documents $d_1, d_2 ..., d_n$ (the Wikipedia articles themselves), we construct a sparse matrix T, called ESA-*matrix*, where each of the n columns corresponds to a concept, and each row corresponds to a term (word). The cell $T[i, j]$ of the matrix represents the TFIDF value of term t_i in document d_j.

After building the ESA-*matrix*, for each term we are able to extract its *semantic interpretation vector* that is the corresponding row in the ESA-*matrix*. A *semantic interpretation vector* for a text fragment (i.e. a sentence, a BOW, an entire document) is obtained by computing the centroid (average vector) of all the *semantic interpretation vectors* related to the terms occurring in that specific text fragment.

ESA is exploited to generate the E-BOW by adding new features to the original TV-show textual descriptions. As the TV-show descriptions in our dataset are in German, we processed the German Wikipedia dump released on October 13th, 2010 (approximately 7.5 GB). After the processing step and the application of the heuristics described in [11] in order to narrow the number of terms and Wikipedia articles in the ESA-*matrix*, we obtained a matrix with 814,013 rows (terms) and 484,218 columns (Wikipedia articles). The input of the feature generation step is the whole BOW considered as a unique text fragment. We adopt this strategy because TV-show descriptions are quite short, and it is difficult to split the text in several fragments (i.e sentence, paragraph, etc.). For each term in the BOW, the corresponding vector from the ESA-*matrix* is extracted, and the centroid of all those vectors is computed. The final step consists in selecting the most important Wikipedia concepts from the centroid vector (those with a higher weight) for adding to the original BOW. The new E-BOW is composed by the keywords in the BOW and the new generated features (Wikipedia concepts) extracted by the centroid vector.

Figure 2 provides an example of a set of features generated for a TV show belonging to the *sports* program genre titled *Rad an Rad - Die besten Duelle der MotoGP (Wheel to wheel - The best duels in the MotoGP)*. We can observe that new concepts related to MotoGP motorcyclists (*Valentino Rossi, Max Biaggi, Shin'ya Nakano, Loris Capirossi*), MotoGP competitions (*großer preis von italien - Italian motorcycle Grand Prix, großer preis von malaysia - Malaysia motorclycle Grand Prix*, etc.), and other generic concepts such as *motogp* have been introduced. Hence, the idea behind the feature generation process is to introduce new concepts allowing an easier identification of the right program genre for a specific TV show. In a recommendation scenario, that representation has several advantages. First of all, representing user interests in terms of (comprehensible) Wikipedia articles allows obtaining a more *transparent* user profile. Furthermore, *serendipitous* (unexpected) recommendations may also be produced: in the previous example the Wikipedia concept *scuderia ferrari* is not directly related to the analyzed TV show (see Figure 2), but it might be interesting for the user.

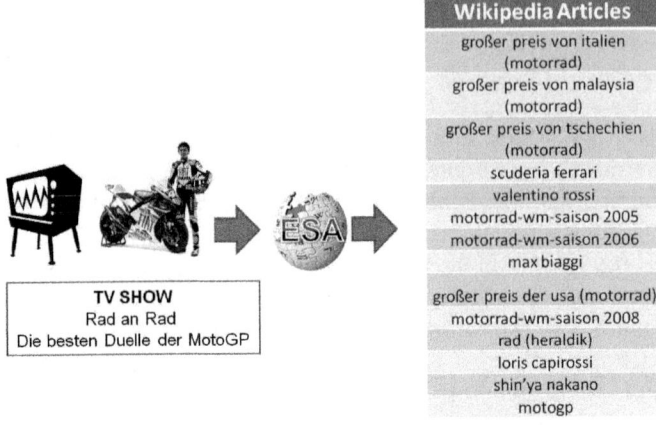

Fig. 2. An example of enrichment by ESA

4   TV-Show Ranked Retrieval

We investigate the application of two different machine learning approaches for the task of TV-show ranked retrieval. The first approach is *random indexing* (RI), a strategy which has been shown to be more effective than the classical *vector space model* (VSM) [17] in a recommendation scenario, while the second approach is *logistic regression* (LR), a gold standard in text classification, which has been adapted for the ranked retrieval task.

Random Indexing. RI is an efficient, scalable and incremental technique for dimensionality reduction. It belongs to the class of so-called *distributional models*, which state that the meaning of a word can be inferred by analyzing its use (that is to say, its *distribution*) within a corpus of textual data. By following this approach, we can represent terms and documents as points in a vector space with a considerable reduction of features to describe them. Through this model we can obtain results comparable to other well-known dimensionality reduction methods (such as singular value decomposition, applied in LSA [7]), but with a substantial saving of computational resources. The goal of RI is to shift the classical VSM representation based on a n-dimensional term-document matrix towards a k-dimensional term-context matrix that is more compact and flexible, since the number of contexts (i.e. the *dimension of the matrix*) is not fixed and could be adapted to the requirements of the specific application domain. The context of a term could be a sliding window of a couple of terms that surround it on the left and on the right, a whole sentence, a paragraph, or the whole document. In this work we exploit the simplest formulation we can provide, namely the context of a term is defined as the *whole document* in which it occurs.

The first step consists of reducing the vector space through the RI algorithm. As in the Rocchio classification algorithm [21], a prototype vector is built for each program genre by summing up all the TV-show vectors belonging to that program genre. Given a prototype vector, we compute the cosine similarity with all TV shows to get the list of the best matching TV-show descriptions for a specific program genre. RI has been extended by means of the quantum negation operator in order to model also the negative evidences for program genres, the terms that typically do not occur in descriptions of a given program genre. The negation operator is useful to get the subspace that will contain the items as close as possible to the positive preference (liked program genre) vector and as far as possible from negative one. It has been already shown that the introduction of the negation operator allows obtaining better results [17].

Logistic Regression. LR is a supervised learning method able to analyze data and recognize patterns. It can be applied in cases where the dependent variable we want to predict can have as value 0 or 1 (i.e., a TV show belongs or does not belong to a specific program genre). The learned model represents the examples as points in a multidimensional space and a logistic function is learned for each class. A logistic function is represented by a sigmoid curve. LR is used for text classification tasks, achieving similar results to *support vector machines* (SVM) [26]. LR has a good accuracy, is robust, and fully automatic, eliminating the problem of manually tuning parameters. LR produces probabilities as output and is preferred over SVM in those scenarios where this aspect has a high relevance. In this work we use the LIBLINEAR library [10], an open-source library for large-scale linear classification (for datasets with a huge number of features and instances) that supports LR and SVM. Given a program genre p, the TV shows are ranked based on their probability to belong to p and are returned in a ranked list. It is possible that the same TV show belongs to the retrieved list of different program genres, but with a different probability value, and a different position in the ranked list. For example, if we have a documentary about horses and equestrian disciplines, it could belong to the retrieved list of "documentary" as well as "sports".

5   Experimental Evaluation

We carried out two distinct experimental sessions: the goal of the first one is to measure the effectiveness of RI and LR in the ranked retrieval task, while the goal of the second session is to investigate the effectiveness of the feature generation process. The dataset used in the experiments contained a set of 133,579 TV-show descriptions, from a set of 47 broadcast channels in the German language. TV shows have been broadcast between April 2009 and April 2011. We assumed that one program genre is specified for each TV show. A TV-show description has an average length of approximately 42 word occurrences.

We run the whole experimental evaluation through a *k-fold cross validation*, with $k=10$. The dataset has been partitioned into 10 subsets of equal size and 10 different runs have been evaluated, each using a different subset for testing and the rest for training.

In Figure 3 the distribution of the TV shows among all the categories is plotted. The dataset is very unbalanced towards some program genres such as

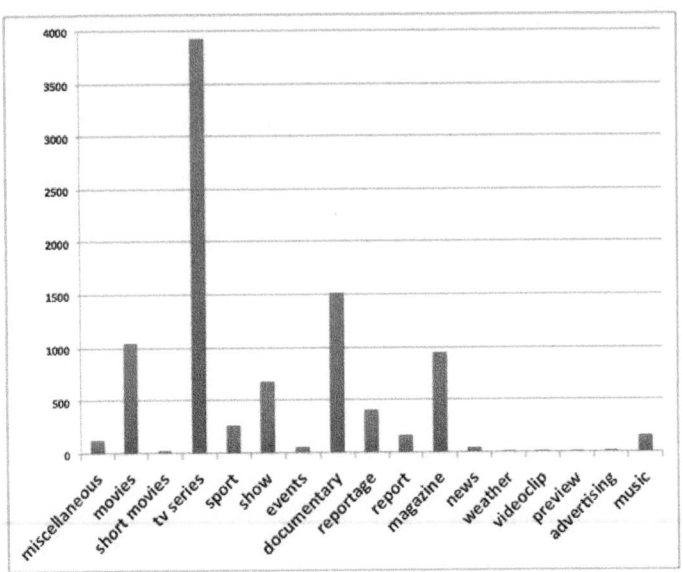

Fig. 3. Distribution of the training examples among the 17 program genres

TV series, movies and *documentary* in comparison to other program genres with a very small number of instances, such as Weather.

We used the precision at $n\%$ with $n = \{5, 10, 25, 50, 75, 100\}$, as metric for evaluating the effectiveness of the proposed model. For a given program genre p, let $L(p)$ be the ranked list of TV shows that are retrieved for program genre p. Let $L(p, n)$ be the *top-n* percent of $L(p)$. Note that the length of $L(p)$ is given by the number of items that actually have program genre p in the given test set. Furthermore, let $C(p, n)$ denote the subset of correctly classified descriptions in $L(p, n)$. Then, the precision at $n\%$, denoted by $P@n\%$ is given by:

$$P@n\% = \frac{|C(p, n)|}{|L(p, n)|} \, . \tag{1}$$

5.1   Experiment 1: Evaluation of the Ranked Retrieval Task

The goal of this experiment is to compare the RI and LR performance for the ranked retrieval task. For RI, we evaluated the performance using different sizes of context vectors (the k parameter in Section 4). More specifically, we evaluated the effect of reducing the dimensionality of vectors representing the TV shows. Indeed, the original size of feature vectors representing TV-show descriptions is $133,579$. In our experiment we considerably reduced the size of those vectors to $500, 1,000, 1,500$ and $2,000$.

Table 1. Results of RI and LR algorithms on the ranked retrieval task ($P@n\%$)

Approach	k	$P@5\%$	$P@10\%$	$P@25\%$	$P@50\%$	$P@75\%$	$P@100\%$
RI	500	0.842	0.791	0.709	0.632	0.578	0.528
RI	1000	0.850	0.802	0.722	0.648	0.591	0.543
RI	1500	0.855	0.806	0.732	0.653	0.599	0.548
RI	2000	0.851	0.810	0.732	0.656	0.600	0.551
LR		**0.920**	**0.903**	**0.884**	**0.864**	**0.820**	**0.747**

Results are depicted in Table 1. It is worth to note that the different size of the context vectors does not affect the performance of the RI algorithm. The most important result is that LR outperforms RI: the larger the number of retrieved items, the larger the gap between the performance of RI and LR. This results confirms that RI is more effective on the retrieving TV shows ranked in the first positions of the list. This is confirmed by observing the loss of performance of RI with an increasing number of retrieved items, as well. On the contrary, LR preserved its accuracy also by considering the whole retrieved list of items ($P@100\%$). We can conclude that LR achieves the best performance, even in the case of large retrieved lists.

5.2   Experiment 2: Evaluation of the Feature Generation Process

In the second experiment we evaluated the impact of the feature generation process described in Section 3 on the performance of the retrieval algorithm. Since LR achieved the best performance in the first evaluation, we decided to run the second evaluation using that algorithm. For each BOW associated to a TV show, we used the ESA-*matrix* to extract the 20, 40 and 60 most related Wikipedia concepts, that we added as new features for enriching the original BOW. Table 2 depicts results of the experiment. It is worth noting that all the configurations using the E-BOW representation outperform the BOW baseline, even though differences between results using 40 or 60 concepts seem to be not statistically significant.

Table 2. Comparison between BOW and enriched BOW ($P@n\%$)

Metric	BOW	E-BOW+20	E-BOW+40	E-BOW+60
$P@5\%$	0.920	0.921	0.941	**0.943**
$P@10\%$	0.903	0.912	0.935	**0.937**
$P@25\%$	0.884	0.902	0.924	**0.927**
$P@50\%$	0.864	0.880	0.901	**0.903**
$P@75\%$	0.820	0.838	0.864	**0.867**
$P@100\%$	0.747	0.764	0.785	**0.786**

Hence, we run the Mann-Whitney Test [20] that, given two sets of observations (obtained by two different approaches) and a single ordering of those results, is able to decide whether the ranked list is achieved by chance or not. We performed the test for each of the following pairs of results by comparing the data points that were obtained in the 10-fold cross validation:

– BOW vs E-BOW+20
– BOW vs E-BOW+40
– BOW vs E-BOW+60

For each level of precision all the results are statistically significant ($p < 0.05$) except the difference between BOW and E-BOW+20 in terms of $Pr@5\%$. We can thus conclude that the ESA-*based* feature generation process allows a better ranking of the most relevant items for each program genre, and this is a very interesting result since in a recommendation scenario a limited number of TV shows is generally suggested.

6   Related Work

The literature in the area of TV recommendation dates back to the 1990s [9]. One of the first attempt in the area of personalized TV that exploits information filtering techniques is presented in [14]. The authors produce a personalized list of TV news according to duration constraint, and solve the problem by an optimization model. Two prototypes were proposed: a category-based system and a keyword-based one. The main differences with respect to our model is that categories are manually assigned to each news, and content was not subjected to any enrichment process. Also in [23], the proposed hybrid personalization techniques produce suggestions according to the program categories a target user has enjoyed in past. In that work a combination of content-based and collaborative recommendation strategies was proposed. However, a problem emerged in that research was the weak diversity of content-based recommendations. The authors proposed a hybrid model for this purpose. To overcome that limitation, in our model we infuse new Wikipedia-based knowledge in the TV-show descriptions.

A collection of research reports on the development of personalized services for Interactive TV is provided in [1], while a thorough overview of current research and trends in the field of personalized TV applications is in [6].

Regarding the dimensionality reduction problem, Berry et al. [4] pointed out the need for dimensionality reduction techniques as a mean to improve the effectiveness and the scalability of VSM. In this context effective techniques for dimensionality reduction such as RI [22] emerged. Semantic vectors[1] is one of the first package [25] implementing a RI algorithm and defining a negation operator based on quantum logic [24]. Some initial investigations about the effectiveness of semantic vectors for retrieval and filtering tasks are reported in [3] and [16], respectively.

---

[1] http://code.google.com/p/semanticvectors/

The use of a semantic representation for TV programs is presented in [5]. The authors propose a hybrid recommender system based on semantic web technologies for addressing the classical problems of both content-based and collaborative approaches. The definition of a semantic similarity between TV shows is an interesting aspect of that work. Structured knowledge represented by means of ontologies was exploited. Conversely, encyclopedic knowledge is used in our research.

Another interesting approach to add semantics to text is proposed in the Wikify! system [15], which has the ability to identify important concepts in a text (keyword extraction), in order to link these concepts to the corresponding Wikipedia pages. The annotations produced by the Wikify! system can be used to automatically enrich documents with references to semantically related information. The Wikify! approach is similar to that implemented by ESA that we used in our work, even though the latter has been effectively used for several tasks, such as text categorization, semantic relatedness and information retrieval. The most recent result is the ESA-*based* retrieval algorithm, called MORAG, which enriches documents and queries with Wikipedia concepts [8]. The authors proved that a feature selection process has a strong impact on the effectiveness of the algorithm. Recently, ESA has been used for automatic music genre classification, in order to represent music samples through a semantic space model [2], while a preliminary work related to the application of ESA in an information filtering scenario is presented in [18].

Recent advances concerning the future of TV are proposed in the NoTube project [13], which aims to demonstrate how semantic web technologies can be used as a tool to connect TV content and the Web through *linked open data,* as part of the wider trend of TV and Web convergence. Semantic representation of digital content is intended to create more intelligent, responsive and personalised applications, in order to filter interesting programmes and advertising. In that project EPG data are linked to semantic entities in the Linked Open Data cloud. As in our work, for a given TV program a set of related Wikipedia concepts are identified. However, the exploited knowledge source is DBpedia, the structured version of Wikipedia.

7 Conclusions and Future Work

In this work we investigated state-of-the-art machine learning methods in the scenario of TV-show retrieval. We compared a statistical method called *logistic regression,* with an incremental and effective technique for dimensionality reduction based on *random indexing.* The motivation behind the choice of these two approaches is that the former is a gold standard in the text categorization area, and the latter is an effective technique for addressing the scalability problem. We also evaluated the impact of a negation operator based on quantum logic that can model in an effective way negative evidence. We investigated the impact of a knowledge-based feature generation process in order to enhance the classical BOW representation and improve the list of interesting items in a personalization scenario. The best learning method in terms of accuracy was LR.

This shows that LR for information retrieval is also effective in situations where text descriptions are very short and where classes may have only few training examples. Furthermore, the Wikipedia-based enrichment process improved the ranking of the retrieved list of TV shows. These results might be efficiently integrated in the platform presented in Section 2, obtaining more accurate personal channels.

In future work, we will investigate the impact of the quantum negation operator to the vector space without any dimensionality reduction and we will try to generalize the results attained by LR, by carrying out an experimental evaluation on videos available in online video repositories such as YouTube. Furthermore, we will adopt an approach where the number of generated features depends on the text length. Finally, the presented model considers only the user preferences expressed in terms of one liked program genre. In the future we will merge the list of interesting items belonging to different program genres, allowing to assign a different weight to each one.

References

1. Ardissono, L., Kobsa, A., Maybury, M.: Personalized Digital Television: Targeting Programs to Individual Viewers. Human-Computer Interaction Series, vol. 6. Kluwer Academic Publishers, Norwell (2004)
2. Aryafar, K., Shokoufandeh, A.: Music genre classification using explicit semantic analysis. In: Proceedings of the 1st International ACM Workshop on Music Information Retrieval with User-centered and Multimodal Strategies, MIRUM 2011, pp. 33–38. ACM, New York (2011)
3. Basile, P., Caputo, A., Semeraro, G.: Semantic vectors: an information retrieval scenario. In: Proceedings of the 1st Italian Information Retrieval (IIR) Workshop, Padua, Italy, January 27-28. CEUR Workshop Proceedings. CEUR-WS.org (2010)
4. Berry, M.W., Drmac, Z., Jessup, E.R.: Matrices, Vector Spaces and Information Retrieval. SIAM Review 41(2), 335–362 (1999)
5. Blanco-Fernández, Y., Arias, J.J.P., Gil-Solla, A., Cabrer, M.R., Nores, M.L., Duque, J.G., Vilas, A.F., Redondo, R.P.D., Muñoz, J.B.: Avatar: Enhancing the Personalized Television by Semantic Inference. International Journal of Pattern Recognition and Artificial Intelligence 21(2), 397–421 (2007)
6. Chorianopoulos, K.: Personalized and mobile digital TV applications. Multimedia Tools and Applications 36(1-2), 1–10 (2008)
7. Deerwester, S., Dumais, S.T., Furnas, G.W., Landauer, T.K., Harshman, R.: Indexing by latent semantic analysis. JASIS 41(6), 391–407 (1990)
8. Egozi, O., Markovitch, S., Gabrilovich, E.: Concept-based information retrieval using explicit semantic analysis. ACM Transactions on Information Systems 29(2), 1–34 (2011)
9. Ehrmanntraut, M., Härder, T., Wittig, H., Steinmetz, R.: The personal electronic program guide - towards the pre-selection of individual TV programs. In: CIKM, pp. 243–250. ACM (1996)
10. Fan, R.-E., Chang, K.-W., Hsieh, C.-J., Wang, X.-R., Lin, C.-J.: LIBLINEAR: A library for large linear classification. Journal of Machine Learning Research 9, 1871–1874 (2008)

11. Gabrilovich, E., Markovitch, S.: Wikipedia-based semantic interpretation for natural language processing. J. Artif. Intell. Res. (JAIR) 34, 443–498 (2009)
12. Iyengar, S.S., Lepper, M.R.: When choice is demotivating: Can one desire too much of a good thing? Journal of Personality and Social Psychology 79(6), 995–1006 (2000)
13. Nixon, L., Aroyo, L., Miller, L.: NoTube: the television experience enhanced by online social and semantic data. In: 1st International Conference on Consumer Electronics (ICCE 2011) (2011)
14. Merialdo, B., Lee, K.T., Luparello, D., Roudaire, J.: Automatic construction of personalized TV news programs. In: Proceedings of the Seventh ACM International Conference on Multimedia (Part 1), MULTIMEDIA 1999, pp. 323–331. ACM, New York (1999)
15. Mihalcea, R., Csomai, A.: Wikify!: linking documents to encyclopedic knowledge. In: Proceedings of the Sixteenth ACM Conference on Conference on Information and Knowledge Management, CIKM 2007, pp. 233–242. ACM, New York (2007)
16. Musto, C.: Enhanced vector space models for content-based recommender systems. In: Proceedings of the Fourth ACM Conference on Recommender Systems, RecSys 2010, pp. 361–364. ACM, New York (2010)
17. Musto, C., Semeraro, G., Lops, P., de Gemmis, M.: Random Indexing and Negative User Preferences for Enhancing Content-Based Recommender Systems. In: Huemer, C., Setzer, T. (eds.) EC-Web 2011. LNBIP, vol. 85, pp. 270–281. Springer, Heidelberg (2011)
18. Narducci, F., Semeraro, G., Lops, P., de Gemmis, M.: Explicit semantic analysis for enriching content-based user profiles. In: Proceedings of the 2nd Italian Information Retrieval (IIR) Workshop, Milan, Italy, January 27-28. CEUR Workshop Proceedings, vol. 704. CEUR-WS.org (2011)
19. Pronk, V., Korst, J., Barbieri, M., Proidl, A.: Personal television channels: simply zapping through your PVR content. In: Proceedings of the 1st International Workshop on Recommendation-based Industrial Applications, RecSys 2009 (2009)
20. Rice, J.A.: Mathematical Statistics and Data Analysis. Duxbury Press (2006)
21. Rocchio, J.: Relevance Feedback Information Retrieval. In: Salton, G. (ed.) The SMART Retrieval System - Experiments in Automated Document Processing, pp. 313–323. Prentice-Hall, Englewood Cliffs (1971)
22. Sahlgren, M.: An introduction to random indexing. In: Methods and Applications of Semantic Indexing Workshop, TKE 2005 (2005)
23. Smyth, B., Cotter, P.: Personalized electronic program guides for digital TV. AI Magazine 22(2), 89–98 (2001)
24. van Rijsbergen, C.J.: The Geometry of Information Retrieval. Cambridge University Press, Cambridge (2004)
25. Widdows, D.: Orthogonal negation in vector spaces for modelling word-meanings and document retrieval. In: ACL, pp. 136–143 (2003)
26. Zhang, T., Oles, F.J.: Text categorization based on regularized linear classification methods. Information Retrieval 4, 5–31 (2000)

Attention and Selection in Online Choice Tasks

Vidhya Navalpakkam, Ravi Kumar, Lihong Li, and D. Sivakumar

Yahoo! Research, 701 First Ave., Sunnyvale, CA 94089
{nvidhya,ravikumar,lihong,dsiva}@yahoo-inc.com

Abstract. The task of selecting one among several items in a visual display is extremely common in daily life and is executed billions of times every day on the Web. Attention is vital for selection, but the end-to-end process of what draws and sustains attention, and how that influences selection, remains poorly understood. We study this in a complex multi-item selection setting, where participants selected one among eight news articles presented in a grid layout on a screen. By varying the position, saliency, and topic of the news items, we identify the relative importance of these visual and semantic factors in attention and selection. We present a simple model of attention that predicts many key features such as attention shifts and dwell time per item. Potential applications of our findings include optimizing visual displays to drive user attention.

1 Introduction

Selecting one among several items in a visual display is a common task — choosing from a lunch menu, from a wardrobe, at a shopping mall, or online at news, media, and portal Web pages. Since visual attention is, in many contexts, necessary for selection, deciphering the complex process of selection requires understanding what *draws* visual attention, what *sustains* it, and how these factors *influence* the selection. This problem is challenging as the process involves a wide range of factors — from low-level visual factors such as visual saliency and the position of items to high-level semantic factors such as the user's interests or preferences for various items.

This work addresses three basic questions: (1) What is the relative importance of position, saliency, and user interest in drawing and sustaining attention in multi-item selection tasks? (2) How do these factors affect the task of selection? (3) Can simple models predict the distribution of eye gaze, shifts of attention, and dwell?

We perform our study by considering the complex task of selecting one among eight news items to read in a heterogeneous display equipped with an eye-tracker. We find that attention shifts are dominated by visual factors such as position and saliency. Contrary to the hypothesis that semantic factors such as user interest (in the content) would matter most for sustaining attention, we find that position plays a dominant role, with significantly higher dwells at top-left positions than other positions. This could be due to two reasons: first, it may reflect the cultural bias of English readers to read from top to bottom, and left

J. Masthoff et al. (Eds.): UMAP 2012, LNCS 7379, pp. 200–211, 2012.

to right. Second, it may stem from the tendency of Web portals to place the important content on the top-left where the user is more likely to notice. We find that the final selection depends mainly on user interest, followed by position, and attention — specifically how *long* the user attends to an item, but not how *quickly* they attend to it. Thus, our work identifies the relative importance of position, saliency, and user interest in drawing and sustaining attention, and in influencing choice in complex, ecological settings.

Based on our empirical findings, we present simple mathematical models of how attention evolves in processing a collection of items in a selection task. The models are based on Markov processes, where the states correspond to the positions of the items and the transition probabilities are used to capture the attention shifts; we make the latter to be a function of the position and saliency. We show that our models are also able to predict key quantities such as the attention shifts, the number of steps to the first fixation on an item, and the per-item dwell time.

2   Related Work

Past studies have shown that while passively viewing displays or searching for objects in displays, attention is initially drawn to visually salient items (i.e., ones that stand out due to differences in motion, brightness, color, orientation, and other visual features) in the display [21,13,22]. Many models have been proposed to formalize saliency and to predict overt attention (eye fixations) on displays during passive viewing of static scenes and videos [9,1,5,10,17]. Studies have also shown that apart from saliency, which is non-volitional, user-independent, and purely display-driven, attention can be drawn by volitional, goal- and expectation-driven factors such as the user goal [4], prior knowledge of the objects in the world and their relation to the display [6,2], and expectation of positions and visual features that are better aligned with the user goal [19,20,23,15]. While the question of what *draws* attention has been studied in depth, little is known about what *sustains* attention. Furthermore, the role of non-visual, high-level, cognitive, and semantic factors such as user interest in attention is less studied. Finally, although it is intuitively clear that position, saliency, and user interest affect attention, their relative importance in selection tasks is unclear.

Previous models of attention shifts focused on the tasks of passive viewing of static display/videos and for visual search of a target object in a display. These involve saliency models [9,16,1] that shift attention in decreasing order of saliency (deterministic attention-shifting strategy), and information-theoretic models [14] that shift attention to maximize global or local information gain about the search target in the display (probabilistic attention-shifting strategy). In our setting, there is no explicit goal for the user. One may argue that the user is searching for *interesting* items to read, but the visual properties of the search target (position, color, etc.) are not known a priori and multiple (or no) interesting target items might be present. Thus shifting attention to maximize information gain, or in decreasing order of saliency is not applicable to our setting. By proposing that attention shifts are probabilistic and a function of the item's position, saliency, and proximity, our model captures attention shifts and eye visits to items on a per-display basis.

Multi-item selection tasks have been explored in the context of Web search result pages. A goal here is to model selection (clicks) based on the relevance of a search result to the user query and the position at which it appears (e.g., [3]). Related eye-tracking studies reveal a "golden triangle heatmap" [7], which is an attention bias towards the top-left positions in the display. These studies typically involve homogeneous pages: a linear list of textual content related to a specific search query of the user. It is unclear if these findings apply to heterogeneous displays (containing both text and images) and to contexts where the user intent is not explicit.

3 Experiment Setup

This section describes the details of the experimental setup. The eye movements of participants were recorded using an eye-tracking equipment while they engaged in the task of selecting one news item to read from a collection of eight article snippets presented in a 2×4 grid. Each item belonged to a different topic. The user interest in the topics ("uninteresting" to "very interesting") was obtained through a post-study survey. For each participant, the position (top-left to bottom-right) and visual saliency (presence/absence of images accompanying the title) of items were varied systematically across treatments. The actual details of content selection and the treatment generation are given below.

Content Selection. We gathered a set of recent news articles where each article is associated with the actual content and metadata that includes an image, a title, a short snippet, and one of the following ten topics: BUSINESS, EDUCATION, ENTERTAINMENT, HEALTH, POLITICS, RELIGION, SCIENCE, SPORTS, TECHNOLOGY, TRAVEL. We collected over 400 random news articles from Yahoo! News, with at least 30 articles for each of the above topics; the metadata for each of the articles was obtained automatically.

Display Generation. A *treatment* is a rendering of eight articles in a 2×4 grid, where each position in the grid is of the same size. Fig. 1 shows an example treatment. For convenience, we number the eight positions in a treatment as 1 (top-left) through 4 (top-right), and 5 (bottom-left) through 8 (bottom-right). Each position has the title and snippet of the article and optionally, the image associated with the article; the articles are called *items*. Clicking on the title of an article will lead to its full content. Given a desired number $k \in \{0, \ldots, 8\}$ of images, a treatment is generated by the following process: first, eight articles are chosen with the constraint that no topic is represented more than once (but the chosen articles are otherwise uniform among all articles on that topic); second, k of the eight articles are chosen uniformly at random to have their images rendered.

Greece hopes for tourism rebound amid crisis

ATHENS, Greece - Many tourists see Athens as a launching pad for visiting the beaches and cute whitewashed buildings of the Greek islands. And the Aegean archipelago can be a great escape, especially during the nation's current economic crisis.

Thousands protest budget cuts at Calif. colleges

 LONG BEACH. Calif. - More than 10,000 people marched, waved signs and occupied buildings at college campuses across California on Wednesday in a show of opposition to state budget cuts to education that could lead to ...

Colin Powell: Obama blew away the birthers

ORANGEBURG, S.C. - Colin Powell told graduates of South Carolina's premier historically black university that they were graduating during a tumultuous time that saw a royal wedding, a pope's beatification and a U.S. military assault that killed Osama bin Laden, "the worst person on earth."

Calif. woman shows off newly transplanted hand

 LOS ANGELES - For the first time in five years, Emily Fennell has two hands.

Writer Harper Lee denies taking part in memoir

 NEW YORK (AFP) - American writer Harper Lee, who rose to fame a half-century ago with her first and only novel, "To Kill A Mockingbird," denied Thursday that she had agreed to take part in a ...

Apple updates software to fix tracking glitch

 SAN FRANCISCO (Reuters) - Apple Inc on Wednesday released a software update to fix a problem that enabled its mobile devices to collect and store customers' location data, making good on a promise it made last ...

Kvitova upsets Azarenka to take Madrid tennis title

 MADRID (AFP) - Petra Kvitova defeated Victoria Azarenka 7-6 (7/3), 6-4 on Sunday to win the ATP-WTA Madrid Masters women's title and earn herself a place in the top 10 in the world rankings.

Obamas attend baptist church on Easter Sunday

WASHINGTON (AFP) - President Barack Obama and his family marked Easter Sunday by attending a service at an African-American baptist church in Washington, standing to clap the 120-strong choir.

Fig. 1. An example treatment. The positions are numbered from 1 to 8 (top-left to top-right, followed by bottom-left to bottom-right).

Procedure. The users were instructed to pick any item of their choice (from each treatment), read it, and rate it on a three-point scale (uninteresting, interesting, very interesting). The study began with a five-point eye calibration, followed by an introductory set of questions on user demographics (gender, age, education-level, and fluency in English). Following this, each user was subjected to 16 treatments in order. For each treatment, they had to select an item to read (based on its title, snippet, and if present, the image), read its contents and rate it, and move to the next treatment. After the user completes all treatments, a survey was conducted to obtain user interest on each of the ten topics, once again on a three-point scale (uninterested, interested, very interested). We logged all the user activities, in particular, the treatments seen, corresponding eye movements and gaze patterns, the item chosen to be read in each treatment, and the time.

Participants. A total of eighteen users participated in our experiments with informed consent. Users were males and females in the age group 18–50, from different professional backgrounds. All users were familiar with the Internet and browsed the web more than once per week. In the experiments, each participant's eye movement patterns were recorded using Tobii 1750 Eye Tracker (sampling rate 50Hz, 17" monitor, 1024 × 768 display resolution).

4 Experimental Results

4.1 Metrics

We parsed the raw eye tracker data to obtain *fixations* (pauses in eye position) and *saccades* (abrupt changes in eye position). As an output of the user study, we obtained, for each user and each treatment, the *fixation sequence* where each fixation was annotated by its (x, y) screen coordinates, timestamp, the item it belonged to, its position, image presence in the item, whether the item was clicked or not, user interest in the item, and number of images in the treatment.

Then, we computed various metrics for each item:

- *time to first fixation*: the earliest time the item was visited (relative to the start of the treatment);
- *dwell time*: the total amount of time spent looking at an item;
- *number of fixations*: the number of times the eye briefly paused on the item;
- *number of visits*: the number of fixations excluding self-loops where the eye stays on the same item (i.e., successive fixations on an item are collapsed into a single visit);
- *shifts of attention/transitions*: the number of visits to item j from item i;
- *click frequency*: the percentage of clicks that occurred on an item; and
- *time to click*: the time when the click occurred relative to the start of the treatment.

The above metrics were decomposed by position, image presence, and user interest in the item.

In addition, we also computed a *saliency* score for each item. We used a saliency model [8] to compute a measure of how visually different an item is from the remaining items in the display.[1] This model is loosely based on the early visual cortex. It assumes that the brain has an internal model of visual input and attracts attention to deviations from the expectation. This is accomplished by considering the difference between the observed log amplitude spectrum of the display and the expected log amplitude spectrum (averaged over several natural scenes), and the residual log amplitude spectrum is used along with the display's phase spectrum to construct the saliency map. For each treatment, we obtained the screenshot and computed its saliency map. We computed the saliency score at each position (1–8) as the total saliency of pixels at that position normalized by the total saliency of pixels in the entire treatment.

4.2   Results

Analysis of the eye movement patterns reveals the influence of each factor — position, saliency, and user interest — on attracting attention (measured by time to first fixation), sustaining attention (measured by dwell time), and in generating selections (measured by click frequency). The statistics are summarized in Fig. 2, and explained in more detail below.

Attracting and Sustaining Attention. In attracting users' attention, measured by the time taken to first fixate the item, position plays a stronger role than saliency, and user interest plays essentially no role (Fig. 2, first column).

---

[1] There are several saliency models based on neurobiology, information theory, natural scene statistics, and deviation from expectation. They yield similar performance for our displays. We chose the model of Hou and Zhang [8] for its computational simplicity.

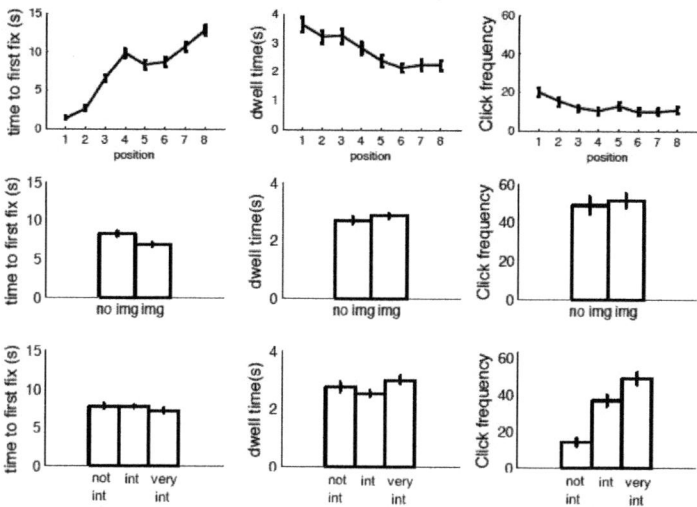

Fig. 2. Data summary. The effect of position, saliency, and interest on time to first fixation (first column), dwell (second column), and clicks (third column).

Attention is drawn to the top-left position 89% sooner on average than the bottom-right position (1.4 ± 0.2s vs. 12.8 ± 0.7s; $t(485) = -16.7, p < 10^{-12}$). In comparison, items with images draw attention only 17% sooner on average than items without images (6.8 ± 0.25s vs. 8.2 ± 0.3s; $t(1754) = 3.3, p < 10^{-4}$).

Although one would expect user interest to dominate sustained attention, our analysis reveals that position plays a stronger role than user interest in sustaining attention (Fig. 2, second column). Top-left positions have 57% ($t(568) = 4.6; p < 10^{-6}$) longer dwells on average compared to bottom-right positions. User interest improves dwell only by 9%, with slightly longer dwells for items reported to be "very interesting" compared to "uninteresting". Finally, image presence does not affect dwell (one-way ANOVA repeated measures, $F(1, 2038) = 0.85, p = 0.36$).

On the flip side, even though position has a strong influence in the onset of attention, saliency can override position bias in all cases, except for the top-left position. For example, an item with an image at position 7 attracts attention almost as early as an item at position 3 without an image: 10 ± 0.9s vs. 8.7 ± 1.2s; $t(137) = -0.93, p = 0.36$. Similarly, position 8 with an image is on par with position 4 without an image: 12.4 ± 1.2s vs. 10.6 ± 1.3s; $t(138) = -1.04, p = 0.30$.

Selection. As expected, selection (i.e., clicks) depend most strongly on user interest, followed by position, and weakly on saliency (Fig. 2, third column). For example, click frequency on "very interesting" items is on average 260% ($t(1345) = 7.1742, p < 10^{-12}$) more than on "uninteresting" items. In comparison, click frequency for the top-left position is only 82% more compared to the bottom-right; and the click frequency gain due to an image presence is still lower at 8% and not significant.

Sustained attention is important for selection — longer dwells are more likely to lead to clicks; namely, $\Pr[\text{click} \mid \text{dwell} > t]$ increases with the time parameter t. For example, click frequency increases by 244% (from 9% to 31%) when dwell increases from less than 5s to 5–10s. Similarly, the median dwell time for clicked items is 200% more than those for unclicked items (3.9s vs. 1.3s), and the dwell distributions for items that were clicked and those that were not clicked are significantly different — the area under ROC curve is 0.79.

5   Predictive Models

We capture the above insights in the form of a mathematical model of how attention evolves in processing a collection of items in a selection task. The model is a discrete-time Markov process [11] with the eight positions of the 2×4 grid as the states; the process is in state $i \in \{1, \ldots, 8\}$ if the user confers visual attention on position i. The initial state distribution π describes the initial focus of user attention, and the state transition probability $P(i, j)$ captures the probability of shifting attention from position i to position j. User attention follows a stochastic process: it starts in some initial state i with probability $\pi(i)$, and then repeatedly switches to another state with probability $P(\cdot, \cdot)$ in a randomized fashion. Since we are interested in studying the shift of attention in different positions, self-loops are avoided in the Markov models; formally, $P(i, i) = 0$ in all our models.

The initial state distribution $\pi(i)$ is intended to capture any biases inherent among users of the system (e.g., top-left bias or centrality bias). It is set to the empirical distribution on various positions observed during the initial one-second duration in our experiments (across all participants and all treatments). Next, proximity, saliency, and position bias are incorporated into the transition probabilities via three specific factors.

5.1   Attention Transition Models

Spatial proximity is incorporated into the Markov process as a factor based on the Gaussian radial basis function:

$$d(i, j) = \exp\left(-\frac{(x_i - x_j)^2/e + (y_i - y_j)^2}{2\sigma^2}\right),$$

where (x_i, y_i) is the coordinate of position i in the 2×4 grid, σ is a scale parameter, and $e > 0$ is an eccentricity parameter. The scale parameter is used to model how fast the transition probabilities decay with greater distances. The eccentricity parameter is used to capture participants' tendency to browse in a row-major or column-major fashion. Thus $e < 1$ implies participants tend to read horizontally, and $e > 1$ the otherwise (vertically).[2]

---

[2] The tendency to browse row-major or column-major can be learned empirically from a subset of the data, but we expect this to be a constant for all sized grid layouts, hence we do not consider it a free parameter.

Position bias is incorporated through a factor $p(i)$, for $i \in \{1, \dots, 8\}$, derived empirically from a subset of the observed data, where $p(i)$ gives the average number of fixations at position i over all user treatments.[3]

Finally, visual saliency is incorporated as a factor $s(i) \in (0, 1)$ for each position $i \in \{1, \dots, 8\}$; this is a score based on a common model of visual saliency [8]. Notice, however, that unlike the proximity factor and the position bias factor, the saliency factor is specific to the treatment.

The above factors result in the following transition probability model:

$$P_{spd}(i, j) \propto s(j)^{\gamma} \cdot p(j) \cdot d(i, j), \tag{1}$$

where $\gamma > 0$ controls the relative importance of saliency in the transition probabilities, compared to proximity and position biases. Since the saliency scores are all between 0 and 1, higher values of γ weaken the effect of saliency. To study the relative contribution of the various factors in model (1), the full model with all factors, and all combinations of the factors $\{s, p, d\}$ were considered. The models are named after the factors they include; for instance, $P_{sp}(i, j) \propto s(j)^{\gamma} \cdot p(j)$.

Finally, in addition to saliency, position, and proximity, an "inhibition of return" memory term [18,12] is incorporated, to avoid revisiting recently visited items. Here, we use a bit vector m to encode the most recently visited cell: $m(j) = 1$ if j is the previous focus of attention and 0 otherwise:

$$P_{spdm}(i, j) \propto s(j)^{\gamma} \cdot p(j) \cdot d(i, j) \cdot (1 - m(j)).$$

5.2 Parameter Fitting

The data was divided into two parts: data from two-thirds of the participants was used for parameter fitting, and data from the remaining one-third was for evaluating how good the fitted parameters are. Parameter estimation was performed on the training set as described below. Predictions were made on the test set, using the best fitting parameters from the training set. For each treatment seen by the user, we simulated the model-predicted fixation sequences for 1000 trials, and computed the likelihood of transitions, visits and dwell as follows. Let $p_{ut}(i, j)$ be the empirical fraction of transitions from position i to j for user u and treatment t, and $\hat{p}_{ut}(i, j)$ be the corresponding model-predicted fraction of transitions. For model M with parameters σ, γ, we computed the likelihood of test data $P(D \mid M, \sigma, \gamma)$ as the expected likelihood of data over all users u and treatments t in the test set; that is

$$\Pr(D \mid M, \sigma, \gamma) = \mathbb{E}_{ut}[\mathbb{E}_{ij}[\hat{p}_{ut}(i, j)]]. \tag{2}$$

Similarly, the likelihood of visits was computed by first finding $p_{ut}(i)$, the empirical fraction of visits at position i for user u and treatment t, and $\hat{p}_{ut}(i)$, the model predicted fraction of visits. Then, Eqn. 2 becomes

---

[3] Alternatively, we could make an assumption that the position bias is focused on the top-left of the display for English readers, and that it decreases linearly as we move to the right or bottom of the display. We would expect similar results in both cases.

$$\Pr(D \mid M, \sigma, \gamma) = \mathbb{E}_{ut}[\mathbb{E}_i[\hat{p}_{ut}(i)]].$$

The likelihood of dwell was computed in a similar fashion, by replacing the fraction of visits at each position in the above equation to the fraction of dwell.

The *spd* model has two free parameters, σ (Gaussian width for proximity calculation) and γ (exponent of saliency). The eccentricity of the ellipse e was a fixed parameter set to 1.4, which is the empirically observed ratio between the number of rightward and vertical saccades. We simulated the *spd* model for various values of $\sigma, \gamma \in \{1/4, 1/3, 1/2, 1, 2, 3, 4\}$. The parameter values that maximized the likelihood of transitions in the training data were chosen as the best fitting parameters. This resulted in $\sigma = 0.5$, and $\gamma = 3$.

5.3   Model Simulations

In this section, we aim at finding simple models that may be used to predict certain key quantities of user behavior.

We first start with the average number of steps it takes for a user to fixate an item for the first time given a display. Note that parameters in the transition models of Section 5.1 can be fit by the procedure described Section 5.2. Here, we ask how consistent these models are with observed data in our user study.

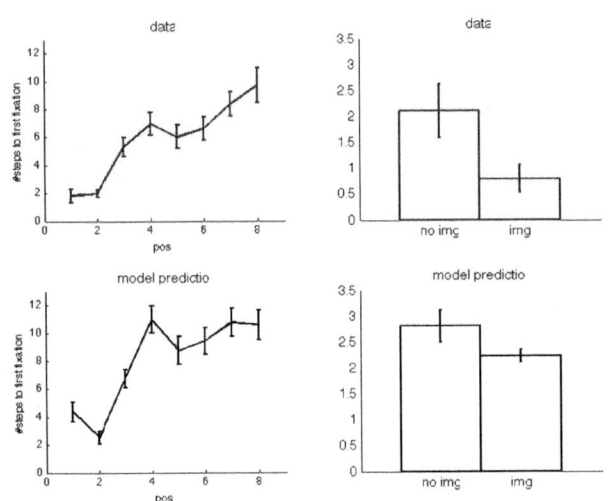

Fig. 3. Comparison between *spd* model prediction and observed number of steps to first fixation. *Left panels:* The model correctly predicts that top-left positions are seen first and the #steps to first fixation increases as we go from left to right, and top to bottom. It also predicts the steeper increase from top-left to top-right positions, and shallower increase from bottom-left to bottom-right positions. *Right panels:* The model correctly predicts that images will be seen earlier than non-images.

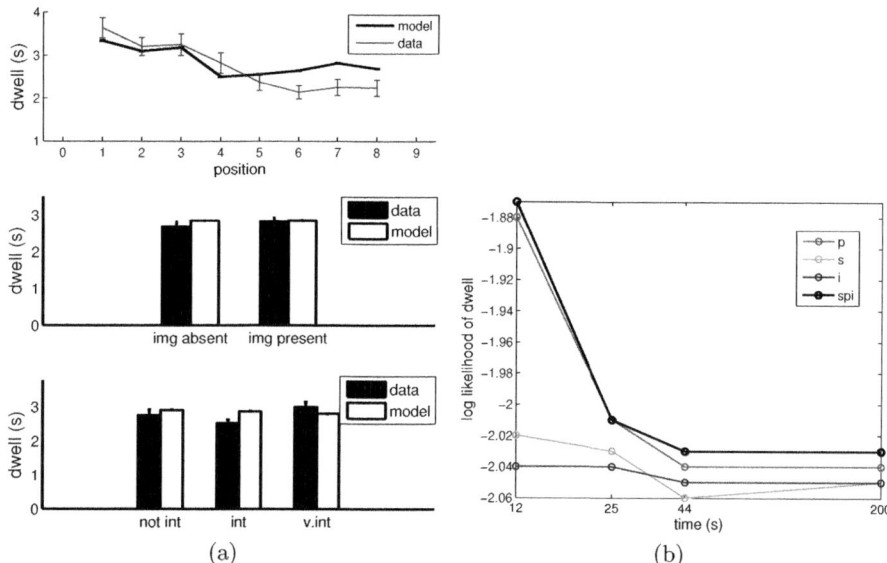

Fig. 4. (a) **Comparison between the linear** *spi* **model prediction and observed dwell.** The model accurately predicts average dwell as a function of position. It also predicts that image presence and user interest do not affect dwell. (b) **Model comparison for predicting dwell per item.** The linear spi model predicts likelihood of dwell better than the baseline and other model variants, over short and long time periods. The performance of the position only model comes close to the spi model, showing that position plays a dominant role in predicting dwell.

Denote by P an arbitrary 8×8 transition matrix of a Markov model, and by π an 8-dimensional row vector containing the initial state occupation distribution. The following steps were used to compute the average first time to fix on position i: we first set the ith row of P to 0 and denote the resulting matrix by P_i; then, the ith component of the vector,

$$\pi \sum_{k-1}^{\infty} k P_i^k = \pi \left(I - P_i \right)^{-2} P_i,$$

will be the average steps to first fixation on i; here, I is the 8×8 identity matrix.

Among the alternatives, the *spd* model is qualitatively accurate in predicting the number of steps to first fixation on an item (Fig. 3). It predicts that images will be seen earlier, which cannot be predicted by models without saliency. It also captures the position bias in the data — that top-left positions will be seen before bottom-right positions. In particular, the model predicts, and the data shows (top panels in Fig. 3), that the increase in the number of steps to first fixation is steeper as we go from top-left to top-right and is shallower as we go from bottom-left to bottom-right.

It is worth noting that although the *spd* model is trained only on a subset of the data and the position bias that it learns is treatment independent, yet it performs well in predicting attention shifts (transitions) and visits on an aggregate basis on the test subset of the data.

Second, we model dwell separately as a linear function of saliency (s), position (p), and interest (i). The parameters of this model (denoted *spi*) are obtained through a linear regression of $\{s, p, i\}$ against the total dwell time per position for various users and treatments in the training data. The resulting parameters are used to predict dwell time for the test data. Fig. 4(a) shows that a linear model predicts dwell on average (as a function of position, image presence, and interest), as well as on a per-treatment basis.

6   Conclusions

In this paper, we studied attention and selection in multi-item setting and identified the relative importance of visual and semantic factors in attention and selection. We also presented a simple model of attention that predicts many key features such as shifts of attention and dwell time per item. Our model was tested on a display with a 2×4 grid layout, but is generalizable and may be used to predict user attention on Web displays with any $m \times n$ grid layout.

These findings advance our understanding of human visual attention in ecological settings, and offer suggestions to improve the design of visual displays to effectively drive user attention, for example, in consumer shopping sites. A simple application of our study is that web content could be personalized by placing the user-relevant content at the top-left positions and including images to make the content both semantically and visually interesting to the user. Other potential applications of our model include display optimization to maximize likelihood of drawing/sustaining user attention.

References

1. Bruce, N., Tsotsos, J.: Saliency based on information maximization. In: NIPS, p. 155 (2006)
2. Chun, M.: Contextual cueing of visual attention. Trends in Cognitive Sciences 4(5), 170–178 (2000)
3. Craswell, N., Zoeter, O., Taylor, M.J., Ramsey, B.: An experimental comparison of click position-bias models. In: WSDM, pp. 87–94 (2008)
4. Egeth, H., Yantis, S.: Visual attention: Control, representation, and time course. Annual Review of Psychology 48(1), 269–297 (1997)
5. Harel, J., Koch, C., Perona, P.: Graph-based visual saliency. In: NIPS, p. 545 (2007)
6. Henderson, J.: Human gaze control during real-world scene perception. Trends in Cognitive Sciences 7(11), 498–504 (2003)
7. Hotchkiss, G., Alston, S., Edwards, G.: Eye tracking study (2005), http://www.enquiroresearch.com/images/eyetracking2-sample.pdf
8. Hou, X., Zhang, L.: Saliency detection: A spectral residual approach. In: CVPR, pp. 1–8 (2007)

9. Itti, L., Koch, C.: Computational modelling of visual attention. Nat. Rev. Neurosci. 2(3), 194–203 (2001)
10. Judd, T., Ehinger, K., Durand, F., Torralba, A.: Learning to predict where humans look. In: ICCV, pp. 2106–2113 (2009)
11. Karlin, S., Taylor, H.M.: A First Course in Stochastic Processes, 2nd edn. Academic Press (1975)
12. Klein, R.: Inhibition of return. Trends in Cognitive Sciences 4(4), 138–147 (2000)
13. Koch, C., Ullman, S.: Shifts in selective visual attention: towards the underlying neural circuitry. Hum. Neurobiol. 4(4), 219–227 (1985)
14. Najemnik, J., Geisler, W.: Optimal eye movement strategies in visual search. Nature 434, 387–391 (2005)
15. Navalpakkam, V., Itti, L.: Search goal tunes visual features optimally. Neuron 53(4), 605–617 (2007)
16. Parkhurst, D., Law, K., Niebur, E.: Modeling the role of salience in the allocation of overt visual attention. Vision Research 42(1), 107–123 (2002)
17. Peters, R., Itti, L.: Applying computational tools to predict gaze direction in interactive visual environments. ACM Trans. Appl. Perception 5(2), 9 (2008)
18. Posner, M., Rafal, R., Choate, L., Vaughan, J.: Inhibition of return: Neural basis and function. Cognitive Neuropsychology (1985)
19. Posner, M., Snyder, C., Davidson, B.: Attention and the detection of signals. Journal of Experimental Psychology: General 109(2), 160 (1980)
20. Torralba, A., Oliva, A., Castelhano, M., Henderson, J.: Contextual guidance of eye movements and attention in real-world scenes: The role of global features in object search. Psychological Review 113(4), 766 (2006)
21. Treisman, A., Gelade, G.: A feature integration theory of attention. Cognitive Psychology 12, 97–136 (1980)
22. Wolfe, J., Horowitz, T.: What attributes guide the deployment of visual attention and how do they do it? Nature Reviews Neuroscience 5(6), 495–501 (2004)
23. Wolfe, J.M.: Guided search 2.0: a revised model of visual search. Psyonomic Bulletin and Review 1(2), 202–238 (1994)

Investigating Explanations to Justify Choice

Ingrid Nunes[1,2], Simon Miles[2], Michael Luck[2], and Carlos J.P. de Lucena[1]

[1] Pontifical Catholic University of Rio de Janeiro - Rio de Janeiro, Brazil
{ionunes,lucena}@inf.puc-rio.br
[2] King's College London, Strand, London, WC2R 2LS, United Kingdom
{simon.miles,michael.luck}@kcl.ac.uk

Abstract. Many different forms of explanation have been proposed for justifying decisions made by automated systems. However, there is no consensus on what constitutes a *good* explanation, or what information these explanations should include. In this paper, we present the results of a study into how people justify their decisions. Analysis of our results allowed us to extract the forms of explanation adopted by users to justify choices, and the situations in which these forms are used. The analysis led to the development of guidelines and patterns for explanations to be generated by automated decision systems. This paper presents the study, its results, and the guidelines and patterns we derived.

Keywords: User Explanation, Guidelines, Patterns, Recommender Systems.

1 Introduction

The popularity of recommender systems has increased significantly in the last decade, with many commercial applications already adopting them. For many years, the main goal of research into such systems has been to improve their *accuracy*, associating this measure with the quality of the recommendation. However, as argued by McNee et. al. [1], the most accurate systems (based on standard metrics) may not be those that provide the most useful recommendations to users. Other aspects, such as trust and transparency, have also been considered, and many of these can be improved by providing users with *explanations* [2]. Such explanations justify the choice of a particular recommendation to users, and their applicability extends to decision support systems [3] and over-constrained problem solvers [4].

There are different existing approaches to generating explanations, from exposing the rationale of the underlying recommendation technique to selecting the essential attributes on which the decision is based. However, there is no consensus on what constitutes a *good* explanation, and what kinds of information must be presented to users in such explanations. Even though existing work [2] provides qualitative arguments that characterise good explanations, there is no extensive research into the kinds of explanation that users expect and need to understand and accept recommendations or decisions made on their behalf and, where work does exist, it is particular to a specific system.

In response, this paper presents a study whose main objective is to give guidance for explanation generation. The study performed consisted of a survey, from whose results we extract types of explanation that people use to justify a choice from a set of available

J. Masthoff et al. (Eds.): UMAP 2012, LNCS 7379, pp. 212–224, 2012.

Table 1. Research questions and their evaluation approach

(a) Research Questions.	(b) Evaluation Approaches.
RQ1. Do users adopt a pattern to justify an option chosen from the set of those available?	**EA1.** Analysis of the arguments given to justify the chosen option and identification of commonalities among arguments given by different users.
RQ2. Is there a relationship between the type of explanation given to support the decision and the chosen option?	**EA2.** Comparison among the arguments given to justify each different chosen option.
RQ3. Do users use a pattern to justify the rejected (not chosen) options?	**EA3.** Analysis of the arguments given to reject options and identification of commonalities among arguments given by different users.
RQ4. Is there a relationship between the type of explanation given to reject options and the rejected or chosen option?	**EA4.** Comparison among arguments given to reject options according to each different chosen and rejected option.

options. As, based on the design of the study, we can assume that the explanations provided by study participants are those that the users would expect to receive, we derive a set of *guidelines* and *patterns*, which are a basis for generating explanations for users as to why particular options are chosen by a recommender system or decision support systems. Therefore, this paper presents three contributions: (i) the design and results of a study into what explanations users expect when justifying choices made; (ii) guidelines for the qualities and forms of explanation needed to best meet user expectations; and (iii) patterns for explanations to be given under different circumstances. The aim of such explanations is to expose to users why a system chose a particular option, thus improving user *satisfaction* and *trust* in the decision.

2   Description

As outlined above, our goal is to identify explanations to be provided to users by recommender systems or automated decision making systems. This section describes our study, including the research questions, procedure and participants. We addressed four research questions, presented in Table 1(a). By answering these questions, we are able to extract patterns for user explanations to be generated by the relevant systems (*RQ1* and *RQ3*), and also the context in which each pattern is adopted (*RQ2* and *RQ4*). These explanations are associated with both chosen and rejected options — the first two questions focus on patterns and their context for explaining the chosen option; and the last two focus on determining why other options were rejected (or not chosen).

2.1   Procedure

Our study consists of collecting information provided by participants through a web-based questionnaire, and its analysis. Our aim is to obtain a high number of participants, so anyone with Internet access could access the questionnaire. The study concerns decision-making and explanation of the decisions made. The choices to be made were between hotels in New York city, a domain chosen because most people are aware of the attributes that characterise hotels; they will have preferences over individual attributes of hotels; New York is a widely known tourist destination, so participants are more likely to have a *known* set of preferences [5]; we have relevant knowledge of the city, so were able to select appropriate options; and there are many New York hotels with available *real data*. The questionnaire was divided into three parts, as follows.

User Data. Our study does not investigate if explanations depend on people's characteristics, such as age or gender. However, we collected some information about the participants in case it was informative, and also to be able to provide demographic information of the participants as a group. The collected participant data is: (i) age; (ii) gender; (iii) location (city and country); and (iv) field of work or study.

Product Choice. Participants are requested to imagine the scenario in which they go to New York on vacation, and must choose a hotel for staying there from a set of options. Hotels are described in terms of attributes associated with hotels and their rooms available at the booking.com website, presented in a table that allows a side-by-side comparison. We took five existing hotels — *Hotel 91*, *Econo Lodge*, *The Hotel at Times Square*, *Comfort Inn*, *Renaissance*, viewing these options as forming three groups (not known to participants), below.

G-1 Dominated Option. Although a dominated option (one that has no advantage and at least one disadvantage with respect to another) is generally not chosen, we add such an option (or at least something close to it) to capture arguments used to reject them. If we ignore small differences in room size, and discount parking price (which typically does not appear in catalogues of features), we can identify one hotel (*Comfort Inn*) dominated by another (*The Hotel at Times Square*) even though *Comfort Inn* actually has better parking price and a slightly better room size than *The Hotel at Times Square*. The assumption (subsequently confirmed by our study) is that most participants focus on the main attributes and ignore small differences, so that *Comfort Inn* is dominated.

G-2 Extreme Options. Extreme options compromise one attribute, e.g. quality, too much in order to improve another, e.g. price. In general, people avoid such options, known as the extremeness aversion principle [6]. We select two extreme options: (i) much lower quality and much lower price (*Hotel 91*); and (ii) much higher quality and much higher price (*Renaissance*).

G-3 Options with Trade-Off. Two options that have relative pros and cons require a trade-off to be made. As this may require a different form of explanation from either category above, we include options that clearly illustrate such a need for trade-off, *Econo Lodge* and *The Hotel at Times Square*.

Reasons for Choice. The participant is asked to state why they choose a particular option, and why they reject the remaining options — we assume that if participants do not choose an option, they automatically reject it. In order to obtain useful responses, we highlight for the participant that *complete* answers should be provided and that arguments should be sufficiently strong to convince another person about the choice made.

In all this, the most important information collected is the provided justifications, expressed in natural language. The analysis part of the study consists of carefully investigating these justifications to identify patterns and define explanation types so that, based on this initial analysis, we can extract quantitative data. Table 1(b) shows our approach to answering our research questions, which is mainly based on a classification of explanation types. In summary, the collected *qualitative* data is: justifications for

Table 2. Demographic Characteristics of Participants

Gender	Male 58 (58%)	Country	Brazil 78 (78%)	United Kingdom 8 (8%)	Age (years)	16-25 4 (4%)	26-35 61 (61%)	Field of Work or	Informatics 54 (54%)	Education 11 (11%)
	Female 42 (42%)		Canada 5 (5%)	Other 9 (9%)		36-45 11 (11%)	>45 24 (24%)	Study	Management 7 (7%)	Other 28 (28%)

acceptance, justifications for rejection, explanation types, and additional characteristics of justifications. The *quantitative* data consists of: chosen hotel, chosen hotel vs. explanation types for acceptance, chosen hotel vs. explanation types for rejection of other hotels, rejected hotels vs. explanation types for their rejection.

2.2 Participants

The participants in our survey are selected using convenience sampling, obtained through the social network of the researchers involved in this study, by means of two forms of publishing the survey: (i) by e-mail, using the contact list of the researcher; and (ii) by Facebook (http://www.facebook.com), the widely known social network. The distributed message consists of an invitation to participate in the survey and a request to forward the invitation for others. The survey was available for participation from 12th to 24th October, 2011 and was completed by 100 people. The demographic characteristics of the participants that completed the survey are described in Table 2. Because we adopted the social network of the lead researcher to perform the study, most participants are aged between 26 and 35 years (61%) and are Brazilians (78%).

3   Results and Analysis

Our collected data consists mainly of justifications expressed in natural language and, as these are qualitative data, we analyse them in a systematic way to extract quantitative information. This section explains how we perform this analysis and provides the results obtained, according to the research questions we aim to answer. Note that, at various points, we label some findings with *"Evidence X,"* in order that we can later refer to them to support our proposed guidelines.

Before proceeding, however, we enumerate the hotels chosen by our participants: *Hotel 91* (18%), *Econo Lodge* (52%), *The Hotel at Times Square* (19%), *Comfort Inn* (7%) and *Renaissance* (4%). As expected, the majority of participants choose a hotel from group G-3. This information is relevant to understanding the relationship between the chosen option and justifications, as indicated by research questions *RQ2* and *RQ4*.

RQ1: Do users adopt a pattern to justify an option chosen from the set of those available? Each participant has to provide five justifications for their choice, from which one explains why they choose a particular hotel. With the analysis of all provided justifications and the principles of grounded theory [7], we derive a classification, which we refer to as *explanation types*, consisting of *six* different types that are described below. We illustrate each of these explanation types for the acceptance scenario in Table 3.

Table 3. Example of Justification for Acceptance and Rejection

Explanation Type	Example of Justification for Acceptance	Example of Justification for Rejection
Critical attribute	H_i is the cheapest option.	There are other options cheaper than H_i.
Dominance	H_i is better in all aspects.	There is no reason for choosing H_i, as it is worse in all aspects than H_j.
Main reason	I chose H_i because it offers the benefit a_i.	I did not choose H_i because it does not offer the benefit a_i.
Minimum requirements	From the hotels that satisfy my requirements, H_i is the cheapest.	H_i is too expensive.
One-sided Reasons	I chose H_i because it provides the benefits a_i and a_j.	I did not choose H_i because it has the disadvantages a_i and a_j.
Pros and Cons	Even though H_i is not the cheapest, it provides the benefits a_i and a_j.	Even though H_i provides the benefits a_i and a_j, its price does not compensate it.

Critical Attribute. For some participants, a single attribute plays a crucial role in the decision-making process, *price* in most cases. In these situations, the justification focuses only on this crucial attribute, and the remaining ones are omitted. The same attribute is used to justify the chosen and all rejected options.

Dominance. The domination relationship can be used as an argument to justify a decision, but the acceptance of an option is justified using dominance only when it dominates all other options. This is an uncommon situation when choosing among products because, due to seller competition, there is typically a trade-off to be resolved, with options presenting both pros and cons. However, if domination *does* arise, the decision is extremely easy: one option may dominate another from a particular participant's perspective, as they might not care about a set of attributes, and the remaining ones create this ideal scenario to make the decision.

Main Reason. Some participants take into account many attributes to make a decision, but a particular option may be chosen (or rejected) when there is one attribute value that, together with its importance, is decisive for the choice. This most important attribute is specific to each option.

Minimum Requirements. People usually have hard constraints, used to filter available options by discarding those that do not satisfy all of them — this can be seen as the establishment of cut-off values. If only one option satisfies all requirements, the decision becomes easy as the justification for option acceptance is that it satisfies all requirements. Furthermore, some participants provide a justification based on minimum requirements but, since more than one option satisfies these requirements, the participants also provide some criterion to distinguish between them, e.g. minimum price.

One-Sided Reasons. Instead of only providing the main reason for acceptance, many participants focus on exposing only positive aspects (or negative, in case of rejection) of the option, even though the chosen option has disadvantages (or advantages) with respect to other options in relation to their preferences. This indicates the existence of a minimal set of attributes that caused the option to be chosen (or rejected).

Pros and Cons. The most complex type of explanation consists of making the option pros and cons explicit, and showing the reasoning process behind the choice. Based on an evaluation of these pros and cons, the participant states that the pros compensate for

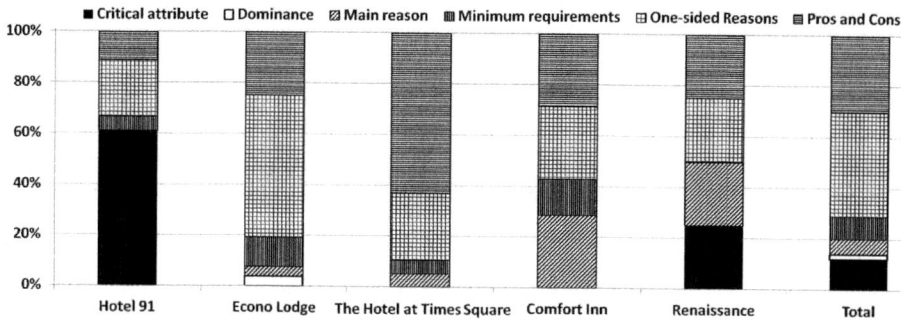

Fig. 1. Explanation types used to justify each chosen hotel

the cons (or do not, in case of rejection). In some cases, participants do not enumerate pros and cons, but only state *"this is (not) the best cost-benefit relationship."*

These explanation types indicate that justifications for choosing an option *do* follow patterns, and these can be used in systems for explanation generation. The right hand side of Figure 1 (which shows the explanation types used to justify each hotel) represents the total number of the different explanation types adopted by the participants, who mostly adopt *one-sided reasons* and *pros and cons* to explain their choices.

RQ2: Is there a relationship between the type of explanation given to support the decision and the chosen option? Given that we have identified patterns used to justify why a particular hotel is chosen, we now investigate if there is any relationship between the type of explanation given and the chosen option. Figure 1 shows how much each explanation type is adopted for each individual hotel.

The distribution of explanation types indicates three norms. First, most of the participants that choose *Hotel 91* (61.11%) justify their decision by referring to a critical attribute, price, indicating that what matters for them is that this hotel is the cheapest. Some participants provide further positive information about the hotel (*one-sided reasons*, 22.22%), in addition to stating that it is cheapest, i.e. they indicate that even though the hotel is the cheapest, the quality that they require is not compromised.

As can be seen in Figure 1, the main adopted explanation types for choosing hotels of the G-3 group are *one-sided reasons* and *pros and cons*, which together has a total of 80.77% for *Econo Lodge* and 89.47% for *The Hotel at Times Square*. The first explanation type is used to show that a whole set of hotel characteristics is responsible for the choice made. In general, participants that choose *Econo Lodge* exclude the cheapest hotel from the set of hotels being considered in the decision, and explain the benefits of this hotel to show that it was suitable for them; i.e. there is no reason to pay more for another option if this hotel already provides what the participant wants. Conversely, participants that choose *The Hotel at Times Square* make a detailed analysis of this hotel against *Econo Lodge*; i.e. they discuss the *pros and cons*, and show that the higher price of the former justifies the benefits it provides, when compared against the latter. With respect to these two options, we make one last observation: two participants (3.85%)

use dominance to justify why they choose *Econo Lodge*, and ignore attributes that are not relevant for them, creating a scenario in which this hotel dominates all others.

Finally, we discuss the results obtained for the dominated option and the most expensive option. It can be seen that there is no explanation type that is most adopted, with participants adopting different explanation types for justifying them. Few participants choose these two options and, since it is not obvious why these options should be chosen, the participants give their particular explanations to justify this decision. In the first case, *Comfort Inn*, some participants are vague and say that they choose this hotel because it has the best cost-benefit relationship, but do not give details. The remaining participants use as arguments the two attributes that this hotel is better than *The Hotel at Times Square*, i.e. parking price and room size. The room size argument is also used as an expression of *intuition*: as the room is bigger, and the price is higher, the hotel "apparently" provides more comfort. For this same reason, some participants choose the 4-star *Renaissance*, as comfort is the most important issue for them, and they are not concerned with price.

RQ3: Do users use a pattern to justify the rejected (not chosen) options? By analysing justifications for rejecting options, we have observed the same explanation types used for justifying the chosen option. The description given for our set of explanation types shows that they can also be applied to reject options. In Table 3, we show examples of how each of these explanation types is used in the context of option rejection.

RQ4: Is there a relationship between the type of explanation given to reject options and the rejected or chosen option? In order to understand how participants choose a particular explanation type, we analyse the relationship between the types adopted to justify rejected options from two perspectives. The first consists of analysing justifications for rejection given for each hotel (Figure 2). The second perspective groups justifications according to the chosen hotel; i.e. we observe which explanation types are adopted to reject other options according to a particular chosen hotel (Figure 3).

Many interesting aspects can be observed. *Critical attribute* is the type of explanation used when the decision is guided by it. For instance, if the participant wants to minimise price, the justification for the rejected hotels is that they are more expensive (than the chosen hotel). Similarly, this situation occurs with the more expensive hotel, when the participant wants to maximise the price (as a proxy for comfort maximisation). *Dominance*, on the other hand, is adopted when the chosen option dominates the rejected option; i.e. the comparison made in the explanation is always for the chosen option against the others. In many situations, preferences (hidden in justifications) of participants who choose *Econo Lodge* indicate that *The Hotel at Times Square* dominates *Comfort Inn*; however, this is not given as an argument to discard the latter, but the participants seek an explanation why *Econo Lodge* is better than *Comfort Inn* (*Evidence A*). Some participants have hard constraints that they require to be satisfied by the chosen hotel, such as a maximum price that they are willing to pay, or a minimum distance from the city centre. In these situations, an option is rejected regardless of the remaining options, and the justification given is that the option does not satisfy the participant's *minimum requirements*.

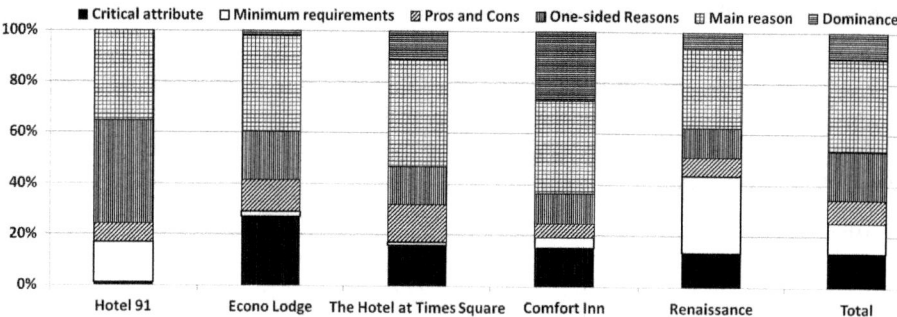

Fig. 2. Explanation types used to justify the rejection of each hotel

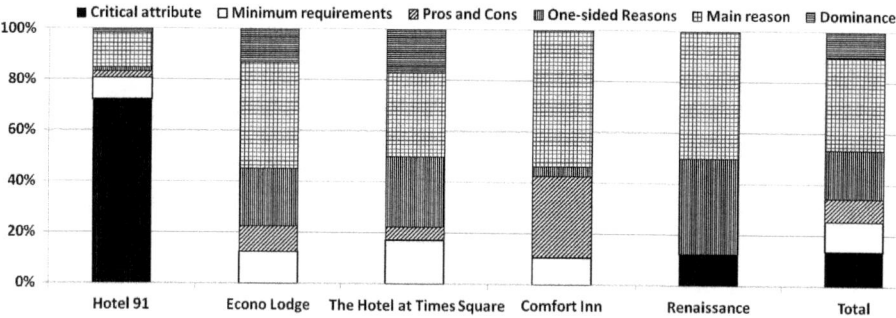

Fig. 3. Explanation types used to justify the rejection of other hotels given a chosen hotel

Main reason and *one-sided reasons* indicate that there is an attribute (or a set of them) that is especially important for the participant and, even though it is not part of a hard constraint, it plays a *decisive role* in the decision; i.e. because of this (these) attribute(s), the option is rejected. This set of attributes is *kept as simple as possible* (*Evidence B*); e.g. some participants that choose *Econo Lodge*, reject *The Hotel at Times Square* and *Comfort Inn* because they do not have a refrigerator and are more expensive (than the chosen hotel). But, to justify the *Renaissance* (which also does not have a refrigerator), they argue only that it is more expensive. It is important to note that the explanations given for *The Hotel at Times Square* and *Comfort Inn* are exactly the same, and there are many other cases in which the same explanation is given for different options rejected for the same reason (*Evidence C*). Finally, *pros and cons* are given as rejection arguments by participants when the decision between two (or three) options is difficult, so they expose these options' pros and cons to show that the chosen option has the best cost-benefit relationship. Thus, *pros and cons* are used only in the *absence of a decisive subset of attributes (Evidence D)*.

In this way, the justification given for rejecting an option depends on both the chosen and rejected options, as the explanation given typically justifies why the rejected option is worse than the chosen one. Only in those cases in which the option is rejected due to a hard constraint (*minimum requirements*), the rejection explanation depends only on the option being rejected.

Further Observations. While analysing the collected data, we also identify other relevant characteristics present in the provided justifications. We describe each of these characteristics below, most of which can be used to suggest informal arguments for systematic approaches to decision-making.

Explicit Trade-Off. Some participants (34%) state that the chosen hotel has the best cost-benefit relationship (or not the best, for rejecting a hotel), and sometimes just provide the argument without any details; e.g. *"For a trip like this, it seems the best cost-benefit among the 3-star hotels."*

Preferences Mentioned. Only a few participants (14%), when requested to justify their decision, provide arguments based on their preferences (*Evidence E*); for example, a participant argued the *"absence of a fitness centre"* to justify a rejection, but this is due to the participant's preference for a hotel *with* a fitness centre — and in some cases, participants make their preference explicit.

Price as a First Class Attribute. The majority of participants (92%) mention the attribute *price* in their justifications, and evaluate options by comparing this attribute with all others. This indicates that *cost* (which can also be time, effort, etc.) is not seen as a disadvantage of an option when compared to another, but as a fixed attribute that should be treated differently in the provided explanations (*Evidence F*).

Irrelevant Attributes. When participants choose a hotel that does not offer as many benefits as the others, they state that those benefits are not important for them and, as a result, there is no reason to pay more for something that will not be used. Irrelevant attributes are mentioned in both acceptance and rejection justifications (34%).

These observations show that cost should be treated as a first class attribute in explanations, as it is a crucial factor considered in the decision. In the cases when a higher price is chosen, and this difference is very small, many participants acknowledge this fact. When the chosen option has a lower price, the benefits provided by other options may be relevant to be mentioned, even though the decision maker does not care about it. In cases where the pros and cons of a set of options make the decision hard, an explicit statement that a particular option has the best cost-benefit relationship might be helpful. Finally, participants typically do not support their arguments with their preferences.

4   Guidelines and Patterns

This study provides us with a means of understanding how users construct arguments to justify a choice, by explaining why an option is chosen and why the remaining ones are rejected. Moreover, based on the results from this study, we are able to contribute to our ultimate goal of providing guidance that serves as a basis for the development of explanation approaches. To this end, we introduce guidelines and patterns derived from our study in this section. For each guideline, we indicate the evidence that supports it.

4.1 Guidelines

1. Provide chosen-option-oriented explanations. (Evidence A) The explanation generation process must be guided by a previously chosen option. The goal of the explanation is not to expose all the reasoning process used to make the decision, but to provide the main arguments that justify a chosen option and reject the remaining ones. After the choice is made, the explanations given should answer two main questions: (i) what makes the chosen option better than the others; and (ii) what makes other options worse than the chosen option.

2. Keep it simple. (Evidence B) The explanation given to a user should be as simple as possible, even justifying the decision with a single sentence; e.g. *A is the cheapest option*. Therefore, the less complex the explanation, the better. The next three guidelines are associated with this, and provide concrete ways of keeping the explanation simple.

3. Focus on the most relevant criteria. (Evidence D) In the given explanation, only the *decisive criteria* should be mentioned; i.e. the minimum set of attributes that causes an option to be selected or rejected. These decisive criteria should be derived from comparison of the chosen option against the others.

4. Group similar options. (Evidence C) An explanation to reject an option can also be given to reject other options. So, rejected options should be grouped when they are rejected for the same reason, and presented as a group and not individually.

5. Back up explanations with preferences, but provide them only if asked. (Evidence E) Characteristics mentioned in explanations are relevant, because of the preferences being considered in the decision-making process; e.g., "I chose this option as it is the cheapest," (explanation) and "I want to minimise costs" (preference). People usually do not explicitly state their preferences to justify their decisions but, if a decision is made on someone's behalf, it is fundamental to back up an explanation with their preferences. As this information is not always needed, and as simpler explanations are better, preferences must be provided as part of explanations only upon request.

6. Use **cost** *as a first class attribute. (Evidence F)* An option is chosen by an individual when they believe that the cost being paid for that option compensates for the benefits it provides. The trade-off between benefits and costs is the key issue in the process of decision-making, so the option attributes that define the option costs should be made explicit and used as first class attributes in the explanation provided to justify a decision.

4.2 Patterns

Based on our study, we derived patterns of explanations, which can be used for supporting a decision made by a software system. Moreover, we identified the components these patterns must have, which comprise a template for an explanation pattern catalog. These components are: (i) a *classification*; (ii) a *context* in which the pattern should be applied; (iii) a *template* for the explanation; (iv) the pattern *description*; (v) an *example*; (vi) *preferences* that back up the explanation; and (vii) optionally, *extensions* to the pattern. Patterns are classified (item (i)) according to three attributes, explained below.

Table 4. Decisive Criteria Pattern

Decisive Criteria Pattern
Classification: *Explanation goal*: both; *Target*: option; *Position*: absolute.
Context: even though there are other attributes that contribute for the option acceptance (or rejection), there is a subset of them that would confirm this decision regardless of the values of the other attributes.
Template: *Option option was [chosen	rejected] because of its set of decisive attributes* .
Description: options, when compared, might have different pros and cons. However, some attributes are the most decisive in the decision (according to their value and importance), while others — which can make a difference in particular cases — do not impact on the decision between two options. Therefore, the only attributes that must be part of the explanation are those that impact on the decision, leaving aside remainder.
Example: three hotel options are given for a user: (i) hotel A is a 3-star hotel, cheaper than the other two options and has a refrigerator in the room; (ii) hotel B is also a 3-star hotel, more expensive than the former, with a better location; and (iii) hotel C is a luxury 4-star hotel, much more expensive than the others and, like hotel B, does not have a refrigerator. While the rejection of B is justified by the absence of the refrigerator *and* its price; the rejection of C is justified only because of its price, as this is the decisive criterion for not choosing it.
Back up preference: preferences over the set of decisive attributes.

- *Goal: accept/reject/both.* An explanation can justify a chosen option (*accept*), a rejected or not chosen option (*reject*), or both (*both*).

- *Target: decision/option.* A pattern can provide guidance to justify the decision as a whole (*decision*), or the acceptance or rejection of a single option (*option*).

- *Position: absolute/relative.* When a pattern target is *option*, the explanation given can be based solely on the target option (*absolute*), or make a statement that explicitly compares the option to another (*relative*).

Due to space restrictions, we do not describe each pattern, but present just one as illustration in Table 4. We also summarise all the patterns in Table 5 (complete description available elsewhere [8]), in which patterns are ordered according to their complexity; i.e. the simpler the explanation associated with a pattern, the earlier it is presented. According to our second guideline, the explanation should be as simple as possible so, if two patterns can be used in a particular situation, the simplest must be applied.

5   Related Work

Recommender systems have different aims that should be achieved beyond accuracy, such as trust, effectiveness and satisfaction, and these have been addressed through explanations that expose the rationale behind the adopted recommendation approach (content-based, collaborative, or hybrid). For example, if a collaborative approach is adopted, the user may receive as an explanation a histogram of ratings of the product given by similar users. McSherry [9] focused on case-based reasoning approaches, in which products are seen as cases from which one should be selected when it is similar to the case provided by the user, and the explanation is based on selected similar cases. Another direction is explanation interfaces [10], which organise recommended products in a way that causes trade-off situations to be resolved explicitly for users, thus facilitating the decision making process.

Even though explanations improve recommender systems, they currently focus on explaining the *means* used to obtain recommendations, but stating that "someone like you chose this product" or "you like similar products" is not sufficient for justifying a recommendation and for users to accept it. This can be seen in a taxonomy recently

Table 5. Explanation Pattern Classification

Pattern	Goal	Target	Position	Template
Critical Attribute	both	decision		*Option __chosen option__ was chosen because it has the best value for __critical attribute__ .*
Cut-off	reject	option	absolute	*Option __rejected option__ was rejected because it does not satisfy constraints associated with __attribute__ .*
Domination	reject	option	relative	*There is no reason to choose option __rejected option__ , as option __chosen option__ is better than it in all aspects, including __cost__ .*
Minimum Requirements⁻	reject	option	relative	*Even though option __rejected option__ satisfies all your requirements, it has a worse value for __attribute__ than option __chosen option__ .*
Minimum Requirements⁺	accept	option	absolute	*Besides satisfying all your requirements, option __chosen option__ has the best value for __attribute__ .*
Decisive Criteria	both	option	absolute	*Option __option__ was [chosen | rejected] because of its set of decisive attributes .*
Trade-off Resolution	both	option	absolute	*Even though option __rejected option__ provides better __pros__ than the chosen option, it has worse __cons__ .* *Even though option __chosen option__ does not have the best value for __cons__ , its values for __pros__ compensate its cons.*

proposed for *classifying explanation generation approaches* [11], whose dimensions focus on the information used to generate the explanation and the underlying recommendation model. Characteristics of *good* explanations have been defined based on the analysis of existing approaches [2], and these can be used as metrics to *evaluate existing approaches*. Our work, on the other hand, identifies *good* explanations that should be given to users, which can be used as guidance for elaborating new explanation approaches, and proposes a template *for classifying explanations*. The challenge of obtaining these explanations from existing recommendation approaches, however, still remains. As our patterns indicate explanations based on option attributes, it may be more straightforward to generate such explanations from approaches based on the relevance of attribute values for users.

6   Conclusion

In this paper, we have presented a study performed to understand how people justify their decisions, by giving explanations why they choose a particular option from the set of those available, and why remaining options are rejected. The study consisted of providing participants (100 people) with a set of carefully chosen hotel options, and requesting them to give reasons for the choice. Based on collected data, we have identified explanation types that are patterns of justifications given by people, and how they are selected to be given as explanation — for both chosen and rejected options. Assuming that explanations given by people are the explanations that users expect to receive as reasons for a choice, our study allowed us to propose a set of guidelines and patterns for the development of explanation approaches. Future work involves producing explanations for choices made by our decision-making technique [12], which takes into consideration this guidance derived from our study.

References

1. McNee, S.M., Riedl, J., Konstan, J.A.: Being accurate is not enough: how accuracy metrics have hurt recommender systems. In: CHI 2006, pp. 1097–1101. ACM (2006)
2. Tintarev, N., Masthoff, J.: A survey of explanations in recommender systems. In: ICDE Workshop, pp. 801–810. IEEE Computer Society, USA (2007)
3. Labreuche, C.: A general framework for explaining the results of a multi-attribute preference model. Artif. Intell. 175, 1410–1448 (2011)
4. Junker, U.: Quickxplain: Preferred explanations and relaxations for over-constrained problems. In: AAAI 2004, pp. 167–172. AAAI Press, USA (2004)
5. Lichtenstein, S., Slovic, P.: The construction of preference. Cambridge Univer. Press (2006)
6. Simonson, I., Tversky, A.: Choice in context: Tradeoff contrast and extremeness aversion. Journal of Marketing Research 29(3), 281–295 (1992)
7. Glaser, B.G.: Emergence vs. Forcing: Basics of Grounded Theory Analysis. Sociology Press, Mill Valley (1992)
8. Nunes, I., Miles, S., Luck, M., Lucena, C.: A study on justifications for choices: Explanation patterns and guidelines. Tech. Report CS-2012-03, University of Waterloo, Canada (2012)
9. McSherry, D.: Explanation in recommender systems. Artif. Intell. Rev. 24, 179–197 (2005)
10. Pu, P., Chen, L.: Trust-inspiring explanation interfaces for recommender systems. Knowledge-Based Systems 20, 542–556 (2007)
11. Friedrich, G., Zanker, M.: A taxonomy for generating explanations in recommender systems. AI Magazine 32(3), 90–98 (2011)
12. Nunes, I., Miles, S., Luck, M., Lucena, C.: User-centric preference-based decision making. In: AAMAS 2012 (to appear, 2012)

The Effect of Suspicious Profiles
on People Recommenders

Luiz Augusto Pizzato, Joshua Akehurst, Cameron Silvestrini,
Kalina Yacef, Irena Koprinska, and Judy Kay

School of Information Technologies
University of Sydney, Australia
`firstname.lastname@sydney.edu.au`

Abstract. As the world moves towards the social web, criminals also adapt their activities to these environments. Online dating websites, and more generally people recommenders, are a particular target for romance scams. Criminals create fake profiles to attract users who believe they are entering a relationship. Scammers can cause extreme harm to people and to the reputation of the website. This makes it important to ensure that recommender strategies do not favour fraudulent profiles over those of legitimate users. There is therefore a clear need to gain understanding of the sensitivity of recommender algorithms to scammers. We investigate this by (1) establishing a corpus of suspicious profiles and (2) assessing the effect of these profiles on the major classes of reciprocal recommender approaches: collaborative and content-based. Our findings indicate that collaborative strategies are strongly influenced by the suspicious profiles, while a pure content-based technique is not influenced by these users.

1 Introduction

There are many online services that enable people to connect with others, such as mentoring systems, social networks and online dating websites. Naturally, it is important that people receive good recommendations to help them find the right person. A particular aspect of recommending people to people is that, because user models are used in both sides of the recommendations (user and item), they can bias the recommender algorithms with a greater role than in traditional recommenders. Therefore it is extremely important to understand and reduce their sensitivity to fraudulent user profiles.

This paper is particularly concerned with online dating. In order to use such service, people have to create a profile that provides information about themselves and the type of people they would like to meet via the website. These profiles can be considered as a personal advertisement, so people can read each other's profiles before deciding to communicate with each other. However, a small number of users are scammers who aim to obtain financial gain by establishing a virtual romantic relationship and such scammers may never meet the other person face to face. As described by the Australian Competition and Consumer

J. Masthoff et al. (Eds.): UMAP 2012, LNCS 7379, pp. 225–236, 2012.

Commission dating and romance scams play on emotional triggers to get people to provide scammers with money, gift or personal details.[1]

Because romance scams work on people's emotions, scammers may need to take a long time to develop a trust relationship with each victim. Scammers may spend months flirting and working on people's feelings and may not give any hint that they seek, would accept or need financial help from the victim before they are sure that the victim trusts them. This means that romance scams are doubly damaging. They exploit people financially and are emotionally traumatic.

In online dating scams, the scammer creates a few *bait-profiles* on dating websites. We define *bait-profiles* as profiles created with the sole purpose of attracting victims for romance scams. Because online dating users are already looking for a partner, they are more susceptible to believe that the information on the bait-profile is genuine.

Email spam detection [14] has long battled email romance scams and other types of fraud and today's detection techniques are highly effective. Despite some similarities between email romance scam and the bait-profiles of scammers on online dating websites, it can be very hard for users to detect a bait-profile. Unlike unrequited email, online dating users are seeking contact with other users, which means that the potential victim might be the one initiating the contact with the scammer. Furthermore, users may not be aware that scamming in online dating even exists. And finally, bait-profiles can be copies of profiles from other online dating websites, and so would appear to users to be perfectly legitimate.

The detection of scamming in the online dating industry is a high priority and requires the recommender systems to ensure that they are not favouring bait-profile over authentic user profiles. This paper is the first work on measuring the effect of bait-profiles on different people recommender systems. This is important as the design of a recommender should take into account that some profiles should be removed from the recommendations. We tackle this using data from a large online dating website. We analysed the profile information of users and their communications. We first establish a mechanism to identify a large number of profile that are highly likely to be bait-profiles. We then examine the effect that these suspicious profiles have on different classes of recommenders.

This paper is organised as follows: Section 2 reviews previous work in online dating and fraud. Section 3 describes the design of our study to investigate the effects of scammers on collaborative and content-based recommenders. Section 4 describes our method for identifying a corpus of suspicious profiles. Section 5 shows the effects of suspicious profiles on recommender systems. Section 6 discusses possible ways to minimise the effect of suspicious profiles and Section 7 summarises our conclusions.

2   Literature Review

Recommender systems for matching people on online dating sites is a relatively new area. One of the first works was conducted by Brožovský and Petříček [2],

---

[1] http://www.scamwatch.gov.au/content/index.phtml/tag/DatingRomanceScams

who compared the performance of two collaborative filtering algorithms. In [15], we have proposed a content-base recommender system for online dating. The recommender extracts the user's implicit preferences (i.e. the preferences that are inferred from their interactions with the other users) and then matches them with the profiles of the other users. Kim et al. [7] proposed a rule-based recommender that also learns from both user profiles and interactions. For a given user, it finds the best matching values for every attribute and then combines them in a rule that can be used to generate recommendations. Cai et al. [3] introduced a collaborative filtering algorithm called SocialCollab based on user similarity in taste and attractiveness. Two users are similar in attractiveness if they are liked by a common group of users, and are similar in taste if they like a common group of users. A hybrid recommender system called CCR was proposed by Akehurst et al. [1]. It combines content-based and collaborative filtering approaches and utilises both user profiles and user interactions.

Using the social networking site Beehive, Chen et al. [4] compared two types of algorithms: based on social network information and based on similarity of user-created content. The results show that all four algorithms were successful in increasing the number of friends for a user but the the first type of algorithms found more known contacts while the second type found more new friends.

Diaz et al. [5] formulated the people matchmaking task as an information retrieval problem, where candidate profiles are ranked based on how well they match the ideal partner profile for a given user. McFee and Lanckriet [9] proposed an approach that learns distance metrics that are optimised for different ranking evaluation measures, e.g. precision and area under the curve.

2.1   Security of Recommender Systems

The security of recommender system algorithms has also been investigated. Mobasher et al. [10] studied the impact of profile injection attacks (a more generic term than the shilling attack that was introduced by Lam and Riedl [8] and O'Mahoney et al. [11]), where the aim is usually to bias the system's behaviour to promote or demote a particular item. They have shown, for example, that hybrid approaches combining item-based and semantic similarity algorithms [10] were more robust against these attacks, even though they could not entirely prevent them. Mobasher et al. [10] also proposed a supervised classification approach for detecting fake profiles in collaborative recommender systems but the general issue of detecting shilling attacks remains an open problem.

Recently Pan et al. [12] analysed the characteristics of the online dating profiles posted on romancescam.com and confirmed as fraudulent. The results showed that the majority of these profiles were of females between 20 and 29 years, contained photos and did not disclose sexual orientation. Many of the profiles also contained the same sentences or certain combinations of words; in addition, the same IP address was used to create more than one profile.

The detection of fraud is very important for online business. Pandit et al. [13] have employed a belief propagation mechanism to detect hidden networks of fraudsters on e-commerce websites. Such detection mechanisms are appropriate when a reputation system is in place (such as on eBay) and fraudsters have the incentive to game the system to improve visibility. Reputation, however, it is not a feature that we can capture or even infer from our online dating data.

We have observed that near duplicate profiles may indicate a scammer, therefore our problem of bait-profile detection is related to the merge/purge problem [6] and data deduplication [16]. However, in our study, we have observed that legitimate users may also have near-duplicate profiles, meaning that the sole detection of near-duplicates does not solve the bait-profile identification problem.

Some legitimate users may create similar looking profile, in order to understand which features are more requested by other users. They may also create small lies on each profile. Toma et al. [17] found that 81% of the users lied about at least one characteristic of their online profile. Men lied more about their height, while women lied more about their weight. However, the inaccuracies were small (2–5.5%) which means that the lies would be difficult to detect face-to-face. Another interesting observation was that the deception was strategic — users lied only about some of their characteristics, the ones that they perceived would make them more attractive. Participants also reported enhancing their photographs (through posing, makeup, lighting or software editing) but being accurate about their relationship status (e.g. single, divorced) and whether they have children. These results indicate that the users strategically balanced their virtual and actual profiles, in anticipation of future face-to-face interaction. Although these findings are hardly surprising, it is important to highlight that, regardless of how truthful someone's profile is, what characterises a bait-profile is not the number of lies they contain but the intent for which these profiles were created.

3   Experimental Design

Our study uses historical data from a major Australian online dating website, containing more than 130,000 users, their profile information and over 2,000,000 messages expressing interest from a user to another user occurring during a one month period. We call these messages Expressions Of Interest (EOI). They are predefined, standard messages, such as "I read your profile and I would like to know you better", to which the recipient can answer, choosing from a set of positive or negative replies. These 2 million EOIs received 15.2% positive replies and 45.7% negative replies.[2] This data was chronologically divided into training and testing sets.

Our first step for investigating the effect of suspicious profiles on the main classes of people recommenders is to assemble a corpus of profiles considered to be highly suspicious: duplicate profiles. We rely on the fact that scammers tend to copy the same or similar versions of the same profile several times for a number of different bait-profiles. Whilst these suspicious profiles do not constitute an exhaustive list of scammers, they nevertherless include the majority of them, hence it is important to measure the resilience of the recommender approaches

---

[2] The remaining interactions (39.1%) had no replies.

against these suspicious profiles. Of course, duplication can in some rare instances be legitimate and can be caused, for example, by a user having forgotten their password and not knowing how to retrieve it. Therefore the construction of our corpus focuses on the identification of profiles which information already appears in other existing profiles and for which we have a strong indication that these profiles are not portraying the same person. These profiles may have been created by different people or even by one person portraying different online dating users. The construction of the corpus is detailed in Section 4.

Once the corpus of suspicious profiles was built, we measure the effect of these profiles on several reciprocal recommenders. We used the following three reciprocal recommender algorithms, implementing the main approaches available in the literature on people recommenders:

1. CF, a collaborative filtering system that uses the user positive responses as an indication of reciprocity;
2. CCR+CF, an hybrid system that combines the CF implementation with the hybrid content-collaborative system CCR [1]; and
3. RECON [15], a content-based system that uses reciprocal preferences to match users.

CF and CCR+CF implement reciprocity by examining the type of response that users had towards the group of users who have sent them an EOI. For instance, these algorithms will favour a user A who has responded mostly positively to a group of users over B who has responded mostly negatively to the same group. The CCR component [1] of CCR+CF deals with the cold-start problem by finding similar users based on profile information.

RECON [15] generates recommendations by giving users a compatibility score with each other. For instance, the compatibility $Compat(Alice, Bob)$ represents how well Bob matches Alice's preferences. RECON presents users with recommendations with higher reciprocal compatibilities. That is, Bob will be recommended to Alice when the harmonic mean between $Compat(Alice, Bob)$ and $Compat(Bob, Alice)$ is higher than between Alice and any other user. The interesting feature of RECON is that even when Alice does not have a preference model, it can recommend on the basis of the people who will like Alice the most (i.e. highest $Compat(X, Alice)$)

4 Corpus of Suspicious Profiles

In order to build a body of suspicious profiles, we need a method of determining whether any given profile is genuine or suspicious. While online dating profiles allow users to provide many of their personal attributes only a few of these will actually prove useful when searching for suspicious profiles.

In an effort to boost the popularity of their bait-profiles, scammers choose a popular range of values for attributes such as age, gender and body type. As there will be many legitimate users who also happen to fall into those categories, we cannot use these as the sole discriminating factors when evaluating the suspiciousness of a particular profile. The only truly uniquely-identifying aspects of the user profile is the profile text, in which the user is meant to write, in their own words, who they are and whom they would like to meet. Therefore, we will regard instances where two profiles have identical profile text as suspicious.

Another identifying characteristic of scammer profiles is their interactions with other users on the dating website. Many such profiles will display suspicious behaviour, such as interacting with an unusually wide range of other users (as opposed to a more normal behaviour of, say, targeting a specific age bracket and sexual orientation) and replying positively to all interaction requests received from other users. However, using such behavioural analysis as a method to detect suspicious is subject to the same cold-start problem that affects recommender systems: we cannot draw any conclusions about a user's behaviour until after they have already begun using the site for a period of time, in which a scammer might have already done significant damage.

Hence we will focus on the comparison of profile text as a method of detecting duplicate bait-profiles in preference to this approach. This has the advantages of not only being used to detect bait-profiles already present in the dating website, but also to detect new bait-profiles the instant they are created.

The process of identifying profiles that are highly similar to, or exact duplicates of, existing profiles is comprised of four main steps:

1. For each user, we process their corresponding profile text and obtain a set of representative keywords for that profile.
2. We then select the 10 most similar profiles for each user, based upon the relevant keyword sets, and compute three different measures of the similarities.
3. We group profiles into sets of near-duplicate profiles, where each profile in the group is a close copy of every other profile in that group.
4. We filter out the profile groups whose member profiles are deemed to be less suspicious, meaning that one legitimate user may have created multiple profiles.

Step 1 — Identifying Representative Keywords. Each profile is indexed using Xapian[3]. During the indexing process, we remove all punctuation, convert upper case characters to lower case and reduce words to their common root form (stemming), so that our process of identifying similar profiles is unaffected by very minor changes in the profile text. We use Xapian's Relevance Set (RSet) function to identify and store a list of 10 key terms that are highly discriminative for each profile, i.e. a selection of terms which, when used as a search query, is most likely to return the profile at hand and hence any duplicates of it. The RSet function selects terms by using the highest maximum term weight after stopwords have been removed. The use of 10 key terms allows the retrieval of a large, but still manageable, number of documents for later processing.

Step 2 — Finding Close Matches. Using the keywords identified in the previous stage, we query the Xapian's index for the 10 closest matches, ignoring

---

[3] Open source information retrieval tool available at http://xapian.org

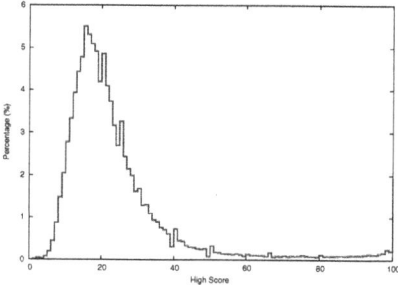

Fig. 1. Distribution of the highest matching score for each user

the user's own profile which would be a perfect match. This search is necessary in order to limit the number of direct profile–profile comparisons that must be performed, due to the size of the database.

For each of the matches found through the Xapian search, we compute three core values which act as a measure of the similarity between the two profiles.

Matching Score represents the Sørensen–Dice coefficient $s(x, y)$, which is a similarity index between two profiles x and y such that:

$$s(x, y) = \frac{2M}{|x| + |y|}$$

where M is the number of matching words between the profiles, where $|x|$ and $|y|$ denote the total number of words in each profile.
Longest Common Subsequence is the length of the longest subsequence of words common to both profiles.
Matching Phrases gives the number of words in the phrases common to both profiles. A phrase in this context is defined to be an n-gram of size three or greater.

We found approximately 23 million profile pairings of the 2.7 million profiles in total. The average of 8.5 pairs per profile shows the normal profiles can be quite unique, and not all profiles can be matched with 10 similar ones.

We then filter these set of matches, keeping only sufficiently close matches Based on the distribution of the highest similarity scores (high scores) for each user, shown in Figure 1, and manual inspection of the profile groups, we determined a set of minimum values for each of the core values that ensures that the two profiles in the match are actual duplicates of each other. Our constraints were: a matching score of 90 or above, a minimum of 25 words in each profile, the longest common subsequence of at least 10 words, and a minimum of 25 words in matching phrases. These constraints reduced the 23 million matches originally found to just under 170,000 *close matches*.

Step 3 — Forming Profile Groups. In this stage, we form groups of profiles such that each profile in the group is a near-duplicate of the others. The set of close matches identified above will determine which profiles are regarded as near-duplicates. If there is a close match between two profiles, they will end up in the same group.

To form the profile groups, we used an agglomerative hierarchical clustering technique with single linkage and used the Sørensen–Dice coefficient as the distance metric. Profiles are merged together into a new cluster provided they have a close match between them (as per the definition of close matches established earlier), and two clusters will be merged provided there is at least one close match between any two profiles within the clusters.

Once all close matches have been exhausted, each cluster represents a profile group of near-duplicate profiles. Profiles that were not able to be clustered are unique profiles and do not get added to any profile groups. We identified more than 22,000 profile groups, consisting of nearly 74,000 different profiles.

Step 4 — Removing Potentially Legitimate Users. In our particular domain, users are able to create duplicate profiles for numerous legitimate reasons, not always maliciously. These reasons can be as simple as a user forgetting their password and being locked out of their original account, to more complex reasons, such as creating a second account to gain access to premium member bonuses for new users. Although these users are not necessarily using the website in its "correct" way, these users are certainly not malicious and their profiles should not be labelled as suspicious or bait-profiles. In order to distinguish these users from suspicious ones, we identified a set of key attributes that would be highly unlikely for legitimate users to change when creating new accounts/profiles. The attributes are: date of birth, gender, sexuality, nationality, ethnic background.

Because profiles assigned to the same group are near-duplicates, we postulate that when profiles in one group contain the same key attributes, they are representing the same user who is likely to be legitimate. On the other hand, if a profile group has more than one distinct value for any of these key attributes, we flag that group as suspicious, and hence all of its member profiles. Two profiles must have duplicate profile text to be in the same group, and so someone who registers a second (or third, fourth, etc.) account that reuses their profile text and yet differs in one or more key attributes should be regarded as highly suspicious. It is impossible to distinguish between the cases where a legitimate user has had their profile copied, where the profile has been copied from an outside source, or where the profile was written from scratch, and therefore we have included the first occurrence of each profile in the suspicious user group.

Our initial set of duplicate groups consisted of more than 74,000 profiles divided into 22,000 groups. From these groups we flagged 83% as suspicious. These suspicious groups contained 89% of the profiles in the original set of duplicate profiles.

Table 1

(a) Top-100 results

	Coverage		% Rec.	
	Target	Cand.	HS	Normal
CF	80.4%	50.1%	11.4%	88.7%
RECON	98.4%	86.1%	2.7%	97.3%
CCR+CF	100.0%	53.7%	12.1%	87.9%
Chance	100.0%	100.0%	2.7%	97.3%

(b) EOI Distribution

	Total Sent	Avg/user
HS	82,372 (7.2%)	23.1
Normal	1,057,020 (92.8%)	8.1
All	1,139,392 (100.0%)	8.5

	Total Received	Avg/user
HS	35,827 (3.1%)	9.9
Normal	1,103,565 (96.9%)	8.5
All	1,139,392 (100.0%)	8.5

5   Effect of Suspicious Profiles on Recommenders

We used historical data from an online dating website containing more than one hundred and thirty thousand users and more than two million interactions among them. These interactions received 15.2% of positive replies and 45.7% of negative replies.[4] For this study, we used the profile information of more than one hundred and thirty thousand users of a major online dating website. We also used more than two million interactions among these users that occur during a one month period. This data was chronologically divided into training and testing sets. From these users we identified 3,567 highly suspicious (HS) users whose profiles were considered to be duplicates of at least one other user.

After running our three recommender systems (CF, CCR+CF, RECON), we computed the following performance measures:

1. The percentage of HS profiles and *normal* profiles (i.e. profiles not in HS) in the top-N recommendations. For comparison, we computed the probability of a profile to be suspicious (i.e. the number of HS profiles versus the total number of profiles) and, similarly, the probability of a profile being a normal profile.
2. Target and candidate coverage. The target coverage is the number of users for whom the system can generate recommendations; the candidate coverage is the number of profiles who were recommended to at least one target user.

Table 1a shows the results for the top-100 recommendations. The results for the first performance measure (percentages of profiles) are also graphically presented in Figure 2a. As can be seen, HS profiles do influence the recommendation lists; however, their effect is different for the different types of recommenders. The content-based recommender RECON is not affected by HS profiles; Figure 2a shows that it is the only system that recommends users from HS at a rate approximately equal to chance.

When comparing CB and CF techniques, the content-based method (RE-CON) has a lower chance of recommending HS profiles than the CF and hybrid methods. If HS profiles had no effect on the recommenders, we would expect the

---

[4] The remaining interactions (39.1%) had no replies.

average number of times an individual profile in HS appears in recommendations to be the same as the average number of times an individual legitimate profile appears. We found that CF and CCR+CF repeatedly recommend the same HS profiles significantly more often than normal profiles (see Figure 2b). However, the higher EOI activity of users in HS, as shown in Table 1b, directly influences the number of times that they appear in the recommendations lists of the CF recommender.

6   Minimising the Effect of Suspicious Profiles on Recommenders

In the previous section, we observed the influence of HS profiles to be higher in recommenders that used collaborative information. The reason for this effect lies on how the CF method works and how reciprocity was implemented.

CF assumes that users who like the same set of items are similar and therefore will also like another item, not yet seen by them. One of the problems with this approach is that it can give preference towards popular items. Although this is not normally a problem for product recommenders unless a shilling attack is in place, for domains such as online dating, it is particularly important that popular users are not recommended to too many people.

The problem with bait-profiles is that they are designed to attract users and therefore designed to be popular profiles. HS profiles have a higher than normal popularity and are more active on the website compared to a normal profile, as shown in Table 1b. Therefore, any method that has a bias (even small) towards popular profiles can be affected by scammers in order to favour their bait-profiles.

The implementation of reciprocity in the CF methods also plays a significant part in boosting the effect of HS profiles. We decided to rank the recommendations based on the difference between the number of positive and negative replies that the candidates have sent to the group of similar users. This ranking method can maximise positive reply rates and minimise negative reply rates, which is one of the main objectives in online dating. However, because scammers have this distinctive behaviour of always replying positively to people, when bait-profiles appear in the CF list, they are likely to appear in the user's recommendations.

Although the number of real bait-profiles in a serious online dating website is quite small, it is still important to build recommenders that do not favour this type of profile over genuine users. The first and most obvious solution to this problem is to build a scam detection method that gives the likelihood of a profile to be a bait-profile. With this information at hand, we can allow the recommender algorithm to promote or demote profiles accordingly.

Because scammers try to attract a wide range of users, bait-profiles tend to have loosely defined preferences. Therefore, in order to minimise the bias towards bait-profiles in content-based methods that account for user preferences (either implicit or explicit preferences), a recommender system may avoid recommending bait-profiles by favouring users whose preferences are more precise. However, this is likely to affect some legitimate users as well.

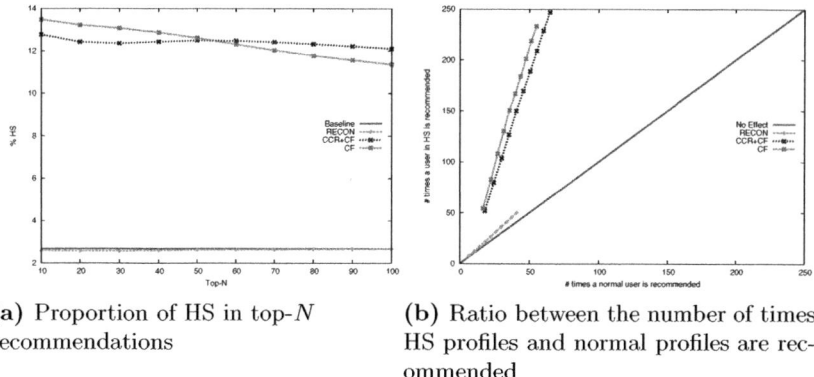

(a) Proportion of HS in top-N recommendations

(b) Ratio between the number of times HS profiles and normal profiles are recommended

Fig. 2. The effect of HS profiles in the recommendations

For CF, if the number of similar users and the number of possible recommendations are large, there is a high chance of recommending a bait-profile. When applying methods for reciprocity such as the ratio between positive and negative interactions as we have done, the chance of bringing bait-profiles within the top-N list also increases. To test this hypothesis, we have performed an experiment where we only varied the number of nearest neighbours used for the CF technique. We confirmed that the effect of bait-profiles is higher when more nearest neighbours are used. Therefore, it is possible to reduce the effect of bait-profiles in CF by using fewer nearest neighbours; however, this will also decrease the accuracy of the recommender.

7 Conclusions

Deceptive people, scams and romance fraud permeates the Internet. Email spamming is a large problem that has affected virtually all email users, and therefore has been addressed by much research. With only a small number of bait-profiles in serious online dating websites, romance scams appears to be a much smaller problem. Nonetheless, this small number of bait-profiles might be highly effective and may cause devastating emotional trauma to people, which alone warrants concerns for the industry.

Reciprocal recommender systems for online dating focus on recommending people who will reciprocate their feeling towards each other. Because scammers are likely to reciprocate their "feelings" towards everyone, recommender systems need to take into account the existence and the characteristics of such fake users. In this study, we have examined the effect of bait-profiles on three reciprocal recommender systems: one CB method (RECON), one CF method, and one hybrid method (CCR+CF). We have observed that the CF method was the most strongly affected by suspicious bait-profiles (HS), while the CB method was seen to be relatively unaffected.

Acknowledgment. This research was funded by the Smart Services Cooperative Research Centre.

References

1. Akehurst, J., Koprinska, I., Yacef, K., Pizzato, L., Kay, J., Rej, T.: Ccr - a content-collaborative reciprocal recommender for online dating. In: Proceedings of the 22nd IJCAI, Barcelona, Spain (July 2011)
2. Brožovský, L., Petříček, V.: Recommender system for online dating service. CoRR abs/cs/0703042 (2007)
3. Cai, X., Bain, M., Krzywicki, A., Wobcke, W., Kim, Y.S., Compton, P., Mahidadia, A.: Collaborative Filtering for People to People Recommendation in Social Networks. In: Li, J. (ed.) AI 2010. LNCS, vol. 6464, pp. 476–485. Springer, Heidelberg (2010)
4. Chen, J., Geyer, W., Dugan, C., Muller, M., Guy, I.: Make new friends, but keep the old: recommending people on social networking sites. In: CHI 2009, pp. 201–210. ACM, New York (2009)
5. Diaz, F., Metzler, D., Amer-Yahia, S.: Relevance and ranking in online dating systems. In: Proceeding of the 33rd SIGIR, pp. 66–73. ACM, New York (2010)
6. Hernández, M.A., Stolfo, S.J.: The merge/purge problem for large databases. SIGMOD Rec. 24, 127–138 (1995)
7. Kim, Y.S., Mahidadia, A., Compton, P., Cai, X., Bain, M., Krzywicki, A., Wobcke, W.: People Recommendation Based on Aggregated Bidirectional Intentions in Social Network Site. In: Kang, B.-H., Richards, D. (eds.) PKAW 2010. LNCS, vol. 6232, pp. 247–260. Springer, Heidelberg (2010)
8. Lam, S.K., Riedl, J.: Shilling recommender systems for fun and profit. In: Proceedings of the 13th WWW, pp. 393–402. ACM, New York (2004)
9. McFee, B., Lanckriet, G.: Metric learning to rank. In: Proceedings of the 27th International Conference on Machine Learning (ICML 2010) (June 2010)
10. Mobasher, B., Burke, R., Bhaumik, R., Williams, C.: Toward trustworthy recommender systems: An analysis of attack models and algorithm robustness. ACM Trans. Internet Technol. 7 (October 2007)
11. O'Mahony, M., Hurley, N., Kushmerick, N., Silvestre, G.: Collaborative recommendation: A robustness analysis. ACM Trans. Internet Technol. 4, 344–377 (2004)
12. Pan, J., Winchester, D., Land, L., Watters, P.: Descriptive data mining on fraudulent online dating profiles. In: Proceedings of the 18th ECIS (2010)
13. Pandit, S., Chau, D.H., Wang, S., Faloutsos, C.: Netprobe: a fast and scalable system for fraud detection in online auction networks. In: Proceedings of the 16th WWW, pp. 201–210. ACM, New York (2007)
14. Pantel, P., Lin, D.: SpamCop: A Spam Classification and Organization Program. In: Workshop on Learning for Text Categorization (1998)
15. Pizzato, L., Rej, T., Chung, T., Koprinska, I., Kay, J.: Recon: a reciprocal recommender for online dating. In: RecSys 2010: Proceedings of the Fourth ACM Conference on Recommender Systems, pp. 207–214. ACM, New York (2010)
16. Sarawagi, S., Bhamidipaty, A.: Interactive deduplication using active learning. In: Proceedings of the 8th ACM SIGKDD, New York, pp. 269–278 (2002)
17. Toma, C.L., Hancock, J.T., Ellison, N.B.: Separating fact from fiction: An examination of deceptive self-presentation in online dating profiles. Personality and Social Psychology Bulletin 34(8), 1023–1036 (2008)

Users and Noise:
The Magic Barrier of Recommender Systems

Alan Said*, Brijnesh J. Jain*, Sascha Narr, and Till Plumbaum

Technische Universität Berlin
DAI Lab.
{alan,jain,narr,till}@dai-lab.de

Abstract. Recommender systems are crucial components of most commercial web sites to keep users satisfied and to increase revenue. Thus, a lot of effort is made to improve recommendation accuracy. But when is the best possible performance of the recommender reached? The *magic barrier*, refers to some unknown level of prediction accuracy a recommender system can attain. The magic barrier reveals whether there is still room for improving prediction accuracy, or indicates that any further improvement is meaningless. In this work, we present a mathematical characterization of the magic barrier based on the assumption that user ratings are afflicted with inconsistencies - noise. In a case study with a commercial movie recommender, we investigate the inconsistencies of the user ratings and estimate the magic barrier in order to assess the actual quality of the recommender system.

Keywords: Recommender Systems, Noise, Evaluation Measures, User Inconsistencies.

1 Introduction

Recommender systems play an important role in most top-ranked commercial websites such as Amazon, Netflix, Last.fm or IMDb [10]. The goal of these recommender systems is to increase revenue and present personalized user experiences by providing suggestions for previously unknown items that are potentially interesting for a user. With the growing amount of data in the Internet, the importance of recommender systems increases even more to guide users through the mass of data.

The key role of recommender systems resulted in a vast amount of research in this field, which yielded a plethora of different recommender algorithms [1, 4, 8]. An example of a popular and widely used approach to recommenders is *collaborative filtering*. Collaborative filtering computes user-specific recommendations based on historical user data, such as ratings or usage patterns [4, 7]. Other approaches include content-based recommenders (recommend items based on properties of a specific item), social recommenders (recommend things based on the past behavior of similar users in the social network) or hybrid combinations of several different approaches.

To select an appropriate recommender algorithm, and adapt it to a given scenario or problem, the algorithms are usually examined by testing their performance using either

---

* Both authors contributed equally to this work.

J. Masthoff et al. (Eds.): UMAP 2012, LNCS 7379, pp. 237–248, 2012.

238 A. Said et al.

artificial or real test data reflecting the problem. The best performing algorithm and parameters among a number of candidate algorithms is chosen. To be able to compare performance, several different measures and metrics were defined. Common measures are precision and recall, normalized discounted cumulative gain (NDCG), receiver operating characteristic (ROC) or the root-mean-squared error (RMSE). RMSE is perhaps the most popular metric used to evaluate the prediction accuracy of a recommender algorithm [11]. It was the central evaluation metric used in the Netflix Prize competition[1]. For the RMSE as performance measure, a recommendation task is typically posed as that of learning a rating function that minimizes the RMSE on a given training set of user ratings. The generalization RMSE-performance of the learned rating function is then assessed on some independent test set of ratings, which is disjoint from the training set. One major drawback of measuring and comparing the performance using only static test data is that user behavior is not always reliable. According to studies conducted by [2, 3, 6] user ratings can be inconsistent (noisy) in the sense that a user may rate the same item differently at different points of time. Following these findings, Herlocker et al. [5] and other researchers coined the term *magic barrier*. The magic barrier marks the point at which the performance and accuracy of an algorithm cannot be enhanced due to noise in the data. Every improvement in accuracy might denote an over-fitting and not a better performance. Thus, comparing and measuring the expected future performance of algorithms based on static data might not work.

While investigations on the magic barrier are important for future recommendation research, only first evaluations on the inconsistency of ratings have been conducted so far. Most importantly, a mathematical characterization of the magic barrier is missing. In this paper, we will present such a mathematical characterization of the magic barrier, based on RMSE , which allows us to assess the actual performance of a recommender as well as the actual room for improvement. In particular, we can identify recommender algorithms that overfit the test set by chance or by peeking at the test set.[2]. We also conducted a first user study with a commercial recommender system, from the German movie recommendation website moviepilot[3], to substantiate our claims and findings in a real-world setting.

Our main contributions are as follows:

- We present a mathematical characterization of the magic barrier. Based on the principle of empirical risk minimization form statistical learning theory, we show that the magic barrier reduces to the RMSE of the optimal (but unknown) rating function. Then we characterize the magic barrier in terms of the expected inconsistencies

---

[1] http://www.netflixprize.com

[2] This occurs when information about the test set is used for constructing a recommender algorithm. For example, when we devise a new recommendation algorithm based on some similarity measure. We train our new algorithm using the cosine similarity and assess its performance on a test set. Then we train the same algorithm using the Pearson correlation and measure its performance on the same test set. Finally, we report the result of the algorithm and the similarity measure with the best prediction performance on the test set rather than choosing the model with the best prediction performance on the training set. Such approaches lead to overly optimistic results.

[3] http://www.moviepilot.de

incurred in the ratings. Since the magic barrier cannot be computed directly, we derive a procedure to estimate it.

- We present and discuss a case study with moviepilot, a commercial recommender system for movies. The case study aims at investigating user inconsistencies in a real-world setting. In addition, we estimated the magic barrier of moviepilot to assess the quality of moviepilot's recommendation engine and to propose a limit on how much moviepilot's recommendations can be improved.

Based on our findings, we propose that a real-world recommender system should regularly interact with users by polling their opinions about items they have rated previously in order to audit their own performance and, where appropriate, to take measures to improve their system.

2 Related Work

Inconsistency in user behavior in the context of recommender systems is a known concept and has been studied on several occasions before. The first mention of inconsistencies in a scope similar to ours was made by Hill et al. [6] in their study on virtual communities. The authors questioned how reliable the ratings were and found a rough estimate by calculating the RMSE between two sets of ratings performed by 22 users on two occasions 6 weeks apart.

Similar reliability issues, e.g. the levels of noise in user ratings, were discussed by Herlocker et al. [5], coining the term *the magic barrier* as an upper level of recommender system optimization.

More recently, Amatriain et al. [2] performed a set of user trials on 118 users based on a subset of the Netflix Prize dataset. The authors attempted to find answers to whether users are inconsistent in their rating behavior, how large the inconsistencies are and what factors have an impact on the inconsistencies. They were able to identify a lower bound, a magic barrier, for the dataset used in the trials.

Following their user trials, Amatriain et al. [3] successfully increased the accuracy of a recommender system by implementing a de-noising step based on re-ratings collected in a study. They presented two re-rating strategies (user-based and data-based) in order to find the *ground truth values* of ratings for the purpose of maximizing accuracy improvements in a recommender system. They concluded that re-rating previously rated items could, in some circumstances, be more beneficial than rating previously unrated items.

Some of the inconsistencies in users' rating behavior can be mitigated by temporal aspects, as Lathia et al. show [8]. This mitigation does however not compensate for all inconsistencies, which Amatriain et al. [3] showed by having different time spans between re-ratings.

The problems of noisy user behavior is connected to the type of evaluation used. Pu et al. [9] present a *user-centric* (as opposed to *data-centric*) evaluation framework which measures the quality of recommendations in terms of *usability, usefulness, interaction quality* and *user satisfaction*, which allows for optimization of recommender systems based on direct user interaction instead of *offline* accuracy metrics such as RMSE, NDCG, etc. User-centric evaluation does however come with a cost in terms of time, additionally it requires a set of users to be available for the evaluation process. Given these drawbacks, most recommender system evaluation still uses traditional information retrieval measures and methods, even though these might not always reflect the actual quality of the recommendation [11] due to the aforementioned inconsistencies in users' rating behavior.

If a model for the maximum level of measure-based optimization would be available, a magic barrier, it could serve as the cut-off point between data-centric and user-centric evaluation.

3   The Empirical Risk Minimization Principle

We pose the recommendation task as that of a function regression problem based on the empirical risk minimization principle from statistical learning theory [12]. This setting provides the theoretical foundation to derive a lower bound (henceforth referred to as the magic barrier) on the root-mean-square error that can be attained by an optimal recommender system.

3.1   The Traditional Setting of a Recommendation Task

We begin by describing the traditional setting of a recommendation task as presented in [4].

Suppose that $\mathcal{R}$ is a set of ratings r_{ui} submitted by users $u \in \mathcal{U}$ for items $i \in \mathcal{I}$. Ratings may take values from some discrete set $\mathcal{S} \subseteq \mathbb{R}$ of rating scores. Typically, ratings are known only for few user-item pairs. The recommendation task consists of suggesting new items that will be rated high by users.

It is common practice to pose the recommendation task as that of learning a rating function

$$f : \mathcal{U} \times \mathcal{I} \rightarrow \mathcal{S}, \quad (u, i) \mapsto f(u, i)$$

on the basis of a set of training examples from $\mathcal{R}$. Given a user u, the learned rating function f is then used to recommend those items i that have largest scores $f(u, i)$. The accuracy of a rating function f is evaluated on a test set, which is a subset of $\mathcal{R}$ disjoint from the training set.

A popular and widely used measure for evaluating the accuracy of f on a set $\mathcal{R}$ of ratings is the root-mean-square error (RMSE) criterion

$$E(f|\mathcal{R}) = \sqrt{\frac{1}{|\mathcal{R}|} \sum_{(u,i) \in \mathcal{R}} \left(f(u, i) - r_{ui} \right)^2}, \tag{1}$$

where the sum runs over all user-item pairs (u, i) for which $r_{ui} \in \mathcal{R}$.[4]

---

[4] For the sake of brevity, we abuse notation and write $(u, i) \in \mathcal{R}$ for user-item pairs (u, i) for which $r_{ui} \in \mathcal{R}$.

3.2 Recommendation as Risk Minimization

Learning a rating function by minimizing the RMSE criterion can be justified by the inductive principle of empirical risk minimization from statistical learning theory [12]. Within this setting we describe the problem of learning a rating function as follows: We assume that

- user-item pairs (u, i) are drawn from an unknown probability distribution $p(u, i)$,
- rating scores $r \in S$ are provided for each user-item pair (u, i) according to an unknown conditional probability distribution $p(r|u, i)$,
- $\mathcal{F}$ is a class of rating functions.

The probability $p(u, i)$ describes how likely it is that user u rates item i. The conditional probability $p(r|u, i)$ describes the probability that a given user u rates a given item i with rating score r. The class $\mathcal{F}$ of functions describes the set from which we choose (learn) our rating function f for recommending items. An example for $\mathcal{F}$ is the class of nearest neighbor-based methods.

The goal of learning a rating function is to find a function $f \in \mathcal{F}$ that minimizes the expected risk function

$$R(f) = \sum_{(u,i,r)} p(u, i, s)\big(f(u, i) - r\big)^2, \tag{2}$$

where the sum runs over all possible triples $(u, i, r) \in \mathcal{U} \times \mathcal{I} \times \mathcal{S}$ and $p(u, i, r) = p(u, i)p(r|u, i)$ is the joint probability.

The problem of learning an optimal rating function is that the distribution $p(u, i, s)$ is unknown. Therefore, we can not compute the optimal rating function

$$f_* = \arg\min_{f \in \mathcal{F}} R(f).$$

directly. Instead, we approximate f_* by minimizing the empirical risk

$$\widehat{R}(f|\mathcal{X}) = \frac{1}{|\mathcal{X}|} \sum_{r_{ui} \in \mathcal{X}} \big(f(u, i) - r_{ui}\big)^2,$$

where $\mathcal{X} \subseteq \mathcal{R}$ is a training set consisting of ratings r_{ui} given by user u for item i. Observe that minimizing the empirical risk is equivalent to minimizing the RMSE criterion.

A theoretical justification of minimizing the RMSE criterion (or the empirical risk) arises from the following result of statistical learning theory [12]: under the assumption that the user ratings from $\mathcal{R}$ are independent and identically distributed, the empirical risk is an unbiased estimate of the expected risk.[5]

---

[5] The set of users and items are both finite. In order to apply the law of large numbers, we may think of $\mathcal{R}$ as being a set of ratings obtained by randomly selecting triples (u, i, s) according to their joint distribution.

4   The Magic Barrier

This section derives a magic barrier (lower bound) on the RMSE that can be attained by an optimal recommender system. We show that the magic barrier is the standard deviation of the inconsistencies (noise) inherent in user ratings. To this end, we first present a noise model and then derive the magic barrier.

4.1   A Statistical Model for Users' Inconsistencies

As shown in user studies [2,3,6], users' rating tend to be inconsistent. Inconsistencies in the ratings could be due to, for example, change of taste over time, personal conditions, inconsistent rating strategies, and/or social influences, just to mention a few.

For the sake of convenience, we regard inconsistencies in user ratings as noise. The following fictitious scenario illustrates the basic idea behind our noise model: Consider a movie recommender with n movies and a rating scale from zero to five stars, where zero stars refers to a rating score reserved for unknown movies only. Users are regularly asked to rate m randomly selected movies. After a sufficiently long period of time, each user has rated each movie several times. The ratings may vary over time due to several reasons ([8]) such as change of taste, current emotional state, group-dynamic effects, and other external as well as internal influences.

Keeping the above scenario in mind, the *expected rating* of a user u on movie i is defined by the expectation

$$\mathbb{E}[R_{ui}] = \mu_{ui},$$

where R_{ui} is a random variable on the user-item pair (u, i) and takes on zero to five stars as values. Then a rating r_{ui} is composed of the expected rating μ_{ui} and some error term ε_{ui} for the noise incurred by user u when rating item i. We occasionally refer to the error ε_{ui} as user-item noise. Thus, user ratings arise from a statistical model of the form

$$r_{ui} = \mu_{ui} + \varepsilon_{ui}, \tag{3}$$

where the random error ε_{ui} has expectation $\mathbb{E}[\varepsilon_{ui}] = 0$.

4.2   Deriving the Magic Barrier

Suppose that f_* is the true (but unknown) rating function that knows all expected ratings μ_{ui} of each user u about any item i, that is

$$f_*(u, i) = \mu_{ui} \tag{4}$$

for all users $u \in \mathcal{U}$ and items $i \in \mathcal{I}$. Then the optimal rating function f_* minimizes the expected risk function Eq. (2). Substituting Eq. (3) and Eq. (4) into the expected risk function Eq. (2) and using $p(u, i, s) = p(u, i)p(s|u, i)$ gives

$$R(f_*) = \sum_{(u,i)} p(u, i)\mathbb{E}\left[\varepsilon_{ui}^2\right] = \sum_{(u,i)} p(u, i)\mathbb{V}\left[\varepsilon_{ui}\right], \tag{5}$$

where the sum runs over all possible user-item pairs $(u, i) \in \mathcal{U} \times \mathcal{I}$ and $\mathbb{V}[\varepsilon_{ui}]$ denotes the variance of the user-item noise ε_{ui}. Eq. (5) shows that the expected risk of an optimal rating function f_* is the mean variance of the user-item noise terms.

Expressed in terms of the RMSE criterion, the magic barrier $B_{\mathcal{U} \times \mathcal{I}}$ of a recommender system with users $\mathcal{U}$ and items $\mathcal{I}$ is then defined by

$$B_{\mathcal{U} \times \mathcal{I}} = \sqrt{\sum_{(u,i)} p(u, i) \mathbb{V}[\varepsilon_{ui}]}.$$

The magic barrier is the RMSE of an optimal rating function f_*. We see that even an optimal rating function has a non-zero RMSE *unless all users are consistent with their ratings.*

Observe that an optimal rating function needs not to be a member of our chosen function class $\mathcal{F}$ from which we select (learn) our actual rating function f. Thus the RMSE of f can be decomposed into the magic barrier $B_{\mathcal{U} \times \mathcal{I}}$ and an error E_f due to model complexity of f giving

$$E_{RMSE}(f) = B_{\mathcal{U} \times \mathcal{I}} + E_f > B_{\mathcal{U} \times \mathcal{I}}.$$

4.3   Estimating the Magic Barrier

As for the expected risk, we are usually unable to directly determine the magic barrier $B_{\mathcal{U} \times \mathcal{I}}$. Instead we estimate the magic barrier according to the procedure outlined in Algorithm 1.

Algorithm 1. Procedure for estimating the magic barrier.

Procedure: Let $\mathcal{X} \subseteq \mathcal{U} \times \mathcal{I}$ be a randomly generated subset of user-item pairs.

1. For each user-item pair $(u, i) \in \mathcal{X}$ do
   (a) Sample m ratings $r_{ui}^1, \ldots, r_{ui}^m$ on a regular basis
   (b) Estimate the expectation μ_{ui} by the sample mean

$$\widehat{\mu}_{ui} = \frac{1}{m} \sum_{t=1}^{m} r_{ui}^t$$

   (c) Estimate the variance of the ratings

$$\widehat{\varepsilon}_{ui}^2 = \frac{1}{m} \sum_{t=1}^{m} \left(\widehat{\mu}_{ui} - r_{ui}^t \right)^2$$

2. Estimate the magic barrier by taking the average

$$\widehat{B}_{\mathcal{X}} = \sqrt{\frac{1}{|\mathcal{X}|} \sum_{(u,i) \in \mathcal{X}} \widehat{\varepsilon}_{ui}^2}. \tag{6}$$

We postulate that all rating functions $f \in \mathcal{F}$ with an empirical risk of the form

$$\widehat{R}(f|\mathcal{X}) \leq \widehat{B}_{\mathcal{X}}^2$$

are likely to overfit on the set $\mathcal{X}$ and consider further improvements on the RMSE below $\widehat{B}_{\mathcal{X}}$ as *meaningless*.

5   Case Study Using a Commercial Movie Recommender

Our experimental case study serves to validate the noise model and to investigate the relationship between the estimated magic barrier and the prediction accuracy of moviepilot. Due to limited resources, we conducted a moderately scaled user study in a real-world setting.

5.1   Moviepilot

moviepilot is a commercial movie recommender system having more than one million users, 55,000 movies, and over 10 million ratings. Movies are rated on a 0 to 10 scale with step size 0.5 (0 corresponding to a rating score of 0, not an unknown rating). The two most common ways to rate movies are either through the "discover new movies" page, shown in Fig. 1(a) or through the "100 movies of your lifetime" page. The former presents a combination of new, popular and recommended movies whereas the latter one presents, like the title suggests, the 100 previously unrated movies deemed most probable to be liked by the user.

The recommendation engine uses a neighborhood-based collaborative filtering approach, with a similarity measure inspired by the cosine similarity, and is retrained regularly, so as to always be able to recommend movies based on an up-to-date model of users' rating histories.

5.2   Data

To estimate the magic barrier, we created a Web-based study for collecting users' *opinions* on movies. An opinion is a score in the same rating scale as standard user ratings. The difference between the two is that ratings are stored in the user profile and used for predictions, whereas opinions do not show up in users' profiles, are only stored in the survey and do, subsequently, not affect the recommendations users are given.

The opinion collection study was implemented as a Web application, Fig. 1(b), mirroring the look-and-feel of moviepilot's rating interface as closely as possible. By emulating the rating interface of moviepilot for opinion polling, we aimed at mitigating any potential distortion of the data due to different interface elements. A comparison of both is shown in Fig. 1.

Users were notified about the study by announcements in newsletters and posts in the community forums. The announcements provided information on timing, duration, process of the opinion collection, the collector, the URL, etc. Users were asked to not to peek at their old ratings when taking part in the study. They were also informed that submitted opinions would not be stored in their profiles.

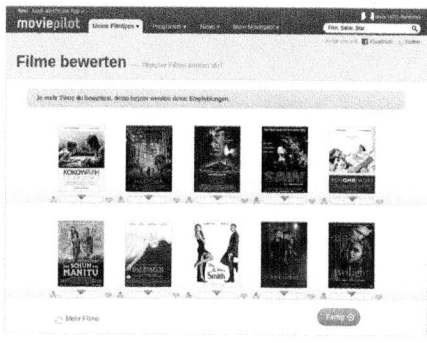 

(a) moviepilot's find new movies page   (b) Opinion interface

Fig. 1. The moviepilot rating interface and the opinion interface used in the user study. The opinion interface mimics the look-and-feel of moviepilot in order to give users a feeling of familiarity lowering the level UI-induced noise.

Whilst taking part in the study, users were presented with a number of movies randomly drawn from the complete set of their rated movies. Each user could submit at most one opinion on each movie. A user could skip any number of movies without providing any opinion. After at least a 20 opinions had been given, the active user could complete the study.

The study ran from mid April 2011 to early May 2011. We recorded only opinions of users that provided opinions on at least 20 movies. A total of 306 users provided 6, 299 opinions about 2, 329 movies.

5.3 Experimental Setup

We estimated the magic barrier according to the procedure described in Algorithm 1. For this, we used the ratings and opinions of those user-item pairs for which the 6, 299 opinions had been recorded.[6] This setup corresponds to sampling two ratings for each of the 6, 299 user-item pairs. The estimate of the magic barrier is the average of the squared sample noise over all 6, 299 user-item pairs.

5.4 Results

Fig. 2 summarizes the outcome of the opinion polling study, it shows the RMSE of moviepilot's recommendation engine and an estimated magic barrier taken over all 6, 299 user-item pairs. The plot also shows the estimated magic barrier restricted to the following subsets of the 6, 299 user-item pairs: (1) user-item pairs with above average rating, (2) user-item pairs with above average opinion, (3) user-item pairs with below average rating, and (4) user-item pairs with below average opinion. The user-specific averages were taken over all ratings given by the respective user.

---

[6] Though opinions differ from ratings conceptually, we treat them equally when estimating the magic barrier.

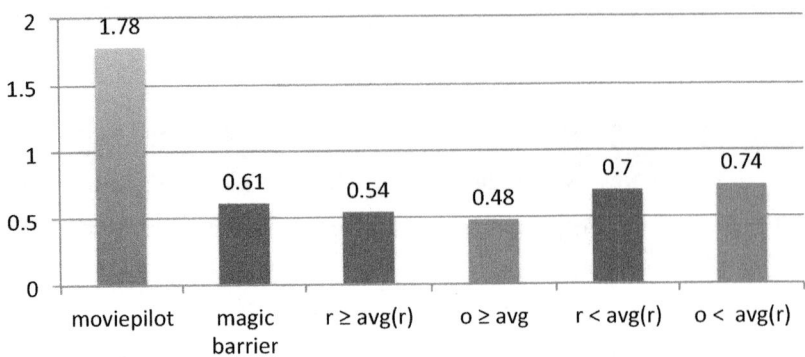

Fig. 2. RMSE of moviepilot and estimated magic barrier, where *all* refers to the estimation computed over all 6, 299 user-item pairs, $r \geq avg(r)$ and $o \geq avg(r)$, resp. refer to the magic barrier restricted to all user-item pairs with ratings and opinions, respectively, *above or equal to* the user-specific average over all user ratings. Similarly, $r < avg(r)$ and $o < avg(r)$, respectively, refer to the magic barrier restricted to all user-item pairs with ratings and opinions, resp., *below* the user-specific average over all user ratings and opinions.

The first observation to be made is that the estimated magic barrier of moviepilot is circa 0.61, which is slightly more than one step in moviepilot's rating scale (± 0.61). In contrast, the RMSE of moviepilot's recommendation engine is about 1.8 which is between three and four rating steps. Under the assumption that the estimated magic barrier is a good estimate of the unknown magic barrier, improvements of a recommender method close to or below the estimated magic barrier are meaningless. Under the same assumptions, there is room for improving the prediction accuracy of moviepilot. These assumptions, however, have to be taken with care due to the limited amount of data for estimating the expected rating of each user-item pair.

The second observation to be made is that our estimate of the magic barrier is lower when restricted to user-item pairs with ratings/opinions above average ratings than for below average ratings. We hypothesize that users tend to be more consistent with their ratings/opinions for movies that they have rated above average. This finding complements the observations of Amatriain et al. [2], i.e. that user ratings seem to be more consistent at the extreme ends of the rating scale.

The results obtained in this as well as in other studies and the theoretical treatment on magic barriers give a strong case for collecting opinions (or re-ratings) in order to

1. estimate the magic barrier for performance evaluation, and
2. improve recommendations based on a set of ratings for each user-item pair rather than on a single rating.

A good estimate of the magic barrier is useful for assessing the quality of a recommendation method and for revealing room for improvements. Recommenders with a prediction accuracy close to the estimated magic barrier can be regarded as 'optimal'. Further improvements of such recommenders are meaningless.

6   Conclusion

The magic barrier is the RMSE of an optimal rating function, and as such, it provides a lower bound for the RMSE an arbitrary rating function can attain. In terms of noise incurred when users rate items, the magic barrier is the square root of the expected variance of the user-item noise. Using this characterization, it is straightforward to derive a procedure for estimating the magic barrier.

In an experimental case study using moviepilot, a commercial movie recommender system, we investigated inconsistencies of user ratings and estimated the magic barrier for assessing the actual prediction accuracy of moviepilot. The results confirm that users are inconsistent in their ratings and that they tend to be more consistent for above average ratings. Our estimate of the magic barrier reveals that there is room to improve moviepilot's recommendation algorithm.

On the basis of our findings we suggest that regularly polling ratings for previously rated items can be useful to audit the performance of the recommendation engine and may, where appropriate, lead to measures taken for improving the existing system.

To obtain statically sound results, a large-scale user study is imperative. In order to regularly poll opinions/ratings of previously rated items, the following issues should be addressed: (1) How to implement a user-friendly interface for polling opinions/ratings without having a deterrent effect on users and unbiased results at the same time? (2) How to present items and sample opinions/ratings to obtain a good estimate of the magic barrier?

Acknowledgments. The authors would like to express their gratitude to the users of moviepilot who took their time to conduct the survey and the moviepilot team who contributed to this work with dataset, relevant insights and support.

The work in this paper was conducted in the scope of the KMulE project which was sponsored by the German Federal Ministry of Economics and Technology (BMWi).

References

1. Adomavicius, G., Tuzhilin, A.: Toward the next generation of recommender systems: A survey of the state of the art and possible extensions. IEEE Trans. on Knowl. and Data Eng. 17, 734–749 (2005)
2. Amatriain, X., Pujol, J.M., Oliver, N.: I Like It.. I Like It Not: Evaluating User Ratings Noise in Recommender Systems. In: Houben, G.-J., McCalla, G., Pianesi, F., Zancanaro, M. (eds.) UMAP 2009. LNCS, vol. 5535, pp. 247–258. Springer, Heidelberg (2009)
3. Amatriain, X., Pujol, J.M., Tintarev, N., Oliver, N.: Rate it again: increasing recommendation accuracy by user re-rating. In: Proceedings of the Third ACM Conference on Recommender Systems, RecSys 2009, pp. 173–180. ACM, New York (2009)
4. Desrosiers, C., Karypis, G.: A Comprehensive Survey of Neighborhood-based Recommendation Methods. In: Ricci, F., Rokach, L., Shapira, B., Kantor, P.B. (eds.) Recommender Systems Handbook, pp. 145–186. Springer, US (2011)
5. Herlocker, J.L., Konstan, J.A., Terveen, L.G., Riedl, J.T.: Evaluating collaborative filtering recommender systems. ACM Trans. Inf. Syst. 22, 5–53 (2004)
6. Hill, W., Stead, L., Rosenstein, M., Furnas, G.: Recommending and evaluating choices in a virtual community of use. In: Proceedings of the SIGCHI Conference on Human Factors in Computing Systems, pp. 194–201. ACM Press/Addison-Wesley Publishing Co. (1995)

7. Koren, Y., Bell, R.: Advances in Collaborative Filtering. In: Ricci, F., Rokach, L., Shapira, B., Kantor, P.B. (eds.) Recommender Systems Handbook, pp. 145–186. Springer, US (2011)
8. Lathia, N., Hailes, S., Capra, L., Amatriain, X.: Temporal diversity in recommender systems. In: Proceedings of the 33rd International ACM SIGIR Conference on Research and Development in Information Retrieval, SIGIR 2010, pp. 210–217. ACM, New York (2010)
9. Pu, P., Chen, L., Hu, R.: A user-centric evaluation framework for recommender systems. In: Proceedings of the Fifth ACM Conference on Recommender Systems, RecSys 2011, pp. 157–164. ACM, New York (2011)
10. Ricci, F., Rokach, L., Shapira, B.: Introduction to Recommender Systems Handbook. In: Ricci, F., Rokach, L., Shapira, B., Kantor, P.B. (eds.) Recommender Systems Handbook, pp. 1–35. Springer, US (2011)
11. Shani, G., Gunawardana, A.: Evaluating Recommendation Systems. In: Ricci, F., Rokach, L., Shapira, B., Kantor, P.B. (eds.) Recommender Systems Handbook, pp. 257–297. Springer, US (2011)
12. Vapnik, V.N.: The nature of statistical learning theory. Springer-Verlag New York, Inc., New York (1995)

Improving Construct Validity Yields Better Models of Systematic Inquiry, Even with Less Information

Michael A. Sao Pedro, Ryan S.J.d. Baker, and Janice D. Gobert

Learning Sciences and Technologies Program, Worcester Polytechnic Institute
{mikesp,rsbaker,jgobert}@wpi.edu

Abstract. Data-mined models often achieve good predictive power, but some-times at the cost of interpretability. We investigate here if selecting features to increase a model's construct validity and interpretability also can improve the model's ability to predict the desired constructs. We do this by taking existing models and reducing the feature set to increase construct validity. We then compare the existing and new models on their predictive capabilities within a held-out test set in two ways. First, we analyze the models' overall predictive performance. Second, we determine how much student interaction data is ne-cessary to make accurate predictions. We find that these reduced models with higher construct validity not only achieve better agreement overall, but also achieve better prediction with less data. This work is conducted in the context of developing models to assess students' inquiry skill at designing controlled experiments and testing stated hypotheses within a science inquiry microworld.

Keywords: science microworlds, science inquiry, inquiry assessment, behavior detector, educational data mining, construct validity, feature selection, J48.

1   Introduction

Feature selection, the process of pre-selecting features before running a data mining algorithm, can improve the performance of data mining algorithms (cf. [1]). Several automated approaches exist for finding optimal feature sets such as filtering redundant features [2], conducting heuristic searches (cf. [3]), using genetic algorithms [4], and clustering [5]. These procedures, though powerful, may yield sets that domain experts would not intuitively expect to align with the target class (construct). An alternative is to select features that specifically improve models' construct validity.

This alternative is motivated by our prior work in developing automated detectors of two scientific inquiry behaviors, designing controlled experiments and testing stated hypotheses, within a science microworld [6]. To build them, we first filtered features that correlated highly with each other, and then constructed J48 decision trees. The resulting detectors worked well under student-level cross-validation. How-ever, upon inspecting them more closely, we noticed some features considered theo-retically important to the constructs [7], [8], [9] were eliminated at the filtering step. Also, other features without theoretical justification remained. We believe this feature

J. Masthoff et al. (Eds.): UMAP 2012, LNCS 7379, pp. 249–260, 2012.

selection process may have yielded a feature set that did not represent all aspects of the behaviors, which in turn may have negatively impacted their predictive performance.

Thus, we explore in this paper whether selecting features with the goal of increasing a model's construct validity and interpretability can also improve a model's predictive ability. We do so by comparing two types of detectors for each behavior. One type is built with an automated feature selection strategy used in our original detectors [6]. The other type is built using a combination of manual selection and statistics to select successful features that theoretically align more closely with the behaviors.

We compare the predictive performance of the two types of detectors against a held-out test set in two ways. First, we compare the detectors' ability to predict behavior at the level of a full data collection cycle. This enables us to measure how well the detectors can be used for assessing performance, or for identifying which students need scaffolding when they claim to finish collecting data. In addition, it is useful to have detectors that can identify a student's lack of skill as quickly as possible so the software can "jump in" and support the student as soon as they need it to prevent frustration, floundering, or haphazard inquiry [10]. Thus, the second way we compare detectors is to determine how much student data is needed before inquiry behavior can be accurately predicted. The faster detectors can make valid inferences, the faster the system can help the students who need it.

2   Background and Datasets

2.1   Learning Environment and Behaviors of Interest

The Science Assistments Phase Change Microworld [6], [10], designed for use in middle school science classes, aims to foster understanding about melting and boiling processes of a substance via semi-structured scientific inquiry. A typical activity requires students to determine if one of four variables (like amount of substance) affects properties of a substance's phase change (like its melting point). Students address this goal by conducting inquiry in four phases: observe, hypothesize, experiment, and analyze data. Each one exercises different inquiry skills. The behaviors of interest for the analyses presented here, designing controlled experiments and testing stated hypotheses behaviors, occur in the experiment phase.

In the experiment phase, students collect data (trials) by designing and running experiments with a phase change simulation. Students can change the simulation's variable values, run, pause and reset the simulation, and view previously collected trials and stated hypotheses. Briefly, when collecting data, students design controlled experiments when they generate data that support determining the effects of independent variables on outcomes. They test stated hypotheses when they generate data with the intent to support or refute an explicitly stated hypothesis. More information about the microworld and constructs can be found in [6].

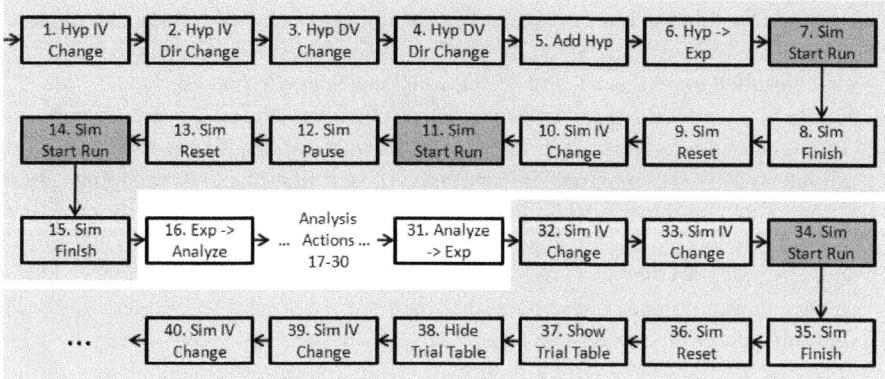

Fig. 1. Example sequence of student actions for a phase change activity. Two clips (shown in light grey) would be generated since the "Experiment" stage was entered twice.

2.2 Labeling Behaviors within the Learning Environment

The first step towards building detectors of these constructs, in both this paper and our previous work, was to employ "text replay tagging" of log files [6]. In this process, low-level student actions within microworld activities are extracted from the database. Next, contiguous sequences of these actions segmented into *clips* (see Figure 1). A clip contains all actions associated with formulating hypotheses (hypothesize phase actions) and designing and running experiments (experiment phase actions). We note that several clips could be generated for a single microworld activity since students could navigate through the inquiry phases many times, as shown in Figure 1. Clips are also the grain-size at which data collection behavior is labeled, and detectors are built.

Once clips are generated, a human coder applies one or more behavior tags to text replays, "pretty-prints" of clips. In this domain, a clip may be tagged as involving designing controlled experiments, testing stated hypotheses, both, or neither. Text replay tagging provides "ground truth labels" from which detectors of the two inquiry behaviors can be built. Next, we describe the datasets generated via text replay tagging student clips from which detectors will be constructed and tested.

2.3 Data Sets

Clips were generated from 148 suburban Central Massachusetts middle school students' interactions within a sequence of four microworld activities. These clips were tagged to create the following training, validation and test data sets:

- *Training Set (601 clips).* Initially, two human coders tagged 571 clips for training and cross-validating the detectors in [6]. Since several clips could be generated per activity, a single, randomly chosen clip was tagged per student, per activity. This ensured all students and activities were equally represented in this data set. Inter-rater reliability for the tags was high overall (κ=.69 for designing controlled experiments, κ=1.0 for testing stated hypotheses). By chance, the stratification yielded few first clips, clips representing students' first data collection within an activity. To have a more representative training set, an additional 30 randomly selected first clips were tagged. In total, 31.4% of the clips were tagged as designing controlled experiments, and 35.6% as testing stated hypotheses.

- *Validation Set (100 clips)*. A special set of clips was tagged by one human coder for engineering detectors with improved construct validity (described in more detail later). This set contained 20 randomly chosen first clips, 20 randomly chosen second clips, up through fifth clips. Clips were not stratified by student or activity. More stringent student or activity-level stratification was not used, because all students and activities were used to build the training set. Stratification would not remove biases already present in this data set. In total, 34.0% were tagged as designing controlled experiments, and 42.0% as testing stated hypotheses.

- *Held-out Test Set (439 clips)*. A human coder tagged all remaining first through fourth clips in the data set for comparing detectors. This set did not contain fifth clips because only 2 remained in the tagged corpus. First clips in which one or no simulation runs occurred were also excluded, because demonstration of the inquiry behaviors requires that students run the simulation at least twice [10]. Such clips would trivially be identified as not demonstrating either behavior and could bias our comparisons. This set had 64.7% tagged as designing controlled experiments and 61.0% as testing stated hypotheses. Note that the data distribution of the behaviors was different in the held-out test set than the other data sets. This occurred due to random chance, but provides an opportunity to conduct stringent validation, since the base rates will be different in this data set than the other data sets.

Feature sets computed over clips, combined with text replay tags, form the basis for training and testing the detectors. Since the aim of this work is to compare models built from different feature sets, we discuss the feature generation and selection processes in more detail in the following section.

3   Feature Selection and Detector Construction

Our original designing controlled experiments and testing stated hypotheses behavior detectors considered 73 features associated with a clip [6]. Feature categories included: variables changed when making hypotheses, full hypotheses made, simulation pauses, total simulation runs, incomplete simulation runs (paused and reset before the simulation finished), complete simulation runs, data table displays, hypothesis list displays, variable changes made when designing experiments, and total actions (any action performed by a student). For each category, counts and timing values (min, max, standard deviation, mean and mode) were computed. In addition, the specific activity number associated with the clip was also included. A pairwise repeat trial count, the number of all pairs of trials with the same independent variable values [9], was also included, as was a unique pairwise controlled trial count, the number of non-repeated trials in which only one independent variable differed between them (cf. [7]). All features were computed cumulatively, taking into account actions in predecessor clips, as in [6]. For example, given the actions shown in Figure 1, the total number of runs for clip 2 would be 5 (assuming no more runs had occurred after action 40).

We added five additional features to this set which seemed to have face validity as potential predictors of the two behaviors, giving a total of 78 features. In specific, we added *adjacent* counts for unique controlled trials and repeats. These are counts of successive trials (e.g. trial 2 vs. 3, 3 vs. 4) in which only one variable was changed (controlled) or all variables were the same (repeated). Since the controlled trials counts excluded repeat trials, we added two additional counts for controlled trials that did allow them, one pairwise and one adjacent. Finally, we added a feature to count when simulation variables explicitly stated in hypotheses were changed.

Two different approaches for feature selection over this set were employed to form behavior detectors. The first approach removed correlated features prior to building detectors (RCF detectors). The second approach involved selecting features geared at improving construct validity (ICV detectors). These procedures are discussed below.

3.1   Removed Correlated Features (RCF) Detector Construction

The original models in [6] were built in RapidMiner 4.6 as follows. First, redundant features correlated to other features at or above 0.6 were removed. Then, J48 decision trees, a Java-based implementation of C4.5 decision trees with automated pruning to control for over-fitting [11], were constructed. The RCF detectors of each behavior developed in this paper were built using this same process. However, they instead were built from the new feature set (78 features), and the enhanced training corpus.

The initial remove correlated features procedure eliminated 53 features. Of the 25 remaining features, 19 were timing values associated with the following feature classes: all actions, total simulation runs, incomplete simulation runs, simulation pauses, data table displays, hypothesis table displays, variables changed when making hypotheses, full hypotheses made, and simulation variable changes. The remaining 6 features were activity number and counts for the following feature classes: all actions, incomplete simulation runs, data table displays, hypothesis list displays, full hypotheses created, and adjacent repeat trials count (one of the new features added). RCF detectors for designing controlled experiments and testing stated hypotheses were then built based on this set of 25 features. Their performance will be discussed later in the Results section.

We note that this procedure eliminated some features which are considered theoretically important to both constructs. For example, counts for controlled trials, total simulation runs, and simulation variables stated in hypotheses changed were all filtered. These features are important, because they reflect theoretical prescriptive models of how data should be collected to support or refute hypotheses. Constructing controlled trials is seen as a key procedural component in theory on designing controlled experiments (cf. [7]). Similarly, running trials and changing values of the variables explicitly stated in the hypotheses both play roles in determining if hypotheses are supported. In addition, some features remaining did not immediately appear to map to theory on these constructs, such as the number of times that the student displayed the hypothesis viewer or data table. As discussed previously, we hypothesize these RCF detectors will not perform as well as detectors, because the remaining features do not theoretically align as well with the behaviors. Next, we describe how we selected features to yield detectors with improved construct validity (ICV detectors), which may in turn improve predictive performance.

3.2   Improved Construct Validity (ICV) Detector Construction

We selected features for the new detectors with increased construct validity (ICV) using a combination of theory and search. We first sought to understand how individual features related to the constructs. This was done by identifying which features had linear correlations to each behavior at or above 0.2. Several features did so with both behaviors: all actions count, total run count, complete run count, variable changes made when designing experiments, changes to variables associated with stated hypotheses when designing experiments, adjacent and pairwise controlled experiments counts (both with and without considering repeats), and pairwise and adjacent repeat trials counts. An additional feature correlated with designing controlled experiments, the number of simulation pauses. From this set of 11 features, the counts for controlled trials, repeat trials, and changing variables associated with stated hypotheses are all features used by others to directly measure procedural understanding associated with the behaviors [7], [8]. The other features, though not directly related, may also help distinguish procedural understanding. Thus, we kept all 11 features for the next round of feature selection.

From here, we reduced the feature set further by performing separate manual backwards elimination search (cf. [1]) for each construct as follows. Features were first ordered in terms of the theoretical support for them by a domain expert. Then, features were removed one at a time, starting with the one with the least theoretical support. From this candidate feature set, a decision tree was constructed using the training set. The resulting model's predictive performance was then tested on the *validation set* of 100 clips. If the candidate model yielded better performance than its predecessor, it was kept. If it did not, the candidate was rejected and another feature with low theoretical support was removed to form a new candidate set. This process was repeated, removing one feature at a time, until performance no longer improved.

Predictive performance was measured using A' [12] and Kappa (κ). Briefly, A' [12], the area under the ROC curve, is the probability that when given two clips, one labeled as demonstrating a behavior and one not, a detector will correctly identify which clip is which. An A' of 0.5 indicates chance-level performance, 1.0 indicates perfect performance. Cohen's Kappa (κ) assesses if the detector is better than chance at labeling behavior. κ of 0.0 indicates chance-level performance, 1.0 indicates perfect performance. When comparing two candidate models, the model with higher κ was preferred. However, if A' decreased greatly and κ increased slightly, the model with higher A' was chosen. If two models yielded the same values, the model with fewer features was chosen.

The best ICV detectors of each construct performed well over the validation set. The best designing controlled experiments ICV detector had 8 features (total run count and pause count were removed) and had A'=1.0 and κ=.84. The best testing stated hypotheses ICV detector had 5 features: variable changes made when designing experiments (both related and unrelated to stated hypotheses), unique pairwise controlled trials, adjacent controlled trials with repeats considered, and complete simulation runs. Its performance on the validation set was also strong (A'=.96, κ=.77).

4   Results: Comparing Predictive Capabilities of Detectors

Having created these two sets of detectors (RCF and ICV), we now can study whether selecting features more theoretically aligned with the two inquiry behaviors will yield better detectors than more traditional approaches. There are two key questions we address. First, which detectors predict best overall? Second, how quickly can detectors identify the two inquiry behaviors? Performance will be compared against the *held-out test set* only, rather than using cross-validation over all datasets. This was done for two reasons. First, the entire training set was used to select features for the ICV detectors. Using the full training set enabled us to understand the relationships between individual features and behaviors more thoroughly. Second, the search procedure for building ICV detectors likely overfit them to the validation set data.

4.1   Comparing Detectors' Overall Performance

We compared detectors' performance at classifying behaviors in the held-out test set, labeled at the clip level. As a reminder, this comparison measures how well the detectors can be used for assessing performance, or identifying which students need scaffolding when they claim to be finished collecting data. Detectors are compared using A' and Kappa (κ). These were chosen because they both try to compensate for successful classification by chance [13], and have different tradeoffs. A' can be more sensitive to uncertainty, but looks at the classifier's degree of confidence; κ looks only at the final label, leading to more stringent evaluation. We note that statistical tests comparing models' A and κ are not performed. This is because students contribute multiple clips in the test set, and thus independence assumptions are violated. Meta-analytical techniques do exist to handle this (e.g. [14]), but our data did not have enough data points per student to employ them.

As shown in Table 1, the detectors with improved construct validity (ICV) detectors outperformed the removed correlated features (RCF) detectors within the held-out test set. For designing controlled experiments, both the RCF (A'=.89) and ICV (A'=.94) detectors were excellent at distinguishing this construct. However, the ICV detector was better at identifying the correct class (RCF κ=.30 vs. ICV κ=.45). Both detectors seem to bias towards labeling behavior as "not designing controlled experiments", as indicated by lower recall rates than precision rates (RCF recall=.46, precision=.90 vs. ICV recall= .58, precision=.95). This suggests that more students would receive scaffolding than necessary upon finishing data collection.

Upon inspecting the results for designing controlled experiments more closely, we noticed a large number of first clips with exactly two simulation runs had been misclassified. These kinds of clips comprised 26.7% of the held-out test corpus. When filtering these out (leaving 322 clips), the performance of the ICV detector was substantially higher (ICV A'=.94, κ =.75, recall=.83). The RCF detector's performance was also higher (RCF A'=.90, κ =.44, recall=.56), but did not reach the level of the ICV detector. The implications of this will be discussed later.

Table 1. Confusion matrices and performance metrics for detectors' overall predictions.

	Designing Controlled Experiments					Testing Stated Hypotheses			
	RCF Detector		ICV Detector			RCF Detector		ICV Detector	
	True N	True Y	True N	True Y		True N	True Y	True N	True Y
Pred N	140	153	146	118	Pred N	142	149	146	37
Pred Y	15	131	9	166	Pred Y	29	119	25	231
	Pc = .90, Rc = .46		Pc = .95, Rc = .58			Pc = .80, Rc = .44		Pc = .90, Rc = .86	
	A' = .89, K = .30		A' = .94, K = .45			A' = .82, K = .24		A' = .91, K = .70	

* Pc = precision; Rc = recall

For the testing stated hypotheses behavior, the ICV detector again showed a substantial improvement over the RCF detector. The ICV detector was around ten percentage points better at distinguishing between the two classes (RCF A'=.82 vs. ICV A'=.91). Furthermore, κ and recall were much higher for the ICV detector than the RCF detector (RCF κ =.24, recall=.44 vs. ICV κ =.70, recall=.86). The ICV detector is therefore quite good at selecting the correct class for a clip, and has much less bias towards labeling behavior as "not testing stated hypotheses".

Though not shown in Table 1, the ICV and RCF detectors were also compared to our original detectors [6], which used the original 73 features and had correlated features removed. Performance on the held-out test set was slightly worse than the RCF detector described here for designing controlled experiments (A'=.86, κ=.28, recall=.42), but slightly better for testing stated hypotheses (A'=.83, κ=.30, recall=.49). The new ICV detectors still outperform these detectors by a substantial amount. In sum, these findings support the idea that improving construct validity can lead to better overall prediction of systematic inquiry. Next, we determine if the ICV detectors can infer behavior with fewer actions.

4.2   Comparing Detectors' Performance Predicting with Less Data

The analyses here determine if detectors can predict behavior labeled at the clip level using less information. Again, these comparisons enable us to determine which detectors are more suitable for identifying which students need support *as they conduct their data collection*. Given our learning environment and approach, there are several ways to define "less information". We chose to look at simulation runs because they are the grain size at which we aim to activate scaffolding. In considering simulation runs, we also had to consider the clip number. Recall that several cycles of data collection could occur in an activity (each cycle represents a clip). Predictive performance could be impacted by the clip number under consideration, because later clips contain all actions associated with predecessor clips. Thus, we compare each detector on predicting behavior labeled at the clip level using actions up to the nth run within the mth clip, for varying numbers of runs and clips.

This approach required new sets of feature values to accommodate the fewer actions. Feature values were computed using all actions from clips $1..m-1$ ($m > 1$), and all actions in the mth clip, up to and including the nth "sim start run" action (actions in dark grey in Figure 1). As an example, the feature values for the action sequence in Figure 1 for clip 2 and two runs would be computed using all actions 1-16 from the first clip, and actions up to and including the second "sim start run" (actions 31-38) in clip 2. Note that the notion of a "full run" actually spans several actions (e.g. actions 11-13 in Figure 1), given that the student could let the simulation run to completion, pause the simulation, or reset it. The "sim start run" action was chosen (rather than "sim finish" or "sim reset") to denote the boundary due to considerations for how we would scaffold students. In particular, we may want to prevent students from collecting of data unhelpful for the subsequent stage of inquiry, where they analyze data. Having the detectors classify behavior at the point where students try to run the simulation enables such an intervention.

We compare detectors' performance using less data by comparing predictions for a given clip-run combination against the ground truth labels at the clip level. The number of clips was varied from 1 to 4, and the number of runs was varied from 1 to 5. A' and κ were computed per combination. Our expectation is that as the number of runs considered increases (and correspondingly the number of actions considered increases), A' and κ will increase. However, since many clips had fewer than five simulation runs, performance metrics may plateau as the number of runs increases. This may occur because no additional information would be available to improve predictions.

As shown in Table 2, the ICV detectors match or outperform the RCF detectors, when both detector variants are given less data on student performance. For clip 1, neither detector performed well for one or two runs ($\kappa \cong 0.0$). This finding associated with one run matched expectations because positive inquiry behavior can only be identified after two or more runs (cf. [7]). For runs 3-5 on the first clip, the RCF detector had A' ranging from .73 to .76, whereas the ICV detector had A' ranging from .93 to 1.0. The RCF detectors' κ remained at chance levels ranging from .06 to .07. The ICV detectors' κ values were better but still low, ranging from .16 to .20.

The designing controlled experiments detectors' poor performance on first clips may be due to misclassifications of such clips with exactly two runs (see Section 4.1). To see if ignoring such clips would impact detectors' ability to classify with less data, we removed them from the test set and re-computed our performance metrics. With only first clips with at least three runs, both detectors' performance using fewer actions, up to the first and second run, remained very low. However, when using actions up to runs 3-5, the ICV detector (run 3: A'=.99, κ=.42; run 4: A'=1.0, κ=.65; run 5: A'=.91, κ=.47) outperformed the RCF detector (A'=.70-.79, κ=.06-.11 for the same values). Additionally, three runs was the level at which the ICV detector could perform as well as classifying when considering all actions in the first clip (ICV all actions A'=.89, κ=.50).

For later clips within an activity, both detectors reach predictive performance equivalent to considering all actions (the "all" columns Table 2) after a single run. However, the ICV detectors outperform the RCF detectors. For example, when looking at clip 2 / run 2, the ICV detector performs better (A'=.97, κ=.82) than the RCF detector (A'=.95, κ=.59). Thus, once students have begun their second data collection cycle within an activity, the ICV detectors can better judge who needs scaffolding after the first run.

Table 2. Designing controlled experiments performance over n-runs and m-clips

			Designing Controlled Experiments										
			RCF Detector						ICV Detector				
Runs	1	2	3	4	5	All	Runs	1	2	3	4	5	All
Clip Num 1	.79 (.00)	.69 (.01)	.75 (.06)	.76 (.07)	.73 (.06)	.71 (.05)	Clip Num 1	1.0 (.00)	1.0 (.04)	1.0 (.16)	1.0 (.20)	.93 (.16)	.93 (.16)
2	.92 (.39)	.95 (.59)	.94 (.59)	.95 (.61)	.95 (.61)	.95 (.61)	2	.98 (.66)	.97 (.82)	.97 (.85)	.97 (.85)	.97 (.85)	.97 (.85)
3	.84 (.22)	.89 (.33)	.89 (.33)	.89 (.33)	.89 (.33)	.89 (.33)	3	.95 (.51)	.93 (.59)	.94 (.66)	.94 (.66)	.94 (.66)	.94 (.66)
4	.89 (.57)	.84 (.46)	.84 (.46)	.84 (.46)	.84 (.46)	.84 (.46)	4	1.0 (.90)	.99 (.79)	.99 (.69)	.99 (.69)	.99 (.69)	.99 (.69)

* Each entry is in the format A' (K)

Table 3. Testing stated hypotheses performance over n-runs and m-clips

			Testing Stated Hypotheses										
			RCF Detector						ICV Detector				
Runs	1	2	3	4	5	All	Runs	1	2	3	4	5	All
Clip Num 1	.70 (.01)	.66 (.06)	.63 (.02)	.63 (.01)	.66 (.04)	.65 (.04)	Clip Num 1	1.0 (.00)	.84 (.37)	.86 (.49)	.91 (.54)	.89 (.53)	.89 (.52)
2	.91 (.40)	.92 (.44)	.90 (.39)	.90 (.39)	.90 (.39)	.90 (.39)	2	.93 (.68)	.95 (.75)	.93 (.73)	.93 (.73)	.95 (.75)	.95 (.75)
3	.88 (.50)	.87 (.47)	.87 (.47)	.87 (.47)	.87 (.47)	.87 (.47)	3	.93 (.86)	.89 (.79)	.87 (.76)	.88 (.76)	.89 (.79)	.89 (.79)
4	.89 (.47)	.91 (.57)	.91 (.57)	.91 (.57)	.91 (.57)	.91 (.57)	4	.90 (.90)	.90 (.79)	.90 (.79)	.90 (.79)	.90 (.79)	.90 (.79)

* Each entry is in the format A' (K)

For testing stated hypotheses, the ICV detector again matched or outperformed the RCF detectors as shown in Table 3. For first clips, the RCF detector had A' values ranging from .63 to .70, and κ values at chance levels. However, the ICV detector performed well at this skill for first clips (ICV all actions A'=.89, κ=.52), a difference from designing controlled experiments. In fact, it could properly identify behavior after just the second run (ICV clip 1, run 2 had A'=.84, κ=.37). By the third run, predictive performance was on par with a detector that could consider all actions. For later clips, the ICV detector outperformed the RCF detector at all run levels. For example, when predicting using actions up to the second run for clip 2, the RCF detector had A'=.92 and κ=.44. Though this performance is good, the ICV detector performed much better with A'=.95 and κ=.75. Thus overall, the ICV detectors can be used to classify testing hypotheses behavior as early as the second run in the first clip, and are better at classification in later clips than the RCF detectors are.

5   Discussion and Conclusions

We investigated whether selecting features based on construct validity improves the predictive capabilities of machine-learned behavior detectors of scientific inquiry behaviors, designing controlled experiments and testing stated hypotheses, within a science microworld [10]. To explore this, we compared two types of detectors. One type removed used an automated approach, removing inter-correlated features (RCF detectors). Another used a partially manual approach to select features theoretically aligned with the behaviors, thereby increasing construct validity (ICV detectors). Models' predictive performance was compared against a held-out test set in two ways. We predicted behavior at the level of a full data collection cycle, the grain size at which behavior was labeled. We also predicted behavior at a finer grain size, micro-world simulation runs, a grain size containing less information.

The results showed that improving construct validity can yield models with better overall predictive performance, even with less data. The ICV detector for testing stated hypotheses reached much higher performance levels than the RCF detector. The current ICV detector can effectively be used to trigger scaffolding when students finish data collection, given its high A'=.91 and κ=.70 values. It also can be used after as few as two runs on students' first data collection to provide fail-soft interventions that are not costly if misapplied. This is evidenced by A' values at or above .84, and κ at or above .37 found when increasing the number of simulation runs (thereby increasing the number of actions available) to make predictions.

The ICV detector for designing controlled experiments also outperformed its RCF counterpart. However, both the ICV and RCF detectors performed poorly when they inferred behavior for students' first data collection within an activity. We discovered this was due, in part, to poor classification of first cycles containing exactly two simulation runs. When ignoring such cycles, the ICV detector's performance improved substantially while the RCF detector remained poor. It could be applied in as few as three runs on students' first data collection. We believe the ICV detector failed on this case because the training set did not contain enough cases of this kind (see Section 2.3 for more details). This issue may be alleviated by adding more of these training clips and re-engineering the ICV detector following our procedure.

This paper offers two contributions towards leveraging feature-based machine-learned detectors to assess behavior. First, we explored the importance of considering construct validity when selecting features. We found that selecting features taking this into account yielded better detectors than selecting features using a more atheoretical approach, by removing inter-correlated features. Second, we described a general process for validating detectors at finer grain-sizes than they were trained and built. For our domain, the finer grain-size was the level of individual simulation runs. We found that detectors with improved construct validity could correctly infer behavior at the finer grain-size. This means we can reuse the ICV detectors as is to trigger scaffolding sooner, without needing to re-tag and retrain detectors to work at this level. In general, grain size and use of the detectors, whether for scaffolding (run or clip level in our domain) or for overall assessment (clip level in our domain), are both important to consider when evaluating detectors' applicability in a learning environment.

There are some limitations to this work. Though we controlled for the data mining algorithm and algorithm parameters, we did not compare the ICV detectors to others built using more sophisticated, automated feature selection approaches (e.g. [4], [5]). In addition, we only used a single data mining algorithm to generate detectors, J48 decision trees. Different data mining algorithms may have yielded different results. Our results are also contingent on the initial set features engineered, since there is no guarantee we computed all possible relevant features for our domain. Finally, we did not consider the notion of broader generalizability. For example, could a detector built for one science domain also detect inquiry skill in other domains? Considering these additional issues will provide more insight into the role construct validity plays in the development and successful use of machine-learned detectors.

Acknowledgements. This research is funded by the National Science Foundation (NSF-DRL#0733286, NSF-DRL#1008649, and NSF-DGE#0742503) and the U.S. Department of Education (R305A090170). Any opinions expressed are those of the authors and do not necessarily reflect those of the funding agencies.

References

1. Witten, I., Frank, E.: Data Mining: Practical Machine Learning Tools and Techniques, 2nd edn. Morgan Kaufmann, San Francisco (2005)
2. Yu, L., Liu, H.: Feature Selection for High-Dimensional Data: A Fast Correlation-Based Filter Solution. In: Proc. of the 20th Int'l Conf. on Machine Learning, pp. 856–863 (2003)
3. Pudil, P., Novovicova, J., Kittler, J.: Floating Search Methods in Feature Selection. Pattern Recognition Letters 15(11), 1119–1125 (1994)
4. Oh, I.-S., Lee, J.-S., Moon, B.-R.: Hybrid Genetic Algorithms for Feature Selection. IEEE Transactions on Pattern Analysis and Machine Intelligence 26(11), 1424–1437 (2004)
5. Bernardini, A., Conati, C.: Discovering and Recognizing Student Interaction Patterns in Exploratory Learning Environments. In: Aleven, V., Kay, J., Mostow, J. (eds.) ITS 2010. LNCS, vol. 6094, pp. 125–134. Springer, Heidelberg (2010)
6. Sao Pedro, M.A., de Baker, R.S.J., Gobert, J.D., Montalvo, O., Nakama, A.: Leveraging Machine-Learned Detectors of Systematic Inquiry Behavior to Estimate and Predict Transfer of Inquiry Skill. User Modeling and User-Adapted Interaction (in press)
7. Chen, Z., Klahr, D.: All Other Things Being Equal: Acquisition and Transfer of the Control of Variables Strategy. Child Development 70(5), 1098–1120 (1999)
8. McElhaney, K., Linn, M.: Helping Students Make Controlled Experiments More Informative. In: Proc. of the 9th Int'l Conf. of the Learning Sciences, pp. 786–793 (2010)
9. Buckley, B.C., Gobert, J., Horwitz, P.: Using Log Files to Track Students' Model-Based Inquiry. In: Proc. of the 7th Int'l Conf. of the Learning Sciences, pp. 57–63 (2006)
10. Gobert, J., Sao Pedro, M., Baker, R., Toto, E., Montalvo, O.: Leveraging Educational Data Mining for Real Time Performance Assessment of Scientific Inquiry Skills within Microworlds. Journal of Educational Data Mining (accepted)
11. Quinlan, J.R.: C4.5: Programs for Machine Learning. Morgan Kaufmann, San Francisco (1993)
12. Hanley, J.A., McNeil, B.J.: The Meaning and Use of the Area under a Receiver Operating Characteristic (ROC) Curve. Radiology 143, 29–36 (1982)
13. Ben-David, A.: About the Relationship between ROC Curves and Cohen's Kappa. Engineering Applications of Artificial Intelligence 21, 874–882 (2008)
14. Fogarty, J., Baker, R., Hudson, S.: Case Studies in the Use of ROC Curve Analysis for Sensor-Based Estimates in Human Computer Interaction. In: Proc. of Graphics Interface, pp. 129–136 (2005)

Inferring Personality of Online Gamers by Fusing Multiple-View Predictions

Jianqiang Shen, Oliver Brdiczka, Nicolas Ducheneaut,
Nicholas Yee, and Bo Begole

Palo Alto Research Center, 3333 Coyote Hill Road, Palo Alto, CA 94304, USA
{jianqiang.shen,oliver.brdiczka,nicolas,nyee,bo}@parc.com

Abstract. Reliable personality prediction can have direct impact on many adaptive systems, such as targeted advertising, interface personalization and content customization. We propose an algorithm to infer a user's personality profile more reliably by fusing analytical predictions from multiple sources including behavioral traces, textual data, and social networking information. We applied and validated our approach using a real data set obtained from 1,040 *World of Warcraft* players. Besides behavioral and social networking information, we found that text analysis of character names yields the strongest personality cues.

Keywords: personality, behavior analysis, social networks, sentiment analysis, virtual worlds.

1 Introduction

Computer systems and devices become "smarter" every day thanks to enhancements in usability and adaptivity. In order for computer systems to further adapt to different users, there is a growing need for fine-grained modeling of preferences and, in particular, the personality of users. Modeling personality based on online behavior could enable better personalization, collaboration and targeted advertising, among others. For instance, personalizing user interfaces and content could improve work efficiency by steering users to the right information. In the workplace, employers could form efficient teams based on compatible personalities. Matching personality types also has commercial applications. For example, if online dating service providers had a better knowledge of a user's personality, they could match him/her with other users with a higher chance of success.

The popularity of online games offers a great opportunity to examine personality inference using significant amounts of data. Indeed, recent online games offer a wealth of behavioral indicators ranging from combat statistics to sociability that could reflect a player's personality. In this paper, we leverage this behavioral richness by attempting to infer the personality of the individual behind a game character. We use data from the popular massively multiplayer online game (MMOG), *World of Warcraft* (WoW), one of the most successful in its genre with close to 11 million subscribers worldwide (http://mmodata.net) who collaboratively accomplish a wide range of activities, from group combat

J. Masthoff et al. (Eds.): UMAP 2012, LNCS 7379, pp. 261–273, 2012.

(against tough computer-controlled "bosses" or other players) to crafting virtual items. Participation in the game world requires considerable time from players [6] and social bonds formed in these virtual worlds often translate to lasting relationships in and out of the game [20].

Recent research has shown that when meeting a stranger face-to-face for the first time, it is possible to quickly assess their personality with some accuracy thanks to verbal and non-verbal cues [14]. In this paper, we attempt a similar personality assessment based on a different set of cues, namely, digital traces generated by a player's activities in the virtual world. To maximize our chances of predicting personality accurately, we consider three data sources: behavioral metrics (e.g. achievements, number of kills), textual data (e.g. names chosen for a character) and social network information (e.g. a player's position in guilds). We build on the intuition that, much like during face-to-face encounters, the activities of the players are cues to their personality. For instance, shy and quiet players might prefer solo activities such as cooking and fishing. Outgoing players might prefer large-scale "raids" involving up to 40 players. Predictions from each data source provides a partial and complementary view of personality, which we then fuse with the others to get the most accurate personality profile possible.

2   Related Work

Personality Profiling. In personality psychology, the Big-5 model is the gold standard. The model measures five traits: Extraversion, Agreeableness, Conscientiousness, Emotional Stability, and Openness to Experience. Personality profiles are usually constructed through surveys based on proven inventories of questions, e.g. International Personality Item Pool [8]. Studies have shown that judgments of personality at zero acquaintance are moderately accurate and based on consensual indicators [14]. For instance [14], observers generally agree that Extraverted individuals speak louder, with more enthusiasm and energy, and that they are more expressive with gestures. Interestingly, personality cues can also be found in the physical world: observers can predict the personality of strangers by looking at their offices and bedrooms [9], or even by examining their top ten favorite songs [19]. There has been some success at predicting personality in a meeting scenario using visual and acoustic indicators [17].

Communication and Personalities. Researchers have started to explore the possibility of predicting personality from electronic cues. It turns out that websites can be used to predict their owner's personality with high levels of consensus and accuracy from the observers [22]. Facebook profiles can be similarly revealing [2] and personality also influences the way one writes electronic text [7] - for instance, the nature and structure of email messages reveals personality traits, down to the simplest indicators: observers were able to infer personality solely on the basis of an email address [1]. We note however that most of these studies rely on human coders to categorize personality from text data. In this paper, we will use automated text analysis techniques instead.

Online Gaming Studies. The depth and breadth of activities available in contemporary MMOGs, coupled with their widespread adoption, has led researchers to use them as "virtual laboratories" for social science research [5]. Research has explored a wide array of issues emerging in these online gaming communities: their unique culture [21], players' motivations and psychology [26], their economic importance [3], their social life [23] - and, most relevant to this paper, the link between a player's online and offline personalities [27]. The latter, however, only considered behavioral indicators available on Blizzard's Armory, a public database of character statistics. In this paper, we extend Yee et al.'s [27] approach by also considering textual and social networking data. We also attempt to predict a player's personality based on information from a single character, whereas Yee et al. grouped information about a player across all their characters. We adopt this more challenging single-character approach since, in general, there is no way to determine if two characters belong to the same player. Only single-character predictions enable practical applications like personalization or targeted advertising.

Our Contribution and Its Implications. Our contribution is threefold. First, instead of aggregating multiple characters, we show it is possible to reliably infer a player's personality based on the activities of a single character. Second, in addition to behavioral features, we explore social networking and textual features. To the best of our knowledge, this is the first attempt at utilizing such rich, multi-pronged information for personality predictions in virtual worlds. Third, we present the constructed features and their predictive power in detail, in order to inform future work on personality. Besides improving personalization and recommendations, incorporating personality estimations into adaptive systems can benefit a wide range of functionalities: for instance, our personality predictor is part of a larger system being developed to detect anomalies and prevent malicious behaviors in corporate networks. Personality profiling enables us to focus on individuals having the motivation and capability to carry out attacks.

3 Personality in Virtual Worlds

To provide some important context for our findings, we give below a brief introduction to the Big 5 personality traits, provide a brief overview of WoW, and discuss our approach to collecting data from the game.

3.1 The Big 5 Model

Personality traits are consistent patterns of thoughts, feelings, or actions that distinguish people from one another [13]. The Big 5 model was developed using factor analytic techniques on adjectives and descriptive phrases of people culled from an English corpus. The corresponding five factors have been shown to account for most individual differences in personality [10,13]:

- **Extraversion** implies an energetic approach to the social world and includes traits such as sociability and positive emotionality. High scorers tend to be sociable, friendly, talkative; low scorers tend to be reserved, shy, quiet.

- **Agreeableness** is a tendency to be compassionate and cooperative rather than suspicious and antagonistic towards others. High scorers tend to be friendly, caring, cooperative; low scorers tend to be critical, rude, suspicious.
- **Conscientiousness** describes socially prescribed impulse control that facilitates task and goal-directed behavior. High scorers tend to be reliable, self-disciplined; low scorers tend to be disorganized, negligent.
- **Neuroticism** relates to emotional stability. High scorers tend to be nervous, sensitive, vulnerable; low scorers tend to be calm, relaxed, secure, confident.
- **Openness** describes the breadth, depth, originality, and complexity of an individual's mental life. High scorers tend to be original, curious, complex; low scorers tend to be conventional, narrow interests, uncreative.

3.2   World of Warcraft

WoW is one of the most popular commercial online games (http://mmodata.net). It is based on a typical leveling up formula seen in many role-playing games. Players start at level 1 and kill monsters to become higher level and acquire better equipment in order to kill bigger monsters. The game encourages players to collaborate - for instance, an important game mechanic is that players must create characters with different skill sets that complement each other: heavily-armored tank classes shield the group from enemy attacks while lightly-armored damage classes deal damage to enemies and healing classes restore health lost in combat. Players must choose to belong to one of two factions: Alliance or Horde. Each faction has five distinct races, e.g., Gnomes or Orcs. A variety of rules dictate where and when players may attack and kill each other. Thus, a distinction is made between PvP (player-vs-player) and PvE (player-vs-environment) activities. PvP activites can range from one-to-one duels to large 40 vs. 40 battlegrounds (BGs). And in general, it is a player's choice as to how much PvP activity they want to engage in. Players in WoW communicate via typed chat and might also use VoIP tools to communicate via speech. The game also provides a modest set of "emotes" (e.g., hug). Players are able to specialize in crafting professions and convert collected raw ingredients into finished goods, such as in tailoring or cooking. There is also a system of Achievements that tracks a variety of combat and non-combat objectives, including Achievements for zones explored, number of hugs given, and cooking proficiency. These Achievement scores provide a sense of how a player chooses to spend their time in WoW. Thus, overall, WoW offers a wide and varied set of rich behavioral cues to draw from. From class choice to amount of PvP activity, from number of emotes used to amount of world exploration, the game context offers a range of measurable behaviors.

3.3   Data Collection

1,040 game players were recruited from WoW forums, mailing lists, publicity on popular gaming sites and social media like Twitter. The age range was 18-65 and the average was 27.03 (SD = 8.21). 26% of participants were women. Participants were asked to list up to 6 WoW characters they were actively playing. This resulted in a total of 3,050 active characters. A 20-item survey measuring the Big-Five was drawn from the International Personality Item Pool [8]. Participants completed a web-based survey that gathered their demographic and personality information. Participants rated themselves on the items using a scale ranging from 1 (Very Inaccurate) to 5 (Very Accurate). For all personality traits, the distributions of participants' scores are roughly Gaussian, with means around 3 and standard deviations around 0.8.

Blizzard, the developer of WoW, provides public access to much of their game data at a website known as the Armory. By searching for a character's name, anyone can view details about their past activities, including how many hugs they have given, their equipment, etc. Using custom data collection software, we collected information about each of our participants' characters on a daily basis from 11/22/2010 to 05/29/2011 (the Armory is updated once a day). Armory profiles consist of hundreds of variables, often in a hierarchy. To avoid being inundated by low-level variables or including overlapping variables, we adopted an analytic strategy of looking at or generating high level variables where possible. This in turn produces more stable variables that map to psychologically meaningful concepts. For example, a notion of geographical exploration would seem to be better tracked by the overall count of zones explored rather than looking at any one particular zone. The resulting variables represent our first data source: behavioral metrics.

Blizzard designed WoW to be extensible through the use of addons: small programs written by players to extend or refine the game's user interface. One addon function can be used to gather limited but valuable data: the *who* command. For a character, typing *who* lists characters in the same game zone who are roughly the same level (±5 levels), with an upper limit of 49 results returned. The intent is to facilitate the formation of groups. The command can be expanded to include additional parameters such as specifying a different game zone or a level range. It therefore becomes possible to conduct a census of the entire population at a given time by progressively cycling through small segments of the population, aggregating batches of 49 players or less to cover all players. Based on rate limits for each *who* query and server load, our designed addon captures a list of all active players on a server every 5 to 15 minutes. We then use this data to create our second data source: social networks, constructed on the basis of which characters are seen playing with each other.

Finally, we build on the intuition that character names are not chosen at random: they are a key marker of identity and players often come up with inventive or humorous uses of names [4]. The same logic applies to guild names. As such, character and guild names constitute our third data source: text data.

4   Personality Inference

We use the three data sources above to build personality predictors and fuse the classifiers. This leverages the different representations of the patterns for classification, which has been shown to increase efficiency and accuracy [15], especially when classifiers are diverse.

4.1 Behavioral Information

To reduce the number of variables to a manageable and meaningful set, we follow the aggregation strategy described by Yee et al. [27]. This yields 68 high-level behavioral metrics that can be extracted from any character's profile on the Armory. The corresponding nine broad categories are as follows:

- Achievements: total achievements, profession achievements (cooking, first aid), achievements from group tasks (10-man dungeons), and their ratios.
- Death: we count the number of deaths in different game areas (such as raids, 10-man dungeon, 25-man dungeon, falling, fatigue, drowning, fire).
- Respecs: a player can switch their character's skill set by paying a fee. We count the corresponding number of these "respecs".
- Travel: we count the uses of each game transportation system (such as summon, flight, portal, hearthed)
- Emote: a character can communicate with other characters through emotes (such as hug, LOL, wave). We count the number of each different emote.
- Equipment and pets: a character can collect or buy equipment and pets in the game. We also differentiate purchased equipments from looted equipment.
- Need/greed rolls: valuable equipment drops from monsters are given to players according to dice rolls. Players select to roll based on "Need" or "Greed", of which the former is given higher priority.
- PvP scenarios: we count participation in PvP events of each type (such as arenas, duels, battlegrounds).
- Damage and healing: we count the sum and ratio of damage/healing points.

We chose to use regression trees to learn personality predictors from those features because of their simplicity, efficiency and accuracy.

4.2 Text Analysis

We use *sentiment analysis, keyword lists* and *n-grams* to generate features from character and guild names. Sentiment analysis is the task of identifying positive and negative opinions, emotions, and evaluations [24]. To do so, we use two sentiment polarity dictionaries. First, we use a dictionary from Wilson et al. [24] containing human-annotated polarity information on 8,221 distinct words. Second, we also use an in-house sentiment dictionary in which the overall polarity of a word was determined by a statistical approach. This dictionary has higher coverage (76,400 words) but lower precision, since the polarities of many words are context dependent. Each dictionary is used to produce separate features. Using these dictionaries, we scan each guild and character name and count how many positive/negative/neutral words appear. A sentiment word can be an adjective, adverb, noun, verb or any part of speech. We count the frequency of each case. We also count the frequency of strongly/weakly subjective words. A word that is subjective in most contexts is considered strongly subjective (e.g., "abusive", "naive") ; otherwise it is weakly subjective (e.g., "accept", "neat").

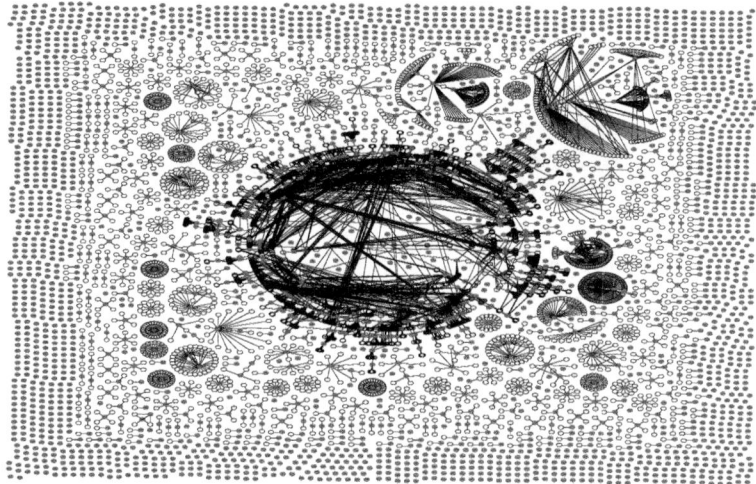

Fig. 1. Part of the constructed social network, including the 3,050 targeted characters and their direct neighbors. Filled nodes are our targeted characters. The entire graph contains more than 135,000 nodes and the frequency threshold to set an edge is 4.

We further created a game keyword list and check if a name contains those keywords. They include race names (e.g., elf, gnome), role names (e.g., priest, warrior), actions (e.g., kill, wave), failures (e.g., drown, fatigue), scenarios (e.g., arena, dungeon) and other frequent words. We currently collect 80 keywords.

In the textual analysis domain, n-gram analysis is a popular technique that uses sliding window character sequences in order to aid classification. To capture other hidden patterns in character and guild names, we also construct n-grams from names. An n-gram is a subsequence of n letters from a given sequence. For example, if the character name consists of 4 letters – ABCD, then we will have bigram AB, BC, CD. We limit n to 4, i.e., we only consider bigrams, trigrams and 4-grams. A larger n adds too much computation complexity and does not improve accuracy much. In many cases, a character's name is related to the player's other choices in virtual worlds, such as race and gender. Thus we include the character's region, virtual gender, race, role and faction as additional features. We train regression trees to profile personality from the text information.

4.3   Social Network Analysis

We hypothesize that personality traits can be detected through the nature and structure of a character's social activities (for instance, [27] shows that Extraverted characters have higher social connectivity on average than Introverts). We therefore attempt to analyze a character's social network to generate predictive features. We use a simple heuristic to build social networks from activity logs: in the networks, each node represents a distinct character; if the frequency

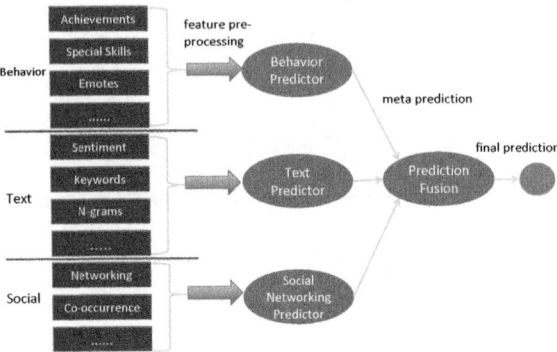

Fig. 2. We fuse several predictions together to get the final prediction of personality

that two characters were observed playing for the same guild, at the same location, at the same time is more than a specified threshold θ, we add an undirected edge between those two characters. By specifying different θ values (we used 9, 6, 4 here), we get different networks. A partial graph by specifying $\theta=4$ is shown in Figure 1. We then analyze the network to compute the following graph characteristics [18] for each node:

- **Degree centrality:** number of edges attached to a node, i.e. a measure of network activity for a node.
- **Betweenness centrality:** nodes that occur on many shortest paths between other nodes have higher betweenness than those that do not. Nodes with high betweenness have greater influence over what flows in the network.
- **Closeness centrality:** nodes that tend to have short geodesic distances to other nodes in the graph have higher closeness. They are in an excellent position to monitor the information flow in the network.

We enhance these social networking features by calculating co-occurrence heuristics. We hypothesize that a socially active person is likely to visit crowded places. For each character, we count the total number of characters playing in the same zone for a given play session. We normalize these values by taking into account the size of zones. We calculate their maximum values, minimum values and histograms as our features and input into regression trees for prediction.

4.4   Fusing Predictors

Classifier fusion has received considerable attention for pattern recognition in the past decade [15,16]. By combining individual outputs, classifier fusion aims for a higher accuracy than that of the best classifier. It has been observed that, although one of the classifiers could yield the best performance, the sets of patterns misclassified by the different classifiers would not necessarily overlap [15]. Thus different classifier designs potentially offer complementary information about the

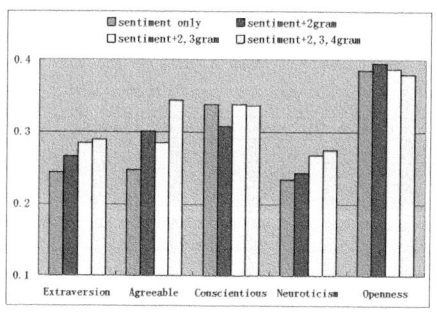
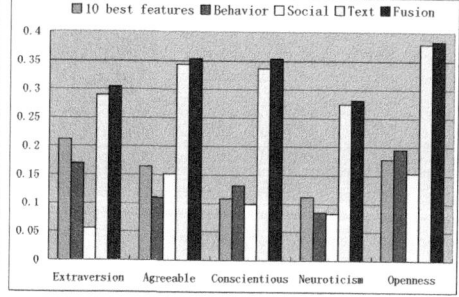

(a) Correlation from text analysis.   (b) Correlation from different methods.

Fig. 3. Correlation of personality predictions with the real values

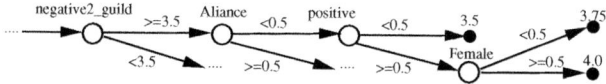

Fig. 4. Part of the regression trees for predicting Openness

patterns to be classified, which could be harnessed to improve accuracy. There-fore, fusing classifiers is particularly useful if they are inherently different - hence our decision to fuse predictors from behavioral information, text analysis and social network analysis. The corresponding diagram is shown in Figure 2. We train a separate predictor on each information source, and predictions from each predictor are then fused into one final prediction through linear regression.

5   Experimental Results

We evaluate our approach with the aforementioned data from 3,050 WoW ac-tive characters. Personalities are coded as real numbers. It is important for the prediction ranking to be close to the real ranking, i.e., if a person has a high "real" value on a personality trait, it is good if the prediction is correspondingly high. We evaluate our approach with the *Pearson correlation* defined as the co-variance of the two variables divided by the product of their standard deviations [11]. Results are based on 10-fold cross validation [12].

We found that character and guild names contain rich information on person-ality. For example, "sin" in names seems to correspond to low Agreeableness, and "hall" and "warrior" seem to correspond to low Extraversion. Sentiment analysis is especially powerful here. The results are plotted in Figure 3(a). We include features from the keyword list in all results, since names are related to the player's other choices in the virtual world. Sentiment analysis plus keyword features generates very good results. Adding n-grams can generally improve ac-curacy. As we increase n, we get better results in most cases except for Openness. But when n is larger than 4, it introduces too many tokens and decreases the

Table 1. Rankings and information gain values of some top informative features

Rank	IG	Feature
		Behavior
1	0.0423	Dungeon-based achievements divided by the sum of all achievements
2	0.0421	Ratio of the count of "need" rolls to the count of all rolls
4	0.0289	Ratio of won duels divided by the count of all duels
5	0.0287	Count of reaching the highest status with a specific faction
8	0.0279	Sum of damage this character created
		Text
1	0.091	Count of negative words in the guild name (in-house dictionary)
2	0.090	Count of positive words in the guild name (in-house dictionary)
3	0.066	Count of negative words in the character name (in-house dictionary)
4	0.057	Count of positive words in the character name (in-house dictionary)
6	0.037	Count of strong subjective words in the guild name (UPitt dictionary)
		Social
1	0.073	Degree centrality when the frequency threshold to set an edge is 1
2	0.041	Frequncy that this character played with fewer than 5 characters
5	0.027	Frequncy that this character played with more than 20 characters
6	0.026	Frequncy that this character played with fewer than 5 guild members
8	0.017	Closeness centrality when the frequency threshold to set an edge is 4

efficiency. We also did not see too much accuracy benefit from large n. Thus we limit n to 4. We reviewed the generated trees and found that parts of them look meaningful. For example, part of the trees for Openness are shown in Figure 4. This tree suggests that if a guild's name contains many negative words from the in-house dictionary, a character with a name containing positive words from Wilson et al.'s dictionary [24] would have higher Openness than other characters.

The complete generated social network when $\theta=4$ contains 135,547 nodes and 30,922 edges. Part of the constructed graph is shown in Figure 1. The graph is relatively sparse and many nodes are singletons. Co-occurrence heuristics are an important supplement and are used to enhance social networking features.

Performance from different methods is shown in Figure 3(b). Yee et al. [27] suggested 10 behavioral features that have highest correlation with each personality trait among all game players. We show results from training a regression tree with those features. Our fusion methods always significantly outperform the "10 best features" method ($p <0.05$).

Text analysis gives better performance than behavioral and social networking information ($p <0.05$). We hypothesize that there could be two reasons. First, behavioral and social networking information were collected from a 6-month period and might not capture the whole picture. Second, behavioral and social networking information can be noisy whereas the character's name, guild, virtual gender, race, role and faction are usually chosen by the player after some careful thinking. Analyzing such relatively clean, stationary data can therefore let us gain some insight about the player's personality. Behavioral features work best for personality traits like Extraversion and Openness, while social network features work best for personality traits like Agreeableness and Openness. Extraversion is reflected in group and solo activities, such as dungeon, raid, questing, and cooking. Agreeableness is related to emotes (e.g. hugs) and player-vs.-player activities such as arenas and duels. Openness is reflected in exploration and also through activities like professions and dungeons. Prediction fusion takes

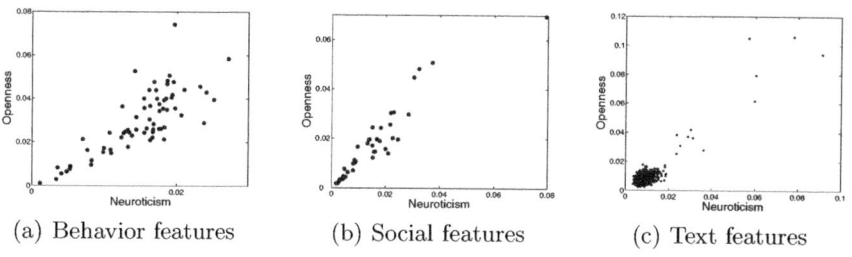

(a) Behavior features   (b) Social features   (c) Text features

Fig. 5. Information gains of different features. Each point corresponds to a feature.

advantage of the diversity of different predictors and gives the best performance in all Big 5 personality traits. Considering this is a difficult problem, it is exciting that the fusion method can achieve correlations higher than 0.35 in general.

Our algorithms can capture common characteristics between characters belonging to the same player and the predictions are well correlated. There are 813 players having at least 2 characters and we randomly sampled two groups. Each group sampled one character from each player and we checked the predictions. The two groups had correlation of 0.538, 0.485, 0.666, 0.480 and 0.623 for Extraversion, Agreeableness, Conscientiousness, Neuroticism and Openness.

Information Gain (IG) [25] is a well-known criterion to measure a feature's power. It calculates the reduction of entropy in the predicted class distribution provided by knowing the value of a feature. We discretize our features by simple binning [12] and measure the information gain for each personality trait. We sort features based on their average IGs of 5 traits. Some top features are shown in Table 1, with some similar features skipped for brevity. We note that different personality traits usually have similar impact on cues, i.e., for most features, their IG values usually have the same magnitude across different traits. We calculated the correlation between features' IGs for different traits and found it is high. For example, for Neuroticism and Openness, the correlation for behavioral features is 0.803, for textual features it is 0.941, and for social features it is 0.934. Figure 5 shows scatter plots with axis values as IGs. It is clear that, in general, good features for Openness are also good for Neuroticism while bad features for Openness are also bad for Neuroticism, although their strength is different, which might contribute to the accuracy difference of predictions. It is also worth noting that though combining n-gram text features together provides good personality cues, many of them alone have weak IGs.

6 Conclusion

Reliable personality inference has important personal and commercial applications. The depth and breadth of activities in online games, coupled with their widespread adoption, make them a good platform to examine personality inference approaches. In this paper, we attempted to infer the personality of the player behind a game character based on data from the popular MMOG, *World of Warcraft.* We profile a person's personality by fusing analytic predictions from multiple sources, including behavioral metrics, textual analysis and social networking information. Each source provides a partial and complementary view about the player's personality. In addition to behavioral and social networking information, we found that names contain strong personality cues.

Acknowledgments. We gratefully acknowledge support for this work from DARPA through the ADAMS (Anomaly Detection At Multiple Scales) program Contract W911NF-11-C-0216. This research was also sponsored by the Air Force Research Laboratory. Any opinions, findings, and conclusions or recommendations in this material are those of the authors and do not necessarily reflect the views of the government funding agencies. We thank Kurt Partridge and anonymous reviewers for the constructive comments.

References

1. Back, M.D., Schmukle, S.C., Egloff, B.: How extraverted is honey.bunny77@hotmail.de? Inferring personality from e-mail addresses. Journal of Research in Personality 42(4), 1116–1122 (2008)
2. Back, M.D., Stopfer, J.M., Vazire, S., Gaddis, S., Schmukle, S.C., Egloff, B., Gosling, S.D.: Facebook profiles reflect actual personality, not self-idealization. Psychological Science 21, 372–374 (2010)
3. Castronova, E.: On virtual economies. Game Studies 3(2) (July 2002)
4. Cherny, L.: Conversation and community: chat in a virtual world. CSLI Pub. (1999)
5. Ducheneaut, N.: Massively multiplayer online games as living laboratories: opportunities and pitfalls. In: Online Worlds: Convergence of the Real and the Virtual. Springer (2010)
6. Ducheneaut, N., Yee, N., Nickell, E., Moore, R.: Building a MMO with mass appeal: a look at gameplay in World of Warcraft. Games and Culture 1(4), 1–38 (2006)
7. Gladis, S.D.: Writetype: Personality Types and Writing Styles. HRD Press (1994)
8. Goldberg, L.R., Johnson, J.A., Eber, H.W., Hogan, R., Ashton, M.C., Cloninger, C.R., Gough, H.C.: The international personality item pool and the future of public-domain personality measures. Journal of Research in Personality 40, 84–96 (2006)
9. Gosling, S.D., Ko, S.J., Mannarelli, T., Morris, M.E.: A room with a cue: Personality judgments based on offices and bedrooms. Journal of Personality and Social Psychology 82(3), 379–398 (2002)
10. Hogan, R., Johnson, J., Briggs, S.: Handbook of Personality Psychology, 3rd edn. Academic Press (1997)
11. Hogg, R.V.: Introduction to Mathematical Statistics, 5th edn. Prentice Hall (1994)
12. Joachims, T.: Learning to Classify Text Using Support Vector Machines. Kluwer (2001)
13. John, O.P., Robins, R.W., Pervin, L.A.: Handbook of Personality: Theory and Research, 3rd edn. The Guilford Press (2010)
14. Kenny, D.A., Horner, C., Kashy, D.A., Chuan Chu, L.: Consensus at zero acquaintance: Replication, behavioral cues, and stability. Journal of Personality and Social Psychology, 88–97 (1992)

15. Kittler, J., Hatef, M., Duin, R.P.W., Matas, J.: On combining classifiers. IEEE Transactions on Pattern Analysis and Machine Intelligence 20, 226–239 (1998)
16. Kuncheva, L.I.: A theoretical study on six classifier fusion strategies. IEEE Trans. Pattern Anal. Mach. Intell. 24, 281–286 (2002)
17. Lepri, B., Mana, N., Cappelletti, A., Pianesi, F., Zancanaro, M.: Modeling the Personality of Participants During Group Interactions. In: Houben, G.-J., McCalla, G., Pianesi, F., Zancanaro, M. (eds.) UMAP 2009. LNCS, vol. 5535, pp. 114–125. Springer, Heidelberg (2009)
18. Newman, M.: Networks: An Introduction. Oxford University Press (2010)
19. Rentfrow, P.J., Gosling, S.D.: Message in a ballad: The role of music preferences in interpersonal perception. Psychological Science 17(3), 236–242 (2006)
20. Seay, A.F., Jerome, W.J., Lee, K.S., Kraut, R.E.: Project massive: A study of online gaming communities. In: Proc. of CHI 2004, pp. 1421–1424 (2004)
21. Taylor, T.L.: Play between worlds. The MIT Press, Cambridge
22. Vazire, S., Gosling, S.D.: E-perceptions: Personality impressions based on personal websites. Journal of Personality and Social Psychology 87(1), 123–132 (2004)
23. Williams, D., Ducheneaut, N., Xiong, L., Zhang, Y., Yee, N., Nickell, E.: From treehouse to barracks: The social life of guilds in WoW. Games and Culture 1(4), 338–361 (2006)
24. Wilson, T., Wiebe, J., Hoffmann, P.: Recognizing contextual polarity in phrase-level sentiment analysis. In: Proceedings of HLT-EMNLP, pp. 347–354 (2005)
25. Yang, Y., Pedersen, J.O.: A comparative study on feature selection in text categorization. In: Proc. of ICML 1997, pp. 412–420 (1997)
26. Yee, N.: The Norrathian Scrolls: A Study of EverQuest, www.nickyee.com/eqt/report.html
27. Yee, N., Ducheneaut, N., Nelson, L., Likarish, P.: Introverted elves & conscientious gnomes: The expression of personality in world of warcraft. In: CHI 2011, pp. 753–762 (2011)

Towards Adaptive Information Visualization: On the Influence of User Characteristics

Dereck Toker, Cristina Conati, Giuseppe Carenini, and Mona Haraty

Department of Computer Science, University of British Columbia
2366 Main Mall, Vancouver, BC, V6T1Z4, Canada
{dtoker,conati,carenini,haraty}@cs.ubc.ca

Abstract. The long-term goal of our research is to design information visualization systems that adapt to the specific needs, characteristics, and context of each individual viewer. In order to successfully perform such adaptation, it is crucial to first identify characteristics that influence an individual user's effectiveness, efficiency, and satisfaction with a particular information visualization type. In this paper, we present a study that focuses on investigating the impact of four user characteristics (perceptual speed, verbal working memory, visual working memory, and user expertise) on the effectiveness of two common data visualization techniques: bar graphs and radar graphs. Our results show that certain user characteristics do in fact have a significant effect on task efficiency, user preference, and ease of use. We conclude with a discussion of how our findings could be effectively used for an adaptive visualization system.

Keywords: User characteristics, User Evaluation, Adaptive Information Visualization.

1 Introduction

Information visualization is a thriving area of research in the study of human/computer communication. Though the field has made substantial progress in measuring and formalizing visualization effectiveness, results and suggestions from the literature are sometimes inconclusive and conflicting [19]. We believe this may be attributed to the fact that existing visualizations are designed mostly around the target data set and associated task model, with little consideration for user differences. Both long term user characteristics (e.g., cognitive abilities and expertise) and short term factors (e.g., cognitive load and attention) have often been overlooked in the design of information visualizations, despite studies linking individual differences to visualization efficacy for search and navigation tasks [1,8], for information seeking tasks [7, 25], as well as anecdotal evidence of diverse personal visualization preferences [3].

Our long term goal is to explore the possibilities of user-centered visualizations, which *understand* that different users have different visualization needs and abilities, and which can *adapt* to these differences. However, before adaptation strategies can be effectively specified, we believe that the influence of user characteristics on visualization effectiveness must be further studied and clarified. As a step in this direction,

J. Masthoff et al. (Eds.): UMAP 2012, LNCS 7379, pp. 274–285, 2012.

we present a user study designed to investigate the impact of different user characteristics on the effectiveness of two common data visualization techniques: bar graphs and radar graphs. With respect to previous work, we expand the set of user characteristics to also include verbal working memory and user expertise (in addition to the prior cognitive measures perceptual speed and visual working memory). Furthermore, we also broaden the set of dependent variables; in addition to user performance, we consider subjective measures such as visualization preference and ease of use.

In the rest of the paper, we first discuss related work, followed by a description of the study design. Next, we look at the impact of user characteristics on visualization effectiveness in terms of completion time, ease-of-use, and user preference, and then present our results. We conclude with a discussion of how our findings could be effectively used in an adaptive visualization system.

2   Related Work

Existing work on identifying the factors that define visualization effectiveness has mostly focused on properties of the data to be visualized or the tasks to be performed, sometimes obtaining inconclusive and conflicting results (see [14] and [19], for an overview). Traditionally, extensive work has been done comparing the effectiveness of graphical data in terms of accuracy and speed across different chart types (e.g., bar, radar), yet this research typically did not take into account individual differences (see [6] and [20]). Notable exceptions were Lewandowsky and Spence [18], who explored the effect of expertise on user performance with scatter plots, discovering that high expertise improved accuracy, but decreased completion time. This was an early indication that the impact of individual user differences should be investigated further.

Only recently, more studies have looked at the role of user differences. [1, 5, 8] have focused on visual displays for information retrieval and navigation in complex information spaces. Velez et al. [22] have explored the link between five spatial abilities and proficiency in a visualization task involving the identification of a 3D object from its orthogonal projections. They found not only a large diversity in the spatial abilities of their study's subjects, but also that these abilities are related to visualization comprehension. Even more recently, there has been a lot of interest in individual differences such as personality traits. In particular, Locus of control has been shown to impact performance across different visualizations relating to the degree to which users have internal and external control (see [15] and [25]). Other cognitive traits too have also been shown to have a strong influence on users' performance. The study by Conati and Maclaren [7] looked at two different visualizations to represent changes in a set of variables: a radar graph and a Multiscale Dimension Visualizer (MDV); a visualization that primarily uses color hue and intensity to represent change direction and magnitude [23]. They found that: (1) a user's perceptual speed was a significant predictor of which of the two visualizations would work better for that user on a specific comparison task, and (2) both perceptual speed and visual spatial working memory were predictors of performance with each visualization for some of the study's tasks. The study we describe in this paper can be seen as an extension of this previous work in at least three fundamental ways. First, in this study we compare radar graphs with bar graphs, a much more common visualization than MDV. Thus, our findings may potentially have a much stronger impact on adaptive information visualization in general. Second, in addition to user performance, we include subjective measures such as visualization preference and ease-of-use as dependent variables in the study. Third, we expand the set of user characteristics (perceptual speed and visual working memory) to include both user expertise and verbal working memory, and in doing so, we broaden the set of user features on which adaptation can be based.

The benefits of user-adaptive interaction have been shown in a variety of tasks and applications such as operation of menu-based interfaces, web search, desktop assistance, and human-learning [16]. However, these ideas have rarely been applied to data visualization, largely due to the limited understanding of which user characteristics are relevant for adaptivity in this domain. Two notable exceptions are the work by Gotz and Wen [14], and by Brusilovsky et al. [4]. Gotz and Wen [14] propose a technique to automatically detect a user's changing goals during interaction with a multipurpose visualization, and adapt the visualization accordingly. In contrast, we focus on adapting the visualizations to other relevant user-dependent factors in addition to goals. In Brusilovsky et al. [4], they adapt the *content* of the visualization to the user's domain knowledge in an educational system, but maintain a fixed visualization technique. By contrast, the research we present is intended to support adaptation that involves both selecting *alternative visualizations* for different users, as well as providing *adaptive help* with a given visualization to best accommodate each user's needs.

3   User Study to Compare Radar and Bar Graphs

The overall goal of the work described in the rest of the paper is to identify what specific user characteristics influence visualization effectiveness, and could therefore be exploited in user adaptive visualization systems. As case studies, we considered two basic visualization techniques: bar graphs and radar graphs (see Figure 1). We chose bar graphs because they are one of the most popular and effective visualization techniques. We chose radar graphs because, even though it has been argued that bar graphs are superior to radar graphs on common information seeking tasks [10], the reality is that radar graphs are still widely used. In our user study, we aim to answer the following questions:

Q1: Are bar graphs better than radar graphs on common information seeking tasks? Does the answer to this question depend on specific user characteristics?

Q2: Do specific user characteristics influence the effectiveness of bar graphs? Likewise for radar graphs?

To answer these questions we assessed three measures of bar graph and radar graph the effectiveness (completion time, ease-of-use, and user preference), on a series of information seeking tasks. In the rest of this section, we first describe the individual characteristics we chose to investigate and then present the study tasks and design details.

3.1   Individual Characteristics Explored in the Study

The individual characteristics we investigate in this study include three cognitive abilities (perceptual speed, verbal and visual working memory), as well as two measures of user expertise, one for each of the two visualizations prior to the study.

User expertise was chosen because expertise is not only a good predictor for performance in general, but it has also been shown to impact visualization effectiveness in complex search tasks [1]. Participants self-reported their expertise by expressing their agreement with the following statement for each visualization type: "I am an expert in using radar(bar) graphs," on a Likert-scale from 1 to 5.

Perceptual speed and visual working memory were selected because they were part of the original set of cognitive measures related to perceptual abilities that were explored by Velez et al. [22]. They were also the only two in the set for which [7] found significant relationships with visualization effectiveness when comparing radar graphs and Multiscale Dimension Visualizer (MDV). Verbal working memory was selected because it may affect performance in processing the textual components of a visualization, which, in our study, include legends, labels, and task descriptions.

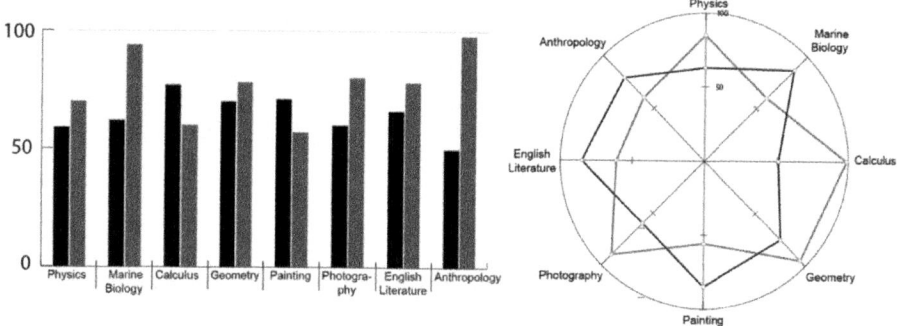

Fig. 1. Example bar and radar graph shown to users in our study

3.2   Participants and Experimental Tasks

Thirty-five subjects (18 females) ranging in age from 19 to 35, participated in the experiment. Ten participants were CS students, while the rest came from a variety of backgrounds, including microbiology, economics, classical archaeology, and film production. Participants were asked to perform a set of tasks evaluating student performance in eight different courses. The tasks were based on a set of low-level analysis tasks that Amar et al. [2] identified as largely capturing people's activities while employing information visualization. The tasks were chosen so that each of our two target visualizations would be suitable to support them. A first battery of tasks involved 5 questions comparing the performance of one student with the class average for 8 courses (single scenario tasks), e.g., *"In how many courses is Maria below the class average?"*. A second battery of tasks involved 4 questions comparing the performance of two students and the class average in order to increase task complexity (double scenario tasks), e.g., *"Find the courses in which Andrea is below the class average and Diana is above it?"*. Arguably, the double scenario tasks are more complex since they involve more comparisons and an increase in visual clutter. Participants repeated each of the 5 tasks in the single scenario with two different datasets that varied in terms of skewness of the value distribution to account for a possible effect of distribution type on visualization effectiveness. Specifically, we compared a spiky distribution with a close-to-uniform distribution, where the spiky distribution was created by alternating student grades between high and low for some of the courses displayed in adjacent positions (Fig. 1). We did not include variations on distribution in the double scenario in order to keep the experiment's length under one hour, as this is generally recommended for studies involving visual attention [13].

3.3   Study Design

The study was divided in two phases corresponding to the task batteries for the single and double scenarios. For single scenario tasks, the experiment used a 2 x 2 x 5 (visualization type x distribution type x task) within-subject design. There were also two orders of presentation for visualization type and two orders of presentations for distribution type, which constitute two between-subject control variables introduced to account for ordering effects. For double scenario tasks, the design was a 2x4 (visualization type x task) within-subject design, with order of visualization type as a between-subject control variable. The experiment was conducted on a generic PC computer running Windows XP, with a 3.20GHZ processor, 2.00 GB RAM, and a 17 inch screen. The experimental software was fully automated and was coded in Python.

3.4   Procedure

The experiment was designed and pilot-tested to fit in a single session lasting at most one hour. It was divided into three components: (1) the cognitive tests, (2) the main sequence of tasks and (3) a post-questionnaire. Participants began by completing the three tests for cognitive measures. They first performed the computer-based OSPAN test for Verbal Working Memory [21] (lasting between 7 and 12 minutes), followed by the computer-based test for Visual Working Memory [12] (10 minutes long) and finally the paper-based P-3 test for Perceptual Speed [9] (3 minutes long). Participants were then stationed in front of the study computer for the main task portion of the experiment. Each participant performed the 14 tasks described earlier two times, once for each visualization type. The presentation order with respect to visualization type and distribution type was fully counterbalanced across subjects. Each task consisted of presenting the participant with a radar/bar graph displaying the relevant data, along with a textual question. Participants would then select their answer from a dropdown menu and click OK to advance to the next task. Upon completion of the task portion of the experiment, participants were given a post-questionnaire consisting of (1) self-reported expertise with each visualization prior to the experiment; (2) items to gauge user preference for each visualization; (3) items to assess the subjective ease-of-use for each visualization.

3.5   Measures

Completion Time: Our software recorded the total amount of time in milliseconds that participants spent on each task. We use this measure as the primary metric for task performance because there is a ceiling effect on task correctness given that subjects could take as much time as they wanted to generate an answer.

Visualization Preference: Preference ratings for each of the two visualizations were collected in the post-questionnaire via the two statements "*I prefer to use bar graph for answering the questions*" and "*I prefer to use radar graph for answering the questions*", rated on a Likert scale from 1 to 5.

Ease-of-Use: A subjective assessment of overall ease-of-use of each visualization was collected in the post-questionnaire by asking participants to rate on a Likert scale from 1 to 5 the two statements: "*In general, radar graph was easy to understand,*" and "*In general, bar graph was easy to understand.*" We used "easy to understand" rather than "easy to use" since the visualizations in the study were not interactive, and thus it was more natural to express usability in terms of understandability.

4   Data Analysis and Results

The goal of this section is to address our study questions Q1 and Q2, by comparing the effectiveness of radar and bar graphs on the tasks described earlier and by investigating whether our selected user characteristics influence this effectiveness. In discussing the results obtained using the General Linear Model and Multivariate analysis, we report statistical significance at the 0.05 level, as well as partial eta squared (η_p^2) for effect size, where .01 is a small effect, .09 is a medium effect, and .25 is a large effect [11]. We separate the analysis of completion time between single scenario and double scenario because in the single scenario phase we have an additional between-subject control for order of distribution type as discussed in section 3.2. We summarize the results of the measured user characteristics in Table 1. The rather large variances for most measures indicate that our user population was quite diverse with respect to these measures.

Table 1. Descriptive statistics of user characteristics collected from the study

Measure	N	Min	Max	Mean	Std. Dev
Percep. Speed	35	54.00	96.00	85.70	11.64
Visual WM	35	0.3	5.4	2.72	1.36
Verbal WM	35	2	6	4.58	1.10
Bar Expert	35	2	5	4.15	0.87
Radar Expert	35	1	5	2.12	1.22

4.1   Completion Time - Single Scenario

In order to study completion time for the tasks in the single scenario phase, we ran a repeated-measures 2 (visualization type) by 2 (distribution type) by 5 (task) general linear model with visualization-type order, and distribution-type order as between-subject factors, and the individual characteristics as covariates. The sphericity assumption was verified for this data set using Mauchly's test. The following points summarize the findings from this analysis:

- There is a large significant effect of visualization type (bar vs. radar), $F(1, 20) = 8.06$, p = .01 $\eta_p^2 = 0. 29$. Completion time was faster with bar graphs (M = 14.25s, SE = 0.6s), than with radar graph   (M = 19.0s, SE = 0.76s).
- There is a large significant main effect of perceptual speed, $F(1,20) = 7.61$, p = .01, $\eta_p^2 = 0.28$, indicating that   the higher the perceptual speed, the faster the completion time for both visualizations. The mean completion time for participants with low vs. high perceptual speed was 18 and 16 seconds, respectively (where high/low is defined based on the median split of perceptual speed values). This result confirms previous findings that differences in cognitive measures can impact general visualization effectiveness and, like in [7], it singles out perceptual speed as a relevant measure.
- There is a medium-large significant interaction effect between visualization type and perceptual speed, $F(1,20) = 4.49$, p < .05 $\eta_p^2 = 0.18$. Even though completion time is always faster with the bar graph, the difference in time performance between bar and radar decreases as a user's perceptual speed increases (See Figure 2-left). This result is important because it confirms the finding in [7] that perceptual speed is a cognitive measure that can impact the *compared effectiveness* of two different visualizations, at least when one of them is a radar graph.

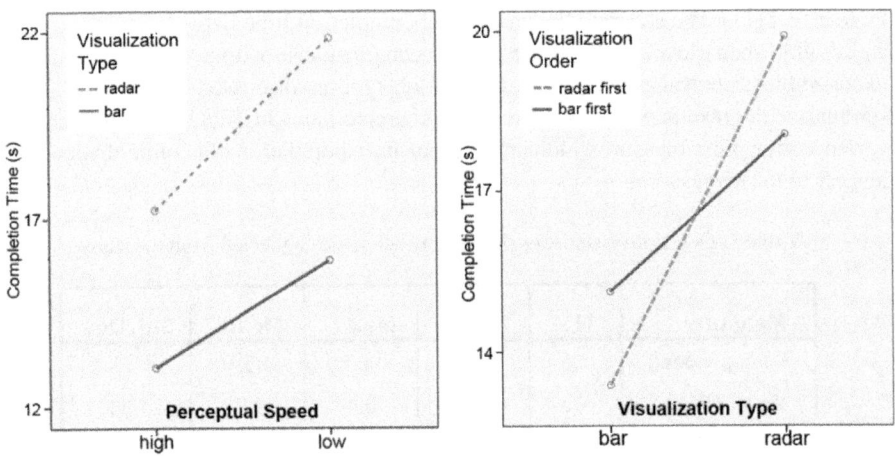

Fig. 2. Charts showing mean completion times for the effect of perceptual speed with graph type (**left**), and the interaction between visualization type and visualization order (**right**)

- There is a large significant interaction effect between visualization type and visualization order, $F(1,20) = 8.66$, p < .01, $\eta_p^2 = 0.30$. Subjects that saw radar graphs first, proceeded to perform better with bar graphs than those who saw bar graphs first. Conversely, subjects who saw bar graphs first, proceeded to perform better on radar graphs than those who saw radar graphs first (see Figure 2-right). Thus, it appears that there is a *training effect* between visualizations, despite the fact that task details are changed from the first to the second visualization provided. What is likely happening is that   the user is becoming familiar with the general task context/domain (e.g., the fact that the user is looking for values of school courses) after seeing it with the first visualization provided, which facilitates task performance with the second visualization.

4.2   Completion Time - Double Scenario

For the double scenario, we ran a repeated-measures 2 (visualization type) by 4 (task) general linear model with visualization order as a between-subject factor, along with the individual characteristics as covariates. The only significant effect found was a medium-sized effect of task, $F(2, 50) = 4.32$, $p < .05$, $\eta p^2 = 0.14$. This effect suggests that, in this phase there is a larger spread of difficulty across tasks as compared to the single scenario phase, resulting in a significant impact of the double scenario tasks on completion time. We find the lack of a significant effect of   visualization type interesting ($p = .465$, $\eta p^2 = 0.02$), because it opens the possibility to challenge claims in the literature that bar graphs are generally superior to radar graphs (e.g., [10, 20]). Given the low effect size, the lack of significant effect for visualization type may be due to a training effect generated by the participants' interactions with the two visualizations in phase one, which managed to eliminate the effect of visualization type detected in phase one. An alternative explanation is that radar graphs are as good as bar graphs for the types of comparison tasks covered in the double scenario phase. While we do not have data to reliably choose between these two explanations, the fact remains that we have encountered a scenario in which radar graphs are as effective as bar graphs, a unique finding to the best of our knowledge. There are also two marginally significant effects that we believe are worth mentioning here because their medium-large effect size indicates a potential for statistical significance given an increased experimental power. First, perceptual speed has a marginally significant main effect, $F(1,26) = 3.87$, $p = .06$, $\eta p^2 = 0.13$, which reflects the influence of this cognitive measure on visualization effectiveness, similar to what was detected in the single scenario phase. Second, radar expertise has a marginally significant main effect, $F(1,26) = 4.01$, $p = .055$, $\eta p^2 = 0.14$, suggesting that for the simpler tasks in the single scenario, the training provided to participants as part of the experimental setup managed to remove differences due to existing expertise, yet for the more difficult tasks in the double scenario phase, expertise starts having an effect. Furthermore, the effect of radar expertise is in terms of overall completion time for both visualization types, which means that radar expertise is linked to both radar graph and bar graph performance.

4.3   User Preference and Ease of Use

Figure 3-left shows the distribution of preference ratings for bar and radar graph. The distribution of ratings for the bar graph is skewed towards high values, whereas it is more uniformly distributed for the radar graph, indicating a higher variance in user preferences for the radar graph visualization. Figure 3-right shows ease-of-use ratings for bar and radar graph. More users give their highest rating to the bar graph than users who do so for the radar graph. However, it is worth noting that both the radar and bar graph are skewed towards high values, indicating that neither visualization is particularly difficult to understand.

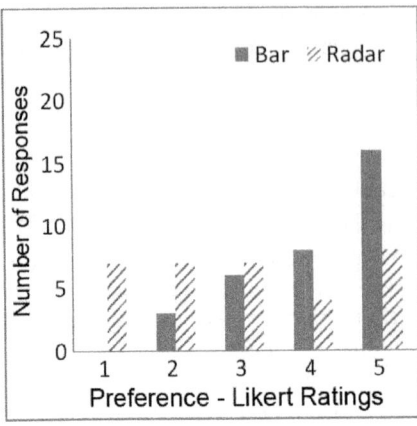 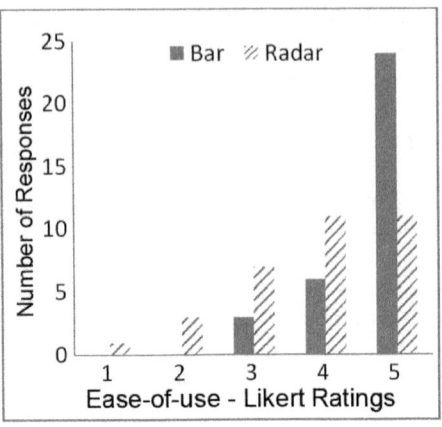

Fig. 3. Likert-scale data collected for graph preference (**left**), and ease-of-use ratings (**right**)

Preference and Ease of use data was collected using a standard 5 point Likert scale, and as such is not suitable for standard parametric analysis due to the lack of normality [17]. We applied the Aligned Rank Transformation (ART) using the ART-Tool [24] to transform our Likert rating scales for Radar Preference, Bar Preference, Radar Ease-of-Use, and Bar Ease-of-Use into normalized distributions which can then be correctly analyzed using standard parametric analysis. We used a multivariate analysis with preference and ease of use ratings as the dependent variables, along with the user characteristics as covariates. The following cognitive measures were found as significant:

- A large significant effect of visual working memory on radar preference, $F(1, 26)$ = 10.65, $p < .01$, $\eta_p^2 = 0.29$. In general, users with higher visual working memory had higher preference ratings for radar graphs.
- A large significant effect of verbal working memory on bar ease-of-use, $F(1, 26)$ = 9.69, $p < .01$, $\eta_p^2 = 0.27$. In general, users with lower verbal working memory had a higher ease-of-use rating for bar graphs.

These findings are extremely interesting, for two reasons. First, they are further evidence that user characteristics in general affect a user's experience with visualizations. Second, they indicate that different characteristics may influence different factors that contribute to the user's overall experience with a visualization. In the case of our study, perceptual speed influenced actual performance (completion time), whereas visual working memory and verbal working memory influenced subjective preference and ease-of-use, respectively.

We also found significant effects for Bar Expertise and Radar Expertise[1]:

- A very large significant effect of Radar Expertise on Radar Preference, $F(1, 26) =$ 45.80, $p < .001$, $\eta^2 = 0.64$, as well as Radar Ease-of-Use, $F(1, 26) = 19.6$, $p < .001$, $\eta_p^2 = 0.43$. We found that users with higher radar expertise had a stronger preference for radar graphs.

---

[1] Computing interaction effects between ART transformed measures is non-trivial, so we leave it to future work for this set of findings.

- A very high significant effect of Bar Expertise on Radar Ease-of-Use, $F(1, 26) = 931.86$, $p < .001$, $\eta_p^2 = 0.97$. Users with a higher bar expertise also had a higher rated ease-of-use for radar graphs.

Whereas it is quite intuitive that expertise should influence degree of preference and perceived ease-of-use, it is interesting that, in our study, expertise influences only subjective measures, and not actual performance.

5   Discussion - Envisioning Adaptive Interventions

Our user study clearly shows that the user characteristics we have considered do influence the effectiveness of bar and radar graphs. The next question is: what are reasonable adaptation strategies with respect to these characteristics? We envision two possible forms of adaptation: one would select different visualizations for different users, and the other would provide only some users with additional support, which they will likely find beneficial when inspecting a given visualization.

To illustrate, let us assume that our adaptive system has a model of the current user that specifies values for her characteristics. Now, if the target visualization is intended to support simple, single-scenario-like tasks, bar charts should be the default choice. However, if the user is low on perceptual speed, she may benefit from adaptive interventions, such as highlighting or arrow pointing to portions of the visualization relevant to the task. In contrast, if the visualization is intended to support more complex, double-scenario-like tasks the adaptation may consist of selecting a different visualization for different user groups. For instance, users with high Visual Working Memory or high Radar Graph Expertise would likely prefer a radar graph, while users with none of these features would be more effective with bar charts.

6   Conclusion and Future Work

This paper presents a user study that investigates the impact of four different user characteristics on the effectiveness of two common data visualization techniques: bar graphs and radar graph. The results of our study confirm and extend preliminary existing findings that individual user characteristics do make a difference in visualization effectiveness. So, we argue, these characteristics should be taken into account when selecting suitable visualization support for each particular viewer.

For the specific comparison between bar graphs and radar graphs, we found that while bar graphs are more effective (in terms of completion time) on simple information seeking tasks, the difference in performance with radar graphs is mediated by perceptual speed, decreasing for users with high perceptual speed. Furthermore, we found that the two visualizations seem to be equivalent on more complex tasks. It is an open question to verify which of the two visualizations would be more effective on a set of tasks more complex than the ones considered in this study.

In terms of impact of user characteristics on visualization effectiveness, in addition to the abovementioned interaction between perceptual speed and visualization type, we found a strong effect of perceptual speed on completion time with each visualization. We also found effects of different user characteristics (visual working memory, self-reported expertise) on subjective measures of user preferences and perceived ease-or-use for each visualization.

In order to apply these results in adaptive visualization, the system must be able to acquire a model of the user characteristics. Furthermore, suitable adaptation strategies must be devised. These are the two problems we are going to work on next.

There are several other interesting ways in which this work could be extended. We plan to re-run a similar study on more complex information visualizations intended to support decision-making. Our hypothesis is twofold: first, we expect the impact of individual differences on time-based performance to be even more pronounced than what we found in this study; second, because of the complexity of the associated tasks, we expect to be able to see effects on task accuracy in addition to completion time. Finally, we will also start experimenting with adaptive visualizations based on our findings on these more complex visualizations.

References

1. Allen, B.: Individual differences and the conundrums of user-centered design: Two experiments. Journal of the American Society for Information Science 51, 508–520 (2000)
2. Amar, R.A., Eagan, J., Stasko, J.T.: Low-Level Components of Analytic Activity in Information Visualization. In: 16th IEEE Visualization Conference, VIS 2005 (2005)
3. Baldonado, M.Q.W., Woodruff, A., Kuchinsky, A.: Guidelines for using multiple views in information visualization. In: Proceedings of the Working Conference on Advanced Visual Interfaces, pp. 110–119. ACM (2000)
4. Brusilovsky, P., Ahn, J., Dumitriu, T., Yudelson, M.: Adaptive Knowledge-Based Visualization for Accessing Educational Examples. In: Proceedings of Information Visualization (2006)
5. Chen, C.: Individual differences in a spatial-semantic virtual environment. Journal of the American Society for Information Science 51(6), 529–542 (2000)
6. Cleveland, W.S., McGill, R.: Graphical Perception: Theory, Experimentation, and Application to the Development of Graphical Methods. Journal of the American Statistical Association 79(387), 531–554 (1984)
7. Conati, C., Maclaren, H.: Exploring the Role of Individual Differences in Information Visualization. In: Proceedings of the Working Conference on Advanced Visual Interfaces (AVI 2008), pp. 199–206. ACM, New York (2008)
8. Dillon, A.: Spatial-semantics: how users derive shape from information space. J. Am. Soc. Inf. Sci. 51(6), 521–528 (2000)
9. Ekstrom, R.B., French, J.W., Harman, H.H.: Kit of factor-referenced cognitive tests. Educational Testing Service. Princeton, NJ (1976)
10. Few, S.: Keep Radar Graphs Below the Radar - Far Below: Information Management Magazine (2005)
11. Field, Hole: How to Design and Report Experiments, p. 153 (2003)
12. Fukuda, K., Vogel, E.K.: Human variation in overriding attentional capture. Journal of Neuroscience (2009)
13. Goldberg, J.H., Helfman, J.I.: Comparing Information Graphics: A Critical Look at Eye Tracking. In: BELIV 2010 (2010)

14. Gotz, Wen: Behavior-Driven Visualization Recommendation. In: ACM International Conference on Intelligent User Interfaces, Sanibel, Florida (2009)
15. Green, T.M., Fisher, B.: Towards the personal equation of interaction: The impact of personality factors on visual analytics interface interaction. In: IEEE Visual Analytics Science and Technology, VAST (2010)
16. Jameson, A.: Adaptive Interfaces and Agents. In: Jacko, J.A., Sears, A. (eds.) Human-Computer Interface Handbook, pp. 305–330 (2003)
17. Kaptein, M.C., Nass, C., Markopoulos, P.: Powerful and Consistent Analysis of Likert-Type Rating Scales. In: Proceedings of the 28th International Conference on Human Factors in Computing Systems, CHI 2010, Atlanta, Georgia, USA, pp. 2391–2394 (2010)
18. Lewandowsky, S., Spence, I.: The perception of statistical graphs. Sociological Methods and Research 18, 200–242 (1989)
19. Nowell, L., Schulman, R., Hix, D.: Graphical encoding for information visualization: an empirical study. In: IEEE Symposium on Information Visualization, INFOVIS 2002, pp. 43–50 (2002)
20. Simkin, D., Hastie, R.: An Information-Processing Analysis of Graph Perception. Journal of the American Statistical Association 82(398), 454–465 (1987)
21. Turner, M.L., Engle, R.W.: Is working memory capacity task dependent? Journal of Memory and Language 28(2), 127–154 (1989)
22. Velez, M.C., Silver, D., Tremaine, M.: Understanding visualization through spatial ability differences. In: Proceedings of Visualization 2005 (2005)
23. Williams, M., Munzner, T.: Steerable, Progressive Multidimensional Scaling. In: Proceedings of the InfoVis 2005, pp. 57–64 (2004)
24. Wobbrock, J., Findlater, L., Gergle, D., Higgins, J.: The Aligned Rank Transform for Nonparametric Factorial Analyses Using Only ANOVA Procedures. In: CHI 2011. ACM Press (2011)
25. Ziemkiewicz, C., et al.: How Locus of Control Influences Compatibility with Visualization Style. In: Proc. IEEE VAST 2011 (2011)

WTF? Detecting Students Who Are Conducting Inquiry Without Thinking Fastidiously

Michael Wixon, Ryan S.J.d. Baker, Janice D. Gobert,
Jaclyn Ocumpaugh, and Matthew Bachmann

Worcester Polytechnic Institute, Worcester, Massachusetts
{mwixon,rsbaker,jgobert,jocumpaugh}@wpi.edu,
bachmann.matt@gmail.com

Abstract. In recent years, there has been increased interest and research on identifying the various ways that students can deviate from expected or desired patterns while using educational software. This includes research on gaming the system, player transformation, haphazard inquiry, and failure to use key features of the learning system. Detection of these sorts of behaviors has helped researchers to better understand these behaviors, thus allowing software designers to develop interventions that can remediate them and/or reduce their negative impacts on user outcomes. In this paper, we present a first detector of what we term WTF ("Without Thinking Fastidiously") behavior, based on data from the Phase Change microworld in the Science ASSISTments environment. In WTF behavior, the student is interacting with the software, but their actions appear to have no relationship to the intended learning task. We discuss the detector development process, validate the detectors with human labels of the behavior, and discuss implications for understanding how and why students conduct inquiry without thinking fastidiously while learning in science inquiry microworlds.

Keywords: student modeling, educational data mining, intelligent tutoring system, science inquiry, off-task behavior.

1 Introduction

In recent years, there has been increasing awareness that the behavior of students learning from educational software can deviate in several ways from the behaviors expected by software designers. Traditional student modeling paradigms tend to assume that a learner is attempting to perform the designated task as intended, and that incorrect performance pertains solely to not knowing the skill [1-3]. However, other researchers have considered the various ways that student behavior may deviate from expected patterns. For example, students may game the system, attempting to succeed in an educational task by systematically taking advantage of properties and regularities in the system used to complete that task, rather than by thinking through the material [4]. Students also may transform the learning task to a different task entirely [5]. Additionally, students may engage in haphazard inquiry, whereby they

J. Masthoff et al. (Eds.): UMAP 2012, LNCS 7379, pp. 286–296, 2012.
© Springer-Verlag Berlin Heidelberg 2012

get closer to and then further from the goal of the task [6], showing a lack of understanding of how to conduct inquiry. Finally, some students may engage in acts wholly disconnected from the goals of the learning system. For example, in an online learning environment in which students were expected to discover what disease is infecting a community of scientists, students instead spent their time in unrelated behaviors, such as placing bananas in the toilet [personal communication, Jennifer Sabourin]. In another example, students plotting points from a function in a Cognitive Tutor for high school mathematics may instead plot a smiley face.

Rowe and his colleagues conceptualize this type of behavior as off-task [7], which they define as "behaviors that are clearly unrelated to the narrative and curriculum." We believe that there are important differences between this behavior and the type of behaviors typically considered to be off-task, whether within educational software [4] or non-computerized learning settings [8]. Whereas off-task behavior in previous accounts is seen as being completely disconnected from the learning task and environment, this "bananas in the toilet" behavior is disconnected from the learning task but occurs within the learning environment. Hence, we propose that this behavior be referred to instead as "WTF behavior." (WTF, of course, stands for "Without Thinking Fastidiously.") WTF behaviors may have negative impacts on learning, as off-task behavior does. However, to the extent that WTF behavior differs from off-task behavior, it may manifest differently in log files, necessitating detectors tailored to this behavior.

Within this paper, we present the first automated detector of WTF behavior, developed in the context of a science inquiry microworld in the domain of Phase Change, within the Science ASSISTments learning software [www.scienceassistments.org; 9-10]. This detector is generated using a combination of feature engineering and step regression, and is cross-validated at the student level (e.g. repeatedly trained on one group of students and tested on other students). We report this detector's effectiveness at identifying WTF behavior, analyze its internal features, and compare it to past detectors of other forms of disengagement.

2   Data Set

The data analyzed in this study were produced by 144 eighth graders (generally ages 12-14), who were using the Science ASSISTments' Phase Change microworld, within their science classes. All attended a middle school with a diverse population in a medium-sized city in central Massachusetts. The student population exhibits substantial economic and educational challenges: 20% of them qualified for free or reduced-price school lunches in the 2009-2010 school year and greater than 50% scored at or below "needs improvement" in the Science & Technology/Engineering portion of the Massachusetts Comprehensive Assessment System (MCAS).

Within the Phase Change microworld, shown in Figure 1, students observe and manipulate a simulation to conduct inquiry regarding the changes between solid, liquid, and gas. Specifically, students form hypotheses regarding the phenomenon, and test their hypotheses by running experiments within the simulation. They then interpret their data, warrant their claims, and communicate findings. At any point during their analysis, they may return to the experiment or hypothesizing phases.

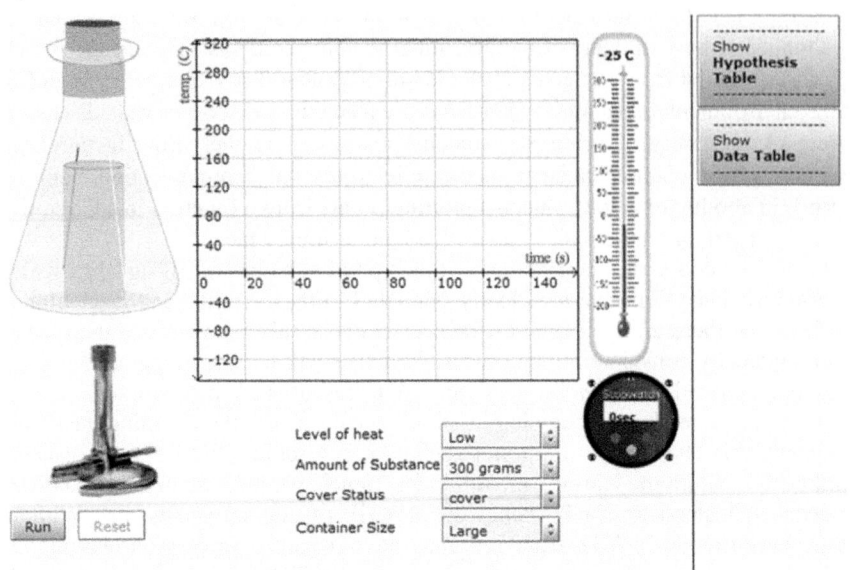

Fig. 1. A screen shot of the Phase Change microworld

Each of the 144 students completed at least one data collection activity in the phase change environment. In this paper, we focus on student actions in the hypothesizing and experimentation phases of the microworld. As students solved these tasks, their actions within the software were logged, including generating hypotheses, designing and running experiments, and switching between hypothesizing, experimentation, and other inquiry activities – for a total of 144,841 actions. Logs included the action type, the relevant simulation variable values, and the time stamp.

3   WTF Detector

3.1   Obtaining Ground Truth Labels of WTF Behavior Using Text Replays

The first step in our process of developing a data-mined detector of WTF behavior, is to develop ground truth labels, using text replays [9, 11]. In text replays, human coders are presented "pretty-printed" versions of log files (as shown in Figure 2). WTF behavior may be difficult to rationally define in log files (and rational detectors of this nature are difficult to validate for generalizability), but behavior that is completely disconnected from the learning task can be identified by humans relatively easily. In past cases, text replays have proved effective for providing ground truth labels for behaviors of this nature [9, 12-13]. Examples of WTF behavior in this data set include running the exact same experiment a large number of times (shown in Figure 2), toggling variable settings back and forth repeatedly, and changing large numbers of variables repeatedly. As can be seen, WTF behavior manifests in several ways, an interesting challenge for developing an automated detector of this construct.

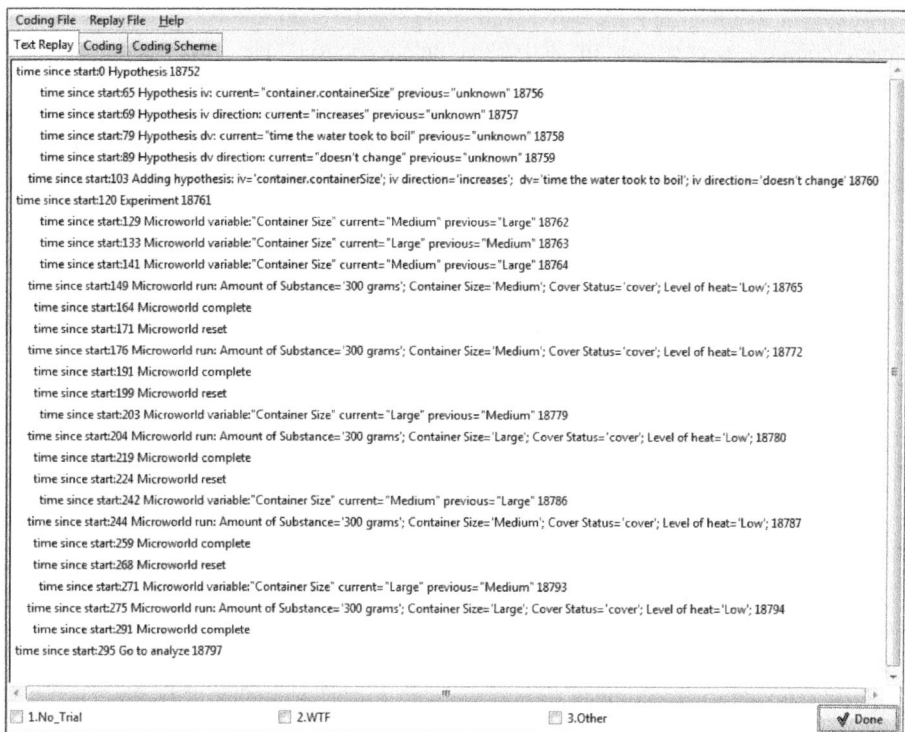

Fig. 2. Text Replay Showing Student Running The Same Trial a Large Number of Times

In order to create text replays, the student data was segmented into "clips", sequences of student behavior. In this paper, we segment student data by sequences of student data collection behavior (experimentation within the microworld), adopting the approach for doing so proposed in [9]. In this approach, a clip begins when a student enters the data collection phase and ends when the student leaves that phase. The typical order of student actions in Science ASSISTments is to create hypotheses, collect data, interpret data, warrant claims, and then communicate their findings, but a student can return to data collection after interpreting data. Thus, a clip may start either after the student makes a hypothesis and decides to collect data, or after the student attempts to interpret data and decides to collect more data.

Clips were coded individually, but not in isolation. That is, coders had access to all of the previous clips the same student produced within the same activity so that they could detect WTF behavior that might have otherwise been missed due to lack of context. For example, a student may repeatedly switch between hypothesizing and experimentation, running the exact same experiment each time. Although repeating the same experiment two or three times may help the student understand the simulation better, doing so more than twenty times might be difficult to explain except as WTF.

Two human coders (the 2nd and 5th authors) practiced coding WTF on two sets of clips which were excluded from use in detector development. In the first set of clips, they coded together and discussed coding standards. Next, the two coders separately each coded a second set of 200 clips independently. The two coders achieved acceptable agreement, with Cohen's [14] Kappa of 0.66.

Afterwards, the 2nd author coded 571 clips, which were used to develop the WTF detector. Since several clips could be generated per activity, a single, randomly chosen clip was tagged per student, per activity (however, not all students completed all activities, causing some student-activity pairs to be missing from the data set). This ensured all students and activities were approximately equally represented in this data set. Seventy of these clips were excluded from analysis, due to a lack of data collection actions on the student's part. Of the 501 clips remaining, 15 (3.0%) were labeled as involving WTF behavior, a proportion similar to the proportions of disengaged behavior studied in past detector development [cf. 12]. These 15 clips were drawn from 15 (10.4%) of the students (i.e., no student was coded as engaging in WTF behavior more than once).

3.2   Data Features

In order to develop an automated detector of WTF behavior from the log files, we distilled features of the data corresponding to the clips of behavior labeled by the coders. An initial set of 77 features was distilled using code that had been previously developed to detect student use of experimentation strategies and testing the correct hypothesis within Science ASSISTments [9]. As many of these features did not appear relevant to detecting WTF behavior and a greater number of features increases the risk of over-fitting [16], this set was manually reduced to 24 features without reference to the labeled data.

All of these 24 features corresponded to information about the set of actions involved in a specific clip and prior actions that provided context for the clip. The first four features involve overall statistics for the clip: (1) the total number of actions, (2) the average time between actions, (3) the maximum time between actions, and (4) the total number of experimental trials run by the student. The next three features were based on pauses: (5) the number of times a student paused the simulation during runs, (6) the average duration of student-initiated pauses of the simulation (i.e., total time spent paused, divided by number of pauses), and (7) the duration of the longest single instance when the student paused the system.

Ten more features relevant to the time elapsed during experimentation were used: (8) the total amount of time spent before running each experimental trial but after performing the previous action, (9) the average time spent by the student before running each experimental trial but after performing the previous action, (10) the standard deviation of the time spent by the student before running each experimental trial but after performing the previous action, and (11) the maximum time spent before running each experimental trial but after performing the previous action.

Several features related to resetting or pausing the experimental apparatus (or the absence of this action), were included. Pausing the simulation can be appropriate in many situations, but doing so large numbers of times may be an indicator of WTF behavior. These include: (12) the number of experimental trials run without either pauses or resets, (13) the average time spent by the student before running each experimental trial which was completed without being reset but after performing the previous action, (14) the number of trials where the system was reset, (15) the average time spent before running each experimental trial that were reset but after performing the previous action, and (16) the maximum time spent before running an experimental trial that was reset before completion but after performing the previous action.

The next set of features involved whether and how a student changed the variables while forming hypotheses. These included (17) the number of times a variable was changed, and three measures of the period of time that elapsed before the student changed a variable (measured from the previous action, whatever it was): (18) the sum total of time elapsed in all these periods, (19) the mean time elapsed across these periods, and (20) the standard deviation of time elapsed across these periods.

The final features consisted of changes to independent variables between experimental trials. These included: (21) the number of times an independent variable was changed during the experiment phase, and three measures of the period of time that elapsed before the student changed a variable (measured from the previous action, whatever it was), namely: (22) the sum total of time elapsed in all these periods, (23) the mean time elapsed across these periods, and (24) the standard deviation of time elapsed across these periods. These features regarding variable changes were useful as extremely large numbers of changes would not map to any reasonable experimentation strategy.

3.3 Detector Development

We attempted to fit detectors of WTF using 11 common classification algorithms, including Naïve Bayes, and J48 decision trees. The best model performance was achieved by the PART algorithm [17], an algorithm that produces rules out of C4.5 decision trees (essentially the same algorithm as J48 decision trees). The implementation of PART from WEKA [18] was run within RapidMiner 4.6 [19]. In this algorithm, a set of rules is built by repeatedly building a decision tree and making a rule out of the path leading to the best leaf node at each iteration. PART has not been frequently used in student modeling, but was used in [20] to predict student course success. These models were evaluated using a process of six-fold student-level cross-validation [21]. In this process, students are split randomly into six groups. Then, for each possible combination, a detector is developed using data from five groups of students before being tested on the sixth "held out" group of students. By cross-validating at this level, we increase confidence that detectors will be accurate for new groups of students.

Detectors were assessed using four metrics, A' [22], Kappa [14], precision [23], and recall [23]. A' is the probability that the detector will be able to distinguish a clip involving WTF behavior from a clip that does not involve WTF behavior. A' is equivalent to both the area under the ROC curve in signal detection theory and to W, the Wilcoxon statistic [22]. A model with an A' of 0.5 performs at chance, and a model with an A' of 1.0 performs perfectly. An appropriate statistical test for A' in data across students would be to calculate A' and standard error for each student for each model, compare using Z tests, and then aggregate across students using Stouffer's method. However, the standard error formula for A' [22] requires multiple examples from each category for each student, which is infeasible in the small samples obtained for each student in our data labeling procedure. Another possible method, ignoring student-level differences to increase example counts, biases undesirably in favor of statistical significance. Hence, statistical tests for A' are not presented in this paper.

The second feature used to evaluate each detector was Cohen's Kappa, which assesses whether the detector is better than chance at identifying which clips involve WTF behavior. A Kappa of 0 indicates that the detector performs at chance, and a Kappa of 1 indicates that the detector performs perfectly. Detectors were also evaluated using precision and recall, which indicate (respectively) how well the model avoids false positives, and how well the model avoids false negatives.

A' and Kappa were chosen because they compensate for successful classifications occurring by chance [24], an important consideration in data sets with unbalanced proportions of categories (such as this case, where WTF is observed 3.0% of the time). Precision and recall give an indication of the detector's balance between two forms of error. It is worth noting that unlike Kappa, precision, and recall (which only look at the final label), A' takes detector confidence into account.

4 Results

The detector of WTF behavior developed using the PART algorithm achieved good performance under 6-fold student-level cross-validation. As shown in Table 1, the detector achieved a very high A' of 0.979, signifying that it could distinguish whether or not a clip involved WTF behavior approximately 97.9% of the time. When uncertainty was not taken into account, performance was lower, though still generally acceptable. The detector achieved a Kappa value of 0.4, indicating that the detector was 40% better than chance. This level of Kappa is comparable to past detectors of other constructs effectively used in interventions [9, 12]. Kappa values in this range, combined with almost perfect A' values, suggest that the detector is generally good at recognizing which behavior is more likely to be "WTF", but classifies some edge cases incorrectly. In general, the detector's precision and recall (which, like Kappa, do not take certainty into account), were approximately balanced, with precision = 38.9% and recall = 46.7%. Thus, it is important to use fail-soft interventions and to take detector certainty into account when selecting interventions – but there is not evidence that the detector has strong bias either in favor of or against detecting WTF behavior.

Table 1. WTF Detector Confusion Matrix

	Clips Coded as WTF by Humans	Clips Coded as NOT WTF by Humans
Detector Predicted WTF	7	11 (false positives)
Detector Predicted NOT WTF	8 (false negatives)	475

The algorithm, when fit on the entire data set, generated the following final model. In running this model, the rules are run in order from the first rule to the last rule.

1) IF the total number of independent variable changes (feature 21) is seven or lower, AND the number of experimental trials run (feature 7) is three or lower, THEN **NOT WTF**.

2) IF the maximum time spent between an incomplete run and the action preceding it (feature 16) is 10 seconds or less, AND the total number of independent variable changes (feature 21) is eleven or less, AND the average time spent paused (feature 5) is 6 seconds or less, THEN **NOT WTF**.

3) IF the total number of independent variable changes (feature 21) is greater than one, AND the maximum time between actions (feature 3) is 441 seconds or less, AND the number of trials run without pauses or resets (feature 12) is 4 or less, THEN **NOT WTF**.

4) IF the total number of independent variable changes (feature 21) is 12 or less, THEN **WTF**.

5) IF the maximum time spent before running each experimental trial but after performing the previous action (feature 11) is greater than 1.8 seconds, THEN **NOT WTF**.

6) All remaining instances are classified as **WTF**.

As can be seen, this detector used 6 rules to distinguish WTF behavior, which employ 8 features from the data set. Four of the rules identify the characteristics of behavior that is NOT WTF, while only two identify the characteristics of WTF behavior. We discuss the implications of the specific rules in the following section.

5   Discussion and Conclusions

In this paper, we introduce a first automated detector that can identify when a student is completely disconnected from the learning task but is still actively using the learning environment. This behavior, which we term WTF behavior ("without thinking fastidiously"), has been reported in multiple online learning environments, but has not yet been modeled or studied to the degree that it merits. Our findings suggest that WTF behavior has prevalence similar to gaming the system, a behavior known to be associated with poor learning [4], and that it can be identified both by human coders and by an automated detector. This opens the possibility of studying how WTF behavior correlates with learning, identifying what factors lead students to engage in WTF behavior, and in turn, developing automated interventions designed to bring students back on track. Work along these lines is currently ongoing in our lab.

Examining the model of WTF behavior obtained provides some interesting implications about this type of behavior. Previous detectors of undesirable behavior have largely focused on identifying the specific undesirable behavior studied [cf. 12, 13, 25]. By contrast, the rules produced by the WTF detector are targeted more towards identifying what *is not* WTF behavior than identifying what *is* WTF behavior. Four of the six rules identify non-WTF behavior. Of the two rules identifying WTF behavior, one simply states that any behavior not captured by the first five rules can be considered WTF. As such, this model suggests that WTF behavior may be characterized by the absence of appropriate strategies and behaviors, in a student actively using the software, rather than specific undesirable behavior.

It is also worth discussing the data feature which is most frequently employed in the model rules: the number of times the student changes a simulation variable (feature 21). Though this feature is used in four of the six rules, there is not a clear pattern where frequently changing variables is simply either good or bad. Instead, different student actions appear to indicate WTF behavior in a student who frequently changes simulation variables, compared to a student who seldom changes simulation variables. Specifically, a student who changes variables many times without stopping to think before running the simulation is seen as displaying WTF behavior. By contrast, a student who changes variables fewer times is categorized as displaying WTF behavior if he or she runs a large number of experimental trials and also pauses the simulation for long periods of time. This may indicate that the student is running the simulation far more times than is warranted for the number of variables being changed, and that his or her pattern of pauses does not seem to indicate that he or she is using the time to study the simulation.

As mentioned earlier, one potential direction for future work is to study the individual differences and situational factors leading students to engage in WTF behavior. This behavior could be expected to emerge for several reasons, including attitudinal reasons such as not valuing the learning task, a goal orientation of work avoidance, or immediate affective states such as confusion, frustration, and boredom. A key first paper investigating this question is Sabourin et al. [26], which showed that when WTF behavior (termed off-task behavior) emerges among students displaying different affect, it has different implications about their affect later in the task. Students who engage in this behavior when they are confused later become bored or frustrated. By contrast, students who engage in this behavior when they are frustrated often become re-engaged. These findings suggest that intelligent tutors should offer different interventions, depending on the affective context of WTF behavior, but further research is needed to determine which strategies are most appropriate and effective for specific learning situations and for learners with specific characteristics. For example, a confused student engaging in WTF behavior may need additional support in understanding how to learn from the learning environment [27]. By contrast, a student who engages in WTF behavior due to boredom or because they do not value the learning task may require intervention targeted towards demonstrating the long-term value of the task for the student's goals [cf. 28].

Automated detectors such as the one presented here have a substantial role to play in understanding the causes of WTF behavior. In specific, these detectors will make it feasible to study WTF behavior across a greater number of situations [cf. 15], helping us to better understand the factors leading to WTF behavior. By understanding the causes of WTF behavior, and how learning software should respond to it, we can take another step towards developing learning software that can effectively adapt to the full range of students' interaction choices during learning.

Acknowledgements. This research was supported by grant "Empirical Research: Emerging Research: Using Automated Detectors to Examine the Relationships Between Learner Attributes and Behaviors During Inquiry in Science Microworlds", National Science Foundation award #DRL-100864. We also thank Michael Sao Pedro for assistance in data distillation and for helpful comments and suggestions, and we thank Arnon Hershkovitz and Adam Nakama for helpful comments and suggestions.

References

1. Corbett, A.T., Anderson, J.R.: Knowledge tracing: Modeling the acquisition of procedural knowledge. User Modeling and User-Adapted Interaction 4, 253–278 (1995)
2. Martin, J., VanLehn, K.: Student assessment using Bayesian nets. International Journal of Human-Computer Studies 42, 575–591 (1995)
3. Pavlik, P.I., Cen, H., Koedinger, K.R.: Performance Factors Analysis – A New Alternative to Knowledge Tracing. In: Proc. of the 14th International Conference on Artificial Intelligence in Education, pp. 531–540 (2009)
4. Baker, R.S., Corbett, A.T., Koedinger, K.R., Wagner, A.Z.: Off-Task Behavior in the Cognitive Tutor Classroom: When Students "Game The System". In: Proceedings of ACM CHI 2004: Computer-Human Interaction, pp. 383–390 (2004)
5. Magnussen, R., Misfeldt, M.: Player transformation of educational multiplayer games. In: Proceedings of Other Players, Copenhagen, Denmark (2004)
6. Buckley, B., Gobert, J., Horwitz, P., O'Dwyer, L.: Looking inside the black box: Assessing model-based learning and inquiry in Biologica. International Journal of Learning Technologies 5(2), 166–190 (2010)
7. Rowe, J., McQuiggan, S., Robison, J., Lester, J.: Off-Task Behavior in Narrative-Centered Learning Environments. In: Proceedings of the 14th International Conference on AI in Education, pp. 99–106 (2009)
8. Karweit, N., Slavin, R.E.: Measurement and Modeling Choices in Studies of Time and Learning. American Educational Research Journal 18, 157–171 (1981)
9. Sao Pedro, M., Baker, R., Gobert, J., Montalvo, O., Nakama, A.: Leveraging Machine-Learned Detectors of Systematic Inquiry Behavior to Estimate and Predict Transfer of Inquiry Skill. To appear in User Modeling and User-Adapted Interaction: The Journal of Personalization Research (in press)
10. Gobert, J., Sao Pedro, M., Raziuddin, J.: Studying the Interaction Between Learner Characteristics and Inquiry Skills in Microworlds. In: Proceedings of the 9th International Conference on the Learning Sciences, pp. 46–47 (2010)
11. Baker, R.S.J.d., Corbett, A.T., Wagner, A.Z.: Human Classification of Low-Fidelity Replays of Student Actions. In: Proceedings of the Educational Data Mining Workshop at the 8th International Conference on Intelligent Tutoring Systems, pp. 29–36 (2006)
12. Baker, R.S.J.d., de Carvalho, A.M.J.A.: Labeling Student Behavior Faster and More Precisely with Text Replays. In: Proceedings of the 1st International Conference on Educational Data Mining, pp. 38–47 (2008)
13. Baker, R.S.J.d., Mitrović, A., Mathews, M.: Detecting Gaming the System in Constraint-Based Tutors. In: De Bra, P., Kobsa, A., Chin, D. (eds.) UMAP 2010. LNCS, vol. 6075, pp. 267–278. Springer, Heidelberg (2010)
14. Cohen, J.: A coefficient of agreement for nominal scales. Educational and Psychological Measurement 20(1), 37–46 (1960)
15. Baker, R.S.J.d., de Carvalho, A.M.J.A., Raspat, J., Aleven, V., Corbett, A.T., Koedinger, K.R.: Educational Software Features that Encourage and Discourage "Gaming the System". Proceedings of the 14th International Conference on Artificial Intelligence in Education, pp. 475–482 (2009)
16. Mitchell, T.M.: Machine Learning. McGraw-Hill, New York (1997)
17. Frank, E., Witten, I.H.: Generating Accurate Rule Sets Without Global Optimization. In: Proceedings of the Fifteenth International Conference on Machine Learning, pp. 144–151 (1998)

18. Witten, I.H., Frank, E.: Data Mining: Practical Machine Learning Tools and Techniques with Java Implementations. Morgan Kauffmann, San Francisco (1999)
19. Mierswa, I., Wurst, M., Klinkenberg, R., Scholz, M., Euler, T.: YALE: Rapid Prototyping for Complex Data Mining Tasks. In: Proceedings of the 12th ACM SIGKDD International Conference on Knowledge Discovery and Data Mining (KDD 2006), pp. 935–940 (2006)
20. Esposito, F., Licchelli, O., Semeraro, G.: Discovering Student Models in e-learning Systems. J. Universal Computer Science 10(1), 47–57 (2004)
21. Efron, B., Gong, G.: A leisurely look at the bootstrap, the jackknife, and cross-validation. American Statistician 37, 36–48 (1983)
22. Hanley, J., McNeil, B.: The Meaning and Use of the Area under a Receiver Operating Characteristic (ROC) Curve. Radiology 143, 29–36 (1982)
23. Davis, J., Goadrich, M.: The relationship between Precision-Recall and ROC curves. In: Proceedings of the 23rd International Conference on Machine Learning, pp. 233–240 (2006)
24. Ben-David, A.: About the Relationship between ROC Curves and Cohen's Kappa. Engineering Applications of Artificial Intelligence 21, 874–882 (2008)
25. Cetintas, S., Si, L., Xin, Y.P., Hord, C.: Automatic Detection of Off-Task Behaviors in Intelligent Tutoring Systems with Machine Learning Techniques. IEEE Transactions on Learning Technologies 3(3), 228–236 (2009)
26. Sabourin, J., Rowe, J.P., Mott, B.W., Lester, J.C.: When Off-Task is On-Task: The Affective Role of Off-Task Behavior in Narrative-Centered Learning Environments. In: Biswas, G., Bull, S., Kay, J., Mitrovic, A. (eds.) AIED 2011. LNCS, vol. 6738, pp. 534–536. Springer, Heidelberg (2011)
27. Roll, I., Aleven, V., McLaren, B.M., Koedinger, K.R.: Can help seeking be tutored? Searching for the secret sauce of metacognitive tutoring. In: Proceedings of the 13th International Conference on Artificial Intelligence in Education, pp. 203–210 (2007)
28. Pekrun, R.: The control-value theory of achievement emotions: Assumptions, corollaries, and implications for educational research and practice. Educational Psychology Review 18(4), 315–341 (2006)

Adapting Performance Feedback
to a Learner's Conscientiousness

Matt Dennis, Judith Masthoff, and Chris Mellish

Department of Computing Science, University of Aberdeen, Aberdeen, AB24 3UE
{m.dennis,j.masthoff,c.mellish}@abdn.ac.uk

Abstract. To keep a learner motivated, an intelligent tutoring system may need to adapt its feedback to the learner's characteristics. We are particularly interested in adaptation of performance feedback to the learner's personality. Following on from an earlier study that investigated the effect of generalized self-efficacy, this study examines how feedback may need to be adapted to the trait Conscientiousness from the Five Factor Model. We used a User-as-Wizard approach, with participants taking the role of the adaptive feedback generator. Participants were presented with a fictional student with a validated polarized level of Conscientiousness, along with a set of marks the student had achieved in a test. They provided feedback to the learner in the form of a short statement. We examined the level to which participants bent the truth as adaptation to the learner's conscientiousness. The study suggests that adaptation to conscientiousness may be needed: using a positive slant for highly conscientious students with failing grades.

1   Introduction

Feedback on progress is an important part of motivating a learner [1, 2, 3]. To produce effective feedback, an intelligent tutoring system may need to adapt this feedback to a learner's characteristics. We are investigating whether adaptation of feedback to the learner's personality is needed. In particular, we are interested in whether giving feedback on learner performance (for example a test score) which has been adapted to the personality of the learner will yield an increase in motivation.

Personality can be measured in many ways, but a popular approach is the trait model which describes the personality of an individual as a series of scores in a set of predefined traits or dimensions [4]. One of the most popular is the Five Factor Model (FFM) – which consists of the traits Extraversion (I), Agreeableness (II), Conscientiousness(III), Emotional Stability (IV) and Openness to Experience(V) [5].[1] This study is the first of a set of studies which will examine each of the traits. It follows on from previous work which looked at a single construct, Generalized Self Efficacy [6], in which we found that participants gave more positive feedback when describing poor performance to learners with low self-efficacy. In this study, we will investigate

---

[1] Psychologists do not agree on the nomenclature of the five traits, and describe them using numerals to avoid confusion between the different sets of terms.

J. Masthoff et al. (Eds.): UMAP 2012, LNCS 7379, pp. 297–302, 2012.
© Springer-Verlag Berlin Heidelberg 2012

the effect of conscientiousness. Conscientiousness (III) describes how efficient, organized, reliable and responsible an individual is [4]. Conscientiousness has strong ties to motivation and has been described as being "the most important trait-motivation variable in the work domain" [7]. Conscientious individuals have been shown to become more stressed when they receive negative feedback on their performance as they are more ambitious [3]. Therefore we would expect feedback given by a tutor towards conscientious students to be more encouraging rather than reproachful when they fail to achieve.

In this study, we examine whether people change the way they tell how a learner has performed on a mock test, depending on how conscientious that learner is. From these studies, we hope to construct an algorithm allowing a tutoring system to adapt its feedback to learner personality.

2   Study Design

The study design follows on from our previous study in which we investigated self-efficacy [6]: participants are asked to take the role of a teacher and give feedback to a student with either high or low conscientiousness. However, we made changes to the design of the study and the method of recruiting participants. In the previous study, we presented participants with one set of 5 percentage scores that a fictional student had achieved in a mock test. These scores ranged from 11% to 91% in roughly 20% intervals. We received comments that this student was not very realistic, so in this study we had two sets of percentage scores: a failing set and a passing set. Thus there were four variants of the study (passing marks with high or low conscientiousness and failing marks with high or low conscientiousness). Participants were recruited from Amazon's Mechanical Turk service, and unlike the last study, were not all trainee teachers. We recognize that the general population may be worse at employing pedagogical strategies than experienced teachers. This may lead to more variation in strategies used, and may make it harder to find statistically significant results. We decided to use the general public nevertheless, given the many participants needed for the planned studies and the need for participants who had not taken part in previous studies. To ensure our findings are valid, we will test the effectiveness of any strategy found on the motivation of students in a future study.

2.1   Design

Participants were presented with a fictional student and a set of percentage scores that the student had achieved on a mock test. Participants then gave feedback to the student on their performance. For each of the topics, participants could say whether the student was above, meeting or below their expectations in that topic. They could also use two modifiers (substantially or slightly) if they wished.

We used a 2x2 between-subject design, with two independent variables: the conscientiousness of the student (high or low), and the grades they had achieved (either passing or failing).

Low Conscientiousness story	High Conscientiousness story
Josh procrastinates and wastes his time. He finds it difficult to get down to work. He does just enough work to get by and often doesn't see things through, leaving them unfinished. He shirks his duties and messes things up. He doesn't put his mind on the task at hand and needs a push to get started. Josh tends to enjoy talking with people.	Josh is always prepared. He gets tasks done right away, paying attention to detail. He makes plans and sticks to them and carries them out. He completes tasks successfully, doing things according to a plan. He is exacting in his work; he finishes what he starts. Josh is quite a nice person, tends to enjoy talking with people, and quite likes exploring new ideas.

Fig. 1. Conscientiousness stories

The conscientiousness of the student was conveyed using a short story (see Figure 1). These stories had been previously validated to express conscientiousness at a polarized level, whilst expressing other traits at normal levels [8].

The achieved grades of the student were expressed as a set of percentage scores on fictional topics (Aromathy, Bartology and Cleropathy) in either a passing set (91%, 69%, 52%) or failing set (9%, 31%, 48%). Participants were told that they expected students to pass their mock test, with 50% being a pass.

The dependent variable was the slant, or bias employed in the feedback that the participants produced. Participants could describe the student's performance on a particular topic in many ways; for example, if they described a score of 91% as 'slightly above' expectations then this constituted a negative slant. Slants were determined in the same way as in the self-efficacy study [6], with the exception of the 48% score, which was not used in that study. Following a similar process to [6] which used three independent judges, we determined the slant for this score. All scores and slants are shown in Table 1.

As in [6], a valid response contained at least one topic and discussed each topic only once. Overall response slant was calculated from the summation of the slants on each topic mentioned (-1 for negative, 0 for neutral, 1 for positive). If a topic was omitted, participants were asked why they did this (to make the response more positive, negative or other) and this was factored into the slant score for the response.

2.2   Participants

Participants were recruited using Amazon Mechanical Turk and paid $0.40. Participants were recruited from the United States, and their English proficiency was tested using the Cloze Test [9] prior to the study with only people who passed the test being able to participate. Participants were asked to indicate their gender, age range and profession (student, teacher or other). We received 99 responses (56% male, 42% female, 2% undisclosed gender; 40% 16-25, 39% 26-40, 1% 26-50, 16% 41-65, 1% over 65, 2% undisclosed; 38% of respondents were students, 11% were teachers, and 50% other) split roughly evenly across conditions (passing grades: 21 high conscientiousness, 27 low; failing grades: 25 high conscientiousness, 26 low).

Table 1. Scores, descriptions, modifiers and resulting slants

Score	Description	Modifier	Slant
91%	above	substantially, none	neutral
		slightly	negative
	meeting	n/a	negative
	behind	all	negative
69%	above	substantially	positive
		none, slightly	neutral
	meeting	n/a	negative
	behind	all	negative
52%	above	substantially	positive
		slightly, none	neutral
	meeting	n/a	neutral
	behind	all	negative
48%	above	all	positive
	meeting	n/a	positive
	behind	slightly, none	neutral
		substantially	negative
33%	above	all	positive
	meeting	n/a	positive
	behind	substantially	negative
		slightly, none	neutral
12%	above	all	positive
	meeting	n/a	positive
	behind	slightly	positive
		none, substantially	neutral

2.3   Hypotheses

We hypothesized that:

- The slant participants employ on feedback will not differ between students with high and low conscientiousness on the passing set of grades (H1)
- The slant participants employ on feedback will differ between students with high and low conscientiousness on the failing set of grades (H2)

These hypotheses were based on our previous study investigating the effect of self-efficacy, where we found that participants tended to only employ slants on poor grades, and the higher stress experienced by highly conscientious people when failing to reach goals [3] (as discussed above).

3   Study Results

3.1   Comparing Slants Where the Grades Are Passing

Figure 2 shows the distribution of the overall slants produced by the participants in the high and low conscientiousness conditions for a student with passing grades.

The slant between the two conditions does not significantly differ ($p = 0.78$, Mann-Whitney test). This supports Hypothesis H1 (though one cannot really prove a hypothesis of this type). Figure 2 also shows that slants employed are very similar.

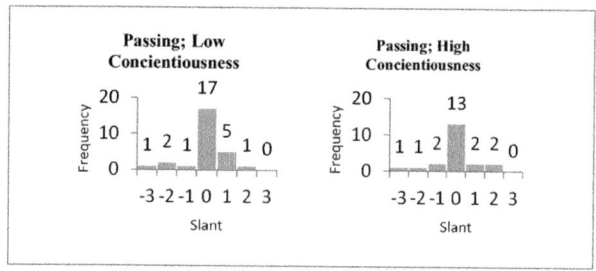

Fig. 2. Comparison of slant of feedback between levels of conscientiousness on passing grades

3.2   Comparing Slants Where the Grades Are Failing

In correspondence with H2, there is a significant difference between the high and low conditions of conscientiousness for a student with failing grades ($p < 0.01$, Mann-Whitney test). Figure 3 shows the distribution of slants across the responses. Participants were more inclined to employ a positive slant when conscientiousness was high.

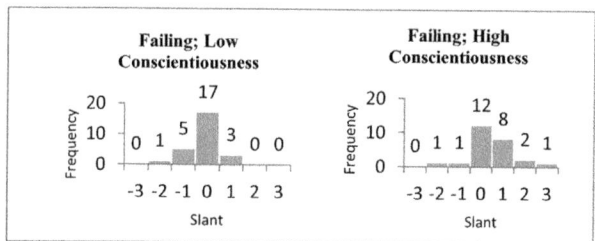

Fig. 3. Comparison of slant of feedback between levels of conscientiousness on failing grades

3.3   Topics

Table 2 shows the slant on each topic for both conditions of the failing grades variant. The difference in responses appears to have come from Cleropathy, with 40% of participants putting a positive slant in the high conscientiousness condition, compared to 11.5% in the low condition.

Table 2. Percentage slants for each topic. A = Aromathy B = Bartology C= Cleropathy

Topic (score)	Low Conscientiousness			High Conscientiousnesss		
	negative	neutral	positive	negative	neutral	positive
A (9%)	0	100	0	0	88	12
B (31%)	19	81	0	8	84	8
C (48%)	8	80.5	11.5	4	66	40

4   Discussion and Future Work

Based on the results of this study, there is no reason to adapt feedback to a learner's conscientiousness for passing grades. This corroborates our earlier findings for self-efficacy. However, there is evidence that adapting feedback to a learner's conscientiousness may be appropriate for failing grades. For these, participants appeared to place a more positive slant on feedback if the student had high conscientiousness than if the student had low conscientiousness.

For the failing student with high conscientiousness, roughly the same number of participants employed a positive slant as employed a neutral slant. The relatively high proportion of neutral slants may be a side effect of using Mechanical Turk: participants work fast and tend to follow instructions very closely, so may consider their responses less deeply. Additionally, the ability of participants to give feedback is likely to vary. Nevertheless, the fact that many participants chose to use a positive slant indicates that this is potentially a good way in which to adapt feedback.

In this study, the positive slant was primarily on the topic that was closest to passing (Cleropathy). However, this may be different with other grades. Additionally, as the study was split into passing and failing variants, we do not know how humans adapt when giving feedback to a student who passed some topics but not others. A further study will investigate this.

Our work so far has investigated how humans adapt feedback to a learner's personality to inspire adaptation algorithms. The next stage will investigate whether this adaptation will indeed impact learners' affective state and motivation.

Acknowledgments. The study was funded by EPSRC platform grant EP/E011764/1.

References

1. Deci, E., Ryan, R.: The empirical exploration of intrinsic motivational processes. In: Berkowitz, L. (ed.) Advances in Experimental Social Psychology, pp. 39–74 (1981)
2. Bandura, A.: Self-Efficacy: The exercise of control. Freeman, New York (1997)
3. Cianci, A., Klein, H., Sejits, G.: The effect of negative feedback on tension and subsequent performance: The main and interactive effect of goal content and conscientiousness. Applied Psychology 95(4), 618–630 (2010)
4. McCrae, R., John, O.: An Introduction to the Five Factor Model and its Applications. Journal of Personality (1992)
5. Goldberg, R.: The structure of phenotypic personality traits. American Psychologist 48(1), 26–34 (1993)
6. Dennis, M., Masthoff, J., Pain, H., Mellish, C.: Does Self-Efficacy Matter When Generating Feedback? In: Biswas, G., Bull, S., Kay, J., Mitrovic, A. (eds.) AIED 2011. LNCS, vol. 6738, pp. 444–446. Springer, Heidelberg (2011)
7. Barrick, M.R., Mount, M.K., Strauss, J.P.: Conscientiousness and performance of sales representatives: test of the mediating effects of goal setting. App. Psy. 78, 715–722 (1993)
8. Dennis, M., Masthoff, J., Melllish, C.: The Quest for Validated Personality Trait Stories. Intelligent User Interfaces, 273–276 (2012)
9. Taylor, W.L.: Cloze procedure: A new tool for measuring readability. Journalism Quarterly 30, 415–433 (1953)

A Multi-faceted User Model for Twitter[*]

John Hannon, Kevin McCarthy, Michael P. O'Mahony, and Barry Smyth

CLARITY: Centre for Sensor Web Technologies,
School of Computer Science & Informatics, University College Dublin, Ireland
firstname.lastname@ucd.ie

Abstract. In this paper we describe an initial attempt to build multi-faceted user models from raw Twitter data. The key contribution is to describe a technique for categorising users and their social ties according to a collection of curated topical categories and in this way resolve much of the preference noise that is inherent within user conversations. We go on to analyse and evaluate this approach on a data set of over 240,000 Twitter users and discuss the applications of these novel user models.

Keywords: Twitter Lists, User Model, Tags.

1 Introduction

Twitter is a real-time sharing and conversation platform that has transformed the way that millions of users communicate and share information online. Today Twitter boasts some 300 million active users generating some 6000+ 140-character messages per second at peak[1]. And the service has evolved from a simple way to keep up with friends to an important platform for information discovery and dissemination[2]. Indeed, recent reports highlight the role that Twitter has played in key events of the 21st century such as the Arab Spring [3].

As a real-time conversational platform Twitter presents a number of interesting user modeling and profiling opportunities and challenges. Twitter users are connected in relatively dense social networks of *followers* and *friends* and these networks can contain communities of users with shared interests. In addition, the conversations that take place within these networks, and the information that is shared through these conversations, has the potential to provide a rich source of user preference and interest data, notwithstanding the 140-character limit that is placed on user posts. For example, user posts are often enriched with tagging information and users often post URLs to pages that they find to be interesting. In recent work [4], the text content of Twitter messages from a user and their followers/friends was used as the basis for text-based profiles as part of a recommendation system to suggest new users to follow. In this work, recommended users were suggested on the basis of term overlaps between the

---

[*] This work is supported by SFI under grant 07/CE/I1147 and by Amdocs Inc.
[1] http://blog.twitter.com/2011/03/numbers.html
[2] http://mashable.com/2009/08/18/mainstream-news-twitter/

J. Masthoff et al. (Eds.): UMAP 2012, LNCS 7379, pp. 303–309, 2012.
© Springer-Verlag Berlin Heidelberg 2012

target user's profile and the profiles of other users. Other researchers have explored Twitter information to model users as the basis for news recommendation [1,6] based on term overlap between news story content and user tweets.

One of the challenges with using tweet content as the basis for profiling is that it can lead to very large but noisy user profiles [8]. Researchers have also explored approaches to couple tags with a user model to enrich a user's experience when using a system [2,7]. In this work we examine an alternative approach that has the potential to generate more focused profiles based on terms that are more categorical in nature. To this end we harness information about the *curated lists* that users have been placed in. In Twitter, users can curate topical lists of other users – for example, a given user might create a list of *technology* people that they follow – and millions of lists have been created on a wide variety of topics. Services like Listorious (http://listorious.com) maintain a category database of these lists with each list hand-annotated with a set of topical tags. Recent research by Kim et al.[5] models a user's characteristics by exploring the tweets produced by users contained within a list. This content-based approach though, can be susceptible to the inherent noise associated with using terms from within tweets. In this paper we describe how using hand-annotated topics/tags associated with lists can be used as the basis for a more focused user profile and how these profiles can be partitioned in a way that helps to emphasize and distinguish core versus peripheral interests.

2   Intentional and Extensional Tag-Based User Models

The user profile that we will describe in this paper associates a weighted set of tags with the target user based on the curated lists that have been categorised by Listorious. Simply put, for each list L_i there are a set of members and a set of tags as shown in Eq. 1 & 2.

$$members(L_i) = \{U_1, ...U_n\} . \tag{1}$$

$$tags(L_i) = \{t_1, ..., t_m\} . \tag{2}$$

For a target user U_T, we can identify the set of lists that this user is a member of (Eq. 3), and the tags applied to this user is the union of the tags that are associated with the user's lists (Eq. 4). Moreover, the weight of a tag for a user is based on the frequency of occurrence of this tag in the user's lists (Eq. 5 & 6).

$$lists(U_T) = \{L_i : U_T \epsilon L_i\} . \tag{3}$$

$$tags(U_T) = \bigcup_{\forall L_i \epsilon lists(U_T)} tags(L_i) . \tag{4}$$

$$weight(U_T, t_i) = \sum_{\forall L_i \epsilon lists(U_T)} count(t_i, L_i) . \tag{5}$$

$$count(t_i, L_i) = \begin{cases} 1 \text{ if } t_i \epsilon tags(L_i); \\ 0 \text{ otherwise.} \end{cases} \quad (6)$$

We call this the user's *intentional* tag profile because it maps a set of tags to the user based on the categories of the Twitter lists that they are members of. Further, it is possible to associate users with tags based on the lists that their friends (people they follow) or followers (people who follow them) are members of; we refer to this type of profile as the user's *extensional* profile. Accordingly, we can readily adapt the above equations to identify and weigh a set of tags that are associated with a list of friends; see Eq. 7 & 8 with corresponding equations assumed for followers. Accordingly we can now profile the target user by the combination of their intentional and extensional profiles as per Eq. 9.

$$friendTags(U_T) = \bigcup_{\forall U_i \epsilon Friends(U_T)} tags(U_i) \,. \quad (7)$$

$$friendTagWeight(U_T, t_i) = \sum_{\forall U_i \epsilon Friends(U_T)} weight(U_i, t_i) \,. \quad (8)$$

$$profile(U_T) = tags(U_T) \cup friendTags(U_T) \cup followerTags(U_T) \,. \quad (9)$$

3 Profile Facets

We propose that this profiling framework has a number of advantages over related research that chooses instead to focus on the content of user tweets [4]. For a start, it provides access to a more limited profile vocabulary, the tags associated with Twitter lists, compared to the words of a tweet. Moreover, the presence of a user in a list requires an explicit assessment and action on the part of the list curator and the subsequent tagging of these lists by Listorious is also a manual collective task. In addition, the overlap and difference between intentional and extensional profile components suggests an opportunity to partition tag-based profiles in a way that helps to emphasis core vs. peripheral interests.

Figure 1 (a) depicts a simple Venn diagram of the intentional and extensional profile elements and divides the tag space of a target user profile up into seven distinct regions. For example, region R_1 is at the centre of the Venn diagram and represents those tags that are common to the user's intentional and extensional profile elements (Eq. 10). This set of tags is interesting because it corresponds to the core interests/expertise of the target user in the sense that these tags have been associated with the target user and also with their followers and friends, and, as such they are a strong indicator of shared topical interests across the users social network. In contrast, region R_6 corresponds to those tags that are unique to the user's intentional profile and as such they represent topics that are of interest to the user that distinguish them from their friends and followers (Eq. 11). Also of particular interest is region R_4, which represents the set of topics that are of interest to both friends and followers but that are not associated

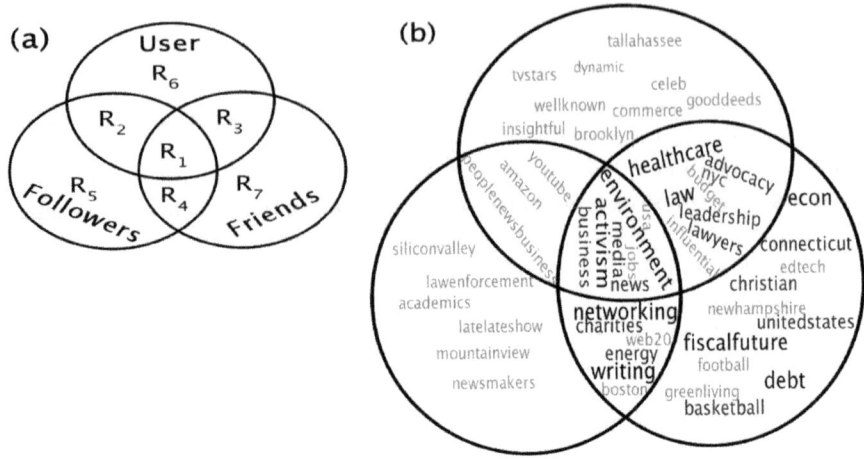

Fig. 1. (a) Intentional and extensional profile regions. (b) Barack Obama's profile showing the tags associated with Obama and his friends and followers.

with the target user (Eq. 12); perhaps these tags represent interests that may be relevant when it comes to expanding the network of the target user, for example.

$$R_1(U_T) = tags(U_T) \cap friendTags(U_T) \cap followersTags(U_T) \,. \qquad (10)$$

$$R_6(U_T) = tags(U_T) - \{friendTags(U_T) \cap followersTags(U_T)\} \,. \qquad (11)$$

$$R_4(U_T) = \{friendTags(U_T) \cap followersTags(U_T)\} - tags(U_T) \,. \qquad (12)$$

We propose that this regioned, multi-faceted approach to profiling Twitter users provides an effective way to model the interests and preferences of users in a way that facilitates a better understanding of core and peripheral interests and also provides for a powerful framework for exploring a space of interests within Twitter's social graph. Figure 1 (b) shows an example of a profile generated for the US President Barack Obama. It is clear that Obama and the people he follows share interests such as *advocacy, law* and *budget* (region R_3). Perhaps a greater insight into the US President's personal interests can be gleaned from the tags in region R_7, which are unique to the people he follows, and include interests such as *basketball* and *greenliving*. Conversely those interests that are unique to Obama's followers, *academics* and *siliconvalley* (see region R_5) highlight the interests of those users that are perhaps most influenced by the US President.

Immediate and obvious applications leading from this approach include, for instance, providing a more powerful recommendation interface to guide users towards other interesting users. For instance, if a user is interested in expanding their own interests they may wish to consider exploring the tags associated with region R_4 since both their followers and friends share these interests. It remains an important part of our future research to explore these opportunities but in what follows we will describe preliminary results based on the construction of profiles for some 246,000 Twitter users.

4   Preliminary Investigation

In order to build our user models we collected two datasets. The first is the lists from Listorious, including membership and tags. In total we gathered 18,000 unique tags from lists covering 1.2 million unique users. We randomly selected a subset of 246k of these 1.2m users, then collected the associated Twitter information of these users, including their follower and friend data. Figure 2(a) shows the distribution of the tags from Listorious across these 246,000 users. We can see that many tags are associated with reasonable numbers of users. For instance, the top 2,000 most frequent tags are found in at least 100 user (intentional) profiles and the top 10,000 tags are found in at least 30 user profiles. Conversely, Figure 2(b) shows the distribution tags across users and we can see that the most tagged users are associated with hundreds of unique tags but in general the top 100,000 most tagged users are associated with at least 6 tags each. To generate the tags for a Twitter user in this experiment we use up to 10,000 of their friends/followers and attempted to retrieve tags for these users from our Listorious dataset. We attained a tag coverage of just under 60% for a user's friends and just under 40% for a user's followers on average, high coverage values given that there are no guarantees that a target user's friends or followers will be contained within tagged Listorious lists. This preliminary investigation suggests that data from Listorious provides a suitably rich source of profile tags.

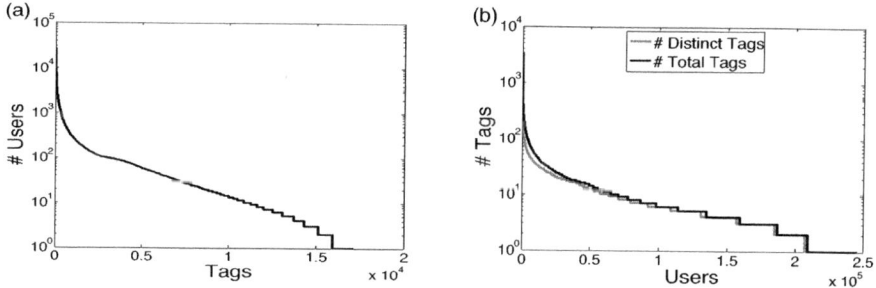

Fig. 2. (a) Distribution of tag occurrences per user. (b) Distribution of the number of total and distinct tags per user.

We were also interested in understanding how frequently we could populate different regions of a user profile with tags. Figure 3 shows the percentage of each user's profiled tags (that is the combination of their intentional and extensional profiles) that are contained in each region of the faceted profile. Clearly there is a

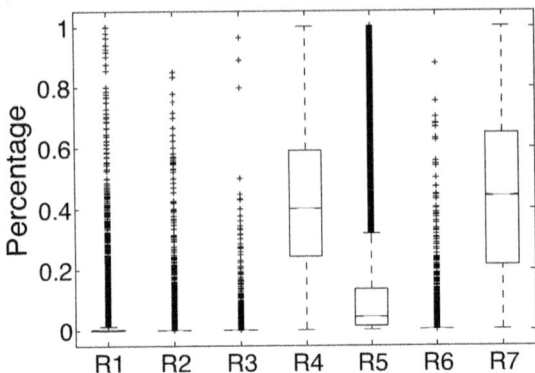

Fig. 3. The percentage of each user's tags in each region of the tag-space

lot of variation here. For a typical user, approximately 40% of their tags fall into region R_4, the user's peripheral interests; these are tags that are not associated with the user directly but that are shared by friends and followers. Region R_7 is also well populated with about 43% of profile tags. These are tags associated uniquely with the users that the target user has opted to follow. Together tags in these two regions represent interesting opportunities to promote content/users to the target user that are likely to be of interest. Interestingly, we find that for most users region R_6 is not well populated. In other words, it is rarely that we find a user whose profile contains a significant proportion of tags that are uniquely associated with the user but not their followers or friends. On the one hand this is perhaps a reasonably intuitive finding – people tend to follow, and are followed by, other people with shared interests; but at the same time, for users who do have well populated R_6 regions, it suggests immediate opportunities to recommend users to follow who share these core interests. More generally it is interesting to consider those users who do have profiles that contain unusually well-populated regions. For example, users who have a lot of unique tags in region R_5 are followed by users with a variety of different interests which are not shared by the target users or their friends. Obama above is an example of such a user and this characteristic seems to be associated with public figures.

5   Conclusions

In this short paper, we have proposed a novel multi-faceted user model for Twitter users. The model profiles users and their social network using tags sourced from curated lists, thereby providing a more robust characterisation of users compared to the more traditional content-based approaches. Our technique partitions the user tag-space into a set of disjoint regions which clearly depicts the niche and shared tags associated with users and their friends/followers.

We believe that the model has the potential to facilitate navigation through the complex domain-space as represented by Twitter, and to provide the basis for personalised topic discovery and friend recommendation.

References

1. Abel, F., Gao, Q., Houben, G.-J., Tao, K.: Analyzing User Modeling on Twitter for Personalized News Recommendations. In: Konstan, J.A., Conejo, R., Marzo, J.L., Oliver, N. (eds.) UMAP 2011. LNCS, vol. 6787, pp. 1–12. Springer, Heidelberg (2011)
2. Carmagnola, F., Cena, F., Cortassa, O., Gena, C., Torre, I.: Towards a Tag-Based User Model: How Can User Model Benefit from Tags? In: Conati, C., McCoy, K., Paliouras, G. (eds.) UM 2007. LNCS (LNAI), vol. 4511, pp. 445–449. Springer, Heidelberg (2007)
3. Dunn, A.: The arab spring: Revolution and shifting geopolitics - unplugging a nation. In: LexisNexis, International And Foreign Law. LexisNexis (2011)
4. Hannon, J., Bennett, M., Smyth, B.: Recommending twitter users to follow using content and collaborative filtering approaches. In: Proceedings of the Fourth ACM Conference on Recommender Systems, RecSys 2010, pp. 199–206. ACM (2010)
5. Kim, D., Jo, Y., Moon, I.-C., Oh, A.: Analysis of twitter lists as a potential source for discovering latent characteristics of users. In: Workshop on Microblogging at the ACM Conference on Human Factors in Computer Systems, CHI 2010 (2010)
6. Phelan, O., McCarthy, K., Bennett, M., Smyth, B.: Terms of a Feather: Content-Based News Recommendation and Discovery Using Twitter. In: Clough, P., Foley, C., Gurrin, C., Jones, G.J.F., Kraaij, W., Lee, H., Mudoch, V. (eds.) ECIR 2011. LNCS, vol. 6611, pp. 448–459. Springer, Heidelberg (2011)
7. Stoyanovich, J., Amer-Yahia, S., Marlow, C., Yu, C.: Leveraging tagging to model user interests in delicious. In: AAAI 2008: Proceedings of the 2008 AAAI Social Information Spring Symposium (2008)
8. Yang, L., Moshtaghi, M., Han, B., Karunasekera, S., Kotagiri, R., Baldwin, T., Harwood, A.: Mining micro-blogs: Opportunities and challenges. In: Social Networks: Computational Aspects and Mining. Springer, TBA

Evaluating Rating Scales Personality

Tsvi Kuflik[1], Alan J. Wecker[1], Federica Cena[2], and Cristina Gena[2]

[1] Information Systems Department, The University of Haifa, Israel
[2] Department of Computer Science, University of Turin, Italy

Abstract. User ratings are a valuable source of information for recommender systems: often, personalized suggestions are generated by predicting the user's preference for an item, based on ratings users explicitly provided for other items. In past experiments that were carried out by us in the gastronomy domain, results showed that rating scales have their own "personality" exerting an influence on user ratings. In this paper, we aim at deepening our knowledge of the effect of rating scale personality on user ratings by taking into account new empirical settings and a different domain (a museum), and partially different rating scales. We compare the results of these new experiments with our previous ones. Our aim is to further validate in a different application context, and domain, and with different rating scales, the fact that rating scales have their own personality which affects users' rating behavior.

Keywords: rating scales, user study, recommender systems.

1   Introduction

User ratings are valuable pieces of information for recommender systems: often, personalized suggestions are generated by predicting the user's preference for an item, based on ratings the users explicitly provided for other items [9]. Nowadays, with the advent of Web 2.0, which has turned users into content producers, almost all the social applications give users the opportunity to rate content (for social or for personalization purposes). Users provides their votes by means of "rating scales", i.e. graphical widgets that are characterized by specific features (e.g. granularity, numbering, presence of a neutral position, etc.). Much work in the field of survey design refers to the possible effects of rating scales on user ratings [7,1,8]. Reviews of psychological literature indicates that expanding the number of choice does not systematically increase scale sensitivity[3,6]. This confirms that how people respond to different rating scales is a primarilyan issue of psychology rather than a mathematical question [5]. In the field of recommender systems there have been few works addressing the problems of how to properly translate ratings given by means of different rating scales. Cosley et al. [4] show that ratings given on different scales correlate well, and thus their approach for ratings translation from one rating scale to another is simply based on mathematical proportion. They implicitly assume that rating scales are neutral tools which do not have any influence on the user ratings themselves. Conversely, in a similar experimental task, where some users were asked to rate the same object on different rating scales [2], Cena et al. observed that 40% of the ratings departed considerably from mathematical

J. Masthoff et al. (Eds.): UMAP 2012, LNCS 7379, pp. 310–315, 2012.
© Springer-Verlag Berlin Heidelberg 2012

proportion. They confirmed this insight in two subsequent experiments [9]. The results have led the authors to define the concept "personality" of the rating scales, which exerts an influence on user ratings. Moreover, for both experiments the authors derived a series of coefficients describing the relationship between the average ratings on each rating scale and the average rating on a reference scale.

In this paper, we aim at deepening our knowledge of the effect of rating scale personality on user ratings by taking into account new empirical settings, a different domain, and partially different rating scales with respect to the experiments described in ([2] and [9]). Instead of having a small number of users rating the same item repeatedly or rating different sets of items with different rating scales, in a controlled lab experiment, we now turned to a realistic setting. We consider the case of museum guides, where real visitors rated multimedia presentations using different rating scales. Aiming at validating our previous experiment in a real setting; we compare the results of this new experiment with the previous ones in order to further validate in a different application context,and domain, and with different rating scales, the fact that rating scales have their own personality which effects users' rating behavior. The paper is organized as follows: Section 2 describes the rating scales features, while Section 3 describes the novel evaluations we carried out, presents the results, and discusses them, comparing them with previous studies. Section 4 concludes the paper with some final remarks and hints for possible future work.

2   The Rating Scales: An Analysis

In [9] Gena et al. defined **rating scales** as complex widgets characterized by: i) *granularity*, i.e. the number of positions on the scale: coarse (e.g., a 3-points scale) or fine (e.g., a 10-points scale); ii) *numbering*, i.e. the numbers, if any, which can be associated with each position (e.g., 3-points rating scales might be numbered 0,1,2; 1,2,3; or -1,0,+1); iii) *visual metaphor*, i.e. the visualization form which influences the emotional connotation of each scale: e.g., a smiley face rating scale is a metaphor related to human emotions; a star rating scale is a metaphor which relies heavily on ranking and scoring conventions (e.g., hotel ratings); both can also convey cultural connotations; iv) *neutral position*, i.e. the presence of an intermediate, neutral point.

According to the authors, all these features contribute to define the **personality** of rating scales, i.e., the way rating scales are perceived by users and affect their behavior. Rating scales personality may cause a certain rating scale to have a specific influence on user ratings, e.g., it stimulates users to express higher/lower ratings than other scales. Rating scale personality may be also measured at two levels [9]. First, at an **aggregate** level, where it is determined according to the behavior of all users of a system, and reflects general tendencies in the use and perception of rating scales. Second, at an **individual** level, where it is determined according to the behavior of a specific user, and it reflects personal idiosyncrasies (e.g., a user might consistently give higher ratings when using a specific rating scale, but her behavior can not be generalized to the whole community). However not only the personality of the rating scale may determine final users ratings. There are at least other two elements influencing the rating, *the item which is being rated* and *the personality of the user who is rating*, e.g., optimistic users may tend to assign positive ratings.

3   The Experiments

In early 2011 a museum visitors guide system was introduced to the Hecht museum[1], a small archeological museum located at the University of Haifa, Israel. The system was an advanced version of the system described in [11]. It is a web-based system that allows users to freely walk around in the museum, wearing a small proximity sensor and carrying an iPod touch. When they are detected at the vicinity of a point of interest, they are offered a selection of multimedia presentations about objects of interest. Once they selected a presentation and viewed it, they are required to provide feedback about their satisfaction from the presentation before continuing the visit (i.e. providing feedback is mandatory before the user continues to use the system).

As part of the design of the user interface 5 different feedback mechanisms designs were implemented and integrated into the system (presented in Fig.1) in order to explore whether the interface design of the rating scales have an impact on the ratings, as suggested by [9].

According to the features seen in the previous section, the rating scales in this experiment differ in granularity (from 2 to 5 points), in metaphors (human emotions: the smiley faces; school marks/degrees: the numerical scale; scoring/ranking: the stars), in the presence of neutral position (present in stars, in 3-points faces, in the numerical scale) and in numbering (there a scale consisting of -1,0,1).

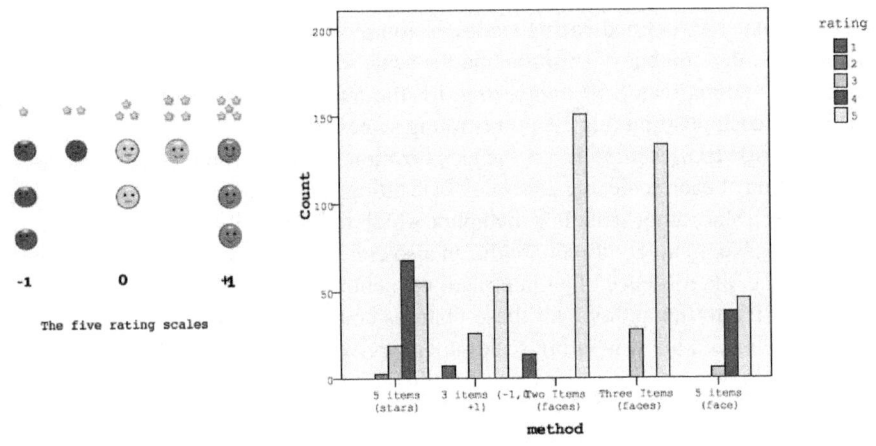

Fig. 1. The used rating scales (left side) and ratings distribution (right side)

Experimental Settings. For experimentation purposes, whenever a visitor logged in and started using the system, a randomly selected rating method was activated for her and used throughout the whole visit. The interactions of the visitors with the system were logged. The experimentation stated in October 2011 and by January 2012 we had

---

[1] http://mushecht.haifa.ac.il/Default_eng.aspx

72 logs of visitors that provided more than 3 ratings[2]. These logs included two groups of visitors: regular visitors (34) and students (38) that participated in a study about indoor navigation and also used the guide to view and rate various presentations during their visit. For every rating scale we got between 14 to 16 user logs that we used for our analysis.

Experimental Results. In general, all visitors scored the presentations high. Table 1 presents the average ratings of the 5 different methods used in the experiment. In order to be able to compare the various scales, all were converted to 1-5 scale in the following way: when there were 2 values, then 1 and 5 were used, when there were 3 values, then 1,3 and 5 were used (for example: $-1 \rightarrow 1$, $0 \rightarrow 3$, $+1 \rightarrow 5$). Looking at the table we can see that the average of the stars (1-5) and numerical values (-1,0,+1) are closer than all the faces, whose ratings are higher. Moreover, while there is little difference between 2 and 3 faces, the average score is a bit lower for 5 faces. This difference is statistically validated by Chi-Square=92.44, df=4, p<0.01 and Levene Test F=15.40, df1=4, df2=641, p<0.01. Using Duncan Homogenous Post Hoc testing we see that the faces form a subgroup (their harmonic means don't significantly differ) with confidence value of at least 90% and the stars and numbers form a subgroup with 78% confidence level.

Considering standard deviation, it seems that numerical values, followed by 2 smiley faces, produce somehow more noisy data (higher STD) than the other rating scales.
It is interesting to note that when considering the use of neutral point, e.g. the 3 smiley faces, users preferred the neutral face instead of using the lower value and they used the neutral value more, as compared to the 2 faces scale (see Fig. 2).

Table 1. Rating scales described according to their personality and experimental results

Rating Scale	Gran.	Numb.	Metaphor	Neutral pos.	Average	STD	Freq.	Coeff.
-1 0 +1	3	x	Marks/Grades	x	4.06	1.294	85	0.921
5 stars	5		Cultural conventions	x	4.21	0.744	145	0.955
2 smiley faces	2		Human emotions		4.66	1.118	165	1.058
3 smiley faces	3		Human emotions	x	4.65	0.760	161	1.055
5 smiley faces	5		Human emotions	x	4.44	0.659	90	1.008

It should be noted that we have considered the average values of the rating scales at the aggregate level, namely the values reflect the behavior of all users of the system, and thus they reflect general tendencies in the use and in the perception of rating scales. However, since ratings may be also influenced by the evaluated item and by the evaluating user, we also have taken into account the following aspects:

In our experiment, visitors watched and rated 43 different presentations and provided 646 ratings for them, giving an average of 15 ratings for presentations. We calculated the average standard deviation, 0.47 (in a 1 to 5 range) with 14% of values higher than 1. Thus, presentations seem to have received quite homogeneous rates, closer to the

---

[2] Visitors that viewed and responded to less than 3 presentations, did not use the guide in practice, so they were discarded from the analysis, there were only a few such cases.

higher values. The 5 score received 64.6% of rates, which could mean, that more often than not, users probably picked and therefore rated presentations they liked.

In order to have a measure of the individual user rating trend, we concentrated on the medium standard deviation, 0.44, with 9% of values higher than 1. Thus users tend to rate presentations they like in a consistent way, namely using the same value while using the same rating scale.

We classified in Table 1, the rating scales, according to their features, their average value, and their coefficient. The *coefficient* has been calculated in order to have a measure of the impact of the rating scale on the way the user rates. It is computed as a ratio between the average ratings of each scale and the average of all the ratings.

As already noted, faces-based rating scales tend to push up the ratings. In particular 2-points and 3-points faces rating scales show a similar medium score. As seen in Fig. 1, the presence of the neutral position (in 3-points smiley face) produce some little distortion in the distribution results, as mentioned in [8]). The neutral face is used more compared to the lower face value in 2 faces scale, while the smiling face is used less compared to the 2 faces scale, thus balancing at the end the final score. In the experiment 2-points and 3-points faces rating scales also seem to correlate with the quantity of ratings, since users using these scales rated more items than other scales (11.8 and 12.6 rates per user vs. 9 rates per users of numbers and 5 faces), except for users using the stars rating scales (13.1 rates per user).

Another interesting finding is related to the low values obtained by the "-1 0 +1" rating scale. [1] found that scales with negative numbers have higher ratings since the negative number is perceived as more negative, so users tend to avoid it. In fact, the negative score has been used 2.6% of times, while the neutral point ("0") has been used 38.5% of times, probably causing the score to be so low.

Discussion. We conclude by providing some insights regarding the features of rating scales as described in Sec. 2: granularity, numbering, metaphor, and neutral position.

Regarding *granularity*, the experiment confirms the result reported in [9] that showed that rating scale characterized by a coarse granularity promoted rates higher than the average. Regarding *numbering*, the experiment shows that the explicit presence of number, even if with negative values, promotes lower ratings, similar to the sliders in the experiment described in [9](-1,0,+1 and 0-10). Regarding *neutral position*, we have observed that particularly 2-point and 3-point faces rating scales show similar score, demonstrating that the presence of the neutral position (in 3-point face) produce some little difference in results. We have noticed that, at least, that the neutral position is probably preferred to its corresponding lower values, probably due to social desirability bias, see [8].

As far as the *metaphor*, looking at the results we could conclude that rating scales sharing the human metaphor seem to correspond with higher results then other scales. Also in [9] the rating scales conveying a metaphor related to human behavior - the thumb - corresponded to rates higher than the average values. In particular, 2-point and 3-point faces, which are very popular on the Web and on social applications, show similar trend and corresponded with the user rating more items. Another rating scale that seems to correspond with higher results is the 5-stars rating scale, which is one of the most used scale in rating-based systems. Thus we may hypothesize that the **popularity** of a rating scale is a another feature that needs to be taken into consideration, and contributes to define the rating personality. This hypothesis needs to be verified in future experiments.

4 Conclusion

In this paper the collected data confirm that that rating scales have a "personality" which exerts an effect on user ratings. While visitors in general favored the presentations they viewed, the average ratings differed (in some cases the differences were statistically significant) between the different rating scales. The implication of our findings is that it is necessary to consider the rating scales personality when translating from one scale to another, since pure mathematical solutions are fundamentally untrustworthy [3]. In fact given the different distributions no linear transformation can exist [10]. This translation can be useful, for example, when users of system can choose the rating scales to vote on items, and thus the system must transpose ratings in a unique scale [2]. A transposition is necessary when systems exchange the user's ratings in a user model interoperability scenario. Finally, sometimes researchers need to compare scores derived from different rating scales [3]. As part of a future work, we are planning to test our ideas with more users. We are also working on finding an approach for translating user ratings that can be used by different applications.

References

1. Amoo, T., Friedman, H.H.: Do Numeric Values Influence Subjects Responses to Rating Scales? Journal of International Marketing and Marketing Research 26, 41–46 (2001)
2. Cena, F., Vernero, F., Gena, C.: Towards a Customization of Rating Scales in Adaptive Systems. In: De Bra, P., Kobsa, A., Chin, D. (eds.) UMAP 2010. LNCS, vol. 6075, pp. 369–374. Springer, Heidelberg (2010)
3. Colman, A., Norris, C., Preston, C.: Comparing rating scales of different lengths: Equivalence of scores from 5-point and 7-point scales. Psychological Reports 80, 355–362 (1997)
4. Cosley, D., Lam, S.K., Albert, I., Konstan, J.A., Riedl, J.: Is seeing believing?: how recommender system interfaces affect users' opinions. In: SIGCHI 2003, pp. 585–592. ACM (2003)
5. Cummins, R.A., Gullone, E.: Why we should not use 5-point likert scales: The case for subjective quality of life measurement. In: Second International Conference on Quality of Life in Cities, pp. 74–93 (2000)
6. Dawes, J.: Do data characteristics change according to the number of scale points used? an experiment using 5-point, 7-point and 10-point scales. International Journal of Market Research 50, 61–77 (2008)
7. Friedman, H.H., Amoo, T.: Rating the rating scales. Journal of Marketing Management 9(3), 114–123 (1999)
8. Garland, R.: The Mid-Point on a Rating Scale: Is it Desirable. Marketing Bulletin 2, 66–70 (1991)
9. Gena, C., Brogi, R., Cena, F., Vernero, F.: The Impact of Rating Scales on User's Rating Behavior. In: Konstan, J.A., Conejo, R., Marzo, J.L., Oliver, N. (eds.) UMAP 2011. LNCS, vol. 6787, pp. 123–134. Springer, Heidelberg (2011)
10. Kaptein, M.C., Nass, C., Markopoulos, P.: Powerful and consistent analysis of likert-type rating scales. In: CHI 2010, pp. 2391–2394 (2010)
11. Kuflik, T., Stock, O., Zancanaro, M., Gorfinkel, A., Jbara, S., Kats, S., Sheidin, J., Kashtan, N.: A visitor's guide in an active museum: Presentations, communications, and reflection. J. Comput. Cult. Herit. 3, 11:1–11:25 (2011)

Automating the Modeling of Learners' Erroneous Behaviors in Model-Tracing Tutors

Luc Paquette, Jean-François Lebeau, and André Mayers

Université de Sherbrooke, Québec, Canada
{Luc.Paquette,Andre.Mayers}@USherbrooke.ca

Abstract. Modeling learners is a fundamental part of intelligent tutoring systems. It allows tutors to provide personalized feedback and to assess the learners' mastery over a task domain. One aspect often overlooked is the modeling of erroneous behaviors that can be used to provide error specific feedback. This is especially true for model-tracing tutors that usually require erroneous procedural knowledge associated to each of the possible error. This process can be automated thanks to a task independent model describing the learners' erroneous behaviors. The model proposed in this paper is inspired by the Sierra theory of procedural error and is developed for ASTUS, an authoring framework for model-tracing tutors.

Keywords: Erroneous behaviors, learner modeling, model-tracing tutors.

1   Introduction

Intelligent tutoring systems (ITS) model different aspects of the learner's interaction with the tutor: how they solve problems [1]; how they manipulate the learning environment's user interface [2]; and how they acquire new knowledge [3]. Those models can be exploited by the tutor to provide personalized feedback.

One aspect of tutoring less frequently modeled is the erroneous behaviors exhibited by the learners. Modeling such behaviors can be benefic for ITSs as it allows them to provide negative feedback on errors, one of Ohlsson's nine learning mechanisms [4]. Constraint based tutors [5] can diagnose errors and provide feedback for them. Baffes and Mooney [6] designed a system to automatically compile bug libraries for classification tasks. Although both those systems can diagnose errors, they are less efficient than model-tracing tutors (MTTs) for modeling the sequence of steps committed by learners while they solve problems [7]. On the contrary, MTTs do not efficiently diagnose the learners' errors and would thus greatly benefit from a model of erroneous behaviors.

The modeling of erroneous behaviors is often neglected in MTTs as it usually requires adding erroneous procedural knowledge to the task's model, a process that requires much effort. In order to solve part of this problem, we took inspiration from computational theories explaining the source of procedural errors. More specifically, we were inspired by Sierra [8], a theory explaining the development of the learners' procedural misconceptions in procedural tasks such as subtraction. This theory provides cognitively plausible explanations for the learners' erroneous behaviors that could be used by MTTs to provide error specific feedback.

J. Masthoff et al. (Eds.): UMAP 2012, LNCS 7379, pp. 316–321, 2012.

Whereas Sierra was designed to simulate the learner's behavior while solving a problem, MTTs are designed to teach how to solve problems. This fundamental difference influences the definition of their task's models. Sierra constructs multiple possible models of the learners' knowledge of the task at different moments during their learning process. MTTs, on the other hand, start with a complete model of the task. This model is designed by an expert to ensure that the tutor can provide efficient pedagogical feedback. Because of this difference, it is not possible to directly apply the Sierra theory in the context of MTTs.

Thus, we defined a model describing how an MTT's procedural knowledge can automatically be disrupted in order to produce erroneous behaviors analogous to those generated by Sierra. We developed this model for ASTUS [9], an authoring framework for MTTs. ASTUS's knowledge representation system was designed so that it can be manipulated by task independent processes such as the automatic disruption of a task's knowledge model.

In this paper we present our model of the learners' erroneous behaviors. First, we show how ASTUS's knowledge representation system respects Sierra's assumptions. Then, we explain how its procedural knowledge can be disrupted using processes inspired by Sierra. Finally, we describe how the repair strategies defined by Sierra can be adapted to ASTUS's knowledge representation system.

2   Knowledge Representation

The first step towards elaborating our model was to make sure that the knowledge representation system used by ASTUS is compatible with the Sierra theory [8]. This theory enumerates assumptions regarding its knowledge representation approach. Even though ASTUS's approach is significantly different from Sierra's, we can show that it is compatible with Sierra's assumptions. In this section, we specify the relevant assumptions for our model and explain how ASTUS implements them.

Sierra is a theory for procedural errors and thus does not define a specific representation for semantic knowledge, but it asserts that the procedural knowledge contains patterns used to access semantic knowledge. The *pattern assumption* indicates that those patterns are defined using a formalism that can be interpreted by the system (Sierra uses predicate calculus). In ASTUS, the patterns are queries that can be used by the procedural knowledge in order to access elements from the knowledge base such as concepts (pedagogically relevant abstraction) and relations (n-ary predicates defined over concepts). Their structure can be manipulated by the system to disrupt a task's procedural knowledge and generate erroneous behaviors.

Sierra's *recurrence assumption* specifies that, during the execution of a task, a goal stack is minimally required to describe its control regime. In ASTUS, the control regime is described using a goal tree, a structure containing more information than a stack. In addition to the current goals and the procedures that can be applied to achieve them, this episodic tree (figure 1) also contains all the previously satisfied goals and goals already planned.

Sierra also specifies the *"goal types" assumption* which asserts that the execution of each goal is determined by its type (AND, OR and FOR-EACH). Those three types were chosen to accurately model the learner's cognitive processes. ASTUS's knowledge representation system also offers multiple execution types, but it differs from Sierra in two main aspects. First, ASTUS separates the goals and the procedures applied to achieve them. Thus, the execution behavior is associated to procedures rather than to goals. Second, ASTUS's execution types were designed to model the teacher's instructions. ASTUS offers different types of procedures such as sequences, equivalent to Sierra's AND goals; selections, equivalent to OR goals; iterations, analogous to FOR-EACH goals; and primitives that represent atomic actions in the learning environment's user interface. Since a procedure's type is explicitly defined, it can be used when disrupting a procedure to generate its possible incorrect executions.

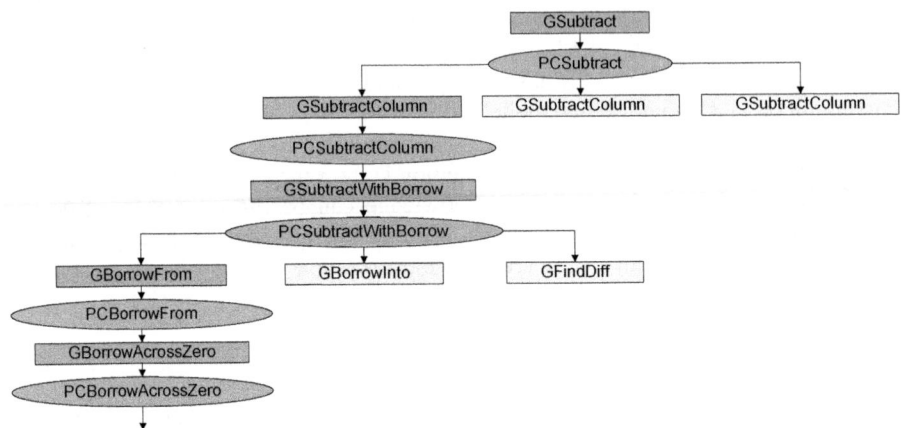

Fig. 1. Part of an episodic tree for a subtraction tutor, rectangles are goals and ovals are procedures. Only the currently active goals are expended.

3   Modeling Erroneous Knowledge

Sierra [8] simulates learning and generates knowledge models that learners could have acquired after a set of lessons. Those models produce the correct solution for problems covered by the lessons used to generate it, but might produce erroneous behaviors when applied to problems from subsequent lessons. The errors might be the result of overly specific patterns or of attempting to solve problems that requires procedures introduced only in subsequent lessons. Sierra also simulates incomplete learning by generating models resulting from the removal of sub goals in AND goals.

ASTUS's knowledge representation system can be used to model erroneous behaviors by disrupting the expert's model of the task to produce incomplete and incorrect models. This objective is achieved by applying principles analogous to Sierra's but adapted to a knowledge representation system designed for MTTs. We first defined, for each type of procedural units, the knowledge required for their correct execution. Then, we enumerated all the disruptions that can be applied to each unit and we described the resulting erroneous behaviors.

This process can be illustrated using conditional procedures which are selection-based procedures where each goal is paired with a logical condition. To successfully execute a conditional procedure, one must know each of these goals and also know the conditions specifying when to use each one of them. During the execution of the procedure, the conditions are evaluated and the goal associated to the first condition that evaluates to true is activated.

Conditional procedures can be disrupted in two ways to represent erroneous behaviors: 1) each sub goal can be removed from the procedure and 2) each condition can be disrupted. When removing a sub goal, its associated condition will also be removed thus preventing it from being selected. There are two different ways to disrupt a condition. First, the disrupted condition can be too specific. In this case, the conditional procedure might not have any active condition for some of the problems. Second, the disrupted condition can be too generic. In this case, the conditional procedure might have more than one active condition at the same time. In both cases, if the number of active conditions is not exactly one, the execution of the procedure will need to be repaired by choosing one goal to achieve.

We illustrate the process of disrupting a procedure with an example from a subtraction tutor. The task of subtraction was chosen since it was used to develop Sierra, but the same process can be applied to any task modeled with ASTUS. The procedure taken as an example is the one that determines how to proceed in order to find the difference of a specific column. Three sub goals are available: find the difference of the column's terms, borrow from the next column before finding the difference or copy the minuend as the difference.

```
Conditional 'PCSubtractColumn' achieves 'GSubtractColumn' {
    if 'c' instanceOf 'TopGreaterColumn'
      goal 'GFindDiff' with 'c'
    if 'c' instanceOf 'TopSmallerColumn'
      goal 'GSubtractWithBorrow' with 'c'
    if 'c' instanceOf 'NoSubtrahendColumn'
      goal 'GCopyMinuend' with 'c'
}
```

Any of the sub goals from this procedure can be removed to produce erroneous behaviors. For example, the 'GSubtractWithBorrow' goal can be removed to produce:

```
Conditional 'PCSubtractColumn' achieves 'GSubtractColumn' {
    if 'c' instanceOf 'TopGreaterColumn'
      goal 'GFindDiff' with 'c'
    if 'c' instanceOf 'NoSubtrahendColumn'
      goal 'GCopyMinued' with 'c'
}
```

When using this version of the procedure, any subtraction problem that requires borrowing will be executed incorrectly. Indeed, there are no conditions that will be evaluated to true when the subtrahend of a column is greater than its minuend. This can lead to errors such as *doesn't-borrow* (described in [8]).

In addition to removing goals, the procedure could be disrupted by modifying its conditions. For instance, the condition for the 'GFindDiff' goal could be made too specific by adding the restriction that the column must also be the units' column:

(c isA TopSmallerColumn) and (c isA UnitsColumn)

This disturbed condition can lead to the *copy-top-except-units error* [8] by causing erroneous behaviors when subtracting any column, except the units, if the subtrahend is not blank.

We applied a similar process for each type of procedures available in ASTUS's knowledge representation system. The result is a specification of how each one can be disrupted in order to model the learners' erroneous behaviors.

The execution of a disrupted task's model can lead to two kinds of erroneous behaviors. A model can be executed apparently without any issue but resulting in an incorrect step sequence or its execution might lead to impasses (situations for which the knowledge model can't be executed furthermore) that will need to be repaired.

4   Repairs

The occurrence of impasses blocks the execution of the knowledge model. In order to resume problem solving when faced with an impasse, learners will try to repair it by applying known procedural knowledge. The Sierra theory [8] includes three repair strategies that learners might use:

- No-op: the goal causing the impasse is not executed. This is achieved by popping the first goal from the goals stack.
- Back-up: very similar to no-op, but pops the goals stack more than once.
- Barge-on: alter the results of patterns in order to obtain a result that enables the execution of the knowledge model.

Each of these repair strategy can be adapted to ATSUS's knowledge representation system. The no-op and the back-up strategies can be simulated by going back to a previous goal in the episodic tree (figure 1). The barge-on strategy requires the modification to the results of queries and to the evaluation of conditions in order to produce results compatible with the execution of the knowledge model.

Examples taken from our subtraction tutor can be used to illustrate how each of the three repair strategies can be applied in ASTUS. If a learner does not know how to borrow from a column containing a zero as its top digit and the current problem is 203-107, the resulting erroneous behaviors will vary depending on the applied repair strategy. Figure 1 shows part of the episodic tree for this problem's initial state.

If the no-op strategy is used, the learner will omit borrowing from the tens column (GBorrowAcrossZero), but will still add ten to the units column (GBorrowInto) and find the column's difference correctly (GFindDiff). The result of the subtraction will be 203-107 = 106. This erroneous behavior is an instance of the *borrow-no-decrement* error described in [8].

If the applied repair strategy is back-up, the learner can go back to any of the previous goal contained in the episodic tree. He might back-up as far as the initial goal (GSubtract) of subtracting the whole problem and skip the units' column. This behavior would produce the answer 203-107 = 10_, an example of the *blank-instead-of-borrow-from-zero* [8] error. He might also back-up to the earlier goal deciding whether he should borrow or not (GSubtractColumn), and try to solve the problem without borrowing for the units' column. This will cause a second impasse since the difference for 3-7 is a negative number.

To repair this second impasse, the learner could use the barge-on repair strategy. This strategy can be used to modify the result of the queries used to find the difference 3-7 by inverting its argument. The new query would then find the difference 7-3, thus subtracting the top number from the bottom one. The use of this repair would produce 203-107 = 104 as its answer and correspond to the *smaller-from-larger-instead-of-borrow-from-zero* error [8].

5   Conclusion

In this paper we showed how an MTT authoring framework can model the learners' erroneous behaviors using task independent processes. This is achieved by specifying how ASTUS's procedural knowledge can be disrupted and how impasses can be repaired to produce behaviors analogous to those generated by Sierra.

The model presented in this paper will have multiple applications in ASTUS. For example, it could be used to help assess the learners' knowledge mastery or to facilitate the development of a simulated learner.

Our next objective will be to validate our model by using it to diagnose the erroneous behaviors of a leaner while solving a problem. It will allow us to evaluate the pedagogical relevance of our approach by providing negative feedback on errors, one of Ohlsson's nine learning mechanisms [4].

References

1. Aleven, V.: Rule-Based Cognitive Modeling for Intelligent Tutoring Systems. In: Nkambou, R., Bourdeau, J., Mizoguchi, R. (eds.) Advances in Intelligent Tutoring Systems. SCI, vol. 308, pp. 33–62. Springer, Heidelberg (2010)
2. Fortin, M., Lebeau, J.-F., Abdessemed, A., Courtemanche, F., Mayers, A.: A Standard Method of Developing User Interfaces for a Generic ITS Framework. In: Woolf, B.P., Aïmeur, E., Nkambou, R., Lajoie, S. (eds.) ITS 2008. LNCS, vol. 5091, pp. 312–322. Springer, Heidelberg (2008)
3. Corbett, A.T., Anderson, J.R.: Knowledge Tracing: Modeling the Acquisition of Procedural Knowledge. User Modeling and User-Adapted Interaction 4, 253–278 (1995)
4. Ohlsson, S.: Deep Learning: How the Mind Overrides Experience. Cambridge University Press, New York (2011)
5. Mitrovic, A.: Modeling Domains and Students with Constraint-Based Modeling. In: Nkambou, R., Bourdeau, J., Mizoguchi, R. (eds.) Advances in Intelligent Tutoring Systems. SCI, vol. 308, pp. 63–80. Springer, Heidelberg (2010)
6. Baffes, P., Mooney, R.: Refinement-Based Student Modeling and Automated Bug Library Construction. Journal of Artificial Intelligence in Education 7(1), 7–116 (1996)
7. Mitrovic, A., Koedinger, K., Martin, B.: A Comparative Analysis of Cognitive Tutoring and Constraint-Based Modeling. In: Brusilovsky, P., Corbett, A.T., de Rosis, F. (eds.) UM 2003. LNCS, vol. 2702, pp. 313–322. Springer, Heidelberg (2003)
8. VanLehn, K.: Mind Bugs: The Origin of Procedural Misconceptions. MIT Press (1990)
9. Paquette, L., Lebeau, J.-F., Mayers, A.: Authoring Problem-Solving Tutors: A Comparison between ASTUS and CTAT. In: Nkambou, R., Bourdeau, J., Mizoguchi, R. (eds.) Advances in Intelligent Tutoring Systems. SCI, vol. 308, pp. 377–405. Springer, Heidelberg (2010)

Using Touch as a Predictor of Effort: What the iPad Can Tell Us about User Affective State

David H. Shanabrook, Ivon Arroyo, and Beverly Park Woolf

University of Massachusetts Amherst

Abstract. Touch is a new and significantly different method of interacting with a computer and it is being adapted at a rapidly increasing rate with the introduction of the tablet computer. We log the characteristics of a student's touch interaction while solving math problems on a tablet. By correlating this data to high and low effort problem solving conditions we demonstrate the ability to predict student effort level. The technique is context free, thus can potentially be applied to any computer tablet application.

Keywords: touch, data mining, statistical analysis, intelligent tutoring systems, human computer interaction, affective computing.

1   Introduction

In a human tutoring situation, an experienced teacher attempts to be aware of a students' affective state and to use this knowledge to adjust his/her teaching[6][8]. For the student who requires a challenge, problem difficulty can be increased. And for the frustrated student, assistance can be provided. Research has shown that affect detection and interventions in the intelligent tutoring environment can also improve learning effectiveness[2][3][4]. But the effectiveness of any intervention based on students' learning state is dependent on the ability to accurately access that state, whether by the human or the computer. In an intelligent tutoring system, real time affect detection is typically attempted either by analyzing student interaction with the system or with sensors[2]. Sensors have the advantage over content specific predictors as they are usually context free; the predictive model is applicable across applications and content. Hardware sensors are used to detect physical actions of the user; camera, chair and mouse sensors can detect facial expressions, posture changes, and hand pressure [4]. And physiological sensors detect internal changes such as heart rate and skin resistance. While sensors have been successfully correlated to student affective state, they are also hard to deploy in real-life situations; they require invasive non-standard hardware and software.

The introduction of computer tablets has produced a new, potentially unique, source of sensory data: touch movements. Tablets, particularly the Apple iPad, are rapidly replacing the traditional PC especially in the education

J. Masthoff et al. (Eds.): UMAP 2012, LNCS 7379, pp. 322–327, 2012.

environment[7][11]. The tablet predominately uses touch interaction; one or more fingers control the interface and provide input by their location and movement directionality. It replaces the mouse and keyboard for control, and the pen in drawing applications. Research has shown differences in cognitive load between keyboard and handwriting input, with increased load for the former method[9]. While touch writing is similar to handwriting, it also feels very different, and we may hypothesize cognitive differences will be found between it and these other input modalities.

This research suggests the touch interaction can be used as a sensor input for affect detection. The advantages over other sensors as a predictor are readily apparent. The tablet platform is inexpensive and becoming widespread, no additional hardware is required. Data collection is straightforward, and the sensor, as integral to tablet use, is non-invasive. Previous research in detecting affect in touch is very sparse. One study attempted to predict emotion comparing mouse and touch screen devices[10]. The results showed good predictive ability using the mouse for one affective state only (irritation). Touch input was less predictive. No other applicable studies were found.

2   mathTouch System

2.1   Description

In this study we demonstrate a method of predicting student effort level using touch data. We implemented a simple iPad 'app' to present problems and record solution input; providing a controlled environment for studying touch as a predictor of affective state. Student activities are used as inputs to models that predict student affective state and thus support tutor interventions.

The touchMath app is an environment that supports detection of student effort through touch. It presents mathematics problems, enables and records the student drawings of the solution, then uploads the solution and touch data to a server. Running on the iPad tablet, touchMath sequentially loads the images, math problems, and instructs students to solve the problem (Figure 1). Below the mathematics problem is a drawing space where students use touch to work on the problem and deliver answers. The student is instructed to 'show all work' as the writing provides the data for affective state detection. Below the working spaced are three action buttons:

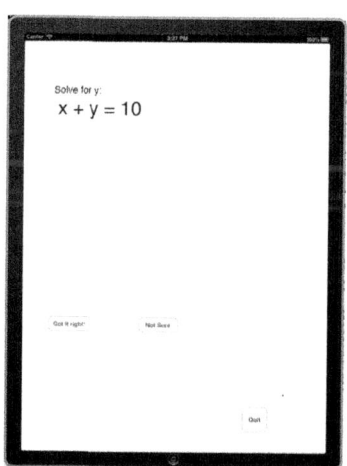

Fig. 1. The touchMath interface

'Got it right!', 'Not sure?' or 'Quit.' By compelling the student to self-report the perceived correctness, we are able to differentiate from actual correctness. The problems are loaded from the server in sequential order until the last problem is completed. New problems can be quickly 'authored' by simply creating an image file, e.g. using a graphics program, hand drawing and scanning, copying from the internet, then uploading the images to the server. This ease of authoring allows rapid and flexible problem creation.

2.2 Implementation

For each problem the app logs the all touch movements; including strokes, uninterrupted touch movements and the points within each stroke. Points are defined by timestamp and x,y,z coordinates, with z the movement of the tablet due to touch pressure (Table 1). The iPad surface is not touch pressure sensitive, however, it contains a hardware accelerometer that detects positive and negative movements along the z axis. The hardware is sensitive enough to roughly replicate the functionality of a pressure sensitive tablet surface[1].

When the student touches the tablet a new stroke recording starts, and continues until the finger is lifted. The stroke time is logged along with the points within the stroke[2]. The series of strokes are logged for each problem solution. When the student completes the problem the strokes log is retained with the problem level information. When the student completes the session, all problem data is retained with the student level information, and the complete data file is uploaded to the server for later analysis. From this data we can derive: stroke time, stroke distance, and stroke velocity.

Table 1. Touch Data

event level	logged data	derived data
student	studentId, problemId, startTime, stopTime	timeElapsed, numReportedCorrect, numActuallyCorrect
problems	strokes, problemId, solutionImage, reportCorrect, startTime, stopTime	timeElapsed, numStrokes
strokes	points, startTime, stopTime	timeElapsed, distance, velocity
points	x, y, z_accel, timeStamp	

---

[1] Also recorded are x_accel and y_accel, although this data is not currently analyzed.

[2] Points are logged by system interrupts with polling determined by an internal algorithm and dependent on hardware and the variability of position change.

2.3   Testing Environment

Preliminary testing was done on a single subject: a male, 12 year old, 7th grade middle school student. The four chosen problems were basic algebra equation simplification problems, a subject chosen as it was similar to the students current math curriculum. The problems were intended to increase in difficulty from easy to beyond ability: *prob0*: x+y=10, *prob1*: 3x + y = 5, *prob2*: $\frac{3}{5}x + \frac{7}{8}y = 4$, *prob3*: $3 = 34y^2 - y - 5.3\,x^3$.

Knowing this students level of algebra knowledge we categorized *prob0, prob1* as low effort, *prob2* as high effort, *prob3* as beyond current ability. The student performed as expected with the first three problems, solving the first two with little difficulty, and the third, *prob2*, with greater effort. The student's approach to *prob3* was to solve for y, but in error, leaving the y^2 variable on the right side of the equation. At the students level of knowledge this was appropriate, as he solved for y assuming it was correct to include

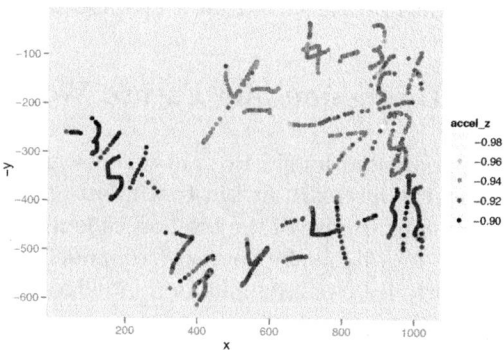

Fig. 2. *prob3* with accel_z

y^2 in the solution, and he indicated this by selecting 'Got it right!'. Therefore, we categorized this solution with the first two as requiring low effort.

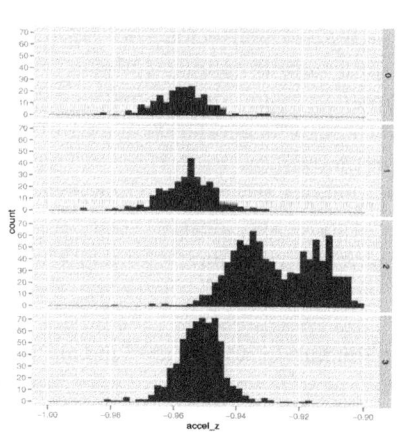

(a) accel_z point distributions

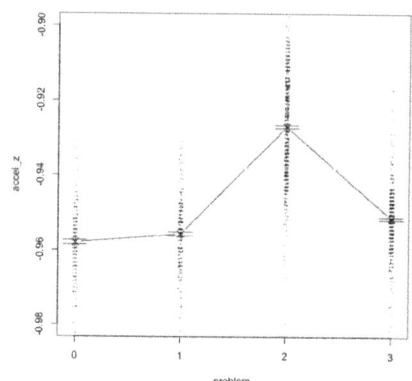

(b) SEM (vertical lines) showing difference significance

Fig. 3. accel_z~problem

3   Findings

Initial visual analysis of the logged data and derived data (Table 1), was performed comparing these metrics across problems. The plots indicated only accel_z differs significantly between low effort *prob0, prob1, prob3* and high effort *prob2* (Figure 3a); with *prob2* plot having more variation and a bimodal distribution[12]. ANOVA results indicate significance for accel_z~problem (p-value 0). And pairwise t-test using Bonferroni adjustment confirmed a significant difference only between the low and high effort problems (Figure 3b) with overlap of SEM intervals except in *prob2*; showing touch pressure as defined by movement on the z axis as a predictor of level of effort in problem solving [5].

4   Discussion and Future Work

The potential implications of this research is profound. We have shown how the students' pressure in the touchMap app while solving mathematics problems can be predictive of the level of student effort. The potential of touch, being the input for tablets, for context-free modeling of user affective state is of significant importance. For example, in a intelligent tutoring environment a natural intervention when a student is answering questions correctly is to increase problem difficulty. However, if this student was working with high effort this would be an incorrect choice and could lead to errors and frustration. A model using touch input to predict effort level would avoid this unadvised intervention.

We will verify this research, conducting a full study with statistically significant sample size, with demographic diversity, varying student ages, sex, ability. Variation across these groups will be analyzed to determine the need for specific models. Problem content will be varied to include geometry, puzzles, other subjects etc. The statistical techniques used in the studies analysis were sufficient to indicate the usefulness of the analysis of touch idea; regression analysis using a combination of touch metrics as predictors and data mining techniques such as unsupervised cluster analysis will be explored to expand on our findings. Other problem metrics will be derived from the data such as acceleration and jitter of touch movements and studied as possible predictors.

Self-reporting to include affective states such as frustration, boredom, and excitement will allow the creation of a general model of affective state. Random sampling could query user affective state or an intelligent questioning mechanism could trigger a query: a student indicating 'Not sure' would trigger the 'Are you frustrated?' query.

A simple intervention model has been implemented, but not used in this study, to change the problem difficulty based on student self-reports. An eraser function will improve the ability of the student to work on solutions, and at the same time, provide new metrics: amount of use, pressure in use, etc. As a very different event than drawing, erasing could be an important predictor of affective state.

In addition to being used as a research tool, we will explore developing math-Touch app as a tutoring system. Used as a homework delivery tool (or for in class testing) a teacher can quickly author homework assignments and upload these to a server; the students' app will present the new problems and collect answers. This is partially implemented as the functionality exists in mathTouch to choose among problem sets.

Publishing touchMath as free app on the Apple App Store, would allow distribution as a math practice tool, emailing the solutions to stakeholders (teacher, tutor, researcher, etc). For our research this will provide data for analysis. As a math intelligence test, the users' anonymous touch data with self-reports will be uploaded to a server providing a potentially large sample size. Applying datamining techniques to a large set of data could yield a refined affect model based on touch input.

References

[1] Arroyo, I., Mehranian, H., Woolf, B.: Effort-based Tutoring: An Empirical Approach to Intelligent Tutoring. In: Proceedings of the 3rd International Conference on Educational Data Mining (2010)

[2] Arroyo, I., Cooper, D.G., Burleson, W., Woolf, B.P., Muldner, K., Christopherson, R.: Emotion sensors go to school. In: Dimitrova, V., Mizoguchi, R., du Boulay, B., Graesser, A.C. (eds.) AIED, vol. 200, pp. 17–24. IOS Press (2009)

[3] Baker, R.S., Corbett, A.T., Koedinger, K.R., Roll, I.: Detecting When Students Game the System, Across Tutor Subjects and Classroom Cohorts. In: Ardissono, L., Brna, P., Mitrović, A. (eds.) UM 2005. LNCS (LNAI), vol. 3538, pp. 220–224. Springer, Heidelberg (2005)

[4] Cooper, D.G., Arroyo, I., Woolf, B.P., Muldner, K., Burleson, W., Christopherson, R.: Sensors Model Student Self Concept in the Classroom. In: Houben, G.-J., McCalla, G., Pianesi, F., Zancanaro, M. (eds.) UMAP 2009. LNCS, vol. 5535, pp. 30–41. Springer, Heidelberg (2009)

[5] Dalgaard, P.: Introductory Statistics with R. Springer, New York (2002)

[6] Lehman, B., Matthews, M., D'Mello, S., Person, N.: What Are You Feeling? Investigating Student Affective States During Expert Human Tutoring Sessions. In: Woolf, B.P., Aïmeur, E., Nkambou, R., Lajoie, S., et al. (eds.) ITS 2008. LNCS, vol. 5091, pp. 50–59. Springer, Heidelberg (2008)

[7] Murphy, G.D.: Post-PC devices: A summary of early iPad technology adoption in tertiary environments. e-Journal of Business Education & Scholarship of Teaching, 18–32 (2011)

[8] Ormond, P., Merry, S., Reiling, K.: Biology students' utilization of tutors' formative feedback: a qualitative interview study. Assessment & Evaluation in Higher Education 30(4), 369–386 (2005)

[9] Read, J.C.: A study of the usability of handwriting recognition for text entry by children. In: Interacting with Computers, pp. 57–69 (2007)

[10] Shuller, B., Rigoll, G., Lang, M.: Emotion Recognition in the Manual Interaction with Graphical User Interfaces. In: ICME, pp. 1215–1218. IEEE Press (2004)

[11] Takahashi, P.: New iPad app for digital textbooks excites Clark County schools. In: Las Vegas Sun, January 19 (2012)

[12] Wickham, H.: ggplot2: Elegant Graphics for Data Analysis. Springer, New York (2009)

Domain Ranking
for Cross Domain Collaborative Filtering

Amit Tiroshi and Tsvi Kuflik

The University of Haifa, Haifa, Israel
{tsvikak,atiroshi}@is.haifa.ac.il

Abstract. In recommendation systems a variation of the cold start problem is a situation where the target user has few-to-none item ratings belonging to the target domain (e.g., movies) to base recommendations on. One way to overcome this is by basing recommendations on items from different domains, for example recommending movies based on the target user's book item ratings. This technique is called cross-domain recommendation. When basing recommendations on a source domain that is different from the target domain a question arises, from which domain should items be chosen? Is there a source domain that is a better predictor for each target domain? Do books better predict a users' taste in movies or perhaps it's their music preferences? In this study we present initial results of work in progress that ranks and maps between pairs of domains based on the ability to create recommendations in domain one using ratings of items from the other domain. The recommendations are made using cross domain collaborative filtering, and evaluated on the social networking profiles of 2148 users. Initial results show that information that is freely available in social networks can be used for cross domain recommendation and that there are differences between the source domains with respect to the quality of the recommendations.

Keywords: cross-domain recommendation, cold-start problem, collaborative-filtering.

1 Introduction

Information overload nowadays prevents us from building information systems following the "one-fits-all" paradigm. In order to provide users with easy access to information, information systems must be adaptable; they should tailor the information served by them to the personal preferences and needs of their users. One approach for adapting content to users' preferences is Collaborative Filtering (CF). The CF approach [1] is based on similarity of users' preferences. It assumes that users which agreed in the past on items they liked will probably agree on more items in the future. For example taking one user's bookshelf and cross checking it with shelves of other users, finding those with similar books, will yield several possible book recommendations for that user. To carry this approach, information needs to be collected from the target user and a large number of other users, regarding their preferences and interests. Having no details at all or an

J. Masthoff et al. (Eds.): UMAP 2012, LNCS 7379, pp. 328–333, 2012.

insufficient amount of them regarding the target user's interests/preferences is defined as the 'Cold-start Problem' [2]. A specific case of the cold-start problem is when a CF for a dedicated target domain does not have the user's preferences in that domain, but do have the user's preferences in other domains. For example, users are requesting recommendations for movies (the target domain), but the CF system only has their books/music preferences. One way to overcome this problem is by making Cross-Domain Collaborative Filtering (CDCF) [3]. In CDCF the system finds users with similar preferences to those of the target user based on domains in which that information is available ('source domains'). Then items from the target domain that were preferred by those users are filtered and recommended to the target user. When considering CDCF application, a major question is how can we decide which source domain to use for what target domain.

2   Background

In order to overcome the sparsity of users to items rating matrices in CF recommendation systems, [3] suggest to mediate ratings across domains. Cross domain mediation works by calculating similarity among users in domains other than the target domain (using methods such as k-nearest neighbors); recommendations are generated based on those similar users taste in the target domain. In their work they have evaluated the mediated recommendations in comparison to regular CF results; separate domains were mimicked by taking a single domain, movies, and splitting it into sub domains based on genres. For example, for recommending an action movie to a target user, that had too few ratings for movies in that genre, the system would take ratings of the user from other genres (e.g., comedy, romance), find similar users based on their ratings for movies in the other genres and for these similar users, and return their most liked movies in the action genre. Results showed that the cross domain based recommendations had even better results than the regular CF ones.

To the best of our knowledge, there was very little work done about domain mapping for the purpose of cross domain recommendations. One example is [4], in that work the authors have mapped between domains using a user study of 144 university students. In their initial analysis they searched for correlation between domains based on shared items, for example "If a user liked the book 'The Devil Wears Prada' did they also like the movie based on it?" or if users enjoyed movies in which a singer they like preformed. This analysis results showed high correlation between song items and movies that were related to each other, and items which involved singers who are also actors. In their second evaluation, domains were mapped using categories similarity; for example, do users who enjoy video games that belong to the action genre, also enjoy action movies? The results of this evaluation showed that users who liked books of a certain genre also enjoyed TV series from the same genre. Their last evaluation method tried to make CF recommendations for a target domain based on items from multiple source domains; in example, making movies and TV series recommendations based on the target user's set of movies, TV series, and CD items combined. The results were that for each combination of source domain items that did not contain items from the target domain, their recommendations ranked last. A related analysis is also shown in [5], in which a community based approach for overcoming the cold start problem has been evaluated. The evaluation was carried on 10,000 users of the social network "imhonet", and two item domains: books and movies. Recommendations were made by splitting the users into communities either based on their social relations or shared items' voting; then CF recommendations were generated for the users, based on the ratings of the members of the community they belong to. The results showed that a community based CF, performs better than taking all users in the user space into consideration. On another example [6], a mapping approach based on Information Retrieval (IR) techniques was suggested and evaluated for measuring the similarity of domains based on Google Directory and Open Directory. A vector of terms frequency was calculated using TF-IDF, for several domains in both web directories (web directories aggregate and categorize websites belonging to the same domain); the cosine similarity between the vector representations of the domains was measured and the results showed that indeed, distances were different between different domains and these results were consistent in the two directories. The authors concluded that inter-domain similarity may help in selecting domains for cross-domain recommendation. Their approach and the one proposed in this work both suggest an automatic way to generate domain mappings. The mapping presented in this work will be based on a larger scale of users (thousands) and from more heterogeneous backgrounds (age, employment, education). We too use CF recommendations and the target user's own set of items from the target domain to evaluate our results, however we do so for any source-to-target domain combinations, creating a full map between available domains. Our results are not refined by domain sub categories, since the dataset lacks that information, but we intend to complete it in future work. This evaluation will be completed by an additional comparison to the recommendations that would have been generated for the dataset using regular CF, as done in [3].

3   Cross Domain Recommendation Using SNS data

The suitability of different domains for CDCF is based on the evaluation of 2148 Facebook[1] profiles, which contained items ("likes") in four domains: Music (artists/bands), Movies, TV shows, and Books. The dataset originally contained 6370 user profiles. However, only 33.72% of them contained at least a single item that belongs to at least one of the domains that were evaluated. The total number of items in each domain, and the average number of items each user liked from each domain are detailed in Table 1.

Table 1. Dataset Statistics

	Music	Movies	TV	Books
Total Amount of Items	7481	5470	3310	4140
Average Amount of Items Per User	6.49	4.68	3.24	2.42
Standard Deviation	13.39	7.78	4.68	3.80

---

[1] http://www.facebook.com

The dataset was collected using the platform's application API and based on users' consent to participate in an online experiment. All profiles and items were loaded into a graph based database system called Neo4j[2]; users and items as nodes connected to each other based on "Likes", with edges labeled by the domain name. A generic cross domain graph walk was then implemented; the walk receives as parameters a source domain and target domain, and returns the various measurements that are described below. The walking method was then performed for each source and target domain combination for the existing domains.

In order to find out which domains are more influential with respect to recommending for other domains in CDCF we have measured the precision of CDCF recommendation using different source and target domains. The process we followed was finding the K-nearest neighbors in a source domain and using these "neighborhoods" for creating recommendations in a target domain. For comparing the results we defined two precision measures. The first was defined as the percentage of items recommended by the system for a user in the target domain, that were included in the items the user actually rated/liked in that domain (PR#1). For example, if music recommendations were made based on movie items, then PR#1 represents the percentage of each user's own music likings that appeared amongst the music recommendations generated by the system. The second measure (PR#2) is the percentage of items appeared in the top 10 items recommended by the CDCF that appeared in the set of recommendations generated for the target domain using *regular* (non cross domain) collaborative filtering; naturally those did not contain the user's own likings in the domain (to continue with the previous example of music recommendations, in this method music recommendations were generated for each user using both CDCF and regular CF, the results of the CF did not contain the user's original preferences in music, and the two sets were intersected). For PR#1 we excluded from the measurements users that did not have items belonging either to the source domain (since no recommendations could be made for them), or that did not have items belonging to the target domain, (since there was nothing to compare to). In PR#2 we excluded users that did not have any recommendation results for the regular CF (since those serve as the basis for the comparison). For both metrics, PR#1 and PR#2, we also filtered out users with less than 5 items in each domain, in order to enable a minimal level of accuracy. An average of 18% of the 2148 users had at least 5 items from the source domain, and 1 item in the target domain, for the various evaluation combinations. Table 2 presents the results of the CDCF recommendation experiment; the rows are grouped by target domain and internally sorted by PR#1. The PR#1 column contains both the number of "hits" and their percentage, averaged for all users that had items in that target domain. As can be seen, although the absolute numbers are low, for nearly every target domain at least 40% of the items a user liked were identified based on the preferences in a different source domain. For example, generating movie recommendations based on similarity in TV series preferences, yielded 5.31 matching items on average, which are 43.56% of the target users' preferred movies. As may be expected, there are noticeable differences between the different domains, it seems that recommending music items based on other domains is more accurate than recommending books. Using a basic co-occurrence ranking, we have capped PR#1's results

---

[2] http://neo4j.org/

to the top 100 returned; the hit rate based on those is given in the 4th column ("PR#1@100"). The drop in the hit rate between PR#1 and PR#1@100 indicates farther work should be done regarding the ranking method of the CDCF returned results (a challenge since users to items rates in Facebook are unary and contain only a "Like" indication). PR#2 shows a similar general behavior to PR#1 – there are domains where CDCF performs better than others, when compared with classical CF.

Table 2. Cross-Domain Collaborative Filtering Domain Ranking

Source Domain	Target Domain	PR #1	PR#1@100	PR #2
TV		6.73 (42.59%)	2.66 (16.87%)	3.25
Movies	Music	6.45 (38.98%)	2.73 (16.54%)	2.92
Books		2.24 (14.02%)	1.29 (08.05%)	1.51
TV		5.31 (43.56%)	2.47 (20.30%)	3.02
Music	Movies	4.45 (39.84%)	2.13 (19.10%)	2.64
Books		2.51 (18.49%)	1.51 (11.13%)	1.23
Movies		3.37 (45.03%)	2.59 (34.53%)	5.48
Music	TV	3.21 (46.51%)	2.29 (33.15%)	5.48
Books		1.90 (24.52%)	1.54 (19.88%)	3.07
TV		1.02 (18.19%)	0.53 (09.55%)	1.60
Movies	Books	1.00 (16.41%)	0.58 (09.54%)	1.48
Music		0.77 (13.63%)	0.40 (07.15%)	0.92

The standard deviations of PR#1 and PR#2 in all cases were higher than the metrics values. It is worth noting, that as can be expected, without filtering out users with at least 5 items in the source domain (e.g. too little information for prediction), the successful prediction percentage drops to 30% for leading source domains in each group.

4   Discussion and Conclusions

This work contributes by suggesting a way for mapping similarity of domains for the purpose of cross-domain collaborative filtering, using available domain-rich users' information. This work gives a unique perspective about CDCF, both because of its scale and the heterogeneity of the user base (multi nationalities/age groups/occupations) and items. Two precision parameters have been used to evaluate the resulted ranking; they demonstrate the ranking both by comparing recommendations to users' previously seen items and unseen ones (e.g. recommended by a community of users in the target domain, applying classical collaborative filtering).

In the future, we intend to further investigate the above mapping. We plan to better understand the differences between domains, in order to be able to suggest how these differences may be taken into account for defining the uncertainty in the CDCF process. We also plan to investigate how the number of ratings in the source domain affects the accuracy of the recommendations in the target domain and the overlap between profiles in the source domain and its potential impact on finding partners for CDCF in the target domain. It is also intended to enrich the dataset using domain knowledge (e.g., Genres) and evaluate its effect on the domain ranks.

Taking a closer look at the dataset, we noticed that sometimes users chose to list all the items they liked as a single long string (there is an option to enter open text on Facebook). Currently we were unable to process this data, but simple parsing may help resolve this problem and further increase the performance of the recommendations.

References

1. Shardanand, U., Maes, P.: Social Information Filtering: Algorithms for Automating "Word of Mouth". In: CHI, pp. 210–217 (1995)
2. Schein, A.I., Popescul, A., Ungar, L.H., Pennock, D.M.: Methods and metrics for cold-start recommendations, pp. 253–260. ACM (2002)
3. Berkovsky, S., Kuflik, T., Ricci, F.: Cross-Domain Mediation in Collaborative Filtering. In: Conati, C., McCoy, K., Paliouras, G. (eds.) UM 2007. LNCS (LNAI), vol. 4511, pp. 355–359. Springer, Heidelberg (2007)
4. Winoto, P., Tang, T.: If you like the Devil Wears Prada the book, will you also enjoy the Devil Wears Prada the movie? A study of cross-domain recommendations. New Generation Computing 26(3), 209–225 (2008)
5. Sahebi, S., Cohen, W.W.: Community-Based Recommendations: a Solution to the Cold Start Problem. In: Workshop on Recommender Systems and the Social Web, RSWEB (2011)
6. Berkovsky, S., Goldwasser, D., Kuflik, T., Ricci, F.: Identifying Inter-Domain Similarities Through Content-Based Analysis of Hierarchical Web-Directories, vol. ECAI, pp.789-790 (2006)

User Modelling Ecosystems:
A User-Centred Approach

Rainer Wasinger, Michael Fry, Judy Kay, and Bob Kummerfeld

School of Information Technologies, The University of Sydney, NSW 2006, Australia
{rainer.wasinger,michael.fry,judy.kay,bob.kummerfeld}@sydney.edu.au

Abstract. The recent exponential growth in mobile applications and
the growing reliance on and awareness of 'user models' by end-users
have led to the need to rethink the functional and end-user requirements
of existing user modelling systems. This paper has two goals. Firstly,
leveraging a functioning user modelling ecosystem that provides anywhere and anytime access to desktop-, web-, and mobile- applications,
this paper identifies a current opportunity (and need) to enhance user interaction with existing user modelling frameworks, by extending beyond
the stereotypical cloud-based user modelling approach to encompass also
a client-based service and an accompanying synchronisation module. Secondly, we draw on an analysis of previous work and a small user study,
to establish the need for a user-centred design focus for user modelling
frameworks. We also identify functionality that end-users (rather than
developers) need and want from a user modelling ecosystem.

Keywords: User modelling ecosystems, client-side and cloud-based user
models, personalisation, framework requirements, user-centred design.

1 Introduction

As described in [7], User Modelling (UM) frameworks have in the past typically
been classified as either: shell systems, in which the UM components exist as
code that can be integrated into a number of different applications; or as user
modelling servers, in which the UM components can be interfaced as a service
running on a server. The review of UM frameworks in [7] also shows that most
applications making use of UM components are either specialty stand-alone applications, as in the case of shell systems, or web-based systems, as in the case
of user modelling servers. However, with the exponential growth in mobile applications, it is no longer just desktop and/or web applications that require the
use of UM components, but also this new breed of mobile application. Mobile
application storefronts like Android Marketplace and the Apple AppStore now
offer in excess of 400,000 and 500,000 applications respectively[1], and for a range
of different device form-factors covering not just communication devices like
smartphones and tablets, but also consumer electronic devices like wrist-watches,

---

[1] Distimo mobile app store analytics, January 2012. http://www.distimo.com/

J. Masthoff et al. (Eds.): UMAP 2012, LNCS 7379, pp. 334–339, 2012.
© Springer-Verlag Berlin Heidelberg 2012

in-car and gaming consoles, and set-top boxes. Mobile devices, especially smart-phones, offer particular promise for personalised applications because they are always on and usually with the user. So, we conclude that it is inevitable that these applications of the future will have significant interaction with feature-rich UM ecosystems and with one another based on such ecosystems. In the context of this paper, the term *user-modelling ecosystem* is used to refer to multiple UM frameworks and their components, each interacting with one another and functioning as a single larger unit.

Another commonality of most previous user modelling frameworks is that they were designed with developers first in mind. This may be partly because most people do not have much understanding of user models, as shown for example in a study on Facebook users [1]. As a result, most UM servers are currently used as backend components in the form of building blocks for larger applications or services. They are accessed by APIs, and their benefits to end-users are the personalised applications and services that UMs enable, rather than the actual UMs themselves. This separation of the user from their UM also contributes to the conflict in themes that are and should be addressed by UM frameworks, like ownership, control, privacy, and the scrutability of user models. However, as end-users continue to become savvier about the benefits and potential uses of their user models, and indeed as they become more reliant on such user models, the need for feature-rich UM ecosystems that have been designed with users (rather than developers) in mind will increase.

In this paper, we outline how a synchronisation module has been used to combine the Personis cloud-based UM server [6] with the PersonisJ client-based UM service for Android [3]. Moreover, we outline how the resulting Personis User Modelling Ecosystem caters for both the functional requirements and the end-user requirements of a modern UM platform. In Section 2, we outline the functional requirements that UM Frameworks have typically followed in past work, as well as the challenges that user models have typically faced due to the conflict between themes such as privacy and personalisation. Then in Section 3, we outline the Personis UM Ecosystem. This is followed by the results of a user experiment conducted to provide insight into the user-centred design requirements for UM Ecosystems in Section 4, and our conclusions in Section 5.

2   Related Work

In his seminal review of generic user modelling systems, Kobsa [7] describes the prominent components of a UM system as incorporating a 'representation mechanism' for expressing the contents of the user model and a 'reasoning' mechanism for deriving assumptions about the user and for detecting inconsistencies in the user model. In that paper, a list of requirements for UM systems is also defined. In particular, it is stated that UM systems should exhibit: generality (i.e. be reusable in as many domains as possible); expressiveness and strong inferential capabilities; support for quick adaptation (i.e. in order to bond with first-time users); extensibility (e.g. to integrate third-party tools); support for importing external user-related information; the ability to manage distributed information; support for open standards; load balancing capabilities; failover strategies; and privacy support. A similar set of requirements is also defined in [2], in which the authors additionally note that there is a disjoint between classical UM research - which looks at themes like generality, domain-independence, expressiveness, and strong inferential capabilities - and UM deployment requirements for real-world environments - which, in contrast, focus on themes like performance, scalability, extensibility, integration of pre-existing data, and privacy protection.

The above reviews place significant focus on the *functional requirements* of UM systems; they are designed with developers in mind, and for systems in which the UM components are a backend feature that is invisible to the end user. Our work by contrast, although aligned with the essential functional requirements of UM systems, as outlined above, has a strong emphasis on *user-centred design*, i.e. the process in which system functionality is optimised to the needs and wants of end-users. In this way, we focus on providing a UM ecosystem with a feature set that caters not just to developers but specifically to end-users of the UM ecosystem. These features, as outlined later in the paper, cover the themes: accessibility, location, ownership, scrutability, user control, model reuse, life logging, application logging, and portability.

Past work on personalisation and adaptive systems (including our own) has also highlighted a range of user-centred themes that can be applied not just to personalisation, but to UM systems in general. These themes cover aspects like a UM's location [3], scrutability, user control and privacy [4], and life logging [5]. Few (if any) past UM frameworks cover all of these end-user requirements, despite - as our study outlines below - these features being classified important to end-users. This is where the Personis UM Ecosystem differentiates itself from the other UM research platforms. In addition to serving as an educational tool, in which UM concepts can be demonstrated to end-users, it has been developed based on a user-centred approach, and as such has been designed to address a growing number of requirements that end-users find important when interacting with their user model and the applications that make use of it.

3   The Personis User Modelling Ecosystem

The Personis User Modelling Ecosystem combines both a cloud-based UM server called Personis [6] and a client-based UM service called PersonisJ that runs on Android devices [3]. Both of these UM platforms provide a mechanism for representing the contents of the user model and a reasoning mechanism for deriving assumptions about the user. So they meet the essential functional requirements identified in [7]. In particular, the representation is based on the accretion/resolution method, in which 'evidence' is accreted or collected and stored in a hierarchical model of 'contexts' and 'components' [3]. Such evidence is supplied to the model via a 'tell' operation and is retrieved from the model using an 'ask' operation. The reasoning mechanism employed by the Personis components is based on inference rules contained in a combination of evidence filters and resolvers. Whereas the filters are used by the system to retrieve a subset of relevant evidence, the resolvers are responsible for interpreting a set of evidence to generate a result.

Some of the user-centred features that are available to end-users of the Personis UM Ecosystem include the ability to view and edit the contents of the model, scrutinise the model, and set permissions for access to it by third-party applications. The end-user is also able to export their user model and be notified when applications attempt to access the model (e.g. to share and/or reuse content). A synchronisation module additionally provides the functionality for an end-user to access their data anywhere and anytime (and regardless of cellular and/or network coverage), and to also visually select which parts of their model should be synchronised with the server. In addition to 'manual' synchronisation, the model can also be 'automatically' synchronised by setting a synchronisation time interval such as 1hr or 6hrs. This executes as part of a background service on the client device. The synchronisation process essentially entails the client and the server exchanging all evidence since a last agreed-upon synchronisation time between those two devices. Since all evidence is time-stamped and contains details on the source of origin, the task of synchronisation becomes a simple comparison of evidence timestamps, and more advanced semantic interpretation of the evidence is left to the filters and the resolvers.

As described earlier, most previous UM frameworks provided only a UM server with which applications can communicate to retrieve user model information from a central repository. With that approach there is a strong requirement for constant and ongoing connectivity to the UM server, which cannot always be guaranteed. This, combined with the increased reliance that end-users now have on UM frameworks, is detrimental to the reliability afforded by ubiquitous and mobile adaptive systems. Other work provides some focus on the replication of a user model from a server onto a mobile device, e.g. [8], which is based on the LDAP protocol, but with this approach the client-side model is always only a derivation of the server-side model (i.e. controlled by the server).

The UM ecosystem described in this paper represents the natural evolution of these earlier approaches. First, it extends on the benefits of the typical UM server as stated in [7] in that by allowing the model to be maintained also on the client-side, true 'anywhere' and 'anytime' access to the model is afforded to end-users, furthermore, the exact same advantages provided to cloud-based UM servers are as a result also afforded to the rich application ecosystems that already exist in today's mobile operating systems, including UM availability, locality, and performance as described in [8]. Additionally, in comparison to the model replication approach used in other work, the use of an entirely distinct client-side UM service provides much increased flexibility that some end-users do deem important to them, e.g. consider the partial synchronisation of a model which, rather than being part of the server model that is replicated to the client, it is the client-model that is only partially synchronised with the server; such a feature would be particularly important in cases where an end user does not have control over a cloud-based UM server.

4   User-Centred Study into UM Design Requirements

In addition to the Personis UM Ecosystem being developed in accordance to end-user requirements that were gathered from past studies and reviews like those described above, the resulting UM ecosystem has also enabled research into better understanding the real-world end-user requirements for such frameworks. In particular, a study was conducted with 8 participants to determine which features of UM ecosystems are important to them. The study is unique in that its end-users interacted in a practical hands-on manner with the UM ecosystem as a frontend component rather than as an invisible backend component, before being asked to quantify the importance of different UM features.

The study had four parts: a background questionnaire; a 5-10 minute tutorial on user modelling; a set of user tasks conducted as a think-aloud; and a questionnaire about the importance of different UM features based on a 7-point Likert scale (which in Table 1 has been collapsed into the values: disagree, neutral, and agree). The participants (5 male and 3 female) ranged in age from 21 to 25 years (mean: 21.6 years), and all were students. Five of the 8 participants were not familiar with the term 'user modelling'/'user models'; though all participants listed at least one social networking site that they actively use, and all participants were aware of their profile data being stored by such websites.

Table 1. Study results on the importance of different UM features to end-users

UM Framework Features	Likert-scale Results
Accessibility: It is important to you that the user model can be used anywhere, anytime, and on any device:	Agree=7; Disagree=1; Neutral=0
Location: You would prefer your user model to be stored client-side (on the mobile device) rather than in the cloud (Internet):	Neutral=4; Disagree=3; Agree=1
Ownership: You would prefer to be the sole owner of your user model rather than allowing access for other services to own your data as well:	Agree=5; Neutral=3; Disagree=0
Scrutability: It is important that users be able to inspect their own user model:	Agree=7; Disagree=1; Neutral=0
User control: It is useful in the user's perspective to create, edit, and delete parts of the user model:	Agree=5; Disagree=2; Neutral=1
Model reuse: Applications should be able to share information in the user model between each other provided that the user has given permission to do so:	Agree=7; Neutral=1; Disagree=0
Life-long logging: It is okay that your user model will store information on you for a long period of time:	Agree=6; Disagree=1; Neutral=1
Application access logging: It is suitable that the user model will log every time an application accesses your user model and the particular content that the applications were trying to access:	Agree=6; Neutral=2; Disagree=0
Portability: The idea of importing and exporting your user models to another user modelling framework is useful:	Agree=6; Disagree=1; Neutral=1

The tutorial component of the study was designed to provide participants with knowledge of the concept of user modelling, including example situations in which user models are commonly used. The tutorial also included the experimenter demonstrating all of the UM functionalities (see Table 1) and allowed time for the participants to ask questions and familiarise themselves with the software. The tasks that the users were asked to complete related to the use of a career organiser application, and the UM model browser and synchronisation module. In particular, users were asked to modify an existing resume contained on a smartphone, and to then perform a (partial) synchronisation of the model from the smartphone to the cloud and then from the cloud to a tablet device. After having completed the tasks, the users quantified the importance of the UM features, the results of which are outlined in Table 1.

The results show that users find it important to access their user models pervasively; that some (but not all) users prefer to store their user models in the cloud rather than locally; that users would like to have sole ownership over their user models; that it is important that users be able to inspect their models and understand the reasons why such information is in the model; that users want full control over their user models; that users would like applications to use their user model (provided that the user has granted permission for this); and that users are okay with information on them being recorded for long periods of time.

5 Conclusions

As described above, this work makes two contributions. First, it introduces the concept of a User Modelling Ecosystem to provide improved user modelling support to mobile-, desktop-, and web- applications; this is achieved by extending the functionality of existing UM server approaches with that of a client-based service and an accompanying synchronisation module. Second, this work highlights the need for user-centred design of UM frameworks by drawing on the views of a small sample of end-users (rather than developers) who provide greater insight into the importance of different UM features.

References

1. Acquisti, A., Gross, R.: Imagined Communities: Awareness, Information Sharing, and Privacy on the Facebook. In: Danezis, G., Golle, P. (eds.) PET 2006. LNCS, vol. 4258, pp. 36–58. Springer, Heidelberg (2006)
2. Fink, J., Kobsa, A.: A Review and Analysis of Commercial User Modeling Servers for Personalization on the World Wide Web. UMUAI 10, 209–249 (2000)
3. Gerber, S., Fry, M., Kay, J., Kummerfeld, B., Pink, G., Wasinger, R.: PersonisJ: Mobile, Client-Side User Modelling. In: De Bra, P., Kobsa, A., Chin, D. (eds.) UMAP 2010. LNCS, vol. 6075, pp. 111–122. Springer, Heidelberg (2010)
4. Kay, J.: Lifelong Learner Modeling for Lifelong Personalized Pervasive Learning. IEEE Transactions on Learning Technologies 1(4), 215–228 (2008)
5. Kay, J., Kummerfeld, B.: Lifelong User Modelling Goals, Issues, and Challenges. In: Lifelong User Modelling Workshop at UMAP, pp. 27–34 (2009)
6. Kay, J., Kummerfeld, B., Lauder, P.: Personis: A Server for User Models. In: De Bra, P., Brusilovsky, P., Conejo, R. (eds.) AH 2002. LNCS, vol. 2347, pp. 203–212. Springer, Heidelberg (2002)
7. Kobsa, A.: Generic User Modeling Systems. In: Brusilovsky, P., Kobsa, A., Nejdl, W. (eds.) Adaptive Web 2007. LNCS, vol. 4321, pp. 136–154. Springer, Heidelberg (2007)
8. Kobsa, A., Fink, J.: An LDAP-based User Modeling Server and its Evaluation. User Modeling and User-Adapted Interaction 16(2), 129–169 (2006)

Adaptive Score Reports

Diego Zapata-Rivera

Educational Testing Service, Princeton, NJ
dzapata@ets.org

Abstract. This paper introduces the idea of adaptive score reports that can be used to provide educational stakeholders with a personalized experience aimed at facilitating student understanding and use of assessment information. These reports can also provide additional learning opportunities for users based on assessment results. An interactive score report for students is used to illustrate opportunities for adaptation.

Keywords: Adaptive score reports, Open student models, Educational assessment, Adaptive learning environments.

1   Introduction

Educational assessment systems generate reports for teachers, students, parents, school administrators or policymakers. Research shows that many educators and administrators have trouble understanding and making appropriate use of score reports [8]. Goodman and Hambleton [6] report that score reports usually include "too much" information and technical jargon which make the reports difficult to understand.

Score reports can be designed and evaluated taking into account the goals, needs, and attitudes of the audience (e.g., [16]). For example, reports for administrators should respond to their need for aggregate level information (across classrooms, schools, or districts) that can be used to make comparisons across these aggregations and between their data and normative data. Teachers on the other hand, are interested in student- and class-level performance data. They want to use these data to inform their instructional strategies. Although this user-centered design approach yields good results, even members of a particular audience may differ in prior knowledge, skills, interests, and attitudes which may result in score report designs that do not meet the needs of particular audience members.

Current efforts on exploring how to communicate standard error of measurement to teachers using various text and graphical representations showed that some teachers may have various misconceptions that interfere with their understanding of measurement error and its implications for making appropriate inferences of score report information [19]. These findings suggest that additional information based on misconceptions can facilitate teacher understanding of score report information.

Researchers in the area of open student models have used a variety of external representations to share student model information, maintained by intelligent tutoring systems,

J. Masthoff et al. (Eds.): UMAP 2012, LNCS 7379, pp. 340–345, 2012.

with teachers, students, and sometimes parents. These representations usually include task- and skill-level information. Some of the representations that have been used include: a hierarchy of topics augmented with student mastery information [10], text descriptions of student performance [4], graphical or tabular representations of the students' strengths and weaknesses [3], Skillometers [1], conceptual graphs [5], Prolog clauses [12], Bayesian networks [17], graphical representations of assessment arguments accompanied by supporting evidence [14,18] and interactive visualization tools for analyzing group performance data [11]. This research has found positive effects on student reflection [2, 17], knowledge awareness [4]; and student learning [7].

Open student models give students control over the adaptation process. However, these systems can also be adaptive and/or adapted to the user needs, knowledge, and goals. For example, Zapata-Rivera & Greer [17] describe how various guidance mechanisms were used to support student interaction with open student models. These supporting mechanisms yielded different levels of student reflection.

As reporting applications become widely used by a wider audience for different purposes, their complexity increases, as well as the chances for misunderstanding and misuse. Thus, personalizing human interaction with these types of tools becomes a good alternative for dealing with these issues [13].

This paper makes the case for adaptive score report applications and describes a use case for adaptive reports based on an interactive score report for students.

2   The Case for Adaptive Score Reports

Score reports are no longer static documents. Score reports are interactive applications that support user interaction with Web-based educational systems. Users have different needs, prior knowledge, and interests. User interaction with these systems may be enhanced by making them adaptive. Adaptive score reports can use information about individual users to adapt interface components and provide additional support to help users understand and make good use of score report information. Hullman, Rhodes, Rodriguez, & Shah [9] suggest that possible dimensions for adapting score reports include: education level, needs for cognition, goals, perceived importance, and self-efficacy.

Implementing adaptive score report applications requires maintaining and keeping track of users' knowledge, goals, and interests, and using this information to adapt user interaction with the system. Some system components that can be made adaptive include: (a) navigation (e.g., maintaining a list of relevant links or questions/answers based on user interests); (b) external representations (e.g., providing annotations and different types of representations based on user prior knowledge and familiarity with particular concepts); (c) explanations and feedback (e.g., definitions, examples based on prior knowledge, current task, and goals) and (d) suggestions (e.g., recommendations for related relevant information based on current task and goals).

By implementing adaptive score report applications, it is expected that individuals will experience a more enjoyable and efficient interaction with online reporting systems. In addition, these adaptive systems may help minimize misuse and misinterpretation of score reports.

The next section presents a use case for adaptive score reports based on an existing interactive score report for students.

3   An Interactive Score Report for Students

Score reports should provide useful information for teachers, students, and parents to guide student learning. However, in some cases score report information may not be clearly communicated or may arrive too late to be useful in guiding instruction (e.g., reports that are only available at the end of the academic year). Assessment results from periodic assessments, formative activities, or online learning and assessment tools are available on time for teachers, students, and parents to guide instruction.

In order for reports to be useful, students need to be engaged in exploring the information included in the score reports and using it in appropriate ways. An interactive score report for middle school students aimed at supporting student engagement by including game-like elements has been designed and evaluated [15]. This interactive student score report implements a guided-instructional activity that involves collecting coins by correctly answering questions about the content of the report. A virtual character guides the students through the score report and provides feedback on their answers (see Figure 1). After they have explored all of the sections of the score report, students write about their performance and propose an action plan.

The report covers the following sections: student identification, purpose and use information (Section 1), overall results (e.g., How you did on all the math tests; Section 2), task-level performance and highlights (e.g., What you did on particular tasks and highlights across tasks; Section 3), and summary and recommendations (e.g., What you did and what you need to do to get the next performance level; Section 4).

Our preliminary data (results of a usability study with 11 middle-school students) show that students find the interactive score report useful and easy to understand. Students (nine out of 11) liked answering the questions about the different areas of the score report and eight out of 11 liked being able to write about what to do to improve their performance. Students (nine out of 11) said that they felt that this activity helped them to learn about the different sections of a score report, and eight out of 11 students felt that the embedded questions helped them to understand the score report. Students had mixed feelings about the dog character that was used to provide feedback. Seven out of 11 students said that they liked the way the dog looked. Two of the students who did not like the dog said that they felt it was more appropriate for younger students. Based on this finding, future versions of the score report might show students several possible characters and let them choose which one they would like to see in the report. Even though several students did not like the way the dog looked, all of them thought the feedback that it gave was helpful [15].

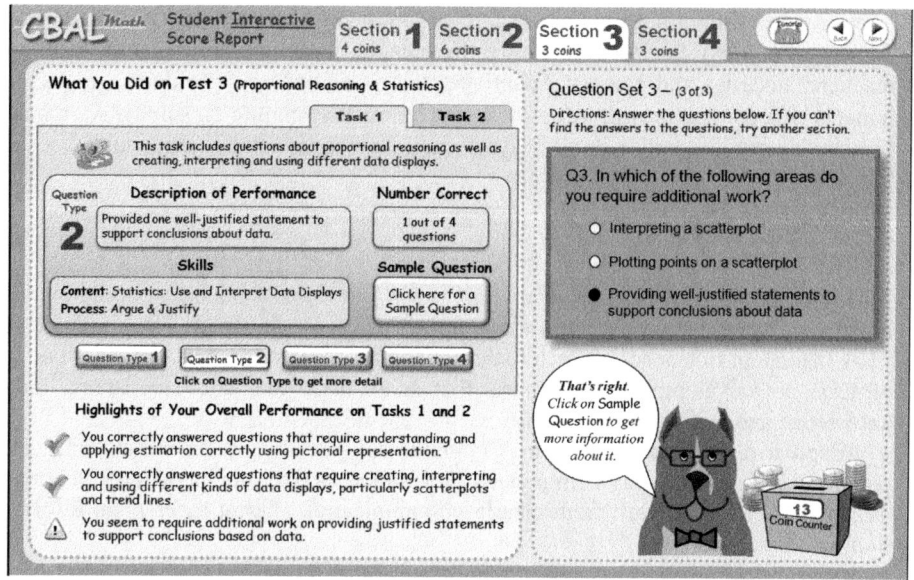

Fig. 1. A virtual dog provides immediate feedback

3.1   Adaptive Features

Several adaptive features that can be implemented in this score reporting application include:

- Adaptive graphical and text representations. Different types of graphical representations can be used to convey assessment information to students. These representations can involve various types of annotations based on students' prior knowledge and familiarity with particular representations.
- Adaptive questions. Students can be provided with questions that are relevant to their own performance (e.g., questions that focused on understanding their weaknesses and strengths). The difficulty of questions can be selected to match the student's knowledge level. The number of points given to students for correct answers can be made proportional to the difficulty level of the question. Feedback and examples may be available for students to learn while interacting with the system.
- Adaptive feedback. Feedback and opportunities for students to learn and practice particular concepts can be made available based on the information in the report and students' performance on additional questions. Feedback may fade out as students demonstrate mastery of relevant concepts. The character could also exhibit various emotions that may be triggered based on students' knowledge and performance on particular questions.
- Adaptive suggestions. Recommendations for additional learning activities can be provided to students based on their knowledge and interests. In addition, teachers can provide a list of activities to be recommended to students that seem to have particular misconceptions.

Score reports should not only communicate assessment information to particular audiences effectively, but they also have the potential to foster communication among teachers, students, and parents. Adaptive score reports can help bridge several components of a comprehensive assessment and learning system (e.g., summative results, formative activities, online tutoring systems, and professional development).

4   Future Work

This line of research opens up several areas for future work, including designing and evaluating adaptive score reports for various audiences. Some examples include reports that adapt to teacher characteristics and can be used to suggest opportunities for professional development and reports that adapt their interaction to parents' prior knowledge and language characteristics.

Adaptive reports can also support communication among teachers, students, and parents. These reports may help parents play a more active role in students' learning. Teachers may also benefit from clearly communicating student assessment information with parents.

Future work also involves evaluating these adaptive reports in terms of user comprehension of assessment information, use, learning support, and user preference.

References

1. Aleven, V., Koedinger, K.: Limitations of Student Control: Do Students Know When They Need Help? In: Gauthier, G., VanLehn, K., Frasson, C. (eds.) ITS 2000. LNCS, vol. 1839, pp. 292–303. Springer, Heidelberg (2000)
2. Bull, S., Brna, P., Dimitrova, V. (eds.): Proceedings of Learner Modelling for Reflection Workshop. AIED 2003 Supplementary Proceedings, vol. V, pp. 209–218 (2003)
3. Bull, S., Nghiem, T.: Helping Learners to Understand Themselves with a Learner Model Open to Students, Peers and Instructors. In: Brna, P., Dimitrova, V. (eds.) Proceedings of Workshop on Individual and Group Modelling Methods that Help Learners Understand Themselves, International Conference on ITS 2002, pp. 5–13 (2002)
4. Bull, S., Pain, H.: Did I say what I think I said, and do you agree with me? Inspecting and questioning the student model. In: Greer, J. (ed.) Proceedings of the World Conference on Artificial Intelligence in Education, pp. 501–508. AACE, Charlottesville (1995)
5. Dimitrova, V., Self, J., Brna, P.: Applying Interactive Open Learner Models to Learning Technical Terminology. In: Bauer, M., Gmytrasiewicz, P.J., Vassileva, J. (eds.) UM 2001. LNCS (LNAI), vol. 2109, pp. 148–157. Springer, Heidelberg (2001)
6. Goodman, D.P., Hambleton, R.K.: Student test score reports and interpretive guides: Review of current practices and suggestions for future research. Applied Measurement in Education 17(2), 145–220 (2004)
7. Hartley, D., Mitrović, A.: Supporting Learning by Opening the Student Model. In: Cerri, S.A., Gouardéres, G., Paraguaçu, F. (eds.) ITS 2002. LNCS, vol. 2363, pp. 453–462. Springer, Heidelberg (2002)
8. Hambleton, R.K., Slater, S.: Are NAEP executive summary reports understandable to policy makers and educators (CSE Technical Report 430). National Center for Research on Evaluation, Standards, and Student Teaching, Los Angeles (1997)

9. Hullman, J., Rhodes, R., Rodriguez, F., Shah, P.: Research on graph comprehension and data interpretation: Implications for score reporting. In: Perspectives from the ETS Score Reporting Conference (ETS Research Report No. RR–11-45). ETS, Princeton (2011)

10. Kay, J.: The UM toolkit for cooperative user modelling. User Modeling and User-Adapted Interaction 4, 149–196 (1995)

11. Mazza, R., Botturi, L.: Monitoring an online course with the GISMO tool: A case study. Journal of Interactive Learning Research 18(2), 251–265 (2007)

12. Paiva, A., Self, J.: TAGUS – a user and learner modelling workbench. User Modeling and User-Adapted Interaction 4, 197–226 (1995)

13. Shute, V.J., Zapata-Rivera, D.: Adaptive technologies. In: Spector, J.M., Merrill, D., van Merriënboer, J., Driscoll, M. (eds.) Handbook of Research on Educational Communications and Technology, 3rd edn. Taylor & Francis, New York (2007)

14. Van Labeke, N., Brna, P., Morales, R.: Opening up the interpretation process in an open learner model. International Journal of Artificial Intelligence in Education 17(3), 305–338 (2007)

15. Vezzu, M., VanWinkle, W., Zapata-Rivera, D.: Designing and evaluating an interactive score report for students. (ETS Research Memorandum No. RM–12-01). ETS, Princeton (2012)

16. Zapata-Rivera, D.: Designing and evaluating score reports for particular audiences. In: Zapata-Rivera, D., Zwick, R. (eds.) Test Score Reporting: Perspectives from the ETS Score Reporting Conference (ETS Research Report No. RR–11-45). ETS, Princeton (2011)

17. Zapata-Rivera, J.D., Greer, J.: Interacting with Bayesian student models. International Journal of Artificial Intelligence in Education 14(2), 127–163 (2004)

18. Zapata-Rivera, D., Hansen, E.G., Shute, V.J., Underwood, J.S., Bauer, M.I.: Evidence-based approach to interacting with open student models. International Journal of Artificial Intelligence in Education 17(3), 273–303 (2007)

19. Zwick, R., Zapata-Rivera, D., Hegarty, M.: Comparing graphical and verbal representations of measurement error in test score reports. Paper Accepted for Presentation at the Annual Meeting of the National Council on Measurement in Education (NCME). Vancouver, CA (2012)

Improving Matrix Factorization Techniques of Student Test Data with Partial Order Constraints

Behzad Beheshti and Michel Desmarais

Polytechnique Montreal

Abstract. Matrix factorization is a general technique that can extract latent factors from data. Recent studies applied matrix factorization to the problem of establishing which skills are required by question items, and for assessing student skills mastery from student performance data. A number of generic algorithms, such as Non-negative Matrix Factorization and Tensor factorization, are used in these studies to perform the factorization, but few have looked at optimizing these algorithms to the specific characteristics of student performance data. In this thesis, we explore how one such characteristic can lead to better factorization: the fact that items are learnt in a constrained order and allow such inferences as if a difficult item is succeeded, an easier one should also be succeeded. In particular, we want to address this question: can a partial order knowledge structure (POKS) be used to guide matrix factorization algorithms and lead to faster or better solutions to latent skills modelling?

1   Introduction

Matrix factorization decomposes a matrix into two or more matrices and it can be used to extract latent factors in some data. This technique plays an important role in different fields such, bioinformatics, recommender systems, and vision, to name but a few. It has achieved great results in each of these fields. For skills assessment, Nguyen et al. [11] have shown that the approach can lead to prediction accuracies comparable and even better than well established techniques such as Bayesian Knowledge Tracing [2]. Matrix factorization can also lead to better means for mapping which skills can explain the success to specific items. For example, in [3], we recently showed that it is possible to derive a *conjunctive Q-matrix* from synthetic test data with NMF and in [1] we introduce some techniques to derive the number of skills. These recent studies lead us to believe that matrix factorization techniques can yield substantial advances to the domain of skills modelling and assessment.

One avenue to improve over current matrix factorization models is to adapt existing algorithms to the specific nature of the domain data. In particular, student performance data is known to be constrained by prerequisite relations among skills or knowledge items [8,7]. This constraint can substantially reduce the space of factorization, both for the purpose of assessing student skills and

J. Masthoff et al. (Eds.): UMAP 2012, LNCS 7379, pp. 346–350, 2012.

for mapping items to skills. The objective of this thesis is to explore how one type of constraints, known as Partial Order Knowledge Structures (POKS), can lead to better factorization techniques for the purposes mentioned.

First, we review the studies that applied factorization techniques in skills modelling.

1.1 Q-Matrix and Matrix Factorization

Matrix factorization is a method to decompose a matrix into two or more matrices. SVD and Non-negative Matrix Factorization (NMF) are well known examples of such methods. We focus our proposal on means to improve the NMF method.

Assume $\mathbf{V}$ is a matrix containing student test results of n items and m students, where a failure is 0 and a success is 1. Factorizing this matrix into two matrices $\mathbf{W}$ and $\mathbf{H}$:

$$\mathbf{V} \approx \mathbf{W} \times \mathbf{H} \qquad (1)$$

leads to a model where $\mathbf{W}$ is an $m \times k$ Q-matrix [10] that maps m items to k skills, and $\mathbf{H}$ is a skills mastery matrix, which indicates the mastery of the k skills by each of the n students. The fewer the number of skills is, the more compact the model is, but, in general, the lower is the accuracy of the matrix derived by the product $\mathbf{W} \times \mathbf{H}$ compared to the original matrix.

1.2 Constraints on the Factorization

Skills will increase the chances of success to items and they never decrease them. Therefore, they should have positive values and this is a first obvious constraint on the factorization. Non-negative Matrix Factorization (NMF) is a well known matrix factorization technique that takes this constraint into account by penalizing negative values in the objective function of the factorization algorithm [9].

As mentioned above, skills are often learnt in a given order. Children learn addition, then subtraction, then multiplication, and so on. This is reflected in the results matrix $\mathbf{V}$ by closure constraints. Defining a student knowledge state as a subset of all items (i.e. a column vector in $\mathbf{V}$), then the space of valid knowledge states is closed under union and intersection according to the theory of Knowledge spaces [6]. In our study, we will relax this constraint to a closure under union, meaning that the union of any two individual knowledge states is also a valid knowledge state. This means that the constraints can be expressed as a partial order of implications among items [4], termed a Partial Order Knowledge Structure (POKS). A few algorithms have been defined to derive such structures from the data in $\mathbf{V}$ [4,5] and the general idea of the thesis is to use this information to guide factorization algorithms.

1.3 Factorization Algorithm

Many algorithms for matrix factorization search the space of solutions to equation (1) by gradient descent. These algorithms can be interpreted as rescaled gradient descent, where the rescaling factor is optimally chosen to ensure convergence. Most of factorization algorithms operate iteratively in order to find the optimal factors. In each iteration of these algorithms, the new value of $\mathbf{W}$ or $\mathbf{H}$ (for NMF) is found by multiplying the current value by some factor that depends on the quality of the approximation in Eq. (1). It was proved that repeated iteration of the update rules is guaranteed to converge to a locally optimal factorization [9].

Changes to the factorization solution and to the search algorithm can be obtained by modifications to the update rule. This is where we can integrate information from the partial order into the search algorithm.

2   Problem Specification

2.1   Hypothesis

Can Partial Order Knowledge Structures improve the Matrix Factorization and Tensor Factorization? We hypothesize that the more a domain is constrained to follow a partial order, the smaller is the space of valid solutions. This will lead to finding better solutions and make the search algorithms more efficient.

2.2   POKS Constraints on the Matrices V, W, and H

Violation of a partial order can be easily detected in matrix $\mathbf{V}$: if an order $I_i \prec I_j$ is defined, meaning that I_i is always learnt before I_j, then we have a violation of this order if and only if I_j is 1 and I_i is 0 in a student column vector (test result). The number of violations indicates the extent to which the data conforms to POKS. A measure will need to be defined for that purpose.

A partial order over items also imposes constraints on $\mathbf{W}$, the matrix that represents Q-matrix. Using the same example $I_i \prec I_j$, if item I_i is linked to a skill S_k, then this skill must also be linked to item I_j. We therefore expect to find a closure under the union operator in the skills column vectors of matrix $\mathbf{W}$ that is consistent with the closure we have for the student knowledge state vectors in matrix $\mathbf{V}$.

As mentioned above, once we have confirmed these constraints and that we can measure their strength, methods to use them for optimizing the matrix factorization algorithm will be developed for the NMF approach.

2.3   Validation

The new algorithms are to be compared over the quality of the $\mathbf{W}$ and $\mathbf{H}$ matrices derived from $\mathbf{V}$, and by the efficiency of the search algorithm.

There are two kinds of validation for this purpose.

- *Validation with synthetic data.*
  The first validation process is to validate with synthetic data using known $\mathbf{W}$ and $\mathbf{H}$ matrices. There are a number of variants to validate the approach.

We could generate a simulated **V** matrix from the product of the predefined matrices **W** × **H** and add slip and guess factors as in [3]. Or we could use a Bayesian network by defining a conditional probability table that is consistent with a given POKS and Q-matrix.

Once the simulated data is generated and an algorithm that uses constraints from partial ordering is defined, we can derive the Q-matrix and skills matrices and compare the factorization **W** × **H** with the original matrices. The hope is that the new algorithm will yield better Q-matrices and skills matrices than the ones derived from standard NMF algorithms.

- *Validation with real data.*

  Besides synthetic data, we should use real data to validate the approach. For such data, we cannot directly compare the Q-matrices and skills matrices since the "real" ones are unknown. However, the measure of quality can be the comparison of the product **W** × **H** for the factorized matrices with the observed data.

3 Conclusion

The goal of this thesis is to develop algorithms to improve matrix factorization for skills modeling and assessment. To do so, we will change the objective function of NMF algorithms according to the partial order constraints that are derived from POKS. If the algorithm does not conform to the partial order constraints, some form of penalty should be applied to the objective function in order to guide the factorization towards a solution compatible with the POKS derived from the same data.

For the evaluation of our work, we should compare the results from normal MF with the aforementioned algorithm both on simulated data and real data to see if we can get any better performance in matrix factorization process.

Matrix factorization is an important technique in different fields of studies and the improvement we are looking for can hopefully be reached by applying partial ordering. In conclusion, we can claim that applying partial ordering into factorization techniques can reduce the result domain in which eventually it can have two potential benefits: a better and faster algorithm that is also compatible with partial ordering.

If the partial order constraints can successfully guide the factorization, the impact should span different fields in addition to skills modeling, namely any domain for which the data follows a partial order structure. In fact, any domain that is subject to a causal structure among observations should contain some form of partial order relations.

References

1. Behesti, B., Desmarais, M.C., Naceur, R.: Methods to find the number of latent skills. In: 5th International conference on Educational Data Mining, EDM 2012, Chania, Greece, June 19-21 (2012) (submitted)

2. Corbett, A.T., Anderson, J.R.: Knowledge tracing: Modeling the acquisition of procedural knowledge. User Modeling and User-Adapted Interaction 4(4), 253–278 (1995)

3. Desmarais, M.C., Behesti, B., Naceur, R.: Item to skills mapping: deriving a conjunctive q-matrix from data. In: 11th Conference on Intelligent Tutoring Systems, ITS 2012, Chania, Greece, June 14–18 (accepted 2012)

4. Desmarais, M.C., Maluf, A., Liu, J.: User-expertise modeling with empirically derived probabilistic implication networks. User Modeling and User-Adapted Interaction 5(3-4), 283–315 (1996)

5. Desmarais, M.C., Pu, X.: A bayesian inference adaptive testing framework and its comparison with Item Response Theory. International Journal of Artificial Intelligence in Education 15, 291–323 (2005)

6. Doignon, J.-P., Falmagne, J.-C.: Spaces for the assessment of knowledge. International Journal of Man-Machine Studies 23, 175–196 (1985)

7. Doignon, J.-P., Falmagne, J.-C.: Knowledge Spaces. Springer, Berlin (1999)

8. Falmagne, J.-C., Koppen, M., Villano, M., Doignon, J.-P., Johannesen, L.: Introduction to knowledge spaces: How to build test and search them. Psychological Review 97, 201–224 (1990)

9. Seung, D., Lee, L.: Algorithms for non-negative matrix factorization. Advances in Neural Information Processing Systems 13, 556–562 (2001)

10. Tatsuoka, K.K.: Rule space: An approach for dealing with misconceptions based on item response theory. Journal of Educational Measurement 20, 345–354 (1983)

11. Thai-Nghe, N., Horváth, T., Schmidt-Thieme, L.: Factorization models for forecasting student performance. In: Conati, C., Ventura, S., Pechenizkiy, M., Calders, T. (eds.) Proceedings of EDM 2011, The 4th International Conference on Educational Data Mining, Eindhoven, Netherlands, July 6–8, pp. 11–20 (2011), www.educationaldatamining.org

Evaluating an Implementation of an Adaptive Game-Based Learning Architecture

Florian Berger

University of Education Weingarten, Kirchplatz 2, 88250 Weingarten, Germany
berger@md-phw.de

Abstract. Current Game-based Learning (GBL) applications often lack features that have been commonplace in conventional e-learning. One of these is the ability to provide players with a personalised experience. The author's dissertation aims at further establishing adaptivity in GBL as a practical feature through three contributions: An adaptive educational game that fulfills key demands for GBL; an architecture that adapts at runtime according to authored references; and a controlled trial to evaluate effects of adaptivity in a statistically sound way.

1 Research Topic: Adaptivity in Game-Based Learning

Digital educational games have been an academic research topic since the early 1980s. But only recently, following an increasing popularity as well as prevalence of computer games as a leisure time activity, so called "serious games" have more widely been accepted as one learning medium among others.

As a result, current Game-based Learning (GBL) applications, while generally providing a more motivating and appealing learning experience [1], often lack features that have been commonplace in conventional e-learning products. One of these is the ability to provide the player with a personalised experience.

It is well understood that non-adapting e-learing tools are less effective in their educational outcome. [2][3] Personalisation, adapivity and reusability are key demands for modern e-learning systems. [4] The author's dissertation intends to help turning adaptivity in Game-based Learning from a "longer-term research vision" [3] into a practical feature.

2 Proposed Contributions

2.1 A Sound Educational Game

Demands. Over the course of the research, an educational game is being developed that shall fulfill two key demands for GBL:

- *Bringing playing and learning together in a meaningful way.* A lot of educational games commercially available fail in this respect, mainly because of the lack of an agreed-upon model how to achieve this fusion. [5] The game to be made will approach this by focussing on simulation aspects, abstaining from text-based learning screens and using *stealth assessment* techniques. [6]

J. Masthoff et al. (Eds.): UMAP 2012, LNCS 7379, pp. 351–355, 2012.

– *Using game mechanics for learning purposes.* While this may seem a trivial demand, a lot of commercial games decouple the learning process from actual gameplay. [7] Tan et al. have isolated components that utilise game features for learning purposes in [8]. Topic, learning outcome and game mechanics of the game to be made will be adjusted to satisfy this design goal.

Synopsis. The educational game aims at training *project management skills*, especially *parallelising tasks*, managing *resource constraints* and *handling breakages and delays*.

The game consists of a series of *scenarios* where the player commands a set of *agents* that are able to fulfill *tasks*. In order to succeed in a scenario, the player has to make the agents complete a given project within given boundaries of time and budget.

Constraints. The constraints for this contribution are the shortage of resources in terms of time, personnel and content production. An academic product, especially when done as part of doctoral research, can provide a well-engineered technical solution, but will inevitably fall behind commercial products regarding the quality of design, content, and testing.

2.2 Adaptivity

In e-learning, there is a number of commonly used techniques to achieve adaptivity: *Pre-learning Assessment* [9], *Assembly On-demand* [4] and *Monitoring* [2]. From these three, the latter is most suitable for the proposed game. Contrary to the former two, the learner can actively participate in the running adaptation process. In addition, the adaptation does not call attention to itself, thus not interrupting the learning process.

The game is planned to adapt to two types of players:

– *Underperformers* who critically lag behind or do not complete the project goals. Here the game will use the technique of an in-game *tutor* who assists these players, effectively rendering it an *Intelligent Tutoring System (ITS)*. These are well described in the research literature. [10]
– *Overperformers* who excel in performing the tasks associated with a project. These will experience increasing *obstacles* that delay the completion of a project and require re-planning. Following an *adaptive testing* approach, difficulty for these players will increase until it matches their abilities. As opposed to conventional game design which consists of a progression of levels of increasing difficulty, as the adaptation will happen in real-time.

There are sophisticated models for adaptive ITS. [10] They however are tailored for e-learning systems with a comparatively low interaction frequency. The key contribution of this part of the thesis will be an adaptation of these models to the high-resolution systems that current games represent.

Charles et al. published a potential framework for adaptive game systems in [11]. It is the author's belief that for *educational* games, this framework has to be extended by an *authored performance reference* as well as an *adaption threshold*. This is necessary because fundamental pedagogical design decisions should be made by a human author. The two cases of adaptation presented above are a consequence of this design, as they represent a positive or negative deviation from the reference, respectively. A flowchart of a framework for adaptive GBL is given in figure 1.

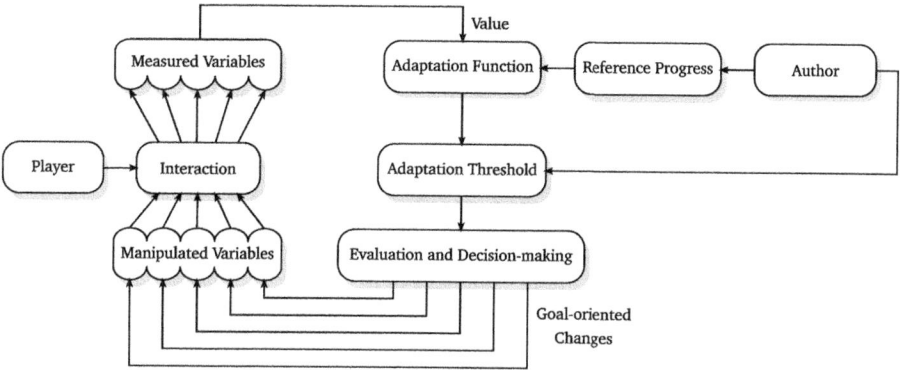

Fig. 1. A flowchart of the framework for adaptive Game-based Learning applications to be implemented

The game to be made will implement this architecture and thus provide a proof of concept. To learn about the feasibility of the architecture itself, further implementations and studies are needed.

2.3 Trial

Not all research projects that propose an adaptive architecture implement a prototype. If they do, its evaluation often uses few test cases, leading to a questionable validity of the results. [12] With adaptive GBL still being a novel topic in adaptive systems research, this problem is even more prevalent.[1]

The author's thesis will verify the implemented architecture by using the method of a controlled trial. After pre-testing to adjust for playing and project management experience, subjects will be assigned randomly to one of three groups: Group I is planned to go through several levels of the game with adaptivity enabled, and then play a final test level. Group II as a control group is planned to play a series of levels with adaptivity disabled, and then also play the final test level. Group III is planned to play only the test level without any prior training to provide control against a training effect. The number of subjects per group is planned to be $n = 50$ to reach statistically meaningful results.

---

[1] See for example chapter 6.6 in [1].

3   Status and Remaining Work

- An *architecture* has been devised, as shown in figure 1. Still lacking is a self-evaluating component that measures the effect of adaptivity at runtime. [11]
- The proposed *game* has been implemented up to the point of underperformer adaptivity. Overperformer adaptivity is still work in progress. Two sub-projects have spawned so far: *Fabula*, an open source game engine for research purposes [13], and *StepSim*, a step-based simulation framework[2].
- A *measured variable* to base the adaptation on has been identified: a vector of percentages of completness for project milestones over time.
- The actual *trial* and its *evaluation* remain to be done. The trial will be carried out using students of business economics, media and education management and computer science from three universities.

4   Research Questions

Questions that the author would like to receive advice on are:

- Is adaptation to under- and overperformers in the same game using the same measurement variable (milestone progress over time) a valid approach, or are these rather two distinct categories that should be measured differently?
- The trial assumes a possible training effect that is enhanced by adaptation, and aims at quantifying it using a test level (see 2.3). There is a number of alternatives to that, e.g. measuring variables related to motivation, time to completion, voluntary repeated playing, and their respective changes over time. How can the effect of adaptivity on learning be measured effectively? What is a sound null hypothesis for the evaluation of adaptive GBL?

References

1. Hodhod, R.: Interactive Narrative for Adaptive Educational Games: Architecture and Application to Character Education. PhD thesis, University of York (2010)
2. Teo, C.B., Gay, R.K.L.: A knowledge-driven model to personalize e-learning. J. Educ. Resour. Comput. 6(1), 3 (2006)
3. Greitzer, F.L., Kuchar, O.A., Huston, K.: Cognitive science implications for enhancing training effectiveness in a serious gaming context. J. Educ. Resour. Comput. 7(3), 2 (2007)
4. Farrell, R.G., Liburd, S.D., Thomas, J.C.: Dynamic assembly of learning objects. In: WWW Alt. 2004: Proceedings of the 13th International World Wide Web Conference on Alternate Track Papers & Posters, pp. 162–169. ACM New York (2004)
5. Weiß, S.A., Müller, W.: The Potential of Interactive Digital Storytelling for the Creation of Educational Computer Games. In: Pan, Z., Zhang, X., El Rhalibi, A., Woo, W., Li, Y. (eds.) Edutainment 2008. LNCS, vol. 5093, pp. 475–486. Springer, Heidelberg (2008)

---

[2] http://florian-berger.de/en/software/stepsim

6. Zylka, J., Müller, W., Berger, F., Rebholz, S.: Assessing Skills and Abilities in Educational Games – Approaches and Perspectives in terms of Game-based Learning. In: Assessment in Game-based Learning: Foundations, Innovations, and Perspectives. Springer, New York (2011)

7. Jantke, K.P.: Digital games that teach: A critical analysis. In: Diskussionsbeiträge. Number 22. Institut für Medien- und Kommunikationswissenschaft, TU Ilmenau (August 2006)

8. Tan, P.H., Ling, S.W., Ting, C.Y.: Adaptive digital game-based learning framework. In: DIMEA 2007: Proceedings of the 2nd International Conference on Digital Interactive Media in Entertainment and Arts, pp. 142–146. ACM, New York (2007)

9. Krichen, J.P.: Dynamically adjusting to learner's competencies and styles in an online technology course. In: SIGITE 2005: Proceedings of the 6th Conference on Information Technology Education, pp. 149–154. ACM, New York (2005)

10. Martens, A.: Ein Tutoring Prozess Modell für fallbasierte Intelligente Tutoring Systeme. Dissertationen zur Künstlichen Intelligenz vol. 281. Akademische Verlagsgesellschaft AKA (2004)

11. Charles, D., Kerr, A., McNeill, M., McAlister, M., Black, M., Kücklich, J., Moore, A., Stringer, K.: Player-centred game design: Player modelling and adaptive digital games. In: Digital Games Research Conference, Selected Papers Publication, pp. 285–298 (2005)

12. Van Velsen, L., Van der Geest, T., Klaassen, R., Steehouder, M.: User-centered evaluation of adaptive and adaptable systems: A literature review. Knowl. Eng. Rev. 23, 261–281 (2008)

13. Berger, F., Müller, W.: Towards an Open Source Game Engine for Teaching and Research. In: Chang, M., Hwang, W.-Y., Chen, M.-P., Müller, W. (eds.) Edutainment 2011. LNCS, vol. 6872, pp. 236–236. Springer, Heidelberg (2011)

Towards a Generic Model for User Assistance

Blandine Ginon

Université de Lyon, CNRS,
INSA-Lyon, LIRIS, UMR5205, F-69621, France

Abstract. This paper aims to present our generic model for user assistance. The approach we propose allows a designer to describe the assistance requested for an application using a common formalism; this description is then used by a generic assistant. A set of epiphyte assistants is then involved to perform assistance actions specified in the assistance description made by the designer.

Keywords: Assistance, user model, formalism, personalization.

1   Introduction

Over the years, computer applications have become more and more complex. Facing the numerous functionalities offered by these applications and their often dense interfaces, a novice user may become confused and give up using them despite the rich possibilities they offer. Otherwise, some users may under-exploit these applications, thus limiting their interest and richness. To overcome this difficulty of handling and use, there are two main ways of working: improving the usability, and assisting the user. First, the establishment of a good ergonomics in an application can increase significantly its usability. For this reason, the quality of ergonomics should be a major concern of application designers. However, this does not resolve all the problems encountered by users. For this reason, assuming that the ergonomics problem can be solved, this PhD thesis is focused towards user assistance.

User assistance, also named help, encompasses everything that can allow users to avoid under-exploit an application, or turn to another user, more expert, to help them overcome their difficulties. It is intended for all users (novice, occasional, standards or expert), addressing both first use and everyday use. The development of an assistance system for an application is a complex but important work. However, developers often neglect it to concentrate on the development the application's functionalities.

The main issue of our thesis is to allow designers to create more efficiently an assistance system suited to a given application and fully customizable according to user models. Our aim is to define generic models to describe assistants and applications' expected assistance. We will use an existing generic model to describe users. It will then be possible to define a broker that will use such descriptions to trigger the appropriate assistant for a given application. The description of the application will help the broker in providing context-sensitive assistance. The user model will make it possible to personalize this assistance according to the user' knowledge, abilities, preferences, goals, experiences…

J. Masthoff et al. (Eds.): UMAP 2012, LNCS 7379, pp. 356–360, 2012.

2   User Assistance

Typology of User Assistance. For the first step of this thesis, we proposed a typology of user assistance, which presents the user needs (whether novice, occasional or expert standards), and compares the different techniques and approaches of assistance that can meet these needs. Assistance needs of users are varied (discovery functionality, guiding, improving practice...). Furthermore, these needs vary depending on the application, its complexity and richness, as well as users, their objectives and their experience of the application. Techniques to meet some assistance needs can be as simple as posting messages, or more elaborate, as the use of patterns or models. Assistance approaches implement different techniques, it may be, for example, systems consultants, tutorials or Context help [**Erreur ! Source du renvoi introuvable.**].

Assistance Model. In order to propose a generic model of user assistance, we are interested in assistance models, and more particularly in generic models, independent from the application where they will be implemented. The generic model of advisor system proposed by [1] allows to designe advisor systems that can be grafted onto an existing application. This approach has been implemented in the Epitalk system, which allows the designer to define, for a given application, a suitable assistance using the advisor system. However, the applications have to be implemented in Smalltalk, and the use of Epitalk requires a good knowledge of Smalltalk and multi-agent programming, which greatly limits its scope.The generic assistance model proposed by [2] aims at actors of distance learning. It consists of a model of the task, a model of the user and the group, and a set of assistance interventions. Assistance interventions can meet the needs of users; it is associated with a set of metadata (user name, goal ...) and a set of rules of the form "If Condition, Then Action". To be reused in the context of our work, the set of proposed actions (change the interface, display messages, change the user model ...) must be enriched to meet the diverse needs of users.

User Model. To allow the personalization of the assistance, we must have information about the users. This information may include knowledge (such as a skill level in using the application), their abilities and possible disabilities (such as a hearing or view rate), and their preferences (such as the mode of assistance they prefer). All this information can be collected, deduced or provided directly by the users themselves. It constitutes a *user model*. To exploit this information about a user, it is necessary that they be expressed in the same formalism. We chose to use the profile modeling language PMDLe [3; 4]. It allows to describe the structure of our user model, *i.e.* the way data are organized in the model, and the data itself. In PMDLe, the structure may be common to several users, for example to all users of an application, while the data is specific to each user. PMDLe is already implemented in an environment able to manage (create, populate and edit) user models [4].

Personalization of the Assistance. To obtain assistance that is effective and accepted by the user, it can be useful to personalize it to suit the context and specificities of the user. Thus, we will not offer the same assistance to a novice user and an expert user, and the proposed assistance will be different for a basic or advanced functionality of the application. An approach to take into account the specificities of users (knowledge, skills, preferences...) consists in defining constraints on the user model. The profile modeling language PMDLe is associated with a model of constraints on profiles cPMDLe [5]. Currently, cPMDLe is implemented for customizing learning activities [6; 5]. Used in another context, cPMDLe can be used to personalize any kind of application using PMDLe for describing user models. For example cPMDLe allows to select users having a knowledge level "novice" for the application, or those whose hearing is between 60% and 80%.

Epiphyte Systems. An epiphyte system is a system that is grafted on another system without interfering with its operation [1]. An assistant system can be grafted to an application, to provide assistance to the users of this application. Several existing systems provide epiphyte assistance [7]. However, these advisor systems are not generic; they can only be applied to their intended applications. However, some studies propose assistance both epiphytic and generic, like the Microsoft companions [8] and the animated conversational agents of WebLéa [9] and Cantoche [10].

3   Our Approach of Assistance to User

In this section, we present our generic model of user assistance. The principle of our approach is to allow in a first step a designer to describe the assistance requested for a given application, and in a second step to provide that assistance, as specified by that description, but also personalized to each user. Our approach involves a set of epiphytes assistants (cf. Ⓐ Fig. 1), such as advisor systems or conversational agents. Thereafter, new assistants may be added to this set. To enable the use of these epiphytes assistants, they must be described using a common formalism, an assistant description language (cf. Ⓑ Fig. 1). This description will later allow our generic assistant to drive these assistants and to graft them onto the target application. This description is made only once by an expert each time a new assistant is added to the system.

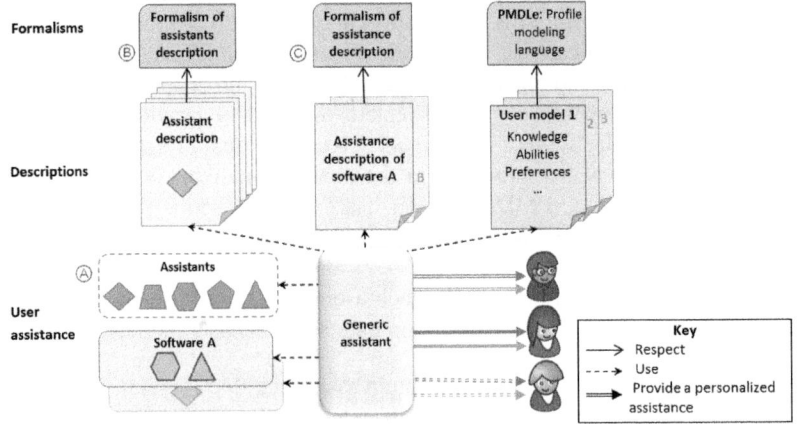

Fig. 1. Generic assistant model

To set up assistance for a given application, the designer should describe the requested assistance, using a common assistance description language, cf. © Fig. 1. Let's take the example of an application with an integrated advisor system and to which a designer wants to add a more complete assistance system, combining several assistance techniques and able to provide each user with personalized assistance. In the description of the requested assistance, the designer can specify for example that a tutorial and a conversational agent must be added to the application. It may also specify that the tutorial is recommended for novice users and available upon request to other users. The choice of the avatar of the conversational agent may depend on the user's preferences. Regarding the advisor system already integrated in the application, the designer can personalize it by specifying for example that the advisor system will frequently intervene to give simple advices on the overall functioning of the application for novice users, while it will intervene less often with expert users, but with an emphasis on very specific advices related to the current task.

The description of the assistance for an application specifies on one hand the assistance techniques that the designer wishes to implement (in addition to any assistance techniques previously integrated to the application) and on the other hand the personalization required for the assistance. To that end, the designer creates assistance rules of the forum "If Condition, then Action". In the specification of conditions, the designer can combine conditions on the user model (such as "If the user is a novice" or "If the user is blind"), with conditions on the context (such as "If the user has completed Stage X" or "If the user has clicked button Y"). In actions, the designer specifies which assistant will perform the action: so this action must respect the assistant description *i.e.*, be a possible action of this particular assistant. For example, if the assistant is a conversational agent whose description states that an action must contain a message and a set of animations (from a list of possible animations), then a possible action could be {message = "Now you can proceed to the next step", animation = "point the finger at the button Next", animation = "smile"}.

Once the assistance designer of an application has specified the description of the requested assistance, our generic assistant will assist each user accordingly. For this purpose, the generic assistant uses together the description of each assistant, the description of the requested assistance, and the user model to control epiphyte assistants when their action is required, but also to personalize any assistance system already integrated into the application as long as it is described using the common assistant description language.

4   Conclusion and Perspectives

With the increasing complexity of applications, a need to assist users of such applications has emerged, because of the wide possibilities they offer.

We presented our generic model for user assistance. This model relies on three description languages, used for describing the available assistants, the assistance requested for the application, and the user model. Then, these descriptions will be used by a generic assistant that will provide the required assistance to each user of the application, in a fully personalized manner according to the designer's choices. For that purpose, the generic assistant can appeal to different epiphyte assistants. We are now defining the formalisms for the description of assistance and for the description of epiphyte assistants. We will then implement these two formalisms in an editor aimed at designers. This editor must enable designers to express their choices but they must also be easy to use and help the designers in their task. We will finally implement a generic assistant, able to provide personalized assistance to user of any application, using the assistance description of this application. We also plan to experiment our propositions, by providing assistance to users of different applications. We will make sure that the editor we provide for designers allows them to express their choices without being too complicated. We will also make sure that the assistance provided to end-users of these applications is a real asset for them.

References

1. Paquette, G., Pachet, F., Giroux, S., Girard, J.: EpiTalk, a generic tool for the development of advisor systems. IJAIED 7, 349–370 (1996)
2. Dufresne, A., Basque, J., Paquette, G., Léonard, M., Lundgren-Cayrol, K., PromTep, S.: Vers un modèle conceptuel générique de système d'assistance pour le téléapprentissage. STICEF 10, 57–88 (2003)
3. Eyssautier-Bavay, C., Jean-Daubias, S.: PMDL: a modeling language to harmonize heterogeneous learners profiles. In: ED-MEDIA, Lisbon, Portugal (2011)
4. Ginon, B., Jean-Daubias, S., Lefevre, M.: Evolutive learners profiles. In: ED-MEDIA, Lisbon, Portugal (2011)
5. Ginon, B., Jean-Daubias, S.: Models and tools to personalize activities on learners profiles. In: ED-MEDIA, Lisbon, Portugal (2011)
6. Lefevre, M., Cordier, A., Jean-Daubias, S., Guin, N.: A Teacher-dedicated Tool Supporting Personalization of Activities. In: ED-MEDIA, Honolulu, Hawaii, pp. 1136–1141 (2009)
7. Kosba, E., Dimitrova, V., Boyle, R.D.: Using Student and Group Models to Support Teachers in Web-Based Distance Education. In: Ardissono, L., Brna, P., Mitrović, A. (eds.) UM 2005. LNCS (LNAI), vol. 3538, pp. 124–133. Springer, Heidelberg (2005)
8. Microsoft, MSAgents (2012),
   `http://www.microsoft.com/products/msagent/main.aspx`
9. Martin, J.-C., Sansonnet, J.-P.: WebLéa (2012),
   `http://perso.limsi.fr/jps/online/weblea/leaexamples/leawebsite`
10. Cantoche, Living Actor (2012),
    `http://www.cantoche.com/index.php?lang=en`

Resolving Data Sparsity and Cold Start in Recommender Systems

Guibing Guo

School of Computer Engineering
Nanyang Technological University, Singapore
gguo1@e.ntu.edu.sg

1 Research Problems

Recommender systems (RSs) are heavily used in e-commerce to provide users with high quality, personalized recommendations from a large number of choices. Collaborative filtering (CF) is a widely used technique to generate recommendations [1]. The main research problems we desire to address are the two severe issues that original CF inherently suffers from:

- *Data sparsity* arises from the phenomenon that users in general rate only a limited number of items;
- *Cold start* refers to the difficulty in bootstrapping the RSs for new users or new items.

The principle of CF is to aggregate the ratings of like-minded users. However, the reported matrix of user-item ratings is usually very sparse (up to 99%) due to users' lack of knowledge or incentives to rate items. In addition, for the new users or new items, in general, they report or receive only a few or no ratings. Both issues will prevent the CF from providing effective recommendations, because users' preference is hard to extract. Although many algorithms have been proposed to date, these issues have not been well-addressed yet.

2 Progress to Date

Due to the popularity of social networks such as Facebook, more and more researchers turn to incorporate the social relationships (e.g. trust[1]) of users to help complement users' preference in addition to item ratings. However, trust has not been well utilized so far since the improved performance of trust-based approaches is marginal. Therefore, we would like to propose a new method that incorporates trust with CF to achieve better performance.

On the other hand, with the advent of virtual worlds such as Second Life, e-commerce in virtual reality (VR) is believed to have a promising future. Since the VR accommodates richer item (product) related information than the traditional online environment, a few works (e.g. [5]) attempt to apply traditional

---

[1] Trust reflects the extent to which users' opinions are valuable in decision makings.

J. Masthoff et al. (Eds.): UMAP 2012, LNCS 7379, pp. 361–364, 2012.

recommendation methods based on the additional information. However, none of them makes good use of the features of VR, such as that users can effectively interact with 3D virtual products and human beings. We believe that VR is more likely and meaningful to be a medium that embraces users' pro-active interactions rather than a mere information source of products. Thus we propose a way to take advantage of these features to enrich the user-item matrix itself.

2.1 Incorporating Trust with Collaborative Filtering

To begin with, we seek a trust-based solution to the concerned issues of CF. Trust relationships of users are often employed in order to correlate more potential raters for the active users who require recommendations, in addition to users' ratings on items. The active user can report his evaluations of trustworthiness towards other users, and each trusted user (neighbor) can also have their own trusted neighbors. Hence a web of trust (WOT) can be constructed. It is reported that trust is positively correlated with similarity [6]. Trust-aware recommender systems [4] attract researchers' attention because trust is able to propagate through the WOT. However, trust propagation is time-consuming and the best length of propagation can only be determined empirically.

Motivated by the previous usage of trust, we propose a simple but effective method to utilize trust to find more similar users whose ratings can be aggregated to generate recommendations [2]. More specifically, the ratings of trusted neighbors will be merged to represent the preference of the active user. Note that the active user is also regarded as a trusted neighbor of himself. Formally, the weighted average of trusted neighbors' ratings on a certain item i will be calculated as follows, used as the new rating for the active user u on this item.

$$\tilde{r}_{u,i} = \frac{\sum_{v \in TN_u} t_{u,v} r_{v,i}}{\sum_{v \in TN_u} t_{u,v}} \tag{1}$$

where $\tilde{r}_{u,i}$ is the merged rating, $t_{u,v}$ is the trust user u has toward user v, and TN_u denotes the set of u's trusted neighbors (including himself).

After that, similar users will be probed using the newly formed rating profile of the active user, and traditional CF is applied to generate recommendations. At the present, only explicit trust information specified by the users themselves is made use of because explicit trust is more reliable than implicit trust in general.

Our method is demonstrated to be effective using three real-life datasets. The results show that our method achieves the best performance in terms of both accuracy and coverage comparing with other benchmarks, especially in the case of cold-start users where the greatest improvement in performance is reached. We also analyze that theoretically, our method is able to function well even in two extreme cases: 1) users have only specified trusted neighbors but not rated any items; and 2) users have only rated items but not identified any trusted neighbors. It will fail to work if and only if both trust and rating information are out of reach. In that case, information other than trust or item ratings is required to model user preference. Furthermore, trust propagation does not provide significant benefits and hence is not necessary for our method, considering the cost and issues it brings. Overall, the data sparsity and cold start problems are largely alleviated.

2.2   Recommender Systems in Virtual Reality

At present we turn to the emerging VR environment in which even richer information is available compared to 2D online environments. For example, the actual products can be represented in the 3D models which enable users to interact with the virtual products, such as viewing from different angles, zooming in and out, touching the surface, customizing the components and even trying them on. It has been reported that the virtual product experience can help users judge the product value and make a better decision prior to purchase [3]. Other features such as the sense of presence, can also enhance user's evaluation of products.

Inspired by those features, we define two new concepts called *virtual rating* and *physical rating*. The former refers to the rating that is reported during or after users' interaction with 3D virtual products prior to purchase whereas the latter corresponds to the rating that is given after users' purchase and experience the actual products. Hence, virtual ratings are the outcomes of product evaluations according to users' virtual product experience. Inversely, physical ratings are the evaluative outcomes of products in the light of real product experience, which in fact are the user-item ratings in traditional RSs. We propose a new RS that makes use of both virtual and physical ratings for recommendations.

For virtual ratings, there could be two approaches for the proposed RS to collect data: manual and automatic. Firstly, the system could provide a user interface to accept users' manual inputs of ratings. Our ongoing research is mainly focused on this approach. Secondly, the system could automatically gather users' ratings according to their emotional responses. More specifically, the positive emotions are captured in the form of electroencephalogram (EEG) signals while users are interacting with 3D virtual products prior to purchase, with the help of a real-time convenient wireless EEG headset. The virtual ratings are then calculated from the averaged relative power of the collected EEG signals.

Recommender systems can benefit from introducing virtual ratings in at least two aspects. Firstly, the data sparsity is reduced because more user-item ratings (virtual and physical) are available. Users can form concrete opinions towards the products they interact with in VR, though they may not have the intention to purchase, which may depend on many other factors in addition to product value, such as consumption need or goal, income or salary, time constraints and so on. Users may interact with lots of products, but only purchase a small portion of them, e.g., users may experience different alternatives before choosing one of them. In most cases, users are not willing to express their opinions about the purchased products unless they are well motivated by good incentive mechanisms. In a word, physical ratings occupy only a small proportion of all products whereas virtual ratings may cover a wider range. The proposed RS will have a sound rating richness and reduce its reliance on incentive mechanisms.

Secondly, the cold start problem is largely alleviated. For users who have virtual and/or physical ratings, their preference can be extracted based on which similar users can be found and recommendations can be generated. Since the preference is more complete, the recommendations generated will be more accurate. Similarly, for the new products, as long as there are some virtual ratings (no need to be purchased) available, they are made possible for recommendations.

3   Future Research

For our trust-based recommender systems, majority strategy is another way to merge the ratings of trusted neighbors, which works well if the ratings are diverse. Thus we would like to investigate how the majority strategy can possibly improve our previous method, especially when the item receives many ratings.

The main future work is to design an effective CF that incorporates both virtual and physical ratings to make better recommendations. Basically, virtual ratings can be utilized at least two ways: 1) separately to form another user-item rating matrix to generate recommendations; or 2) transformed into physical ratings somehow and integrated into the original user-item rating matrix to fill in the missing values. In order to determine the best way to utilize virtual ratings, we need to understand them more deeply. In principle, there are two fundamental research concerns. The first is the method that users use to evaluate product values in VR and the factors that are taken into considerations. The other is the connections and distinctions between virtual and physical ratings. To validate the soundness and effectiveness of the proposed method, we may need to build up a prototype of virtual malls and recruit real users for ratings collection.

Since VR also supports users' interaction with other users in real time and face to face, another line of future research focuses on the social (trust) relationships among users. Although we have successfully employed explicit trust, it is not clear whether the method is applicable to VR. Furthermore, now that virtual ratings are introduced, it is worth investigating whether trust can be built upon virtual ratings. In that case, trust usage will be even more complex.

References

1. Adomavicius, G., Tuzhilin, A.: Toward the next generation of recommender systems: A survey of the state-of-the-art and possible extensions, pp. 734–749 (2005)
2. Guo, G., Zhang, J., Thalmann, D.: A Simple But Effective Method to Incorporate Trusted Neighbors in Recommender Systems. In: Masthoff, J., et al. (eds.) UMAP 2012. LNCS, vol. 7379. Springer, Heidelberg (2012)
3. Jiang, Z., Benbasat, I.: Virtual product experience: Effects of visual and functional control of products on perceived diagnosticity and flow in electronic shopping. Journal of Management Information Systems 21(3), 111–147 (2004)
4. Massa, P., Avesani, P.: Trust-aware recommender systems. In: Proceedings of the ACM Conference on Recommender Systems, pp. 17–24 (2007)
5. Shah, F., Bell, P., Sukthankar, G.: A destination recommendation system for virtual worlds. In: Proceedings of the Twenty-First International Florida Artificial Intelligence Research Society Conference (2010)
6. Ziegler, C., Golbeck, J.: Investigating interactions of trust and interest similarity. Decision Support Systems 43(2), 460–475 (2007)

Data Mining for Adding Adaptive Interventions to Exploratory and Open-Ended Environments

Samad Kardan

Department of Computer Science, University of British Columbia
2366 Main Mall, Vancouver, BC, V6T1Z4, Canada
skardan@cs.ubc.ca

Abstract. Due to the open ended nature of the interaction with exploratory environments (EE) for learning, it is not trivial to add mechanisms for providing adaptive support to users. Our goal is to devise and evaluate a data mining approach for providing adaptive interventions that help users to achieve better task performance during the interaction with an EE.

Keywords: Educational Data Mining, Adaptive User Interfaces, Adaptive Interventions, Exploratory Environments.

1   Background and Motivation

Advances in HCI continuously aid the creation of novel interfaces to support education and training. For example, Interactive Simulations (IS hereafter) are increasingly used as Exploratory/open-ended Environments (EE henceforth) for learning. These environments are designed to foster exploratory and active learning by giving students the opportunity to proactively experiment with concrete examples of concepts and processes they have learned in theory. However, it has been shown that some students may not learn well from this relatively unstructured and open-ended form of interaction (e.g., [2]), because they lack the skills needed to explore effectively and thus end up being overwhelmed by the large amount of available options compared to more structured learning activities (e.g., [1]). These students can benefit from having additional guidance when they interact with an IS (e.g., [3]). We plan to provide this guidance in the form of adaptive interventions. Implementing adaptive interventions requires adding two components to an EE: *(i)* a **user model** that determines if and when to intervene, with additional information on which interventions are appropriate at a given time, and *(ii)* an **intervention mechanism** that can deliver different types of interventions based on the assessment of the user model.

A user modeling approach that has been extensively used in learning environments that support structured problem solving activities is to rely on domain experts to identify the relevant knowledge and behaviors to include in the model. This expert-based approach, however, has several disadvantages. First, it can be costly and time consuming (e.g., [4]). Second, it may be unfeasible in EE because the novelty of these systems makes it difficult to judge a priori which ensemble of user interaction behaviors are conducive to better/worse learning and should be represented in the user model. Finally, expert-based user models tend to be domain and application-specific

J. Masthoff et al. (Eds.): UMAP 2012, LNCS 7379, pp. 365–368, 2012.

and thus have limited transferability. All these issues make an expert-based approach less likely to succeed for EE (e.g., [5], [6]).

The alternative method for user modeling which is less reliant on expert knowledge, is to use machine learning techniques on user-related data. This approach has become very popular recently leading to a great increase in publications in Educational Data Mining (EDM) [7]. A common source of data that has been used to build user models in EDM is interface action logs (e.g., [8, 9]). More recently, there has been increasing interest in exploring eye-tracking data as an additional source of information in user modeling for ELE. (e.g., [6, 10, 11]). However, there has been so far very limited work on how to user these data-based user models to provide adaptive support within an EE. Data mining approaches have been used for generating hints during more structured problem solving activities (e.g., [12]). Intention to use generated models/patterns for providing a personalized experience in an interactive learning environment is stated in some works (e.g., [8, 9]), but to the best of our knowledge there is no educational EE in which both adaptive interventions and the user model activating them are generated by mining the user interaction data. Our proposed research aims to fill this gap.

2   Goals and Objectives

The goal of our research is to devise and evaluate a framework for adding adaptive support to EE. Our approach relies on using data mining techniques to *(i)* cluster users into classes that correspond to different levels of task performance and *(ii)* identify distinctive behaviours of each class. These clusters and the corresponding behaviours are then used to create a *user model* that can classify new users as they interact with the target EE. The output of the user modeling process (i.e. predicted user performance along with the interaction behaviours that cause it) will be used by an *intervention mechanism* that provides adaptive support during the interaction if the detected user behaviours are associated with suboptimal task performance. We expect that an EE with user-adaptive interventions will be more effective compared to its non-adaptive counterpart. To achieve the aforementioned research goal, we need to answer following questions:

- **Q1:** Is it possible to cluster users into different performance groups based on the similarity of their behaviours, and find which patterns are responsible for the different performance levels?
- **Q2:** Given interface actions and gaze data as two sources of user data, how do they compare as predictors of user performance?
- **Q3:** When both sources are available, is there any benefit in combining them? If so, how can they be combined effectively?
- **Q4:** How can suitable *types* of adaptive interventions be derived from the detected interaction patterns
- **Q5:** What are suitable ways of delivering the types of adaptive interventions identified in Q4 (e.g., subtle vs. assertive delivery)?
- **Q6:** How effective are these adaptive interventions?

So far, we have conducted a user study to collected both interface and eye-gaze data for an EE. We have also developed a user modeling framework [13] that showed positive findings in relation to Q1 for both user actions [13] and eye-gaze data [14].

3   Approach and Expected Contributions

This work extends existing work in the EDM community by using a data-based user modeling approach to provide adaptive, real-time interventions in EE. This involves covering all four steps of the cycle of applying EDM to a domain [15]:

— **Collecting user-related data**, in our case both interface actions and eye-gaze data, by running appropriate user experiments.
— **Pre-processing** the collected data. In our research, this step will require new methods for *(i)* validating inherently noisy gaze data, and *(ii)* meaningfully combine interface and gaze data [Q3].
— **Applying data mining techniques** to identify clusters of users with effective vs. ineffective interaction patterns, and use these to build an online user model that can assess in real-time the effectiveness of a user's interactions with an EE. [Q1, Q2, Q3]. Some of the challenges we face in this step include: *(i)* clustering of sparse feature vectors, *(ii)* defining an appropriate multi-criteria objective function to identify meaningful user clusters with similar behaviours and learning performance, and *(iii)* using association rule mining for building user models that can accurately classify users in real time during interaction with the ELE
— **Interpret, evaluate and deploy the results:** In our work, this step includes *(i)* analyzing the discovered behaviour patterns and evaluating the performance of the generated user models; *(ii)* devising a method to derive effective adaptive interventions based on the discovered patterns (e.g. providing *explicit help* on how to use at best the available EE functionalities, vs. scaffolding adequate usage via *interface adaptation*) [Q4, Q5]; *(iii)* evaluating the effectiveness of this approach by conducting a user study to compare an adaptive and a non-adaptive version of the same EE [Q6].

To summarize, this work is expected to make the following contributions:

— An in-depth and inclusive evaluation of using data mining on user interaction data for providing adaptive interventions within an EE. We will quantitatively evaluate our method in different stages of the process including: *(i)* meaningfulness of user clustering based on the interaction data; *(ii)* performance of generated user models; *(iii)*, effectiveness of the adaptive interventions derived by the proposed approach .
— Novel insights on using eye-gaze data for modeling user performance in EE, including: *(i)* identifying and validating meaningful eye-gaze features, *(ii)* evaluating gaze data as a predictor of user performance with an EE and *(iii)* comparing/combining gaze and action data as performance predictors.
— A dataset containing the interface actions and eye-gaze data of 45 users interacting with an EE that will be made available to the EDM research community.

Acknowledgement. This research is done under the supervision of Dr. Cristina Conati at the Computer Science Department of the University of British Columbia. It is funded by the GRAND NCE network (projects AFFEVAl and SIMUL)

References

1. Ploetzner, R., Lippitsch, S., Galmbacher, M., Heuer, D., Scherrer, S.: Students' difficulties in learning from dynamic visualisations and how they be overcome. Computers in Human Behavior 25, 56–65 (2009)
2. Shute, V.J.: A comparison of learning environments: All that glitters. In: Computers as Cognitive Tools, pp. 47–73. Lawrence Erlbaum Associates, Inc., Hillsdale (1993)
3. De Jong, T.: Technological Advances in Inquiry Learning. Science 312, 532–533 (2006)
4. Beck, J., Stern, M., Haugsjaa, E.: Applications of AI in education. Crossroads 3, 11–15 (1996)
5. Ting, C.-Y., Zadeh, M.R.B., Chong, Y.-K.: A Decision-Theoretic Approach to Scientific Inquiry Exploratory Learning Environment. In: Ikeda, M., Ashley, K.D., Chan, T.-W. (eds.) ITS 2006. LNCS, vol. 4053, pp. 85–94. Springer, Heidelberg (2006)
6. Amershi, S., Conati, C.: Combining Unsupervised and Supervised Classification to Build User Models for Exploratory Learning Environments. Journal of Educational Data Mining 18–71 (2009)
7. Romero, C., Ventura, S.: Educational Data Mining: A Review of the State of the Art. IEEE Transactions on Systems, Man, and Cybernetics, Part C: Applications and Reviews 40, 601–618 (2010)
8. Köck, M., Paramythis, A.: Activity sequence modelling and dynamic clustering for personalized e-learning. User Modeling and User-Adapted Interaction 21, 51–97 (2011)
9. Shanabrook, D.H., Cooper, D.G., Woolf, B.P., Arroyo, I.: Identifying High-Level Student Behavior Using Sequence-based Motif Discovery. In: Proceedings of 3rd International Conference on Educational Data Mining, Pittsburgh, PA, USA, pp. 191–200 (2010)
10. Eivazi, S., Bednarik, R.: Predicting Problem-Solving Behavior and Expertise Levels from Visual Attention Data. In: The 2nd Workshop on the Eye Gaze in Intelligent Human Machine Interaction, Palo Alto, California, USA, pp. 9–16 (2011)
11. Perera, D., Kay, J., Koprinska, I., Yacef, K., Zaïane, O.R.: Clustering and Sequential Pattern Mining of Online Collaborative Learning Data. IEEE Trans. on Knowl. and Data Eng. 21, 759–772 (2009)
12. Barnes, T., Stamper, J., Lehman, L., Croy, M.: A pilot study on logic proof tutoring using hints generated from historical student data. In: Educational Data Mining 2008: Proceedings of 1st International Conference on Educational Data Mining (2008)
13. Kardan, S., Conati, C.: A Framework for Capturing Distinguishing User Interaction Behaviours in Novel Interfaces. In: Proceedings of the 4th International Conference on Educational Data Mining, Eindhoven, The Netherlands, pp. 159–168 (2011)
14. Kardan, S., Conati, C.: Exploring Gaze Data for Determining User Learning with an Interactive Simulation. In: Masthoff, J., et al. (eds.) UMAP 2012. LNCS, vol. 7379. Springer, Heidelberg (2012)
15. Romero, C., Ventura, S., García, E.: Data mining in course management systems: Moodle case study and tutorial. Computers & Education 51, 368–384 (2008)

Formalising Human Mental Workload as Non-monotonic Concept for Adaptive and Personalised Web-Design

Luca Longo

School of Computer Science and Statistics, Trinity College Dublin
longol@scss.tcd.ie

Abstract. Web Design has been evolving with Web-based systems becoming more complex and structured due to the delivery of personalised information adapted to end-users. Although information presented can be useful and well formatted, people have little mental workload available for dealing with unusable systems. Subjective mental workload assessments tools are usually adopted to measure the impact of Web-tasks upon end-users thanks to their ease of use and are aimed at supporting design practices. The Nasa Task Load Index subjective procedure has been taken as a reference technique for measuring mental workload, but it has a background in aircraft cockpits, supervisory and process control environments. We argue that the tool is not fully appropriate for dealing with Web-information tasks, characterised by a wide spectrum of contexts of use, cognitive factors and individual user differences such as skill, background, emotional state and motivation. Furthermore, in this model, inputs are averaged without considering their mutual interactions and relations. We propose to see human mental workload as non-monotonic concept and to model it via argumentation theory. The evaluation strategy includes coparisons with the NASA-TLX in terms of statistical correlation, sensitivity, diagnosticity, selectivity and reliability.

Keywords: Human Mental Workload, Non-monotonic Reasoning, Argumentation Theory, Human-Computer Interaction, Web Design.

1 Introduction

Interaction and Web Design have been continuously evolving with Web-sites becoming more complex and structured. This shift is mainly caused by the increasing degree of personalisation of information presented to end-users and by the increasing adaptivity new interactive Web-based systems incorporate. Although information presented can be useful, interesting and well formatted, people have little mental workload available for dealing with unusable interfaces [1]. A burdensome interface has a negative impact on the analysis of data and decision-making processes of individuals consuming information over the Web. Similarly, boring and monotonous interfaces are skipped and avoided by end-users as not

J. Masthoff et al. (Eds.): UMAP 2012, LNCS 7379, pp. 369–373, 2012.

engaging. Designers are usually focused on creating user-friendly interfaces. However, poor usability impedes individuals to properly seek and consume information, and in turn Web-sites loose visitors [2]. If designers can measure the mental workload of end-users, during interaction, then specific structural interface or system changes can be evaluated in the design process. Interfaces that generate low mental workload on end-users (underload), are usually perceived being boring and not interesting. High mental workload (overload), instead, is synonymous of complex and tiresome interfaces. Both the levels should be avoided, bringing workload to proper fitting load. Mental workload assessment techniques can be small scale, representing a discount and cheap method for enhancing testings of usability. Nasa Task Load Index [3] is a subjective mental workload assessment technique adopted in Web-based systems. Although it has been taken as a reference tool for its simplicity, it has a background in aircraft cockpits, supervisory and process control environments. In this proposal, we argue the tool is not fully appropriate for dealing with Web-information tasks, characterised by a wide pool of cognitive and environmental factors affecting mental workload. NASA-Tlx a multi-dimensional rating procedure that infers an overall workload index based on a weighted average of ratings on six sub-scales: mental, physical and temporal demands, own performance, effort and frustration. We argue that this set of factors is limited to properly assess workload on Web-tasks because it does not consider individual differences such as the skills, the background and the motivation of operators along with the context of use. Furthermore, in this model, inputs are averaged without considering their mutual interactions and relations.

1.1   Human Mental Workload

Human Mental Workload (MWL) is a multifaceted complex construct mainly applied in psychology. A plethora of definitions exists in the literature [4,5,6,7]. Intuitively, mental or cognitive workload is the amount of mental work necessary for a person to complete a task over a given period of time. Generally, it is not a inherent property, rather it emerges from the interaction between the requirements of a task, the circumstances under which it is performed, and the skills, behaviour and perceptions of the operator [3]. All these factors can be combined in different ways, supporting and contradicting each other. Some of them can be uncertain and contraddicting. For this reason we propose to see the construct of mental workload as a non-monotonic concept. The basic idea of non-monotonic inferences is that, when more information is obtained about a concept, some inference that were earlier reasonable may be no longer so. In modeling mental workload, pieces of evidence can be aggregated following a defeasible reasoning process, and the conclusion they support can change in the light of new evidence. For instance, if the time spent for executing a task is known to be high, this is a reason to believe that the mental workload elicited is high as well. However, if the objective activity on the same task is also available, and it is known to be low, then there is a new reason to infer the mental workload is low. Yet, if the end-user is known to be not skilled, then is believed that workload is high, thus justifying the high time for executing the task. Further evidence can be part of this reasoning process [8], known to be defeasible due to the fact that arguments are not infallible, instead they can be defeated by new information.

1.2 Argumentation Theory

Argumentation theory has become an important topic in the field of Artificial Intelligence and Computer Science, resulting from a multi-disciplinary approach at the intersection of Philosophy and Law, and with elements drawn from Psychology and Sociology. It systematically studies how pieces of evidence, built as arguments, can be expressed, sustained or discarded in a defeasible reasoning process, as well as the validity of the conclusions reached [9]. Argumentation theory gained importance with the introduction of formal and computable models, inspired by human-like reasoning. These models extended classical reasoning models based on deductive logic that appeared increasingly inadequate for problems requiring non-monotonic reasoning, commonly used by humans, as well as explanatory reasoning, not available in standard non-monotonic logics such as default logic [10]. Argumentation Theory implements non-monotonic reasoning [11] that differs from standard deductive reasoning because in the former a conclusion can be retracted in the light of new pieces of evidence, whereas in the latter the set of conclusions always grows. Argumentation lends itself to explanatory reasoning because argumentative reasoning is composed of modular and intuitive steps, thus avoiding the monolithic approach of many traditional logics for non-monotonic reasoning. *The reasoning required in defining and modeling the concept of human mental workload is both non-monotonic and explanatory.* Argumentation theory is also suitable when the available information may be uncertain and conflicting. This is the case of mental workload, where there may be relevant but partially uncertain and conflicting evidence.

2 Proposal

We propose to extend the well-known work of Dung, on abstract argumentation frameworks [10], for rationally measuring mental workload and for aggregating available evidence, in a given Web-context, towards a unique representative level of workload. Practically, we propose to design a context-aware and user-centered framework in which human mental workload can be defined, measured, analysed and explained taking into consideration individual differences and contexts of use. The research question **RQ** is:

> **As human mental workload can be seen as a non-monotonic complex construct, what is the impact of non-monotonic reasoning techniques in approximating it as a usable computational concept and in enhancing the quality of human mental workload assessments?**

Two sub-research questions can be defined: **sRQ1**: To what extent can Argumentation Theory support the measurement of subjective mental workload? **sRQ2**: To what extent can an argument-based model foster/enhance the assessment of subject mental workload in Web-based information systems?

3   Evaluation Strategy

The evaluation is aimed at assessing the quality of the outcomes of the arguments-based computational model by means of comparisons against the outcomes of the Nasa-TLX model in terms of statistical correlation and differences in sensitivity, diagnosticity, selectivity and reliability. This evaluation process is as following:

1. selection of a set of Web-interfaces X;
2. design of a set T of Web-tasks for each x in X;
3. implementation of structural changes on each x in X resulting in a set X^{mod};
4. execution of designed tasks T by two groups of end-users on X & X^{mod};
5. subjective assessment of workloads, after execution of tasks T, both by the designed arguments-based model (AM) and the Nasa-TLX;
6. evaluation of AM comparing its outputs against the ones of Nasa-TLX's (on X & X^{mod}) by means of statistical correlation;
7. evaluation of the sensitivity, diagnosticity, selectivity and reliability of AM.

4   Key contributions

The research will contribute to the field of Web design, proposing a novel executable paradigm capable of human mental workload assessments in the field of Web-based information systems. The expected outcomes are to produce an applicable context-aware and user-centered methodology more appropriate for assessing subjective mental workload in Web scenarios. The contribution will provide reference and case studies for the application of a tool useful for promoting mental workload-aware Web systems contributing to the appreciation and support of design, personalisation and adaptation practices in HCI.

References

1. Redish, J.: Expanding usability testing to evaluate complex systems. Journal of Usability Studies 2(3), 102–111 (2007)
2. Nielsen, J.: Designing Web Usability: The Practice of Simplicity. New Riders Publishing, Indianapolis (1999)
3. Kantowitz, B.: Development of nasa-tlx (task load index): Results of empirical and theoretical research. Human Mental Workload 51, 139–183 (1988)
4. Hancock, P.A., Meshkati, N.: Human Mental Workload. North Holland Ed. (1988)
5. Wickens, D., McCarley, J.: Applied Attention Theory. CRC (2008)
6. Cain, B.: A review of the mental workload literature. Report (2007)
7. Gopher, D., Donchin, E.: Workload: An examination of the concept. Handbook of Perception and Human Performance 2(41), 1–49 (1986)

8. Baroni, P., Guida, G., Mussi, S.: Full non-monotonicity: a new perspective in defeasible reasoning. In: European Symp. on Intelligent Techniques, pp. 58–62 (1997)
9. Toni, F.: Argumentative agents. In: Proc. of Multiconference on Computer Science and Information Technology, pp. 223–229 (2010)
10. Dung, P.M.: On the acceptability of arguments and its fundamental role in non-monotonic reasoning, logic programming and n-person games. Artificial Intelligence 77, 321–357 (1995)
11. Brewka, G., Niemel, I., Truszczynski, M.: Non-monotonic reasoning. In: Handbook of Knowledge Representation, pp. 239–284 (2007)

Detecting, Acquiring and Exploiting Contextual Information in Personalized Services

Ante Odić

University of Ljubljana Faculty of Electrical Engineering,
Tržaška 25, Ljubljana, Slovenia
ante.odic@ldos.fe.uni-lj.si

Abstract. The PhD research presented in this paper addresses some of
the problems involved in creating a context-aware personalized service.
Our main interest is in the steps of defining, detecting, acquiring and
using real and relevant context of users. Our goals are to: collect and
publish a context-rich movie recommender database, add theoretical requirements for contextual information in existing definitions of context,
develop a methodology for relevant-context detection and inspect the
impact of relevant and irrelevant context on the rating prediction using
the matrix-factorization algorithm. This paper presents the work done
so far and future plans with open issues.

Keywords: user modeling, recommender systems, contextual information.

1 Introduction

Incorporating contextual information in recommender system (RS) has been a
popular research topic over the past decade. Contextual information is defined
as information that can be used to describe the situation and the environment
of the entities involved in such a system [1], and has shown to improve the
recommendation results in context-aware recommender systems (CARS), as well
as other personalized services [2].

However, there are still a number of issues concerning the definition, acquisition, detection and modeling of these dynamic information [3]. It is not easy to
decide which contextual information to use. Information that is relevant in one
system might be irrelevant in others [4]. Contextual information that does not
have a significant contribution to explaining the variance in the ratings could degrade the prediction, since it could play the role of noise [5]. For that reason, we
should be able to predict and later detect whether a specific piece of information
should be acquired and used or not.

The issue of assessing the usefulness of certain contextual information has
been already addressed. The authors in [6] used the paired t-test to detect which
contextual information is useful in their database; however, this test can be used
only if certain assumptions are met by the data. In [7] the χ^2 test was used for the
detection of the relevant context; however, this test could be inappropriate for

J. Masthoff et al. (Eds.): UMAP 2012, LNCS 7379, pp. 374–377, 2012.

small sample sizes, i.e., for new systems and the cold-start problem. The authors in [8] conducted a context-relevance assessment to determine the influence of some contextual conditions on the users' ratings in the tourist domain, by asking users to imagine a given contextual condition and evaluate the influence of that condition. However, as they state, such an approach is problematic, since the users rate differently in real and supposed contexts [9].

In addition, several discussions on the context-aware topic were raised at the RECSYS2011 conference's workshops [10] and [11]. The question remains which pieces of contextual information should be included in the databases and how to assess the context quality in the existing databases, such as Moviepilot, Yahoo! Music, Movielense, etc.

The aim of this study is to provide the theoretical background that will help predict which information is contextual and, as such, could be used in a context-aware service. In addition we will provide a methodology for the detection of relevant pieces of contextual information in the early stage of the data acquisition, that will not have the limitations of the aforementioned related work, and inspect the impact of the context relevancy on the recommendations.

2   Goals to Achieve

Contextual information can improve the recommendations since it takes the description of the situation, in which the user consumed the item, into account. However, from all the available pieces of contextual information we should be able to identify the relevant ones, which do contribute to explaining the variance in the users' decision making process. For this reason we are interested in achieving the following goals in our study:

Extending the Definition of Context. We identified several important issues concerning the time dimension of contextual information during our studies (e.g., specific context changes several time during the consumption of the item, different stages during the user-item interaction which all have different context, etc.). Since these issues can lead to the acquisition of the irrelevant contextual information, we would like to extend the existing definition with the list of requirements that should insure avoiding the irrelevant information in some extent.

Acquiring a Context Rich Database. The existing databases are scarce in contextual information so a real data with multiple contextual variables is needed for our research.

Context Relevancy Detection. Contextual variables that explain the part of the unexplained variance in users' decision (i.e., ratings) should be detected by using statistical methods with power analysis that are appropriate for a specific dataset.

Assessment from Users' Opinion vs. Detection on the Data. We are interested in inspecting whether users are aware of what influences their decision and could the assessment from users' opinion provide the insight on which pieces of contextual information to use.

Impact of the Detection on the Rating Prediction. We want to evaluate the impact of the different detection methods on the recommendation results, by using the real (not hypothetical) consumption data.

3 Work Done So Far

We created an online application for rating movies (`www.ldos.si/recommender.html`). In addition to providing a rating for a movie consumed, users fill in a questionnaire created to explicitly acquire the contextual information describing the situation during the consumption stage of the user-item interaction. Ratings and contextual information are provided immediately after the consumption. Our context movie database (LDOS-CoMoDa) [12] has been in development since 15.9.2010. It contains three main groups of information: general user information, item metadata and contextual information. The pieces of the contextual information in our database are: **Time, Day, Season, Location** (home, public, friend's), **Weather, Social** (alone, partner, friend/s, colleagues, parents, public, family), **End Emotion, Dominant Emotion** (six basic emotions and neutral), **Mood, Physical State** (healthy, ill), **Decision** (user's choice, other) and **Interaction** (first, n-th). Up to this date we collected 2001 ratings from 112 users for 1109 items. The database is available for other researches.

In order to acquire the users' opinion on which contextual information is relevant, we created an online survey, which was answered by 72 subjects. Once the survey data was acquired we assessed which contextual information is relevant and which is irrelevant.

The relevancy of each contextual variable in the LDOS-CoMoDa database was tested by statistical testing. We also used the power analysis which proved to be important in order to avoid rejecting relevant context. For the detection, we used the Pearson's χ^2 test, the Freeman-Halton test, and the Kruskal-Wallis ANOVA test. The decision which test to use depends on the data and the assumptions of each test.

The problem of determining how well the results from the assessment and the detection match, is basically the problem of determining the inter-annotator agreement with two annotators: assessment from survey and detection from rating data. We also measured how well does each approach determine relevant context. From these results we concluded that the users are not always aware of what influences their decisions, and that detection performs much better than the assessment.

We inspected the impact of relevant and irrelevant context on the rating prediction by incorporating context in the matrix factorization (MF) algorithm. We have implemented and tested different contextualized models with MF, each piece of contextual information at the time and multiple context at once.

4 Contributions

By addressing the described problems we believe we can improve the understanding of the contextual information and its' impact on the recommendations. We believe that our findings and the methods developed will help answer the question which data to acquire, how to insure the quality of the acquired contextual information, how to avoid using and spending resources on acquiring those pieces of information that are irrelevant and could deteriorate the results of CARS, and how to incorporate such relative contextual information into the recommendation algorithms.

Acknowledgments. I would like to thank my supervisor Andrej Košir and colleague Marko Tkalčič for all the guidance. I also thank my colleagues Matevž Kunaver and Tomaž Požrl for the help with creating the online application.

References

1. Abowd, G.D., Dey, A.K., Brown, P.J., Davies, N., Smith, M., Steggles, P.: Towards a Better Understanding of Context and Context-Awareness. In: Gellersen, H.-W. (ed.) HUC 1999. LNCS, vol. 1707, pp. 304–307. Springer, Heidelberg (1999)
2. Toutain, F., Bouabdallah, A., Zemek, R., Daloz, C.: Interpersonal Context-Aware Communication Services. IEEE Communications Magazine, 68–74 (January 2011)
3. Yujie, Z., Licai, W.: Some Challenges for Context-aware Recommender Systems. In: 2010 5th International Conference on Computer Science and Education (ICCSE), pp. 362–365 (2010)
4. Dey, A.K.: Understanding and Using Context. Personal and Ubiquitous Computing 5(1), 4–7 (2001)
5. Baltrunas, L., Ludwig, B., Ricci, F.: Matrix Factorization Techniques for Context Aware Recommendation. In: Proceedings of the Fifth ACM Conference on Recommender Systems, pp. 301–304 (2010)
6. Adomavicius, G., Sankaranarayanan, R., Sen, S., Tuzhilin, A.: Incorporating contextual information in recommender systems using a multidimensional approach. ACM Transactions on Information Systems (TOIS) 23(1), 103–145 (2005)
7. Liu, L., Lecue, F., Mehandjiev, N., Xu, L.: Using Context Similarity for Service Recommendation. In: 2010 IEEE Fourth International Conference on Semantic Computing, pp. 277–284 (September 2010)
8. Baltrunas, L., Ludwig, B., Peer, S., Ricci, F.: Context relevance assessment and exploitation in mobile recommender systems. In: Personal and Ubiquitous Computing, pp. 1–20 (June 2011)
9. Ono, C., Takishima, Y., Motomura, Y., Asoh, H.: Context-Aware Preference Model Based on a Study of Difference between Real and Supposed Situation Data. In: Houben, G.-J., McCalla, G., Pianesi, F., Zancanaro, M. (eds.) UMAP 2009. LNCS, vol. 5535, pp. 102–113. Springer, Heidelberg (2009)
10. 2nd challenge on context-aware movie recommendation of the 5th acm recsys conference (October 2011), http://2011.camrachallenge.com.
11. 3rd cars workshop of the 5th acm recsys conference (October 2011), http://cars-workshop.org
12. Košir, A., Odic, A., Kunaver, M., Tkalcic, M., Tasic, J.F.: Database for contextual personalization. ELEKTROTEHNISKI VESTNIK 78(5), 270–274 (2011)

Multi-source Provenance-aware User Interest Profiling on the Social Semantic Web

Fabrizio Orlandi

Digital Enterprise Research Institute,
National University of Ireland, Galway
fabrizio.orlandi@deri.org

Abstract. The creation of accurate user profiles of interest across heterogeneous websites is a fundamental step for personalisation, recommendations and analysis of social networks. The opportunities offered by the Web of Data and Semantic Web technologies introduce new interesting challenges. In particular, the main benefits for user profiling techniques are given by the extensive amount of already available and structured information and the solution to the "cold start" problem. On the other hand it is difficult to manage a massive "open corpus" such as the Web of Data and select only the relevant features and sources from an heterogeneous collection of datasets. Hence we propose semantic technologies for interlinking social websites and provenance management on the Web of Data to retrieve accurate information about data producers. The goal is to build comprehensive user profiles based on qualitative and quantitative measures about user activities across social sites.

Keywords: Social Web, Semantic Web, User Modelling, User Profiles, Web of Data, Provenance of Data.

1 Introduction

The extraction, analysis and representation of information about users' knowledge and activities on the Web plays an important role for software systems providing personalisation and recommendations to their users. The demand for personalisation on social media websites, search engines, e-commerce websites, etc. is clearly growing and becoming an essential part of every relevant web service. The challenges for web service providers are to provide accurate recommendations and personalisation without having to explicitly ask for users' input or make users wait for valuable recommendations only after a long initial training period on the system (the "cold start" problem). To overcome these challenges it is important to create accurate user models and integrate relevant information about users from different sources on the Web [3]. In this regard the Web of Data is certainly a valid and extensive source of information for profiling and recommendation algorithms. The Web of Data offers structured data from different domains and communities. It provides easily accessible and machine readable data that can help solving the "cold start" problem and enriching the level of detail of user profiles. However one of the main challenges in dealing

J. Masthoff et al. (Eds.): UMAP 2012, LNCS 7379, pp. 378–381, 2012.

with the Web of Data is to select only the relevant features and sources [2]. Especially in the social web context, where content is usually created by users themselves, it changes frequently and it is spread across multiple heterogeneous social sites. In this context *provenance of data* is a building block for: establishing data trust and quality measures, the knowledge acquisition/filtering process and the user profiling phase [4]. Moreover, semantic annotations and reasoning provide a solution to the problem of selecting only the relevant information.

Research Goals

The purpose of our research is to investigate: (i) how to extract relevant information from social media websites and make it available following the Linked Data principles; (ii) how to use the Web of Data as a global open corpus for personalisation purposes; (iii) the role of provenance on the Web of Data and how to use it for user profiling; (iv) how to improve the current user profiling and personalisation techniques leveraging the potentialities of Linked Data, provenance of data and Social Web Science.

2   Research Contributions

Following a state of the art review for the research areas of user modelling and personalisation, especially in relation with the Semantic Web field, our contributions in the first two years of research focused on the following:

1) The development of a framework for the semantic representation and data management of wikis. In particular we built and efficient application with a simple user-interface enabling semantic searching and browsing capabilities on top of different interlinked wikis. We described how we designed a common model for representing social and structural wiki features and how we extracted semantic data from heterogeneous wikis [6].

2) A solution for representing and managing provenance of data from Wikipedia (and other wikis) using Semantic Web technologies. In particular we provided a specific lightweight ontology for provenance in wikis. Then, a framework for the extraction of provenance data from Wikipedia has been implemented, as well as an application for accessing the generated data in a meaningful way and exposing it to the Web of Data.

3) An approach for modelling and managing provenance on DBpedia (one of the largest datasets on the Web of Data) using Wikipedia edits, and making this information available on the Web of Data. For this purpose a modelling solution, an information extraction framework and a provenance-computation system have been implemented [7].

4) A Semantic Web approach to filter public microblog posts matching interests from personalised user profiles. Our approach includes automatic generation of multi-domain and personalised user profiles of interest, filtering Twitter stream based on the generated profiles and delivering them in real-time [5].

5) A system that allows users to set fine-grained privacy preferences for the creation of privacy-aware faceted user profiles on the Social Web.

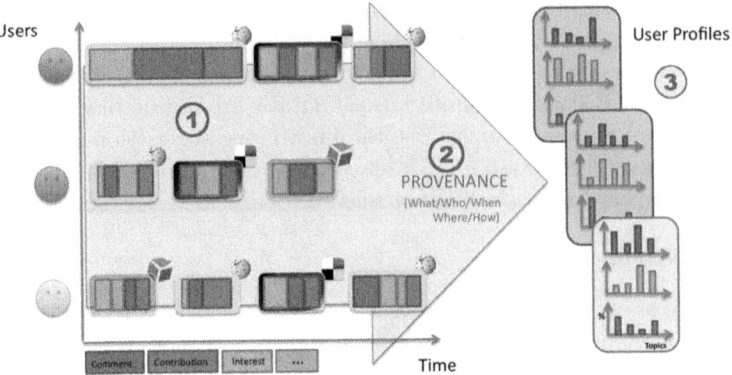

Fig. 1. The complete profiling process: from user activities on heterogeneous social media websites (1), to their provenance representation (2), do the data aggregation and analysis (3)

3   Current and Future Work

The studies conducted on the use of semantics for interlinking social websites and subsequently on provenance on the Web of Data provide us the necessary baseline for our current work. In particular we focus on building comprehensive user profiles based on quantitative and qualitative measures about user activities across different social websites. Provenance of data is particularly useful to evaluate on each different website and/or dataset the type and amount of contributions to be attributed to a particular user. This would allow us to infer expertise, interests and qualitative estimations on users' activities.

More in detail, we are now focusing on user profiling algorithms for Wikipedia users that take into account the different possible types of contributions on that wiki. The different types of contributions are not only those that involve changes in Wikipedia articles' content but also those that result in changes on the Web of Data, in this case in the DBpedia dataset. Every edit in Wikipedia that involves structural features of the Wikipedia articles, results in a change in the DBpedia dataset. Hence we are currently investigating the relevancy of those edits compared to the other types.

Moreover one of our current activities involves the real-time user profiling and personalisation on Twitter. The aim is to provide a user profiling framework building user profiles of interests across different social websites. These user profiles can then be used for personalising and filtering social web streams of messages such as the Twitter stream (see also [1]). We plan to implement a framework that manages user models from different applications starting from Wikipedia and integrating it to other social media websites. Specific ontologies will be used to represent and connect user models from different applications in an interoperable way. The application will be capable of collecting information from the Web of Data and use it to enrich the user models. Approaches to automatically aggregate ontology-based user models will be explored.

4   Conclusions and Future Research Questions

The aforementioned research plan is expected to be completed in two more years. One of the main important challenges is the evaluation of the user profiling algorithms implemented. In particular, at the moment a corpus for measuring the quality of the developed methods is not available and user based evaluations are demanding and require a large number of participants.

Another challenge is the study on the different sets of features for a user profiling algorithm that have to be implemented depending on the use case, the application and the source. For example, the profiling algorithm should adapt to the personalisation scenario or the use case, whether it is for music recommendations or for filtering a microblog stream. Moreover, the user model should also adapt to the source where the user information is extracted from. Users use different sites for different purposes, hence the activities performed and the interests expressed on social websites should be captured adopting different criteria. Thus, the profile information originated from different sources may have different importance for the application that requires the aggregated profile and this issue needs to be investigated.

Finally, as our background is closer to the Semantic Web area of research, a more accurate investigation on the user modelling topics will be beneficial. Especially on the automatic aggregation and representation of user models which is crucial to our research, it is still a research challenge but extensive work has been done already in the past.

References

1. Abel, F., Gao, Q., Houben, G.-J., Tao, K.: Semantic Enrichment of Twitter Posts for User Profile Construction on the Social Web. In: Antoniou, G., Grobelnik, M., Simperl, E., Parsia, B., Plexousakis, D., De Leenheer, P., Pan, J. (eds.) ESWC 2011, Part II. LNCS, vol. 6644, pp. 375–389. Springer, Heidelberg (2011)
2. Aroyo, L., Houben, G.: User modeling and adaptive Semantic Web. Semantic Web Journal (2010)
3. Carmagnola, F., Cena, F., Gena, C.: User model interoperability: a survey. User Modeling and User-Adapted Interaction (2011)
4. Hartig, O., Zhao, J.: Publishing and Consuming Provenance Metadata on the Web of Linked Data. In: McGuinness, D.L., Michaelis, J.R., Moreau, L. (eds.) IPAW 2010. LNCS, vol. 6378, pp. 78–90. Springer, Heidelberg (2010)
5. Kapanipathi, P., Orlandi, F., Sheth, A., Passant, A.: Personalized Filtering of the Twitter Stream. In: SPIM Workshop at ISWC 2011, pp. 6–13. CEUR-WS (2011)
6. Orlandi, F., Passant, A.: Semantic Search on Heterogeneous Wiki Systems. In: International Symposium on Wikis (WikiSym 2010). ACM (2010)
7. Orlandi, F., Passant, A.: Modelling provenance of DBpedia resources using Wikipedia contributions. Journal of Web Semantics 9(2) (2011)

User Feedback and Preferences Mining

Ladislav Peska

Department of software engineering
Charles University in Prague
Malostranske namesti 25, Prague, Czech Republic
peska@ksi.mff.cuni.cz

Abstract. In this paper, we present our vision and some initial experiments on how to anticipate significance, similarity or polarity of various types of (preferably implicit) user feedback and how to form individual user preference for recommendation. Throughout the corporate web, we can observe the same patterns or actions in user behavior (e.g. page-view, amount of scrolling, rating or purchasing). Recorded user behavior – user feedback – is often used as base for personalized recommendation, but the connection between the feedback and user preference is often unclear or noisy.

Our goal is to analyze user behavior in order to understand its relation to the user preference. We report on some initial experiments on a real-world e-commerce application. We describe our new models and methods how to combine various feedback types and how to learn user preferences.

Keywords: User preference, user behavior, implicit feedback, recommender systems.

1 Introduction, Motivation, Contribution and Related Work

Recommending and estimating user preferences on the web are both important commerce application and interesting research topic. Traditionally the most time and effort was spent on the explicit feedback based research, mainly on the single feedback factor – rating the objects. Probably the most important reason for that is a very straightforward link between user's feedback and user's preference. However on the other hand user rating is often too rare to provide reasonable output alone.

While moving to the implicit feedback, where user behavior is recorded without user cooperation, we may receive abundant amount of data, but the link between feedback and preference becomes less clear, especially if we record various feedback factors (e.g. time on page, amount of scrolling, mouse clicks, etc.). There are several questions linked: Should we use more various implicit factors? Are there any advantages? If so, how should we combine or evaluate them?

Motivation Example: a travel agency site employing tours recommendation. The site can record several types of implicit user feedback see [6] and want to use it in their collaborative based recommending methods. Recommending methods typically expects user preference to the objects he knows as their input. Our mission is then to

J. Masthoff et al. (Eds.): UMAP 2012, LNCS 7379, pp. 382–386, 2012.

provide recommending methods with such preference composed from the feedback. Such composed system can thereafter produce recommendation (top-k objects) based on combined feedbacks.

The **main contribution** of our work will be:

- Proposing new models and methods how to combine various feedbacks into the preference (Fig. 1,2).
- Online experiments and comparison of our methods against baselines and other recommenders. Generate data for further offline experiments.
- Improve recommending by embedding our methods into the existing systems e.g. [2], [6].

Related Work: The majority of the research on recommender systems focused on explicit or only one implicit feedback type. This is probably because, that many publicly available datasets (Netflix, Last.fm etc.) contains only a few different types of user feedback. There are several review articles e.g. Xiao and Benbasat [7] provide in-depth study of e-commerce recommender systems.

We extend the work of Eckhardt and Vojtas on combining various user modeling methods [2]. Lee and Brusilovsky [5] used implicit negative feedback in their job recommender. Claypool et al. [1] compared *Scrolling, Mouse Clicks, Mouse Move* and *Time on Page* implicit factors against explicit *Rating* using adapted browser. Several other authors compare implicit behavior against explicit rating e.g. Jawaheer et al. [3] on an online music server.

Important for our research is work of prof. Kiessling et al. on Preference SQL system e.g. [4] as we use their combination operators in our models. Our first results and the *UPComp* recommender are published in [6].

2   Models of User's Preference and Methods How to Learn Them

Preference on the Single Feedback Type: We assume, that for arbitrary fixed user any feedback is in the form *Feedback(object, feedback type, value)*. First we need to establish link between the feedback value and user's preference. We illustrate our approach on handling two implicit factors (see Fig. 1a,b). We look for rules of type Fig 1c composing feedback factor and purchases to the preference (using various rule learning methods like Apriori algorithm, Bayesian networks, ILP adapted to the preference). The result of this phase will be the user preference mined from single feedback factor e.g. value from [0,1].

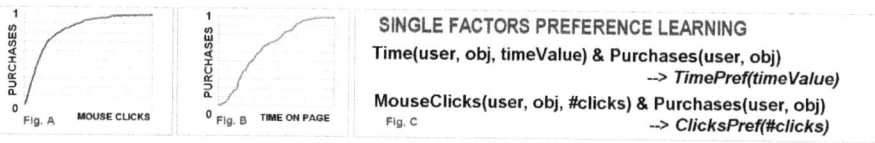

Fig. 1. Example of mouse clicks on object vs. purchases (Fig. 1a) and time on page vs. purchases distribution function (Fig. 1b) recorded on SLAN tour travel agency (see [6]). Pseudocode rules of how to learn single factor preferences (Fig. 1c).

Models of User Preference: Having user preference mined from single factor we can form a preference cube $[0,1]^{|F|}$, where $(1,...1)$ is the ideal object. In our previous work we used (heuristically) weighted average as combination method. This idea can be generalized into the *Ranking model*, where the user's preference is the result of a ranking function keeping partial order over single factor preferences.

A valuable extension to the *Ranking model* provides Kiessling's et al. [4]. Their model works on a data cube of object attributes. The user's conjunctive queries are transformed into the soft conditions (rules made by a domain expert) and then combined with *Priorization, Pareto* or *Ranking operator*. We use their operators over our single factor preferences to form the *Preference algebra model*. As an addition to the Kiessling's models, we will formulate methods to learn combination function over single factor preferences. We also plan to compare original [4] with our new methods.

Both previous models expect that the single feedback preference is equally important in all its values, which does not have to be true (e.g. "user spent 10sec on page" is probably not as interesting as "user spent 1500sec on page"). We will enhance *Preference algebra model* to cope with such situations e.g. by employing work of Zimmermann and Zysno [8].

Interesting task could be also to employ preferences of the site owner into our models (especially in e-commerce).

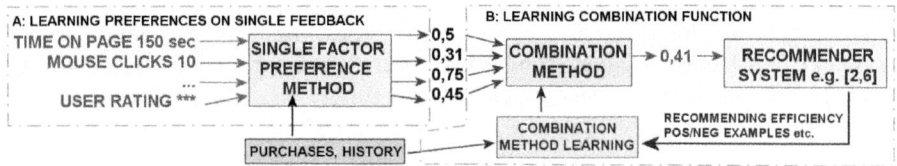

Fig. 2. Overview of the proposed system for combining user feedback

Learning Preference Model

There are several ways how to learn the preference models: from recommending efficiency, similarity between explicit and implicit feedback, positive and negative examples etc. Due to the space reasons, we present only one of our proposed methods to learn *Preference algebra* model from pos/neg examples (Fig. 2b).

If we have an empty system, we will start with a heuristic function e.g. average. We define user actions distributing objects into the positive/neutral/negative groups. This is e.g. purchasing (positive), rating the object or immediate leaving (negative). Iteratively, we will compare factors values for objects in each group. Then we will combine factors with *Priorization* or *Ranking* operator according to their resolution or *Pareto* if results are similar (again, there are several methods to distinct factor usefulness e.g. mean and variance analyzes or evolutionary algorithms). This step can be done for aggregated values of all users, certain user clusters or for single user only.

Table 1. Results of single factor recommending efficiency, online experiment on SLAN tour travel agency (see [6]); in total 7760 unique users

Factor	Click through rate	Conversion rate
Random recommending (baseline)	3.02%	0.97%
Time on object	4.50%	1.71%
Amount of scrolling	4.94%	1.98%
Mouse actions on object	4.15%	0.98%

Experiments on Learning Preference Models: Our primary domain for experiments is the e-commerce sites, where we can benefit from large number of different feedback types and well defined utility functions like *click through* or *conversion rate*. Our previous experiments were made on cooperating sites measuring recommending efficiency (see Tab. 1). However we would like to introduce a browser plug-in recording user feedback to extend our research to non-cooperating sites.

The social networks are also important domain, where we can benefit from explicitly specified connections between users and rich user profiles. We can use user data from *sitit.cz* portal and e.g. measure differences in user behavior between groups of users based on their profile or connections.

3   Conclusions and Future Work

We have presented our vision on how to understand various types of user feedback, how to model user preferences and some methods to learn the preference models. Our key problem is how to combine more types or sources of feedback together. Another interesting challenge related to implicit feedback is how to model negative preference.

There was not enough space to discuss more aspects of our work like the process model, other ways to express feedback, temporal aspect of user's preference, owner preferences or events causing changes in user preferences and/or behavior etc.

This work was supported by the grant SVV-2012-265312 and GACR 202-10-0761, with thanks to my advisor Peter Vojtas.

References

1. Claypool, M., Le, P., Wased, M., Brown, D.: Implicit interest indicators. In: Proc. of IUI 2001, pp. 33–40. ACM, New York (2001)
2. Eckhardt, A., Vojtáš, P.: Combining Various Methods of Automated User Decision and Preferences Modelling. In: Torra, V., Narukawa, Y., Inuiguchi, M. (eds.) MDAI 2009. LNCS, vol. 5861, pp. 172–181. Springer, Heidelberg (2009)
3. Jawaheer, G., Szomszor, M., Kostkova, P.: Comparison of implicit and explicit feedback from an online music recommendation service. In: Proc. of HetRec 2010, pp. 47–51. ACM, New York (2010)
4. Kießling, W., Endres, M., Wenzel, F.: The Preference SQL System - An Overview. IEEE Data Eng. Bull. 34, 11–18 (2011)

5. Lee, D.H., Brusilovsky, P.: Reinforcing Recommendation Using Implicit Negative Feedback. In: Houben, G.-J., McCalla, G., Pianesi, F., Zancanaro, M. (eds.) UMAP 2009. LNCS, vol. 5535, pp. 422–427. Springer, Heidelberg (2009)
6. Peska, L., Eckhardt, A., Vojtas, P.: UPComp - A PHP Component for Recommendation Based on User Behaviour. In: Proc. of WI-IAT 2011, pp. 306–309. IEEE Computer Society, Washington, DC (2011)
7. Xiao, B., Benbasat, I.: E-commerce product recommendation agents: use, characteristics, and impact. MIS Q. 31(1), 137–209 (2007)
8. Zimmermann, H.J., Zysno, P.: Latent connectives in human decision making. Fuzzy Sets and Systems 4, 37–51 (1980)

Ubiquitous Fuzzy User Modeling
for Multi-application Environments
by Mining Socially Enhanced Online Traces

Hilal Tarakci and Nihan Kesim Cicekli

[1] Tubitak Uzay Space Technologies Research Institute, Ankara, Turkey
[2] Department of Computer Engineering, Middle East Technical University,
Ankara, Turkey

Abstract. In this paper, we propose an interoperable ubiquitous user model which illustrates different aspects of the individual's interests, preferences and personality. It is constructed by mining socially enhanced online traces of the user and aggregating the partially obtained profiles. Those traces include actions performed and relationships established in the social web accounts in addition to the local machine traces such as bookmarks and web history. Moreover, we claim that mining the content in a context-aware approach and computing fuzziness values during the process results in a more reliable user profile.

Keywords: ubiquitous user model, social web mining, user profiles, user modeling.

1 Introduction

In this paper, we propose a ubiquitous fuzzy user model which illustrates different aspects of the individual's interests, preferences and personality. The proposed model is constructed by mining socially enhanced online traces of the user and aggregating and aligning the partially obtained profiles. Those traces include actions performed and relationships established in the social web accounts in addition to the local machine traces such as bookmarks and web history. Moreover, we claim that mining the content in a context-aware approach and computing fuzziness values during the process results in a more reliable user profile.

In our study, we not only consider explicitly stated form based information in social networks, but also activities performed such as sharing or commenting on a video about a certain topic and clicking the 'like' button on a sports team page etc. When advanced activity types are taken into account, more sophisticated user model structures are required. [2] models high order relations in the social network as a unified hypergraph. Influenced by this idea we employ unified fuzzy hypergraph[4] structure which is able to model high order relations naturally in addition to supporting applications with different data reliability requirements. For instance, the reliability of whether an individual is a fan of a specific rock band is more important for a find-best-gift-for-your-friend program than a music recommendation application.

J. Masthoff et al. (Eds.): UMAP 2012, LNCS 7379, pp. 387–390, 2012.

A generic user modeling library for the social semantic web is proposed in [1]. Similarly, we aim to tailor the constructed user model in accordance with the needs of the requester applications. Furthermore, we intend to manage whole life cycle of an individual's user model by considering not only the construction of the profile but also the necessary information updates to the profile.Moreover, the constructed user model is mapped to supported ontologies by external links during construction phase enabling export of the required portion of the profile partially in the form of the ontology supported by the consumer application.

2   User Model Construction by Mining Socially Enhanced Online Traces

The information which is required in order to construct the user profile is synthesized from two main sources: (i)distributed user profiles embedded in the social accounts and (ii)the traces left on the devices of the individual. In the proposed work, Facebook, Twitter and LinkedIn accounts of the individual are going to be mined in order to obtain long and short term interests of the user besides his/her relationships with other people. Exploitation of the user's smart phone, home and work computers in the user model construction process is optional and requires the user to install a client application to analyze information such as his web usage data and bookmarked web sites. The user model construction and consumption process is illustrated in Fig. 1. The first task in the construction of the user model is finding the social web accounts of the user. The social web mining component is responsible for mining the activities in the discovered accounts in a context-aware fashion. The context in this work consists of place and time. Current context information is extracted from check-in declarations on social web accounts or mobile phone GPS. Besides, future context is available when the user declares to attend an event on his/her social web account. As an

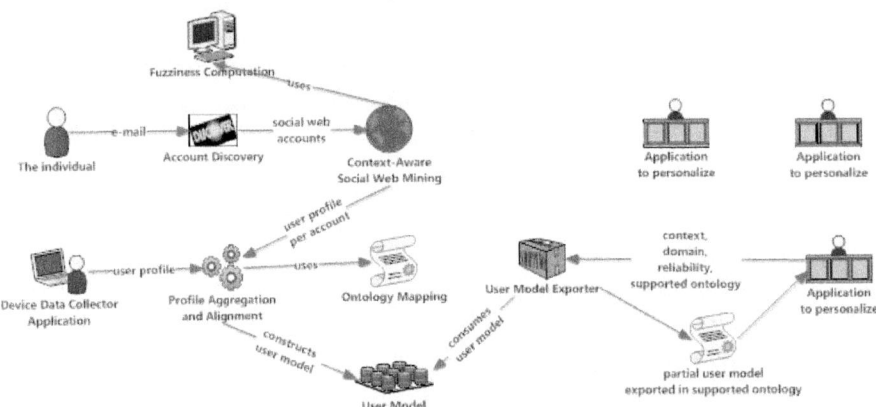

Fig. 1. User Model Construction and Consumption Process

example use of the context, suppose the user liked the page for Adidas products and currently in Ankamall. In this scenario, an advertisement application is able to inform the user about the discount in Adidas store in Ankamall. On the other hand, fuzziness values for the findings is computed by assessing the reliability which usually depends on how the information is supplied. For instance, in a Facebook account, the information page where the user specifies his work and school information and explicit likes on several categories such as music, movie, hobbies and etc. are highly reliable especially for long term interests, whereas the concepts the shared, liked or commented posts are about gives less trustful clues about the user's short term interests. In an analogical manner, the professional interests obtained from LinkedIn profile of the individual are more reliable than those on Facebook account.Afterwards, the constructed profiles from separate data sources are aggregated and aligned to create a holistic user model which is modeled and stored by unified fuzzy hypergraph structure. Following the profile aggregation process, the concepts used are externally linked to supported ontologies including GUMO [3] and Wikipedia categories, whereas semantic for users are supplied by generating and linking hCard profiles.

3   Unified Fuzzy Hypergraph User Model Structure

A hypergraph is the generalization of an ordinary graph by introducing hyperedges which are nonempty subsets of the vertex set. Vertices of a hypergraph represents the entities to be modeled such as people, resources, tags, organizations, concepts etc. in social networking domain. Hyperedges represent the high order relations between those entities. For instance, a hyperedge connecting a user with a resource and a tag models the situation that the resource is assigned with the tag by the user. In a fuzzy hypergraph, each vertex in the hyperedge is assigned a fuzziness value in the range $[0,1]$ representing the reliability of the entity belonging to the relation modeled by the hyperedge. For instance, suppose the following information is mined from Facebook: (i)Feride liked Lady Gaga page, (ii) Munise declared to attend Lady Gaga concert, (iii) Munise liked Sertab Erener page, (iv) Kamuran shared a music video of Sertab and (v) three Lady Gaga videos recently. The following is an incidence matrix of a fuzzy hypergraph which accords with the given scenario:

$$
\begin{array}{c c c c}
 & LadyGaga & SertabErener & popmusic \\
Feride & 1 & 0 & 0 \\
Munise & 3/4 & 1 & 3/4 \\
Kamuran & 3/4 & 1/2 & 1/2
\end{array}
$$

The fuzziness value of Feride's interest on Lady Gaga is determined as 1, since she explicitly stated this on her Facebook page in (i). Similarly, Munise-Sertab Erener like relation fuzziness is also 1 based on (iii). Since Munise is going to attend Lady Gaga concert, there is a strong possibility that she likes her music, which is stated as 3/4 fuzziness in the incidence matrix. Similarly, by judging (iv), Kamuran may like Sertab Erener, but there is no strong evidence for this information. However, he probably likes Lady Gaga since he shared three videos recently. The fuzziness values for pop music interest is determined by examining interests on Lady Gaga and Sertab Erener, since both are pop music singers. If the user has an interest on both singers, fuzziness value for pop music is taken as the minimum of the two.

The subset of the fuzzy hypergraph which supports a reliability level can be extracted by using the c-level hypergraph [4]. In the above incidence matrix, the subset of hypergraph with reliability 1 includes edges Lady Gaga{Feride} and Sertab Erener{Munise} whereas the subset with reliability 1/2 consists of Lady Gaga{Feride, Munise, Kamuran}, Sertab Erener{Munise, Kamuran}, pop music{Munise, Kamuran}. The c-level hypergraph with a strict reliability requirement has less number of elements, since elements with lower reliability than required trust level are filtered.

4   Conclusion

In this paper, we propose an ubiquitous user model for multi application environments which is constructed by mining the user's activities on social web accounts. Furthermore, we anticipate that computing fuzziness values and modeling the user in a context-aware manner will reinforce the reliability of the user profile. In order to accomplish this, fuzzy hypergraph data structure, which naturally represents high order relations and defines fuzzy membership values for each element of hyperedges, is used to model the user. In future work, we perform extensive analysis on social web mining methodology by providing several fuzziness computation and context-awareness approaches in order to evaluate the effect of fuzziness and context-awareness on the reliability of the ultimate user profile.

References

1. Gao, Q., Abel, F., Houben, G.J.: GeniUS: Generic User Modeling Library for the Social Semantic Web. In: Joint International Technology Conference. Springer (2011)
2. Tan, S., Bu, J., Chen, C., Xu, B., Wang, C., He, X.: Using rich social media information for music recommendation via hypergraph model. ACM Trans. Multimedia Comput. Commun. Appl. 7S(1), 1–22 (2011)
3. Heckmann, D., Schwartz, T., Br, B., Kroner, E.: Decentralized User Modeling with UserML and GUMO. In: 10th International Conference on User Modeling, pp. 61–65 (2005)
4. Goetschel Jr., R.: Introduction to Fuzzy Hypergraphs and Hebbian Structures. Fuzzy Sets and Systems 7, 113–130 (1995)

Facilitating Code Example Search on the Web through Expertise Personalization

Annie T.T. Ying*

School of Computer Science, McGill University, Montreal, Canada
annie.ying@cs.mcgill.ca

1 Research Problem and Solution Outline

The Web is an important resource for a programmer: as much as 20% of a programmer's time is spent on the Web [2]. When a programmer searches for information on the Web, two distinct information needs arise depending on the programmer's previous knowledge of a library's Application Programming Interfaces (APIs[1]): *learning* how to invoke a software library versus *reminding* the programmers themselves the details deemed not worth remembering [2].

Of the various types of documentation programmers find on the Web, code examples are one of the most effective because they demonstrate the usage of APIs [8]. Researchers in Software Engineering, a field aiming at improving productivity in software development, have proposed recommendation systems for code examples (e.g., work by Bajracharya et al [1]). The problems with these systems and general search engines in addressing the learning and reminding cases for code search are two-fold: **1-Re-finding code examples:** A programmer retrieving a known example may need to go through a search engine result page and possibly click on multiple pages to re-find the code example. **2-Connecting a code example to known knowledge:** Existing code example recommendation systems do not attempt to provide explanations on why a recommendation is made. Providing appropriate explanations can increase a recommendation system's effectiveness, efficiency, and user satisfaction.[2] To alleviate these two problems, we personalize code example search on the Web by taking into account each programmer's expertise, by addressing the following:

RQ1: How do we generate a user profile that captures a programmer's expertise?
RQ2: How do we help a programmer identify known code examples more effectively?
RQ3: How do we provide explanation on a code example for a programmer to make decision about whether the example is relevant more efficiently?

For RQ1, we propose to use the interaction of a programmer with APIs as a way to measure the expertise in the short-term: the more a programmer interacts with an API, the more expertise the programmer has on a particular API and

---

* Supervisor: Martin Robillard, McGill University.
[1] The mechanism (e.g., method calls) to invoke a functionality of the library.
[2] Tintarev and Masthoff surveyed on explanation in recommendation systems [11].

J. Masthoff et al. (Eds.): UMAP 2012, LNCS 7379, pp. 391–394, 2012.

the more likely it is the reminding scenario. Our expertise measure is adapted from previous work [7,5] which calculated the measure by analyzing logs from programming environments (e.g., Eclipse[3]) and from the version history of the source code. To represent more long-term programming expertise, we use existing work in ontological-based user profile [10]. The ontology is inferred from tags from a community-based programming question-answering site, StackOverflow.[4] For RQ2, we propose a summary snippet generation method that displays the code example a programmer is re-finding to directly satisfy the information need. For RQ3, we adapt a tag-based explanation approach [13] to programming tags.

These solutions are mostly contributions in Software Engineering. For the User Modeling community, our contribution is in showing Software Engineering as a promising domain to apply User Modeling (RQ1). In this thesis, we extend Ye and Fischer's work [4], one of a few in applying User Modeling to Software Engineering, for a more comprehensive representation of programming expertise. Our work highlights the diversity of information sources (e.g., from source code to tags from StackOverflow on programming questions), the availability of structured information (e.g., source code), and the abundance of existing data (e.g., version history of source code) in Software Engineering, enabling an unusually rich user profile representation. For the rest of the paper, we focus on solutions to RQ1 on generating user profiles (Section 2.1) and briefly describe RQ2 and RQ3 in Section 2.2. Section 3 outlines progress to date.

2   Proposed Solutions

2.1   User Profiles Based on Programmer Expertise (RQ1)

To better understand code search information needs on the Web, we turn to the seminal work on search goal taxonomy [3] and its extension [9]. From analyzing queries from the log of a code search engine, we map the learning and reminding scenarios from the programming context to the search goal taxonomy: **navigational** (the goal is to "go to a known website the user has in mind", and in programming context, to a library or a package, for both *learning* or *reminding* purposes) and **informational** (the goal is to "learn something by reading or viewing Web pages") which includes **directed informational** (the goal is to "learn something in particular about my topic", and in the programming context, about a specific code element, e.g., the query *http_get_request_body*, for *reminding* purposes) versus **undirected informational** (the goal is to "learn anything and everything about my topic," and in the programming context, a general programming concept and functionality, e.g., the query *red black tree,* for *learning* purposes). Previous work in inferring query search goals exist for certain types of queries but suggests that the search goal for software-related queries is usually ambiguous [6], because depending on the searcher's knowledge, the goal can be different. Hence, we need to model the expertise of the programmer in a user profile.

---

[3] www.eclipse.com

[4] www.stackoverflow.com

Code Expertise (short-term): The rich body of previous work has shown differences in programming experts and newcomers (e.g., by Wiedenbeck [14]). However, these results are dated and on source code in general, not specifically on API methods and their usage, of which code examples are targeted to demonstrate. Therefore, we examined programmer interaction logs on the Eclipse programming environment on over 4000 programming tasks and found that project experts (those with commit rights to a project) navigate less to commonly-known code, such as APIs, and navigate less to code they have interacted with a lot.

This difference in experts and newcomers motivated us to model API usage expertise at the fine-grained code element level. We use an expertise notion called usage expertise [7]: the more a programmer has authored code that uses an API code element (as evident from the version history of the source code), the higher the usage expertise. We adapted this measure to analyze interaction history in addition to version history [5]. Our contribution is in the novel use of this type of measure in a user profile.

Area Expertise (long-term): Code expertise is appropriate for short-term, more specific representation in a user profile. To model the long-term expertise of a programmer, we use a more general notion of expertise, in which we make use of existing tags in the programming question-answering site, StackOverflow. Researchers in Software Engineering have started to study these tags [12]; our contribution is in using these tags to represent the type of knowledge a programmer has and use this representation in a user profile.

First, we build a training set that maps for each API method (e.g., *Frame.-addWindowListener*) mentioned in a question or an answer, the tags associated with the corresponding question (e.g., tags *java* and *awt*). Although the tags from StackOverflow do not form a hierarchy, we can construct one by analyzing tag co-occurrences.[5] We create a supervised classification model that distinguishes the terms which distinguish API methods associated with a tag versus methods which are not. With this model, we can predict for a new API method, which tags are associated with the method. The same algorithm can be used to associate tags to API methods that are called in source code authored by a programmer: the more code authored by a programmer containing *Frame.addWindowListener*, the more knowledge on *java* and *awt* the programmer should have.

We use an ontological user profile as in the work by Sieg et al. [10]. The way to populate the user profile is by "passive observation of a user's information access activity," in our case, looking at the code authored by a programmer that contains a given API method.

2.2   Applying the User Profiles (RQ2 and RQ3)

Snippet Generation: When a programmer enters a query for a reminding purpose, the summary textual snippet should ideally satisfy the programmer's information need right away.

---

[5] The tags *perl* and *AWT* seldom appear together, but when *AWT* appears, *java* appears but not vice-versa. We can conclude that *AWT* is a child node of *java*.

Tag-Based Explanation Generation: We use the tag-based explanation generation ideas proposed by Vig et al [13] to enable a programmer make decision about whether a code example is relevant more efficiently. Vig et al. showed that if we want to use tags (in our case, of programming areas from StackOverflow) as a way to explain the recommendations, the way that will maximize the level of "justification" is to sort by tag relevance but showing user expertise in the programming area.

3   Progress to Date

Work in progress include the mapping the code search information needs (learning versus reminding) to the search goal taxonomy and the short-term code expertise user profile generation. User profile generation regarding expertise in general programming areas and the application of user profile are work that remains.

References

1. Bajracharya, S.K., Ossher, J., Lopes, C.V.: Leveraging usage similarity for effective retrieval of examples in code repositories. In: Proc. of Int'l Sym. on Foundations of Software Eng., pp. 157–166 (2010)
2. Brandt, J., Guo, P.J., Lewenstein, J., Dontcheva, M., Klemmer, S.R.: Two studies of opportunistic programming: interleaving web foraging, learning, and writing code. In: Proc. of Int'l SIGCHI Conf., pp. 1589–1598 (2009)
3. Broder, A.: A taxonomy of web search. SIGIR Forum 36(2), 3–10 (2002)
4. Fischer, G., Ye, Y.: Personalizing Delivered Information in a Software Reuse Environment. In: Bauer, M., Gmytrasiewicz, P.J., Vassileva, J. (eds.) UM 2001. LNCS (LNAI), vol. 2109, pp. 178–187. Springer, Heidelberg (2001)
5. Fritz, T., Ou, J., Murphy, G., Murphy-Hill, E.: A degree-of-knowledge model to capture source code familiarity. In: Proc. of Int'l Conf. on Software Eng., pp. 385–394 (2010)
6. Lee, U., Liu, Z., Cho, J.: Automatic identification of user goals in web search. In: Proc. of Int'l Conf. on World Wide Web, pp. 391–400 (2005)
7. Ma, D., Schuler, D., Zimmermann, T., Sillito, J.: Expert recommendation with usage expertise. In: Proc. of Int'l Conf. on Software Maintenance (2009)
8. Robillard, M.: What makes apis hard to learn? answers from developers. IEEE Software 26(6), 27–34 (2009)
9. Rose, D., Levinson, D.: Understanding user goals in web search. In: Proc. of Int'l Conf. on World Wide Web, pp. 13–19 (2004)
10. Sieg, A., Mobasher, B., Burke, R.: Web search personalization with ontological user profiles. In: Proc. of Conf. on Info. & Knowledge Mgmt., pp. 525–534 (2007)
11. Tintarev, N., Masthoff, J.: Designing and evaluating explanations for recommender systems. In: Recommender Systems Handbook, pp. 479–510 (2011)
12. Treude, C., Barzilay, O., Storey, M.: How do programmers ask and answer questions on the web? In: Proc. of Int'l Conf. on Sw. Eng, pp. 804–807 (2011)
13. Vig, J., Sen, S., Riedl, J.: Tagsplanations: explaining recommendations using tags. In: Proc. of Int'l Conf. on Intelligent User Interfaces, pp. 47–56 (2009)
14. Wiedenbeck, S.: Novice/expert differences in programming skills. Int'l. Journal of Man-Machine Studies 23(4), 383–390 (1985)

Author Index

GPSR Compliance

The European Union's (EU) General Product Safety Regulation (GPSR)
is a set of rules that requires consumer products to be safe and our
obligations to ensure this.

If you have any concerns about our products, you can contact us on
ProductSafety@springernature.com

In case Publisher is established outside the EU, the EU authorized
representative is:

Springer Nature Customer Service Center GmbH
Europaplatz 3
69115 Heidelberg, Germany

Batch number: 09490872

Printed by Printforce, the Netherlands